William Dalrymple

was born in Scotland and brought up on the shores of the Firth of Forth. He wrote the highly acclaimed bestseller *In Xanadu* when he was twenty-two. The book won the 1990 *Yorkshire Post* Best First Work Award and a Scottish Arts Council Spring Book Award; it was also shortlisted for the John Llewellyn Rhys Memorial Prize. In 1989 Dalrymple moved to Delhi where he lived for six years researching his second book, *City of Djinns*, which won the 1994 Thomas Cook Travel Book Award and the *Sunday Times* Young British Writer of the Year Award. *From the Holy Mountain*, his acclaimed study of the demise of Christianity in its Middle Eastern homeland, was awarded the Scottish Arts Council Autumn Book Award for 1997; it was also shortlisted for the 1998 Thomas Cook Award, the John Llewellyn Rhys Prize and the Duff Cooper Prize. A collection of his writings about India, *The Age of Kali*, was published in 1998.

William Dalrymple is a Fellow of the Royal Society of Literature and of the Royal Asiatic Society, and in 2002 was awarded the Mungo Park Medal by the Royal Scottish Geographical Society for his 'outstanding contribution to travel literature'. He wrote and presented the television series *Stones of the Raj* and *Indian Journeys*, which won the Grierson Award for Best Documentary Series at BAFTA in 2002. He is married to the artist Olivia Fraser, and they have three children. They now divide their time between London and Delhi.

From the reviews:

'The most touching love story to have come out of India since Shah Jehan and Begum Mumtaz, whose death inspired the Taj Mahal . . . It is far more romantic than any work of fiction could be, and more tragic in its outcome, with a final twist guaranteed to make the eyes dazzle. Dalrymple is the most perceptive and sympathetic observer of the Asian scene writing today, and for the Indophile, the lover of romance and the lover of the written word, *White Mughals* is nothing less than a *kush bagh*, a garden of delights . . .' CHARLES ALLEN, *Literary Review*

'Love and war are usually thought to inhabit different spheres and, except in Tolstoy, we do not expect them to mix. Part of the achievement of this magnificent book is the way William Dalrymple effortlessly melds the two motifs so that the public story of the British conquest of India and the poignant tale of a love affair interpenetrate, with each adding a dimension to the other. Much of Dalrymple's narrative has the pace of a thriller ... [but] above all this book is a bravura display of scholarship, writing and insight. No brief review can do justice to its manifold excellence and all one can say is that Dalrymple manages the incredible feat of outpointing most historians and novelists in one go' FRANK McLYNN, *Independent on Sunday*

'William Dalrymple's story of a colonial love affair will change our views about British India' MIRANDA SEYMOUR, *Sunday Times*

'Imaginatively conceived, beautifully written, intellectually challenging and a passionate love story – this is Dalrymple's lifetime achievement and the best book he has ever written. He has done for India and the British what Edward Said did for the meeting between the West and the Arab world in *Orientalism*. Despite its setting in the eighteenth century, this is a hugely important contemporary book. Dalrymple has broken new ground in the current debate about racism, colonialism and globalisation. The history of the British in India will never be the same after this book' AHMED RASHID

'Moving, wide-ranging and richly textured ... Through massive research blessed with serendipity, and through imagination and empathy, Dalrymple has evoked the world of the British in late-eighteenth-century India as no one has before ... A wonderful book, a story of love and the humanity we share'
FRANCIS ROBINSON, *Times Literary Supplement*

'Anyone who fails to read William Dalrymple's *White Mughals* owing to a lack of interest in India, will be losing a rich reward. By following the love story of a British Resident in Hyderabad and a Muslim noblewoman, he goes deep into the relationship of East and West in the late eighteenth century when the twain did most certainly meet. A devoted and – in this case – uncannily lucky researcher, Dalrymple offers a feast of often astonishing information and a cast of men and women ranging from the comic to the heart-rending, but above all he writes in a way that draws you into his own enthusiasm for the subject. This is an irresistible book'

DIANA ATHILL, *Guardian* Books of the Year

'Dalrymple's subject is the unlovely term "transculturation", but his book has some lovely stuff about race, diplomacy, warfare and, especially, sex ... A witches' brew of deviousness, desire, ambition and astonishment'   ROBIN BLAKE, *Financial Times*

'A masterpiece'   *New Statesman* Books of the Year

'Technically ambitious ... There is a scholarly seriousness here; also a moral passion. This capacious book is never more engaging than when Dalrymple describes, with a novelist's compassion, the tragic costs of Kirkpatrick's rebellion'   PANKAJ MISHRA, *Guardian*

'The Deccan plateau's monumental grandeur is the proper setting for Dalrymple's cliffhanging historical thriller, a book profoundly faithful to the poignancy of love briefly consummated amidst conflicting cultures. The pulsating true chronicle of a British Resident's tempestuous romance with a Muslim aristocrat's teenage daughter in Hyderabad two hundred years ago is the result of diligent research, presented with Dalrymple's trademark wit and penned in a stylishly expository manner: superbly structured, each chapter ends on a note of suspense. The plot is offset by the regional politics of the Deccan, and whether it is war, sex, intrigue or astrology, Dalrymple is a sound and willing guide. This is a classic work on a heroic theme that also rescues one of India's most noble but least regarded landscapes from shameful neglect'

BILL AITKEN, *Outlook*

'*White Mughals* stands as a convincing indictment of imperialism and an affecting story of a love affair ... Dalrymple is one of the most captivating writers of non-fiction at work today'

HUGH MACDONALD, *Herald* (Glasgow)

'A history book of the highest academic standards ... well written, well researched and worldly wise ... A huge historical *tableau vivant* of the courtly, decadent, poetic world of eighteenth-century India, when Mughal princes lived in glittering palaces and the British lived like Rajahs. Most accounts of the British in India dwell on the Victorian era and because of this we tend now to think that Victorian attitudes were the only attitudes held by our compatriots out there. This is one of the few books to deal with the century or two before the Victorians and to set the record straight. The underlying purpose is to highlight how liberal and un-Victorian were the mores of the earlier period. But this message is conveyed through a stirring tale of battles, plots, sex, love and betrayal, without ever straying from the historical facts ... Dalrymple's genius is to bring the characters and drama richly to life as engrossingly as a good novelist'

JONATHAN LORIE, *The Traveller*

'There is much that is universal about the story – of love against the odds, of a loyalty that transcended the barriers of race and ethnic background – but Dalrymple has written a considerably broader work of history too. It displays impressive scholarship, drawing on many previously untapped primary sources, combining a minute dissection of end-of-the-eighteenth-century Anglo-Indian relations with a history of the mercantile and political landscape. Dalrymple after a successful career as a travel writer and an essayist, has now demonstrated himself a master historian'

EDWARD MARRIOTT, *Evening Standard*

'A bare outline of the plot gives little idea of the zest and energy with which Dalrymple has managed to reconstruct this extraordinary story, ransacking every major repository of British Indian records from Edinburgh to Hyderabad itself, nor of the infectious enthusiasm and affection for India and its ways which are evident on every page ... *White Mughals* is a remarkable achievement: illuminating, thought-provoking, moving – and entertaining. Despite its length, anyone even superficially interested in the British in India will find it hard to put down' SIR DAVID GOODALL, *The Tablet*

'Fascinating and enthralling ... William Dalrymple unscrolls a wide panorama: a vivid and often turbulent panorama of India during the eighteenth century. Impressively researched, and written with vigour and panache ... Dalrymple is a gifted narrator who brings vividly to life the dealings between the Indian princes and the East India Company. He brilliantly depicts some of the leading characters SELINA HASTINGS, *Daily Mail*

'An ambitious piece of revisionist history ... Long after India was painted as an area of darkness it is heartening that an erudite writer with a nose for history, a yearning for travel and a pen soaked in the best traditions of writing holds up a different India to the world ... Dalrymple's book, which turns established theories and perceptions topsy-turvy, is bound to create a lot of ripples among historians and give us a perspective we never knew existed' BINOO JOHN, *Indian Express*

'Combines the "what next?" tension of a good novel with the archival sleuthing of the true historian. A magnificent achievement shedding new light on the East India Company and elite England' *Independent* Books of the Year

'Brilliant, poignant and compassionate, *White Mughals* is not only a compelling love story, but it is also an important reminder, at this perilous moment of history, that Europeans once found Muslim society both congenial and attractive, and that it has always been possible to build bridges between Islam and the West' KAREN ARMSTRONG

'That William Dalrymple's books are exhaustively researched, well-documented, excellent reads is a given. So when even hard-nosed critics say he has surpassed himself with his latest book about India, looking forward to grabbing a copy is the least fans of his writing could do. And he doesn't disappoint. The book is on a more ambitious scale than Dalrymple's earlier writings and though ostensibly about the love shared by an East India Company official and a young Begum at Hyderabad at the end of the eighteenth century, the book is also a document against the popular notion of the "Clash of Cultures". The book ends with almost a plea for co-existence, for an adaptation of the spirit of "tolerance and understanding" so well embodied by these White Mughals, an example the current polarised world would be well advised to follow'

SUMAN TARAFDAR, *Hindustan Times*

'*White Mughals* is well researched — so much so that it reads like a novel, ironically a Victorian one. But nothing in the book is made up. Dalrymple's exhaustive research of documents, letters and diaries from the eighteenth century puts him squarely inside the world of his subject. The writing is crisp and the footnotes resonate with Dalrymple's acerbic wit . . . [Most of all] Dalrymple wants to make a point: that the theory of the clash of civilisations is simplistic, convenient, racist and untrue. He does this spectacularly well'

SHAILJA NEELAKANTAN, *Far East Economic Review*

'A superlative, groundbreaking story that fully justifies all the effort, all the costs, all the risks [it took to write] . . . At a time when Islamophobia is rising to danger levels in the West we need this reminder more than ever that once, however briefly, East and West met in tolerance and peace — and love'

DAVID ROBINSON, *Scotsman*

WHITE
MUGHALS

Love and Betrayal in
Eighteenth-Century India

WILLIAM DALRYMPLE

Flamingo
An Imprint of HarperCollins*Publishers*

Flamingo
An Imprint of HarperCollins*Publishers*
77–85 Fulham Palace Road,
Hammersmith, London w6 8jb

The HarperCollins website address is:
www.harpercollins.co.uk

Published by Flamingo 2003
17 16 15 14 13 12 11

First published in Great Britain by
HarperCollins*Publishers* 2002

ISBN 0 00 655096 7

Set in PostScript Linotype Minion with
Spectrum display

Printed and bound in Great Britain by
Clays Ltd, St Ives plc

For Sam and Shireen Vakil Miller
and
Bruce Wannell

CONTENTS

ILLUSTRATIONS

William Kirkpatrick in Madras as Wellesley's Private Secretary in late 1799, by Thomas Hickey. *(Courtesy of the National Gallery of Ireland)*

James Achilles Kirkpatrick, the British Resident at Hyderabad, 1799. *(Private collection)*

The Nizam and his durbar ride out on a hunting expedition *c*.1790, by Venkatchellam. *(Salar Jung Museum, Hyderabad)*

Aristu Jah at the height of his powers, *c*.1800, by Venkatchellam. *(V&A Picture Library, I.S. 163–1952)*

Henry Russell, *c*.1805, by Venkatchellam. *(Collection of Professor Robert Frykenberg)*

The two youngest sons of the Nizam, princes Suleiman Jah and Kaiwan Jah, *c*.1802, by Venkatchellam. *(Private collection)*

Nizam Ali Khan consults Aristu Jah and his son and successor Sikander Jah, *c*.1800, by Venkatchellam. *(Private collection)*

Ma'ali Mian, Aristu Jah's eldest son and the husband of Farzand Begum, by Venkatchellam. *(Private collection)*

The young Maratha Peshwa Madhu Rao with his guardian and effective jailor, the brilliant and ruthless Maratha Minister Nana Phadnavis. By James Wales, 1792. *(Royal Asiatic Society/Bridgeman Art Library)*

Tipu Sultan, the Tiger of Mysore, *c*.1790. *(V&A Picture Library, I.S. 266–1952)*

Richard Colley Wellesley, 1st Marquess Wellesley, by J. Pain Davis, *c*.1815. *(By courtesy of the National Portrait Gallery, London)*

Mir Alam. *(Salar Jung Museum, Hyderabad)*

James Achilles Kirkpatrick, *c*.1805, attributed to George Chinnery. *(Courtesy of the Hongkong and Shanghai Banking Corporation Ltd)*

General William Palmer in old age, *c*.1810. *(Courtesy of the Director, National Army Museum, London)*

General William and Fyze Palmer with their young family in Lucknow, painted by Johan Zoffany in 1785. *(OIOC, BL)*

James and Khair's children, Sahib Allum and Sahib Begum, painted by George Chinnery in 1805. *(Courtesy of the Hongkong and Shanghai Banking Corporation Ltd)*

The mercenary Alexander Gardner in his tartan *salvar kemise*.

The tomb of Michel Joachim Raymond.

The hill of Maula Ali.

Hyderabad state executioners in the 1890s.

Medicine men.

Amazon harem guards and band members.

Raymond's Bidri-ware hookah. *(Private collection)*

William Kirkpatrick. *(Strachey Trust)*

William Linnaeus Gardner.

William Fraser.

James Achilles Kirkpatrick as a young man. *(Strachey Trust)*

William Palmer the Hyderabad banker as a disillusioned old man.
   (Private collection)

Kitty Kirkpatrick.

Henry Russell on his return to England.

Thomas Carlyle. *(Strachey Trust)*

The south front of the Hyderabad Residency in 1805. *(Strachey Trust)*

The south front of the Residency today.

The north front of the Residency today.

The *naqqar khana* gateway into Khair un-Nissa's *zenana*.

Hyderabad's Char Minar in the 1890s.

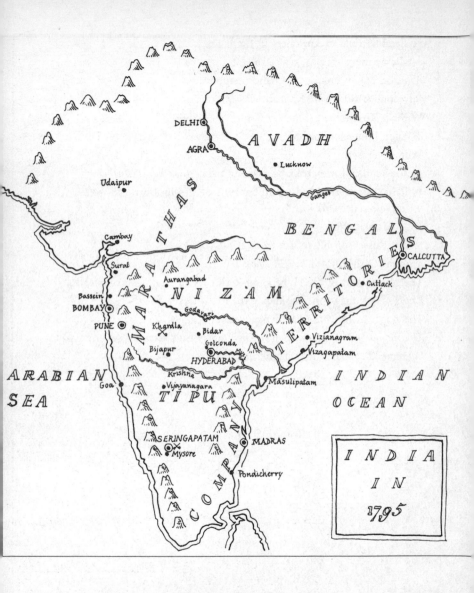

INDIA
IN
1795

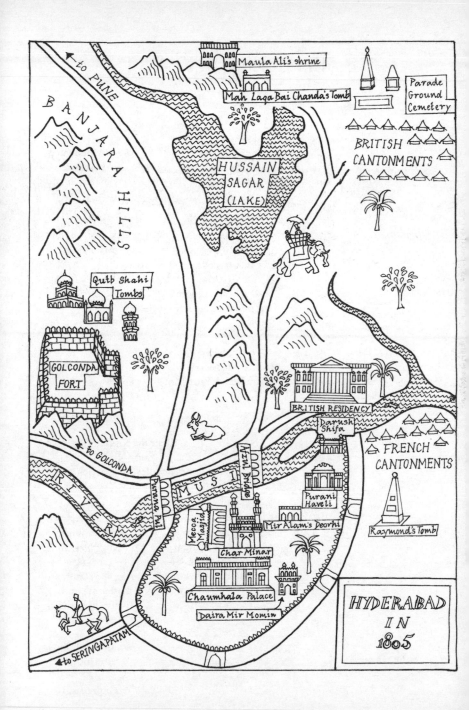

THE SHUSHTARIS

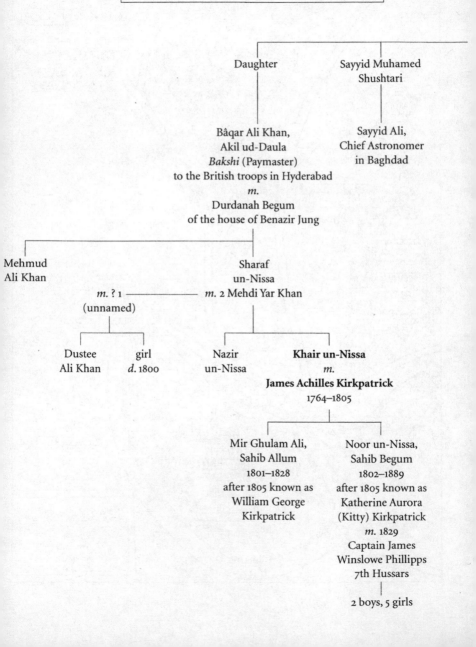

Daughter   Sayyid Muhamed
Shushtari

Bâqar Ali Khan,
Akil ud-Daula
Bakshi (Paymaster)
to the British troops in Hyderabad
m.
Durdanah Begum
of the house of Benazir Jung

Sayyid Ali,
Chief Astronomer
in Baghdad

Mehmud
Ali Khan

m. ? 1 ———————— *m.* 2 Mehdi Yar Khan
(unnamed)

Sharaf
un-Nissa

Dustee
Ali Khan

girl
d. 1800

Nazir
un-Nissa

Khair un-Nissa
m.
James Achilles Kirkpatrick
1764–1805

Mir Ghulam Ali,
Sahib Allum
1801–1828
after 1805 known as
William George
Kirkpatrick

Noor un-Nissa,
Sahib Begum
1802–1889
after 1805 known as
Katherine Aurora
(Kitty) Kirkpatrick
m. 1829
Captain James
Winslowe Phillipps
7th Hussars

2 boys, 5 girls

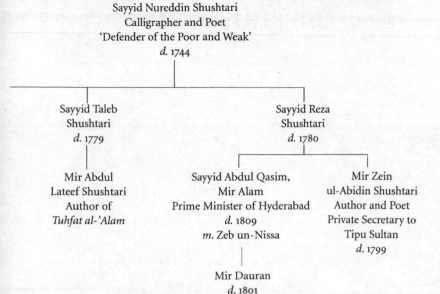

Sayyid Nureddin Shushtari
Calligrapher and Poet
'Defender of the Poor and Weak'
d. 1744

Sayyid Taleb
Shushtari
d. 1779

Mir Abdul
Lateef Shushtari
Author of
Tuhfat al-'Alam

Sayyid Reza
Shushtari
d. 1780

Sayyid Abdul Qasim,
Mir Alam
Prime Minister of Hyderabad
d. 1809
m. Zeb un-Nissa

Mir Dauran
d. 1801

Mir Zein
ul-Abidin Shushtari
Author and Poet
Private Secretary to
Tipu Sultan
d. 1799

THE KIRKPATRICKS

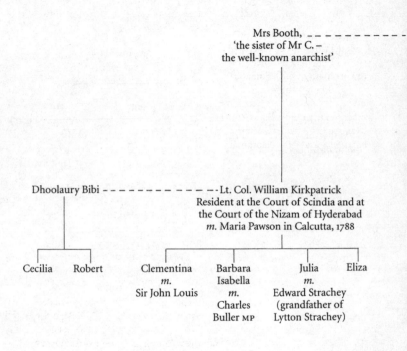

Mrs Booth, _ _ _ _ _ _ _ _ _ _
'the sister of Mr C. –
the well-known anarchist'

Dhoolaury Bibi – – – – – – – – – – –Lt. Col. William Kirkpatrick
Resident at the Court of Scindia and at
the Court of the Nizam of Hyderabad
m. Maria Pawson in Calcutta, 1788

| Cecilia | Robert | | Clementina | Barbara | | Julia | Eliza |

Cecilia   Robert

Clementina
m.
Sir John Louis

Barbara
Isabella
m.
Charles
Buller MP

Julia
m.
Edward Strachey
(grandfather of
Lytton Strachey)

Eliza

James Kirkpatrick, MD
author of *Putrifaction*
1701–1770
m.
Creole Lady from Georgia
|
– – – – – – Col. James Kirkpatrick
'the Handsome Colonel'
Commander in Chief
of Fort Marlborough, Sumatra
1729–1818
m.
Katherine Munro in Madras, 1762
(daughter of Dr Andrew Munro,
founder of the Madras Hospital)

George Kirkpatrick
1763–1838
m.
Eleanor Metcalfe

Major James Achilles Kirkpatrick – – – – 'The
1764–1805   Dark Girl'
Resident at the Court of the
Nizam of Hyderabad, 1798–1805
m.
Begum Khair un-Nissa, 1800

Mir Ghulam Ali,   Noor un-Nissa,   'The
Sahib Allum   Sahib Begum   Hindoostanee
1801–1828   1802–1889   Boy'
after 1805 known as   after 1805 known as
William George   Katherine Aurora
Kirkpatrick   (Kitty) Kirkpatrick
                         m. 1829
                         Captain James
                         Winslowe Phillipps
                         7th Hussars
                         |
                         2 boys, 5 girls

DRAMATIS PERSONAE

1. THE BRITISH

THE KIRKPATRICKS

Colonel James Kirkpatrick ('The Handsome Colonel', 1729–1818): *The raffish father of William, George and James Achilles. A former colonel in the East India Company army, at the time of James's affair he had retired to Hollydale, his estate in Kent.*

Lieutenant Colonel William Kirkpatrick (1756–1812): *Persian scholar, linguist and opium addict; former Resident at Hyderabad and in 1800 Military Secretary and chief political adviser to Lord Wellesley; illegitimate half-brother of James Achilles Kirkpatrick.*

George Kirkpatrick (1763–1818): *James's elder brother, known as 'Good honest George'. A pious and humourless man, he failed to make a success of his career in India and never rose higher than the position of a minor Collector of taxes in Malabar.*

Major James Achilles Kirkpatrick (1764–1805): *Known in Hyderabad as Hushmut Jung – 'Glorious in Battle' – Nawab Fakhr-ud-Dowla Bahadur; the thoroughly Orientalised British Resident at the Court of Hyderabad.*

William George Kirkpatrick (1801–1828): *Known in Hyderabad as Mir Ghulam Ali, Sahib Allum. After arriving in England, he fell into 'a copper of boiling water' in 1812 and was disabled for life, with at least one of his limbs requiring amputation. He lingered on, a dreamy, disabled poet, obsessed with Wordsworth and the metaphysics of Coleridge, before dying at the age of twenty-seven.*

Katherine Aurora Kirkpatrick (1802–89): *Known as Noor un-Nissa, Sahib Begum in Hyderabad and subsequently as Kitty Kirkpatrick in England;*

daughter of James and Khair un-Nissa; sent to England 1805; married Captain James Winslowe Phillipps of the 7th Hussars on 21 November 1829; died in Torquay in 1889 at the age of eighty-seven.

THE WELLESLEYS

Richard Colley Wellesley, Marquess Wellesley (1760–1842): *Governor General of India. Originally a great hero of James Kirkpatrick, his bullying imperial policies came to disgust James and led him to resist with increasing vigour the Company's attempts to take over the Deccan.*

Colonel Arthur Wellesley (1769–1852): *Governor of Mysore and 'Chief Political and Military Officer in the Deccan and Southern Maratha Country'. Greatly disliked the Kirkpatrick brothers. Later famous as the Duke of Wellington.*

Henry Wellesley (1773–1847): *Assistant to his brother the Governor General, and Governor of the Ceded Districts of Avadh.*

THE PALMERS

General William Palmer (d.1814): *Friend of Warren Hastings and James Achilles Kirkpatrick, and Resident at Poona until he was sacked by Wellesley. Married Fyze Baksh Begum, a begum of Oudh. Father of William, John and Hastings.*

Fyze Baksh, Begum Palmer (aka Sahib Begum, c.1760–1820): *Daughter of 'a Persian Colonel of Cavalry' in the service of the Nawabs of Oudh. Her sister Nur Begum was married to General Benoît de Boigne. Fyze married General Palmer and had four sons and two daughters by him, including William Palmer the banker, whom she lived with in Hyderabad after the General's death. Best friend of Khair un-Nissa: when the latter died, she locked herself up for a month, saying 'she had lost the only real friend she ever had'.*

John Palmer (1767–1836): *'The Prince of Merchants'. General Palmer's son by his first wife Sarah Hazell.*

Captain William Palmer (1780–1867): *Son of General Palmer by Fyze Palmer. Initially James Kirkpatrick found him a job in the Nizam's service, where he wrote a letter to Wellesley criticising the Governor General's treatment of James under the* nom de plume *Philothetes.*

William subsequently became a powerful banker in Hyderabad, before suffering a catastrophic bankruptcy.

THE RUSSELLS

Sir Henry Russell (1751–1836): *Chief Justice of Bengal and father of Henry and Charles.*

Henry Russell (1783–1852): *Kirkpatrick's Private Secretary and assistant. Later a lover of the Begum.*

Charles Russell: *Commander of the Resident's bodyguard and obedient younger brother to Henry.*

THE RESIDENCY STAFF

Captain William Hemming: *Commander of the Resident's bodyguard. Named by Henry Russell as the principal enemy of James in the Residency.*

Samuel Russell: *'The Engineer'. Son of Academician John Russell, and no relation to Henry and Charles. Briefly the Nizam's engineer, he helped James finish the Residency.*

Thomas Sydenham: *Secretary to the Resident. James came to distrust him, and called him 'Pontifex Maximus'. On James's death he became Resident, attempting to weed out James's 'Mughalisation' of the Residency, and sacking many of James's key staff.*

Munshi Aziz Ullah, Munshi Aman Ullah: *Two highly educated brothers from Delhi who became James's trusted* munshis.

Dr George Ure: *Surgeon to the Residency.*

Mrs Ure: *Wife of Dr Ure and a fluent Urdu speaker, she was a vast woman with an apparently unquenchable appetite. She accompanied James's children to England in 1805.*

THE SUBSIDIARY FORCE

Lieutenant Colonel James Dalrymple (1757–1800): *Commander of the Subsidiary Force.*

Lieutenant Colonel Samuel Dalrymple: *Cousin of James Dalrymple and friend of Henry Russell. Was on board ship with James Kirkpatrick on his final journey. His wife Margaret was generally regarded as 'odious'.*

Dr Alexander Kennedy: *The Subsidiary Force doctor.*

OTHER MISCELLANEOUS BRITISH

Edward, Lord Clive (1754–1839): *Son of Robert Clive ('Clive of India'), he was the notably unintelligent Governor of Madras.*

Mountstuart Elphinstone (1779–1859): *Traveller and East India Company civil servant who rose to be Governor of Bombay; visited Hyderabad with Edward Strachey in August/September 1801 en route to a position in Pune.*

Edward Strachey (1774–1832): *Traveller and civil servant; visited Hyderabad with Mountstuart Elphinstone in August/September 1801 en route to a position in Pune. In 1808 he married Julia, the youngest and prettiest daughter of William Kirkpatrick.*

2. THE FRENCH

Michel Joachim Marie Raymond (1755–98): *Mercenary commander of the French Battalion in Hyderabad.*

Jean-Pierre Piron: *Raymond's successor.*

3. THE HYDERABADIS

THE NIZAM'S FAMILY

Nawab Mir Nizam Ali Khan, Asaf Jah II (1761–1803): *Nizam of Hyderabad, father of Sikander Jah. The fourth son of the first Nizam, Nizam ul-Mulk, he succeeded his father having dethroned and imprisoned his brother Salabat Jung.*

Bakshi Begum: *First wife of Nizam Ali Khan and adoptive mother of*

Sikander Jah. *Very powerful: 'in charge of the Privy Purse and control of all Mahal disbursements'. In 1800 was considered 'elderly'.*

Tïnat un-Nissa Begum: *Wife of Nizam Ali Khan and mother of Sikander Jah. Also old and powerful: according to James Kirkpatrick she had custody over the family jewels.*

Ali Jah (d.1798): *Son of Nizam Ali Khan who rebelled in 1798. Ali Jah surrendered near Bidar to Mir Alam and General Raymond, and shortly afterwards 'committed suicide' in somewhat suspicious circumstances.*

Dara Jah: *Son-in-law of Nizam Ali Khan who revolted against him in 1796. Dara Jah was recaptured by James Dalrymple at Raichur and returned to Hyderabad, where he subsequently disappears from the record.*

Nawab Mir Akbar Ali Khan, Sikander Jah, Asaf Jah III (1771–1829): *Nizam of Hyderabad; only surviving son of Nizam Ali Khan.*

Jahan Pawar Begum: *Also known as Hajji Begum. Daughter of Ma'ali Mian and Farzand Begum, granddaughter of Aristu Jah from whom she inherited Purani Haveli, and wife of Nizam Sikander Jah. Mistreated by Sikander Jah, she warned James of Sikander Jah's plan to assassinate him.*

Mama Barun, Mama Champa: *Aseels at the court and the principal attendants at the durbar of Nizam Ali Khan. Also commanded the female regiment – the Zuffur Plutun – at the Battle of Khardla.*

ARISTU JAH'S HOUSEHOLD

Ghulam Sayyed Khan, Aristu Jah, Azim ul Omrah (d.9 May 1804): *The Nizam's Minister, dubbed 'Solomon' by the Kirkpatrick brothers. Started his career as* qiladar *(fortress-keeper) in Aurangabad, and after the assassination of Minister Rukn-ud-Dowlah became First Assistant Minister, then Minister. Following the defeat at Khardla, he was sent in March 1795 as a hostage to Pune. After his return in 1797 he resumed office, a position he held until his death in 1804. His granddaughter Jahan Pawar Begum married Nizam Sikander Jah.*

Sarwar Afza, Nawab Begum: *Aristu Jah's chief wife. Mir Alam plundered her of all her property after the death of her husband.*

Ma'ali Mian: *Son of Aristu Jah; died young in 1795 on the Khardla campaign.*

Farzand Begum: *Sister of Munir ul-Mulk and the Minister's daughter-in-law, married to Ma'ali Mian, and close friend of Sharaf un-Nissa. According to some sources she put pressure on Sharaf un-Nissa to marry Khair to James Kirkpatrick.*

THE SHUSHTARIS

Sayyid Reza Shushtari (d.1780): *Shi'a divine who travelled from Shushtar first to Mughal Delhi then to Hyderabad, where he was given land by Nizam ul-Mulk. Sayyid Reza 'refused all public office, even the post of Chief Judge', retiring to a life of prayer. His reputation for integrity was the foundation upon which his son, Mir Alam, and so the rest of the Shushtari clan, rose to power in Hyderabad.*

Mir Abul Qasim, Mir Alam Bahadur (d.8 December 1808): *Aristu Jah's vakil and representative of the Nizam in Calcutta; led the Nizam's army on the Seringapatam campaign (1799); exiled in 1800; restored to favour and made Prime Minister in July 1804 to succeed Aristu Jah; first cousin of Bâqar Ali Khan. Until his death from leprosy in 1808 he was in receipt of a pension from the British government of two thousand rupees a month.*

Mir Dauran (d.1801): *Son of Mir Alam. Died of leprosy in 1801.*

Mir Abdul Lateef Shushtari: *Cousin and colleague of Mir Alam. His representative at the court after Mir Alam's disgrace. Author of the Tuhfat al-'Alam.*

Bâqar Ali Khan, Akil ud-Daula: *A native of Shushtar in Iran. First cousin of Mir Alam: he was the son of the sister of Mir Alam's father. Accompanied Mir Alam on his embassy to Calcutta. Later became the* bakshi *or Paymaster of the Subsidiary Force, in which capacity he accompanied the Subsidiary Force to Seringapatam; father of Sharaf un-Nissa and grandfather of Khair un-Nissa. Following Khair's marriage to James, Aristu Jah 'exalted the head' of Bâqar Ali Khan, 'awarding him a title and an estate consisting of some villages'. Said to be defective in sight and hard of hearing.*

Durdanah Begum: *Wife of Bâqar Ali Khan, mother of Sharaf un-Nissa, grandmother of Khair un-Nissa. From the family of Mir Jafar Ali Khan.*

Sharaf un-Nissa Begum (c.1765–21 July 1847): *Daughter of Bâqar Ali*

Khan; mother of Khair un-Nissa, and much younger second wife of Mehdi Yar Khan, who died in the late 1780s or 1790s, leaving her a widow with two unmarried teenage daughters, after which she returned to her family deorhi. Following Khair's marriage to James, she was given an estate by the government 'and maintained it herself'. In her old age her estates were confiscated and she died in poverty.

Mehdi Yar Khan: Son of Mirza Qasim Khan; father of Khair un-Nissa; husband of Sharaf un-Nissa. Died sometime in the late 1780s or 1790s leaving his much younger widow with two unmarried teenage daughters.

Khair un-Nissa Begum: The daughter of Sharaf un-Nissa and granddaughter of Bâqar Ali Khan; wife of James Achilles Kirkpatrick. She was originally engaged to Mohammed Ali Khan, son of Bahram ul-Mulk.

Nazir un-Nissa Begum: Sister of Khair un-Nissa.

Dustee Ali Khan: Half-brother of Khair un-Nissa and son of Mehdi Yar Khan by an earlier wife.

OTHER HYDERABADI OMRAHS

Rajah Ragotim Rai: Brahmin nobleman in the circle of Aristu Jah. James disliked him: 'This enormous vulture must be got rid of somehow.' Sacked and plundered by Mir Alam after the death of Aristu Jah.

Rajah Chandu Lal: Protégé first of James then of Mir Alam, whom he succeeded in power. Long-time diwan of Nizam Sikander Jah, he was responsible for confiscating the estates of Sharaf un-Nissa. Great patron of poetry.

Mah Laqa Bai Chanda: Poet, historian and courtesan, initially attached to the durbar of Aristu Jah. Became the lover of both Mir Alam and Mustaqim ud-Daula.

4. LONDON, 1820

Charles Buller MP, Barbara Isabella Buller: William Kirkpatrick's daughter and son-in-law. James died in their house in Calcutta; later it was at their house that Kitty met the young Thomas Carlyle.

Julia Kirkpatrick: *Daughter of William Kirkpatrick, wife of Edward Strachey, friend and cousin of Kitty Kirkpatrick.*

Thomas Carlyle (1795–1881): *Savant; tutor to the sons of Charles Buller, in whose Calcutta house James died.*

DYNASTIC LISTS

THE NIZAMS OF HYDERABAD
Nizam ul-Mulk 1724–48

Civil war 1748–62

Nizam Ali Khan 1762–1803

Nizam Sikander Jah 1803–29

Nizam Nasir ud-Daula 1829–57

MINISTERS
Aristu Jah 1778–1804

Mir Alam 1804–08

Munir ul-Mulk 1809–32

Rajah Chandu Lal 1832–43

BRITISH RESIDENTS
John Kennaway 1788–94

William Kirkpatrick 1794–98

James Achilles Kirkpatrick 1798–1805

Henry Russell (Acting) October–December 1805

Thomas Sydenham 1805–1810

Charles Russell (Acting) June 1810–March 1811

Henry Russell December 1811–1820

Sir Charles Metcalfe 1820–1825

GOVERNORS GENERAL
Warren Hastings 1774–85

Marquis Cornwallis 1786–93

Sir John Shore (Acting) 1793–98

Lord Wellesley 1798–1805

Marquis Cornwallis (again) 1805

George Barlow (Acting) 1805–07

Lord Minto 1807–13

ACKNOWLEDGEMENTS

I began work on this book in the spring of 1997. Over the five years – and many thousands of miles of travel – since then, innumerable people have been incredibly generous with their hospitality, time, expertise, advice, wisdom, pictures, editing skills, bottles of whisky, family papers, camp beds and cups of tea. They range from the nameless Sufi in a tomb in Bijapur who was kind enough to wave a peacock fan over me while I sat writing notes in the shade of his shrine, through to the best Biryani cook in Hyderabad (he's called Salim and you can find him in the *dhaba* facing the Chowk Masjid), to the old shepherd in Bidar who led me up a cliff face to show me the best view of the necropolis of Ashtur. Then of course there are the historians who explained the intricacies of Company, Maratha or Nizami politics, and the large number of very patient librarians in India and Britain who put up with my incessant manuscript queries. Perhaps most important of all, I should mention the descendants of James Achilles and Khair un-Nissa Kirkpatrick who, while choosing to remain anonymous, let me have unconditional access to their unique archive.

I would also like to thank the following by name:

In the UK: Bob Alderman, Charles Allen, Chris Bayly, Mark Bence-Jones, Richard Bingle, Richard Blurton, Jonathan Bond, Anne Buddle, Brendan Carnduff, Lizzie Collingham, Patrick Conner, Jeremy Currie, Jock Dalrymple, Philip Davies, Simon Digby, Alanna Dowling, Jenny Fraser, Sven Gahlin, Nile Green, Charles Grieg, Christopher Hawes, Amin Jaffer, Rosie Llewellyn Jones, Wak Kani, Paul Levy, Jerry Losty, John Malcolm, Sejal Mandalia, Peter Marshall, Gopali Mulji, Doris Nicholson, Henry Noltie, Alex Palmer, Iris Portal, Kathy Prior, Addie Ridge, Mian Ridge, Mahpara Safdar, Narindar Saroop, Ziaduddin Shakeb, Nick Shreeve, Robert Skelton, Fania Stoney, Allegra Stratton, Susan Stronge, Fariba Thomson, David and Leslie Vaughan, Philippa Vaughan, Brigid Waddams, Lucy Warrack, Theon Wilkinson, Amina Yaqin and the late Mark Zebrowski. Particular thanks are due to Mary-Anne Denison-Pender of the wonderful Western & Oriental Travel, who covered much of the cost of my various peregrinations around the Deccan, and also to the Scottish Arts Council whose generous travel grant covered a long research trip to the Delhi National Archives.

In the US: Indrani Chatterjee, Sabrina Dhawan, Michael Fisher, Bob Frykenberg, Durba Ghosh, Navina Haidar, Ali Akbar Husain, Maya Jasanoff, Omar Khalidi, Elbrun Kimmelman, Karen Leonard, Nabil Matar, Gail Minault, Eleni Phillon, Robert Travers, Sylvia Vatuk, Stuart Cary Welch and Peter Wood.

In India: Javed Abdulla, Mohamed Bafana, Rohit Kumar Bakshi, Pablo Bartholomew, V.K. Bawa, Vijay Shankar Dass, John Fritz, S. Gautam, Zeb un-Nissa Haidar, Elahe Hiptoola, Princess Esra Jah, Mir Moazam Husain, S. Asmath Jehan, Bashir Yar Jung, J. Kedareswari, A.R. Khaleel, Nawab Abid Hussain Khan, Pradip Krishen, Jean-Marie Lafont, Narendra Luther, George Michell, Jagdish Mittal, Sarojini Regani, Arundhati Roy, Laeeq Salah and Prita Trehan. I would especially like to thank Bilkiz Alladin for her generosity in sharing her Khair un-Nissa research, and also Nausheen and Yunus Jaffery for their help with Persian and Urdu sources.

David Godwin and Giles Gordon both worked incredibly hard in pushing this book forward. For their energy and enthusiasm many, many thanks. My different publishers have all been full of good advice – Robert Lacey, Helen Ellis, Arabella Pike and Aisha Rahman at HarperCollins; Ray Roberts and Paul Slovak at Penguin Putnam; David Davidar at Penguin India; Paolo Zaninoni at Rizzoli. Most of all I would like to thank Michael Fishwick, who has been as frank, funny, generous and wise in his guidance with this, our fifth book together, as he was with our first, *In Xanadu*, which he took on some sixteen years ago now.

Olivia has, I think, found living in a *ménage à trois* with Khair un-Nissa a little more trying than she did previous cohabitations with Byzantine ascetics, taxi-stands full of Sikh drivers and the courtiers of Kubla Khan, but she has borne the five-year-long ordeal with characteristic gentleness and generosity. To her – and to Ibby, Sam and Adam – a million thanks and much, much love yet again.

I would like to dedicate this book to Sam and Shireen Vakil Miller for their constant affection and friendship, first in Delhi and then in London, over the course of more than a decade; and to Bruce Wannell whose incredibly wide-ranging scholarship and wonderful translations from the Persian have done more than anything else to make this book quite as unfeasibly long as it is.

WILLIAM DALRYMPLE
Page's Yard, 1 July 2002

The British Residency complex that James Achilles Kirkpatrick built in Hyderabad, now the Osmania Women's College, is recognised as one of the most important colonial buildings in India, but its fabric is in very bad shape and it was recently placed on the World Monuments Fund's list of One Hundred Most Endangered Buildings. A non-profit-making trust has now been set up to fund conservation efforts. Anyone who would like more information, or to make a donation, should contact Friends of Osmania Women's College, India, Inc., a tax-exempt 501(c)3 not-for-profit organisation aimed at restoring the Osmania/British Residency buildings and site:

800 Third Avenue, Suite 3100
New York, NY 10022
Telephone: (00 1) 212/223 7313
Facsimile: (00 1) 212/223 8212
E-mail: osmaniafoundation@hotmail.com
Donations may be sent by wire to:
Bank of New York
530 Fifth Avenue, New York, NY 10036
ABA #: 021-000018 Account #: 630-1601059
In the name of: Friends of Osmania Women's College, India, Inc.

INTRODUCTION

I FIRST HEARD ABOUT James Achilles Kirkpatrick on a visit to Hyderabad in February 1997.

It was the middle of Muharram, the Shi'a festival commemorating the martyrdom of Hussain, the grandson of the Prophet. I had just finished a book on the monasteries of the Middle East, four years' work, and was burnt out. I came to Hyderabad to get away from my desk and my overflowing bookshelves, to relax, to go off on a whim, to travel aimlessly again.

It was spring. The stones of the mosques were warm underfoot, and I wandered through the shrines of the old city, filled now with black-robed Muharram mourners reciting sinuous Urdu laments for the tragedy of Kerbala. It was as if Hussain had been killed a week earlier, not in the late seventh century AD. This was the sort of Indian city I loved.

It was, moreover, a relatively unexplored and unwritten place, at least in English; and a secretive one too. Unlike the immediate, monumental splendour of Agra or the Rajput city states of the north, Hyderabad hid its charms from the eyes of outsiders, veiling its splendours from curious eyes behind nondescript walls and labyrinthine backstreets. Only slowly did it allow you in to an enclosed world where water still dripped from fountains, flowers bent in the breeze, and peacocks called from the overladen mango trees. There, hidden from the streets, was a world of timelessness and calm, a last bastion of gently fading Indo-Islamic civilisation where, as one art historian has put it, old 'Hyderabadi gentlemen still wore the fez, dreamt about the rose and the nightingale, and mourned the loss of Grenada'.[1]

From the old city, I drove out to see the craggy citadel of Golconda. For six hundred years Golconda was the storehouse of the apparently ceaseless stream of diamonds that emerged from the mines of the region, the only known source of these most precious of stones until the discovery of the New World mines in the eighteenth century. Inside the walls you passed a succession of harems and bathing pools, pavilions and pleasure gardens. When the French jeweller Jean-Baptiste Tavernier visited Golconda in 1642 he found a society every bit as wealthy and effete as this architecture might suggest. He wrote that the town possessed more than twenty thousand registered courtesans, who took it in turns to dance for the Sultan every Friday.

This richly romantic and courtly atmosphere had, I soon discovered, infected even the sober British when they arrived in Hyderabad at the end of the eighteenth century. The old British Residency, now the Osmania University College for Women, was a vast Palladian villa, in plan not unlike its exact contemporary, the White House in Washington. It was one of the most perfect buildings ever erected by the East India Company, and lay in a massive fortified garden just over the River Musi from the old city.

The complex, I was told, was built by Lieutenant Colonel James Achilles Kirkpatrick, the British Resident – effectively Ambassador – at the court of Hyderabad between 1797 and 1805. Kirkpatrick had apparently adopted Hyderabadi clothes and Hyderabadi ways of living. Shortly after arriving in the town, so the story went, he fell in love with the great-niece of the *diwan* (Prime Minister) of Hyderabad. He married Khair un-Nissa – which means 'Most Excellent Among Women' – in 1800, according to Muslim law.

Inside the old Residency building, I found plaster falling in chunks the size of palanquins from the ceiling of the former ballroom and durbar hall. Upstairs the old bedrooms were badly decayed. They were now empty and deserted, frequented only by bats and the occasional pair of amorous pigeons; downstairs the elegant oval saloons were partitioned by hardboard divides into tatty cubicles for the college administrators. As the central block of the house was deemed too dangerous for the students, most of the classes now took place in the old elephant stables at the back.

Even in this state of semi-ruination it was easy to see how magnificent the Residency had once been. It had a grand, domed semi-circular bay on the south front, reached through a great triumphal

arch facing the bridge over the Musi. On the north front a pair
of British lions lay, paws extended, below a huge pedimented and
colonnaded front. They looked out over a wide expanse of eucalyptus,
mulsarry and casuarina trees, every inch the East India Company at
its grandest and most formal. Yet surprises lurked in the undergrowth
at the rear of the compound.

Here I was shown a battered token of Kirkpatrick's love for his
wife in the garden at the back of the Residency. The tale – apocryphal,
I presumed, but charming nonetheless – went as follows: that as
Khair un-Nissa remained all her life in strict purdah, living in a
separate *bibi-ghar* (literally 'women's house') at the end of Kirkpatrick's garden, she was unable to walk around the side of her
husband's great creation to admire its wonderful portico. Eventually
the Resident hit upon a solution and built a scaled-down plaster
model of his new palace for her so that she could examine in detail
what she would never allow herself to see with her own eyes. Whatever
the truth of the story, the model had survived intact until the 1980s
when a tree fell on it, smashing the right wing. The remains of the
left wing and central block lay under a piece of corrugated iron, near
the ruins of the Mughal *bibi-ghar*, buried deep beneath a jungle of
vines and creepers in the area still known as the Begum's Garden. I
thought it was the most lovely story, and by the time I left the garden
I was captivated, and wanted to know more. The whole tale simply
seemed so different from – and so much more romantic than – what
one expected of the British in India, and I spent the rest of my
time in Hyderabad pursuing anyone who could tell me more about
Kirkpatrick.

I did not have to look far. Dr Zeb un-Nissa Haidar was an elderly
Persian scholar who taught her veiled women students in one of the
less ruinous wings of the old Residency. Dr Zeb explained that she
was a descendant of Rukn ud-Daula, a Hyderabadi Prime Minister
of the period. She said she was familiar not only with the outlines
of the story but with many of the contemporary Persian and Urdu
sources which mentioned it.

According to Dr Zeb, these Hyderabadi sources were explicit about
the fact that Kirkpatrick had converted to Islam to marry his bride.

They also mentioned that despite the scandal Kirkpatrick had been very popular in Hyderabad, mixing freely with the people, and taking on the manners of the city. Dr Zeb remembered one sentence in particular from a history called the *Tarikh i-Khurshid Jahi:* 'by an excess of the company of the ladies of the country he was very familiar with the style and behaviour of Hyderabad and adopted it himself'. Several of the Persian sources also hinted that, by the end, Kirkpatrick's political allegiances had lain as much with the Nizam, or ruler, of Hyderabad as with the British. None of these sources had ever been translated into English, and so were virgin territory for those unfamiliar with either nineteenth-century Deccani Urdu or the heavily Indianised Persian that the manuscripts were written in – which meant virtually everyone bar a handful of elderly Hyderabadi Islamic scholars.

One night I visited the tomb of Kirkpatrick's great rival, General Michel Joachim Raymond. Raymond was a Republican French mercenary in the service of the Nizam who had, like Kirkpatrick, adopted the ways of Hyderabad. Just as Kirkpatrick's job was to try to ease the Hyderabadis towards the British, Raymond had tried to persuade the Nizam to ally with the French. After his death, he was buried next to an obelisk, under a small classical Greek temple on the hilltop above the French cantonments beyond the city, at Malakhpet.

While Raymond had definitely abandoned Christianity – something that seemed to be confirmed by the absence of any Christian references or imagery on his tomb – his Hyderabadi admirers were uncertain whether he had turned Hindu or Muslim. His Hindu sepoys Sanskritised the name Monsieur Raymond to Musa Ram, while his Muslims knew him as Musa Rahim, Rahim being the personification of the merciful aspect of Allah. The Nizam, who was as uncertain as everyone else, decided to mark the anniversary of Raymond's death on 25 March in a religiously neutral way by sending to his monument a box of cheroots and a bottle of beer. The custom had apparently survived until the last Nizam left for Australia after Independence; but as I happened to be in Hyderabad on the date of his anniversary I was intrigued to see if any memory of Raymond had survived.

Raymond's monument was originally built on a deserted moun-
taintop several miles outside the walls of Hyderabad. But the recent
rapid growth that has turned Hyderabad into India's fourth-largest
city has encroached all around the site, so that only the very top of
the hill around the monument is now empty of new bungalows and
housing estates. I left my taxi at the roadhead and climbed up towards
the temple. It was clearly silhouetted against the sulphur-red of the
city's night sky. As I walked I saw shadows flitting between the pillars,
vague shapes which resolved themselves as I drew closer into the
figures of devotees lighting clay lamps at the shrine at the back of the
temple. Maybe the figures saw me coming; whatever the reason, they
had vanished by the time I reached the monument, leaving their offerings behind on the tomb: a few coconuts, some incense sticks, some
strings of garlands and a few small pyramids of sweet white *prasad*.

Back in London, I searched around for more about Kirkpatrick. A
couple of books on Raj architecture contained a passing reference to
his Residency and the existence of his Begum, but there was little
detail, and what there was seemed to derive from an 1893 article in
Blackwood's Magazine, 'The Romantic Marriage of James Achilles
Kirkpatrick', written by Kirkpatrick's kinsman Edward Strachey.[2]

My first real break came when I found that Kirkpatrick's correspondence with his brother William, preserved by the latter's
descendants the Strachey family, had recently been bought by the
India Office Library.* There were piles of letter books inscribed 'From
my brother James Achilles Kirkpatrick' (the paper within all polished
and frail with age), great gilt leather-bound volumes of official
correspondence with the Governor General, Lord Wellesley, bundles

* The India Office Library originally comprised the library and records of the East India
Company. It later became the library of the British government's India Office, and is
now a separate annexe of the British Library in London.

of Persian manuscripts, some boxes of receipts and, in a big buff envelope, a will – exactly the sort of random yet detailed detritus of everyday lives that biographers dream of turning up.

At first, however, many of the letters seemed disappointingly mundane: gossip about court politics, requests for information from Calcutta, the occasional plea for a crate of Madeira or the sort of vegetables Kirkpatrick found unavailable in the Hyderabad bazaars, such as – surprisingly – potatoes and peas. This was interesting enough, but initially seemed relatively unremarkable, and I found maddeningly few references either to Kirkpatrick's religious feelings or to his personal affairs. Moreover, much of the more interesting material was in cipher. No sooner did Kirkpatrick begin to talk about his amorous adventures, or the espionage network he was involved in setting up, than the clear and steady penmanship would dissolve into long lines of incomprehensible numbers.

It was only after several weeks of reading that I finally came to the files that contained the Khair un-Nissa letters, and some of these, it turned out, were not encoded. One day, as I opened yet another India Office cardboard folder, my eyes fell on the following paragraph written in a small, firm, sloping hand:

> By way of Prelude it may not be amiss to observe that I did once *safely* pass the firey ordeal of a long nocturnal interview with the charming subject of the present letter – It was this interview which I alluded to as the one when I had full and close survey of her lovely Person – it lasted during the greatest part of the night and was evidently *contrived* by the Grand-mother and mother whose very existence hang on hers to indulge her uncontrollable wishes. At this meeting, which was under my roof, I contrived to command myself so far as to abstain from the tempting feast I was manifestly invited to, and though God knows I was but ill qualified for the task, I attempted to argue the Romantic Young Creature out of a passion which I could not, I confess, help feeling myself some-thing more than pity for. She declared to me again and again that her affections had been irrevocably fixed on me for a series of time, that her fate was linked to mine and that she

should be content to pass her days with me as the humblest
of handmaids . . .

Soon after this I found some pages of cipher which had been
overwritten with a 'translation', and the code turned out to be a
simple one-letter/one-number correspondence. Once this was solved,
the whole story quickly began to come together.

I had one more major break when I stumbled across a secret East
India Company Enquiry into the affair, with sworn testimony taken
from witnesses and detailed, explicit questions getting astonishingly
frank and uninhibited answers; as I held the Enquiry in my hands
any lingering doubts I had disappeared: there was wonderful material
here for a book.

For four years I beavered away in the India Office Library, returning
to Delhi and Hyderabad occasionally to examine the archives there.
Inevitably, in India there were problems. In Delhi, in the vaults of the
Indian National Archives, someone installing a new air-conditioning
system had absent-mindedly left out in the open all six hundred volumes of the Hyderabad Residency Records. It was the monsoon. By the
time I came back for a second look at the records the following year,
most were irretrievably wrecked, and those that were not waterlogged
were covered with thick green mould. After a couple of days a decision
was taken that the mould was dangerous, and all six hundred volumes
were sent off 'for fumigation'. I never saw them again.

That same monsoon, the River Musi flooded in Hyderabad and the
BBC showed scenes of archivists in the old city hanging up to dry on
washing lines what remained of their fine collection of manuscripts.

Gradually, despite such setbacks, the love story began to take shape.
It was like watching a Polaroid develop, as the outlines slowly
established themselves and the colour began to fill in the remaining
white spaces.

There were some moments of pure revelation too. On the last day
of my final visit to Hyderabad, after three trips and several months in
the different archives, I spent the afternoon looking for presents in the
bazaars of the old city behind the Char Minar. It was a Sunday, and the
Chowk was half-closed. But I had forgotten to buy anything for my

family, and with my eye on my watch, as the plane to Delhi was due to take off in only five hours' time, I frantically trailed from shop to shop, looking for someone who could sell me some of Hyderabad's great speciality: decorated Bidri metalwork. Eventually a boy offered to take me to a shop where he said I could find a Bidri box. He led me deep into the labyrinth behind the Chowk Masjid. There, down a small alley, lay a shop where he promised I would find 'booxies booxies'.

The shop did not in fact sell boxes, but books (or 'booksies', as my guide had been trying to tell me). Or rather, not so much books as Urdu and Persian manuscripts and very rare printed chronicles. These the proprietor had bought up from private Hyderabadi libraries when the great aristocratic city palaces were being stripped and bulldozed throughout the sixties and seventies. They now lay stacked from floor to ceiling in a dusty, ill-lit shop the size of a large broom-cupboard. More remarkably still, the bookseller knew exactly what he had. When I told him what I was writing he produced from under a stack a huge, crumbling Persian book, the *Kitab Tuhfat al-'Alam*, by Abdul Lateef Shushtari, a name I already knew well from James Kirkpatrick's letters. The book turned out to be a fascinating six-hundred-page autobiography by Khair un-Nissa's first cousin, written in Hyderabad in the immediate aftermath of the scandal of her marriage to James. There were other manuscripts too, including a very rare Hyderabadi history of the period, the *Gulzar i-Asafiya*. I spent the rest of the afternoon haggling with the owner, and left his shop £400 poorer, but with a trunkload of previously untranslated primary sources. Their contents completely transformed what follows.*

---

* It is one of the quirks of modern Indian historiography that the Deccan remains still largely unstudied: little serious work has been done on any of the Deccani courts, and this remains especially true of its cultural history: Deccani paintings are still routinely misattributed to the Mughal or Rajput *ateliers*. In an age when every minute contour of the landscape of history appears to be rigorously mapped out by a gridiron of scholarly Ph.D.s, this huge gap is all the more remarkable. The history of Hyderabad and the wider Deccan remains a major lacuna: for every book on the Deccan sultanates, there are a hundred on the Mughals; for every book on Hyderabad there is a shelf of Lucknow. As the historian George Michell recently noted in the introduction to a Deccani volume of *The New Cambridge History of India*, 'few scholars, Indian or foreign, have worked extensively in the Deccan, which remains little visited and surprisingly unexplored'. See George Michell and Mark Zebrowski, *The New Cambridge History of India 1.7: Architecture and Art of the Deccan Sultanates* (Cambridge, 1999).

By 2001, four years into the research, I thought I knew Kirkpatrick so well I imagined that I heard his voice in my head as I read and reread his letters. Yet there still remained important gaps. In particular, the documents in the India Office gave no more hint than the original article in the 1893 *Blackwood's Magazine* as to what had happened to Khair un-Nissa after Kirkpatrick's death. It took another nine months of searching before I stumbled across the heartbreaking answer to that, in the Henry Russell papers in the Bodleian Library in Oxford. The tale – which had never been told, and seemed to be unknown even to Kirkpatrick's contemporaries – bore a striking resemblance to *Madame Butterfly*. Day after day, under the armorial shields and dark oak bookcases of the Duke Humfrey's Library, I tore as quickly as I could through the faded pages of Russell's often illegible copperplate correspondence, the tragic love story slowly unfolding fully-formed before me.

Finally, only a few months before I began writing, family papers belonging to the great-great-great-grandson of Kirkpatrick and Khair un-Nissa turned up a couple of miles from my home in West London. This extended the story through to the no less remarkable tale of Khair un-Nissa's daughter, Kitty Kirkpatrick. She had initially been brought up as Sahib Begum, a Muslim noblewoman in Hyderabad, before being shipped off to England at four years old, baptised on her arrival in London and thenceforth completely cut off from her maternal relations. Instead she had been absorbed into the upper echelons of Victorian literary society, where she had fascinated her cousins' tutor, the young Thomas Carlyle, and formed the basis for the heroine Blumine, 'a many tinted radiant Aurora ... the fairest of Oriental light-bringers', in Carlyle's novel *Sartor Resartus*.

This last set of family papers told the story of the series of remarkable coincidences which brought Kitty, as an adult, back into contact with her Hyderabadi grandmother, and the emotional correspondence which reunited the two women after a gap of nearly forty years. They were letters of great beauty and intense sadness as the story emerged of lives divided by prejudice and misunderstanding, politics and fate. One wrote in English from a seaside villa in Torquay; the other replied from a Hyderabadi harem, dictating in Persian to a scribe who wrote on paper sprinkled with gold dust and enclosed the letter in a Mughal *kharita*, a sealed gold brocade bag. Her grandmother's letters revealed to Kitty the secret of how her parents had met and fallen in love, and led to her discovering for herself the sad truth of Khair un-Nissa's fate.

The story of a family where three generations drifted between Christianity and Islam and back again, between suits and *salvars*, Mughal Hyderabad and Regency London, seemed to raise huge questions: about Britishness and the nature of Empire, about faith, and about personal identity; indeed, about how far all of these mattered, and were fixed and immutable – or how far they were in fact flexible, tractable, negotiable. For once it seemed that the normal steely dualism of Empire – between rulers and ruled, imperialists and subalterns, colonisers and the colonised – had broken down. The easy labels of religion and ethnicity and nationalism, slapped on by generations of historians, turned out, at the very least, to be surprisingly unstable. Yet clearly – and this was what really fascinated me – while the documentation surrounding Kirkpatrick's story was uniquely well-preserved, giving a window into a world that few realise ever existed, the situation itself was far from unusual, something the participants were themselves well aware of.

The deeper I went in my research the more I became convinced that the picture of the British of the East India Company as a small alien minority locked away in their Presidency towns, forts and cantonments needed to be revised. The tone of this early period of British life in India seemed instead to be about intermixing and impurity, a succession of unexpected and unplanned minglings of peoples and cultures and ideas.

The Kirkpatricks inhabited a world that was far more hybrid, and with far less clearly defined ethnic, national and religious borders, than we have been conditioned to expect, either by the conventional Imperial history books written in Britain before 1947, or by the nationalist historiography of post-Independence India, or for that matter by the post-colonial work coming from new generations of scholars, many of whom tend to follow the path opened up by Edward Said in 1978 with his pioneering *Orientalism*.[3] It was as if this early promiscuous mingling of races and ideas, modes of dress and ways of living, was something that was on no one's agenda and suited nobody's version of events. All sides seemed, for different reasons, to be slightly embarrassed by this moment of crossover, which they preferred to pretend had never happened. It is, after all, always easier to see things in black and white.

This was something I became increasingly sensitive to when, in the course of my research, I discovered that I was myself the product of a similar interracial liaison from this period, and that I thus had Indian blood in my veins. No one in my family seemed to know about this, though it should not have been a surprise: we had all heard the stories of how our beautiful, dark-eyed Calcutta-born great-great-grandmother Sophia Pattle, with whom Burne-Jones had fallen in love, used to speak Hindustani with her sisters and was painted by Watts with a *rakhi* – a Hindu sacred thread – tied around her wrist. But it was only when I poked around in the archives that I discovered she was descended from a Hindu Bengali woman from Chandernagore who converted to Catholicism and married a French officer in Pondicherry in the 1730s.

It also became increasingly clear to me that the relationship between India and Britain was a symbiotic one. Just as individual Britons in India could learn to appreciate and wish to emulate different aspects of Indian culture, and choose to take on Indian manners and languages, so many Indians at this period began to travel to Britain, intermarrying with the locals there and picking up Western ways.

The Mughal travel writer Mirza Abu Taleb Khan, who published in Persian an account of his journeys in Asia, Africa and Europe in 1810, described meeting in London several completely Anglicised Indian women who had accompanied their husbands and children to Britain, one of whom had completed the cultural transformation so perfectly that he 'was some time in her company before I could be convinced that she was a native of India'.[4] He also met the extraordinary Dean Mahomet, a Muslim landowner from Patna who had followed his British patron to Ireland. There he soon eloped with, and later married, Jane Daly, from a leading Anglo-Irish family. In 1794 he confirmed his unique – and clearly surprisingly prominent – place in Cork society by publishing his *Travels*, the first book ever published by an Indian writing in English, to which half of Ireland's gentry became subscribers. In 1807 Dean Mahomet moved to London where he opened the country's first Indian-owned curry restaurant, Dean Mahomet's Hindostanee Coffee House: 'here the gentry may enjoy the Hooakha, with real Chilm tobacco, and Indian dishes in the highest perfection, and allowed by the greatest epicures to be unequalled to any curries ever made in England'. He finally decamped to Brighton where he opened what can only be described as Britain's first Oriental massage parlour, and became 'Shampooing Surgeon' to Kings George IV and William IV. As Dean Mahomet's biographer, Michael Fisher, has rightly noted, 'Mahomet's marriage and degree of success as a professional medical man stand as warnings against simple projections backward of later English racial categories or attitudes.'[5]*

This seemed to be exactly the problem with so much of the history written about eighteenth- and early-nineteenth-century India: the temptation felt by so many historians to interpret their evidence according to the stereotypes of Victorian and Edwardian behaviour and attitudes with which we are so familiar. Yet these attitudes were clearly entirely at odds with the actual fears and hopes, anxieties and aspirations of the Company officials and their Indian wives whose voluminous letters can be read with the greatest of ease in the fifty miles of East India Company documents stored in the India Office Library. It is as if the Victorians succeeded in colonising not only

---

* On a smaller scale the same is true of France. As early as 1761 Anquetil-Duperron mentions the Indian wife of a French officer accompanying her husband back to Europe, after which many others followed, such as Bannou Pan Dei Allard, who settled with her mercenary husband at Saint-Tropez, and Fezli Azam Joo Court with hers at Marseilles.

India but also, more permanently, our imaginations, to the exclusion of all other images of the Indo–British encounter.

Since the late-twentieth-century implosion of Empire and the arrival in the West of large numbers of Indians, most of whom have, as a matter of course, assumed Western clothes and Western manners, this East-to-West cross-fertilisation of cultures does not surprise us. But, perhaps bizarrely, the reverse still does: that a European should voluntarily choose to cross over – and 'turn Turk' as the Elizabethans put it, or 'go native' or 'Tropo', to use the Victorian phrases – is still something which has the capacity to take us aback.

Only seventy-five years after the death of James Achilles Kirkpatrick, and indeed within the lifetime of his Anglo-Indian, Torquay-Hyderabadi, Islamo-Christian daughter, it was possible for Kipling to write that 'East is East and West is West and never the twain shall meet'. There is a tendency to laugh at Kipling today; but at a time when respectable academics talk of a Clash of Civilisations, and when East and West, Islam and Christianity appear to be engaged in another major confrontation, this unlikely group of expatriates provides a timely reminder that it is indeed very possible – and has always been possible – to reconcile the two worlds.

I

O N 7 NOVEMBER 1801, under conditions of the greatest secrecy, two figures were discreetly admitted to the gardens of Government House in Madras.

Outside, amid clouds of dust, squadrons of red-coated sepoys tramped along the hot, broad military road which led from the coast towards the cantonments at St Thomas's Mount. Waiting in the shade of the gates, shoals of hawkers circled around the crowds of petitioners and groups of onlookers who always collect in such places in India, besieging them with trays full of rice cakes and bananas, sweetmeats, oranges and *paan*.

Inside the gates, beyond the sentries, lay another world: seventy-five acres of green tropical parkland shaded by banana palms and tall tamarind trees, flamboya, gulmohar and scented Raat-ki-Rani, the Queen of the Night. Here there was no dust, no crowds and no noise but for birdsong – the inevitable chatter of mynahs and the occasional long, querulous, woody call of the koel – and the distant suck and crash of the breakers on the beach half a mile away.

The two figures were led through the Government Gardens towards the white classical garden house that the new Governor of Madras, Lord Clive, was in the process of rebuilding and enlarging. Here one of the two men was made to wait, while the other was led to a patch of shade in the parkland, where three chairs had been arranged around a table. Before long, Lord Clive himself appeared, attended by his Private Secretary, Mark Wilks. It was a measure of the sensitivity of the gathering that, unusually for a period where nothing could be done without a great retinue of servants, all three men were unaccompanied. As Clive administered an oath, Wilks began to jot down a detailed record of the proceedings which still survives in the India Office Library:

> The Rt. Hon. the Lord Clive having required the presence of Lieut. Col Bowser at the Government Garden for the purpose of being examined on a subject of a secret and important nature, and having directed Captain M Wilks to attend his Lordship for the purpose of taking down the minutes of the examination, addressed Lieut. Col Bowser in the following manner:
>
> The object of the inquiry which I am about to institute involves considerations of great importance to the national interest and character. I am therefore instructed by His Excellency the most Noble Governor General to impress this sentiment on your mind and to desire that you prepare yourself to give such information on the subject as you possess with that accuracy which is becoming [to] the solemnity of the occasion . . .[1]

The oath taken, Clive proceeded to explain to Bowser why he and his colleague, Major Orr, had been summoned four hundred and fifty miles from their regiments in Hyderabad to Madras, and why it was important that no one in Hyderabad should know the real reason for their journey. Clive needed to know the truth about the East India Company's Resident at the court of Hyderabad, James Achilles Kirkpatrick. For two years now rumours had been in circulation, rumours which two previous inquiries – more informal, and far less searching – had failed to quash.

Some of the stories circulating about Kirkpatrick, though perhaps enough to raise an eyebrow or two in Calcutta, were harmless enough. It was said that he had given up wearing English clothes for all but the most formal occasions, and now habitually swanned around the British Residency in what one surprised visitor had described as 'a Musselman's dress of the finest texture'. Another noted that Kirkpatrick had hennaed his hands in the manner of a Mughal nobleman, and wore Indian 'mustachios . . . though in most other respects he is like an Englishman'.[2]

These eccentricities were, in themselves, hardly a matter for alarm. The British in India – particularly those at some distance from the main presidency towns of Calcutta, Madras and Bombay – had long adapted themselves to Mughal dress and customs, and although this had lately become a little unfashionable it was hardly something which on its own could affect a man's career. It was certainly not enough to give rise to a major inquiry. But other charges against Kirkpatrick were of a much more serious nature.

Firstly, there were consistent reports that Kirkpatrick had, as Clive put it, 'connected himself with a female' of one of Hyderabad's leading noble families. The girl in question was never named in the official inquiry report, but was said to be no more than fourteen years old at the time. Moreover she was a Sayyeda, a descendant of the Prophet, and thus, like all her clan, kept in the very strictest purdah. Sayyeds – especially Indian Sayyeds – were particularly sensitive about the purity of their race and the chastity of their women. Not only were they strictly endogamous – in other words they could never marry except with other Sayyeds – in many cases Sayyed girls would refuse even to mix with pregnant women from outside, lest the unborn child in the stranger's womb were to turn out to be male and thus unwittingly contaminate their purity.[3] Despite these powerful taboos, and the precautions of her clan, the girl had somehow managed to become pregnant by Kirkpatrick and was recently said to have given birth to his child.

Early reports in scurrilous Hyderabadi newsletters had claimed that Kirkpatrick had raped the girl, who was called Khair un-Nissa, then murdered a brother who had tried to stand in his way. There seemed to be a consensus that these accounts were malicious and inaccurate, but what was certain – and much more alarming for the Company – was that news of the pregnancy had leaked out and had caused widespread unrest in Hyderabad. Worse still, the girl's grandfather was said to have 'expressed an indignation approaching to phrenzy at the indignity offered to the honour of his family by such proceedings, and had declared his intention of proceeding to the Mecca Masjid (the principal mosque of the city)'.[4] There he promised to raise the Muslims of the Deccan against the British, thus imperilling the British hold on southern and central India at that most sensitive period when a Napoleonic army was still at large in Egypt and feared to be contemplating an audacious attack on the British possessions of the subcontinent.

Finally, and perhaps most shockingly for the authorities in Bengal, some said that Kirkpatrick had actually, formally, married the girl, which meant embracing Islam, and had become a practising Shi'a Muslim. These rumours about Kirkpatrick's alleged new religious affiliation, combined with his undisguised sympathy for, and delight in, the Hyderabadi culture of his bride, had led some of his colleagues to wonder whether his political loyalties could still be depended on at all. More than a year earlier, the young Colonel Arthur Wellesley, the future Duke of Wellington, had written to his elder brother Richard, the Governor General in Calcutta, expressing exactly this concern. As Commander in the neighbouring state of Mysore, Colonel Wellesley had heard reliable reports that Kirkpatrick now seemed to be so solidly 'under the influence' of the Hyderabadis that 'it was to be expected that he would attend more to the objects of the Nizam's court than those of his own government' – that Kirkpatrick might, in other words, have 'gone over' to the other side, to have become, to some extent, a double-agent.[5]

The question of how to respond to these allegations was one that the Governor General, Lord Wellesley,* had agonised over for some time. There were several complicating factors. Firstly, despite all the stories in circulation, Kirkpatrick had an exceptional record in the East India Company's Political [diplomatic] Service. Without a drop of blood being shed, he had succeeded in expelling the last serious French force from southern India and had successfully negotiated an important treaty with the Nizam of Hyderabad. This had, for the first time, brought the Nizam's vast dominions firmly into alliance with the British, so tipping the delicate balance of power in India firmly in Britain's favour. For this work Wellesley had, only a few months earlier, recommended Kirkpatrick to London for a baronetcy.

But this was not the only complication. Kirkpatrick's elder brother

* Before 1800, Richard Colley Wellesley was known as Lord Mornington. For the purpose of clarity and continuity, he will be referred to throughout as Lord Wellesley.

William was one of the Governor General's closest advisers in Calcutta, indeed was credited by Wellesley himself as being one of the principal architects of his policy. While Wellesley was determined to find out the truth about the younger Kirkpatrick, he wished to do so, if possible, without alienating the elder. Finally, he knew it was going to be difficult openly to investigate any of these sensitive stories without causing a major scandal, and possibly inflicting considerable damage on British interests not only in Hyderabad, but all over India. Yet the rumours were clearly too serious and too widespread to ignore.

For all these reasons, Wellesley decided to fall back on the strategy of holding a secret inquiry in Madras, and there to solicit the sworn testimony of the two most senior British soldiers in Hyderabad, Lieutenant Colonel Bowser and Major Orr, both of whom had come into close contact with Kirkpatrick, without either of them being close enough friends for their veracity to be compromised.

It was not a perfect solution, especially as Wellesley did not much admire the new Governor of Madras, Edward, Lord Clive. He was son of the more famous Robert Clive, whose victory at Plassey forty-four years earlier had begun the East India Company's astonishing transformation from a trading company of often dubious solvency to a major imperial power with a standing army and territorial possessions far larger than those of the country which gave it birth. After their first meeting, Wellesley wrote that Clive was 'a worthy, zealous, obedient & gentlemanlike man of excellent temper; but neither of talents, knowledge, habits of business, or firmness equal to his present situation. How the devil did he get here?'[6] Yet Wellesley realised it would be impossible to conduct an inquiry in Calcutta without involving Kirkpatrick's brother, and that there was little option but to delegate the job to Clive.

Moreover, as the future of Britain's relationship with the largest independent Muslim state in India now hinged at least partly on the exact details of Kirkpatrick's relationship with the girl in question, it would clearly be necessary during the course of the inquest to ask a series of the most intimate and searching questions.

The whole business, Wellesley concluded, would no doubt prove horribly embarrassing for all concerned, and be much better sorted out by Clive in Madras. So, on 30 September 1801, Wellesley formally wrote to Lord Clive telling him to prepare a secret inquiry into Kirkpatrick's conduct, while simultaneously sending orders to Hyderabad for Bowser and Orr to be discreetly, and promptly, despatched to the coast.

Over the course of the following few days 'Orr and Bowser answered, under oath, a series of questions of such intimate and explicit nature that the finished report must certainly be one of the most sexually revealing public documents to have survived from the East India Company's India: to read it is to feel a slightly uneasy sensation akin to opening Kirkpatrick's bedroom windows and peering in.

The two witnesses, whose bright soldierly blushes are clearly visible through the formal lines of Captain Wilks's perfect copperplate handwriting, were asked how Kirkpatrick had come to meet and have an affair with a teenage Muslim noblewoman who was kept in strict purdah, especially when she was engaged to be married to another man. Was it Kirkpatrick or the girl who had taken the initiative: who seduced whom? When did they first sleep together? How often? When did it become a matter of public record? How did the story get out? What was the reaction in Hyderabad? The way the document is written – exactly like a modern trial report or Parliamentary Inquiry – heightens this sense of immediacy and familiarity:

> *Question:* Do you understand that the young lady was seduced by the Resident, or do you rather believe that he became the dupe of the interested machinations of the females of her family?
>
> *Answer:* I cannot state to which of these suppositions the public opinion most inclines. It is said that the lady fell in love with the Resident, and that the free access very unusual in Mohammedan families which had been allowed to him by the females of that family may appear to confirm the opinion of design on their part.
>
> *Question:* What is the date of the first supposed intercourse between the Resident and the young lady?

Answer: I first heard it whispered about the beginning of the year. Every day afterwards it became more publicly spoken of and universally believed until the period of the complaint.

Parts of the story that unfolds through the pages of the examination are so strikingly modern that it is sometimes hard to believe it was written two hundred years ago. There is much talk of the embarrassing pregnancy, the family's desperate attempts to procure an abortion, Kirkpatrick's last-minute intervention to stop the termination, and the girl's mother's heartfelt cry that if only the sectarian religious divisions which had plagued the whole affair did not exist, this man could have had her daughter 'in the same manner that he might have had her before the distinctions introduced by Musa [Moses], Isa [Jesus] and Mohamed were known to the world'. There is also Kirkpatrick's unembarrassedly romantic declaration (relayed by Bowser) that 'whatever might be the ultimate result of these investigations, he was determined never to desert the lady or her offspring'. The remoteness of history evaporates: these are immediately recognisable and familiar human situations.

But, equally, reading through the report there are other moments when the sensation of familiarity dissolves and it is as if we are back in some semi-mythical world of Scheherazade and the *Arabian Nights*: we read of discreet interviews taking place through bamboo harem screens, of hunting expeditions where cheetahs are let slip at grazing gazelles, of spies following palanquins through the bazaars, and of a threat by the girl's grandfather 'to turn fakeer' – become a wandering ascetic – as the only recourse to save the family honour.

Above all, one is also confronted with the unexpected sight of a senior British official who was believed, not least by his Hyderabadi in-laws, to be a practising Muslim, who routinely wore Indian clothes and who – even before this liaison – clearly kept his own harem at the back of his house, complete with Mughal maidservants, *aseels* (wetnurses), midwives and harem guards. It is all a very surprising world to find in such close and intimate association with official British India. It is certainly unfamiliar to anyone who accepts at face value the usual rigid caricature of the Englishman in India, presented over and over again in films and cheap TV dramas, of the Imperialist Incarnate: the narrow-minded, ramrod-backed sahib in a sola topee and bristling moustache, dressing for dinner despite the heat, while raising a disdainful nose at both the people and the culture of India.

Yet the more one probes in the records of the period, the more one realises that there were in fact a great many Europeans at this period who responded to India in a way that perhaps surprises and appeals to us today, by crossing over from one culture to the other, and wholeheartedly embracing the great diversity of late Mughal India.

Beneath the familiar story of European conquest and rule in India, and the imposition of European ways in the heart of Asia, there always lay a far more intriguing and still largely unwritten story: the Indian conquest of the European imagination. At all times up to the nineteenth century, but perhaps especially during the period 1770 to 1830, there was wholesale interracial sexual exploration and surprisingly widespread cultural assimilation and hybridity: what Salman Rushdie – talking of modern multiculturalism – has called 'chutnification'. Virtually all Englishmen in India at this period Indianised themselves to some extent. Those who went further and converted to Islam or Hinduism, or made really dramatic journeys across cultures, were certainly always a minority; but they were probably nothing like as small a minority as we have been accustomed to expect.

Throughout, one has a feeling that people are being confronted by an entirely new type of problem as two very different worlds collide and come into intimate contact for the first time. There are no precedents and no scripts: reading the letters, diaries and reports of the period, it is as if the participants are improvising their way through problems, prejudices, tensions and emotions that people have simply never experienced in this way before.

India has always had a strange way with her conquerors. In defeat, she beckons them in, then slowly seduces, assimilates and transforms them.

Over the centuries, many powers have defeated Indian armies; but none has ever proved immune to this capacity of the subcontinent to somehow reverse the current of colonisation, and to mould those who attempt to subjugate her. So vast is India, and so uniquely resilient and deeply rooted are her intertwined social and religious institutions, that all foreign intruders are sooner or later either shaken off or absorbed. The Great Mughals, as one historian memorably observed, arrived in India from central Asia in the sixteenth century as 'ruddy men in boots'; they left it four centuries later 'pale persons in petticoats'.[7] Until the 1830s, there was every sign that India would have as dramatic a transforming effect on the Europeans who followed the Mughals. Like all the foreigners before them, it seemed that they too would be effortlessly absorbed.

This 'crossing over' was a process that dated from the very beginning of the European presence in India. The Portuguese were the first to make the transition. After the conquest of Goa in 1510 – some sixteen years before the arrival of the Mughals in north India – the Portuguese commander Afonso de Albuquerque made a point of ordering his men to marry the widows of the Muslim defenders they had massacred during the taking of the city. Albuquerque himself presided at the weddings of these 'fair Mooresses of pleasing appearance'[8] and provided them with dowries. The fair Mooresses were then forcibly converted to Christianity, and after baptism, many were made to receive the rudiments of the Catholic faith. But this crude attempt at force-feeding unadulterated Portuguese culture to India proved as short-lived, and as unsuccessful, as previous attempts to impose unadulterated Turkish, Sassanian Persian or Greek culture had been during the preceding centuries.

Over the course of the next fifty years, the women, the environment and the sheer distance of Goa from Europe all worked on the new arrivals, so that gradually, generation by generation, the conquistadors began abandoning the ways of Portugal and taking on instead the customs of India. Already, by the time the Portuguese Inquisition arrived in India in 1560, Goa much more closely resembled the Mughal capitals of Delhi and Agra than it did Lisbon or any city in Portugal. As one shocked Jesuit reported back to Rome, 'the Inquisition is more necessary in these parts than anywhere else, since all the Christians here live together with the Muslims, the Jews and the Hindus and this causes laxness of conscience in persons residing therein. Only with the curb of the Inquisition will they live a good life.'

By 1560, the Portuguese grandees of Goa dressed ostentatiously in silks, shielding themselves with umbrellas, never leaving their houses except accompanied by vast retinues of slaves and servants. Travellers reported how the Goan aristocracy kept harems and that even the Christian women wore Indian clothes inside the house and lived as if in purdah, 'little seene abroad'.[9] If they had to go out, they did so veiled or in modestly covered palanquins.

Their menfolk chewed betel nut, ate rice (but only with their right hand) and drank arrack; they rubbed themselves with 'sweet sanders',[10] and their hospital doctors prescribed the old Hindu panacea of cow's urine three times a day to their patients 'in order to recover their colour, one glass in the morning, one at midday, and one in the evening'.[11] They drank water from the pot in the Indian fashion 'and touch it not with their mouths, but the water running from the spout falleth into their mouthes, never spilling a drop ... and when any man commeth newly from Portingall, and then beginneth to drink after this manner, because he is not used to this kinde of drinking, he spilleth it in his bosome, wherein they take great pleasure and laugh at him, calling him Reynol, which is a name given in jest to such as newlie come from Portingall'.[12]

Even the ecclesiastical establishment showed signs of taking on the ways of its Indian environment: from 1585 a bizarre edict was issued commanding that only Indo-Portuguese with Brahminical (Hindu priestly) blood would be accepted in the colony's seminaries to train for the priesthood of the Roman Catholic Church: 'all this they have learned and received from the Indian heathens,' wrote a surprised Dutch traveller, Jan van Linschoten, 'which have had these customs of long time.'[13]

By 1642, the governor of the Dutch East India Company Anthony van Diemen could report that 'most of the Portuguese in India look upon this region as their fatherland, and think no more about Portugal. They drive little or no trade thither, but content themselves with port to port trade as if they were natives and had no other country.'[14] His compatriot, van Linschoten, came to the same conclusion: 'The posteritie of the Portingales, both men and women, doe seeme to be naturall Indians, both in colour and in fashion.'[15]

These early descriptions of Indo-Portuguese culture set the tone for what was to come over the next three hundred years, in a wide range of encounters between different Indian peoples and various colonial intruders. It is clear from the start that what was happening was not so much a wholesale substitution of one culture for another, so much as a complex process of fusion. Indo-Portuguese society was neither purely Portuguese nor wholly Indian, but a hybrid mixture of the two: a European template adapted to the climate and social mores of India, or, from the opposite perspective, an Indian environment tinct with European institutions, Indo-Portuguese architecture and an amalgam of increasingly Indianised European cultural importations. The Portuguese in India, and their Indo-Portuguese descendants, did not leave one culture to inhabit another, so much as live in both at the same time, accommodating in their outlook and lifestyles rival ways of living in and looking at the world.

To the Dominican fathers of the Goan Inquisition, of course, this process of acculturation was always unacceptable. Any signs that Hindu customs were being followed in a Christian house were enough to get the entire family and their servants arrested and put to torture. A list was drawn up by the Inquisition of banned Indian practices, which can now act for the social historian as a useful index of the different ways in which the Portuguese picked up the habits, tastes and superstitions of their Indian neighbours.

Included in this list are such shockingly heretical practices as 'cooking rice without salt as the Hindus are accustomed to do', wearing a *dhoti* (loincloth) or *choli* (short, often transparent Indian bodice), and refusing to eat pork. Even certain trees, plants and vegetables were proscribed. It was forbidden, for example, to grow a Tulsi plant, considered by many Hindus to be a talisman against the Evil Eye.*

Perhaps partly because of the Inquisition, a surprisingly large number of Portuguese made the decision to emigrate from Portuguese territory and seek their fortunes at different Indian courts, usually as gunners or cavalrymen. Again this was a process whose origins dated from the very beginning of the Portuguese presence in India: in 1498, on his famous first journey to India, Vasco da Gama found that there were already some Italian mercenaries in the employ of the various rajahs on the Malabar coast; and before he turned his prow homewards two of his own crew had left him to join the Italians in the service of a Malabar rajah for higher wages.[16] Sixty years later, by 1565, according to the Portuguese chronicler Barros, there were at least two thousand Portuguese fighting in the armies of different Indian princes. By the early seventeenth century, another Portuguese writer thought the number must have reached at least five thousand.[17]

The men who 'went over' were often from the very margins of Portuguese society. They were attracted by the remarkable religious freedom of India, and also by the better prospects, and higher and more regular pay. Others were no doubt lured from Portuguese service by the delights of a society in which slavery, concubinage and polygamy were widespread and entirely accepted, and where they could emulate the curious figure some British sailors encountered at the beginning of the seventeenth century living it up on the Moluccas 'with as many women as he pleaseth . . . he will sing and dance all day long, near hand naked . . . and will be drunk two days together'.[18] By contrast, conditions of service in the Goan army were very harsh, especially during the monsoon rains, when inactive soldiers, unhoused and often unpaid, could be seen wandering the red earth roads of Goa 'seeking alms'.[19]

---

* Hence the story told by one traveller, that when he was dining with a Goan host a messenger arrived from the Inquisition with a note for the householder. The man 'blanched, and with great foreboding and trembling opened the letter', expecting to be summoned to prison. But in fact the Inquisitor merely wished for some mangoes from the man's orchard. The mangoes were duly picked and sent without delay; 'and that very evening the man chopped down his trees to make sure that nothing in his house ever again brought him to the attention of the Inquisition'. For a Hindu nationalist view of the Inquisition see A.K. Priolkar, *The Goa Inquisition* (Bombay, 1961). See also, as a balance, Sanjay Subrahmaniyam, *The Portuguese Empire in Asia: A Political and Economic History* (London, 1993), pp.83–4.

Whatever the reason, many thousands of Europeans took service in Indian courts all over the subcontinent. Nor was it just the Portuguese. At the height of the Mughal Empire, so many Europeans took service in the Mughal army that a special suburb was built for them outside Delhi called Firingi Pura (Foreigners' Town). The inhabitants of Firingi Pura included renegade Portuguese, Englishmen and French, many of whom chose to convert to Islam, and who formed a distinct Firingi (or Foreigners') regiment under a Frenchman titled Farrashish Khan.[20]

The Mughals had no monopoly on these renegades: their rivals, the four great Deccani Muslim sultanates that controlled much of southern and central India, were also keen to make use of their services. Attached to the Adil Shahi court of Bijapur, for example, there was Gonçalo Vaz Coutinho, formerly a powerful landowner in Goa, who was imprisoned on a murder charge before escaping to Bijapur where he converted to Islam. Here he was given 'lands with great revenues, where he remained as a perfect Moor, with his wife and children'.[21]

It was also often to these sultanates of the Deccan that English renegades tended to make their way when, a century later, large numbers of Englishmen first started arriving in India. An eyewitness account of one of the earliest defections was written by the early English trader Nicholas Withington. His account gives a clear picture of the number of independent Europeans on the loose in India at the beginning of the seventeenth century, all of them intent on making their fortunes and quite prepared, if necessary, to change and change again their clothes, their political allegiance and their religion. It also shows the dangers that were inherent in undergoing circumcision – the biggest single obstacle for many potential converts to Islam. 'There came likewise unto us one that had formerlye rune awaye from our shippes to the Portugales, and agayne from them to us,' wrote Withington.

> In this way passing through the Decannes countrye, he was perswaded by another Englishmen (that was turned Moore and lived there) to turne Moore; which hee did and was circumsized, the Kinge allowinge him 7s 6d per daye and his diett at the Kinge's own table; but within eighte dayes after his cirumsizion he dyed.

Likewise another of our companie, [a trumpeter] called
Robert Trullye ... went to [the] Decanne to the King thereof,
carryinge along with him a Germayne for his interpritor that
understoode the language; and coming there, offred bothe to
turne Moores, which was kyndlye accepted by the Kinge. So
Trullye was circumsized, and had a newe name given to him
and a great allowance given to him by the King, with whom
he continued. But they cominge to cutt the Germayne, founde
that hee had ben formerly circumcised (as he was once in
Persia) but thought nowe to have deceaved the Deccannes,
whoe, fyndinge him allreddy a Moore, would not give him
entertaynment; soe hee retorned to Agra and gott himselfe
into the service of a Frenchman, and is turned Chrystian
againe, going usually to Mass with his master ... So there is
with the King of the Decanne fower Englishemen which are
turned Moores, and divers Portungales allsoe.[22]

From the margins of their own society, these early European renegades became important mediators between the world of Europe
and the world of India. They also demonstrated the remarkable
porousness and fluidity of the frontier which separated the two. From
the mid-sixteenth century, with the advent of wholesale defections
from Portuguese Goa, followed a century later by a new wave of
renegades from the British East India Company bridgehead at Surat
in Gujerat, the borderlands of colonial India had taken up the role
they would continue to occupy over the next three hundred years:
as spaces where categories of identity, ideas of national loyalty and
relations of power were often flexible, and where the possibilities for
self-transformation were, at least potentially, limitless.

Contrary to the Imperial mythology propagated by the Victorians, the British were initially no more immune than any other nation to the social forces that transformed the Portuguese in India. Indeed it was one of the distinguishing marks of the ragtag assortment of Englishmen who first ventured into the Mughal Empire during the seventeenth century that they excelled in accommodating themselves to what must at first have appeared to them a profoundly foreign society.

Unlike the Portuguese, who usually came out to Goa with the intention of settling in India for good, the English did in general envisage returning home at the end of their postings, and this profoundly affected the way they looked at the country in which they lived.* Nevertheless, the success of the East India Company in its formative years depended as much on contacts across the lines of race and religion as it did on any commercial acumen, and to varying extents the traders, soldiers, diplomats and even the clergymen who ventured eastwards had little choice but to embrace Mughal India. Nor should this tendency surprise us: from the wider perspective of world history, what is much odder and much more inexplicable is the tendency of the late-nineteenth-century British to travel to, and rule over, nearly a quarter of the globe, and yet remain resolutely untouched by virtually all the cultures with which they came into contact.

There was, however, nothing very new in this crossing of cultures. English merchants trading in the Middle East had been mixing with Muslims and converting to Islam for centuries.† Much of the initial

---

* Though this was not necessarily true of the poorer white soldiers, who often had little desire (or even opportunity) of returning home.

† There are also, of course, numerous examples of crossing cultures and 'going native' at this period outside the Islamic world: Sir William Johnson, 'the Mohawk Baronet', and his two Iroquois wives in New York State; various dubious Scots setting themselves up as rulers in Honduras; 'Samurai William' Adams's life in the service of the Shogun in seventeenth-century Japan; and the 'White Rajah' James Brooke in Sarawak. See J.T. Flexner, *Mohawk Baronet: Sir William Johnson of New York* (New York, 1959); Kirk Swineheart, *Molly's War* (forthcoming, 2003); Giles Milton, *Samurai William* (London, 2002); Steven Runciman, *The White Rajahs: A History of Sarawak from 1841 to 1946* (Cambridge, 1960); also John Demos's gripping *The Unredeemed Captive: A Family Story from Early America* (New York, 1994).

contact between Britain and the wider Islamic world took place against a background of seventeenth-century naval skirmishes, where Muslim technological superiority at sea led to the capture and sinking of large numbers of British vessels. Between 1609 and 1616 it was reported that 466 English ships were attacked by Ottoman or Barbary galleys, and their crews led away in chains. By May 1626 there were more than five thousand British captives in the city of Algiers and a further 1500 in Sali, and frantic arrangements were being made in London to redeem them 'lest they follow the example of others and turn Turk'.

By the 1620s the Turkish naval presence was no longer confined to the Mediterranean, and had extended its reach into the waters of the British Isles: in August 1625, 'The Turks took out from the Church of "Munnigesca" in Mounts' Bay [Cornwall] about 60 men, women and children, and carried them away captives.'[23] What was more worrying still were reports that some of these raids were being led by Englishmen who had converted to Islam and 'turned Turk': for example, in September 1645 seven ships 'from Barbary' landed in Cornwall and their crews were led inland 'by some renegade of this country'.[24]

It was reports that very large numbers of British captives were converting to Islam that really rattled the Stuart authorities. Worse still, while some of these conversions were forced, many were clearly not, and British travellers of the period regularly brought back tales of their compatriots who had 'donned the turban' and were now prospering in the Islamic world: one of the most powerful Ottoman eunuchs during the late sixteenth century, Hasan Aga, was the former Samson Rowlie from Great Yarmouth,[25] while in Algeria the 'Moorish Kings Executioner' turned out to be a former butcher from Exeter called 'Absalom' (Abd-es-Salaam).[26] Equally, a *dragoman** encountered by some English travellers first in Constantinople, then later in Aden, was described as 'a Turk, but a Cornishman born'.[27] There was also the Ottoman general known as 'Ingliz Mustapha': in fact a Scottish Campbell who had embraced Islam and joined the Janissaries.[28]†

* An interpreter and guide in Ottoman lands.

† When Charles II sent one Captain Hamilton to ransom a group who had been enslaved on the Barbary Coast his mission was unsuccessful, as they all refused to return: the men had converted to Islam, risen in the ranks, and were now 'partaking of the prosperous Successe of the Turks', living in a style to which they could not possibly have aspired

The English Ambassador to the Ottoman court, Sir Thomas Shirley, purported to have little time for these renegades, describing them as 'roagues, & the skumme of people, whyche being villaines and aethiests are fledde to the Turke for succour & releyffe'. But his reaction is undoubtedly as much a reflection of English anxiety and insecurity at this period as it is of any incipient Imperial arrogance. Certainly those who 'turned Turk' seemed to include a fairly wide cross-section of British society, including arms dealers and money counterfeiters, sea captains and soldiers of fortune as well as a 'trumpeter', 'divers English gentlemen' working as pirates out of the North African Barbary Coast, and a lone Englishwoman who became one of the wives of the Dey of Algiers.[29]

As Shirley pointed out in one of his despatches, the more time Englishmen spent in the East, the closer they moved to adopting the manners of the Muslims: 'Conuersation with infidelles doeth mutch corrupte,' he wrote. 'Many wylde youthes of all nationes, as well Englishe as others ... in euerye 3 yeere that they staye in Turkye they loose one article of theyre faythe.'[30] Islam overcame the English more by its sophistication and power of attraction than by the sword: in 1606 even the English Consul in Egypt, Benjamin Bishop, converted and promptly disappeared from public records.[31]*

It was thus very much with the weary expectation that large numbers of English traders were bound to be tempted to swap religions and cultures, and to desert the Company in order to join

---

back home, in a society they found to be every bit as sophisticated as their own, and a great deal more tolerant. The frustrated Captain Hamilton was forced to return empty-handed: 'They are tempted to forsake their God for the love of Turkish women,' he wrote in his official report. 'Such ladies are,' he added, 'generally very beautiful.' Nabil Matar, *Islam in Britain 1583–1685* (Cambridge, 1998), p.37.

* All this, of course, went down very badly at home, and the treacherous 'renegade' soon became a stock character on the English stage. Indeed, jibes about circumcision and men who converted to Islam expecting harems and who instead ended up as eunuchs became something of a Jacobean equivalent of the mother-in-law joke; see e.g. Daniel J. Vitkus (ed.), *Three Turk Plays from Early Modern England* (New York, 2000). It also caused a problem for the Church authorities when former apostates began returning home in large numbers, some wishing readmission to the Church, others apparently wishing to keep to their new faith. In 1637 the matter was the subject of a full-scale parliamentary debate when Archbishop Laud presented to the House *A Form of Penance and Reconciliation of a Renegado or Apostate from the Christian Religion to Turcism*; see Matar, *Islam in Britain 1558–1685*, p.69.

Mughal service, that the first British treaty with the Mughal Empire was drawn up in 1616. Its author, the Jacobean ambassador Sir Thomas Roe, was quite clear about the potential danger posed to the Company by the defection of renegades, and insisted as point eight of the treaty that all 'English fugitives were to be delivered up to the factory'.* The Mughal Prince Khurram – later Shah Jehan – disputed this article – 'a stand was made against the surrender of any Englishman who might turn Moor' – but Roe stood firm, realising from his experience of the Ottoman Middle East the crucial importance of the provision. In the end, according to the report sent back to England, the vital 'point was yielded to the ambassador's insistence'.[32]

The great Mughal port of Surat on the coast of Gujerat was the focus for the first contacts between British traders and the peoples of the Mughal Empire. Here the British 'factors' as they called themselves, inhabited a building that combined elements of both an Oxbridge college and a Mughal caravanserai. On one hand, the day started with prayers and ended at a communal meal presided over by both the President and the Chaplain, whose job it was to monitor the behaviour of the factors, ensure regular attendance at chapel and prevent un-Christian behaviour. On the other hand, this cosy English collegiate scene took place within a 'Moor's building', and after dinner the factors could wash and unwind in a 'hummum'[33] (Turkish bath). In the absence of European goods, the factors quickly adapted themselves to the material culture of India, and very soon such specifically Indian luxuries as 'a betle box, two pigdanes [from the Hindi *pikdan*, a spittoon], and a rose-

---

* At this period the English called their trading posts 'factories', though little or no manufacturing ever went on there.

water bottle' begin to turn up in the inventories of the factories.[34]

The best descriptions of the daily life of the Surat factory are contained in travel accounts, for although the official correspondence of the factors is almost entirely extant,* most of the letters are concerned with the minutiae of trade and touch only very obliquely on the way the factors are actually living their daily lives. Yet occasionally there are hints as to the degree to which the factors are adapting themselves to the world outside their walls.

One such slip occurs in 1630 when President William Methwold admits that the factors have almost completely given up using the Western drugs that the Company was in the habit of sending out to Surat, preferring to take the advice of local Mughal doctors: 'The utility of the drugs is not to be doubted,' writes Methwold, 'but being farr fecht and longe kept, applied by an unskilful hand, without the consideration of the temprature of a mans body by the alteration of climats, they peradventure have small or contrary effects.' Rather sheepishly he then admits: 'wee for our parts doe hold that in things indifferent it is safest for an Englishman to Indianize, and, so conforming himselfe in some measure to the diett of the country, the ordinarie phisick of the country will bee the best cure when any sicknesse shall overtake him'.[35]

Only when an articulate traveller turns up is it suddenly possible to colour in the hard commercial outlines revealed in these carefully phrased public letters. John Albert de Mandelslo, the Ambassador of the Duke of Holstein, visited the English factory at around the same time as President Methwold was writing his medical letter to London. His account reveals that despite the attempts of the factors to portray their establishment as a sort of sober, pious outpost of Trinity College, Cambridge, washed up on the shores of Gujerat, the life of the factors was in fact much more lively than anyone was prepared to let on to London. The factors may have kept to the rule that they should remain unmarried – indeed there is only one reference in the earliest years to a factor formally marrying an Indian girl, and that caused

* Indeed much of it is in print in a massive set of thirteen huge volumes (ed. William Foster) called *The English Factories in India 1618–1669* (London, 1906–27).

a major scandal* – but this did not stop them dressing in Indian clothes and being serenaded of an evening by troupes of Mughal dancing girls and courtesans. North of Surat, the British had rented a 'lodge' attached to a garden tomb, or as Mandelslo puts it, 'a mausoleum of a person of quality of the country'. One evening during Mandelslo's visit, the factors drove out, and after first taking 'two or three turns about the garden' they – presumably well out of sight of their Chaplain – laid on

> the greatest entertainment imaginable, and to come to the height of that country's endearments, they sent for some *Benjan* women, who were very desirious to see my cloaths, which I still wore after the *Germane* fashion, though the *English* and *Dutch* who are settled in the *Indies* go ordinarily according to the mode of the country, and would have obliged me to put them off; but perceiving I was unwilling to do it, and withal that I made some difficulty to accept of the profers they made me to strip themselves naked, and to doe anything that I would expect from persons of their sex and profession, they seem'd to be very much troubled, and so went away.[36]

The further the factors went from the English base in Surat, the more they found themselves adapting to Indian ways. At the end of the seventeenth century Job Charnock, the founder of Calcutta, adopted the Bengali *lungi* and married a Hindu girl whom he allegedly saved from the funeral pyre of her first husband. The story is told in one of the first English travel books about India, Alexander Hamilton's *New Account of the East Indies*:

> Mr *Channock* choosing the Ground of the Colony, where it now is, reigned more absolute than a *Rajah* . . . The country

---

* The first ever reference to a love affair between an Englishman and an Indian girl is in a letter of 20 February 1626: 'John Leachland having for some years past privately kept a woman of this country and refusing to put her away, in spite of all persuasions, it is debated whether to dismiss him from the Company's service; but as this would only lead to his marrying her and forsaking his country and friends, it is resolved not to adopt this extreme course, in the hope that time will reclaim him, "being otherwise a man of fayre demeanour, sufficient abilities, and clear of accounts with the Honourable Company in India".' *The English Factories in India 1618–1669*, Vol. 3, p.119; see also Vol. 5, pp.35, 39, 61.

about being overspread with *Paganism*, the Custom of Wives burning with their deceased Husbands is also practiced here. Mr *Channock* went one Time with his ordinary guard of Soldiers, to see a young widow act that tragical Catastrophe, but he was so smitten with the Widow's Beauty, that he sent his guards to take her by Force from her Executioners, and conducted her to his own Lodgings. They lived lovingly many Years, and had several children. At length she died, after he had settled in *Calcutta*, but instead of converting her to *Christianity*, she made him a Proselyte to *Paganism*, and the only Part of *Christianity* that was remarkable in him, was burying her decently, and he built a Tomb over her, where all his Life after her Death, he kept the anniversary Day of her Death by sacrificing a Cock on her Tomb, after the *Pagan* Manner.[37]

It was in the Mughal capital of Agra, however, that the factors found themselves most profoundly challenged both by the might and prosperity of the Mughal Empire, and by the seductive elegance of Mughal civilisation at its zenith. According to one of them, 'heere in the heart of the city we live after this country in manner of meat, drink and apparel . . . for the most part after the custom of this place, sitting on the ground, at our meat or discourse. The rooms are in general covered with carpets and with great, high round cushions to lean on.'[38] One of the very first English envoys, William Hawkins, even accepted a wife offered to him by the Emperor and 'in his howse used altogether the customes of the Moores or Mahometans, both in his meate and drinke and other customes, and would seeme to bee discontent if all men did not the like . . . he was very fickle in his resolucion, as alsoe of his religion'.[39]

It was not long before one of these factors made a formal conversion. On 5 April 1649, Francis Breton, the East India Company's most senior official in Asia, took up his quill and began to write a letter to the Directors back home. He had some bad news to break: 'And heere we wish to our penn might bee sylent,' he wrote, 'but to our griefe it must imparte unto you a sad story, itt tending not only to the losse of a man, but the dishonour of our nation, and (which is incomparably worse) of our Christian profession; occasioned in Agra by ye damned apostasy of one of your servants, Josua Blackwelle.'

Breton went on to describe how after prayers one Sunday, Blackwell had 'privately conveighed himselfe to the Governor of ye citty, who, being prepaired, with the Qazi [judge or senior lawyer] and others attended his comeing; before whome hee most wickedly and desperately renounced his Christian faith and professed himself a Moore, was immediately circumcised, and is irrecoverably lost'.*

Blackwell was only twenty-three, the son of 'the King's Grocer' at the Court of St James. He had left home at the age of seventeen and early on had been sent to oversee the East India Company's trading post at the Mughal court. It was an important appointment, for this was the apex of India's Mughal golden age, and from Agra the Emperor Shah Jehan ruled an empire that covered most of India, all of Pakistan and great chunks of Afghanistan; across the river from the small English community, the great white dome of the Taj Mahal was already rising from its plinth above the River Jumna. Blackwell was ambitious, and he knew that the wealth of the Mughal Emperor surpassed that of any prince in Europe; moreover the sheer size, sophistication and beauty of the Mughal capital at this point could not but profoundly challenge any notions Blackwell may ever have entertained of the superiority of Christendom. The pain of circumcision, he reckoned, was a small price to pay for gaining access to such a bountiful fount of patronage.[40] The letters sent after Blackwell by his colleagues are explicit about his motives, namely: 'idle hopes of worldly preferments' and 'the vaine suggestions of the Devill' which led him to hope for rapid enrichment.[41] As far as the other factors were concerned, it was ambition, not religious conviction, that led Blackwell to cross.

Blackwell was soon joined by many more British renegades, most

* Intriguingly, Breton himself went on to be buried in an entirely Muslim-looking octagonal tomb, with a dome, Tughluk-style arches and a Mughlai filial on top. It survives today, surrounded by grim 1960s blocks of flats on the northern outskirts of Surat. A picture of it can be seen in Christopher Ridgeway and Robert Williams (ed.), *Sir John Vanbrugh and Landscape Architecture in Baroque England* (London, 2000), p.126, plate 87. In a fascinating essay in this book, Robert Williams shows how Vanbrugh as a young Company factor in Surat admired and sketched Breton's tomb, and is later thought to have used the ideas he collected in the Surat cemeteries when planning his domed mausolea at such quintessentially English country houses as Blenheim and Castle Howard.

of whom headed into the service of the Deccani sultanates. In 1654, twenty-three East India Company servants deserted Surat in a single mass breakout. Others soon followed, having first run amok in Surat in the manner of many later groups of English hooligans on a night out abroad: 'Their private whorings, drunkenesse and such like ryotts ... breaking open whorehouses and rackehowses [i.e. arrack bars] have hardened the hearts of the inhabitants against our very names,' wrote a weary William Methwold. Little wonder that the British were soon being reviled in the streets 'with the names of Ban-chude* and Betty-chude† which my modest language will not interprett'.[42]

As with the Portuguese before them, the willingness of so many Britons to defect to the Mughals was partly a reflection of the disgusting conditions in which the British kept their ordinary soldiers and sailors, many of whom had not chosen to come to India of their own volition in the first place. The correspondence of the Madras Council is often full of complaints that the recruits the Company was sending out to India were the lowest detritus of British society: 'It is not uncommon to have them out of Newgate [prison], as several have confessed,' reads one letter, 'those however we can keep pretty much in order. But of late we have had some from Bedlam.'[43]

Men like this, often from the furthest geographical and social margins of British society, had little reason to feel any particular loyalty to the flag of a trading company owned by rich London merchants, and to such people the prospects offered by Mughal service often proved irresistible. In the 1670s the British were disturbed to discover that the Mughals had set up an active network of covert recruiting agents in Bombay, and by the 1680s such was their success that Charles II of England found it necessary to call home from India 'all Englishmen in indigenous service there'.[44] Few heeded his words. By the end of the century desertion had become a critical

---

* 'Sister-fucker'.
† 'Daughter-fucker'. Yule, incidentally, includes both terms in *Hobson-Jobson: A Glossary of Colloquial Anglo-Indian Words and Phrases* (London, 1903). He avoids giving direct translations of these still-popular Hindustani endearments, saying merely that 'Banchoot and Beteechoot [are] terms of abuse which we should hesitate to print if their odious meanings were not obscure "to the general". If it were known to the Englishmen who sometimes use the words we believe there are few who would not shrink from such brutality.'

problem for the Company as more and more Britons fled into Indian service, sometimes to the Mughal court, but increasingly, like the trumpeter Robert Trullye, to the rich and tolerant sultanates of Bijapur and Golconda which between them still controlled much of southern and central India.

This Deccani context is significant, for the great city states of the Deccan – like those of their contemporaries in Renaissance Italy – were always more eclectic and open to outsiders than even the cosmopolitan Imperial Mughal court in Agra. Relations between Hindus and Muslims had always been easier in the Deccan than in the more polarised north, and it had long been a Deccani tradition that the Hindu kings of Vijayanagar should make the gesture of dressing in public in Islamic court costume,[45] while every Muslim sultan in the region made a point of employing a Hindu Chief Minister.*

Into this ethnic and religious confusion was thrown a fantastic influx not just of Portuguese and other European mercenaries, but also galleys full of Middle Eastern immigrants who arrived at the Deccani ports direct from Persia, the Yemen and Egypt. These Middle Eastern immigrants turned the Deccan into the greatest centre of Arabic learning and literary composition outside the Levant, and brought with them a taste for the tilework of the Ottomans and the architectural innovations of Persia and Transoxiana.

This hybridity is immediately apparent in Deccani paintings. Typical is a miniature painted by Rahim Deccani around 1670.[46] On one side a prince is shown seated in profile wearing Deccani court dress; on the other are two female attendants, one playing a vina, the other looking on, bare-bellied, her dark nipples visible through the light covering of a diaphanous silk *choli*. So far no surprises: it is a conven-

---

* Some sultans even took on Hindu customs: early in his reign, Sultan Ibrahim Adil Shah II of Bijapur adopted the *rudraksha* rosary of the Hindu sadhu, assuming the title of *Jagat Guru*, or Teacher of the World. In his writings the Sultan used highly Sanskritised language to shower equal praise upon Sarasvati and the Prophet Muhammad, and at one point more or less described himself as a Hindu god: 'He is robed in saffron coloured dress . . . Ibrahim whose father is God Ganesh, whose mother is Sarasvati, has an elephant as his vehicle.' For Sultan Ibrahim Adil Shah see Richard Maxwell Eaton, *Sufis of Bijapur 1300–1700* (Princeton, 1978), pp.95–106; also George Michell and Mark Zebrowski, *The New Cambridge History of India 1.7: Architecture and Art of the Deccan Sultanates* (Cambridge, 1999), pp.162–7.

tional seventeenth-century Indian garden scene, an arcadia of culti-vated indulgence. But placed in the centre of the picture is a fourth courtesan, wearing gorgeous silk knickerbockers and the plumed, wide-brimmed hat and tumbling locks of a Jacobean dandy; at her feet is an Indian rendering of a King Charles spaniel. She serves her prince wine in a European glass.

A miniature where the world of Shah Jehan's harem comes into collision with the wardrobe of Guy Fawkes indicates the astonishingly eclectic tone of the Deccani courts, and helps explain why so many Europeans found themselves so easily absorbed into the ethnically composite élites of the region. Here former Portuguese artillerymen might find themselves in court beside Persian poets and calligraphers, turbaned Afghan warlords, reformed Shirazi sailors, ex-camel cavalrymen from the Hadramaut, renegade French jewellers and, not least, a smattering of newly ennobled English trumpeters.

The courts of the Deccan retained this ability to seduce and assimi-late outsiders. One hundred and fifty years after Robert Trullye was circumcised at the court of Golconda, James Achilles Kirkpatrick submitted to the same operation in the court of the dynasty which succeeded the Qutb Shahis: the Asaf Jahi Nizams of Hyderabad.

It was the long campaign of conquest against the Deccan sultanates, begun in 1636 by Shah Jehan and completed half a century later by Aurangzeb in 1687, that fatally overstretched the Mughal Empire, initiating its gradual 150-year-long decline. This in turn created a vast vacuum of power at the heart of India – a vacuum that some among the British were determined to fill.

In the course of the eighteenth century, as British power steadily increased, and that of the Mughals gradually declined, the incentives to cross cultures for financial betterment steadily diminished; as a result open conversions to Islam seem to have become correspondingly less common. But in India at least, as the East India Company slowly transformed itself from a mercantile organisation into a colonial government, discreet conversions did continue, albeit for rather different motives: by the late eighteenth century conversion was usually a precondition for marriage to any well-born Muslim lady.[47]

There were also a significant number of forced conversions. Between 1780 and 1784, following the disastrous British defeat by Tipu Sultan of Mysore at the Battle of Pollilur, seven thousand British men, along with an unknown number of women, were held captive by Tipu in his sophisticated fortress of Seringapatam.* Of these over three hundred were circumcised and given Muslim names and clothes.[48] Even more humiliatingly, several British regimental drummer boys were made to wear *ghagra cholis* and entertain the court as dancing girls.[49] At the end of ten years' captivity, one of these prisoners, James Scurry, found that he had forgotten how to sit in a chair or use a knife and fork; his English was 'broken and confused, having lost all its vernacular idiom', his skin had darkened to the 'swarthy complexion of Negroes', and he found he actively disliked wearing European clothes.[50] This was the ultimate colonial nightmare, and in its most unpalatable form: the captive preferring the ways of his captors, the coloniser colonised.

Nevertheless, during the last quarter of the eighteenth century, around the time that James Kirkpatrick first arrived in India, British power was growing steadily, and with it the attitudes of the British in India were beginning to change too. With their new confidence and growing power, the British cities of the coast were becoming more and more un-Indian: every year new English theatres and libraries were being built alongside churches modelled on St Martin-

---

* Tipu Sultan of Mysore (1753–99) was the most formidable enemy faced by the British in India in the late eighteenth century. He was the son of Haidar Ali, a former cavalry subaltern in the Nizam of Hyderabad's forces, who had displaced the Hindu Wodiyar rulers of Mysore and seized their throne for his own. Tipu was an energetic ruler and a military genius, though the British tended to dismiss him as an 'infamous tyrant', a 'usurper', and ruler of 'the most perfect despotism in the world'. After succeeding to the throne at his father's death in 1782, Tipu twice defeated the British and seized Coorg, Canara, Malabar and great chunks of the Nizam's dominions, before being slowly beaten back by the British under Cornwallis. He was finally killed during the storming of his river island fortress of Seringapatam in 1799 (see pp.192–3).

in-the-Fields. English newspapers were opened, English card games were played and English balls and masquerades were thrown. The Freemasons opened a Lodge, the Old Etonians started an annual cricket match, and by 1774 there was even a Calcutta Hunt Club.[51] It was not an immediate or complete change, and throughout the eighteenth century elements of the old intercultural hybridity continued. Indian dress, for example, remained popular in private and in informal public situations, as a form of casual 'undress' (as it was then called). Until the 1770s it was not unknown even for members of the Council in Calcutta to wear it for meetings; apart from anything else it was, of course, much better suited to the climate.*

The ease with which so many Company servants continued to take on Indian ways is in part a reflection of the receptive age at which so many of them arrived in India: according to the statutes of the East India Company no one was allowed to join after the age of sixteen, so that any official who had reached the age of thirty had usually spent at least half his life in India. As the disapproving British missionary the Rev. Claudius Buchanan put it, expressing the fears and anxieties of many generations of Imperial and religious officials in Britain: 'What was to be looked for in a remote and extensive Empire, administered in all its parts by men, who came out boys, without the plenitude of instruction of English youth in learning, morals, or religion; and who were let loose on their arrival amidst native licentiousness, and educated amidst conflicting superstitions?'[52]

Yet for all this an important distinction was beginning to develop between the British who lived in the increasingly European ambience of the three coastal cities and those who lived in – and to varying

---

* Certainly in eighteenth-century Madras idle young factors could still be found loafing around at midday 'in long draws, a banian coat, and slippers' and attending both church and the parade ground in 'Moormen's suits', while as late as 1788 Eliza Davidson noted the growing fashion for turbans among the women of the colony, writing of 'caps, Hats &c, &c, all now given away for this more convenient Asiatic head dress'. See Amin Jaffer, *Furniture from British India and Ceylon* (London, 2001), p.40. The Madras wills and inventories for the period show the quantity of such clothes in Britons' wardrobes. Captain James Cope for example bequeathed 'all my Moors clothes' to his *dubash*. Captain d'Illens had 'a pair of Moorman's slippers, 3 ditto coats, and 3 tappets and a sash', while Captain Callender had two complete 'Moormens' suits, and Achilles Preston five. Henry Dodwell, *The Nabobs of Madras* (London, 1926), p.184.

extents became part of – the real Indian India beyond the walls of the Presidency towns. The degree to which an individual was exposed to this very different and initially very foreign world depended increasingly on where he was posted, just as the extent to which he reacted to such influences was determined by his individual sympathies and temperament.

As before, the greatest transformations took place amongst those completely cut off from European society, notably those East India Company officials who were posted to the more distant Indian courts. James Kirkpatrick's counterpart as British Resident in Delhi was the Boston-born Sir David Ochterlony, an old friend of Kirkpatrick's elder brother William. Ochterlony was a man already well used to walking the cultural faultlines between different worlds. His father was a Highland Scot who had settled in Massachusetts. When the American Revolution broke out, the family fled to Canada, and thence to London where David entered the Company's army in 1777. He never returned to the New World, and having made India his home vowed never to leave.

When in the Indian capital, Ochterlony liked to be addressed by his full Mughal title, Nasir-ud-Daula (Defender of the State), and to live the life of a Mughal gentleman: every evening all thirteen of his consorts used to process around Delhi behind their husband, each on the back of her own elephant.[53] With his fondness for hookahs and nautch girls and Indian costumes, Ochterlony amazed Bishop Reginald Heber, the Anglican Primate of Calcutta, by receiving him sitting on a divan wearing a '*choga* and *pagri*' while being fanned by servants holding peacock-feather *punkhas*. To one side of Ochterlony's own tent was the red silk harem tent where his women slept, and on the other side the encampment of his daughters, all, according to the Bishop, 'hung around with red cloth and thus fenced in from the eyes of the profane'.

Ochterlony's cortège, which the Bishop later spotted on the move through the country of Rajputana, was equally remarkable: 'There was a considerable number of horses, elephants, palanquins and covered [harem] carriages,' wrote Heber. '[long lines of regular army sepoys], and I should guess forty or fifty irregulars, on horse and foot, armed with spears and matchlocks of all possible forms; the string of camels [and elephants] was a very long one ... [it might have been] an Eastern prince travelling. Sir David himself was in a carriage and four. He is a tall and pleasing looking old man, but was so wrapped up in shawls, Kincob fur and a Mogul furred cap, that his face was all that was visible ... He has been absent from his home country about 54 years; he has there neither friends nor relations, and he has been for many years habituated to Eastern habits and parade. And if he shows no sign of retiring and returning to Britain who can wonder that he clings to the only country in the world where he can feel himself at home?'[54]

Every bit as assimilated into their Indian surroundings were those European mercenaries who fought for Indian rulers. A pair of Irish mercenaries who both came out to India in the mid-eighteenth century as common seamen, and who separately jumped ship and worked their way across India training the sepoys of Indian rulers, show how far these transformations could go.

Thomas Legge, from Donaghadee in Ulster, developed an interest in Indian alchemy and divination and ended his days as a fakir living naked in an empty tomb in the deserts of Rajasthan outside Jaipur. He had travelled through central India and Hindustan to Sindh, occasionally taking up work as a cavalry officer and cannon-maker, before heading on again up the Indus into the Pamirs and exploring Kabul and Badakshan. At some point he returned to India where he married a granddaughter of Favier de Silva, a celebrated Portuguese astrologer who was sent out to India by the King of Portugal to advise Maharajah Jai Singh of Jaipur – builder of the great Delhi observatory, the Jantar Mantar – on matters astrological.

At one point Legge met James Tod, the author of the *Annals and Antiquities of Rajasthan* whose almost complete absorption into Rajasthani culture led even the Indophile Ochterlony to complain that Tod was 'too much of a Rajpoot himself to deal with Rajpoots'. Tod, who clearly recognised in Legge a kindred spirit, was fascinated by the ragged visionary who appeared at this camp, and the two men talked deep into the night as the Irishman told Tod of his studies in Indian alchemy and divination, and revealed that in his travels he believed he had discovered the Garden of Eden deep in the Hindu Kush – giving Tod a Hibernian version of one the most ancient legends of central Asia: 'Deep down in the heart of a mountain,' Legge told Tod, 'was situated a beautiful garden, filled with delicious fruit, with piles of gold bricks at one end, and of silver at the other.' At length Tod delivered Legge back to his deserted tomb, where he resumed his life as a fakir. He died not long afterwards, in 1808, and was buried in the tomb in which he had lived.[55]

Another of Legge's contemporaries, George Thomas, had his roots in the opposite end of Ireland, but like Legge took service among the rajahs of the north of India. In due course, at the end of the eighteenth century, Thomas succeeded in carving out his own state in the Mewatti badlands west of Delhi, and was a possible model for Peachey Carnehan in Kipling's *The Man Who Would be King*. 'The Rajah from Tipperary', as he was known back home, was referred to in India as 'Jehaz Sahib' – a name which may have derived from an Indian mangling of George, or be a reference to his naval past, *jehaz* being Urdu for ship.

Once established in his Haryana kingdom, Jehaz Sahib built himself a palace, minted his own coins and collected about him a harem, but in the process totally forgot how to speak English; when asked at the end of his career to dictate his autobiography, he said he would be happy to do so as long as he could speak in Persian, 'as from constant use it was become more familiar than his native tongue'.[56] William Franklin, who eventually took down Thomas's dictated memoirs, said that though Thomas was uneducated 'he spoke, wrote and read the Hindoostany and Persian languages with uncommon fluency and precision'; indeed his Anglo-Indian son, Jan Thomas, became a celebrated Urdu poet in the *mohallas* of Old Delhi, and is depicted in miniatures of the period wearing the extravagant dress and raffish haircut of a late Mughal *banka* or gallant.[57]

Such transformations might still have been common in the interior, but by the 1780s if an East India Company official stayed in Calcutta, Madras or Bombay, or indeed one of the big Bengal cantonments, his exposure to Indian customs could sometimes be very limited indeed. Eighteenth-century Calcutta in particular struck visitors as a dislocated outpost of Europe, as if Regency Bath had been relocated to the Bay of Bengal.

'Calcutta,' wrote Robert Clive, 'is one of the most wicked places in the Universe . . . Rapacious and Luxurious beyond conception.'[58] If it was a city where great wealth could be accumulated in a matter of months, it was also one where it could be lost in minutes in a wager, or at the whist table. Death, from disease or excess, was a commonplace, and the constant presence of mortality made men callous: they would mourn briefly for some perished friend, then bid drunkenly for his horses and buggies.

At the centre of Calcutta lay the Writers' Building, where the young Company officials were lodged while they underwent their initial training. In form it was little different from the British public schools from which most of the Writers had recently been drawn, and its inhabitants continued to behave as if the building occupied a loop of the Thames rather than a bend in the Hoogly. The favourite after-dinner toast was to turn the traditional ditty 'Alas and Alack-the-Day' into 'A Lass and a Lakh* a Day' – a succinct comment on the motives that led most of these Writers to come out to India in the first place.

In time, almost all of these Calcutta-based Writers would take on a few superficial glosses of Indianness. These might include riding in a palanquin, attending nautches (Indian dance displays) or smoking a hookah: indeed in the 1780s hookah-smoking became the height of fashion, even for the very few British women resident in Calcutta.†

---

* i.e. One hundred thousand rupees.
† The diarist William Hickey records that he was told on arrival that 'Here everyone uses a hookah, and it is impossible to get on without [it].' He added: 'I have frequently heard men declare that they would much rather be deprived of their dinner than their hookah.' William Hickey (ed. A. Spencer), *The Memoirs of William Hickey* (4 vols, London, 1925), Vol. 2, p.136. Such was their popularity that special places had to be allotted for them in boxes at the theatre in Calcutta. Making little carpets for the hookahs to rest upon even came to be regarded as a suitable pastime for bored British memsahibs.

Nevertheless in this insular world the only way that a Briton in Calcutta could come into close or intimate contact with Indians and Indian society was if he took an Indian *bibi*, or companion. In the second half of the eighteenth century the majority of Company servants still seem to have done this: of the Bengal Wills from 1780 to 1785 preserved in the India Office, one in three contains a bequest to Indian wives or companions or their natural children.[59] It can safely be assumed that many more kept Indian mistresses without wishing to leave a formal legal record of the fact.

The practice became so common that the Urdu poets in Lucknow began abandoning the old time-honoured formula of Hindustani romantic poetry – Muslim boy meets Hindu girl with fatal consequences – and began composing *masnavi* where Hindu girls fell for English men, though with the same time-honoured dénouement. In Rajab Ali Beg Suroor's *The Story of Wonders*, the love-struck Englishman ('a handsome youth of noble lineage and high rank; in his head the ardour of love; in his heart the fire of passion . . .') falls so deeply in love with the beautiful daughter of a Hindu shopkeeper that he lapses into love-induced insanity before dying of heartbreak when the girl's parents forbid the romance ('he dropped on the bed of dust, crying in anguish . . .'). The story ends with a scene reminiscent of a modern Bollywood movie when his Hindu lady-love throws herself onto his coffin from a second-floor window as the funeral procession winds its way past her door, leaving her mortally injured. Suroor concludes:

> The attraction of passionate love united the separated ones. All who had witnessed this scene shuddered in awe and the more compassionate ones fainted. Rumours about the misfortune spread through the city. The girl's parents were so grief-stricken that they soon died. This is what Love the troublemaker has done: it laid to rest, side by side in the dust, the victims of separation as well as those responsible for it. People in their thousands would come to look at their tomb . . .[60]

Many wills from the period rather touchingly confirm the impression of Suroor's *masnavi* in suggesting that ties of great affection and loyalty on both sides were not uncommon at this time. Certainly many contain clauses where British men ask their close friends and family to care for their Indian partners, referring to them as 'well beloved', 'worthy friend' or 'this amiable and distinguished lady'. The wills also show that in many cases the *bibis* achieved a surprising degree of empowerment. A few refer to contracts – something like eighteenth-century prenuptial agreements – and many women inherited considerable sums and households full of slaves from their English partners on their death. When Major Thomas Naylor died in 1782, for example, he bequeathed to his companion Muckmul Patna forty thousand rupees,* a bungalow and a garden at Berhampore, a hackery, bullocks, jewels, clothes and all their male and female slaves.[61] Another East India Company merchant, Matthew Leslie, left each of his four wives a house and twenty thousand rupees, a very considerable bequest.[62]

Having an Indian concubine did not of course lead to any automatic sympathy with India or Indian culture on the part of a Company servant – far from it. But it was recognised at the time that in practice cohabitation often did lead to a degree of transculturation, even in the transplanted Englishness of Calcutta. Thomas Williamson for one was quite clear as to the effect that taking a *bibi* had on a newly arrived Englishman: '. . . in the early part of their career', he wrote, 'young men attach themselves to the women of this country; and acquire a liking, or taste, for their society and customs, which soon supersedes every other attraction'.[63] The explorer Richard Burton echoed a similar idea a little later: an Indian mistress taught her companion, he wrote, 'not only Hindustani grammer, but the syntaxes of native Life'.[64]†

---

* At least £240,000 in today's currency.

† Again, this was a two-way process. The few surviving wills of the *bibis* (Durba Ghosh, in her extensive search through archives in England and India, 'Colonial Companions', found only thirty-seven) indicate that just as their consorts were picking up Indian habits and Indian ways in this hybrid milieu, so the women were undergoing a similar journey in reverse, and picking up European manners and ways of living. According to Ghosh, many of them 'wore European clothes, owned European furniture, ate European food, [but they also] had brass pots and pans, hookah implements, betel eating accessories and wore saris and shawls'; a few even converted to Christianity. As with the world inhabited by the Indo-Portuguese of Goa two centuries earlier, we are clearly in a hybrid environment of overlapping practices: a fecund multicultural, multi-ethnic and multi-religious confusion of different ways and modes of living.

At a time when the British showed no particular enthusiasm for cleanliness, Indian women for example introduced British men to the delights of regular bathing. The fact that the word shampoo is derived from the Hindi word for massage, and that it entered the English language at this time, shows the novelty to the eighteenth-century British of the Indian idea of cleaning hair with materials other than soap.[65] Those who returned home and continued to bathe and shampoo themselves on a regular basis found themselves scoffed at by their less hygienic compatriots: indeed it was a cliché of the time that the British in Bengal had become 'effeminate'.[66] A few Calcutta men were known to have had themselves circumcised to satisfy the hygienic – and presumably religious – requirements of their Indian wives and companions.[67]

As a result of similar influence, some East India Company servants were even persuaded to become vegetarians. A novel of the period paints an intriguing portrait of a returned Calcutta nabob* tormented by depression following the premature death of his Hindu bride. He had become 'a person neither English nor Indian, Christian nor Hindu. In diet he was a rigid disciple of Brama', eating rice, fruit, potatoes and other vegetables while 'looking upon the slaughter of a cow as only next to the murder of a human being'.[68] That this tendency was not restricted to fiction is clear from the writings of several vegetarian nabobs from the period, including the Mayor of Calcutta and survivor of the Black Hole, John Zephania Holwell, as well as the enigmatic Irish General whose collection of sculptures forms the core of the British Museum Indian Collection, Major General Charles 'Hindoo' Stuart. Stuart, who travelled around the country with his Indian *bibi* beside him, his buggy followed by a cavalcade of children's carriages 'and a palkee load of little babes',[69] went as far as employing a group of Brahmins whose ritual purity he regarded as essential for properly dressing his Hindu family's food.[70]

---

* Old India hands who returned to England with their fortunes came to be known as 'nabobs' in the eighteenth century, especially after Samuel Foote's 1779 play *The Nabob* brought the term into general circulation. The word is a corruption of the Hindustani *nawab*, literally 'deputy', which was the title given by the Mughal emperors to their regional governors and viceroys.

Not all the relationships recorded in the wills of the period make such happy reading, and there are many in which Indian *bibis* are treated with a chilling carelessness: Alexander Crawford, writing his will in Chittagong in 1782, goes into extravagant details as to how he wants his executors to care for his dogs and horses. After several pages of this sort of thing he adds, almost as an afterthought, 'To my girl I desire that two thousand rupees may be given for her care of my children provided that she places them under your charge without any further trouble.' Unlike the animals, no name is given for her, and there are certainly no last endearments recorded.[71] Judging by the wills they left, many Englishmen were serial monogamists, moving on from one partner to another, sometimes at speed, and a substantial number kept two *bibis* simultaneously. A few indeed had large harems, even by contemporary Indian standards. Such a case is recorded by Thomas Williamson, whose *East India Vade Mecum* was the standard guide to life in Calcutta for young Company officials coming out to India, and which was to the eighteenth-century Company servant what the *Lonely Planet* guide is to the modern backpacker. Williamson writes of the case of one Company servant who kept no fewer than sixteen concubines. When asked what he did with them all, he merely muttered: 'Oh I just give them a little rice and let them run around.'[72]

William Hickey's relationship with his Bengali *bibi* Jemdanee is a good example of the sort of relationship a Calcutta nabob might form with an Indian woman at this time. The relationship started as one of simple concubinage. Hickey makes no bones about the way he inherited Jemdanee after a neighbour returned home to England: 'I had often admired a lovely Hindustani girl who sometimes visited Carter at my house,' he writes in his *Memoirs*. '[She] was very lively and clever. Upon Carter's leaving Bengal I invited her to become an intimate with me, which she consented to do.'[73] Yet the relationship quickly developed into something deeper: 'From that day to the day of her death Jemdanee lived with me, respected and admired by all my friends for her extraordinary sprightliness and good humour. Unlike many of the women of Asia she never secluded herself from the sight of strangers; on the contrary she delighted in joining my male parties, cordially joining in the mirth though never touching wine or spirits of any kind.'

Jemdanee was also a great favourite with one of Hickey's best friends, Ben Mee: 'My love and good wishes to the gentle and every way amiable Jemdanee,' Mee wrote in one letter. 'Would that her good natured countenance and sweet temper were here ... [We would share] some nice highly peppered curries.'[74] Hickey's *Memoirs* are interspersed with these occasional letters from Mee, who soon absconds to Europe on the run from his debtors, from where he sends presents to Jemdanee. From Paris he writes: 'I lately met with some ornaments, fresh from Paris, which from being so I think likely she will admire and cry "Wah! Wah!" [Hurrah! Hurrah!] at; they consist of bracelets, necklace and earrings. My best love to her and I beg her to wear them for my sake.'[75]

When Hickey is ill 'my kind hearted and interesting favourite ... sat by my side anxiously watching my varying countenances as the agonizing pain I endured increased or diminished'.[76] When he is better, they buy a 'large and commodious Residence in Garden Reach, about seven miles and a half from Calcutta, beautifully situated within a few yards of the river, affording us the advantage of water as well as land carriage'. Here Hickey takes four apartments 'for my sole use, that Jemdanee and her female attendants might be sufficiently private and retired ... Jemdanee was so pleased with the novelty of the thing that nothing would satisfy her but remaining there entirely. She therefore sent for her establishment and settled herself in our upper rooms.'[77]

After a while Jemdanee became pregnant, 'regularly increasing in bulk ... expressing her earnest desire that it might prove "a chuta William Saheb"'.

She remained in uninterrupted health and the highest flow of spirits until the 4th of August when having laughed and chatted with her after my breakfast, I went to the Court House to attend a case of considerable importance. I had not been there more than an hour when several of my servants in the utmost alarm ran over to tell me that the Bibee Sahib was dying. Instantly going home, I found my poor girl in a state of insensibility, apparently with a locked jaw, her teeth being so far clenched together that no force could separate them. She had just been delivered of a fine healthy looking child which was remarkably fair.

Hickey discovered that Jemdanee had become terrified when 'after an hour in violent agony' she gave birth to a child, only to be told by the Bengali midwife – Hickey's European doctor Dr Hare then being absent on business – that she should lie still for she was going to have twins 'and another child was coming. This so terrified the poor suffering girl, that giving a violent screech, she instantly went into strong convulsions . . .'

> Doctor Hare arrived in five minutes after I got home, and was greatly surprised and alarmed at the state in which he found her, for which he could in no way account. By the application of powerful drugs which the Doctor administered, she, in half an hour, recovered her senses and speech, appeared very solicitous to encourage and comfort me, saying she had no doubt she should do very well. Doctor Hare also gave me his assurances that the dangerous paroxysm was past and all would be as we could wish. With this comfortable assurance I again went to attend my business in Court, from whence I was once more hastily summoned to attend to my dying favourite, who had been suddenly attacked by a second fit from which she never recovered, but lay in a state of confirmed apoplexy until nine o'clock at night when she, without a pang, expired.

'Thus,' wrote a heartbroken Hickey, 'did I lose as gentle and affectionately attached a girl as ever a man was blessed with.'[78] It was several months before he had recovered sufficiently from the death to resume his work in the Calcutta courts.

Hinduism, and Hindu culture in general, proved less accessible to the British than Islam, at least partly because many Hindus regarded the British as untouchable, refusing to eat with them, so restricting somewhat the possibilities for social intercourse. Yet this did not put off many of Hinduism's more ardent British admirers, and as a subject for intellectual study, Hinduism took precedence over Islam amongst the early British in Calcutta.

In March 1775 a twenty-three-year-old Company official, Nathaniel Brassey Halhed, published his translation of *A Code of Gentoo Laws*.[79] The response in Britain to this first revelation of 'the wisdom of the Hindoos' was electric. As the reviewer in the *Critical Review* put it:

> This is a most sublime performance ... [we] are persuaded that even this enlightened quarter of the globe [i.e. Europe] cannot boast anything which soars so completely above the narrow, vulgar sphere of prejudice and priestcraft. The most amiable part of modern philosophy is hardly upon a level with the extensive charity, the comprehensive benevolence, of a few rude, untutored Hindoo Bramins ... Mr Halhed has rendered more real service to his country, to the world in general, by this performance, than ever flowed from all the wealth of all the *nabobs* by whom the country of these poor people has been plundered ... Wealth is not the only, nor the most valuable commodity, which Britain might import from India.[80]

Edmund Burke agreed. He read Halhed's book and, according to Charles James Fox, thereafter 'spoke of the piety of the Hindoos with admiration, and of their holy religion and sacred functions with an awe bordering on devotion'; in Parliament Burke declared that 'Wherever the Hindu religion has been established, that country has been flourishing.'[81] This was still the Age of Reason, and loss of faith in the more intolerant and narrow aspects of Christianity combined with a growing interest in non-European civilisations to create an intellectual climate deeply receptive to the sort of ideas Halhed claimed lay at the heart of Hinduism.

Into this arena of intellectual excitement sailed, on 15 January 1784, the Justice of the new Supreme Court at Calcutta, Sir William Jones. Less than six weeks after he had landed, Jones had gathered together a group of thirty kindred spirits, to institute 'a Society for enquiring into the History, Civil and Natural, the Antiquities, Arts, Sciences and Literature of Asia'. Its patron was the most enlightened of all the British Governors General, Warren Hastings, who shared the new enthusiasm for Hinduism and who declared: 'in truth I love India a little more than my own country'.[82] Under Jones and Hastings, the Asiatic Society of Bengal quickly became the catalyst for a sudden explosion of interest in Hinduism, as it formed enduring relations with the local Bengali intelligentsia and led the way to uncovering the deepest roots of Indian history and civilisation. In this way it was hoped to educate Europe about this relatively unknown civilisation; as Hastings put it, 'such studies, independent of utility, will diffuse a generosity of sentiment . . . [after all, the Indian classics] will survive when British dominion in India shall have long ceased to exist, and when the sources which it once yielded of wealth and power are lost to remembrance'.[83]

Before long Jones had decamped to Krishnagar, sixty miles up the Ganges from Calcutta, where he adopted the local Indian dress of loose white cotton and rented a bungalow built 'entirely of vegetable materials'. Here he surrounded himself with Brahmins who helped him learn Sanskrit, a language which he soon realised was 'more perfect than Greek, more copious than Latin, and more exquisitely refined than either'. As for Sanskrit literature, Jones was agog at the wonders he daily uncovered: 'I am in love with the *gopis*,' he wrote soon after his arrival, 'charmed with Krishna and an enthusiastic admirer of Rama. Arjun, Bhima and the warriors of the *Mahabharata* appear greater in my eyes than Ajax or Achilles appeared when I first read the *Iliad*.'

Many of Jones's letters seem to have been written from here. 'I concur with you,' he writes to one friend, 'in paying adoration to springs and rivers; and I am going soon up the great stream Ma Gunga and towards the Holy banks of the God Jumna.' He congratulates one correspondent on finding a well-preserved copy of the Gita, another on the way he has learned to sing 'Hindoostanee airs'. One day he is sending letters up country requesting information from the Pundits of Benares on the different names and avatars of a particular god, on the next recommending the Calcutta doctors to try out various ayurvedic cures. In India, Jones wrote that he had discovered Arcadia.[84] Valmiki was the new Homer, the *Ramayana* the new *Odyssey*. The possibilities seemed endless.

Nevertheless, despite their enthusiasm, few of the Calcutta Sanskritists let their interest in Hinduism stray far beyond the intellectual. Jones himself remained a practising member of the Church of England, albeit one who showed an attachment to the idea of reincarnation: 'I am no Hindu,' he wrote, 'but I hold the doctrines of the Hindus concerning a future state to be incomparably more rational, more pious and more likely to deter men from vice than the horrid opinions inculcated by the Christians on punishment without end.'[85] But there were some others who went further. Technically it is impossible to convert to Hinduism: as much a social system as a religion, to be a Hindu you must be born a Hindu; traditionally there was no ceremony for conversion. No one, however, seems to have told this to 'Hindoo Stuart'.

Not much is known about this strange Irishman who in the 1780s came out to India while still in his teens; but he seems to have been almost immediately attracted to Hinduism, and within a year of his arrival in Calcutta had adopted the practice – which he continued to his death – of walking every morning from his house to bathe in and worship the Ganges according to Hindu custom. As his obituary in the *Asiatic Journal* put it: 'General Stuart had studied the language, manners and customs of the natives of this country with so much enthusiasm, that his intimacy with them, and his toleration of, or rather apparent conformity to their ideas and prejudices, obtained for him the name *Hindoo* Stuart, by which, we believe, he is well known to our readers.'[86] In his writings he explicitly refers to himself as a 'convert' to Hinduism.*

* The inventory of goods that Stuart left behind him when he died gives a powerful picture of someone strung between two different worlds. On the one hand he clearly has the normal paraphernalia of a Georgian gentleman – sugar tongs, toast racks and billiard cues, along with the usual camp tables, map cases and portable furniture you might

Stuart's military contemporaries, even those who were enthusiastic Indophiles themselves, never quite knew what to make of their General. At one point Hindoo Stuart was given command of the largest cavalry cantonment in central India, where he found that his deputy was an old acquaintance of James Kirkpatrick's, William Linnaeus Gardner, who like Kirkpatrick himself was almost certainly a convert to Islam. Gardner's letters to a cousin give a flavour of life in this bizarre outpost of the East India Company military establishment commanded by a pair of converts to India's two rival religions.

The first reference to Hindoo Stuart in his deputy's letters occurs just as the previous General is leaving and it has been announced that Stuart is to take over. 'General Watson left us this morning,' wrote Gardner, 'and, good and kind as he is, I am happy he is off for the farewell dinners are most appalling events, particularly where a Man's loyalty is measured by the number of Bottles he can gulp down. General Stuart, his successor, I suppose does not pride himself on the capacity of his stomach or the strength of his head as he regularly performs his *pooja* and avoids the sight of Beef.'

From this point Stuart features regularly in the Gardner correspondence, under the pet name 'General Pundit' or 'Pundit Stuart'. On one occasion Gardner remarks: 'The General is an odd fish. He wrote to me to come to him at Chukla Ghat where the Hindoos bathe – particularly the women! He has the *Itch* beyond any man I ever knew. On this spot he is going to build a pagoda [temple]! Every Hindu he salutes with Jey Sittaramjee!' On another occasion Gardner says he is going to have to take command as the General is planning to go off for a week to bathe at the Kumb Mela. On another he reports how a friend had just returned from the weekly horse fair held at Saugor. In the midst of it he found Stuart sitting 'surrounded by a

---

expect from a campaigning soldier of the period; he also clearly enjoyed his *shikar* (hunting). On the other he owns a quite amazing amount of 'Hindoostanee' clothes and objects: pointed slippers, Mughal water flagons, yak-tailed flywhisks, spittoons for betel, hookahs and so on. The list also details a huge collection of statues of Hindu deities which Stuart appears to have worshipped. Certainly he built a Hindu temple at Saugor, and when he visited Europe he took his Hindu household gods with him. Inventory of goods of the late Major Genl. C. Stuart, OIOC L/AG/34/27/93–765: pp.745–63 [museum] and 765–87 [personal].

dozen naked faqueers who, joining their hands over his head, gave him Benediction'.[87]

Stuart was not just an admirer of the Indian religions, he was also an enthusiastic devotee of Hindu women and their dress sense. In the early years of the nineteenth century he wrote a series of improbable articles in the Calcutta *Telegraph* in which he tried to persuade the European women of the city to adopt the sari, on the grounds that it was so much more attractive than contemporary European fashions, and warning that otherwise Englishwomen had no hope of competing with the beauty of the women of India:

> The majority of Hindoo women are comparatively small, yet there is much voluptuousness of appearance: – a fulness that delights the eye; a firmness that enchants the sense; a sleekness and purity of skin; an expression of countenance, a grace, and a modesty of demeanour, that renders them universally attractive ... The new-mown hay is not sweeter than their breath ... I have seen ladies of the Gentoo cast, so exquisitely formed, with limbs so divinely turned, and such expression in their eyes, that you must acknowledge them not inferior to the most celebrated beauties of Europe. For my own part, I already begin to think the dazzling brightness of a copper coloured face, infinitely preferable to the pallid and sickly hue of the European fair.*

If Stuart's extreme passion for all things Hindu was definitely unusual, showing respect for Hinduism and participating in its rituals was not, and there are frequent references in the sources of the period

---

* Stuart was also perhaps the first recorded devotee of what the Bollywood film industry now knows as the wet-sari scene: 'For the information of ladies recently arrived in this country, it may be necessary to state that the Hindoo female, modest as the rosebud, bathes completely dressed ... and necessarily rises with wet drapery from the stream. Had I despotic power, our British fair ones should soon follow the example; being fully persuaded that it would eminently contribute to keep the bridal torch for ever in a blaze.' Stuart's articles were anonymously reprinted in *A LADIES' MONITOR Being a series of letters first published in Bengal on the subject of FEMALE APPAREL Tending to favour a regulated adoption of Indian Costume; and a rejection of SUPERFLUOUS VESTURE By the ladies of this country: with Incidental remarks on Hindoo beauty; whale bone stays; iron busks; Indian corsets; man-milliners; idle bachelors, hair powder, side saddles, waiting-maids; and footmen. By the author of A VINDICATION OF THE HINDOOS* (Calcutta, 1809).

to Company officials attending pujas, presenting gifts in temples and participating in sacrifices. James Grant, for example, gave a bell to the Durga temple in Benares after the priests there had prayed for his safety when he and his wife and children were caught in a whirlpool in the Ganges immediately opposite the temple.[88] About the same time the British celebrated the Treaty of Amiens by marching with military bands to the Temple of Kali.[89]

Hindu texts confirm this open-minded attitude. At the suggestion of some Brahmins, General Richard Matthews is recorded in a Tamil history of the period as praying to a Hindu deity at a temple in Takkolam in order to be cured of some crippling stomach aches. According to the anonymous author of the history, Matthews was successfully cured of his pains and thereafter gave generously to the temple. The story opens with the General camped near the temple, where his troops hope to make use of the water from the temple spring. But after his 'pariahs and lower [caste] attendants' have entered the temple, the water supply which 'usually fell through the Cows Mouth [in a jet] the size of an elephant's trunk with great noise' mysteriously fails:

> The general then promised money to defray the expenses of *Homa* [fire ceremonies for the purification] that water might fall from the Cow's Mouth as before; but the Brahmins replied that they could not make the water to fall as before, whereupon the Gentleman was angry at the Brahmins, & gave them leave to return to their Houses and he returned to his tent –
>
> That night the gentleman was seized with a terrible pain in his bowels, which threatened to endanger his life, and believing that it was owing to his forcibly entering into the pagoda & looking into every place, he sent for the Poojaries and questioned them. They recommended him to pray to the God, thro' whom he would be cured. Next morning General Matthews came & stood in the Pagoda in the presence of the God, and there prayed to the God; he then returned to his tents & in that same moment he recovered from his pain; therefore that gentleman presented a bag of 1000 pagodas to the God and ordered them still to continue to worship; he

also added some villages to the allowances of the God. There-
upon the Poojaries brought a number of cows into the pagoda
& performed the *Pooniacharum*, or ceremony of purification;
and they assembled the Brahmins & entertained them all for
the sake of the God; whereupon the water which before fell
from the Cows Mouth in a stream of the size of an elephants
trunk, fell again.

'General Matthews,' adds the author, 'remained six months in that
place; and he used to have the water that fell from the cows mouth
brought to him for his own drinking ... When the general went
away he left his concubine at this place.'[90]

Not all Company officials shared the enthusiasm of Generals Stuart
and Matthews either for India in general, or for Hinduism in particular.

Most powerful of the critics was one of the Company's Directors,
Charles Grant. Grant was among the first of the new breed of Evangelical Christians, and he brought his fundamentalist religious
opinions directly to the East India Company boardroom. Writing
that 'it is hardly possible to conceive any people more completely
enchained than they [the Hindus] are by their superstitions', he
proposed in 1787 to launch missions to convert a people whom
he characterised as 'universally and wholly corrupt ... depraved as
they are blind, and wretched as they are depraved'.[91] Within a few
decades the missionaries – initially based at the Danish settlement
of Serampore – were beginning fundamentally to change British perceptions of the Hindus. No longer were they inheritors of a body of
sublime and ancient wisdom, as Jones and Hastings believed, but
instead merely 'poor benighted heathen', or even 'licentious pagans',
some of whom, it was hoped, were eagerly awaiting conversion, and
with it the path to Civilisation.

The Rev. R. Ainslie was typical of Grant's missionaries. In *British Idolatry in India*, a sermon printed and disseminated to the Evangelical faithful back home, the excitable Ainslie wrote of his visit to a temple in Orissa: 'I have visited the Valley of Death!' he told a hushed congregation. 'I have seen the Den of Darkness!' The sermon goes on for nearly twenty pages, describing the 'sinful and disgusting scenes' the Rev. Ainslie had witnessed. These 'sinful scenes', rather disappointingly, turn out to be nothing more than Company officials assisting the Hindus in their rites. Of the great Juggernaut procession in Orissa, Ainslie comments: 'The cloths and mantles are furnished for the idol pageantry by British servants. The horrors are unutterable ... Do not European gentlemen encourage these ceremonies, and make presents to the idol, and often fall down and worship?'[92]

One of the most outspoken of the missionaries was the Rev. Alexander Thompson, who after a lifetime of denouncing the evils of Hinduism devoted his retirement to writing a long and intemperate tract entitled *The Government Connection with Idolatry in India*.[93] According to Thompson, the enthusiasm of Company officials of the late eighteenth century had become one of the main causes of a major Hindu revival. Looking back to the 1790s, he reminds his readers that

> the chief officers of the Government [at that time] belonged to a peculiar class. Those who between 1790 and 1820 possessed the greatest experience, and held the highest offices in India, were on the whole an irreligious body of men; who approved of Hinduism much more than Christianity, and favoured the Koran more than the Bible. Some hated Missions from their dread of sedition; and others because their hearts 'seduced by fair idolatresses, had fallen to idols foul'.*

* Thompson gives a fascinating list of examples of Company participation in Hindu rituals. At Cuddapah 'prayers for rain (*Varuna Pujam*) were ordered by the Collector to be presented at the various temples in seasons when drought and famine were feared', and '150 star pagodas' of government revenue put aside to finance the pujas. In Madras the Collector had revived the defunct 'festival of the idol Yeggata', and given presents to the idol in the name of the Company. On another occasion Thompson tells how a missionary acquaintance of his discovered that at the salt warehouses at the mouth of the Ganges, the Company employed a full-time Brahmin to perform prayers to the

The 'Brahminised' British – as they came to be known – did not go down before the missionary onslaught without a fight. It was to combat the intolerance of these Evangelicals that Hindoo Stuart anonymously published a pamphlet called *A Vindication of the Hindoos.*[94] In this text he tried to discourage any attempt by European missionaries to convert the Hindus, arguing that, as he put it, 'on the enlarged principles of moral reasoning, Hinduism little needs the meliorating hand of Christianity to render its votaries a sufficiently correct and moral people for all the useful purposes of a civilised society'. On the subject of Hindu mythology, which the missionaries ridiculed at every turn, Stuart wrote: 'Whenever I look around me, in the vast region of Hindoo Mythology, I discover piety in the garb of allegory: and I see Morality, at every turn, blended with every tale; and, as far as I can rely on my own judgement, it appears the most complete and ample system of Moral Allegory that the world has ever produced.' He also pointed out that the *Vedas* were 'written at that remote period in which our savage ancestors of the forest were perhaps unconscious of a God; and were, doubtless, strangers to the glorious doctrine of the immortality of the soul, first revealed in Hindostan'.

The reaction that Stuart generated by writing his defence of Hinduism is a measure of how attitudes were beginning to change at the close of the eighteenth and the opening years of the nineteenth century. A full-scale pamphlet war broke out, with furious attacks made on the anonymous 'Bengal Officer' who produced the work, denouncing him as an 'infidel' and a 'pagan'.[95]

Nor was it just missionaries who took against Stuart: his own

---

goddess Laxmi 'to secure the Company's trade in salt against loss'. The same missionary later discovered that there was a similar arrangement in place at 'the Opium agency in Behar', where Brahmins were retained to pray for a good harvest and the safe arrival of the first opium boats. Rev. A. Thompson, *Government Connection with Idolatry in India* (Cape Town, 1851), pp.4, 17, 29, 32. Other sermons of the period contain many other such tales, for example the case of the commanding officer of a regiment near Tanjore giving his sepoys money to sacrifice a sheep to Kali, and the commander himself coming and bowing down before the image to eradicate cholera from his ranks. James Peggs, *A Voice from India: The British Connection with Idolatry and Mahomedanism, particularly the Government grant to the Temple at Juggarnarta and numerous other temples in India. A letter to Sir J.C. Hobhouse* (London, 1847).

colleagues were becoming equally scathing. 'Incredible as it may sound reader,' wrote one horrified officer, 'there is at this moment a British general in the Company's service, who observes all the customs of the Hindoos, makes offerings at their temples, carries about their idols with him, and is accompanied by fakirs who dress his food. He is not treated as a madman, but would not perhaps be misplaced if he had his idols, fakirs, bedas, and shasters, in some corner of Bedlam, removed from its more rational and unfortunate inmates.'[96]

Even passing travellers began to take potshots at the increasingly isolated Stuart: 'There was one circumstance which staggered my incredulity,' wrote Elizabeth Fenton in her journal. 'There was here an Englishman, born and educated in a Christian land, who has become the wretched and degraded partaker of this heathen worship, a General S— who has for some years adopted the habits and religion, if religion it be named, of these people; and he is generally believed to be in a sane mind, rather a man of ability.' Pausing in her horror only to add a second semi-colon to her breathless rant, she continued; 'it makes you pause and in vain attempt to account for such delusion. Those whom it is the will of God to be born in Darkness are not accountable, but that any who ever lived in the light of Christianity should voluntarily renounce its hopes is truly awful.'[97]

Hindoo Stuart was not alone in facing criticism. All over India, as the eighteenth century gave way to the nineteenth, attitudes were changing among the British. Men who showed too great an enthusiasm for Hinduism, for Indian practices or even for their Indian wives and Anglo-Indian children, were finding that the climate was growing distinctly chilly.

David Hare, a Scottish watchmaker who founded the Hindu College in Calcutta, was actually denied a Christian burial when he died of cholera, on the grounds that he had become more Hindu than Christian.[98] Many others found their Indianised ways led to a block on their promotion. When Francis Gillanders, a British tax-collector stationed in Bihar, was found to be involving himself too closely in the temple at Bodh Gaya, to which he donated a bell in 1798, the Directors of the Company back in London wrote to the Governor General expressing their horror that Christians should be, as they put it, administering 'heathen' rites.[99] A little later Frederick Shore found that his adoption of native dress so enraged the increasingly self-righteous officials of Calcutta that a government order was issued explicitly forbidding Company servants from wearing anything except European dress. The following year the army issued similar orders forbidding European officers from taking part in the festival of Holi. 'Pagan festivals', along with gambling, concubinage, peculation and drunkenness, were all things to be firmly discouraged in this new climate. The shutters were beginning to come down.

Ideas of racial and ethnic hierarchy were also beginning to be aired for the first time in the late 1780s, and it was the burgeoning mixed-blood Anglo-Indian community which felt the brunt of the new intolerance. From 1786, under the new Governor General, Lord Cornwallis, a whole raft of legislation was brought in excluding the children of British men who had Indian wives from employment by the Company. Cornwallis arrived in India fresh from his defeat by George Washington at Yorktown. He was determined to make sure that a settled colonial class never emerged in India to undermine British rule as it had done, to his own humiliation, in America.

With this in mind, in 1786 an order was passed banning the Anglo-Indian orphans of British soldiers from travelling to England to be educated, so qualifying for service in the Company army. In 1791 the door was slammed shut when an order was issued that no one with an Indian parent could be employed by the civil, military or marine branches of the Company. In 1795, further legislation was issued, explicitly disqualifying anyone not descended from European parents on both sides from serving in the Company's armies except as 'pipers, drummers, bandsmen and farriers'. Yet, like their British fathers, the

Anglo-Indians were also banned from owning land. Thus excluded from all the most obvious sources of lucrative employment, the Anglo-Indians quickly found themselves at the beginning of a long slide down the social scale. This would continue until, a century later, they had been reduced to a community of minor clerks and train drivers.[100]

Faced with limited prospects in India, those Company servants rich enough to send their Anglo-Indian children home tended to do so, and many mixed-blood children were successfully absorbed into the British upper classes, some even attaining high office: Lord Liverpool, the early-nineteenth-century Prime Minister, was of Anglo-Indian descent.[101] Much, however, depended on skin colour. As the Calcutta agent John Palmer wrote to Warren Hastings, when discussing what to do with his three orphaned Anglo-Indian step-grandchildren: 'the two eldest [who] are almost as fair as European children . . . should be sent to Europe. I could have made no distinction between the children if the youngest was of a complexion that could possibly escape detection; but as I daily see the injurious consequences resulting from bringing up certain [darker-skinned] native children at Home, it is become a question in my own mind how far I should confer a service in recommending the third child' to proceed to England. It was decided in the end that the 'dark' child should stay in India and try to make his way as a clerk, while the others were shipped to Britain to try their luck there.[102]*

It was not just Anglo-Indians who suffered from the new and quickly-growing prejudices in Calcutta. Under Cornwallis, all non-Europeans began to be treated with disdain by the increasingly arrogant officials at the Company headquarters of Fort William. In 1786,

---

* After the two 'fair' boys had arrived, Hastings wrote around his friends to find a school where their 'birth and complexion would be no impediment to admission'. When a school was found in Edinburgh, there remained but 'one great objection to such plans of education . . . I mean the Scotch language which Boys cannot help acquiring . . . [Let us hope] it may be rubbed off by their removal to England before it is too completely fixed.' Colour prejudice, it seemed, was far more acute among the British in India than at home, where, as late as 1805, Hastings clearly believed that a Scots accent was at least as damaging for someone's prospects as any Indian blood or a swarthy complexion. Hastings Correspondence, BL Add Mss 45,418, Vol. II, p.132, Letter from Hastings to Anderson, Daylesford House, 23 July 1805.

John Palmer's father, General William Palmer,* who later became one of Kirkpatrick's closest friends and allies, wrote to his friend David Anderson expressing his dismay at the new etiquette regarding Indian dignitaries introduced to Calcutta by the recently-arrived Cornwallis. They were received, he wrote, 'in the most cold and disgusting stile, and I can assure you that they observe and feel it, and no doubt they will resent it whenever they can'.[103]

These new racial attitudes affected all aspects of relations between the British and Indians. The Bengal Wills show that it was at this time that the number of Indian *bibis* being mentioned in wills and inventories began to decline: from turning up in one in three wills in 1780 and 1785, the practice went into steep decline. Between 1805 and 1810, *bibis* appear in only one in every four wills; by 1830 it is one in six; by the middle of the century they have all but disappeared. The second edition of Thomas Williamson's *East India Vade Mecum*, published in 1825, had all references to *bibis* completely removed from it,[104] while biographies and memoirs of prominent eighteenth-century British Indian worthies which mentioned their Indian wives were re-edited in the early nineteenth century so that the consorts were removed from later editions: for example John Collins, known as 'King Collins', who was the Resident at the court of the Marathas' leader Scindia, was deprived of the harem mentioned in the first edition of Major Blackiston's *Twelve Years Military Adventures in Hindustan*.[105]

Englishmen who had taken on Indian customs likewise began to be objects of surprise – even, on occasions, of derision – in Calcutta. In the early years of the nineteenth century there was growing 'ridicule' of men 'who allow whiskers to grow and who wear turbans &c in imitation of the Mussulmans'.[106] Curries were no longer acceptable dishes at parties: 'the delicacies of an entertainment consist of hermetically sealed salmon, red-herrings, cheese, smoked sprats, raspberry jam, and dried fruits; these articles coming from Europe, and being sometimes very difficult to procure, are prized accordingly'.[107] Pyjamas, for the first time, became something that an Eng-

---

* William Palmer did not become a General until 1805, and in 1786 was only a humble Major. But to avoid confusion, I will refer to him throughout as General Palmer.

lishman slept in rather than something he wore during the day. By 1813, Thomas Williamson was writing in *The European in India* how 'The hookah, or pipe . . . was very nearly universally retained among Europeans. Time, however, has retrenched this luxury so much, that not one in three now smokes.'[108] Soon the European use of the hookah was to go the way of the *bibi*: into extinction.

Yet what was true of Calcutta was not necessarily true of Company servants who lived outside the walls of the three Presidency towns. If a young Writer was bright, learned the languages and did well in his exams, he might still be posted to one of the Residencies attached to the various independent Indian courts. There he could find himself the only educated European for several hundred miles. In that case – and especially if he found himself in a centre of hybrid Indo-Islamic culture such as Hyderabad or Lucknow, or one of the more lively Rajput courts like Udaipur – he would by necessity be forced to draw his closest friends, his ways of speaking and thinking, and his sexual partners, from his Indian surroundings.[109]

Wearing Indian costume, marrying Indian wives and living a hybrid Anglo-Mughal lifestyle had always been more popular, and the transformations more dramatic, in these great centres of Mughal culture than they were in the insular world of the Presidency towns. From the 1790s until the 1830s, however, a division grew up between what was considered acceptable and proper in Calcutta, and the ways of behaviour that were still thought perfectly appropriate in the Residencies attached to the different Indian courts: for example, when the formidable Lady Maria Nugent, wife of the British Commander-in-Chief in India, visited Delhi she was horrified by what she saw there. It was not just the Resident, Sir David Ochterlony who had 'gone native', she reported, his Assistants William Fraser and Edward Gardner were even worse. 'I shall now say a few words of Messrs. Gardner and Fraser who are still of our party,' she wrote in her journal. 'They both wear immense whiskers, and neither will eat beef or pork, being as much Hindoos as Christians, if not more; they are both of them clever and intelligent, but eccentric; and, having come to this country early, they have formed opinions and prejudices, that make them almost natives. In our conversations together, I endeavour to insinuate every thing that I think will have any weight with them. I talk of the religion they were brought up in, and of their friends, who would be astonished and shocked at their whiskers, beards, &c. &c. All this we generally debated between us,' concluded Lady Nugent, 'and I still hope they will think of it.'[110]

Two worlds were growing apart – and it was into that growing chasm of cultural misunderstanding that James Achilles Kirkpatrick fell. If that gap widened into an abyss during the first years of the nineteenth century, it was largely due to the influence of one man.

On 8 November 1797, Lord Wellesley, a minor Irish aristocrat, set out from England to take up his appointment as Governor General of Bengal and head of the Supreme Government of India. For nearly three hundred years Europeans coming out to the subcontinent had been assimilating themselves to India in a kaleidoscope of different ways. That process was now drawing to a close. Increasingly Europeans were feeling they had nothing to learn from India, and they had less and less inclination to discover anything to the contrary. India was perceived as a suitable venue for ruthless and profitable European expansion, where glory and fortunes could be acquired to the benefit of all concerned. It was a place to be changed and conquered, not a place to be changed or conquered by.

This new Imperial approach was one that Lord Wellesley was determined not only to make his own, but to embody. His Imperial policies would effectively bring into being the main superstructure of the Raj as it survived up to 1947; he also brought with him the arrogant and disdainful British racial attitudes that buttressed and sustained it.

II

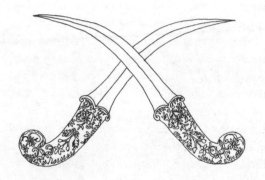

W HEN HE STEPPED ASHORE at the Cape of Good Hope on a January day in 1798, Richard Wellesley was a short, self-possessed and ambitious young man of thirty-seven with a high forehead, thick, dark eyebrows and a straight Roman nose. He had compelling blue eyes and a firm chin, the prominence of which was emphasised by his three-quarter-length sideburns. There was a purposeful set to his small mouth and an owlish gleam in his expression that hinted at brilliance, and perhaps also at ruthlessness. But there was also a vulnerability and even a paranoia there too, apparent in all his portraits. It was a weakness that he increasingly came to disguise with a mask of arrogance.

Wellesley's perceptive host, Andrew Barnard, the Commander of the Cape garrison, spotted this flaw immediately and predicted to his wife Anne that there were 'inconsistencies in his character, as he is clever but weak [and] proud ... he will get thro' the task of what is entrusted to him to the satisfaction of his employers, but that in doing it he will get himself more looked up to than beloved'.[1] It was an accurate prophecy. Wellesley made no intimate friends in India, and his colleagues, including his younger brother Arthur, frequently found him impossible to deal with; but few ever doubted his genius or his abilities.

Barnard was however wrong about one thing: Wellesley did not satisfy his nominal employers, the Directors of the East India Company. Indeed he did not even attempt to do so, and his private letters to the President of the Board of Control, the government body set up in 1784 to oversee the Company, make little secret of his 'utter contempt' for the opinions of 'the most loathsome den of the India House'.[2] Though he won the Directors an empire, Wellesley came within a whisker of bankrupting the Company to do so, and it was clear from the beginning that he had set his sights on far more ambitious goals than maintaining the profit margins of the Company he was supposed to serve, but whose mercantile spirit he actually abhorred.

Unknown to the Company Directors, Richard Wellesley had come out East with two very clear goals in his mind. He was determined to secure India for British rule, and equally determined to oust the French from their last foothold on the subcontinent. In this he was following the bidding of Henry Dundas, the Board of Control's President, whose Francophobe ideas were transmitted to a receptive Wellesley at a series of lengthy briefings before the new Governor General embarked for India. In particular Dundas had instructed Wellesley to 'cleanse' those pockets of Indian power that had been 'contaminated' by French influence: namely the courts of Tipu Sultan of Mysore, Nizam Ali Khan of Hyderabad, and those of that network of rival Hindu chiefs who ruled the great Maratha Confederacy – all of whom had raised sepoy armies trained by Francophone mercenaries and renegades, and all of whom could, potentially, be used against the British and in favour of the French.

As his ship was being refitted and its sails remodelled – HM's frigate *La Virginie* had 'become dangerously overmasted before they were cut lower'[3] – Wellesley used his enforced leisure at the Cape to recover from the dreadful passage from England and to learn what he could about India. Every day began with a 'Bengal levée' of jaundiced old India hands, many of whom had come to the Cape to try to recover their health: Anne Barnard called them the 'yellow generals'. They limped in one by one and competed with each other 'to pour the riches of their knowledge and experience' on the new Governor General. There were others passing through the Cape, too, who could bring Wellesley up to speed with the latest developments in Bengal. According to Anne Barnard's *Journal*, as well as the yellow generals there were also 'Captains from India with despatches to the

Government [who] stop here and finding his Excellency at the Cape deliver up their official papers which he opens, peruses, and by such means will arrive instructed on the present position of affairs there, and will appear a prodigy of ability in being Master of all so soon after his arrival'.

After these meetings and briefings were over, the evenings were occupied with a series of heavy dinners given in Wellesley's honour by the local Dutch community. Their culinary abilities left much to be desired: 'They begin their dinners *piano, piano* with stewed cows heel,' wrote Barnard,

> a favourite dish [of theirs, eaten with] Tripe and Macaroni ... But they increase the size and number of their dishes with every course, ending at last with enormous Joints ... [One family] received us all with open countenances of gladness and hospitality ... but the most resolute grin was born by a Calf's head as large as that of an ox, which was boiled entire and served up with ears whole and a pair of gallant young horns ... the teeth were more perfect than any dentist ever made ... [The meal concluded with] a Tureen of Bird's Nest Soup ... a mess of the most aromatic nastiness I ever tasted.

On his return to the Barnards after this ordeal, Wellesley diplomatically avoided commenting on the fare beyond venturing that 'I would not have missed the sight of my worthy friend with the white teeth for twenty pounds.'[4]

In her diaries and letters, Anne Barnard gives a detailed record of the entertainments and diversions she organised for her distinguished guest. She names the various admirals, judges and governors who were called to dine with Lord Wellesley, the Dutch burghers who invited them to supper, even 'His Excellency the Governor of Mosambique, a stately well-stuffed Portuguese ... [attended by] a black dwarf 34 high', who tried to bribe Wellesley with a gold-tipped cane. But a figure she never mentions is the one who undoubtedly had the most influence on Wellesley of all the people he met at the Cape: Major William Kirkpatrick.

By 1798 William Kirkpatrick, elder brother of James Achilles, looked much older than his forty-four years. Disappointments in his career, marital difficulties and years of painful illness all showed on his features. Two fine paintings of him by Thomas Hickey survive. In the first, painted in 1787, he looks an awkward if determined figure, holding in one hand the deeds of the orphanage he had just set up in Calcutta. There is a searching, slightly uncertain and quizzical expression on his features, as if he is trying to size up the viewer; he also looks a little impatient, as if he has much better things to do than sit around having his portrait painted. Only twelve years separate this from the second portrait,[5] painted in 1799, a year after Kirkpatrick met Wellesley at the Cape; but from the transformation that has taken place in the sitter you might guess it was thirty years. The tangle of unruly hair in the first portrait has retreated far from the forehead; there are bags under Kirkpatrick's eyes; and he has lost a great deal of weight. He looks weary and perhaps a little disillusioned; only the upturned nose, the determined set of the lips and the slightly impatient expression echo the earlier figure.

Wellesley's first letter to Dundas in London, written three weeks after his arrival at the Cape, is almost entirely concerned with William Kirkpatrick; indeed his conversations with Kirkpatrick take up not only the entire thirty-page despatch, but also a further forty pages of enclosures. The letter details a matter that was to be a central concern not just of Wellesley and Dundas, but of both Kirkpatrick brothers in the months ahead: the growing French influence in the courts of India.

'Among the subjects you recommended to my early consideration upon my arrival in India,' wrote Wellesley,

> you particularly urged the necessity of my attending with the utmost degree of vigilance to the system, now persued almost universally by the native princes, of retaining in their service numbers of European or American officers, under whom the native troops are trained and disciplined in imitation of the corps of seypoys in the British service.
>
> By accident I found at this place, on account of his health, Major Kirkpatrick, lately Resident at the Court of Hyderabad, and formerly at that of Scindia, and I have endeavoured during the period of my detention here to collect from him whatever

information he could furnish respecting the European or American officers and the corps commanded by them in the service of the Nizam.[6]

Wellesley had asked William Kirkpatrick to provide written answers to a range of questions about the French mercenary forces employed by the Nizam, notably 'one commanded by a Frenchman by the name of Raymond' and officered by 'Frenchmen of the most virulent and notorious principles of Jacobinism . . . an armed French party of great zeal, diligence and activity'. The answers he received so impressed him that he not only forwarded them, unedited, to Dundas, he also begged Kirkpatrick to abandon the plans he had been making to return to England, and to take up a job at his side in Calcutta, as his Military Secretary.

William had serious health problems which had developed in India – he was suffering in particular from a severe and very painful combination of gout and rheumatism – but when Wellesley made him the offer he promised to consider it, subject to the success of a cure at 'the hot mineral baths about 70 miles from here'.[7] His ultimate acceptance of Wellesley's largesse changed the course not only of his career, but also that of the man he had left as Acting Resident at Hyderabad: his younger brother James.

Several years later, after William had retired to England, Wellesley looked back to that meeting at the Cape and wrote that he 'had no hesitation in declaring that to [William Kirkpatrick] I am indebted for the seasonable information' which enabled the Governor General to pull off the remarkable successes of his first two years in office. He went on:

> Kirkpatrick's skill in Oriental languages, his acquaintance with the manners, customs and laws of India are not equalled by

any person whom I have met in this country. His perfect knowledge of all the native courts, of their policy, prejudices and interests, as well as of all the leading political characters among the inhabitants of India, is unrivalled in the Company's Civil or Military service . . . These qualifications recommended him to my particular confidence. He possessed no other recommendation, or introduction to my notice.[8]

Kirkpatrick, Wellesley emphasises, rose on his merits, not on the influence of his birth or his patrons. Yet even Wellesley probably did not know quite how far William had come in his life, nor from what inauspicious beginnings. For William Kirkpatrick was not in fact James Achilles' full brother, but an illegitimate half-brother,* born in Ireland to a Mrs Booth, 'the sister of Mr C– the well known anarchist', with whom William's father had had a brief affair. Throughout their entire childhood, William's legitimate half-brothers, George and James Achilles, were totally unaware of his existence.

The father of the Kirkpatrick brothers was Colonel James Kirkpatrick of the Madras Cavalry, known universally as 'the Handsome Colonel'. This name was apparently a reference not only to his good looks and 'very dark brown eyes', but also to his rackety love-life. The Bloomsbury matriarch Jane Maria Strachey, mother of Lytton, was married to William Kirkpatrick's grandson, and spent many months researching the Handsome Colonel's roots as part of her obsessive mapping of the Stracheys' genealogy. A pious Victorian lady much given to displays of public devotion,† she was not entirely pleased by what she discovered. The Handsome Colonel, it turned out, was born in 1730 on a plantation in Charlestown, South Carolina, to which his family had fled from Dumfriesshire after being implicated in the failed 1715 Jacobite uprising. More alarming still to Lady Strachey was the discovery that the Colonel's mother was 'probably a Creole'. Sometime around the middle of the eighteenth century

---

* Not an unusual state of affairs in eighteenth-century England, where as many as a third of all births were illegitimate. See Peter Laslett (ed.), *Bastardy and its Comparative History* (London, 1980).

† For a wonderful picture of the Strachey family lined up at prayer, girls to one side, boys facing them, in descending order of age, see the cover of *Bloomsbury Heritage: Their Mothers and Their Aunts* (New York, 1976), by Elizabeth French Boyd.

the family returned to Britain,* where the Handsome Colonel embarked on what Strachey described as 'an adventurous and irregular life' more distinguished for its amorous conquests than its military ones.[9]

William Kirkpatrick was born when his father was a bachelor of twenty-four; he was raised at boarding school in Ireland, supported but publicly unacknowledged by the Colonel. When William was only four, the Colonel set off for India where he joined the Company's Madras Cavalry as an ensign. In due course, when William was old enough, the Handsome Colonel purchased his illegitimate son a military cadetship in the Company; but they never met in India, for the Colonel's career there lasted only eight years, and by the time William arrived in 1771 the Colonel had long since left.

Before returning to England, the Handsome Colonel had married in Madras Katherine Munro, the eldest daughter of Dr Andrew Munro, the founder of the new Madras hospital. Dr Munro was a controversial figure in the Madras Presidency. He had, by all accounts, great belief in the efficacy of his 'Hysterick drafts', but was renowned for his short temper and violent dislike of anything he thought might approach hypochondria. At one point 'nineteen covenanted [Company] servants' took out a formal complaint against him for his conduct; in particular they noted that when one of them wanted a powder to cure him of a severe case of scurvy in the teeth, Munro had written to his deputy, 'Sir, pray give that impudence what he wants and let me not be plagued with his nonsense.'[10]

A contemporary account of Dr Munro's hospital shows that the doctors' attitude to hospital management reflected his no-nonsense approach: 'I never heard of such irregularities as at present exist in the Presidency hospital,' wrote a visiting surgeon.

> I have frequently, during my short attendance, found in visiting
> the sick two or three of them lying in a state of intoxication, and
> I have heard of others who were not under my charge being in
> a similar condition. It is not an uncommon practice of the
> patients to form parties, often with the sergeant of the guard, to

---

* On their return from America the Kirkpatricks apparently ceased to think of themselves as Scottish, settling in Kent and becoming church-going Anglicans.

go into the Black Town [the Indian quarter of Madras] where they generally remain during the greater part of the night, committing every kind of enormity. The hospital in consequence becomes a scene of riot and confusion during the night, and the shade and other unoccupied parts of the hospital are places of resort for gaming and boxing during the day.[11]

For all this, the marriage between the Handsome Colonel and Munro's beautiful daughter was apparently a passionate one, and within two years Katherine had given the Colonel two sons, George, born on 15 July 1763, and James Achilles, born thirteen months later, on 22 August 1764. Both were baptised in St Mary's Church in the Fort of Madras, where Katherine and the Colonel had been married. But when James Achilles was eighteen months old, his mother died of a sudden fever aged only twenty-two, despite – or perhaps partly because of – the ministrations of her father. James and George must presumably have been brought up by Indian *ayahs* until their father returned home to England three years later. Never one to miss an amorous opportunity, the Handsome Colonel fathered yet another illegitimate child – this time a daughter – on the boat home in a brief affair with a Mrs Perrein,* the wife of a Portuguese Jewish mercenary in the service of the Nawabs of the Arcot.[12]

There is a gap in the archives concerning the period James and George spent in England as boys. While their father set off East again, this time to command Fort Marlborough in Sumatra, all that is known is that the two brothers were briefly sent to Eton, where they must have been younger contemporaries of Richard Wellesley, and that their schooling was finished off in 'various seminaries' in France.† In between terms, they spent the holidays with their Kirkpatrick grandfather at Hollydale near Bromley in Kent. Their grandfather had by now sold his Carolina plantations, abandoned his Jacobite sympathies, and belatedly – and somewhat unsuccessfully –

---

* The source material gives the name 'Perrein', but this is surely a mis-rendering of the common Indo-Portuguese surname Perreira.

† The word 'seminary' at this period did not necessarily suggest a religious establishment; and as the Kirkpatricks were Anglicans, not Roman Catholics, it is highly unlikely that the word was being used in that sense. It is much more likely that the writer meant merely 'boarding schools'.

embarked on the life of an author: his political works were judged 'very dull',[13] and his most notable production was a slim volume of medical research entitled *Putrifaction*. In March 1779, at the age of fifteen, after just eleven years in Europe, James returned to India, the land of his birth. As he had done with James's elder half-brother, the Handsome Colonel had obtained for him an East India Company cadetship, based in Madras.

It was inevitable now that William and James would meet. Lady Strachey had in her possession the Handsome Colonel's diaries and letter books, all now lost, which gave an indication of the manner in which it happened. She reported her discovery in a letter to a relation:

> When James Achilles had gone to India & was about to go to the same part in which William was, their father wrote to desire him to form the acquaintance of a young gentleman of the same name who he cannot do better than model himself upon; shortly after this he is writing to J.A. of William as 'your brother'. In a subsequent letter in which he reproves J.A. of negligence towards a natural [i.e. illegitimate] son of his own, he enters somewhat at large into the question; he says in his opinion there is no difference in the duty a parent owes to his legitimate and illegitimate children; & that he thinks James will agree with him that they both know an instance in which the natural son was superior in capacity & attainments to the legitimate.[14]

Despite the ten-year gap in their ages and the strangeness of their meeting, which seems to have taken place in 1784 or 1785, the two half-brothers immediately became close. Judging from the tenor of their often moving and heartfelt letters, the relationship seems to have given a much-needed emotional prop to both men. Of the two, William was the senior, but he seems also to have been the more vulnerable and insecure; hardly surprising perhaps when the loveless and institutionalised nature of his childhood is taken into account.

A strong impression of William at the beginning of his career – a lonely and melancholy teenager washed up in India without money, backers or patrons – survives in the letters he wrote throughout the

1770s and eighties to his great friend John Kennaway.[15] Kennaway was a grammar-school boy, the son of an Exeter merchant who came out to India in 1772 with his brother after being presented with a cadetship each by their East India Company cousin, Richard Palk. The brothers had nearly died on arrival when their ship was wrecked in the mouth of the Ganges, and they 'presented themselves to Governor Hastings with nothing but the clothes on their backs'.[16] Despite this inauspicious beginning, the Kennaways were well-connected, and John quickly overtook William Kirkpatrick – who was a year his senior – in the race for preferment. This did not get in the way of their friendship, however, and letters William wrote to Kennaway are surprisingly deeply felt.

In the first, dated 18 January 1774, Kirkpatrick writes warmly that he is 'pleased with the proof you have given me of your affection . . . and I do assure you I regretted your absence as much as my amiable friend did mine'. A year later, the tone is more emotional: '*You* know yourself and (I hope) *me* too well to doubt the sincerity of my affection for you,' he writes. By 1777, the tone has become close to the romantic: 'I am dull, stupid and melancholy,' writes an anguished Kirkpatrick. 'In a word I am low spirited . . . [and] I have been low spirited ever since I left you: I am still low spirited: and low spirited shall I continue.' He talks of 'all I have suffered since my separation from you', and how 'my promised bliss' has been snatched from him by Kennaway's departure.

Kirkpatrick finally declares himself to Kennaway in a letter of the period which is dated only '12 Dec'. The two boys have had a tiff, and Kirkpatrick sits up late writing to his friend attempting to explain his feelings:

> My dear Jack,
>
> You had not been gone last night two minutes when I wished to see you again. I thought I had a hundred things to tell you, which had not occurred to me while you were with me. To say the truth you left me but half happy: for though our mutual and renewed assurances of invariable friendship were productive of the greatest pleasure I ever felt – yet it was damp'd considerably by your hasty departure. Ah my dear

friend! Had you known my nature you would not have doom'd me to suffer a whole nights uneasiness without having been thoroughly convinced of the capaciousness of my disposition.

I have a heart which though it is capable of the most tender attachment, cannot silently brook the least appearance of slight or indifference in its master – you my dear Jack are *its master*, and while you govern it like a sincere and affectionate friend, it will be in all situations obedient to your pleasure.

Thus I have told you my mind with that frankness which ever attends true affection.

Adieu my dear Jack

W Kirkpatrick

Monday night.

It is difficult to know how to interpret these tortured letters, given that at the same time as he was writing them, William was living with an Indian women, Dhoolaury Bibi, by whom he fathered two Anglo-Indian children, and with whom he maintained a relationship until the end of his life, despite being married to an Englishwoman – Maria Pawson – for twelve years in the middle. There is no evidence that Kirkpatrick had any sort of physical relationship with Kennaway, and it is perfectly possible – even probable – that the boys' romantic friendship was entirely platonic; but equally the possibility must remain that part of William's melancholy came from suppressing an unresolved and apparently unconsummated bisexuality.*

In 1784, after thirteen years in India, William returned to England to consult doctors and recover his health. He brought with him his two Anglo-Indian children, Robert and Cecilia, then aged seven and four, whom he placed in the care of the Handsome Colonel. The

---

* Certainly, William comes across as a vulnerable and lonely man who craves affection, and he is especially articulate about his bouts of depression. 'By gravity,' he writes to Kennaway on 13 June 1779, 'I intended to express that kind of shadow or image of calm sorrow or grief which is observable sometimes in the air, sometimes in the speech, and sometimes in the writing of a person . . . I have a thousand times, Jack, when low spirited, almost been blind and deaf to all around me – wholly absorbed in my painful reflections – and possibly so extravagant in my remarks and assertions as . . . to incur the reproach of a dull and mad fellow.' Kennaway Papers, Devon Records Office, Exeter, B961M ADD/ F2, William Kirkpatrick to Kennaway, 13 June 1779.

Colonel had recently retired from Sumatra to Hollydale, where James and George had been brought up, but which William had apparently never seen. Though his father agreed to take in the children, the meeting between father and son was not a success: 'I found my father and all my other connections in perfect health,' William wrote to Kennaway from London, 'but I was so unhappy as not to find the former in that temper of mind necessary to his own and my felicity. Disappointments and other accidents of fortune not merited by him, have so far formed his disposition that, did nothing else make my speedy return to India proper, that consideration alone would render my continuance in this country exceedingly unpleasant.'

In stark contrast to the pain of visiting his father, William spent a happy month with Kennaway's family in Exeter, writing to his friend that he would 'reserve the history of my visit, and my account of the family, for the happy moment when I shall again have the pleasure of embracing my dear Jack. Suffice it for the present to inform you that I passed near a month among them with a satisfaction that nothing but your presence could have increased.' Nevertheless, the visit to England brought home to William as nothing else the constraints under which he was forced to live. In India his talents and position had gradually brought him status and respect; but in England he was no one, still the unacknowledged and illegitimate son of a rakish nabob. More to the point he was poor. In India the friends he had made were of a different class and a different economic bracket to him. Visiting the Kennaways, he realised suddenly the impossibility of ever returning to England, unless he were first to make his fortune. In a letter to Kennaway he tried to explain to his friend how he felt:

> . . . It is impossible for me to describe how impatient I am to return to India – not that were I in possession of the means, I could not live more to my satisfaction in England: but without those means England instead of being a paradise must be a Hell to every man who returns from India with a grain of feeling or virtuous pride. Here have I a few friends (the only substantial solace or blessing that life affords) whom I love and esteem very heartily: but from whose society I should be

obliged to banish myself were I to stay in England another year: for they being men of fortune, how could I approach them, or associate with them when not worth a groat? Which situation therefore is irksome – is painful – beyond expression. I will therefore return to India as early as possible: and there I will live the remainder of my days, unless by acquiring a fortune (which, by the bye, it is hardly possible I ever should) I shall be defended from the cruel necessity of cutting myself off from the society of all those whom I love.[17]

William's letters are invariably written with great grace and beauty, and with numerous classical and Oriental literary allusions: with Kennaway in particular he frequently discusses Persian literature, the rival translations of Hafiz, and the beauties of the *Shahnama*. He worked hard at perfecting his Persian, Bengali and Hindustani; but throughout the entire correspondence, and despite all his Orientalist learning, there is little feeling for India evident in William's letters.*

Indeed, in some quarters William Kirkpatrick had already got a reputation for haughtiness towards Indians. The Indophile General William Palmer, who had been Warren Hastings' Military Secretary, then Resident in Lucknow, was alarmed when he heard in November 1786 that William Kirkpatrick had been made Resident at the camp of the Maratha leader, Mahadji Scindia. 'I am suprized that Kirkpatrick should have sought that Station,' wrote Palmer. 'His mind is strongly prejudiced against India.'[18]

As General Palmer had predicted, William Kirkpatrick's tenure as Resident at the court of Scindia was not a success, and for exactly the reasons he had foreseen. Kirkpatrick's childhood made him especially sensitive to anything that might appear a slight. In a letter written

---

* William's languages seem to have been merely a valuable tool that in due course would give wings to his career: in 1779 he was promoted to Persian interpreter to the Commander in Chief of the Bengal army, and in 1781, only ten years after his arrival in India, was promoted to captain. Increasingly he used his language skills to make intelligence-gathering a speciality, carefully collating Persian newsletters from the different Indian courts and forming contacts with men like George Cherry, one of the Company's most senior intelligence officers. In time these contacts would become central to the careers of both Kirkpatrick brothers. But William's slightly businesslike attitude to Orientalist learning is in no way complemented by the pleasure, surprise or enjoyment of India that one finds in many other letters of the period, notably those of his younger half-brother James.

by the then Resident, James Anderson, to William when the news of his posting was made public, William was warned that the Maratha's Hindu peasant manners were very different from those of the courtly Muslim Mughals with whom he had been used to dealing:

> in an early period of my residence in this camp I could not help thinking that Scindia was sometimes guilty of petty neglects and inattention towards me, which as experience has since warned me were to be ascribed only to the difference of the Maratha modes and customs from those of the Musalmens to which I had been accustomed . . . [Scindia] appeared to be deficient in the minutiae of attention, such as in frequent messages and enquiries and other little intercourses of civility which are so rigidly practiced by the politer Mussalmen . . .[19]

The warning, however, fell on deaf ears. Within a month of his arrival at Delhi, where Scindia was then encamped, William was complaining to the Governor General Lord Cornwallis that Scindia and his court were rude and neglectful: 'his general object [is to subject] the English Resident at his Durbar [court] to humiliating situations'. Scindia in turn formally complained to Calcutta of William's arrogance and haughtiness.

Cornwallis was planning a war against Tipu Sultan, and had no wish at that moment to see any sort of hostilities break out between the Company and the Marathas; rather he wished to conclude some sort of defensive alliance with them. So he wrote back to William saying that he was 'exceedingly sorry to hear of a coldness between you and Scindia', and instructed him to live 'on a footing of friendship and good humour' with the Maratha durbar. At the end of the letter he made his position even more frank: 'Your good sense will immediately point out to you the substance and the intention of this dispatch. I wish to avoid a public breach with Scindia, and therefore should he, from any motives whatever, continue the slights and inattentions of which you complain . . . you will treat them as much as possible as matters of personal offence only.'[20]

The letter could not have been more clearly expressed; but it was already too late. Things had reached a head on 24 January 1787. One of William's escort had gone to swim in the Jumna, where he met a *dhobi* (a laundryman) who was cleaning the clothes of Scindia's son-in-law on the ghats. The sepoy demanded that the washerman – an untouchable – move away while he took his swim. The washerman refused to do so. He was promptly attacked by the sepoy, who beat him over the head with a *lathi* (truncheon or stick). A troop of Marathas happened to be passing by and joined in on the side of the *dhobi*, leaving the sepoy badly wounded. The incident escalated, and by the afternoon, after several soldiers on either side had been severely wounded, William was forced to leave his quarters in a crumbling palace in Old Delhi for his own safety. From a temporary camp in the garden of Safdarjung's tomb, six miles outside the city, he demanded that the offenders should be arrested and that there should be a formal apology. None was forthcoming.

In October, after an impasse lasting ten months, William wrote to Kennaway: 'Finding it impossible to live on terms of good humour with Scindia without taking certain measures not agreeable to the policy thought necessary by Ld Cornwallis, I have come to the resolution of resigning from my present office.' He duly did so, in a rather tentative way, and was surprised to find it immediately accepted by the Governor General. His surprise turned to alarm when, once he had left his position and set off towards Calcutta, it became increasingly clear that Cornwallis blamed William, not Scindia, for what he regarded as a wholly unnecessary breach in relations with a powerful neighbour.

A year later, Kirkpatrick still had no new appointment, and the full scale of the disaster that had overtaken his career began to sink in. When Kennaway was appointed Resident at Hyderabad, William wrote to congratulate him, adding: 'the disgraceful and mortifying situation in which I at present stand must operate to the ruin of both my character and fortunes.'[21]

From his new appointment in Hyderabad, Kennaway replied sympathetically. To his brother William, however, he confided that he thought Kirkpatrick's behaviour honourable, but suicidal: 'Kirk's prospects in this country are now very unpromising,' he wrote in December 1788.

In quitting a similar rather more lucrative situation than that which I at present hold and sacrificing his interest to the rigidity of his principles, he gave up a certainty of a handsome independency [i.e. sufficient capital to allow him to retire to England on the interest] in the course of four or five years ... In a single and unencumbered state I certainly should not have acted in the same manner. Perhaps I should have been wrong in not doing so, but I think I could have preserved my virtue without sacrificing my interest.[22]

What made matters worse was that William Kirkpatrick was now very far from 'single and unencumbered'. Three years earlier, on 26 September 1785, only a few months after his return from England and after a very brief courtship, he had married Maria Pawson, whom Lady Strachey describes as 'being of the Yorkshire gentry'. A portrait of Maria by Romney shows a pretty, sensual woman with full lips, long reddish hair and an intelligent, knowing expression. She and Kirkpatrick quickly had four children in as many years; but the marriage was not a success.

Maria had initially accompanied her husband to Scindia's Delhi camp, but soon departed to Agra where she tried, without success, to pull strings with the Mughal court in order to get permission to live in Taj Gunj, immediately beside the Taj Mahal. When her request was formally turned down she became angry at what she regarded as a humiliating rebuff, and headed off with her infants towards Calcutta. Kirkpatrick was forced to admit to John Shore, Cornwallis's deputy* (and eventual successor), that 'by personal argument and insistence I may possibly be able to get her consent [to return]', but that he could not guarantee it. He then promised that 'I should take care that nothing of an embarrassing nature should arise,' perhaps implying that public rows were already a feature of the marriage.[23] By the end of 1788 it was decided that Maria should return to England with the children, and settle in Bath.

The marriage struggled on, with William continuing to write

* Shore's official job description was 'the senior and presiding member of the Calcutta council', until he formally succeeded Cornwallis as Governor General of Bengal. After 1792 he was awarded a baronetcy and became Sir John Shore. In 1798 he was made Lord Teignmouth.

affectionate letters to his wife for a further nine years; but her replies became shorter and increasingly perfunctory. By 1794 William was complaining that Maria's letters were 'wholly inadequate . . . scribbled in haste, often illegible, very inaccurate and what is worst of all (with regard to the feelings of a husband and a father) extremely deficient in those details which it is so easy for you to furnish, and which I must naturally wish for. Let me entreat you, therefore, my dear girl, to discontinue this hurry-scurry mode of conducting your correspondence with me, and to recollect that you are not writing by the penny post but by a conveyance that seldom offers, and to a husband at some thousand miles distance from you.'[24] The following year Maria ceased to reply to his letters at all. By 1797 a legal separation was agreed to, due to Maria's 'misconduct'.[25] The four girls from the marriage were packed off to live with their various cousins at the Handsome Colonel's. There is no evidence that William and Maria ever met again; certainly William's grandchildren were all told that Maria had died after the birth of her youngest child, and after his death were astonished to discover a bequest to her in William's will, which she duly received.[26] Ironically, she turned out to be living in India, apparently with a new lover.

For five years, from 1787 until 1792, during Maria's absence in Bath, William Kirkpatrick's career languished, and he wrote irregularly to Kennaway, explaining that he had not put pen to paper more often as 'my disappointments were so near my heart that I could have handled no other subject, and as you could give me no relief, I determined to give you no pain'.[27] Depressed and dejected, he returned to badly-paid regimental duties.

William's linguistic talents brought him a second break, however, in 1792, when he was appointed to head a mission to Nepal. Travelling through previously unexplored parts of the Himalayas, he was the first European to reach Nayakote, where the Nepalese rajahs then held court. Though the mission yielded no diplomatic results, it was regarded as an important sortie into new territory, and William later produced a book on his travels – *A Description of the Kingdom of Nepaul* – which was widely applauded. The expedition moreover brought about his reconciliation with Cornwallis, who went on record saying of William that 'no one could have acquitted himself with more ability, prudence and circumspection'.[28]

The expedition returned Kirkpatrick to favour, and in March 1793 he was able to write an excited note to Maria in England revealing that 'my friend Kennaway' was retiring due to ill-health in December, and that if 'my friend Mr Shore' got appointed Governor General to replace Cornwallis, as looked likely, 'there can be little doubt of my succeeding [Kennaway] at the Residency at Hyderabad. God bless you my dearest girl. I am not allowed to add more.'[29] By November both appointments had come through, and Kirkpatrick wrote to Bath that his prospects had suddenly dramatically changed. His income would now be substantial, and 'I am hopeful by the practice of a proper economy to be in a few years in possession of what I consider a competency.' It would also now be possible to give the girls 'a private education'.

He saved for last the news that he was due to set off overland down the east coast of India from Calcutta the following week, and that 'the place where my brother James commands lies on my route to Hyderabad. It is my wish he should proceed thither with me, to fill an appointment the succession to which has been secured for him by Sir John Kennaway . . . With his talents and the chance before him of getting the assistantship under me sooner or later it will introduce him with great advantages into the diplomatic line. I am strongly of the opinion he ought not to decline the offer.'[30]

In 1793 James Achilles Kirkpatrick appeared at first sight to be a very different figure from his tortured, complex half-brother. Easy-going and generous, with an effortless gift for friendship, James was blessed with his father's good looks, though with his mother's much fairer Scottish colouring. He had full lips, startling blue eyes and a mop of straw-coloured hair which he swept back foppishly over his forehead and wore rather longer than was usual at the period. He was considered by his contemporaries to be tall and well proportioned as well as unusually handsome. But he was a sensitive man and, like his brother, he felt the need for continual reassurance; indeed his letters are full of expressions of affection for his correspondents which sometimes read like cries for reciprocation.

At the age of twenty-nine James had spent fourteen years in the Company's Madras army without in any way distinguishing himself as a soldier; but he shared William's gift for languages, and as well as having complete mastery of Persian and Hindustani, he seems to have spoken the languages of the south – notably Tamil and Telegu – with some fluency. If, as seems likely, James had been brought up by Indian *ayahs* after his mother's death, it is quite possible that this fluency may have dated back to his Madras childhood; certainly there are frequent reports that many British children of the period alarmed their parents by speaking the Hindustani (or in this case, presumably, Tamil) of their *ayahs* as their first language.

As with William, it was this linguistic ability that would in time be James's escape route from the drudgery of the military line; but in contrast to William, whose Orientalist learning had not stopped him from adopting a straightforwardly John Bull attitude towards India, James from the beginning had a far more affectionate view of the country where he was born and where he had spent the early years of his childhood. In an anonymous autobiographical fragment which he submitted to the *Madras Courier* in 1792 he described himself as 'an officer who from his proficiency in the Persian and Hindoostanee tongues, and conversancy in the manners and customs of the race of men by whom those languages are spoken, had contracted a certain degree of partiality towards them'.[31]

One aspect of this 'partiality' was a relationship with an Indian *bibi* with whom he had lived for many years and by whom he fathered a son. In 1791 James brought the boy back to England during a year's sick leave, after which the child joined the multi-ethnic household of children, legitimate and illegitimate, presided over by the Handsome Colonel in Kent, no doubt to the growing puzzlement of his country neighbours.

As well as a 'partiality' towards Indians, James also had an over-whelming aesthetic feeling for the sheer beauty of India, something that is apparent throughout his correspondence. Again and again his letters praise the landscape through which he is passing, writing home soon after his return to the Deccan in February 1792 about the 'charming verdure that cloathes the whole country and renders it so delightful to the eye . . . you may walk bare headed in the sun without inconvenience almost any hour of the day'. He particularly admired Tipu Sultan's Mughal-style pleasure gardens near Bangalore: 'They please me very much . . . and are laid out with taste and design, the numerous cypress trees that form the principal avenues are the tallest and most beautiful I ever saw.'

A month later, when his regiment was involved in the siege of Tipu's island capital Seringapatam during the Third Mysore War, even the 'alarming mortality' among the European troops and the 'infectious exhalations from millions of putrid carcases that cover the whole surface of the earth for twenty miles around the capital' could not blind James to the astonishing loveliness of the city he was engaged in besieging: 'The palaces and gardens upon the island with-out the city far exceed the palace and gardens at Bangalore in extent, taste and magnificence, as they are said to fall short of the principal ones within the city. Of this last we have an exterior view from our trenches, and considering how much it overtops the lofty walls and battlements of the city, its height must be as considerable as its extent is great.'

He had seen Tipu's magnificent Mughal-style garden palace 'Lall Baug [the Red Garden], in all its glory' the day before: 'Alas!' he writes to his father, 'it fell sacrifice to the emergencies of war.' The palace was made hospital for the wounded and the garden 'toppled to supply materials for the siege. The whole avenues of tall and majestic cypresses were in an instant laid low, nor was the orange, apple, sandal tree or even the fragrant bowers of rose and jasmine spared in this indiscriminate ruin. You might have seen in our bat-teries fascines of rose bushes, bound with jasmine and picketed with pickets of sandal wood. The very pioneers themselves became scented . . .'

He even dodged enemy shells to make a visit to the newly erected tomb of Tipu's father Haidar Ali, which he greatly admired, though judging it 'in every respect inferior to the Taj at Agra'. Intriguingly he adds: 'I herewith enclose you some of the plaister I picked up, which had fallen from Hyder's tomb stone. It is said to be composed with earth from Mecca, or as it is called, the Scrapings of the Dust from the Holy Tomb of the Prophet, and consequently must possess many rare and invaluable virtues.'[32] In another writer these remarks might be taken as satirical; but it is clear from the context that James was being perfectly serious, though 'Scrapings of the Dust from the Holy Tomb of the Prophet' was certainly a strange choice of gift for the Handsome Colonel, who throughout his career had shown little interest in religious matters, less still in Muslim relics.

If, aesthetically and emotionally, James's letters show a great love of India that remained fixed and constant throughout his life, his political views were at this stage less clearly formed. Later in life he would come to regard the East India Company as an untrustworthy and aggressive force in Indian politics. But in the early 1790s he still subscribed to the conventional English view which tended to see Indian rulers as 'effeminate' and 'luxurious' tyrants, whose 'unorganised despotism' sapped their countries of strength and the possibility of progress. This was perceived as a direct contrast to the Company, whose introduction of Western ways to India, protected by an army of 'undaunted spirit and irresistible ardour', was believed by most of the British in India to bring unambiguous blessings to the subcontinent.

In his letters home at this time James duly writes of Tipu's 'boundless ambition and unrelenting cruelty', but even at this early period he was unusual among his compatriots in that he saw many qualities to admire in the Sultan of Mysore. He writes that, 'born and bred in camp, and tutored in the science of war under a great master [i.e. his father Haidar Ali], Tipoo possesses all the characteristic valour and hardiness of the soldier while his achievements in the Fields of Mars are far from discrediting the precepts inculcated by his father'. The various British reverses and defeats bore ample witness to Tipu's 'skill in arms. If he is at all addicted to, or versed with the arts of peace it has scarcely been in his power to cultivate them ... his whole reign having been one continued state of military preparations or actual warfare'. Moreover, James was astonished by Tipu Sultan's bravery and his spirit of resistance. Despite the Company's successful counterattack there was no evidence that Tipu's 'firmness is shaken or his perseverance abated', and although four armies were now advancing in strength towards him, 'if he has as yet made any offers of submission it is more than I have heard of'.[33]

In contrast, James's elder brother William saw Tipu merely as a caricature: a one-dimensional monster, the worst possible incarnation of 'Oriental despotism'. For him Tipu was a 'cruel and relentless enemy', an 'intolerant bigot', a 'furious fanatic', an 'oppressive and unjust ruler ... [a] sanguinary tyrant, [a] perfidious negociator', and, to top it all, a 'mean and minute economist'.[34] In these very different perceptions of Indian rule lay the seeds of much future disagreement between the two brothers.

James survived the bloodshed of the Third Mysore War quite unscathed, only to be badly wounded three months later, in bed, by his own orderly. One morning he woke on his camp bed to find the man, 'who was of Mughal descent', stealing from his trunk. The orderly rushed out, then reappeared shortly afterwards with two of James's own swords. James wrote an anonymous third-person account of the incident for the *Madras Courier*:

> ... defenceless and nearly naked as he had risen from his bed ... two deadly blows were warded by his hands which though cut deeply were saved from absolute amputation by a letter which happened providentially to be clenched in it. Thus maimed and incapable of further resistance, his last resource was in flight, in attempting which two other wounds inflicted with a deadly aim brought him down. When the blood thirsty and insatiable miscreant thinking he had dispatched him, turned about in search of more victims but not finding any within his reach, and having worked as he doubtless thought at the time mischief hopeless of pardon, he drew his dagger, and in a frenzy of despair, plunged it eight successive times into his own remorseless bosom.[35]

The attack shook James, and made him fundamentally review his life in India. During his convalescence he wrote to the Handsome Colonel, weighing up where he stood in the service after fourteen years. He was not optimistic: 'My prospects of promotion,' he wrote, 'are as distant at this moment as when I embarked, there being at this moment a hundred Lieutenants above me on the infantry list [who would all receive promotion before him]. Should matters remain on this present footing I cannot reasonably expect more than ten steps yearly, at which rate ten long years must elapse before I attain the rank of Captain – that is to say after a service or rather servitude of three and twenty years.'[36] It was a promotion his talented elder brother had managed after just a decade in India.

James had had some letters of introduction at the beginning of the war, but they did not seem to have had the slightest effect. He had given General Sir William Meadows his letter, but 'the little general was too deeply engaged storming forts and other warlike achievements to acknowledge their receipt, so I can say nothing as to the benefits I may expect to reap from them'. He had letters 'from Col. Fullarton to his relation Col. Maxwell still unused, and Col. Maxwell is said to have great influence with Lord Cornwallis'. But all in all, James acknowledged, his prospects were not promising, and he pleaded with his father to exert his influence somehow to improve his lot.[37] Suddenly missing the comforts and facilities of home, he also asked the Colonel to send out 'a few dozen of Velna's Vegetable Syrup, the efficacy of which I was made fully sensible of in my passage out. The want of vegetables during a long campaign has occasioned a return of my old scorbutic complaint.'

At this point, just when he least expected it, influence was exerted on James's behalf only just four months later; and it came from a totally unexpected and quite unsolicited quarter. In July, his brother's friend, the newly knighted Sir John Kennaway, wrote to him out of the blue from Hyderabad inviting him to stay, and offering to help him in any way he could. At James's request, Kennaway intervened with James's commanding officer, and by August had got him the command of the distant fort at Vizianagram, in tribal territory thirty miles north-west of the important east-coast port of Vizagapatam.[38]

Vizianagram is, even today, a remote and impoverished spot, surrounded by barren hills and scrappy, scattered tribal outposts. At the end of the eighteenth century it was even more inaccessible, far removed from the centre of things. But at least it was a command, a start.

Then, only three months after James's appointment at Vizianagram, William wrote to him from Calcutta with the news of his new appointment as Resident at Hyderabad. He invited his brother to join him in some capacity there, telling him to think about the offer, and that they would discuss it when they met: William would be passing Vizagapatam on his way from Bengal in six weeks' time.

William's journey down the east coast was a slow one. French privateers working out of Mauritius made it impossible for him to travel by boat,[39] much the quickest route: ten days on a good wind could have taken him to the port of Masulipatam, then a week's journey up the old Golconda road would have brought him to Hyderabad. But as this was impossible, he was forced to travel by camel and elephant, and to make his way slowly down the spine of the Eastern Ghats, between the peaks and teak forests of the ghats and the blue coves and inlets of the Bay of Bengal. The brothers met at Vizagapatam, on the northern reaches of the Coromandel coast.*

It was a warm Christmas Eve, and James took little persuading to give up his garrison duties and throw in his lot with William. That night, on James's instructions, the two brothers drafted a letter in William's name to James's commanding officer asking him to approve a transfer to Hyderabad.

The brothers spent Christmas together, probably for the first time. But it quickly became clear that James's discharge would take longer than hoped to wind its way through the Company's military bureaucracy. It was agreed, therefore, that for the time being he should stay

---

* Although not mentioned in the letters of either brother in Vizagapatam, in 1793 carpenters of the Kamsali caste were busy making some of the most beautiful objects ever to come out of the fusion of Western tastes and Eastern skills, for which Vizagapatam had quickly become internationally famous: superbly delicate furniture where ivory was inlaid in sandalwood and ebony in a dazzling efflorescence of Anglo-Indian marquetry. For a superb study of Vizagapatam furniture, see Armin Jaffer, *Furniture from British India and Ceylon* (London, 2001), pp.172–221.

in Vizianagram, and William should head on to Hyderabad alone. After a long period of truce and even friendship, war was again said to be brewing between the Nizam of Hyderabad and his old enemies the Marathas, and it was vital for William to get to Hyderabad as soon as possible to do what he could to forestall it.

William arrived in Hyderabad a month later to find – ominously – that Nizam Ali Khan, the elderly ruler of Hyderabad, was not in his city, but had decamped to the ancient Deccani capital of Bidar, the impregnable fortress that most closely abutted the Hyderabad–Maratha frontier. There it was said he was already engaged in amass-ing a grand army. Stopping in Hyderabad only long enough to order 'wax candles, Patna potatoes, some raspberry and cherry brandy, garden peas, good coffee, a pipe of hock and some good red port',[40] William got back on his elephant and set off on the eighty-mile journey to Bidar.

The road passed through a landscape whose wasted state testified to the unstable and violent history of the region over the previous 150 years. The flat expanses of neglected and untilled former cotton fields were dotted with heavily fortified villages and burned-out fortlets. A contemporary English traveller described the same journey in pessimistic terms: 'as for the country I have passed through, nothing can be more melancholy than the appearance of it. Deserted villages, unfrequented roads, and the traces of former cultivation, make the scene more painful than it otherwise would be, by showing what it has once been, and aggravating the look of the present misery, by the contrast of former blessings.' The same observer also men-tioned passing 'some bodies of predatory horse plundering the country we have passed through', though the freebooters avoided tangling with him due to his armed escort.[41]

Nor was this just an English view of the country. According to the

Iranian traveller Abdul Lateef Shushtari, who was related to one of
the most powerful clans in Hyderabad and in 1794 was acting as the
Nizam's *vakil** in Calcutta, the countryside around the capital grew
more and more ruinous the closer you got to the Maratha frontier:
'Now, because of rebellious enemies and oppressive tax-collectors,
the whole country has become a ruin, its inhabitants scattered and
miserable; those few unable to flee are afflicted with famine. Leadership has broken down, the laws of governance are disrupted . . .
There are so many ruins and abandoned homes, that though the
region has a peerless climate, nevertheless the country is now worse
than in most other places in India.'[42]

After a four-day journey through this increasingly war-blackened
landscape, William saw rising ahead of him the grim battlements of
Bidar.

Even today, after a century and a half of decline and neglect, Bidar
is still one of the most magnificent fortresses in India. Then it was
unmatched. It was built on a great plug of dark brown basalt rising
steeply out of the flat planispheres of the Deccan plateau. In every
direction, great loops of bleak black crenelations swept for miles over
hills and down steep valleys, a seemingly endless expanse of towers
and walls, gateways and bastions, arch-shaped merlons and fortified
escarpments. Within the embrace of these battlements lay a perfect
oasis: white-budded cotton fields and gardens filled with rich well-
watered black earth, where bullocks ploughed small neatly-tilled strips
edged in palm groves and guava orchards, a great green splash of
fertile farmland and a stark contrast to the wasteland immediately
outside the walls.

To one side, by the river, lay the dhobi ghats from which came
the splash and thud of washermen slapping their clothes on the basalt
steps, while in the distance was a small lotus-choked lake punctuated
at its corners by domed *chattri* pavilions. Beyond, in the barren wastes
outside the walls and the reach of the irrigation runnels, a scattering
of bulbous whitewashed domes signalled the presence of the medieval
royal necropolis of Ashtur; in the scrub around it stood two rambling

---

* In this context, ambassador or representative, though in common usage it means
'lawyer'.

Sufi shrines packed with pilgrims and miracle-seekers come to solicit the aid of long-dead sheikhs.

On the evening of 10 February 1794, three months after he left Calcutta, William Kirkpatrick and his escort passed by the necropolis and entered Bidar under the dogleg of the massive Golconda Gate. They crossed through ring after ring of town and citadel walls, and over a series of deep ditches cut out of the living rock by gangs of medieval slaves. All around in the narrow, crowded streets, between the ancient shrines and the spice souk, the horse and the diamond merchants, the textile sellers and the *karkhanas* (workshops) where the town's craftsmen were hammering away at their Bidri-ware pots and hookahs, the newcomers saw evidence of the gathering army, as hordes of freelances from all over India congregated on the city to seek service.

At the best of times the bazaars of the Deccan were filled with a mix of peoples from all over the East; but at this moment Bidar was bursting with a particularly diverse group of mercenary cavalry: Arabs from the Hadramaut, bearded Sikhs from the Punjab, knots of tur-baned Afghans and Pathans from the frontier and their Rohilla cousins from the Ganges plains. Wandering through the bazaars too were groups of the Nizam's regular infantry, the red-jacketed sepoys trained by the French commander, Michel Joachim Raymond, with their black tricorn hats, white shirts and short shin-length boots.[43] William's new Assistant, William Steuart, whom William had just met for the first time in Hyderabad, was impressed: 'The Nizam's army ... looked larger than ever I saw Scindia's,' he wrote. 'He maintains few foot soldiers, but his cavalry are reckoned 40,000. Such as I have seen are excellent; the men are well dressed & the chiefs pride themselves in giving a uniform long gown to their troopers to distinguish them, some having jackets with two crossed swords in the way of chintz, others with one sword and some plume of yellow or red.'[44]

The cosmopolitan mix in the bazaars was reflected in the architec-ture of the streets through which these crowds surged. While the bazaars and the fortifications were entirely Indian in style, many of the structures within the city looked for their inspiration to the heart of the Islamic world, bypassing the experiments of the Mughals in northern India to borrow direct from the tilework of the distant Ottomans, or the architectural models of Transoxiana. From atop his elephant Kirkpatrick could see what appeared to be displaced fragments of Timurid Bukhara and Samarkand: melon-ribbed domes that might happily have topped the tomb of Timur himself; delicate lozenges of highly coloured Iznik-like tilework with blues as startling as a sapphire in an Ottoman dagger; even a *madrassa* which would not look in the least bit out of place in the maidan of Safavid Isfahan.

By late evening, having passed slowly through miles of choked bazaars, the English party finally reached the inner courtyard of the citadel. William's first letter from Bidar is brief and official, noting only that the Minister, Aristu Jah,* had abandoned precedent and etiquette and had personally conducted him straight to the Nizam's durbar in an effort to be friendly, and to impress upon him 'the anxious desire of the Nizam to connect himself as closely as possible with our government'.[45]

William Steuart, however, left a much fuller description of the Nizam's durbar at around this time. The Nizam and his Minister he mentions only briefly: 'The Nizam is polite and extremely attentive,' he wrote, 'but his mermidons are haughty and overbearing in a high degree. His Minister is a clever but lazy hound whose avowed maxim is to distress all the subjects in order to please the avaricious disposition of his master whose beard he holds with both hands & with it can manage as he likes.'[46]

This assessment by Steuart greatly underestimated the achievement of the two men who between them saved their kingdom from almost certain extinction: when Nizam Ali Khan acceded to the throne thirty-two years earlier in 1762, few would have guessed that, almost alone of the contending forces of the Deccan, it would be Hyderabad that would survive the vicissitudes of the next seventy-five years.

Although he underestimates the Nizam Ali Khan and his Minister,

---

* The Nizam's Minister, Ghulam Sayyed Khan, was not in fact awarded the title Aristu Jah ('the Glory of Aristotle') until 1796; at this point he was known as Mushir ul-Mulk ('Advisor to the Kingdom'). But as Aristu Jah is the name by which he is almost universally known in contemporary histories, for purposes of clarity and continuity he will be referred to by this title throughout.

Steuart gives a revealing account of what it was actually like to attend the Nizam's durbar, and the telling way it mixed Indian with Middle Eastern custom: eating paan, for example, in the Indian fashion, while drinking small cups of coffee *à la Turque*: 'The chiefs after presenting Nuzzirs [symbolic offerings] retire to the *adab gah* & make their humble obeisance,' he wrote.

> Afterwards [they] have permission to approach but seldom sit down. There is more state and pomp here than I ever saw at [the Mughal Emperor] Shah Alam's durbar. Agreeably to the custom of the Nizam's family he [Nizam Ali Khan] never smokes but swallows large balls of paun which as he has no teeth he cannot chew; he drinks a great deal of coffee, & extremely warm, having a fire in the middle of the durbar to heat it & cup bearers who deliver it in quick rotation in small agate cups. He keeps a great many women, has had or rather they have had 200 children of which number 30 are still alive & of these seven are sons & 23 daughters. The heir apparent looks as old as his father (who is 62) but I imagine is not above 37.
>
> The durbar usually assembles at night; silver candlesticks wax & tallow candles, a constant supply of blue lights one after another held up on blue poles have a pretty effect; some amber tapers are kept burning near his Highness but their smell is so strong that I imagine it serves more to drown that of the tallow which certainly is not agreeable; one stink to drown away another.
>
> Jewels are worn by all the chiefs, such as sarpèches [turban ornaments], pearl necklaces, bazoo bunds [armbands], & even those kurrahs over the wrist which women only in Hindustan wear. The Mussulmens here look like Hindoos, shave close & wear small turbans, long gowns like peishwas and cut the hair near the ear in the regular way of the uncut [i.e. uncircumcised] fellows.

The buildings in which the durbar took place reflected the magnificence of the gathering. William Kirkpatrick was very struck by the stark contrast between the grimness of the outer fortress and the intricate decoration of the private mosques and the apartments of the palaces in the inner citadel. Deccani craftsmen always compensated for their forbidding building material by filling their interiors with fantasies of tilework or stucco, carved woodwork and *trompe-l'oeil* wall paintings. Of nowhere was this more true than the Rangin Mahal, one of the most sublime medieval interiors in India, where William must have had his private audience with the Nizam. Here the walls were covered alternately with intricate tilework and sculpted panels of arabesques, the hard volcanic granite manipulated as easily as if it were as soft as plaster and as delicate as a lace ruff.

This atmosphere of sophisticated courtly sensuality is found in its most concentrated form in the Deccani miniatures which were being painted in the *ateliers* of the Nizam's palaces.* In the images produced in these workshops, water drips from fountains, parakeets fly to roost and peacocks cry from the mango trees.

Nothing about these charmed garden scenes indicates that the Marathas might ride into the outskirts of the city at any minute, burning and pillaging. Indeed, this calm artistic idyll stood in complete and direct contrast to the political reality of upheavals and traumas across the entire eighteenth-century Deccan. The Nizam's father, Nizam ul-Mulk, had founded the semi-independent state of Hyderabad out of the disintegrating southern provinces of the Mughal Empire in the years following 1724. He was an austere figure, like his idol, the puritanical Mughal Emperor Aurangzeb, instinctively disapproving of the arts and especially of the un-Koranic skill of miniature portrait-painting. A close watch was kept on his nobles, and those who held illicit parties during Muharram were reported to him by his spies. Permission for dance displays and nautches had to be sought from the durbar and was only granted on the occasion of festivals and marriages.[47]

Nizam ul-Mulk was an ingenious general but an even more talented statesman, using bribery and intrigue to achieve what his old-fashioned and outmoded Mughal armies could not. While breaking from the direct control of Delhi, he made a point of maintaining

---

* Nizam Ali Khan's two great court painters were Rai Venkatchellam and Tajalli Ali Shah, both of whom, significantly enough, had the status of senior nobles in the Hyderabad durbar.

his nominal loyalty to the Mughal Emperor, and throughout the eighteenth century the people of Hyderabad continued to refer to themselves as Mughals and saw their state as a semi-detached fragment of the old empire of Akbar and Shah Jehan. Nizam ul-Mulk also kept a careful watch on the Marathas, using spies and diplomacy to keep them in check. He warned his followers: 'The Emperor Aurangzeb with his immense army and the expenditure of the entire treasure of Hindustan could not defeat them. Many families were ruined and yet no benefit came out of this campaign. I have made them obedient and faithful to me through diplomacy.'[48]

At his death in 1748, this carefully-created structure tottered towards collapse as Nizam ul-Mulk's sons fought among themselves and tried to establish themselves as rulers by entering into rival alliances with the neighbouring powers, notably the Marathas to the north and west and the French at Pondicherry to the east. It was fourteen years before Nizam Ali Khan – an illegitimate younger son – finally established himself on the throne, throwing his elder brother Salabat Jang into the dungeons of Bidar, where he was strangled.

By this time, the state looked as if it stood on the verge of extinction as the Marathas, the French, the English and the armies of Haidar Ali of Mysore swooped down on the extremities of Hyderabad like vultures, seizing chunks of the Nizam's dominions for their own purposes. Yet Hyderabad did not collapse, thanks largely to the diplomacy and the carefully-constructed system of alliances created by Nizam Ali Khan. Militarily, Hyderabad was the weakest of the competing states of the Deccan when he took control, but only it and the East India Company would remain important powers by the time of his death. It was his extraordinary achievement to turn the state from the Sick Man of Late Mughal India into the vital strategic asset of the eighteenth-century Cold War, without whose friendship and support no power could gain dominance in India.

In 1794, when the Kirkpatrick brothers first met him, the Nizam was over sixty years old, a tall, gaunt figure who had lost his teeth and hair, but who retained his watchfulness and his skill at manipulating both the rival factions at his court and the weaknesses of his external enemies. A contemporary miniature of him shows him as an old man – emaciated, lightly freckled and clean-shaven – leaning back on the bolsters of his *musnud*;* to one side are placed a sword and a spittoon.[49] He is depicted as wise yet cautious, deep in conversation with his Minister in front of a white marble pavilion. He wears a semi-transparent *jama* of white muslin, and a tight white turban out of which emerges a jewelled aigrette. He has a gilded cummerbund, and a band of large pink gems gleam on his turban. James Kirkpatrick, who got to know him well, left a detailed pen portrait of him:

> His stature is of the tallest and his frame still retains indications of that robustness, for which in his youth he was remarkable. His complexion is dark and his features, though never handsome, are by no means deficient in expression, bespeaking a thoughtful and not unintelligent mind. His mien is graceful and dignified, and his address replete with that princely courtesy and condescension, which while sufficiently calculated to inspire ease and confidence in all who approach him, bespeaks him not forgetful of his own dignity, or of the illustrious lineage he lays claim to and professes to set a high value upon.
>
> He has generally I believe, been considered as a Prince who though not endowed with either splendid talents or great mental resources, has proved himself on some trying occasions not deficient in those arts which are considered in the East as constituting the essence of Government ... His defects as a warrior are amply compensated by his skill as a politician.[50]

Most contemporary observers, however, attributed the extraordinary skill with which the Hyderabadis had manoeuvred their way through the minefields of Deccani politics less to Nizam Ali Khan than to his brilliant and wily Prime Minister, Aristu Jah, 'the Glory of Aristotle'. Though a ruthless politician, Aristu Jah was a deeply civilised man, and his extensive patronage of both painters and poets led to a revival in both arts after the austere rule of Nizam ul-Mulk. Perhaps partly because of this, a great many miniatures of him survive. They show a tall, cunning-looking man, heavily built with a

---

* The low arrangement of cushions and bolsters which formed the throne of Indian rulers at this period.

wily expression, a hooked nose and a carefully trimmed beard. He is always shown towering over his contemporaries with a small red turban, a simple string of pearls over his chest, and another pearl bracelet around his right wrist; in his hand, invariably, is the snake of a gold hookah. Contemporary Hyderabadi chronicles say he never left this pipe for a second, and that 'the smell of his scented tobacco' was one of the great features of the Minister's durbar. This passion for his pipe was something that also struck Edward Strachey when he met Aristu Jah:

> The minister was smoking in the proper oriental style. He neither laid hold of his hookah nor did he open his mouth purposely to receive the mouthpiece, but his servant watched him, and put the point of it close to his lips. Now and then he stroked the minister's whiskers with it and when a good opportunity offered [itself] poked it a little way into his mouth. The minister who did not appear to have observed it before took a whiff. When he began to speak, the man took it out again, stroked his whiskers with the mouthpiece and again put it to his master's mouth at the proper time. When the minister made a movement as if he was disposed to spit, one of his faithful attendants held out both hands and received a huge mouthful of spittle, with great care he then wiped it on a cloth which was by him and wrapped it up carefully, appearing then ready to receive in his hands any such deposit however precious, which his master might think fit to place there.[51]

In the durbar, alongside Aristu Jah and the Nizam, there was a third figure who would play a major role in the lives of both Kirkpatrick brothers, and indeed in time was to become a close relation by marriage of James. Mir Alam had risen to power from respectable but impoverished origins as the Private Secretary to Aristu Jah. When John Kennaway arrived in Hyderabad he saw Mir Alam merely as a sycophant in the train of the Minister: 'I do not think he has much influence even with the Minister whose every sentiment and opinion he adopts with a blind servility,' he wrote in 1788.[52]

Since then, however, Mir Alam had led a successful embassy to

Calcutta, had befriended Lord Cornwallis and been made the Nizam's *vakil* to the Company, through whom the Nizam's relations with the British were to be channelled. As a result the Mir was beginning to show signs of increasing independence from Aristu Jah, his former patron, especially in the matter of the looming conflict with the Marathas, which he openly opposed, and compared to needlessly 'throwing sand in a hornets' nest'.[53]

For much of his reign, Nizam Ali Khan had indeed avoided making war with the Marathas, and followed his father's advice to woo them with diplomacy rather than challenge them with arms. Now however, partly under the influence of the Minister, he had decided to change his policy, and with the aid of his new infantry regiments trained by General Raymond, had allowed himself to be persuaded that it might finally be possible for his troops to meet the Marathas in battle. For this reason he and Aristu Jah were very anxious to forge an alliance with the English through William, and to enlist the armies of the Company on their side. Aristu Jah was the most Anglophile of the Nizam's advisers, and alone in the durbar realised the real and growing military strength of the Company. His ideas, however, were not widely shared, and another powerful faction at court, led by the Paigah nobles who made up the Nizam's praetorian guard, made no secret of the fact that they would have liked Hyderabad to ally with the Marathas and against the English. A third faction wished the Nizam to make an alliance with Tipu and the French.

What no one at court knew yet was that Sir John Shore, the new Governor General, had already decided to reject the Nizam's request to the Company to unite against the Marathas. Before he set off to Hyderabad, Shore had briefed William Kirkpatrick to stick to the existing Triple Alliance, signed four years earlier in 1790, which bound the Marathas, the Nizam and the Company together as allies, and which isolated the Company's great enemy Tipu Sultan, who remained outside the alliance. Events would show that this was a crucial error of judgement by Shore, and one that very nearly destroyed both the state of Hyderabad and the Company's still fragile presence in southern and central India.

William Kirkpatrick initially made a very good impression on the

Nizam's court, not least for his exceptional linguistic abilities. Gobind Krishen, the Maratha *vakil* at the Hyderabad durbar, reported to Pune: 'This Kirkpatrick has wonderful intelligence and mastery of Persian speech, is equally careful in writing, understands accounts, and is well informed in public business and is versed in astronomy. In this way he is expert in everything.'[54] William realised, however, that his popularity at the Nizam's court would greatly diminish as soon as the Minister realised that he would not be persuaded to join in the projected campaign against the Marathas. As negotiations between the Nizam and the Marathas continued over the course of the next few months, and with the two sides openly preparing for war, William wrote to Shore that he was resisting all the attempts of Aristu Jah and the Nizam to lure the British 'from our system of moderation and neutrality'.

He also did his best to persuade the Hyderabadis that in his opinion their army was simply not up to taking on the celebrated infantry regiments of the Marathas. These were trained in the latest French military techniques by one of the greatest military figures of eighteenth-century India, Comte Benoît de Boigne, and famed for their 'wall of fire and iron', which had wreaked havoc upon even the best-drilled Indian armies sent against them.[55] Aristu Jah, wrote Kirkpatrick, did not seem to think 'the danger so imminent, as I should be inclined to do, were a brigade of De Boigne's to be actually employed against him, for in this case I am afraid that the business would be over before the people at home would be able to send out the necessary orders for our taking this state under our protection'.[56]

By December, however, Kirkpatrick realised that he was failing to get his message across: not only the Nizam, but the entire camp at Bidar had convinced themselves that victory against the Marathas was within their grasp. Every night the dancing girls sang songs about the forthcoming triumph, and Aristu Jah even announced to the court that when they took Pune he would send his Maratha counterpart Nana Phadnavis, 'the Maratha Machiavelli', off to exile in Benares 'with a cloth about his loins, and a pot of water in his hands, to mutter incantations on the banks of the Ganges'. 'There would appear to be a storm brewing in the head of [Aristu Jah],' William

Kirkpatrick wrote to Shore, 'which may possibly burst at no great distance of time ... Whenever it takes place I shall dread its consequence; and not be without my fears of these consequences being ere long.'[57]

Kirkpatrick was right to be anxious. In December 1794, just as news arrived that his brother James had finally succeeded in getting transferred from Vizianagram to Hyderabad and was already on his way, the order was given. The Nizam's huge army lumbered out of the safety of Bidar and headed off to war in the direction of the Maratha capital of Pune.

The campaign was as short as it was disastrous.

For three months the Nizam's army advanced slowly towards Pune along the banks of the Manjirah River. The Marathas advanced equally slowly towards the Mughals (as the Hyderabadis called themselves*). Of the two armies, the Marathas' was slightly larger – around 130,000 men against the Mughal total of around ninety thousand; the Maratha force was also much the more experienced and better led. Both armies were equally divided between cavalry and infantry, though only the Hyderbadis had a regiment of female infantry dressed in British-style redcoats, brought along primarily to protect the Nizam's harem women, who also came along on the trip in a long caravan of covered elephant howdahs.[58]

The slow march towards Pune was marked by frequent courtly but inconclusive negotiations between the two sides; to the end the Nizam insisted that he was not invading the Maratha territories, merely enjoying a prolonged hunting expedition along the marches of his territory. At every stage, negotiation was preferred to fighting,

---

* The Hyderabadis considered themselves a semi-detached fragment of the old Mughal Empire, and always referred to their forces as 'the Mughal army'. This is also how they are referred to in Maratha documents.

and intrigue to outright war. Like the baroque social etiquette of the Nizam's court, the military strategy of the Nizam seemed like an elaborate and courtly charade, a slow and penetrating game of chess rather than a real campaign with living soldiers suffering actual fatalities.

While negotiations continued, both sides spent much of their energies on attempts at destabilising the army of the other through bribes and covert intelligence work. Aristu Jah spent a vast sum – rumoured to be around one crore rupees* – trying, unsuccessfully, to persuade Scindia and his famous de Boigne brigades to desert the Maratha army, while Nana Phadnavis spent a smaller sum – reportedly around seven lakh rupees† – trying to encourage the pro-Maratha and pro-Tipu factions in the Hyderabad durbar to betray Aristu Jah. Mir Alam, Aristu Jah's former protégé, was believed to be among those who received Nana bribes.[59] The British Resident in Pune, Sir Charles Warre Malet, thought Mir Alam's behaviour particularly suspicious when he came to the Maratha court to negotiate, and he relayed his suspicions back to William: 'He appears to have done little else since his arrival at Pune,' wrote Kirkpatrick to Shore, 'but complain and insinuate perpetual suspicions [of Aristu Jah] to Sir Charles Malet, the utility of which I have never been able to discover. On the contrary they only serve to perplex and procrastinate matters.'[60]

Aristu Jah, meanwhile, concentrated all his efforts on trying to persuade Kirkpatrick to throw in his lot – and more specifically the armies of the East India Company, especially the two British regiments stationed at Hyderabad – with the Nizam. But William refused to alter his position: in this war, he maintained, the Company was to be strictly neutral. He even rather stiffly refused to answer Aristu Jah's question as to which route the Hyderabad army would do best to take, saying it was 'against all sense of propriety' for him to give advice on such a matter.

Finally, on the evening of 14 March 1795, the Nizam's army arrived at the top of a ridge known as the Moori Ghat, and looked down to see the Maratha army encamped a day's march below them. At eight

---

* A crore is ten million – so around £60 million in today's currency.
† Around £4.2 million.

o'clock the following morning, 15 March, the Nizam gave the order for his troops to descend from the heights of the ghat. The Marathas were waiting for them at the bottom.

Firing began soon after lunch, at around 2 p.m. It was the two rival battalions of French-trained infantry that came into contact first, with the 'Corps Français de Raymond' fighting under the French Republican tricolore and making steady progress into the centre of their Maratha counterparts, the famous de Boigne brigades, who fought under the French Bourbon emblems. To William's great surprise, Raymond's twelve newly raised infantry regiments used their higher altitude to great effect, showering de Boigne's flanks with sprays of grapeshot. Kirkpatrick was more surprised still when the Mughal Women's Regiment, the Zuffur Plutun or Victorious Battalion, advanced equally steadily downhill with their muskets, and succeeded in holding their own against the Maratha right wing.* By nightfall, Raymond's force, deserted by their Paigah cavalry escort, had been forced to retreat a little in the face of a fierce cannonade from de Boigne's artillery. But the bulk of the Nizam's army had succeeded in reaching their designated campsite on the banks of a rivulet three miles on from the slopes of Moori Ghat. There they dug in for the night, well positioned for the expected battle the following morning.

No one was quite sure at the time what went wrong, but just after eleven o'clock that night, a sudden panic broke out in the Nizam's camp. Looking back on the rout the following morning, William wrote:

> The events appear to me like a kind of dream, so unexpected, so unaccountable, and so amazing were they. Nothing in the least can be reasonably said to have gone wrong on the part of the Nizam's army that was slightly engaged with the enemy. A couple of Sirdars [noblemen] of some note were killed, and

---

* British commentators who saw the Zuffur Plutun on parade tended to make snide remarks about their 'ridiculous appearance'. Those who saw them in action, however, were always surprised by the women's ferocity, discipline and effectiveness: Henry Russell later quoted 'an officer of high rank in the King's Army [who] once said on seeing a party of them that they would put half the native corps in India to the Blush'. From 'Henry Russell's Report on Hyderabad, 30th March 1816', reprinted in *Indian Archives*, Vol. IX, July–December 1955, No. 2, p.134.

perhaps a hundred men: but His Highnesses troops were in quiet possession of the ground they wanted to occupy for the night at 11pm, when the pusillanimity of the Nizam or of his Minister, or of both together, led to the fatal resolution of falling back ... The consequences were such as might be expected: universal trepidation and great loss of baggage: – but these were only the immediate consequences. Those that are likely to follow threaten very seriously the future independence of this state, since it seems but too probable that His Highness will be obliged to yield to all the demands of the Pune government.[61]

What in fact had happened, as Kirkpatrick later learned, was that an intermittent cannonade by the Marathas had panicked the Nizam's women, and especially Bakshi Begum, the Nizam's most senior wife, who threatened to unveil herself in public if the Nizam did not take his entire *zenana* (harem) into the shelter of the small and half-ruined moated fort of Khardla. This lay at the very bottom of Moori Ghat, just over three miles behind the front line. During the confusion of the Nizam's inexplicable retreat, a small party of Marathas looking for water stumbled across a Mughal picket, and the brief exchange of fire in the dark was enough to throw the remaining Hyderabadi troops into a complete panic. They rushed back to the walls of the Khardla Fort, leaving all their guns, baggage camels, ammunition wagons, stores and food behind them.

When dawn broke the following morning, the Marathas found to their amazement that the Mughals had not only thrown away their strategic advantage, but left their arms, ammunition and supplies scattered over the battlefield while taking shelter in an utterly indefensible position. Charles Malet wrote in his official report that morning that 'we are necessarily astonished at the important consequence that ensued in the unaccountable flight of the Nizam's army, by which not only the respectability of his personal character and government was sacrificed, but the very existence of himself and his army endangered'.[62] Their amazement did not, however, stop the Marathas from taking full advantage of the Mughal reverse: by ten o'clock in the morning they had brought in four hundred abandoned Mughal ammunition carts, two thousand camels and fifteen heavy cannon. By eleven they had completely surrounded the army of Hyderabad, and began raining shot down on the fort from the sixty cannon which they managed to manoeuvre onto the lower slopes of Moori Ghat. There had hardly been a battle; but already it was all over for the Nizam.[63]

By the following morning provisions in the fort were already beginning to run low, and the Marathas had sent in an envoy to settle terms. 'The distress of the army for water and forage is increasing hourly,' wrote William, who had taken shelter with the rest of the Nizam's entourage,

> its quarters being so straightened that it can procure but little of either without such exertions as it does not appear disposed to make. The Maharatta durbar publickly holds a very moderate language on occasion of its late extraordinary success: but it remains to be seen whether its demands will correspond with its professions . . . Gobind Krishen [the Maratha envoy] has arrived to settle the terms of an accommodation . . . for the rest however I fear the approaching negotiations will be far from terminating in a manner favourable to the political interests of the Company.[64]

In the event negotiations rambled on for twenty-two days. Each day the situation grew worse in the Hyderabad camp as the Marathas tightened the siege. Each day, as the Nizam hesitated, the Marathas raised their demands. Many in the Nizam's camp suspected that the lack of any serious resistance or any attempt to break the siege was due to treachery within the Hyderabad ranks, with suspicion later falling on both Mir Alam and the pro-Maratha Paigah nobles. These suspicions increased when it emerged that the key Maratha demand was the disgrace and surrender of the presumed plotters' principal enemy, the Nizam's pro-English Minister, Aristu Jah. Whatever its cause, the scale of the disaster for Hyderabad was now increasingly clear: 'The Nizam is obliged to yield to all the demands of the M[aratha]s,' wrote William, 'and ceases to be an independent prince.'[65]

Many of the letters that William wrote at this period are lost, as the messengers who carried them failed to make it through the Maratha lines, and were cut down by the patrolling Pindary horsemen. The few which have survived show that the situation within the fort was insupportable, and that Kirkpatrick's small English party was suffering as badly as the rest.

The water in the old fort was green and brackish and gave the defenders dysentery, but despite this sold for a rupee* a cup. By the end of the first week all spare supplies of forage and food were finished, and the price for even a handful of lentils rose astronomically. The defenders cut down the Tamarind trees in the fort and ate their leaves and bark and unripe fruit. After these were exhausted, starvation began to set in: some died of hunger, others of thirst, and the squalor led to an outbreak of cholera.[66] By the end of the second week, a third of William's escort and servants were dead. On 30 March he wrote to Calcutta:

> The distress I am witness to hourly goes to my soul, and yet
> I am unable to relieve it even among my own narrow circle.
> I assure myself that Sir John Shore will not turn a deaf ear to
> the petition I have offered up on behalf of some of my sufferers
> – yet God only knows when or where their hardship will end.
> I have buried at least 14 or 15 of my people since the rout and
> we are very sickly. I have held up wonderfully well: but a trip
> to the sea is necessary to my restoration after what I have
> lately suffered from Rheumatism.[67]

William was in fact playing down the seriousness of his own illness. Before the siege, the effect of spending the entire monsoon under canvas had already taken its toll, and he had had to spend more and more time flat on his camp bed, taking opium to relieve his pain. The rest of his party and their pack animals had also found the going hard. Even before they left Bidar, Kirkpatrick had lost two of his elephants and two of his camels. Now all of his escort and servants who were not dead were seriously ill, and there was little the Residency's English doctor, George Ure, could do for them. Particularly

---

* Approximately £6 in today's currency.

badly affected was William's Assistant, Steuart, who was languishing with a high fever. He never completely recovered, lingering on until October when his strength finally ebbed away.

For the Nizam, the end came on 17 April. A treaty was signed, giving the Marathas the crucial fortresses of Daulatabad,* Ahmednagar and Sholapur as well as great swathes of Hyderabadi territory worth an annual thirty-five lakh rupees of revenue. The Nizam was left with a fragment of his old territories and an indefensible frontier, as well as a bill of two crore rupees† in war reparations. The amount of territory to be ceded was reduced by nearly half at the last minute, but the price was the surrender of Aristu Jah, who was handed over as a hostage into the hands of his old enemy, the Maratha Prime Minister Nana Phadnavis. The contemporary Hyderabad historian Ghulam Husain Khan has left an account of the meeting of the two old rivals:

> The first words Nana spoke to Aristu Jah were: 'Nawab Sahib, the one crore [rupees] you spent [in bribes] didn't achieve anything much, did it? Whereas the 7 lakhs I spent bribing the nobles in your government had a considerable effect – it even led to this our happy meeting!'
>
> Aristu Jah answered grimly: 'Such is fate!'
>
> 'Your Excellency,' continued Nana, 'you undertook in this campaign to despatch me with *dhoti* and *lota* [water-pot] to Benares . . . now that it's worked out rather differently, what are your intentions?'
>
> 'Well, why don't you send me on pilgrimage to God's holy house at Mecca?' replied Aristu Jah.
>
> 'God willing, we will send your Excellency to the house of God, and this sinner to Benares, whereby we shall both gain spiritual credit. But first you must be the guest of our government for a few days, to observe and be entertained, isn't that so?'
>
> 'That is indeed so,' replied Aristu Jah.
>
> Then they both rose and went towards the [Maratha] camp,

---

* The spectacular citadel near Aurangabad that had once been the Muslim bridgehead in the Deccan and the capital of the Delhi Sultanate.
† Say £120 million in today's currency.

the two prime-ministers hand in hand ... From there, stage by stage, they went to Pune, where Aristu Jah was imprisoned in an old ruined garden which had been appointed for him to reside in. One thousand youths trained in the English manner bearing muskets [sepoys from de Boigne's brigades] and a thousand Arab mercenaries were posted around the garden to guard him, with several carpet-spreaders, bearers and servers, altogether about 100 attendants to keep him company, men of no rank who were the only ones allowed to enter the camp in the garden. Everyone coming in or going out was searched and any paper with writing on it was confiscated.[68]

On 24 April 1795, William Kirkpatrick and his escort limped back into Hyderabad, a few days ahead of the Nizam's defeated army. He found his brother James waiting for him at the Residency.

The two brothers had last seen each other sixteen months earlier, at Christmas in Vizianagram on the east coast, in the most optimistic circumstances. William's career had suddenly revived and he had been able to use his influence and new powers of patronage to help his younger half-brother. Hyderabad was a major posting, and there was every reason to think that the brothers would have good opportunities for advancing their careers by increasing British influence there.

Now things were very different. The scale of the defeat suffered by the Hyderabadis raised a serious question mark about the long-term viability of the Nizam's dominions, while the failure of the British to help their allies in any way had destroyed the Nizam's confidence in the reliability of the Company; instead he now looked upon Raymond and the French as his real protectors, thus entirely changing the balance of power in the eighteenth-century precursor to the later Great Game. This was a disastrous development for the Company at a time when Britain and France were at war and victorious French armies were occupying Belgium and Holland, and were now menacing north Italy. Moreover, with the exile and imprisonment of Aristu Jah, the British had lost their main advocate at the Hyderabad court, and the durbar was now dominated by nobles deeply antagonistic to the Company. William was severely ill, and needed to leave Hyderabad to convalesce and recover his health in peace. Worse still, his Assistant, Steuart, was clearly beyond recovery. In such circumstances it was not a happy reunion.

Within a month of the Nizam's return, it began to be apparent that the French were successfully filling the place once occupied by the English. The Nizam said he was seriously considering disbanding the two English battalions which were stationed at Hyderabad, pointing out to William, with some justification, that there was no point in maintaining them at such a heavy cost when they could not be used to defend him from his prime enemy, the Marathas. On 13 May, William and James went together to see the Nizam, and reported that 'his discourse chiefly consisted of enquiries and observations relative to the posture of affairs in Europe . . . From the whole tenor it was easy to perceive that some Frenchman had been taking considerable pains by utterly false or highly exaggerated accounts, to impress him with a firm belief that nothing could any longer resist his nation . . .'[69] Subsequent despatches were filled with details of the growing French power at court and the serious threat to British interests posed by Raymond's French brigades, which the Nizam had now authorised him to increase in size to ten thousand men.

In November, after Raymond swiftly and efficiently put down a revolt by the Nizam's younger son, Ali Jah, his rise became even more irresistible. William wrote to his friend Jonathan Duncan in Bombay that only

> three years ago [Raymond] was an obscure partisan, but is now at the head of a disciplined force of at least 10,000 infantry with a well equipped train of artillery, pretty well officered with Europeans who are of his own nation and principles. This man who, I have reason to think, is very ill-disposed towards our nation is, you will easily conceive, in more respects than one the source of much uneasiness to me.[70]

The Nizam rewarded Raymond for his suppression of Ali Jah's revolt by raising him to a position of new eminence within the durbar and giving him two Persian titles – Azdhar e-Jang, the Dragon of War, and Mutahwar ul-Mulk, the Bravest in the State.[71] He was also awarded a huge estate, located in the strategically vital region immediately next to the Hyderabadi citadel Golconda.*

Over the following year, things went from bad to worse. Already the British were alarmed by reports that the French Republican officers in Tipu Sultan's island fortress of Seringapatam had founded a Mysore Jacobin Club 'for framing laws conformable with the laws of the Republic', which had planted a 'Liberty Tree' in the Sultan's capital.[72] Now 'Citizen Tippoo' was discovered by British interceptions to be in communication with Napoleon Bonaparte, whom he formally invited to visit India to liberate the country and expel the British. He had even sent ambassadors to Paris along with a draft treaty in which he proposed an alliance to drive the British out of India.[73]

It also became clear that Raymond was in regular touch not only with the French officers who drilled Tipu's infantry, but also with the French Revolutionary command in Pondicherry and Mauritius. On 16 December 1796, William wrote in cipher to Shore, the Governor General, that his spies in the French camp had discovered that 'Raymond has very lately received a commission from the French Directory; and also that it has been given out in his camp that Tippoo has despatched a large quantity of provisions to Mangalore for the use of the French armament daily expected to arrive at that Port. The accounts may be false, but they are at least an indication of the wishes and disposition of the French party here.'[74]

Shore replied, also in cipher, by asking if it was possible to use subterfuge somehow to 'frame' or discredit Raymond so as to make him appear suspect in the Nizam's eyes – a proposal which might

* William tried in vain to persuade the Nizam to reconsider the grant, reporting that 'The Nizam was either too grateful for his recent services, or too fearful to refuse the remuneration he required. The artifices of our enemies, joined to what HH is pleased to consider our coldness with regard to his interests – manifested as he thinks by declining to meet all his unreasonable expectations [during the Khardla campaign] – have rendered him of late more unmanageable on certain points than would be wished.' OIOC, Kirkpatrick Papers, F228/5, p.8, 17 January 1796, William Kirkpatrick to James Duncan.

imply that the Kirkpatrick brothers already had experience in such covert intelligence operations. But William replied that he thought the plan too risky, and 'attended with much more hazard of discredit to myself, than danger to him'.[75] There was, he advised, only one way of overturning Raymond's influence: to negotiate a treaty with the Nizam unambiguously promising British support in the event of a Maratha attack. Only then might the Nizam possibly consider himself safe enough to dispense with the support of his French regiments. As before, Shore dithered, and eventually refused permission for William to explore the possibility of such a treaty.[76]

This was the position when William's health forced him to resign his post as Resident. By early summer 1797 he knew that, despite the precariousness of the British position in Hyderabad, he was simply too ill to continue in the job. For several months he had been telling Shore of his extreme 'sufferings from rheumatism and a disordered stomach . . . I might perhaps be able to go on for a year at H[ydera-bad], yet so much and so often do I suffer from the pains that have so long afflicted me; and so firmly fixed does the constant coldness of my extremities and especially my hands appear to be that I think I should be little better than a dead weight in a situation requiring not only much mental exertion but also a good deal of bodily fatigue.'[77] By the end of 1796 Shore had given him permission to retire to the coast whenever he felt the need. Writing to the Handsome Colonel in November, William stated that 'I wait for nothing but the return of Peace in Europe (on which all our politics in this part of the world continually hinge) in order to see what a change of air will do for my shattered frame . . . The Cape would afford me the best chance.'[78]

But it was not just peace William was waiting for. There was one thing more to be resolved with Shore before he could leave: his brother's succession to his job. Since the death of Steuart in October 1795, James had been William's deputy at the Residency – a huge jump in rank for a humble lieutenant who prior to his arrival in Hyderabad had been commanding an obscure garrison in the tribal belt on the modern Andhra–Orissa border. But James had flourished in Hyderabad, where his unusual linguistic skills combined with his instinctive sympathy and liking for Mughal culture had proved a major asset to William.

James had immediately struck up an excellent relationship with the Nizam, and by simple courtesy gained first his ear, and then, later, his trust. Several years later he explained what he believed to be the secret of his success in Hyderabad: 'The people at Madras I am told are at a loss to conceive by what magic I always continue to work my ends out of the durbar, and if you wish to know what the magic consists in, I will inform you in a few words, that it consists in treating old Nizzy with a great deal of respect and deference, humouring him in all his innocent whims and wishes.'[79] Typical was James's idea of ordering a special quilt for the old man as the Hyderabadi winter set in: 'I am glad to hear the pelisse for old Nizzy is on its way hither,' he wrote to Calcutta. 'It will arrive in very good season as the cold weather is just setting in, when the old gentleman requires warm clothing. You have no idea how kindly these marks of attention are taken by him; I may truly say that by such attentions I have gained his warm heart.'[80]

James had also proved himself adept at the kind of intelligence work essential in so faction-ridden and strategically sensitive a posting, where the spies of each rival grouping eavesdropped on each other in a rapid merry-go-round of espionage. As events subsequently showed, in his first two years at Hyderabad James had succeeded in setting up an extensive network of spies and contacts in the court and the French camp, ranging from sweepers and harem guards to various senior Begums in the Nizam's *mahal*, some of Raymond's officers and the Nizam's official court historian and artist, Tajalli Ali Shah.

William was impressed – and a little surprised – by the performance of his younger brother: 'I will honestly own,' he wrote to Shore, 'that I was a stranger, as I believe he himself also was, to the fullest extents of his talents and capacity for this business, till by being left a few months to himself they had the opportunity of developing themselves.'[81] He and James had become very close in the time they spent living together in the Hyderabad Residency. William confided to Shore that if his brother got the job of Resident he felt quite sure that he would support him financially if the change of air at the Cape failed to mend his wretched health and he was forced to retire altogether from the Company: 'Such is my reliance on his fraternal affection, and on his attachment to my children, and so infinitely better a life is his than mine, that I should consider myself as much more securely provided for by his obtaining [the job of Resident], than I would be by my aiming to retain this situation for another year or two.'*

In the event, James was made Acting Resident – effectively put on probation and given a chance to prove himself – while William was despatched to the Cape to recover his health sometime in the middle of the hot summer of 1797. William was still far from recovered the following January when he was introduced to the incoming Governor General, Lord Wellesley, at Anne Barnard's house. The two immediately hit it off, sharing a common Francophobia and a similarly bullish attitude to the future of British rule in India.

Writing to his friend Colonel John Collins in Calcutta shortly after he had been offered the job of Wellesley's Military Secretary, William confided: 'I have had many conversations with his Ldship since his arrival here [the Cape], in the course of which I have satisfied all his enquiries relative to the politics at the court of Hyderabad ... he appears to be extremely well informed for a stranger to Indian affairs [and] to be of pleasing easy manners.'[82] More importantly, William wrote that he had persuaded Wellesley of the necessity of signing an unambiguous treaty of friendship and support with the Nizam,

---

* William was not mistaken in his estimation either of James's gratitude or of his affection for him. As James wrote to him the following year, after laying aside 'Rs. 10,000 a year for the use of my dear little nieces ... setting aside our close connection by blood – our strong – nay, I will add, unbounded mutual affection and attachment, and the many, many juvenile obligations I owe you (and which made an impression on my heart never to be effaced) setting aside as I say all these considerations, could I possibly have done less than this to the Man to whom I am not only indebted for my present high station with all its concomitant advantages, but even for the very share of acquirements which have enabled me hitherto to acquit myself therein to the satisfaction of my superiors? Such has been my invariable attachment to you from the time that I began to know and appreciate your virtues and talents, that there was nought in my possession or power that I would not at any time have resigned most joyfully upon the smallest hint from my dearest and best beloved brother.' OIOC, Kirkpatrick Papers, F228/11, p.112, 4 April 1799, James Kirkpatrick to William Kirkpatrick.

something Shore had always refused to do. In due course William wrote a long letter to James explaining how to open negotiations with the Nizam; and a few days after this Wellesley wrote himself. James was thrilled at the chance to take on the French, and wrote back flattered and elated by the new Governor General's 'wise and liberal propositions' and 'masterly' instructions.

To William he wrote a more heartfelt reply: 'I need not, I am sure my dear Will, say anything to you on the subject of my gratitude to that most worthy nobleman [Lord Wellesley] for his uniform condescension and kindness towards me. You know my heart, and can form a good idea of my feelings on the occasion . . .'[83]

III

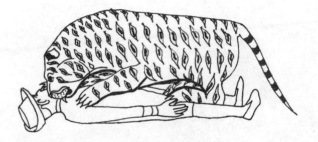

F ROM THE PARAPET of the wall that surrounded the British
Residency in Hyderabad, James Achilles Kirkpatrick could look
down over the River Musi, a raging torrent during the monsoon,
but a gentle, fordable stream in summer. On the far bank of the river
rose the great city of Hyderabad: a seven-mile loop of walls, and over the
top of its watchtowers, stretching far into the distance, a magnificent
panorama of white mosques and palaces, monuments and tombs,
domes and minarets, their gilt filials glinting in the summer sunlight.

For one hundred years from the late sixteenth century, thanks at
least partly to the profits of the diamond trade, Hyderabad had been
one of the richest cities in India; it was certainly the most prosperous
town outside the Mughal Empire. Sultan Quli Qutb Shah had planned
his new city in 1591 as 'a metropolis which would be unequalled the
world over and a replica of paradise itself'.[1] When the French traveller
M. de Thevenot passed through in the late 1650s he described how far
the Sultan's plans had succeeded: elegant, clean, opulent and well
planned, the still-young city of Hyderabad was filled with grand houses
and gardens, and miles of bazaars humming 'with many rich merchants, bankers and jewellers and a vast number of very skilful artisans'.

Beyond the walls, the scene was equally seductive. The pleasure
gardens and the country retreats of the rich extended for miles in
every direction; beyond, to the south-west, lay the citadel of Golconda
with the swelling hemispheres of the great Qutb Shahi tombs at its
base. European merchants flocked there 'and make great profits . . .
the Kingdom may be said to be the Country of Diamonds'.[2] One of

these merchants was William Methwold, the English factor at the sultanate's seaport of Masulipatam. On his first visit to Golconda he was astonished by what he saw, describing it as

> a citie that for sweetnesse of ayre, conveniencie of water and fertility of soyle, is accounted the best situated in India, not to speake of the Kings Palace, which for bignesse and sumptuousnesse, in the judgement of such as have travelled India exceedeth all belonging to the Mogull or any other Prince ... built of stone, and, within, the most eminent places garnished with massie gold in such things as we commonly use iron, as in barres of windowes, bolts and such like, and in all other points fitted to the majesty of so great a King, who in elephants and jewels is accounted one of the richest Princes of India. [The Sultan] married the daughter of the King of Bijapur, and hath beside her three other wives, and at least 1000 concubines: a singular honour and state amongst them being to have many women, and one of the strangest things to them I could relate, and in their opinions lamentable, that his excellent Majesty our Gracious Sovereigne should have three kingdoms and but one wife ...[3]

After a prolonged rivalry between Golconda and Mughal Delhi, the Mughal Emperor Aurangzeb finally captured and sacked Hyderabad in 1687, stabling the horses of his cavalry in the Shi'ite mosques and *ashur khanas* (mourning halls) as a deliberate insult to the city's Shi'a (and thus, in Aurangzeb's orthodox Sunni eyes, heretical) establishment.*

---

* Shi'ism lay at the heart of the identity of Qutb Shahi Hyderabad. The origins of the divide between Sunni and Shi'a go back to the very beginnings of Islam in the period immediately after the death of the Prophet, when the Muslim community was split over the succession. One group, the Sunnis, recognised the authority of the Medinan (and subsequently Ummayad) Caliphs. The other major group, the Shi'as, maintained that sovereignty was a matter of divine right and resided in the descendants of the Prophet, starting with his son-in-law, Ali (*Shi'at Ali* meaning 'the Party of Ali' in Arabic). Ali was murdered in 661 AD, and his son Hussain died at the hands of the Ummayad Caliph al-Yazid at the Battle of Kerbala nineteen years later, in 680. Thereafter Shi'ites remained almost everywhere an Islamic minority until the start of the sixteenth century, when the Iranian Safavid dynasty made Shi'ism the sole legal faith of their Persian empire. Soon after this, a series of Shi'ite leaders came to power in the Indian Deccan, among them the Qutb Shahis, who dedicated their new capital, Hyderabad, to Ali, Hyder being one of his names. They also accepted the nominal overlordship of the Iranian Safavids of Isfahan, the mortal enemies of the Sunni Mughals of Delhi.

After this, the city underwent a temporary eclipse. The focus of the region moved to Aurangzeb's new Mughal headquarters town at Aurangabad, and for eighty years Hyderabad was left a melancholy shadow of its former glory, with whole quarters of the city deserted and ruined. But on the accession of Nizam Ali Khan in 1762, Hyderabad was again made the capital of the region, and this time of a domain which now embraced a far wider slice of central and southern India than the old Qutb Shahi sultanate of Golconda had ever done.

Despite the intermittent warfare of the period, the city quickly began to recover its former wealth and splendour. The ruins of the Qutb Shahi palaces and public buildings were renovated and restored, the mosques rebuilt, the gardens replanted and, crucially, the city walls were strengthened and patched up. By the 1790s Hyderabad, with a population of around a quarter of a million, was once again both a major centre of commerce and the unrivalled centre of the hybrid Indo-Muslim civilisation of the Deccan, the last link in a cultural chain stretching back to the foundation of the first Muslim sultanates in the region in the fourteenth century.

At Hyderabad's centre stood the great Char Minar, a monumental gateway formed by a quadrant of arches rising to four domed minarets. The Char Minar marked the meeting of the city's two principal bazaars, where the road from the craggy citadel of Golconda crossed with that coming from the great port of Masulipatam: 'There are drugs here of all sorts,' wrote one visitor, 'every kind of spice, book, paper, ink, pens, gingham, cloth, silk fabrics and yarn of all colours, swords and bows, arrows and quivers, knives and scissors, spoons and forks, thimbles and dice, needles large and small, gems fine and false – in short, all that one may desire.'[4]

Here merchants and traders from all over the Middle East as well as from France, Holland, England and even China came to buy from the spice bazaar where mountains of cloves, pepper, ginger and cinnamon were all on display, the necks of hessian sacks rolled down to reveal shiny black carob sticks, lumpy ginger stems, aromatic slivers of sandalwood or small hillocks of bright orange turmeric. Other merchants came to Hyderabad to purchase silver and copper, the famous blades of its unrivalled 'Damascus' swords, exquisite gold brocades and *shatranji* (chessboard) carpets.

In the streets crowds of Persians and Arabs in flowing robes joined turbaned Mughals from Delhi and Lucknow, Portuguese horse-traders from Goa and parties of Dutch jewellers up from their base on the coast at Masulipatam. Together they explored the bazaars, testing the delicacies of the city's famous confectioners or lingering before the fragrant stalls of the perfumers, where the scents and aromatic oils were mixed to suit the season, and their ingredients altered depending on the heat or the degree of humidity.*

Beyond stretched the shops of the filigree-dotted gold and silver merchants, which led in turn into the richest of all the bazaars: that of the jewellers and the diamond mart. The great Golconda diamond mines – from ancient times until the early eighteenth century the world's sole supplier of these most coveted of all precious stones – were not yet exhausted, and the same seams that had produced the legendary Koh-i-Noor as well as the Hope and the Pitt diamonds were still active enough in 1785 for Nizam Ali Khan to send King George III the newly discovered 101-carat Hastings Diamond as a small diplomatic gift.[5] Stones of that size were always rare, even in Hyderabad, but the heavily guarded workshops nevertheless groaned with lesser treasures: gleaming rubies the colour of pigeon's blood and scatterings of lizard-green emeralds, superbly inscribed spinels and jewelled daggers, champlevé scabbards and manuscripts of the Koran, their bindings inlaid with burnished gold and empurpled ebony. There were other more effete fopperies too: bejewelled and enamelled flywhisks, and *bazubands* (armbands) set with the Nine Auspicious

---

* The appreciation of scent was especially dear to Deccani Muslim culture, and a matter of great connoisseurship. Many texts on scented gardens, on erotic scents, on the art of incense and perfumery survive, but two in particular stand out. The '*Itr-I Nawras Shahi* is a treatise on perfumery written for the great syncretic Bijapur Sultan, Ibrahim Adil Shah II, which describes how to prepare volatile oils and vapours to scent bedrooms and other contained spaces, as well as the hair and the clothes; it also details the preparation of massage oils, gargles, dentrifices and breath-fresheners. The other great surviving Deccani perfumery manual is the *Lakhlakha*, a Hyderabadi text of the early nineteenth century which goes into incredible detail on the preparation of ambergris, camphor, musk and scented candles. See Ali Akbar Hussain, *Scent in the Islamic Garden* (Karachi, 2000), Chapter 5.

Gems, including yellow topaz and the rarest chrysoberyl cats' eyes.[6]

Palaces stretched off down the narrow sidestreets towards Mughal-pura, Shah Gunj and Irani Gulli, some magnificent, but most plain on the street frontage, hiding their richly latticed treasures for those admitted within. Many were huge – 'some of them are three times the length of Burlington House', reported one astonished British traveller[7] – and contained within them wide expanses of garden, cool and quiet after the bustle of the streets. Throughout ran rippling runnels punctuated by slowly dribbling marble fountains and filled with 'rows of mango trees, date-palms, coconuts, fig trees, bananas, oranges, citrons, with some yew trees ... and very fine circular reservoirs. Around the reservoir are dotted pots of fragrant flowers'.[8]

Where there are the rich in India, there are always the poor too. The magnificent architecture of Hyderabad's palaces and mosques created a façade of order and grandeur which hid the thieving, the sickness, the hunger and the pain that lay behind. On his arrival in the city several years earlier William Steuart had been very struck by its extremes of wealth and poverty – something that travellers in the Nizam's dominions continued to notice right up until the middle of the twentieth century: 'There is perhaps a stronger contrast of extravagant profusion & of wretchedness at this durbar than any-where in India,' Steuart wrote in 1790.

> By the former I mean the Nizam's pomp & state: he has a swaree* of 400 elephants, several thousand of horsemen near his person who receive upwards of 100 Rs nominal pay who are extremely well mounted & richly caparisoned. His other chiefs also show marks of pomp. But I have to observe that except the chiefs all are wretched & miserable; grain seldom cheeper than 15 seer a rupee & since my arrival never above 12 – the poor devils are sadly put to it for a livelihood.[9]

Leading out from behind the grand bazaars ran a warren of filthy lanes and unswept sidestreets – the preserve of the rats, the

---

* Elephant stables (and the whole establishment and paraphernalia related to the keeping of elephants).

pickpockets and the lower sort of prostitute. Even the lane leading to the royal stabling yard was known as 'Muthri Gulli' – Urinating Lane – and the road that led from the main gate of the palace was 'fit for horse and carriage traffic only'.[10] Along this route sat the beggars, the lepers, the lame, the halt and the blind. Maimed sepoys flanked landless peasants and the mentally ill, ejected from the Sufi shrines as unhealable and beyond the powers even of the city's renowned exorcists. From the palace to the gates of the Mecca Masjid they sat in lines, crying for alms and raising their bandaged hands in supplication to passing palanquins, out of which, if they were lucky, might be thrown a small shower of silver annas.

For these people, as for the other Hyderabadis, there were the festivals. To one side of the Char Minar was the Maidan-i-Dilkusha, or Heart-Rejoicing Square, where on holidays such as *Id* and the Prophet's birthday the ground would be swept clean and *bhistis* (water-carriers) sprinkle the warm earth with water. After this canopies and awnings would be raised and food provided free to the entire populace. Elaborate displays of fireworks would round off the evening.[11]

Nearby was the city's renowned Dar ul-Shifa, or 'house of healing', a four-hundred-bed teaching hospital open to all for no charge and famous as one of the most sophisticated centres of yunani* and ayurvedic medicine. Beside it stood a wide garden, the Bagh i-Muhammed Shahi, specially planted with healing herbs and aromatic plants, as well as with flowers whose purifying and uplifting scent was believed to help the patients recover.[12]

There were other scents too, as well as the gardens, the whiff of spices from the bazaars and the darker smells emanating from Muthri Gulli. From nearby street stalls came the all-pervading smell of grilling kebabs, and another smell still more specific to Hyderabad: the scent of slowly-cooking *biryani*: 'In truth,' admitted a patriotic Delhi-wallah, abandoning for a moment his metropolitan Mughal hauteur, 'no better dish is cooked anywhere throughout India.'[13]

One of General Raymond's French officers found this smell par-

---

* Ionian or Byzantine medicine, passed to the Islamic world through Byzantine exiles in Persia.

ticularly irresistible: 'There are dishes consisting of bread made *à la manteque* [*naan*], stew, and the liver of fowls and kids, very well dressed,' he wrote, '[but most renowned of all is the] rice boiled with quantities of butter, fowls and kids, with all sorts of spicery . . . which we found to be very good, and which refreshed us greatly.'[14]

In his conversations with Wellesley at the Cape, James's brother William Kirkpatrick painted a straightforward picture of Anglo–French rivalry in Hyderabad, where the beleaguered Union flag of the Residency fluttered bravely against a rising tide of French Revolutionary tricolore. The reality on the ground was a little different.

It is clear from a variety of sources that by the late 1790s both the French officers of the Corps de Raymond and their counterparts in the British detachments stationed in Hyderabad, as well as the staff of the British Residency, had all, to different extents, begun acclimatising themselves to their Hyderabadi environment and to Hyderabadi ways of living.

By 1797, when William left Hyderabad, his brother James had already begun wearing what Arthur Wellesley described as 'a Mussulmen's dress of the finest texture' for all occasions 'excepting when he was obliged to receive the officers of the [British military] detachment, or upon certain great occasions when the etiquette of the Nizam's durbar required that the English Resident should appear there in the dress of an Englishman'.[15] He smoked a hookah, wore Indian-style 'mustachios [and] has his hair cropped very short & his fingers dyed with henna', as one surprised visitor recorded in his diaries. Moreover, James had taken on the Eastern habit of belching appreciatively after meals, which sometimes took visitors to the Residency aback, as did his tendency to 'make all sorts of other odd noises', possibly a reference to him clearing his throat (or even nostrils) in the enthusiastic and voluble Indian manner.[16] According to the contemporary Hyderabadi historian Ghulam Imam Khan in his *Tarikh i-Khurshid Jahi*:

> I must mention that the Resident [James Kirkpatrick] had a great liking for this country, and especially for the people of Hyderabad. He was very close to the Prime Minister and a great favourite of the Nizam who used to call him 'beloved son'. It is said that in contrast to many of the English who are often proud, haughty and snobbish, Kirkpatrick was a very cordial and friendly person. Anyone who had spent a little time with him would be won over by his pleasant manners. In the very first meeting, he would make the other person feel he had known him for years, and take him for an old friend and acquaintance. He was completely fluent in the language and idiom of these parts, and followed many of the customs of the Deccan. Indeed he had spent so much time in the company of the women of Hyderabad that he was very familiar with the style and behaviour of the city and adopted it as his own. Thanks partly to these women he was always very cheerful.[17]

Over at the French cantonments on the other side of the Musi, there was a similar situation. Raymond was believed to be a practising Muslim by many of his sepoys, though a few took him to be a Hindu; his deputy Jean-Pierre Piron was also reported to be 'wanting to turn mussulman', though it is unclear if he ever did so.[18] The doctor of the French corps, Captain Bernard Fanthôme, seems to have special-ised in ayurvedic and yunani cures, and had seven Indian *bibis*, the most senior of whom was a daughter of the Mughal Prince Feroz Shah. Fanthôme, who was known at court as Fulutan Sahib due to his wisdom – 'Fulutan' is the Persian name for Plato – later became a doctor in the service of the Mughal Emperor Akbar Shah II, and fathered a dynasty of notable Urdu and Persian poets, including 'Jargis', 'Shaiq' and 'Sufi', most of whom were pious Muslims and whose *masnavi* were treasured in the royal libraries at Lucknow and Rampur.[19] Like Fanthôme, most of the French, and a great many of the British, had married or lived with Hyderabadi women, by whom they had large families and through whom they gained Hyderabadi roots.[20]* The image conveyed by William Kirkpatrick's official despatches of two fiercely opposed national camps soon fractures on examination into a more nuanced reality of a pair of isolated European outposts slowly assimilating themselves with their surroundings, while retaining their national rivalries and a few other features of their European origins.

In the British Residency this unlikely amalgam of Mughal and European cultures was particularly striking: one visitor in 1801 wrote that 'Major Kirkpatrick's grounds are laid out partly in the taste of Islington & partly in that of Hindostan.'[21] The Hindustani part of the compound was defined by the remains of the ancient pleasure garden in which the Residency was built. In its centre was a large Mughal-style *baradari*† pavilion which the British had turned into 'a dining hall and place of public entertainment', while nearby stood a Mughal-style *mahal* or sleeping apartment from which led a pair of mature cypress avenues. From this axis ran various runnels, fountains, pools and flowerbeds, all of which had survived from the garden's earlier incarnation as a pleasure retreat.[22]

During the sixteenth century, under the rule of Hyderabad's founders, the Qutb Shahi sultans, the entire bank of the River Musi at this point had been decorated with long lines of elegant Mughal-style gardens and country houses, cascades and *chattris*.‡ The remains of this crumbling Arcadia stretched northwards as far as the eye could see, though during the chaos of the early eighteenth century a number of the gardens had been encroached upon by villagers and turned into paddy fields. The whole area was dominated by the vast skeleton of Tana Shah's pleasure palace. According to Edward Strachey:

---

* Raymond's magnificent hookah, which survives in a private collection in London, is emblematic of the cultural fusion of the period: it is a masterpiece of Bidri work, with superbly controlled silver inlay decoration curling around the bell of the black zinc water-pot; but this most Mughal of objects is decorated with Raymond's 'JR' monogram, while the ornament that surrounds it – all classical swags and scrolls – is more French Empire than Deccani.

† Literally 'twelve doors': the open garden kiosks with arcades of three arches on each side popularised by the Mughals.

‡ A domed kiosk supported on pillars; often used as a decorative feature on top of turrets and minarets.

Near the Residency, within a mile, are the ruins of a palace and garden which were formerly celebrated for their elegance and magnificence. It is now known by the name of Tannee Shah's garden. Tannee Shah was the last of the Kuttub Shah Kings. It is related of him that after hunting, his tent being pitched at this place, he slept and in a dream he saw a beautiful palace and garden with fountain and aquaduct. When he awoke he gave orders that a similar palace and garden should be begun immediately.[23]

If the remains of ruined Qutb Shahi Gardens gave the British Residency the 'Hindustani' part of its character, a scattering of elegant neo-classical bungalows and stable blocks provided the other, Islington, part of its identity. The most prominent of these buildings was a two-storey house intended for the personal use of the Resident. William Kirkpatrick had had it made during his absence on the Khardla campaign; but, unsupervised, it had been quickly and cheaply built, and though barely four years old was already in a semi-ruinous condition. Within a year James was writing to William seeking his help to get the funds out of Calcutta to renovate it:

The upper storey you built to the house at the Residency is now scarcely habitable, as it leaks in all parts so that I am obliged to proof it to prevent it falling in on the lower storey, which itself gives strong symptoms of decay. I have been for these two or three months past patching up what the rains have caused to moulder away, but this patchwork is neither durable, comfortable nor creditable, and as I cannot suppose that it is wished that my accommodations should be either uncomfortable or uncreditable, it must end in my sending in an estimate.[24]

Although the bungalows provided for the Residency staff were Western in design, they had one very Eastern feature which would perhaps have surprised Lord Wellesley, or at least his masters in London: all had separate *zenana* wings for the Indian wives and mistresses attached to the staff. James complained to one friend that these were much smaller than necessary for the accommodation of the full *zenana* apparatus – the enormous entourage of *aseels*,* eunuchs, handmaids, *ayahs* and wetnurses which seems to have been the norm at this period: one of Kirkpatrick's English visitors, for example, turned up to stay with 'at least a dozen females', although how many of these were *bibis*, and how many the *bibis*' families and attendants, is unclear.[25]

These *bibis* came from across the Indian social spectrum, and the relationships they formed with the Residency staff varied accordingly. At the most basic level, there was a mechanism in place for procuring common bazaar prostitutes – or possibly the city's famously refined courtesans – from the city for passing British travellers: when Mountstuart Elphinstone stopped in at the Residency in August 1801 on his way to Pune he wrote in his diary that the 'whore whom I am going to keep was to have come to be looked at but did not'. (This, incidentally, was probably just as well for the woman in question as Elphinstone was then suffering from a bad attack of clap and spent much of his time rubbing sulphur and mercury into the affected area, though he remarked in his diary that 'I ereqtate comfortably enough considering.'[26]†)

Other British officials and soldiers in Hyderabad, however, had more serious monogamous relationships with educated women from the upper reaches of Indian society. Lieutenant Colonel James Dalrymple, the commander of the British troops in Hyderabad (and a cousin of Anne Barnard, Lord Wellesley's host at the Cape), was married to Mooti Begum, the daughter of the Nawab of Masulipatam. It seems to have been a measure of the equality of their marriage that the two agreed to split the upbringing of their five children

---

* *Aseels* were the key figures in a *zenana*. Usually slave girls by origin, they performed a number of essential administrative and domestic tasks within the women's quarters. In the Nizam's *zenana* the senior *aseels* were important figures of state.

† All the younger members of the Residency seem to have suffered from severe attacks of venereal disease at different points. In June 1805, James's then Assistant Henry Russell wrote to his brother Charles, who had gone to the coast to recover from a particularly painful bout, to tell him the news that another of the younger Assistants, 'Bailey has proved himself, and has communicated that fashionable disease to his girl . . . they are now amusing themselves together with Ure's fine [mercury] ointment.' A week later Henry Russell himself went down with a painful attack. See Bodleian Library, Russell Correspondence, Ms Eng Letts C155, p.98, 25 June 1805.

according to sex: the boys were sent to Madras to be brought up as Christians, eventually to be sent back to East Lothian to join the ranks of the Lowland Scottish gentry, while the only girl from the marriage, Noor Jah Begum, was brought up as a Hyderabadi Muslim and remained in India where she eventually married one of her father's sepoys, a 'Cabulee havildar* named Sadue Beig'.[27]

Likewise, William Linnaeus Gardner, who began his freelance career in the Nizam's army in 1798, was married to Begum Mah Munzel ul-Nissa, the daughter of the Nawab of Cambay, and Gardner seems to have converted to Islam to marry her. The two had met in Surat a year earlier, whence the fourteen-year-old Begum had fled with her mother from a palace coup. Gardner had glimpsed the Princess while he was sitting through the interminable negotiations of a treaty:

> During the negotiations a *parda* [curtain] was gently moved aside, and I saw, as I thought, the most beautiful black eyes in the world. It was impossible to think of the Treaty; those bright and piercing glances, those beautiful black eyes completely bewildered me.
>
> I felt flattered that a creature so lovely as she of those deep black, loving eyes must be should venture to gaze upon me . . . At the next Durbar, my agitation and anxiety were extreme again to behold the bright eyes that haunted my dreams by night and my thoughts by day. The *parda* was again gently moved, and my fate was decided.
>
> I asked for the Princess in marriage; her relations were at first indignant, and positively refused my proposal . . . however on mature deliberation, the hand of the young Princess was promised. The preparations for the marriage were carried forward: 'Remember,' said I, 'it will be useless to attempt to deceive me, I shall know those eyes again, nor will I marry any other.'
>
> On the day of the marriage I raised the veil from the countenance of the bride, and in the mirror that was placed between

---

* According to *Hobson-Jobson*: '*Havildar*: a sepoy non-commissioned officer corresponding to a sergeant.'

us, beheld the bright eyes that had bewildered me; I smiled –
and the young Begum smiled also.[28]

It was a happy and long-lasting marriage. Years later, living with
his Anglo-Indian family on his wife's estates at Khassgunge near Agra,
with his son James married to a niece of the Mughal Emperor,
Gardner wrote to his cousin Edward:

> At Khassgunge I anticipate very great happiness. I am fond
> of reading and I am fond of my garden and (there's no
> accounting for taste) have more relish in playing with the
> little brats than for the First Society in the World. The Begum
> and I, from 22 years constant contact, have smoothed off each
> other's asperities and roll on peaceably and contentedly ...
> Man must have a companion, and the older I get the more I
> am confirmed in this. An old age without something to love,
> and nourish and nurse you, must be old and uncomfortable.
> The house is filled with Brats, and the very thinking of them,
> from blue eyes and fair hair to ebony and wool makes me
> quite anxious to get back to them again.[29]

He added: 'Few [men] have more occasion to congratulate themselves on their domestic comfort.'[30] Eight years later he was able to
joke how 'my having been married some thirty years and never having
taken another wife surprises the Musselmans very much, and the
ladies all look upon me as a pattern: they do not admire a system
of having three or four rivals, however well pleased the gentlemen
may be with the custom'.[31]

If there appears to have been no shortage of beautiful Muslim
Begums in Hyderabad, their European counterparts seem to have
been in shorter supply – and to have been something of a mixed
blessing. Hyderabad at this period was no place for a demanding, or
fashionable, or socially ambitious European woman. Unlike Calcutta,
Madras or Bombay, there were no milliners or portrait painters, no
dancing or riding masters, no balls, no concerts, no masquerades.
Boredom and loneliness led to depression, or dissipation, or that
sour, embittered *ennui* that Kipling depicted in his Mrs Hauksbees
and Mrs Reivers a hundred years later: 'Among the nations of the

world, the charms of our fair countrywomen are unrivalled,' wrote the young Henry Russell, one of James's Assistants at the Residency, on his arrival at Hyderabad. 'Unfortunately for us [in this city] we possess but the very dregs . . . Mrs S— contaminates the atmosphere which she breathes and pollutes the very earth on which she treads.'[32] Her friend Margaret Dalrymple, wife of James Dalrymple's cousin Samuel, seems to have been little better, and struck Elphinstone as 'an affected, sour, supercilious woman'.

Mrs Ure, the wife of the Dr George Ure who had been besieged with William Kirkpatrick at Khardla, was less poisonous than these two – James thought she was 'perfectly unassuming and more devoid of affectation than almost any woman I ever met with'; but her drawback was her vast and apparently unquenchable appetite.[33] Together with her portly husband, she ate up as much as the rest of the Residency staff altogether: 'The young couple's consumption of tea and sugar alone is at least double mine,' wrote Kirkpatrick soon after their marriage, when Mrs Ure first became a regular at the Residency dining table. 'The *khansaman** tells me a couple of grilled chickens were regularly served up by their direction at their breakfast table. And two fowls boiled down into Mollygotauny soup for their tiffin!! The consequence of which is, as might well have been expected, that the lady was seized with a fever which according to Greene's and Ure's account absolutely endangered her life. It has now however left her, and though extremely weak, the *khansaman* has received directions to provide daily calve's feet jelly's until further orders. You may recollect from experience what a costly dish these calves feet jelly's are at Hyderabad . . .' Later Kirkpatrick reported that during her illness, Mrs Ure complained of a lack of appetite but still managed to put away every day 'poultry, rice, milk, butter, vegetables &c, &c, &c, &c' as well as 'two plum cakes, a goose, a turkey and ducks innumerable besides fowls and mutton'.[34]

Judging by this list, it would seem that the cooking at the Residency was overwhelmingly European in character; however, the Nizam knew that James personally preferred Indian food, and took to regu-

---

* Butler (literally 'master of the household gear'). Today, when butlers are sadly in short supply, the word is more often used of cooks.

larly sending him a Hyderabadi speciality made from *brinjauls* (aubergines), for which he had expressed a particular liking.[35] Moreover,
despite the European cuisine, the Residency kitchens were run so as
not to break any Indian notions of purity, with strict caste rules in
operation, presumably so as not to put off Indian guests. Years later,
when Henry Russell was made Resident, he wrote to his brother
that he planned to bring back the regulations that James had put
in place: 'Among other improvements,' he wrote, 'pray take great
pains to purify every place in the Residency from the pollution of
dhains, chamars [i.e. sweepers and untouchables] and other vagabonds of that type. Upon that subject I intend to be quite as particular as Colonel Kirkpatrick was. Your cooks are all that they ought
to be; but Rakeem Khan tells me that *dhains* are still allowed to go
where they ought not to go, and to touch what they ought not to
touch.'[36]

The pastimes of the Residency staff also intriguingly mixed the
customs of Georgian England with those of late Mughal India. There
was a great deal of obsessive card-playing and gambling, as if the
Residency were a gentlemen's club in St James's: whist, dunby and
'Pope Joan' alternated with backgammon and billiards as a way of
transferring winnings and debts from one member of the Residency
to another, and so filling the long, hot Indian nights. But Georgian
pursuits often dovetailed with Mughal ones: after a Saturday morning
spent shooting sand grouse ('The Resident is a capital shot,' reported
Elphinstone[37]), Kirkpatrick would go hunting the black buck with
his tame cheetahs: 'The cheetahs are kept hood winked on a cord,'
wrote Edward Strachey,

> and when they get near enough to the deer the hood is taken
> off and they are slipped at the game. They run perhaps two
> or three hundred yards. If they don't catch the animal, (which
> they have singled from the herd) in that time, then they crouch
> and do not attempt to take another. The first time the cheetah
> failed but a second attempt had better success; he ran a con-
> siderable way after a deer, then sprang on him. When we
> came up he had the deer's throat in his mouth & its body
> between his legs. He gave up his prey more readily than one

would expect & it was lain on the cart with him but out of his reach.[38]

In the evenings after returning from the hunt, Kirkpatrick would invite troops of Hyderabad's famous nautch girls to the camp to perform. In matters of Deccani dance and music, many members of the Hyderabad Residency became connoisseurs – so much so that Mah Laqa Bai Chanda, Hyderabad's most celebrated dancer and courtesan as well as the first major woman poet in Urdu, dedicated her *divan* to one of Kirkpatrick's Assistants, Captain John Malcolm. This was a matter of some political delicacy: Mah Laqa Bai was the lover of Mir Alam, and may also have been, at different times, the inamorata of Nizam Ali Khan and possibly Aristu Jah too. How Mir Alam felt about Mah Laqa giving her *divan* to Malcolm – the dedication took place at a private nautch at Mir Alam's house – is not recorded.[39]*

An alternative to nautches were the *bhands* (buffoons or mummers), whom Elphinstone was particularly taken with when they performed after one of James's hunting expeditions: 'They played many parts such as a woman trying to force her way into a zenana, a profligate nephew and his uncle, a foolish horseman wheedled out of his money and clothes by singers.'[40] Such entertainments alternated with more conventional Georgian fare such as 'reading Dryden out loud' and 'Mrs. Hewitt singing after dinner aires'.

Kirkpatrick – and no doubt many others on the Residency staff – spent other evenings visiting friends in the old city, though it was necessary to get the express permission of the Minister for members of the Residency to enter the city after sunset. James was especially fond of visiting his friend Tajalli Ali Shah, the Nizam's court painter, poet and historian, whose grand courtyard house – or *deorhi* as they are known in Hyderabad – was 'the coffee house of Hyderabad' according to James, and the place where everyone came to exchange political gossip.[41] With Shah's help, he collected Hyderabadi minia-

---

* The *divan* given by Mah Laqa Bai Chanda is now in OIOC, Islamic Ms, 2768. The book contains an inscription: 'The Diwan of Chanda the celebrated Malaka of Hyderabad. This book was presented as a nazr from this extraordinary woman to Captain Malcolm in the midst of a dance in which she was the chief performer on the 18th Oct 1799 at the House of Meer Allum Bahadur.'

tures, and attended *mehfils* and *mushairas* – poetic symposia. He also regularly attended the Tuesday cockfights at Aristu Jah's mansion, and visited the Minister at other times to play chess and fly pigeons.

Under James the Residency also participated in the life and yearly cycle of seasons and festivals of Hyderabad to an extent that it was never to do again. James saw to it that the Residency gave regular donations to the Sufi shrines of the city. He also took parties to join in the festivals: to break the Ramadan fast by eating *'iftar* with the Nizam or the Minister, to travel with the durbar up to the Shi'a shrine of Maula Ali during its annual *'urs* (festival day), and to present himself, head covered, at the city's *ashur khana* during Muharram.

If, under James Kirkpatrick, the Residency's participation in the social and cultural life of Hyderabad led to much cross-fertilisation of ideas and the growth of a number of deep friendships between the Residency and the *omrahs* (nobles) of the court, it also led to some very real political benefits. European ignorance of the complex codes of Mughal etiquette often caused unexpected and diplomatically disastrous offence at Indian courts: in 1750 for example the Hyderabad durbar completely broke off relations with the French after the Nizam received an inadequately deferential letter from the Governor of Pondicherry. The Hyderabad Prime Minister of the time wrote a curt note to the Governor, returning the offending letter and noting: 'Your letter was not politely written. Even the Sultan of Rum* writes respectfully [to the Nizam]. How great the difference between you, the master of one seaport and [the Nizam], the Governor of the entire Deccan! Should you not therefore treat him with due deference?'[42] James's increasing absorption into Mughal society meant that he would never make such basic errors of etiquette.

Likewise his personal knowledge of harem life meant that he avoided the crucial mistake made by many of his contemporaries: of regarding Muslim harems merely as places of pleasure, and so underestimating the power of the Nizam's women in the Hyderabad

---

* The Ottoman Emperor. The Muslims always called the Byzantines, correctly enough, 'the Romans', and when the Seljuk Turks conquered 'Roman' Anatolia in the eleventh century, they renamed themselves the 'Seljuks of Rum'. When the Ottomans succeeded the Seljuks and conquered Constantinople in 1453 the Ottoman Sultan became known across the Islamic world as the Sultan of Rum.

political process. In his very first report for Wellesley, James wrote not only about the Nizam and his advisers, but also devoted many pages to analysing the distribution of power within Nizam Ali Khan's harem:

> Among the wives and concubines of the Nizam, two dominate the zenana. These are the Bukshee Begum and Tînat un-Nissah Begum, the former of whom has the charge of the privy purse, and control of all Mahl [*zenana*] disbursements, and the latter the custody of the family jewels which are valued at the lowest at two crores of rupees. They are both advanced in years . . . and are thought to possess much influence with the Nizam, which they have never been known (it is said) to exert to bad purposes, and they are both much respected. For some years past the Bukshee Begum has entirely refrained from all interference in public matters, employing the whole of her time in acts of charity and devotion. Tînat un-Nissa on the other hand, takes a deep interest in the affairs of the state, and has not failed to avail herself of the share she enjoys in the Nizam's confidence, and of that weight which her rank in the Mahl gives her at court, where her influence is all pervading.[43]*

James's writings show that he correctly understood the very precise and intricate hierarchy in the Nizam's harem, where elderly post-menopausal women, particularly those with adult male princely children, had considerable influence – much more so, perhaps surprisingly, than their younger, more sexually active rivals.[44] This know-

* In time, that influence would become irresistible. Tînat un-Nissa had risen from the position of Bukshee Begum's serving girl 'to the honour of the Nizam's bed'. Her rise had been due as much to her intelligence and talent for intrigue as to her beauty, and as she grew older she became both more powerful and more ruthless. She also became increasingly opposed to British influence. James's later Assistant Charles Russell found it almost impossible to win any point she opposed, and wrote to Calcutta that she was a 'haughty, tyrannical, rapacious, cunning and officious woman'. Indeed he complained that she interfered with every arrangement of government, from the most important to the most trivial. Each Minister or noble of rank felt obliged to seek her patronage, without which his career had no hope of survival. New Delhi National Archives, Foreign Political Consultations, Charles Russell to Minto, 4 August 1810, FPC 6 September 1810, No. 23. Also Hyderabad Residency Records, Vol. 38, pp.79–90. See also Zubaida Yazdani, *Hyderabad During the Residency of Henry Russell 1811–1820: A Case Study of the Subsidiary Alliance System* (Oxford, 1976), p.83.

ledge enabled him successfully to predict the outcome of power struggles and succession disputes.*

Kirkpatrick's intimate knowledge of Mughal society also allowed him to participate in Hyderabadi court ritual in a way that earlier Residents had been unqualified to do, and later generations would find impossible. So when the Nizam recovered from an illness, James did not just go and congratulate him as other diplomats of the period might have done. Instead, as he reported to Calcutta:

> After paying my respects to his Highness and expressing my Joy in his happy Recovery, I passed a Bag containing a thousand Rupees with the usual ceremony thrice round his Highness's head, and then desired that it might be considered as a *Tussaddookh* or health-offering on the present Joyful Occasion; a mode of manifesting the interest which the Government I represent takes in his Highness's welfare, that was highly applauded by all present, and appeared to excite a pleasing emotion even in his Highness himself as far as could be perceived in his low and listless condition.[45]

It was a small gesture, but clearly one that was appreciated. By wearing Islamic dress, using Mughal styles of address, larding his speeches with the Persian aphorisms of 'the wise Shaikh Sady', and accepting and using Persian titles, James Kirkpatrick made himself intelligible in the political *lingua franca* of the wider Mughal world. Equally important was his willingness to submit to the ritual subordination of Mughal court procedure – the giving of *nazrs* (symbolic gifts) and the accepting of *khilats* (symbolic court dress supposedly taken from the Nizam's own wardrobe) all had profound political significance in Mughal court ritual.

By mastering the finer points of etiquette of the court and submit-

---

* One of the Nizam's most talented and popular sons was Feridun Jah, but Kirkpatrick discounted the possibility of him succeeding his father, since 'the Mother of this promising young Prince is probably a woman of very obscure birth, as it would not appear that she ranks amongst the Begum's or even Khanums of the Nizam's Mahl – that is, she is neither acknowledged as a wife, nor distinguished as a concubine'. Instead, Kirkpatrick was able correctly to predict that it would be the unpopular and mean-minded Sikander Jah, rather than one of his more charismatic half-brothers, who would eventually succeed his father on the *musnud*.

ting to procedures that some other Residents refused to bow to, James quickly gained a greater degree of trust than any other British Resident of the period, and so was able to reap the diplomatic rewards.

In the crucial period immediately after William Kirkpatrick left for the Cape, and General Raymond's rise at court seemed irresistible, these small diplomatic advantages were much needed.

By 1797 Raymond's personal income was vast – his estates on their own yielded fifty thousand rupees a year – and according to one observer, 'in the style of his domestic life he collected around him every luxury and elegance within the reach of a European in India'.[46] Indeed Raymond's corps was so well financed that he was able to outbid the British not only for the services of their best sepoys, but was even able to bribe several senior British officers to defect from the two British battalions stationed in Hyderabad to take up service with the French corps for increased wages. These defections were a great blow to both British morale and British prestige in the city. In August 1797 James reported that three more Englishmen had deserted and that something must quickly be done to stop 'the growing power and influence of the French here which if not speedily overthrown will be productive of the most serious mischief for us . . . Surely no one in his senses can doubt that the French will now bend the whole of their own exertions and those of their allies to shake our power in India to the very foundations.'[47]

In the early months of 1798 Raymond persuaded the Nizam again to increase the size of his force, this time to over fourteen thousand men, with a complete train of cannon and its own bespoke gun foundry, all drawn by five thousand of its own bullocks. The force also manufactured its own swords, muskets and pistols besides its excellent artillery; there was even a small cavalry group numbering six hundred. To make matters worse, Raymond was personally very popular in the durbar. One of the most senior of the princes, Sikander Jah, who since the rebellion and subsequent suicide of his brother Ali Jah was now one of the two possible heirs apparent, was so enamoured of the Frenchman that he went as far as swearing 'by the head of Raymond'.[48]

Moreover there were worrying signs that Raymond was planning some sort of pre-emptive strike on the two British battalions in Hyderabad. As James reported to his brother: 'Three nights ago Raymond sent between the hours of eleven and twelve a *Moheer* (answering to a *havildar* major) with six sepoys to reconnoitre the English camp, which he did accordingly and returned with his report to his chief. R has a spy in our lines. I hope he will soon be apprehended.'[49]

James had good reason to believe that Raymond's loyalty to France far outweighed his loyalty to the Nizam. After all, the French corps fought under the Revolutionary tricolore rather than the insignia of the Nizam, and Raymond himself made no secret of the fact that he regarded his troops not as Hyderabadi but instead 'a French body of troops employed and subsidised by the Nizam'. Raymond personally owned all the guns and military equipage used by his force, and could in principle walk away with both the arms and the men at any time he wished. It would, James feared, be very easy for him to use his force to attempt some sort of *coup d'état* against the Nizam.

The news that Raymond was scouting out the English camp and clearly considering an attack on the English in Hyderabad confirmed all Lord Wellesley's suspicions. He was quick to see a wider French conspiracy behind the moves, writing to James that 'the junction between the French officers with their several corps in the respective services of the Nizam, of Scindiah, and of Tippoo might establish the power of France in India upon the ruin of the states of Poonah [the Marathas] and of the Deccan [Hyderabad]'.[50]

Although many of Wellesley's writings at this period have an air of Francophobe paranoia to them, the new Governor General was in fact quite correct about the threat posed by Raymond. As a recently discovered cache of papers has shown, Raymond was indeed in correspondence both with the French officers of de Boigne's corps in Scindia's service and with those working for Tipu at Seringapatam, where Raymond had himself been employed before entering the Nizam's service fourteen years earlier.

The scale of Raymond's ambitions is revealed in a series of passionately patriotic letters he wrote in the early 1790s to the Compagnie des Indes Orientales headquarters at Pondicherry, pledging his loyalty to France and the Revolution: 'I am ready to sacrifice all,' he wrote to the Count de Conway, the Governor of Pondicherry, 'if I am so fortunate that circumstances may ever put it in my power to prove the zeal for my country which animates me.' A later letter was even more explicit about his hopes that the different French corps in India might one day be able to act in concert: 'My troops are the only ones in the capital ... I pray that my fellow citizens may place at your disposal in India the means for acting on the first necessity. Then, my General, the modest strength of the machine which I have put together may display itself.'

To the Chevalier de Fresne, Governor of the important French base on the Île de France (modern Mauritius), Raymond was even more explicit about his aims and intentions: 'As for me, my General, I shall always follow as my first duty whatever [orders] you wish to give me ... If ever I can still be useful to France I am ready to pour my blood once more for her. I labour only to discharge this duty and gain your good opinion.'[51]

In the late summer of 1797, just as things seemed to be spinning out of James's control, the increasingly fragile position of the British in Hyderabad was suddenly steadied when Aristu Jah, the former Prime Minister who had been imprisoned in Pune for over two years, sent some extraordinary news to the Nizam: not only had he succeeded in negotiating his own release, he had managed to get the Marathas to agree to return almost all the land and fortresses that had been ceded to them after the Battle of Kharlda. They had even waived the enormous indemnity owed to them by the Nizam.

So astounding was the news, and so remarkable was Aristu Jah's achievement in negotiating it from confinement, that many of his contemporaries assumed that he could only have achieved this major diplomatic coup with the aid of sorcery. Even Abdul Lateef Shushtari, one of the most intelligent and least credulous Muslim observers of the period, believed that Aristu Jah was a master of the dark arts, and that 'the balance of his mind was overthrown by his obsession with alchemy to make gold and magic to have power over angels'.[52] The historian Ghulam Husain Khan was more explicit. In the *Gulzar-i-Asafiya* he wrote how for two years Aristu Jah was imprisoned in his garden outside Pune, forgotten by the Nizam's durbar and ignored by the Marathas, until eventually he decided that his only hope of escape was by using his occult arts:

> He began the litanies of the Prayer of the Sword breathing on a bowl of water, which he then threw over a desiccated wood apple tree in the hope that, if after 20 days the tree started sprouting green shoots, then after completing the 40 days of the litanies, this obstinate misfortune would turn out according to his wishes. So he began reciting and indeed after twenty days, the desiccated wood apple, whose branches were withered as if they had not had any rain for many years, suddenly put out green shoots and fresh leaves – a miraculous demonstration of the power of the Almighty! Those who knew of Aristu Jah's vow praised God and grew hopeful that his prayers would be granted. Then Aristu Jah, his heart fortified with hope in God's merciful grace, stopped eating meat and in a constant state of purification, recited his litanies with devout sincerity and brought his 40 days' devotions to completion.
>
> It is said that on the very day the 40 days were completed, in the first watch of the day, a messenger suddenly brought the news that [the young Maratha Peshwa] Madhu Rao had fallen off the roof and was dead. While flying a kite, he had slipped from the parapet and toppled onto the fountain below, whose spout had pierced him to the liver. Aristu Jah was

astonished, for the secret intention of his reciting the litanies had been that there should be a revolution in the leadership in Pune so that he could be freed. For without a change of ruler and the ensuing squabbles among the nobles, it was uncertain how he could be released. God most Holy, who has power over all things, realised his desires and manifested a miracle according to his prayers.[53]

British observers in Pune took a different view. They believed that the young Peshwa's death was neither an accident nor an act of black magic, but a very deliberate suicide brought on by Madhu Rao's frustration at the restrictions imposed on him by his guardian, the Maratha Minister Nana Phadnavis. Though Madhu Rao was now twenty-one and old enough to rule in his own name, the Minister had kept him from all real power and left him to play impotently in the gilded cage of his palace, his every move watched by Nana's spies. Madhu Rao's suicide was his ultimate revenge on his jailer, for without his ward, Nana instantly lost his authority to govern.

From his garden prison, Aristu Jah realised his chance had come and expertly exploited the confusion, playing the different factions in Pune against each other with a talent for intrigue and manipulation that came close to genius. The day after Madhu Rao's death he managed to lure Nana's young rival, Daulat Rao Scindia, to come and visit him by offering him as a gift a celebrated stallion which Scindia had once expressed an admiration for. Alerted by his spies, as Aristu Jah knew he would be, Nana soon paid a visit to Aristu Jah's garden prison to try to discover the purpose of Scindia's visit. He suspected that Scindia had been trying to get the backing of Hyderabad in the coming succession struggle. According to Ghulam Husain Khan:

> Nana asked Aristu Jah: 'What was all this? Why did Daulat Rau come to see you?'
>
> Aristu Jah replied 'Your spies were present, no doubt they heard my peerless stallion mentioned. He came to fetch it, nothing more!'
>
> Nana refused to believe this. 'For God's sake, tell me the essence of the matter, and so calm my worries!'

However much Aristu Jah denied, Nana didn't stop insisting. Finally Aristu Jah hinted that Scindia was plotting Nana's ruin. Nana was aghast: 'As your Excellency is my friend and the wisest of this generation,' he said, 'tell me whatever you think is advisable for me to do at this time, and don't hold back.'[54]

Aristu Jah duly advised Nana to flee to a remote fort for his own safety. Terrified, Nana left Pune that night, taking the Arab troops which guarded Aristu Jah as his escort. By the following morning, Aristu Jah found himself left unguarded and in a perfect position to escape. But rather than fleeing back to Hyderabad, he chose to stay in Pune, continuing to play faction off against faction, promising each the support of the Nizam. By the time the succession dispute was finally resolved in the summer of 1797, and Nana reinstated as Minister at Aristu Jah's express request, the latter had managed to persuade all the different parties in the Maratha court to annul the humiliating Treaty of Khardla and release the Nizam from nearly all his obligations. Aristu Jah left Pune with full honours and headed off towards Hyderabad, where he was received as a national hero. The Nizam reinstated him as Prime Minister and showered him with titles, estates and jewels.

Aristu Jah's release came just in time for Kirkpatrick. A week earlier, the Nizam had finally given way to pressure from the pro-French and pro-Tipu parties at court, and announced that he was going to dismiss the English troops from Hyderabad. Aristu Jah heard the news midway between Pune and Hyderabad, and sent an urgent message for the Nizam to rescind the order, which the indecisive Nizam duly did. The Company sepoys who were already on their way to the coast marched back to their old camp and the British presence in Hyderabad was saved; but Aristu Jah made it immediately apparent to James that there was a price to pay for this. The Company would have to decide whether or not it was a full ally of the Nizam, and whether in future it would be prepared to defend Hyderabad against the Marathas. Only then would Aristu Jah be able to persuade the Nizam to jettison Raymond and disband the French corps. James was able to reply to the Minister's 'very earnest proposal' that he had already been given the authority to begin negotiations by the Governor General, and lost no time in presenting a draft treaty to the Minister.

For others in Hyderabad, Aristu Jah's release was less good news. Raymond had secretly conspired with the pro-French nobles at the Hyderabad durbar to bribe the Maratha court to prolong Aristu Jah's captivity in Pune.[55] There was also evidence that Aristu Jah's former protégé Mir Alam was involved: after all, he had been one of the principal beneficiaries of the Minister's absence, and had assumed many of his administrative functions. Aristu Jah had learned about their treachery from Nana, and returned to Hyderabad determined to exact revenge on all his enemies.

The Minister was particularly angered by Mir Alam's behaviour: though he owed his position at court entirely to Aristu Jah's patronage, throughout the latter's entire captivity, Mir Alam had not once written to him. From now on, Aristu Jah's considerable talent for intrigue would be dedicated single-mindedly to revenging himself on Mir Alam. James could have little inkling how far he himself would be caught in the trap Aristu Jah began to lay to accomplish this aim.

From the moment Aristu Jah arrived back in Hyderabad, events began to move quickly. Only the tortuous weeks it took to get letters and drafts of the new treaty to and from Calcutta, and the need for extreme secrecy, slowed the frenetic pace of negotiations, as James worked to replace Raymond as the centre of influence in the Hyderabad durbar.

Lord Wellesley, by May 1798 installed in Calcutta and anxious to get on with what he saw as his principal task of reducing French influence in the subcontinent, sent James a series of lengthy despatches minutely laying down the exact boundaries within which

James was to work. He did not approve when James allowed himself the slightest discretion to verge even marginally from these guidelines, and at one point wrote to General William Palmer, the new Resident at Pune: 'I find that Captain Kirkpatrick has departed very widely both from the spirit and letter of my instructions to him.'[56] But as the treaty neared the moment of signing, and as the Nizam agreed one by one to almost all of Wellesley's terms, James gradually returned to favour with his irascible new master. By the end, the Nizam was holding out on only one of Calcutta's demands: that the French corps be immediately dismissed. Raymond was personally well liked by the old man, and he was determined not to lose him, despite the urgings of his Minister. He seemed oblivious to the fact that destroying Raymond was the Company's principal aim.

As the negotiations gathered pace, both Wellesley and James remained worried that events on the ground might overtake their schemes. The main worry remained a French coup, possibly combined with an attempt to assassinate the elderly Nizam and replace him with one of his more pliable sons. One son, Ali Jah, had revolted in October 1795; another senior family member, Dara Jah, had come out in rebellion the following March, raising the flag of revolt from the reputedly impregnable hill fort of Raichur until dislodged and captured by Lieutenant Colonel James Dalrymple on 20 April.[57]

Then in September a plot was uncovered in the palace aiming to do away with the Nizam with the aid of black magic. This was taken every bit as seriously as the two rebellions. To the great alarm of the Minister and the Nizam's *zenana*, it was found that (as James reported to Calcutta)

> malignant sorcery was being practised against the Nizam ...
> inquiries are still being prosecuted to get to the bottom of the
> necromantic practices being used against His Highness.
> Images of paste have been dug up [in the palace] with pow-
> dered glass in their bodies & dogs hair. Since they have been
> discovered His Highness says he feels better, eats better and
> sleeps better. But they have not yet found the promoter of
> the sorcery.[58]

However much the British might dismiss the sorcery as hocus pocus, it added to the growing perception in Hyderabad that the Nizam's days might well be numbered.

Hyderabad in 1798 had something of the feel of post-war Berlin or Vienna: a city alive with intrigue and conspiracy, where no one could trust anyone else. At the centre of the city, like the spider at the heart of his web, lay the Nizam himself, assisted by a very efficient intelligence network.* Nizam Ali Khan kept a secret 'intelligencer' known as a *khufia navis* in every fort, village and city in his dominions, as well as in the palaces of the more important nobles; like his father he probably also received information from the *pirs* (holy men) of the Sufi shrines across his territory.[59] From outside his lands, from the Mughal capital of Delhi and the Maratha court in Pune, he was sent a daily newsletter from a professional Hyderabadi *akhbar navis*, or 'news-writer'.[60] This intelligence department had a considerable budget. One of Aristu Jah's successors as Prime Minister, Rajah Chandu Lal, was to spend at least 'seven lakhs of rupees annually' getting sensitive information from Calcutta alone.[61]

Nor was it just a question of information: abductions, assassinations and poisonings were regularly used by the spies of Indian rulers at this period to accomplish their aims. Poisoning in particular has a long history in India, being recommended as a vital instrument of statecraft by ancient India's Machiavelli, the great political philosopher Chanakya† (c.300 BC), who in his *Artha Shastra* suggested that court-esans were particularly useful for administering slow-acting toxins to selected clients when they were asleep.[62] Certainly there is evidence that

---

* Its voluminous archives survive in the records of the *Daftar-i-Dar ul-Insha*, now in the Andhra Pradesh State Archives.
† Also known as Kautilya. In modern New Delhi, the diplomatic quarter is named in his honour Chankyapuri; rather muddlingly, it also contains a Kautilya Marg.

Aristu Jah was prepared to consider more dramatic forms of intelligence work than simply spying. At one point two prominent figures from Hyderabad escaped from the Nizam's territories to Pune, from where Aristu Jah discovered that they were plotting to have him assassinated. He responded by proposing the sort of operation more usually associated with modern intelligence agencies, ordering that 'the motions of both these intriguers [should be] most strictly watched for the purpose of having them carried off if a fair opportunity should offer, and conducted on horses or camels with all expedition to Hyderabad'.[63]

The Nizam was not the only one who employed informers in Hyderabad: several different groups kept networks of spies at work. Raymond, for example, had successfully placed a spy in the English military camp, who had yet to be apprehended although the fact of his existence was acknowledged – through Kirkpatrick's own agents in the French camp. Moreover, quite unknown to James, Tipu Sultan had succeeded in placing a paid informer within the Residency staff who throughout this period was busily copying sensitive documents from the Residency *daftar* or chancellery, and despatching them to Seringapatam via 'the Fakir', a nephew of the Nizam named Imtiaz ul-Omrah who was the head of the pro-Tipu faction at court.* In his more facetious moments, James referred to 'the Fakir' as 'the Doctor of Divinity',[64] but he did not underestimate Imtiaz, recognising him as his most formidable enemy within the durbar.[65]

James was aware that intelligence leaks were occurring somewhere between Calcutta and Hyderabad, though he did not yet realise his own office was responsible for them. For this reason he took the precaution of writing almost all of his politically sensitive letters in cipher.†

Perhaps James might have done well to employ such precautions,

---

* Imtiaz was known as the Fakir as 'during a temporary disgrace he assumed the habit of a Fakir or holy mendicant which he still continues to wear'. For 'the Fakir' see James Kirkpatrick, 'A View of the State of the Deccan, 4th June 1798', Wellesley Papers, BL Add Mss 13582, f.38, pt 11.

† He was not however forced to go as far as his predecessor, his brother William's friend John Kennaway. During the Mysore Wars, to be sure of avoiding Tipu's agents, letters from Residents were, according to Kennaway, 'obliged to be written on a piece of paper that might be inserted in a quill' and then inserted into the person of the courier; and they were not even then very secure. Kennaway Papers, Devon Records Office, Exeter. Kennaway to Lieutenant Colonel Harris, 16 August 1790.

for he continued to discover evidence of the lack of security surrounding the Residency's affairs. He was horrified when Mir Alam's cousin, Abdul Lateef Shushtari, told him of a letter James was about to receive from Calcutta before it actually arrived. More worrying still, William Gardner, then a new recruit in the Nizam's irregular cavalry, managed to discover some of Wellesley's decisions on details of the new treaty before James did.[66] James thought the leaks were occurring in Madras, and wrote angrily to his brother William about the lack of security there, especially when the details of his plans to take on Raymond came quickly to be an open secret in Hyderabad.* It was not for another year that James realised he had a mole at work in his own staff.[67]†

Kirkpatrick was however no innocent in the game of espionage. One of his first jobs in Hyderabad had been to set up his own network of informers. Within the Nizam's *mahal* he had spies, probaby *burarun*: 'female domestics or slaves of the seraglio who collect a daily budget of [often scandalous] tittle tattle not always of a description to be given to the world', as another British intelligence officer of the period described them.[68] He also bribed the palace sweepers to pass on information and documents from the Nizam's inner apartments, and his letters are full of references to 'my information from the interior of the palace'.‡

But it seems unlikely, judging by his letters, that James would have been prepared to contemplate more devious and Machiavellian methods of conducting his business. So when, on the morning of 25

* In September 1798 James wrote to William saying that: 'Considering the strict secrecy observed by Lord [Wellesley] in his communication of his plans to General Harris [the military commander in Madras], and the reserve of the latter to everyone about him on the subject, the only way I can account for the affair having got out so completely as it has done, is by supposing that General Harris entrusted Lord W's letter to be deciphered by someone in office [in Madras], who let the secret out.'

† A year later, at the fall of Seringapatam, carefully-made copies of much of James's private and public correspondence were found in the Tipu's palace. See OIOC, F228/11, p.192, 5 August 1799.

‡ Certainly it was a secret letter from the British sepoys in Hyderabad to the Nizam, brought to the Residency from the palace dustbins by one of the Nizam's sweepers, that allowed James's immediate successor to nip a major conspiracy in the bud in 1806. New Delhi, National Archives, Hyderabad Residency Records, vol. 71, from Neil Edmonstone to Thomas Sydenham, 14 October 1806. See also Sarojini Regani, *Nizam–British Relations 1724–1857* (New Delhi, 1963), p.197. Also Delhi National Archives, Secret Consultations, Foreign Dept, 1800, No. 20, p.1.

March 1798, General Raymond was found dead aged only forty-three, in highly suspicious circumstances, all the evidence pointing to the use of some agonising slow-acting toxin or poison, there is every reason to believe that James was as surprised as everyone else.

Everyone else, that is, except perhaps Aristu Jah, who without blinking announced the confiscation of Raymond's extensive estates that same evening.

Raymond was buried in a perfect classical Greek tomb on a hilltop at Malakpet, just outside the city of Hyderabad. It lay immediately above the French cantonments he had founded and supervised. Beside it was raised an obelisk. Both tomb and obelisk were left free of the iconography of any religion; only the same simple monogram which can be found on Raymond's hookah – a looped and italicised 'JR' – breaks the purity of its line.*

Raymond was succeeded by his deputy Jean-Pierre Piron, a rougher and less sophisticated man than his former commander. Piron lacked Raymond's great charm, and was less clever at concealing both his feelings and his ambitions. His first action on succeeding Raymond was to send his counterpart in Scindia's service a republican silver tree and a Cap of Liberty. This, once reported back to Calcutta by British spies in Pune, fed Wellesley's increasingly paranoiac belief that a worldwide republican conspiracy was afoot, encouraging him to speed up his plans to topple the French party at Hyderabad.[69]

Reporting the death of Raymond to Calcutta, James wrote that the French corps remained formidable despite its founder's death:

> The officers commanding this numerous and in a comparative
> view, well disciplined and appointed Body of Infantry, are not
> only most of them violent Republicans themselves, but have

---

* The tomb was mysteriously destroyed in March 2002. The Archaeological Society of India has promised to rebuild it.

even contrived (I think) to infuse some of their spirit and animosity towards the English in their Men, many hundreds of whom, particularly the Native officers, are old Pondicherry sepoys. The arms commonly used by these French Corps are certainly not of the best, but according to information I have received, there are complete spare sets in store, ready to be issued to them in cases of emergency.[70]

In fact the French corps was later discovered to have in store enough equipment to arm twelve thousand more troops – a measure of Raymond's hopes and ambitions.[71] Yet James soon realised that Raymond's death was going to make his job much easier. He first detected signs of laziness creeping into the routine of the French camp in the middle of the summer. Reviewing his intelligence on the French cantonments six months later, just after the text of his new treaty had finally been agreed by Calcutta, he wrote to William: 'Things in Piron's lines go on as usual, and the daily detail of duty continues without any alteration since Piron succeeded to the Command of the Party. During Raymond's time, however, there was more vigilance for he always kept spies abroad to advise him what was doing, but Piron has not a single Harkarrah [runner or spy] employed.'

This, wrote James, was just as well, as the news from outside Hyderabad was far from heartening: 'The report of the day is that the French are triumphant in Europe, have entirely humbled the English, and that Tippoo is prepared for war, having been joined by 12,000 Frenchmen who landed at one of his ports.'

The reports turned out to be exaggerated; but some French soldiers and sailors had indeed turned up, and Tipu quickly wrote to the French commander in Mauritius asking for more.

Aristu Jah, meanwhile, was pressing ahead with his own schemes to ease the removal of the French officers from Hyderabad. His plan was to establish two new mercenary regiments under a pair of Irish and American adventurers who had formerly guarded him in his garden prison in Pune. He hoped that in due course, after the treaty with the Company had been signed and the French officers were rounded up, most of the rank and file sepoys of Raymond's corps could be re-assigned to these two new English-speaking corps.

One regiment, of five thousand men, was raised by the thirty-six-year-old Michael Finglas, an Irish mercenary 'possessed of very little talent or education', according to James, but blessed with what in James's eyes was the great redeeming quality of not being French. Aristu Jah had lured him to Hyderabad from Pune and given him the singularly inappropriate title of Nawab Khoon Khar Jung, 'the Falcon'.[72]* James approved of the move, and at first regarded Finglas as a good-natured if slightly ineffective figure, only later coming to deprecate what he termed Finglas's 'deplorable weakness and infirmity both mental and bodily'.[73]

Finglas appointed as his deputy the young William Linnaeus Gardner, now newly married to his Cambay Begum. Gardner had been born in Livingstone Manor in New York State, between the Catskills and the Hudson, a godson of the Swedish botanist and a nephew of the British Admiral Alan Gardner, Baron Uttoxeter. At the age of thirteen he had had to flee the New World after the Patriot victory in the War of Independence, in which his father had fought prominently – and initially very successfully – for the British government. James at first thought William Gardner 'a young man of honour as well as ability'; but the two men – so similar in many ways, with their Indian wives and shared love of Mughal culture – fell out after Gardner began manoeuvring to replace Finglas as head of the newly formed corps. By November James was writing that Gardner had planned a series of 'unjustifiable and villainous intrigues with a view to terrifying his chief [Finglas] into a resignation of his Command, [and so] has disorganised the whole Party'.[74] By the end of the year Gardner had secretly slipped out of Hyderabad to try his luck elsewhere.[75]†

---

* Literally 'drinker of blood'.
† William Linnaeus Gardner eventually founded the Company's irregular cavalry regiment Gardner's Horse, which still exists in the modern Indian Army.

Aristu Jah's second regiment was raised by another independent-minded American exile: an intermittently violent and short-tempered Yankee from Newburyport, Massachusetts named John P. Boyd.[76] Boyd raised and trained a corps of 1800 men before being discharged by Aristu Jah in July 1798 due to his 'refractoriness, disobedience and unreasonableness'.[77] He promptly stormed back to Pune with his corps, where he rejoined the Peshwa's service.*

The freelances and adventurers in Maratha service from which Aristu Jah had plucked Boyd, Finglas and Gardner were, in general, a markedly unmanageable and unreliable lot of ruffians. William Gardner was a rare exception in coming from an educated background: most of his fellows were ne'er-do-wells from the furthest margins of Western society, men like Michael Filoze, 'a low-bred Neapolitan of worthless character' who had formerly been employed as muleteer in the Apennines; or Louis Bourquoin, a part-time firework salesman and former French pastrycook, 'his skill in culinary matters being superior to his skill in military ones'.[78] These adventurers almost all came to India to seek their fortunes, and moved employers and changed sides as they wished; as James put it, 'Europeans in the native services acquire such a spirit of wandering' that they were impossible to keep track of. One of the most prominent, the raffish Chevalier Dundrenec, changed sides no fewer than seven times in fifteen years.

Most freelances adopted Indian ways of living, and several converted to Islam: Colonel Anthony Pohlmann, originally from Hanover, 'lived in the style of an Indian prince, kept a seraglio, and always travelled on an elephant, attended by a guard of Mughals, all dressed alike in purple robes, and marching in file in the same way as a British Cavalry regiment'.[79]†

---

* Boyd later fell out with the Peshwa as well, and eventually returned to America, where he disgraced himself in the War of 1812 in which he led two thousand Americans to defeat at the hands of eight hundred British Canadians. His entire campaign was described as having 'no redeeming incident', while his character was described by one colleague in that war as 'a compound of ignorance, vanity and petulance'. Another of his brothers-in-arms was equally withering, describing him as amiable and respectable in a subordinate position, but 'vacillating and imbecile beyond all endurance as a chief under high responsibilities'. *The Dictionary of American Biography.*

† Even those who did not formally convert, and who retained some of their European way of life, ended up mixing it to an extent with Mughal culture. This is most strikingly

The white Mughals

PREVIOUS PAGE: John Wombwell, a Yorkshire chartered accountant, smokes his hookah on a Lucknow terrace *c*.1790 as the River Gomti flows behind him.

TOP: Sir David Ochterlony relaxes with his *nautch* girls at the Delhi Residency *c*.1820 while (BELOW) Antoine Polier admires his troupe in Lucknow some thirty years earlier. Fireworks explode in the background.

A Lucknow dinner party *c.*1820. The gentleman at the head of the table smokes his hookah and wears a Lucknavi *jama* over his British military uniform. On his head he appears to be wearing some sort of Scots tam o'shanter.

The bibis

OPPOSITE, TOP LEFT: Bengali *bibi*, 1787, by Francesco Renaldi.

TOP RIGHT: Boulone Elise, the *bibi* of Claude Martin; 'she Chused never to quit me . . . We never had word or bad humour one against another'.

BELOW: Jemdanee, the companion of William Hickey, 1787, by Thomas Hickey. Two years later Jemdanee died while giving birth to a '*chuta* William Saheb'. The child survived his mother, and was devotedly nursed by Hickey, only to perish a month later.

ABOVE: The only contemporary image of Khair un-Nissa, painted in Calcutta *c.*1806-7. The portrait was always regarded as something of a disappointment: 'She is so much handsomer than her picture,' wrote Henry Russell soon after it was completed.

The Deccani pleasure garden

ABOVE LEFT: Afternoon *raag*: a begum listens to music under a *chattri* in her garden while her attendants look on. Hyderabad, *c.* 1760.

ABOVE: A love-sick Hyderabadi begum consults an *aseel* while waiting in the moonlight for the arrival of her lover *c.*1750 .

LEFT: The Deccani princess goes hawking. An image of the legendary Chand Bibi (d.1599), Bijapur's answer to Joan of Arc, from the collection of Henry Russell. Painted in Hyderabad, *c.*1800.

TOP: A Deccani prince with his women. While one plays music, another looks after a pet deer, while a third, dressed in Jacobean silk knickerbockers and a plumed, wide-brimmed hat, passes her prince a glass of wine. At her feet is an Indian rendering of a King Charles spaniel. From Bijapur, *c.*1680, by Rahim Deccani.

BELOW: Nizam Ali Khan crosses the causeway from Hyderabad to his citadel of Golconda, *c.*1775. To one side of the Nizam's yellow-caparisoned royal elephant, women bathe in the Musi, while on the other side Sufis and *sadhus* look on.

ABOVE: The Handsome Colonel with George and James Kirkpatrick at Hollydale, *c.*1769. James is on the right of the picture with the mischievous expression on his face. 'Worthy George', James's elder brother, is already, at the age of seven, as serious-minded as he was to remain the rest of his life.

BELOW: William Kirkpatrick in Madras as Wellesley's Private Secretary in late 1799, soon after the victory over Tipu Sultan. To William's left stand his Persian *munshis* and Hindu assistants, as well as two Bengal sepoys.

A few of these men became distinguished poets in Urdu – one, whose pen name was Farasu, was the son of a German Jewish soldier of fortune, Gottlieb Koine, by a Mughal Begum; according to a contemporary critic this unlikely poet left behind him a 'camel load of poetic works'.[80] Others continued to write in their native European languages, and their letters give wonderful glimpses of the enviably anarchic and at times almost piratical life they led. As Pohlmann wrote to a freelance friend while trying to decide whether to move on from one prince to another: 'I believe this part of the country will be given away to some rajahs, and if that takes place I am inclined to volunteer to take [service in] the Cachmeere country, where the best and handsomest ladies are ... As soon as I get the order for returning I shall be with you in a jiffy, as the cold nights are setting in and I dare say you join in my opinion that a beautiful Cashmereian woman would not be a bad acquisition. I really think it would be a very agreeable amusement.'[81]

It was this wildness, this resolute refusal to play by the rules, that made the mercenaries' relationship with the Company officials so difficult and complicated. On the one hand they had much in common: they were from the same culture and had both learned to accommodate themselves to another. On the other, a Resident like James lived on his prestige at court, and could not afford to mix too intimately with the deserters, criminals and charlatans who tended to make up the freelance battalions. As James observed rather stiffly at the time to William:

> I have always and ever shall make it a rule to maintain the consequence and respectability of my station towards all descriptions of men; my invitations to anyone whatever of Finglas's corps have and shall continue to be very rare indeed; not only because it is what I think I owe to myself as Resident,

---

evident in the Catholic graveyard in Agra where many of the mercenaries ended up. Here they lie side by side, buried in one of the strangest necropolises in Asia, filled with line upon line of small Palladianised Taj Mahals, some authentically late Mughal, but most covered with a crazy riot of hybrid ornament: baroque *putti* cavorting around Persian inscriptions; latticed *jali* screens rising to round classical arches. At the four corners at the base of the drum, where on an authentic Mughal monument you would expect to find minarets or at least small minars, there stand instead four baroque amphorae.

but to them as servants of this state which I know does not relish any close intercourse between us. I have abundant means without seeing any of them very often, of keeping the party in proper order.[82]

As well as adventurers, criminals and runaways, a sizeable minority of the freelances in Finglas's battalions, as elsewhere, were Anglo-Indians. Since Cornwallis had passed legislation banning Anglo-Indian children of British soldiers from entering the East India Company's army between 1786 and 1795, increasing numbers of the unemployed sons of Indian mothers and British soldiers too poor to send their children 'home' sought out service with one of the Indian princes. The increasingly racist and dismissive attitude of the British to their mixed-race progeny was something that struck the French General Benoît de Boigne, who had been one of the first to recruit adventurers and to train them into formidable fighting units for Scindia. Sending a newly orphaned Anglo-Indian recruit to one of his officers who was then the *qiladar* (fort keeper) at Agra, de Boigne observed that the boy had no introduction, but 'appears to have good will and inclination [and] you may try him ... I have already sent you many of these young men, sons of European officers which can't prevent me from observing how few [British] fathers can leave anything to their [Anglo-Indian] children at their death. There are hundreds more at Calcutta who wish to enter into the service, but have no friends to recommend them and no other means to go up [to Agra from Calcutta].'[83]

One rather unusual Anglo-Indian who turned up in Hyderabad around this time looking for a commission in Finglas's regiment was the young William Palmer. He was the Anglo-Indian son of James Kirkpatrick's opposite number in Pune, General William Palmer, by his beloved Mughal wife Begum Fyze Baksh of Delhi. As fluent in Persian and Urdu as he was in English and French, and educated in both India and England, where he had attended Woolwich Military Academy, William was equally at home in Mughal and English culture, and was able to switch from one to the other as easily as he changed from his jacket to his *jama*. He was also extremely intelligent, with a flair for entrepreneurial innovation that would later blossom into a banking fortune of almost unparalleled magnitude.

At the time, with the confrontation with the French corps looming imminently, James hardly took in Palmer's arrival in Hyderabad, beyond noting that 'he is dark but clever and cultivated'.[84] In due course, however, William Palmer was to play a major role not only in Kirkpatrick's story, but that of his entire extended family.

Nizam Ali Khan finally signed the Preliminary Treaty with the East India Company on 1 September 1798. The treaty authorised the Company to provide six thousand regular East India Company troops for the Nizam's use, in addition to the two battalions already stationed in Hyderabad. The troops were to be under British officers, but available to the Nizam both for internal peacekeeping and tax-collecting work, and for campaigns outside the state in the event of aggression by a third party. In return the Nizam was to pay the Company an annual subsidy of £41,710, and to dismiss the French corps, whose officers – along with the British deserters under them – were all to be transported to Europe as prisoners of war. Exactly how or when this was to be done, however, was not made explicit in the text of the treaty document.

Following the signing, an uneasy month passed as the new British force of four full-strength battalions – some six thousand troops along with a train of artillery – made its way up the 150 miles from Guntur. This was the nearest Company-controlled town, where Wellesley had ordered them to collect two months earlier in readiness to seize the moment and march to Hyderabad to confront the French.[85]

As rumours of the secret treaty began to leak out, Aristu Jah moved Finglas's two English-officered battalions to camp beside the Residency compound, and so offer some protection in the event of a pre-emptive French attack – a prospect which began to look increasingly likely.

Despite having obtained the Nizam's signature on the treaty, James remained unconvinced that the Nizam would actually disband the French forces when the new Company battalions arrived, and began to make contingency plans in case the Corps Français put up resistance. On 26 September he wrote in cipher to William:

> I am prepared for difficulties being made when things come to a pinch (both by Aristu Jah and others, both from fear and from other motives) not only as to the delivering up to me of the French officers but also to my using any coercion for the purpose of bringing the delicate business to an early and completely successful issue. You may depend on it however that should this prove the case, I will be as firm and inflexible as you could wish me. I have always felt the importance of securing as many of the French officers as possible and for this reason have always thought that it was better to run the risk of resistance by drawing the whole party together at Hyderabad than by dispersing it to run the hazard of both officers and sepoys going off to Tippoo and to Scindeah where they would leave no stone unturned to be revenged on us.[86]

For this reason James got Aristu Jah to concentrate the French troops in their cantonments in Hyderabad, and to avoid sending any out on tax-collecting missions, or any other assignment.

It was, of course, a risky strategy. If there was serious resistance, concentrating the French forces would make the task of disarming them all the more difficult.

At this crucial moment, on 6 October 1798, with the British reinforcements just three days' march from Hyderabad, the extraordinary news arrived in the city of Napoleon Bonaparte's landing in Egypt, and his subsequent spectacular capture of both Alexandria and Cairo. Napoleon was quite clear as to his aims. In a book about Turkish warfare he had scribbled in the margin before 1788 the words, 'Through Egypt we shall invade India, we shall re-establish the old route through Suez and cause the route by the Cape of Good Hope to be abandoned.' Nor did he anticipate many problems: 'the touch of a French sword is all that is needed for the framework of mercantile grandeur to collapse'.[87] From Cairo he sent a letter to Tipu, answering the latter's pleas for help and outlining his plans:

> You have already been informed of my arrival on the borders of the Red Sea, with an innumerable and invincible army, full of the desire of releasing and relieving you from the iron yoke of England. I eagerly embrace this opportunity of testifying to you the desire I have of being informed by you, by the way of Muscat and Mocha, as to your political situation. I could even wish you could send some sort of intelligent person to Suez or Cairo, possessing your confidence, with whom I may confer. May the Almighty increase your power, and destroy your enemies!
>
> Yours &c &c
> Bonaparte[88]

It was exactly the sort of imaginative coup against British interests in the East which Raymond had long been waiting for, and which came just three months too late for him. Nevertheless, it immediately changed the complexion of events in Hyderabad, galvanising the sinking spirit of the French in their cantonments, and creating great anxiety for James and the British. In Pune, too, the French mercenaries in Maratha service prepared themselves to aid their motherland; their new republican commander even sent a detailed invasion plan to Bonaparte. As one of the Pune Frenchmen, the former pastrycook Louis Bourquoin, wrote many years later:

> Several Frenchmen discussed this expedition and the feasibility of giving it some support ... General Bonaparte, following the footsteps of Alexander would have entered India not as a devastating conqueror ... but as a liberator. He would have

expelled the English forever from India so that not one of them would have remained and by depriving them of the inexhaustible wealth of this vast country would have restored independence, peace, and happiness to Asia, to Europe, and to the whole world. These projects were no idle dreams. All the Princes in India were longing for French intervention, and that formidable enemy of the English, Tipu Sultan, was still alive . . .[89]

Though they would have disputed the Anglophobe invective, the British in Hyderabad were under no illusions as to how easily Bonaparte's ends could be achieved. Not only was there no effective British naval unit guarding the Malabar ports, the journey down the Red Sea was an easy one. Indeed, as James wrote to his brother William, it was the very route by which William Linnaeus Gardner had come to Hyderabad only a few months earlier: 'The more I think of this damned Egyptian Expedition of the French the more uneasy it makes me,' wrote James.

I shall not be surprised at the French who will attempt anything to wreak their vengeance, coming down the Red Sea in large boats and landing at Mangalore. They can get thousands of *donies* [rafts] I understand at Suez and could I am told without any great effort have small *gollies* [transports] dragged across the isthmus. Captain Gardner who himself came down the Red Sea in a *doney* tells me that two frigates would block the straits Babelmandel, and that there is moreover an uninhabited island three or four miles in circumference at the mouth of it, strong by nature, and which might be rendered exceedingly so by art. It appears to me to be a material object to us under present circumstances, to get possession of that island with all possible dispatch, and to render it as strong as possible; but the stationing of some ships of war there without a moments loss of time appears still more indispensably requisite.[90]

Three days later, on 9 October, the new British troops finally marched into Hyderabad. With them came Captain John Malcolm, who was to be James's new Assistant, and who joined him that night for dinner at the Residency. Malcolm was one of seventeen children of a Scottish farmer. He had attracted Wellesley's attention with a political essay he had sent to Calcutta, and which Wellesley had judged 'very promising'. He got on well with James, but the two had very different political views. Malcolm was an enthusiastic and unrepentant supporter of Wellesley's new 'Forward Policy', that believed in expanding British dominion and influence in India wherever and whenever possible. It was an approach James came to be increasingly uneasy with, and as his political views changed so did his relations with Malcolm.[91]

News soon arrived of a further mishap which seriously endangered James's fast-fading hopes of intimidating the French into peacefully laying down their weapons. The British had marched into Hyderabad in two parties, and the first regiment forded the Musi in heavy rain on the evening of the fourteenth. But the following morning when the second regiment came to the river they found that it had risen dramatically overnight. There was no way they could join the first regiment. One was on the Residency bank, the other on that of the city and the French cantonments. At the same time, James learned from his spies that Piron had finally learned the full terms of the treaty, including the clause abolishing his corps.[92] If ever he was going to make a pre-emptive move on the British, now would be his moment.

At this vital juncture, when they were at their most vulnerable, the British forces in Hyderabad found themselves split in two.

For the next uneasy week the waters of the Musi remained too high for the artillery to be safely transported across it. Yet still the French – apparently paralysed by indecision – made no attempt to attack the divided British force.

With no sign yet emerging from the palace that the Nizam was ever going to issue the order instructing the French to disarm, James decided to take the initiative and wrote to Aristu Jah, formally asking him to fulfil the terms of the treaty. For several days no reply was received, and no action was taken beyond the Nizam opting to leave Hyderabad and take shelter within the more defensible walls of his fortress of Golconda. On the sixteenth James wrote to his brother: 'I wait impatiently for an answer to my last letter to the Minister, which I think you will allow is as strong as it could be. If it fails of the success I look for from it, I shall make a point of seeing him immediately, and of not leaving him until I have gained my point.' By the nineteenth there was still no reply, and James had become convinced that the inaction was deliberate, that the news of Bonaparte's triumphs in Egypt was leading the Nizam seriously to reconsider his decision to sign the treaty with the Company.

Knowing that any hesitation could now be fatal, James finally went in person to Golconda on the evening of the nineteenth and gave an ultimatum to an anxious-looking Aristu Jah: if the Nizam hesitated any longer he would have no option but to order an attack on the French cantonments. He also set his spies to work, telling William in cipher: 'I am employing every engine both to prevent the possibility of stubborn resistance and to render it ineffectual even in case of its being attempted.'[93] To this end he arranged for a small mutiny to take place in the French lines on the morning of the twenty-first, calculating that the chaos it caused would disrupt any attempt at resistance. He had other plans for subterfuge too, writing to William that 'I shall take good care the night preceding this business that the [French] party be unable either to move one way or the other with its guns as I have provided for the bullock traces [harnesses] being all cut to pieces.'[94]

The threat of violence had the effect James calculated it would have. On the following night, 20 October, at about ten o'clock, the Nizam finally issued a formal order to the troops of the French corps that he had dismissed their European officers, and that the troops had thus been released from their obedience to their superiors. If they continued to obey them, wrote the Nizam, they would be shot as traitors.

What James had not calculated on was the speed with which Piron decided to make terms. That same evening he sent two French officers to the Residency to tell Kirkpatrick that he was ready to surrender, 'well knowing that, though the general policy might dictate their removal from the Deccan, they [hoped they] would be individually considered to every justice and indulgence that could with propriety be extended to them'.[95] With this single proviso, they meekly asked for a British officer to go to the French lines the following morning to take charge of their property. It was at this point that things began to go badly wrong.

James was unable to get word to his spies in the French camp about the offer to surrender, so that when Malcolm turned up as arranged on the following morning, the twenty-first, expecting to oversee the collection of French arms, he found instead that the mutiny which James had arranged had indeed taken place – but in a form very different to that which James had planned. The sepoys had arrested and imprisoned their superiors just as they were about to leave the camp to surrender, and were now making attempts to defend the cantonments. Worse still, Malcolm was seized by the rebellious sepoys and taken into custody along with Piron and all the other French officers.

For the rest of that day, James waited to see whether the sepoys would release their captives and surrender. By nightfall there was no sign that they were planning to do so. He came to a decision: the only remaining hope of a peaceful surrender would be for him to seize the initiative and frighten the sepoys into laying down their arms. This decision was confirmed when John Malcolm, accompanied by Piron and several other French officers, turned up at the Residency at midnight, having been sprung from their confinement by a small group of the sepoys, deserters from British regiments who had once, by pure good fortune, served under Malcolm and had remained fond of their former officer.

Before first light on the twenty-second, the half of the British force on the French side of the Musi surrounded the French cantonments, arranging their guns on the ridge above the French lines, not far from Raymond's tomb. The other half of the British force, that on the Residency side, brought up their guns to what Malcolm described as 'a strong post, about four hundred yards in the rear of Monsieur Piron's camp, between which and him there was the River Moussy, which could only be forded by infantry; the guns could however play from the bank of the river with excellent effect, on the principal [French] magazine, and right of the camp'.[96]

When dawn broke, the French corps woke up to find themselves completely surrounded. At nine o'clock James offered the mutineers payment of all money owing to them, and employment in Finglas's corps if they would now surrender. They had 'one quarter of an hour to stack their arms and march off to a cowle or protection flag, which was pitched by one of the Nizam's principal officers, about half a mile to the right of the camp. If they did not comply with the terms of the summons, they were immediately to be attacked.'[97] For thirty minutes the sepoys remained undecided. Two thousand cavalry massed under Malcolm on the right flank; five hundred more waited on the right. In the centre were four thousand infantry. There was complete silence. Then, just after 9.30, to James's great relief, the sepoys finally sent out word that they accepted the terms.

The British cavalry rode in quickly and took possession of the magazine, storehouses, powder mills, gun foundries and cannon, while the French sepoys fled to the flag under which they were to surrender themselves: 'at once a glorious and piteous sight', thought James.[98] Within a few hours, the largest French force in India, more than sixteen thousand men strong, was disarmed by a force of less than a third that number. Not a single shot had been fired, or a single life lost.

James watched the soldiers laying down their arms all afternoon by telescope from the roof of the Residency. That evening, in a state of mixed exhaustion and elation, he wrote to William that 'I am too much fagged to write you a long letter . . .', but he wanted William to know that the 'turning adrift of thousands of Raymond's troops, all of which I saw this evening from the roof of my house with my spy glasses as plain as if I had been on the spot, was the *finest sight I ever saw in my life*'.

In a postscript written two hours later, there came even better news: had William heard yet the report that had just arrived from

Bombay, 'of Admiral Nelson's glorious naval action'? In the Battle of the Nile, Nelson had sunk almost the entire French fleet in Aboukir Bay, wrecking Napoleon's hopes of using Egypt as a secure base from which to attack India. It was a quite amazing turn of events. For two weeks it had suddenly looked quite possible that India was going to become a French colony. Now, equally suddenly, that threat was extinguished. As James wrote to Calcutta, it was extraordinary to think that 'only three days ago things wore a very dismal appearance'.[99]

In the weeks that followed, Wellesley wrote to congratulate James, formally appointing him Resident in his brother's place, and recommending him to London for a 'mark of Royal Favour', in other words a baronetcy. Wellesley was delighted – as well he should have been, as the Company granted him £500 a year for twenty years as a reward for what James had done: 'I am happy to express my entire approbation of the judgement, firmness and discretion you have manifested,' he wrote to James. In the meantime Wellesley made James an honorary ADC, then an almost unique honour.

The news of this arrived on Christmas Day 1798, and James wrote back to William, 'pray make my most grateful acknowledgement to my Noble Patron and Master [Wellesley] for this new mark of approbation he has been pleased to confer on me, and which I assure you I am not a little proud of'.[100]

It was about this time, sometime in December 1798, that something of even greater significance to James took place, an event that would in due course utterly change the course of his life, as well as completely undermine his newly forged relationship with Wellesley.

Two years earlier, while Aristu Jah was still in captivity in Pune and Mir Alam had taken over the management of the Nizam's British affairs, the Mir had appointed as *bakshi* or paymaster of the British detachment in Hyderabad an elderly Persian cousin of his. This was

Bâqar Ali Khan, titled Akil ud-Daula, the Wisest of the State. The old man was a little deaf and short-sighted, but a good-natured and jovial figure who quickly became popular with the British officers in Hyderabad. William Kirkpatrick and he had become great friends, and before he left Hyderabad William had written a pen portrait of him to a friend in Masulipatam:

> This gentleman is deservedly a great favourite with all the officers; on which account, as well as because he is a relation of Meer Allum, and a very hearty friend of our nation, I beg you to pay him every attention in your power. You will find him a very jolly conversable man; and if you have any relish for Persian poetry a mighty pleasant companion since he has all the anacreontic tribe at his finger ends. He drinks (*under the rose*) three glasses of wine after dinner, provided there be no black-visaged lookers on: and among the ladies is a very gallant fellow. In short, though you have visited the Court of Lucknow, I think you will allow when acquainted with him, that his equal is rarely to be met with among the Asiatics.[101]

Bâqar Ali Khan had one daughter, a young widow named Sharaf un-Nissa, who had – unusually – returned to the family *deorhi* with her two teenage daughters after the death of her husband Mehdi Yar Khan.[102] Like her father, Sharaf un-Nissa appears to have been very well disposed towards the British, and used to invite the wives of the Company officers to visit her in her *zenana*. They in turn reported that she was 'unusually free of the prejudices of her sect'.[103]

Although Bâqar Ali was only the maternal grandfather of Sharaf un-Nissa's two daughters, and so under no legal obligation to be responsible for them, the old man had generously taken upon himself the business of arranging his granddaughters' marriages: as always an expensive business in India.* By the end of 1798 Bâqar Ali Khan had negotiated marriages for both girls with members of the Hyderabad nobility, and the wedding ceremony of the elder of the two, Nazir

* The fact that Sharaf un-Nissa returned to her father's *zenana*, and that it was Bâqar Ali Khan rather than her late husband's clan – particularly her senior brother-in-law, Mir Asadullah – who arranged the marriage of the two girls, may suggest some sort of rupture between Mehdi Yar Khan's clan and the intelligent and independent-minded Sharaf un-Nissa.

un-Nissa, was celebrated sometime in December. James attended the marriage party.

His own account of it is very brief and gives little away. Indeed he only mentions it to William in an aside when he writes that Bâqar's wife, Durdanah Begum, had asked for a loan to help meet the expense of the wedding, and that, in view of the family's loyalty to the British, James had 'sent the sum requested as a *loan*, as a marriage portion for the Begum's granddaughter – say, did I do wrong?'[104]

But James almost certainly had other things in his mind when he arrived at the celebrations. For, according to Sharaf un-Nissa, he had already heard about the extraordinary beauty of her newly betrothed younger daughter, Khair un-Nissa, from one of the Company officers' wives who had met her in her mother's *zenana*. Forty years later, as an old woman of eighty, Sharaf un-Nissa remembered that

> my father was the *bakshi* appointed by the Nizam's government to attend the English Gentlemen. In consequence of the appointment which he held, several of the English Gentlemen were in the habit of coming to entertainments at his house. On one occasion an entertainment was given to Colonel Dallas and about twenty gentlemen and their ladies came to my father's house. Colonel Dallas's lady came to the women's *zenana* apartments, and visited us ladies. She greatly admired my daughter; and said she reminded her strongly of her own sister. After this on her return to her own house she praised the beauty of my daughter to Hushmut Jung Bahadur [James Kirkpatrick]. After this Colonel Kirkpatrick sought out my daughter.[105]

Only one contemporary picture of Khair un-Nissa survives, and it dates from 1806, a full eight years after the entertainment Bâqar Ali Khan gave for Colonel Dallas. Yet even then, when she was aged about twenty, Khair un-Nissa still looks little more than a child: a graceful, delicate, shy creature, with porcelain skin, an oval face and wide-open, dark brown eyes. Her eyebrows are long and curved, and she has a full, timidly expressive mouth that is about to break into a smile; just below it, there lies the tiny blemish that is the mark of real beauty: a tiny red freckle, slightly off-centre, immediately above the point of her chin. Yet there is a strength amid the look of over-whelming innocence, a wilfulness in the set of the lips and the dark-ness of the eyes that might be interpreted as defiance in a less serene face.

A later Hyderabadi source reveals that it was at the wedding of Nazir un-Nissa that Khair un-Nissa first saw James Kirkpatrick, from behind a curtain:

> Accidentally the Resident and [Bâqar Ali Khan's younger granddaughter] the Begum [Khair un-Nissa] saw one another and they immediately fell deeply in love . . . It is related by elderly persons that Mr Kirkpatrick was very handsome and [Khair un-Nissa] was renowned throughout the Deccan for her beauty and comeliness . . . on account of differences in religion marriage was out of the question. According to Mohamadan law a Mohamadan man can marry a Christian woman but a Mohamadan woman cannot be given in mar-riage to a Christian. [Moreover Khair un-Nissa was already engaged to someone else.] When the story of their amours became public, a general sensation took.
>
> The relations of the Begum were naturally very furious and for a time the life of the lovers was in danger, but their passion for one another was not of a character as could be restrained by fear or disappointment. Every obstacle thrown in their way only seemed to make it stronger & stronger . . .[106]

IV

T HE ANCIENT PERSIAN TOWN of Shushtar lies on the
borders of modern-day Iran and Iraq, in the badlands to
the far south-west of the country. Flanked on one side by
the marshes leading down to the River Tigris and on the other by
the dry and rocky Zagros mountains, Shushtar clings to the edge of
a narrow plateau, just below the confluence of the Karun River with
one of its tributaries.

The town was of great importance during the classical period. The
Roman Emperor Valerian, enslaved by the Persian Emperor Shahpur
I after being defeated in AD 260, spent the rest of his life in captivity
in Shushtar, labouring at the construction of a colossal dam. The
dam still stands; but the region has been in decline since then, and
its once-rich agricultural land has long been exhausted. Yet for all
its poverty, Shushtar somehow managed to retain its high culture.
For generations the town exported its highly educated clan of black-
turbaned Sayyids across the Shi'ite world, from Kerbala to Lucknow
and Hyderabad. They distinguished themselves by their knowledge
of mathematics and astronomy, yunani medicine and Shi'a jurisprudence, as well as other more obscure forms of esoteric learning. They
were also renowned for their talents as poets and calligraphers.[1]

Around 1730, Sayyid Reza, a young Shushtari *mujtahid** left
Shushtar to seek his fortune in the Mughal Empire. The road east
was a well-worn route: the mosque in Shushtar, one of the oldest in

---

* A cleric; one who does *ijtehad*, the interpretation of religious texts.

Persia, dating back to AD 868, was constructed in shisham wood brought from India by medieval Shushtari traders. In the centuries following those first trading contacts, generations of Persians had been welcomed to the various Muslim courts of India, where they were honoured as bearers of high culture and inheritors of a sublime literary tradition.*

Following in the footsteps of this long succession of émigré Persian scholars, soldiers and confidence tricksters, Sayyid Reza found his way to Delhi. There he took service in the household of the Prime Minister of the Mughal Emperor, another Persian exile named Abul Mansur Khan Khorasani, who later took the title Safdar Jung, and whose magnificent tomb is the last great Mughal monument in Delhi.

For two decades Sayyid Reza worked in the palaces of the Mughal capital; but as the Empire began to shatter and fragment under a succession of incompetent emperors, and as Delhi slowly descended into chaos, Sayyid Reza decided to return home to Shushtar. Because the land route by Kabul and Kandahar was blocked by fighting, he made the decision to head south to the Deccan, from where he hoped to catch a ship up the Gulf to Persia. But by chance, in Hyderabad, he met Nizam ul-Mulk, the father of Nizam Ali Khan. The Nizam was impressed by Sayyid Reza's learning and integrity, and persuaded him to stay on in India under his patronage. Sayyid Reza settled in Hyderabad, in Irani Gulli, a small colony of Persian exiles not far from the Char Minar, tucked in behind the narrow lanes of the Burkha Bazaar. There his wife gave birth to a son, Abul Qasim, known to history by his later title, Mir Alam.

In his old age Sayyid Reza gave up worldly attachments and dedicated his life to prayer and fasting. According to his nephew, the old

---

* They were also known for 'favouring their own nation', and for exaggerating greatly about themselves and their origins: stories were told of how, once over the Indian border, the humblest salt-sellers would try to pass themselves off as Persian noblemen and would duly be honoured with huge estates by the Great Mughal. Ellison Banks Findly (trans. William Irvine), *Nur Jehan: Empress of Mughal India* (New Delhi, 1993), p.9; and Niccolao Manucci, *Storia do Mogor, or Mogul India, 1653–1708* (London, 1907), Vol. 1, p.171. Abdul Lateef Shushtari, Sayyid Reza's grandson and our source for his travels, has himself been accused of exaggerating the importance of his clan in the *Tuhfaat al'Alam*. See the essay by Ahmad Kasravi, '*Ham dozd ham dorugh*' (Not Only a Liar but a Plagiarist), in *Peyman*, Vol. 1, No. 3, 1312AH.

man 'refused all public office: however much Nizam ul-Mulk urged him to accept a position in the Hyderabad government, even the post of Chief Judge, he turned the offer down. Some fifteen or sixteen years before his death, the desire for retreat became dominant in his character, and he increasingly cut himself off from other people. He spent his days alone in his prayer room, donned an ascetic's cloak and spent his life in worship, seeking the True God.'[2] He died in 1780, and was buried in the sanctified burial ground of Daira Mir Momin, beside the tomb of the great Shi'a saint Shah Chirag.

It was during the forty days of mourning for Sayyid Reza that the young Mir Alam met Aristu Jah for the first time. Aristu Jah was already in his fifties and the most powerful official in Hyderabad; Mir Alam was in his late twenties, the penniless but talented son of a respected divine. The Minister had come in person on the third day of mourning to attend the *soyem* ceremony at the house of Sayyid Reza, and when he took the young man aside and confirmed him in possession of his father's estates, Mir Alam replied with a fine Persian couplet praising the wisdom of the Minister. Aristu Jah, who had both a discerning eye for talent and a great love of poetry, realised that Mir Alam was a youth of unusual promise, and invited him to attend his durbar. Before long, he had appointed him his Private Secretary, and given him the job of preparing his correspondence and journals.[3]

Physically, Mir Alam was a slight youth, and seemed especially so when he stood beside Aristu Jah, whose remarkable height and bulk emphasised his new Secretary's lean and wiry build. Mir Alam had a serious, intelligent face, with a long, straight nose and a thin, finely waxed moustache. His complexion was strikingly fair, a legacy of his Persian ancestry; but it was his watchful, alert expression that people always remarked upon. It was as if he were constantly vigilant, awake for an opening or an opportunity, and few Europeans who met him failed to come to the conclusion that here was an unusually clever and ambitious young man. James Kirkpatrick was very struck by him on their first meeting, and wrote to Wellesley that 'as a scholar he stands unrivalled, and as a man of business he would have few equals . . . his stile is remarkable for its strength and perspicuity, as well as elegance, and his pen is consequently always employed when state papers requiring extraordinary care and attention are called for'.[4]

Muslim chroniclers, by contrast, singled out Mir Alam's qualities of *ferasat*, which is sometimes translated as intuition but which has far greater resonance in the Persian, referring to that highly developed sensitivity to body language that almost amounts to mind-reading, and which was regarded as an essential quality for a Muslim courtier. It is still an admired feature in the social and political life of the Muslim East.[5]

Despite Mir Alam's intuition, intelligence and abilities, however, there always seemed to be a strange absence of feeling in the man, as if there were a chilling numbness somewhere in his heart. As the Mir grew older and increasingly powerful, this potential for callousness became more marked. James's Assistant Henry Russell, who later got to know him well, had no doubts about the Mir's qualities, writing of his 'extraordinary capabilities'. But he was also under no illusions about his unusual ruthlessness, describing him as 'utterly deficient in qualities of the heart', and 'strangely without emotions . . . He neither remembers his obligations, nor forgets his adversaries. Though he always craves to be popular and expects gratitude from others, he is devoid of any sympathy or compassion towards his fellow beings, be it individually, or collectively.'[6]

Mir Alam was, nevertheless, a generous patron to his friends and family, and when the news of his growing power and success in Hyderabad reached his relations in Shushtar, several of them decided to emigrate from Iran to Hyderabad and seek service there on his staff. Among these was his first cousin, Bâqar Ali Khan, the son of Sayyid Reza's elder sister, who was around twenty years older than Mir Alam. Bâqar Ali was generously received by Mir Alam, made a *mansabdar*,* and married to a Hyderabadi beauty named Durdanah Begum, the daughter of one of the city's most powerful families.[7] In due course two children were born of the marriage, a boy, Mehmud Ali Khan, and a girl, Sharaf un-Nissa, the mother of Khair un-Nissa.

---

* An office-holder whose rank was decided by the number of cavalry he would supply for battle – for example, a *mansabdar* of 2500 would be expected to provide 2500 horsemen when the Nizam went to war.

When in 1787 Aristu Jah sent his Secretary on an important embassy to Calcutta, Bâqar Ali accompanied Mir Alam to the Company's Bengal headquarters along with a large escort of cavalry, seven caparisoned war elephants and seventy camels laden with gifts and supplies. In Calcutta, the embassy was received by Lord Cornwallis, and Mir Alam struck up an enduring friendship with the Governor General, who was impressed by his 'straightforward good sense and intuitive understanding, as well as by his easy eloquence'. At their parting, Cornwallis presented the Mir with a diamond-encrusted walking stick.[8]

Mir Alam and his cousin stayed three years in Calcutta, learning about the English and making a wide variety of contacts among the officials and Orientalists of the city. They became especially friendly with Neil Edmonstone, later to become Wellesley's Private Secretary and the head of the Company's Intelligence Service, whom they regarded, somewhat unexpectedly, as 'a good musician and mathematician'.[9] They were particularly impressed by the military arsenals they saw in Fort William: 'Three hundred thousand rifles hung up in good order and easy to collect, ammunitions factories hard at work, and two to three thousand cannons in place with five to six thousand more in reserve and ready for use.'[10] It was a visit that made a profound impression on Mir Alam. After what he had seen, he remained convinced throughout his career that the British were effectively invincible in India, and that the best interests of the Hyderabad state – and of Mir Alam – lay in allying with them as strongly and as closely as possible.

While Mir Alam and Bâqar Ali were in Calcutta, they heard a rumour that another member of their clan had just arrived from Persia, aboard an English vessel. Mir Abdul Lateef Shushtari, another first cousin of Mir Alam, and the son of one of Sayyid Reza's brothers, had like Bâqar Ali Khan made the journey from Persia with a view to hitching his career to that of Mir Alam; unlike his cousin Bâqar Ali, however, he left a detailed and entertaining account of his Indian travels and impressions, the *Tuhfat al-'Alam*, or 'Gift to the World':

'I had just arrived in India,' he wrote,

and as soon as he heard of this, Mir Alam spent two or three
days inquiring of my whereabouts and sought me out. While
he was in the city I spent most of my time in his company:
his brotherly kindness made up for the dreadfulness of being
in India . . . My cousin had become one of the great amirs
of the Deccan, resorted to by petitioners from all over the
Arab and Persian world. However pressing this crowd, he
never became bad-tempered, and always tried to solve their
problems. He is particularly remarkable for his resolution
and quick-thinking, which cuts through difficulties like a
sword.[11]

Shushtari's *Tuhfat al-'Alam* is one of the most fascinating texts
to survive from the period: a strikingly immediate and graphic
account of late-eighteenth-century India as perceived by a disdainful,
fastidious and refined émigré intellectual – a sort of eighteenth-
century Persian version of V.S. Naipaul. Written in 1802, when Shushtari was under house arrest in the immediate aftermath of the scandal
of James Kirkpatrick's liaison with Khair un-Nissa, and the entire
Shushtari clan was in deep disgrace, it gives a highly jaundiced
account of India, which Abdul Lateef regards with all the *hauteur*
that high Persian culture was capable of: 'Since I came to this country,
I cannot begin to recount all that has happened to me by way of
suffering, deception and diseases, with no one intelligent to talk to
. . . Alas, alas, how could I know that matters would come to this
present sorry state – broken and stuck in the hellish climate of
Hyderabad!'

In this spirit he compares his book to 'the flutterings of a uselessly
crying bird in the dark cage of India', remarking that 'to survive
in Hyderabad you need four things: plenty of gold, endless hypocrisy,
boundless envy, and the ability to put up with parvenu idol-
worshippers who undermine governments and overthrow old
families'. Yet for all its sectarian animosity and intellectual arrogance,
the *Tuhfat* is a perceptive and observant account, which brings the
intrigue and faction-ridden world of courtly Hyderabad into sharper
focus than any other surviving text.

It also, more pointedly, provides the best source for how

Khair un-Nissa's wider family felt about her affair with James Kirkpatrick.

Abdul Lateef's visit to the subcontinent started badly. On arrival in India, the easily-disgusted Persian recorded his horror at the sights that greeted him at Masulipatam, his first port of call. Welcomed by a group of Iranian Qizilbash* traders who lived there, he remarks that he was 'shocked to see men and women naked apart from an exiguous cache-sex mixing in the streets and markets, as well as out in the country, like beasts or insects. I asked my host "What on earth is this?" "Just the locals," he replied, "They're all like that!" It was my first step in India, but already I regretted coming and reproached myself.'[12]

Calcutta Shushtari liked better. He admired the Company merchants' beautifully whitewashed villas, some of them 'painted and coloured like marble'. Appalled by the dirt of Masulipatam, he was especially appreciative of Calcutta's exceptional cleanliness: 'Seven hundred pairs of oxen and carts are appointed by the Company to take rubbish daily from streets and markets out of the city and tip it into the river,' he noted appreciatively.

Shushtari's account is throughout surprisingly Anglophile, as he takes an interest in European science and admires the technological achievements of the British: the *Tuhfat* discusses such diverse subjects as polar exploration, gravity, magnetism, the scientific comparisons then being made between men and monkeys, and even sceptical

---

* Literally, *qizil* = red, *bash* = head, a reference to the Qizilbash's coloured turbans rather than their hair-colour. The Qizilbash were followers of Isma'il Shah Safavi, and formed the bulk of the troops of Shi'ite Iran from the sixteenth century, spreading to Afghanistan with the Safavid rule in Herat and Qandahar, and in the eighteenth century to northern India with the armies of Nadir Shah. Colonies of Qizilbash are still scattered in Kabul, Peshawar and Lahore. By the time Shushtari was writing, the term no longer referred only to soldiers but also to traders.

atheism, which he touches on but prefers not to discuss in detail, regarding it as 'inappropriate for this book'.[13] He is also impressed by the fact that the British at this period were still profoundly respectful to Indian men of learning:

> They treat the white-beard elders and old-established families, both Muslim and Hindu, courteously and equably, respecting the religious customs of the country and as well the scholars, sayyids, sheikhs and dervishes they come across ... More remarkable still is the fact that they themselves take part in most of the festivals and ceremonies of both the Muslims and the Hindus, mixing with the people; in Muharram they even enter the *tazia-khane* mourning-halls though they do not join in the mourning [of the death of Mohammed's grandson Hussain at the Battle of Kerbala in AD 680]. They pay great respect to accomplished scholars of whatever sect.[14]

Deferential and enquiring the British might have been, but according to Abdul Lateef they had a lot to learn from the Persians in terms of personal hygiene, as well as in matters of high culture. Shushtari was particularly horrified by what the British did to their hair, 'shaving their beards, twisting their hair into pony-tails, and worst of all, using a white powder to make their hair look white.' Not content with these enormities, 'neither men nor women remove pubic hair, accounting comely to leave it in its natural state'.[15]*

Shushtari was of the opinion that European women were particularly bizarre, immoral and headstrong creatures: 'most European women have no body-hair,' he notes,

> and even if it does occur, it is wine-coloured, soft and extremely fine ... By reason of women going unveiled and the mixed education of boys and girls in one school-house, it is quite the thing to fall in love. I have heard that well-born girls sometimes fall in love with low-born youths and are

---

* This is something that has always horrified educated Muslims who have come into intimate contact with Westerners: the twelfth-century Arab intellectual Usama ibn Munquid complained of the same unattractive trait in Crusader Syria, telling a story about a visit to a bath-house at Ma'arra in the course of which he notes with some disgust that a Frank he comes across in the baths kept his pubic hair 'as long as his beard'. See Francesco Gabrieli, *Arab Historians of the Crusades* (London, 1969), p.78.

covered in scandal which neither threats nor punishment can control, so their fathers are obliged to drive them out of the house; the girl follows her whims, and mingles with whom she fancies. The streets and markets of London are full of innumerable such well-bred girls sitting on the pavements. Brothels are advertised, with pictures of prostitutes hung at the door, and the price of one night is written up with all the furnishings required for revelry . . .[16]

This, believes Shushtari, is largely the fault of the Americans; indeed Abdul Lateef must go down in history as the first Muslim writer to take up cudgels against the United States, which, 180 years ahead of his time, he already regards as the Great Satan:

No man [in the West] can prevent his wife from mixing with strange men . . . but it was only after the conquest of America that the disgraceful habit of allowing women to sit unveiled in public became common in France and then spread to the rest of Europe. Similarly, tobacco, the pox and burning venereal diseases were all unknown in the world five years ago, except in America, and the problem spread to the rest of the world from there.

India is, however, fully a match even for the horrors of America. There are many things that disgust Shushtari about the subcontinent, but his real venom is reserved for the Muslims of India who have, as he sees it 'gone native', and by intermarrying with Hindus – or Muslim converts from Hinduism – assimilated not just their customs but their very un-Islamic morality: 'They accept water from the hands of Hindus, use the oil they buy from them, eat their cooked foods – whereas they flee from all contact with the English, who at least in appearance are People of the Book and who respect religion and the law.'[17]

The only thing that appalls Abdul Lateef Shushtari more than the men in India is the behaviour of the women, Hindu and Muslim alike, who in his eyes have no idea about proper modesty, and take every imaginable liberty. He discusses at some length the case of Muni Begum, who was the effective ruler of the state of Murshidabad in Bengal: 'she is neither the mother of the present ruler, nor even from a good family, but was a singer kept by Ja'far [Ali Khan, the ruler of Bengal] who became completely infatuated with her and the Supreme Giver opened the doors of good fortune for her'.

Shushtari's surprise at the power of women in late Mughal India is very significant. Islam has never been monolithic and has always adapted itself to its social and geographical circumstances. The Hindu attitude to women, to their place in society, to their clothing and to their sexuality has always been radically different from that of Middle Eastern Islam. But over centuries of Hindu–Muslim co-existence in India, much mutual exchange of ideas and customs took place between the two cohabiting cultures, so that while Hinduism took on some Islamic social features – such as the veil worn by upper-caste Rajput women in public – Indian Islam also adapted itself to its Hindu environment, a process accelerated by the frequency with which Indian Muslim rulers tended to marry Hindu brides.

As this happened the cultural gap between the court culture of Mughal India and Safavid Iran widened ever larger. Women in Iran were more confined and less able to act in the public sphere than in India where, thanks to the influence of Hinduism, notions of purdah, and ideas about the seclusion and protection of women, were always less deeply entrenched and less central to notions of male honour.[18] As a result, Muslim women in India have always played a more prominent role in politics than their sisters in the Middle East. Indian society, both Hindu and Muslim, was certainly very patriarchal and hierarchical; yet there are nevertheless several cases of very powerful Indian Muslim queens: Razia Sultana in thirteenth-century Delhi; or Chand Bibi and Dilshad Agha, the two warrior queens of sixteenth-century Bijapur, the first of whom was famous for her horse-womanship, while the latter was renowned for her prowess as an artillerywoman and an archer, personally shooting in the eye from atop her citadel Safdar Khan who had the temerity to attack her kingdom.[19]*

Moreover Mughal princesses tended to be richer, and to possess far greater powers of patronage, than the secluded Iranian noblewomen Shushtari would have been familiar with in Iran: half the most important monuments in Shah Jehan's Mughal Delhi were built by women, especially Shah Jehan's favourite daughter Jahanara, who independently constructed several mansions (including one in the Red Fort which alone cost 700,000 rupees,† a garden, a bath-house and a palatial caravanserai; she also laid out the whole of the principal avenue of the city, Chandni Chowk.[20]

Aristocratic Mughal women also tended to be much better educated than their Iranian cousins: almost all of them were literate, and were taught at home by elderly male scholars or 'learned matrons'; the curriculum included ethics, mathematics, economics, physics, logic, history, medicine, theology, law, poetry and astronomy.[21] As a result there were many cases of highly educated Indian Muslim princesses who became famous writers or poetesses: Gulbadan, the sister of the second Mughal Emperor Humayun, wrote her brother's biography, the *Humayun Nama*, while her great-great-great-niece Jahanara wrote a biography of the celebrated Indian Sufi, Mu'in ud-Din Chisti, as well as several volumes of poetry and her own epitaph.[22] More scholarly still was Aurangzeb's daughter, Zeb un-Nissa. According to the *Maasir i-Alamgiri*, the history of Aurangzeb's reign, Zeb un-Nissa had learned the Koran by heart and 'completely mastered the Arabic and Persian languages, as well as the art of writing all the various styles of calligraphy. Indeed her heart was set on the collection, copying and reading of books. The result was that she collected a library the likes of which no man has seen; and a large number of theologians, scholars, pious men, poets, scribes and calligraphists by this means came to enjoy the bounty of this scholarly lady.'[23]

This sort of thing was dangerous enough, thought Shushtari; but

---

* There are also a number of rare cases of queens in the Arab world, such as Asma Bint Shihab al-Sulayhiyya of eleventh-century Yemen. See Fatima Mernissi's fascinating study *The Forgotten Queens of Islam* (Cambridge, 1993).
† Around £4.2 million in today's currency.

more shocking still was the way these over-educated and independent-minded Indian women behaved. He was particularly horrified at the number he came into contact with on his travels who had had affairs – or even intermarried – with the English:

> The women of the immoral Hindus and the Muslims they have corrupted, of their own accord and desire enter into the bonds of wedlock with the English. These English do not interfere with their religion nor compel them to leave *purda* veiling; when any son born of the union reaches the age of four, he is taken from his mother and sent to England to be educated. Some daughters are left with their mothers to be trained by them in their own way before being married off to a Muslim who is then given some appointment; the fathers also leave the girls something of their inheritance. When children reach the age of discretion, they are free to choose their religion themselves.[24]

This approach was not in fact some radical colonial departure, but was part of an old Indian tradition: providing wives or concubines for rulers had long been a means of preferment in courtly India. As the British rose to power across the subcontinent it became increasingly politically opportune to marry princely Indian women to them, so binding the British, and especially the British Residents, into the Indian political system and gaining a degree of access and leverage over them: William Linnaeus Gardner for example is quite open about the fact that his application to marry his Begum was ultimately agreed to by her family as 'on mature deliberation, the ambassador [i.e. Gardner] was considered too influential a person to have a request denied, and the hand of the young princess was promised'.[25]

Behind these frequent liaisons between British men and Indian women – and Shushtari's horrified attitude to such connections – lay not just different approaches to gender, but radically differing approaches to both romantic love and sexuality between India and Iran. Sexuality in India was always regarded as a subject of legitimate and fascinated enquiry, and looked upon as an essential part of the study of aesthetics: *srngararasa* – the erotic *rasa* or flavour – being one of the nine *rasas* comprising the Hindu aesthetic system. Such was the lack of embarrassment in both Hindu and Muslim courts that numerous miniatures were commissioned and painted showing exactly how the fullest possible pleasures of this *rasa* might be attained. It was a world away from the rigid ban on the depiction of images of any sort that defined the strictest interpretations of Middle Eastern Islam.

Between the fifteenth and the eighteenth centuries many of the classics of Hindu writing on love and eroticism were translated into Persian for the use of the princes and princesses of Indian Muslim courts. Significantly, it was in the more cosmopolitan and less comprehensively Islamicised courts of the Deccan such as Bidar, Bijapur and Golconda that much of this work of translation and dissemination took place: erotic treatises such as the famous *Kama Sutra* and the *Srngaramanjari* (literally 'The Bouquets of Sexual Pleasure') were translated into Persian or Deccani Urdu, while Indian Muslim authors added new studies to the erotic shelves of the palace libraries such as the *Lazat al-Nissa* (or 'Delights of Women') and the *Tadhkirat al-Shahawat* ('Book of Aphrodisiacs'), both of which were much read and copied throughout the eighteenth-century Deccan.

Other texts advised on how to plant a pleasure garden with sensually stimulating plants as an aid to seduction, or even, in the case of the *'Itr-i Nawras Shahi*, how to 'charge' a palace bedroom with scents appropriate to prolonging and heightening sexual pleasure: as well as placing bouquets of tuberoses and other strongly scented flowers at varying heights in the room, the writer suggests burning varieties of citron- and jasmine-derived incense, and lifting the bedspread so that the sheets can absorb the fragrance, which will be 'enticing, invigorating, and pleasure giving'.[26]

Nor was it just a matter of erotic theory: judging by the evidence of travel accounts, sexuality played a significantly more open role in daily life and gossip in India than it did in Iran. Travellers to the subcontinent regularly brought back tales of romantic liaisons in the palaces of the Mughals, especially with the *khanazads* or *salatin*, the palace-born princes who moved freely about the harem as children and whose entry as adults was restricted but not entirely forbidden. The *salatin*, who tended to marry into the royal household and lived in the precincts of the Mahal, were said to have taken full advantage of their status: certainly, according to the seventeenth-century Venetian quack Niccolao Manucci, 'under cover of this title, these princesses and many great ladies gratify their desires'.[27]

If this is true of Mughal India in general, it is especially true of late Mughal India between the early eighteenth and the mid-nineteenth century. After the end of the enforced puritanism of Aurangzeb and Nizam ul-Mulk's period, attitudes changed completely: Nizam Ali Khan even founded a department of his civil service to oversee and promote the business of dancing, music and sensuality, the *Daftar Arbab-i-Nishaat* (the Office of the Lords of Pleasure).[28] At the same time there was an explosion of unrestrainedly sensual art and literary experimentation: in Delhi, Lucknow and Hyderabad, poets at this time wrote some of the most unblushingly amorous Indian poetry to be composed since the end of the classical period seventeen hundred years earlier.

This was the age of the great courtesans:* in Delhi, Ad Begum would turn up stark naked at parties, but so cleverly painted that no one would notice: 'she decorates her legs with beautiful drawings in the style of pyjamas instead of actually wearing them; in place of the cuffs she draws flowers and petals in ink exactly as is found in the finest cloth of Rum'. Her rival, Nur Bai, was so popular that every night the elephants of the great Mughal *omrahs* completely blocked the narrow lanes outside her house; yet even the most senior nobles had to 'send a large sum of money to have her admit them ... whoever gets enamoured of her gets sucked into the whirlpool of her demands and brings ruin in on his house ... but the pleasure of her company can only be had as long as one is in possession of riches to bestow on her'.[29]

Nur Bai's counterpart in Hyderabad was Mah Laqa Bai Chanda, the mistress of Mir Alam, and the most celebrated beauty of the age.[30] She was as renowned for her intelligence as her matchless

* The most famous courtesan of all was the great Umrao Jan Ada of Lucknow, immortalised in the eponymous novel by Mirza Mohammad Hadi Ruswa, and more recently in the film by Mozaffer Ali. A good English translation of Ruswa's novel was recently produced by Khuswant Singh and M.A. Husaini.

dancing; and on meeting her, according to Shushtari, the young Mir Alam immediately 'fell in love with this moon-faced beauty* and threw off the gravitas of the scholar. In the days of the full springtime flush of his youth, his mind was unsettled by her seductive beauty and ravishing charm, so that he could only think of love and poetry, and soon fell ill. It took him more than three months to recover and get back to studying and teaching the Islamic curriculum.'[31]

Mah Laqa Bai was not just glamorous and seductive: she was widely regarded as Hyderabad's greatest contemporary poet, whose works were collected as far away as Delhi and Lucknow. She built a famous library filled with books on the arts and sciences, and commissioned the *Mahanama*, a major new history of the Deccan; later she became an important patron of poets in her own right.[32] Such was the Nizam's reliance on her wisdom that alone of the women of Hyderabad she was given in her own right the rank of a senior *omrah*, so that she could attend the durbar and advise the Nizam on state policy.[33] She also accompanied him to war, dressed in male clothing, and gained a reputation for her riding skills, her accomplishments with the bow, and even with the javelin. No wonder Kirkpatrick's Assistant John Malcolm called her 'an extraordinary woman', or the Hyderabadi sage Qadrat Ullah Qasim wrote that she was 'a unique combination of body and soul'.[34]

The poetry of Mah Laqa was typical of much of the verse of the period in being concerned largely with the joys of love. At this time a whole new specialist vocabulary of Urdu and Deccani words and metaphors developed to express the poet's desires: the beloved's arms were likened to lotus stalks, her nose to a champa bud, her thighs to banana stems, her plaited hair to the Ganges, and her *rumauli* – a word that was coined to describe the faint line of down which ran from below a woman's navel – to the River Godavari. In this spirit, the Avadhi poet Shauq (1783–1871) wrote a whole series of *masnavis* on amorous subjects entitled *Fareb-i-Ishq* ('The Wiles of Love') and the *Bahar-i-Ishq* ('The Spring of Love'), while his contemporary Nasik summed up his life's work with the epitaph:

---

* A rather weak pun by Shushtari: Mah Laqa's pen name, 'Chanda', means moon.

I am a lover of breasts
Like pomegranates;
Plant then no other trees
On my grave but these.

This sort of thing was not to everyone's taste: the great Delhi poet
Mir expressed his view that most Lucknavi poets could not write
verse, and would be better-advised to 'stick to kissing and slavering'.
But this mood of fleshy decadence crossed from the *mushairas* (poetic
symposia) of the poets to the workshops of other artists: to the tailors,
for example, where *derzis* laboured to produce ever more transparent and revealing *cholis* with weaves of wondrous lightness named
baft hawa ('woven wind'), *ab-e-rawan* ('running water') and *shabnam*
('evening dew').

Similar concerns inspired the scriptoria of the miniaturists. In
Hyderabad, the artists of Nizam Ali Khan's period were producing
miniatures that tapped into the old erotic pulse of so much pre-
Islamic Indian art and which were concerned above all with the
depiction of aesthetic bliss in the Arcadia of the scented Deccani
pleasure garden. Here courtesans as voluptuous as the nude *yakshis**
and *apsaras*† of south Indian stone sculpture attend bejewelled
princes who seem to have walked off the walls of the ancient Hindu
cave sculptures of nearby Badami. These women smoke hookahs and
swim in long garden pools, they drink wine and play with pigeons
or while away the moonlit monsoon nights on swings, listening to
music and carousing in marble pavilions. The hunting and battle
scenes of high Mughal art have disappeared. As one rather surprised
Indian art historian has commented, 'it is difficult to account for
their sudden absence from the painters' list of themes, but it shows
that women and not hunting or war were important for their
patrons'.[35]

There was nothing to compare with this pleasure-loving spirit in
Shushtari's Persia. For in strong contrast to the sensual decadence
of late Mughal India, the Iranian and Middle Eastern attitude to

---

* Female Hindu fertility nymphs, often associated with sacred trees and pools.
† The courtesans and dancing girls of the Hindu gods; heavenly dispensers of erotic
bliss.

romantic love lay much closer to Eastern Christian notions (the environment in which so many early Islamic attitudes developed), which emphasised the sinfulness of the flesh, the dangers of sexuality and even, in extreme cases, the idealisation of sexual renunciation and virginity. In Iranian literature love is usually portrayed as a hazardous, painful and dangerous condition: typically, in the great Persian epic *Layla and Majnun*, Majnun is driven mad by his love for Layla, and ends up dying wasted, starving and insane.*

This is the attitude to romantic love that Abdul Lateef Shushtari subscribes to, and the *Tuhfat* contains a discussion of the subject in which he emphasises the derivation of the Persian word for romantic love – *'Ishq* – as coming from 'the bindweed that strangles . . . doctors call it a melancholy distemper of black bile, curable only by sexual union with the desired object'.†

As Shushtari wrote on this subject, the notorious affair between his cousin's granddaughter Khair un-Nissa and James Kirkpatrick must have been at the back of his mind. At the time he was writing the affair had led to the destruction of all his hopes – and those of much of his family – of wealth, success and power in India: romantic love and sexual fulfilment had indeed turned into a kind of poisonous bindweed dragging down all who had become entangled in it.

The liaison was thus a most sensitive and scandalous subject, and Shushtari refuses to discuss it directly, remarking only that 'a detailed account of this notorious affair is not appropriate to these pages, indeed even a summary mention of it would provoke horror and disgust in the reader'; but what is intriguing about his account is the fact that he clearly does not in any way blame Kirkpatrick for what happened. Instead he describes him in the warmest terms: 'The Company representative, Major James Kirkpatrick, is a man of good

---

* The devotional Hindu attitude to love was different again, regarding it not so much a matter of pain as a metaphor that eased one's submission before an omnipotent power.
† He then tells an anecdote to illustrate this, which he says was related to him 'by reliable sources, of an [Iranian] Qizilbash boy in Benares who, a few years before I came to India, fell in love with a Brahmin girl and made a hut of reeds by the bathing ghats to watch the girl coming to the river. They became lovers, but were soon separated by her parents. So they joined in a suicide pact and drowned in the River Ganges, where their bodies appeared momentarily clasping each other, before disappearing, in spite of all the searches of swimmers and divers. Shushtari, *Kitab Tuhfat al-'Alam*, p.554.

character and firm friend of mine. He has made a garden on the outskirts of Hyderabad where he lives: it is a beautiful garden and I occasionally went there in his company and found him a man of great intuition and understanding, second only to my older brother.' As far as Shushtari is concerned, James did not initiate the affair, and so was not responsible for what happened.

Over and over again in his book, Shushtari emphasises the uniqueness of his clan of Sayyids, the importance to them of endogamy, and the central duty of Sayyid men to look after their women and to guard their virtue. Yet here was a case of a good Shushtari Sayyid – his own first cousin, Bâqar Ali Khan – coming to India, intermarrying with an Indian Muslim family, and so in Shushtari's eyes picking up immoral Indian ways. The result: Bâqar's granddaughter throwing herself not just at a non-Sayyid, but at a non-Muslim, a *firangi*.

The initiative, he implies, came from Khair un-Nissa's side, and it was there that lay the shame.

In January 1799, about a month after the wedding of Nazir un-Nissa, serious disagreement broke out in the household of Bâqar Ali Khan about the match intended for the younger of his two granddaughters, Khair un-Nissa.

An engagement had been arranged by Bâqar Ali for the girl, who was then probably not much older than fourteen. The man in question is never named, but he was from the clan of one of the most powerful Hyderabadi nobles, Bahram ul-Mulk, and the son of a close friend and ally of Mir Alam, a prominent nobleman named Ahmed Ali Khan.[36]

It is not clear what the women of the family objected to in the match: maybe Ahmed Ali Khan's son was violent, drunken or untrustworthy; maybe they just disliked him or thought him insuf-

ficiently grand for the girl; maybe it was simply that Bâqar Ali Khan
had arranged the marriage without consulting the women when, as
maternal grandfather, his legal right to matchmake was open to
question: after the death of Khair un-Nissa's father, Mehdi Yar Khan,
legal responsibility for the girl's marriage would normally have fallen
first to Sharaf un-Nissa, her mother, then to Mehdi Yar Khan's
surviving brother, Mir Asadullah Khan and his close male relations.*
Bâqar Ali Khan would not normally have been expected to involve
himself in such matters.

Possibly the disaffection of the women of the household was due to
a mixture of all these reasons. But whatever the cause, it is quite clear
that they strongly disagreed with the match; and it is also clear that
in eighteenth-century Hyderabad there was an understanding that the
women of an aristocratic family – and especially the bride herself – did
have a real right to veto any marriage arranged for them: a decade
earlier, for example, the women of Nizam Ali Khan's *zenana* had joined
together to reject a proposal from Tipu Sultan that his brother-in-law
might marry one of the Nizam's daughters. The women argued that
Tipu and his clan were *parvenu* Indian-born commoners with no noble
blood in their veins, that even Tipu himself was the son of an illiterate

---

* According to the *Nagaristan-i-Asafiya* and the *Yadgar-i-Makhan Lal*, Sharaf un-Nissa's
husband, Mehdi Yar Khan, and his brother Mir Asadullah were the sons of Mirza Qasim
Khan, the *faujdar* (fort-keeper) of Bhongir and a prominent supporter of Nizam ul-Mulk's
great rival, Mubariz Khan. Mirza Qasim Khan was killed when the Nizam defeated
Mubariz Khan at the Battle of Sheker Khera on 11 October 1724, so winning the Deccan
and frustrating the designs of the Sayyid brothers – the real power behind the Mughal
Emperor Muhammad Shah Rangila – to topple him from power. Mirza Qasim Khan's
family were however quickly forgiven by Nizam ul-Mulk for supporting the wrong side,
and Sharaf un-Nissa's husband Mehdi Yar Khan prospered under both Nizam ul-Mulk
and Nizam Ali Khan, before dying sometime in the 1780s or nineties. Sharaf un-Nissa
must however have been at least forty years younger than her husband. She was certainly
not Mehdi Yar Khan's only wife, as Khair un-Nissa had an older half-sister, from a
different (and probably older) mother, who died in early March 1800 'in consequence
of medicines she repeatedly took to procure pregnancy'. See entries for Bâqar Ali Khan
in the *Nagaristan-i-Asafiyya* and the *Yadgar-i-Makhan Lal* (no page numbers), and Yusuf
Husain, *The First Nizam: The Life of Nizam ul-Mulk Asaf Jah I* (Bombay, 1963), p.137.
For the death of Khair un-Nissa's half-sister, see OIOC, Kirkpatrick Papers, F228/11, p.338,
9 March 1800, James Kirkpatrick to William Kirkpatrick. It is interesting to speculate
whether Sharaf un-Nissa's experience of being married to an old man, and the possible
unhappiness this caused her, led her to view more sympathetically Khair un-Nissa's
resistance to her grandfather's attempt to impose a marriage upon her.

soldier of fortune, and that it would dishonour the blood of the Asafiya dynasty to mix it with such peasant Indian stock – after all, Tipu's father had been a humble soldier in the Nizam's army. Despite the political benefits that an alliance with Mysore might bring to Hyderabad, Nizam Ali Khan eventually agreed to the women's demands, and Tipu's ambassador was sent back to Seringapatam empty-handed.[37]

By the end of January 1799, the women of Bâqar Ali Khan's household appear to have despaired of persuading the old man to cancel the engagement of his own volition. Some sort of public engagement ceremony* had been performed 'which rendered it impossible to break off the match without disgrace to the parties', and Bâqar dug his heels in, saying that he refused to shame the family by withdrawing from the contract.[38] But the women did not admit defeat, and in mid-February they seized an opportunity to take matters into their own hands when Bâqar and Mir Alam had to leave Hyderabad for several months to go off on campaign.

The cause of their departure was the Nizam's decision to join the British in their new war against Tipu Sultan. This was the next stage in Lord Wellesley's aggressive campaign to extinguish the last remnants of French influence in India and to establish the British not only in their place, but as the undisputed pre-eminent power in the subcontinent. From captured correspondence, Wellesley now had solid proof of what he had always suspected: that Tipu was seeking French troops and supplies from the Governor of Mauritius, and was actively plotting with Bonaparte to bring down British rule in India. Wellesley was determined he would never allow either Bonaparte or Tipu a second chance. The captured letters were the excuse

---

* Presumably this was the ceremony known as a '*mangni*', or more picturesquely the '*lahri bel*' (green creeper), at which first contracts were exchanged. In this ceremony the mother of the groom, accompanied by her relatives and friends, pays a visit to the house of the girl, bringing with her trays full of gifts for the bride and her parents, including dresses, ornaments, perfumes and betel leaves. The girl would then be unveiled and her face shown to the visitors for the first time. This initial meeting with a future mother-in-law was often a very traumatic experience for the bride, and it is quite possible that one of the major attractions of life with Kirkpatrick in Khair's eyes was that she would be mistress of her own *zenana* and not under the authority of a possibly cruel or unpleasant older woman. See Zinat Kausar, *Muslim Women in Medieval India* (New Delhi, 1992), pp.25–7.

he needed to open hostilities and to play the checkmate in the forty-year-long struggle between the sultans of Mysore and the East India Company.

Now that the Corps Français de Raymond had been disarmed in Hyderabad, and the news had come through of the defeat of the French fleet at Aboukir Bay, Wellesley began making detailed logistical preparations for a major assault on Tipu's well-fortified river-island capital of Seringapatam. He wrote personally to Tipu in a vein of deepest sarcasm, breaking the news to him of Nelson's devastating victory at the Battle of the Nile: 'Confident from the union and attachment subsisting between us that this intelligence will afford you the deepest satisfaction, I could not deny myself the pleasure of communicating it.'[39] Meanwhile he worked late into the night preparing the logistics for Tipu's destruction.

On 3 February 1799, everything was in place and General Harris, the Commander in Chief, was ordered to mobilise and 'with as little delay as possible ... enter the territory of Mysore and proceed to the siege of Seringapatam'.[40] A message was also sent to the Nizam to call up his troops to assist his British allies, as had been agreed in the Preliminary Treaty he had signed five months earlier.

Bâqar Ali Khan, as *bakshi* to the British troops in Hyderabad, had to go with the army and act as liaison between the British and the Hyderabadis. Mir Alam came too, as overall commander of the large contingent of Hyderabad troops, though as his younger brother, Sayyid Zein ul-Abidin Shushtari, was Tipu's Private Secretary and a senior Mysore courtier,* he must have felt a certain ambivalence about the campaign.[41] More ambivalent still must have been the attitude of the (at least) four thousand Hyderabadi infantry soldiers who had formerly been sepoys of Raymond's corps until they were reassigned to British-officered regiments after the French capitu-

---

* Mir Zein ul-Abidin Shushtari was as remarkable a figure as his brother Mir Alam and first cousin Mir Abdul Lateef Shushtari. Like these two, he was a poet, writer and scholar as well as a successful and prominent courtier who led several diplomatic missions for Tipu. He rose to power in Mysore after composing for Tipu an army manual, a verse history and an epic in praise of fighting the jihad against the *firangi* infidels, the *Zad ul-Mujahedin*. See Kate Brittlebank, *Tipu Sultan's Search for Legitimacy: Islam and Kingship in a Hindu Domain* (New Delhi, 1997), pp.27, 35.

lation. Ironically, they were now under the direct command of James
Kirkpatrick's Assistant Captain John Malcolm, who had played such
a major role in their surrender only four months earlier.[42]

Realising that his situation was now very serious, Tipu wrote a
desperate plea to the Nizam warning him that the English 'intended
extirpating all Mussulmans and establishing Hat Wearers* in their
place', and arguing that the Nizam and he, fellow Muslims, should
join together to resist the Company; but it was too late.[43]

On 19 February, the six East India Company battalions in Hyderabad under the command of Lieutenant Colonel James Dalrymple,
along with the four battalions of Hyderabadi sepoys under John
Malcolm, and over ten thousand Hyderabadi cavalry under the command of Mir Alam, joined up with General Harris's huge Company
army, which had marched up from Vellore. On 5 March, with some
thirty thousand sheep, huge stocks of grain and a hundred thousand
carriage bullocks trailing behind them, the two armies crossed the
frontier into Mysore.[44] In their wake were at least a hundred thousand
camp followers. Wellesley, who had moved south to Madras to see
the army off, believed it to be 'the finest which ever took the field
in India'; but it was a huge and unwieldy force, and it trundled
towards Seringapatam at the agonisingly slow place of five miles a
day, stripping the country bare 'of every article of subsistence the
country can afford', like some vast cloud of locusts.[45]

* 'Hat wearers', or *topi wallahs*, was a common Indian term for Europeans, especially
the notably behatted English at this period; Indians were of course *pagri wallahs*, or
turban-wearers. Half a century earlier, Tipu's father, Haider Ali, at the very beginning
of his career, had captured a Madras clerk named Stuart and forced him to train his
infantry. When Stuart pointed out that he was an accountant and had not the faintest
clue how to drill troops, Haider replied that he 'never doubted the soldiership of a man
who wore a hatt'. From *Mr Stuarts Travels in Coromandel and the Dekan, 1764*, quoted
in Kate Brittlebank, *Tipu Sultan's Search for Legitimacy: Islam and Kingship in a Hindu
Domain* (New Delhi, 1997), p.21. Intriguingly, in certain circumstances, hats also seem

Whatever the new war might mean for Hyderabad, Sharaf un-Nissa was quite clear about the opportunities it presented her in her efforts to outflank her father on the issue of the unsatisfactory marriage which had been arranged for her younger daughter. At Nazir un-Nissa's wedding, James Kirkpatrick had seen Khair un-Nissa, and they had apparently made a deep impression on each other. Now the women of the *zenana* seem to have decided that Kirkpatrick was the answer to their problem, and to have persuaded themselves that he was a far more appropriate suitor for the girl than the unpopular son of Ahmed Ali Khan.

With this in mind, according to James, 'every inducement had been held out to him by the females of the family: the young lady had been shown to him when she was asleep, his portrait had been given to her by her mother, or grandmother, and she had been encouraged in the partiality which she expressed for the original from a view of the portrait, that he had been perpetually importuned with messages from the ladies to visit at the house of the Khan, and on an occasion of his indisposition he had received daily messages from the young lady herself to inquire after his health – [indeed] that occasions were even afforded her of seeing him from behind a curtain, and that latterly she was permitted in that situation to converse with him. In conclusion they were purposely brought together at night in order that the ultimate connection might take place.' For this to happen, according to the testimony of Lieutenant Colonel Bowser, 'the ladies of Bauker's family paid a visit of two days to those of the Resident'.[46]

About Khair un-Nissa's motives there is little dispute: James Kirkpatrick certainly believed that the girl had fallen in love with him, and he may have been right: certainly nothing in her behaviour contradicts this view. To his brother William, James later wrote that

---

to have been important to Europeans as expressions of their distinctiveness from Indians: when Lieutenant John Lindsay was captured by Tipu he spent his time in prison manically making hats from material he begged from his jailers, as a sort of symbol of resistance against the circumcisions and forced conversions to Islam that several of the British prisoners were forced to undergo. See Linda Colley, 'Going Native, Telling Tales: Captivity, Collaborations and Empire', in *Past and Present*, No. 168, August 2000, p.179.

'[among] all the ranks and descriptions of people here, the story of B[âqar Ali Khan]'s grand daughter's long cherished partiality for me [is] perfectly known'. James's belief was echoed by Bowser in the Clive Report: he stated under oath that 'it is said that the lady fell in love with the Resident'.[47] James also claimed that Khair un-Nissa had threatened to take poison unless he helped her escape from a 'hateful marriage'.[48]

Exactly why Sharaf un-Nissa and her mother, Durdanah Begum, were so keen on the match is, however, a much more difficult question to answer. It could of course have been a mother's sympathy with her lovelorn daughter, and a wish to save her from unhappiness and possible suicide. But Khair un-Nissa was a descendant of the Prophet, a Sayyida, and so part of a strictly endogamous clan who never married their women to non-Sayyids, and whose prestige and notions of honour depended largely on this stricture being rigorously observed. Moreover, there was no tradition of love marriages in eighteenth-century Indian society – indeed at that period it was a fairly novel concept even among aristocratic families in the West – and yet it is clear that Sharaf un-Nissa not only gave her assent to Khair un-Nissa's attempt to seduce Kirkpatrick, she and Durdanah Begum went out of their way to help her achieve it; indeed if James is to be believed, the two women more or less pushed the girl into his bed. Why would they do this?

The most likely explanation is that they realised that such a connection would be hugely advantageous to their family. James was not only a powerful British diplomat; since February 1798 he had also been an important Hyderabadi nobleman, with a series of titles given to him by the Nizam – Mutamin ul-Mulk, Hushmat Jung ('Glorious in Battle'), Nawab Fakhr ud-Dowlah Bahadur – and an elevated place in the Nizam's durbar.

Other Indian women who had married British Residents at this time had found that marriage brought them prestige, wealth and rank. James's opposite number at the Maratha court, General William Palmer, for example, was married to a Delhi begum named Fyze Baksh who would later become Khair un-Nissa's best friend. Fyze's father was an Iranian immigrant and a captain of cavalry who had moved from Delhi, where Fyze was born, to Lucknow. On her marriage to William Palmer, she was formally adopted by the Mughal Emperor Shah Alam and loaded with titles: the spectacular gilt *sanad* awarding her the title Sahib Begum survives in the India Office Library, and there can be little doubt that it represented a considerable jump in rank for a woman who was from a respectably aristocratic but hardly imperial background.[49]

An even more dramatic transformation in status was experienced by General Sir David Ochterlony's senior *bibi*, Mubarak Begum. Though Ochterlony is reputed to have had thirteen wives, one of these, a former Brahmin slave girl from Pune who converted to Islam and is referred to in his will as 'Beebee Mahruttun Moobaruck ul Nissa Begume, alias Begum Ochterlony, the mother of my younger children',[50] took clear precedence over the others.[51]

'Generalee Begum', as she was also known, occasionally appears in contemporary letters, where she is frequently accused of giving herself airs. She offended the British by calling herself 'Lady Ochterlony' – in one letter it is recorded that 'Lady Ochterlony has applied for leave to make the Hadge to Mecca' – and also offended the Mughals by awarding herself the title Qudsia Begum, previously that of the Emperor's mother.[52*] Much younger than Ochterlony, she certainly appears to have had the upper hand in her relationship with the old General, and one observer remarked that Ochterlony's mistress 'is the mistress now of everyone within the walls'.[53]

Mubarak Begum ultimately overplayed her hand: after Ochterlony's death she inherited Mubarak Bagh, the Anglo-Mughal garden tomb he had built in the north of the city, and she used part of her considerable inheritance to build a mosque and a *haveli* for herself at Hauz Qazi in the old city of Delhi.[54] But her profound personal unpopularity, combined with her dancing-girl background, meant that no Mughal gentleman would ever be seen using her structure.

---

* She even seems to have set herself up as a power in her own right, and to have engaged in her own independent foreign policy: at one point it was reported that 'Mobarruck Begum alias Generalee Begum fills the [Delhi] papers with accounts of the Nizars and Khiluts [gifts and dresses of honour] given and taken by her in her transactions with the vaqueels [ambassadors] of the different [Indian] powers' – an extraordinary liberty if true. Gardner Papers, National Army Museum, Letter 87, p.226, 10 August 1821.

It is still, to this day, referred to in the old city as the 'Rundi-ki-Masjid', or Prostitute's Mosque.*

Mubarak Begum's extreme social and political ambitions led to her nemesis. But her story is nevertheless a graphic illustration of quite how powerful a woman could become by being the wife or even the senior concubine of a British Resident. Sharaf un-Nissa was a widow whose father was pressuring her to marry her daughter to a man neither mother nor daughter thought suitable. Kirkpatrick clearly represented a very eligible escape route.

Yet there is one further possible explanation for Sharaf un-Nissa's willingness to indulge her daughter's wishes. Sharaf un-Nissa's great friend was Farzand Begum, the daughter-in-law of Aristu Jah, and the moving force in the Prime Minister's *zenana*.† Over and over again in the records, we hear of Sharaf un-Nissa visiting Farzand Begum, and Sharaf un-Nissa later insisted that Farzand Begum had encouraged her to marry Khair un-Nissa to the British Resident.[55] Farzand Begum seems to have been involved in encouraging the liaison from the outset, for it was later reported that Aristu Jah had supervised it from its commencement, and in Mughal society the only way he could have done this would have been through the women in his *zenana*.[56] It is also unclear whether Aristu Jah or Farzand Begum offered Sharaf un-Nissa any inducements to make her daughter available to Kirkpatrick; but it is known for sure that following the marriage Sharaf un-Nissa was indeed granted lucrative *jagirs* (estates) of fifty thousand rupees per annum by the Nizam.[57]

---

* It is an interesting question if there is any etymological link between the Hindustani 'rundi', a prostitute or dancing girl, and the modern English word 'randy'. *The Oxford English Dictionary* says the derivation of the word is 'obscure', and suggests it may have come from the Dutch; but an Indian link seems equally likely.

† Farzand Begum, a granddaughter of the previous Prime Minister Rukn ud-Daula, was the widow of Aristu Jah's only son Ma'ali Mian, who had died in 1795 as the Hyderabadi army was on the way to the Battle of Khardla. She was also the sister of Zaman Ali Khan, Munir ul-Mulk, one of the most important Hyderabadi *omrahs*, who succeeded Aristu Jah and Mir Alam as Prime Minister. Henry Russell described him as 'having all the vices of a man of weak understanding, timid, ignorant and bigoted . . . incapable of warm and steady attachments, never refusing the smallest bribe . . . not quite illiterate'. 'Henry Russell's Report to Lord Moira, reprinted from the Russell Papers in the Bodleian Library', in *Indian Archives*, 9, 127, p.143. Farzand Begum clearly had more charm and talents than her brother.

If this was part of a deal, a *quid pro quo* for giving Khair un-Nissa to the British Resident, it would follow that the affair between Kirkpatrick and Khair un-Nissa was to some extent planned – or at least manipulated – by Aristu Jah, a tactician of genius who realised how far he could use the relationship for his political advantage. As later events would show, Aristu Jah also clearly hoped that if he played his cards carefully, the relationship might be the weapon he had been looking for to revenge himself on his great rival, Khair un-Nissa's first cousin once removed, Mir Alam. If this is the correct interpretation – and it was certainly what Mir Alam later believed to be the case[58] – then it would follow that Khair un-Nissa was made available to Kirkpatrick as what (in the parlance of modern spy novels) is known as a 'honey trap'.

If this is the case, how should we judge Sharaf un-Nissa's actions? Was she effectively prostituting her daughter for her own ends and ambitions? However we may regard it today, this is certainly not how the women of the family would have looked at it themselves. Sexuality was a key asset and weapon for women in Mughal India, and subtly finding a way of making the women of a family available to powerful rulers and officials was a recognised means of achieving advancement and preferment at court and in society.[59] All Sharaf un-Nissa was doing was adapting this ancient tradition to the new semi-colonial environment – and here lay her problem.

Even with the most Mughalised British official, there were big differences between setting up a marriage alliance with a British Resident, and doing the same with a senior Mughal courtier, as the women would in due course discover. What might be regarded as normal courtly behaviour in a Mughal environment could be misconstrued by Europeans as procurement or pimping; moreover British Residents moved quickly from court to court before, in most cases, returning home to Britain. Alliances that in a Mughal environment would be permanent often became dangerously short-term in a colonial one. At first Sharaf un-Nissa's strategy to gain influence through marrying her daughter to the British Resident seemed to work. Only time would reveal the scale of the difficulties involved in trying to cross such sensitive cultural frontiers.

In the end, motives are always difficult to establish. But what is certain is that with Bâqar Ali Khan away on campaign with the army, Sharaf un-Nissa was free to follow her own plan to bring her daughter and the British Resident together. She did not hesitate to take full and immediate advantage of that opportunity. According to Mir Alam's later testimony, it was shortly after he and Bâqar Ali 'took the field against Tippoo Sultaun [that] Kirkpatrick debauched this girl'.[60]

It was several months before James admitted to his elder brother that he was sleeping with Khair un-Nissa. Indeed he only did so explicitly long after the scandal had broken and William had written to him repeatedly demanding to know exactly what truth lay behind the ever more outrageous rumours emanating from Hyderabad.

The two brothers had lived closely together in Hyderabad, and each knew that the other was involved in a long-term relationship with at least one Indian woman. Some time after his wife Maria's return to England, William had re-established his relationship with Dhoolaury Bibi, by whom he had earlier fathered two children, Robert and Cecilia, both of whom were now teenagers and living with the Handsome Colonel in Kent. Dhoolaury Bibi had joined William in Hyderabad when he became Resident, and after William had left to recover his health at the Cape, James had written to his brother assuring him that his mistress was well and happy, and that he was looking after her. After William returned to India, Dhoolaury Bibi followed him to Calcutta, and was still living there, with her son Robert, twelve years later when she received a substantial legacy in William's will.[61] It seems to have been a serious and loving relationship; it was certainly longstanding: as their first child, Robert, was born in 1777, the two appear to have lived together for at least twenty-three years, except for the brief interlude between 1785, when William married Maria Pawson, and 1788, when Maria left India to return to England.

James, meanwhile, was also living with at least one Indian girl, by whom he had had a son. Neither her name nor that of the child has survived, and all that is known of the girl is that she was significantly darker-skinned than Khair un-Nissa, and so was perhaps of Tamil or Telugu origin.[62] James seems to have treated the relationship in a rather offhand manner: there are explicit references in the Clive Report – and in some of the Indian sources – to James's women in the plural,[63] and stories of his amorous adventures at this period reached even Arthur Wellesley in Seringapatam three hundred miles away: 'About three years ago he is supposed to have debauched a young Mogul woman by pretending to be a Persian from Iran,' the future Duke of Wellington reported to his brother Lord Wellesley, '[and it is said] that he has her now in his house.'[64] He also reported that Mir Alam had told him that this sort of adventure was far from unusual for Kirkpatrick, and that if he were to come to Hyderabad 'he would hear enough to make him ashamed that such a man was an Englishman' – much the same sort of thing as had long been said of James's oversexed father, the Handsome Colonel.[65]

After Khair un-Nissa appeared on the scene the 'dark girl' – and any other women then living in the Resident's *zenana* – simply disappear from James's letters, and the 'dark girl' is referred to only once, as 'my old inmate'.[66] It is possible that she died; certainly she received no legacy or any mention at all in James's will. James's apparent indifference to the girl seems to have extended to her child. Even the Handsome Colonel, never one to take the business of parenting too seriously, was a little shocked by James's apparent lack of interest in his 'Hindustani boy', and wrote to admonish him, saying that 'in his opinion there is no difference in the duty a parent owes to his legitimate and illegitimate children'.[67] When the child tragically caught a fever and died in the Handsome Colonel's arms in the summer of 1804, James wrote correctly but a little distantly to his father about 'that much lamented youth', saying how 'the estimation as well as regard in which my departed son was held by all who knew him, and by him in particular [i.e. the Handsome Colonel] who from his superior discernment, as well as opportunities, is so eminently qualified to form a just opinion, is the highest compliment that his memory could receive'.[68]

This was very different from the sort of deeply felt and emotional language James would use about Khair un-Nissa and his children by her, and perhaps illustrates how far the British brought with them to India a morality that was determined as much by class as by race: there was one way you were expected to behave with a mistress from the lower classes, and quite another set of rules for educated girls from the top drawer of society, irrespective of their skin colour or nationality.[69]

Certainly, it was precisely Khair un-Nissa's aristocratic birth and connections that led to James's reticence on the subject to William. Seducing Mir Alam's cousin had clear political implications, and initially James responded evasively to William's questions about the relationship by merely denying that he had any intentions of marrying Khair: it was, he maintained, 'an absurd report' that William had heard.[70] But William could see that he was not getting straight answers to the questions he was asking, and in letter after letter he kept up the pressure on James: was it true – had he seduced the girl or not? James was eventually forced to respond by giving William a full account of exactly how and where he had first slept with 'B[âqar]'s granddaughter', as he refers to her. In this letter he tried to clear himself of the charge of having taken the initiative in 'debauching' the girl: on the contrary, he maintains, it was Khair un-Nissa who had come to visit him – bringing her mother and granny along to his *zenana*, ostensibly as part of a visit to his women: 'My dearest Will,' he wrote,

> When I declared myself to you in my former letter unre-
> servedly with respect to what passed between B's granddaugh-
> ter and myself I did so because towards you I have never
> known what concealment was, though it may admit of a ques-
> tion how far I had *right* to open myself even to you in the
> present instance. It being now however at all events too late
> to recall what has passed, and placing as I do the most implicit
> reliance on your discretion as well as affection, I shall proceed

to answer without even a shadow of reserve the enquiries you are so anxious to have satisfied.

By way of Prelude it may not be amiss to observe that I did once *safely* pass the firey ordeal of a long nocturnal interview with the charming subject of the present letter. It was this interview which I alluded to as the one when I had full and close survey of her lovely Person – it lasted during the greatest part of the night and was evidently *contrived* by the Grandmother and mother whose very existence hang on hers to indulge her uncontrollable wishes. At this meeting, which was under my roof, I contrived to command myself so far as to abstain from the tempting feast I was manifestly invited to, and God knows but ill qualified for the task, attempted to argue the Romantic Young Creature out of a passion which I could not, I confess, help feeling myself something more than pity for – She declared to me again and again that her affections had been irrevocably fixed on me for a series of time, that her fate was linked to mine and that she should be content to pass her days with me as the humblest of handmaids. These effusions you may possibly be inclined to treat as the ravings of a distempered mind but when I have time to impart to you the whole affecting tale you will then at least allow her actions to have accorded fully with her declarations.

Until the above time (which might be a fortnight or three weeks before the interview spoken of in my former letter[71]) the young lady's person was inviolate but was it human nature to remain proof against another such fiery trial? No, will perhaps be your reply, but wherefore you will probably ask, expose yourself to it? In answer I have nought to plead but human feelings, or if you please human frailty, which would not withstand the heart rending account of this interesting young females state of desperation and the pressing message from her grandmother to fly to her relief.

Here again however I did not act but on the fullest previous conviction founded on numerous collateral circumstances as much as actual information, that the grandfather and the mother (though they kept aloof on the occasion) were privy to the assignation – I went then and when I assure you, which I do most solemnly, that the Grandmother herself plainly intimated the design of this meeting and the grand-daughter in faint and broken accents hinted that the sacrifice she was about to make me was the only chance (as she fondly persuaded herself) of avoiding a hateful marriage I think you cannot but allow that I must have been *something more or less than man* to have held out any longer. Deliberate female seduction I hold in as much contempt and detestation as any man, but whatever charge of imprudence (and who is at all times wise?) may be considered as attaching to my conduct on this trying occasion, or unwarrantable as it may be if tried by the rigid rules of morality, I can on no account endure the slightest whisper of it having being dishonourable or ungenerous . . .

I could say a great deal more on the foregoing subjects – [but] I must entreat you, my dear Will, to spare me if possible the pain of any further discussion of them,

Ever your faithful brother,

JAK[72]

While the affair with Khair un-Nissa dominated James's private life, his official time was fully occupied with coordinating the Hyderabad end of Lord Wellesley's war with Tipu Sultan.

James's task was to help keep the massive Company army supplied with sheep and grain, horses and carriage bullocks, a particularly important job now that Tipu had resorted to scorched-earth tactics in the hope of starving the advancing British army into retreat. James also tried to encourage Aristu Jah to send more cash for his sepoys' salaries, as well as further reinforcements to the front. In the former logistical task he had some success; but cash and reinforcements were not to be had, and the more he pressed the wily Minister on the matter, the more the 'perverse' Aristu Jah fobbed him off, often quickly changing the conversation to his greatest passion, cock-fighting.[73] By April James seems to have come to the conclusion that the most likely way to get anything out of the Minister was to hold out the offer of some prime English fighting cocks as long as Aristu Jah would commit some of his élite Paigah cavalry units to the war effort in return: 'The Minister is passionately fond of game cocks and very desirious of getting some English ones of the true game breed,' he wrote urgently to William a month after the Hyderabad forces set off on the road to Mysore. 'Are any of this kind to be had at Madras?'[74]

News from the front indicated that the campaign was about to reach its climax. By early April, General Harris had already taken several key forts, and Tipu had been forced to retreat within the great walls of Seringapatam. With only thirty-seven thousand troops, he was heavily outnumbered by the allies, but he remained a formidable enemy. In the three Anglo–Mysore Wars that had preceded the current conflict, the Mysore forces had frequently defeated the East India Company, and two of the most prominent Company commanders in the campaign, Sir David Baird and his cousin James Dalrymple, had both been prisoners of Tipu, having been captured and imprisoned after the disastrous British defeat at Pollilur in 1780 – 'the most grievous disaster which has yet befallen the British arms in India', as a contemporary called it at the time.[75]*

Tactically the Mysore forces were fully the match of those of the East India Company, and Tipu's sepoys were every bit as well trained by their French officers as those of the Company were by theirs; and the steely discipline of the Mysore infantry amazed and worried many British observers.[76] Moreover the sepoys' rifles and cannon were based

---

* When Sir David Baird's Scottish mother heard that her son had been captured by Tipu at the Battle of Pollilur in 1780, and that the prisoners had been led away handcuffed two by two, she remarked, 'I pity the man who was chained to oor Davie.' Quoted by Denys Forrest in *Tiger of Mysore: The Life and Death of Tipu Sultan* (London, 1970), p.48. A letter from James Dalrymple to his father, Sir William Dalrymple, smuggled out of the prison of Seringapatam, survives in the India Office. According to a note written by James's Anglo-Indian grandson, G. Wemyss Dalrymple, 'The paper was rolled up, and put into a quill, then passed into the person of a native, and so brought into the prison. With the same quill, he wrote the letter, the ink was solid Indian ink, and was also in the quill, and the letter was brought out of the prison, by the same native in the same manner.' OIOC, Eur Mss E330.

on the latest French designs, and their artillery had a heavier bore and longer range than anything possessed by the Company's armies. Indeed in many respects the Mysore troops were more innovative and technologically advanced than the Company armies: firing rockets from their camel cavalry to disperse hostile cavalry, for example, long before William Congreve's rocket system was adopted by the British army.[77] More worrying still for Wellesley, the defences of Seringapatam were designed by French engineers on the latest scientific principles, following Sébastian de Vauban's research into artillery-resistant fortification designs, as adapted by the Marquis de Montalembert in his book *La Fortification Perpendiculaire*.* These provided the most up-to-date defences that the eighteenth century could offer, and took into account the newly increased firepower of cannon, bombs and mines, as well as the latest developments in tactics for storming and laying siege to forts.[78]

By mid-April the siege of Seringapatam had begun, and Tipu was showing every sign of resisting with his characteristic ingenuity and tenacity. As one British observer wrote, he 'gave us gun for gun . . . [and night-time skirmishes were] made with desperate exertion . . . Soon the scenes became tremendously grand; shells and rockets of uncommon weight were incessantly poured upon us from the SW side, and fourteen pounders and grape from the North face of the Fort continued their havoc in the trenches; while the blaze of our batteries which frequently caught fire . . . was the signal for the Tiger sepoys [Tipu's élite forces, dressed in tiger-striped uniforms] to advance, and pour in galling vollies of musketry.'[79] It was a brave and skilful defence. But by 3 May, after the guns of the Nizam's contingent had been brought up to within 350 yards of the weakest west corner of the walls, a substantial breach was made, and Harris set the following day for the assault.[80]

At 1 p.m., in the heat of the day, most of Tipu's sepoys went off

---

* Choderlos de Laclos, author of *Les Liaisons Dangereuses*, studied fortifications directly under Montalembert before, in 1793, being offered the job of Governor General of the French settlements in India. He was however arrested before he could take up the post. It is fascinating to speculate about the effect both on the fortifications of Seringapatam, and on the literature of India, if he had made it to Pondicherry. See Jean-Marie Lafont, *Indika: Essays in Indo–French Relations 1630–1976* (New Delhi, 2000), p.186 and p.200 n57.

to rest for the afternoon. In the Company trenches, David Baird, who had spent forty-four months in Tipu's dungeons, roused himself and gave his troops 'a cheering dram and a biscuit'. He then drew his sword, jumped out of the trench and led a storming party – which included two hundred of Mir Alam's best Hyderabadi sepoys – over the River Cauvery and straight into the breach. His two columns scrambled over the glacis and into the city, swinging right and left along the ramparts amid fierce hand-to-hand fighting. Within a few hours the city was in British hands. Baird was later taken to Tipu's body by one of his courtiers. It lay amid a heap of dead and wounded, with three bayonet wounds and a shot through the head. Tipu's eyes were open and the body was so warm that for a few moments, in the torchlight, Baird wondered whether the Sultan was still alive; but feeling his pulse, he declared him dead.*

Already the Mysore casualties hugely outnumbered those of the allies: some nine thousand of Tipu's troops were dead, as opposed to around 350 of the Company and Hyderabadi sepoys. But that night the city of Seringapatam, home to a hundred thousand people, was given over to an unrestrained orgy of rape, looting and killing. Arthur Wellesley told his mother:

> Scarcely a house in the town was left unplundered, and I understand that in camp jewels of the greatest value, bars of gold etc etc have been offered for sale in the bazaars of the army by our soldiers, sepoys and followers. I came in to take command of the army on the morning of the 5th and with the greatest exertion, by hanging, flogging etc etc in the course of that day I restored order ...[81]

The prize committee, whose job it was to distribute the booty, began to collect what was left of Tipu's possessions and the contents

---

* Some secondary sources erroneously have Tipu's body being discovered by Arthur Wellesley. That it was Baird who found him is made quite clear in the letter Baird wrote to General Harris; it can be found in Montgomery Martin (ed.), *The Despatches, Minutes and Correspondence of ... Wellesley* (London, 1836), Vol. 1, pp.687–9. Arthur Wellesley's role in the taking of Seringapatam has been exaggerated by some historians, who have slightly inflated his importance with the benefit of hindsight and in view of his subsequent European triumphs. Baird and Harris were the two ranking officers who at the time were credited with defeating Tipu.

of his treasury: around £1.1 million of gold plate, jewellery, palanquins, the Sultan's solid-gold tiger throne, arms and armour, silks and shawls – 'everything that power could command or money could purchase'.[82]

It was nearly a fortnight later, on 17 May, that one of James's *harkaras** finally galloped into Hyderabad with the news of the great victory. James's confidential *munshi*, or Private Secretary, Aziz Ullah, was already on his way

> to the Durbar to pay his respects to the Minister and His Highness on the occasion of the Feast of Sacrifices [*Bakra 'Id*]. He immediately took with him the substance of the News, and upon him communicating it to the Nizam and Solomon [as James dubbed Aristu Jah], the former immediately put a string of his own pearls on the Munshi's neck, and the latter got up and threw his arms around him. Uzeez Oolah had some difficulty in prevailing on them to postpone a *feu de joye* until I should announce to them the happy event officially, which thank God! I am now enabled to do ... [The Nizam] is in prodigious high spirits [and I was welcomed into the old city] ... by a continued firing of cannon for an hour together from the walls of the city and of Golcondah.[83]

It was a great moment, and a vindication of the Anglo–Hyderabadi alliance James had worked so hard to build. But in the sheer scale of the victory and the stupendous quantity of riches seized by the victorious army lay the seeds of much future dissent, not only between the British and the Nizam, and between Aristu Jah and his victorious general Mir Alam, but also between Wellesley and his masters back in London, and, indirectly, between James Kirkpatrick and all these others.

Wilkie Collins' wonderful Victorian detective story *The Moonstone* opens at the fall of Seringapatam when the narrator's cousin, John Herncastle, seizes 'the Yellow Diamond ... a famous gem in the native annals of India [once] set in the forehead of the four-handed Indian God who typifies the Moon'. To do this Herncastle, 'a torch

---

* Literally 'all do-er': a messenger, runner or newswriter; a spy (or 'intelligencer').

in one hand, and a dagger dripping with blood in the other', murders the Moonstone's three guardians, the last of whom tells him as he dies that the diamond's curse will follow Herncastle to his grave: 'The Moonstone will have its vengeance yet on you and yours!' In the course of the novel, the diamond brings death and bad luck to almost everyone who comes into contact with it, before being seized back by its mysterious Hindu guardians.[84]

The story is of Collins' own invention, and does not pretend to be based on fact. Yet strangely enough, the looting of Seringapatam did act like a curse on many of the leading participants in the plunder, and, remarkably, a hoard of diamonds seized from Tipu's treasury did indeed fatally dog the career of Mir Alam from that moment onwards.*

It was a full five months before the victorious Hyderabadi army marched back to Golconda, where it received a heroes' welcome. On 11 October, according to Abdul Lateef Shushtari, who was in the

---

* Legends of 'cursed' gems were very common in India, the Koh-i-Noor ('Mountain of Light') being the most famous example, as it was reputed to bring disaster on all its male owners. It was taken from Mughal India by the Persian adventurer Nadir Shah, who was assassinated less than a decade after seizing the diamond. Four kings succeeded to the Shah's throne in as many years, the last of whom, Shahrukh Mirza, was blinded and tortured to get possession of the Koh-i-Noor. Several other subsequent rulers were also dethroned and imprisoned before the diamond was eventually taken from the treasury in Lahore and given to Queen Victoria in 1850, a little before the death of Prince Albert. The traveller Richard Burton was appalled when he heard that the Koh-i-Noor was to be given to the Queen, and quoted a Hyderabadi friend of his who asked, 'Are they going to send that accursed thing to the Queen? May she refuse it! All natives spit with horror when they hear it mentioned.' Victoria also appeared to have believed the legend, and gave orders that the stone should only be worn by women. It currently rests in the crown of the late Queen Mother. Another Golconda stone, the 112.5-carat violet-coloured Hope Diamond, has left an even more bloody trail of death, disease, execution, palace coups, revolutions, nervous breakdowns and car crashes behind it, though its current owner, the Smithsonian Institution in Washington, seems to have survived its presence in its galleries without too many fatalities. See Omar Khalidi, *Romance of the Golconda Diamonds* (Ahmedabad, 1999).

crowd to greet his cousin, 'Mir Alam returned to Hyderabad, and the Nizam sent his personal elephant for him to make a triumphal entry. He even ordered the nobility to come 2 or 3 *farsakhs* out of the city to greet him.'* Other Hyderabadi accounts confirm this picture: 'When Mir Alam returned from Seringapatam,' wrote Ghulam Husain Khan, 'his fame reached the skies.'[85] But beneath the surface, tensions were already beginning to become apparent about Mir Alam's behaviour after the victory over Tipu. As Shushtari put it, 'This moment of triumph was also the beginning of his downfall, as courtiers itched with envy and started plotting his downfall.'[86]

The Mir Alam who returned from Seringapatam was a markedly different figure to the man who had set off nine months earlier. Physically, he was weaker, indeed he had been so ill in Madras that his formal audience with Lord Wellesley had had to be delayed, and some even thought he was dying.[87] This severe sickness was the first sign that he had caught the leprosy that would slowly eat away at him over the next decade. But for all his ill-health, the Mir had a new self-confidence – even a distinct arrogance – about him. The spectacular victory over Tipu, the close friendships he had forged with the senior British commanders, and his meeting with Lord Wellesley had all combined to give him a new sense that his rapid rise to power was firmly backed by the Company, and rumours quickly began to spread that he was now intent on overthrowing his old master Aristu Jah, who had irritated the Company officials in Calcutta by his lack of urgency in sending reinforcements and funds to the front in Mysore. Certainly, James noticed a big change in Mir Alam's manner, and soon wrote to William that 'the whole train of MA's conduct from the time of his return to Hyderabad has been a heap of inconsistencies & improprieties, and I really believe that his Lordships distinguished reception of him has turned his head'.[88]

Nor was James the only one to be offended by the Mir's behaviour. Even before his triumphant return, on 14 September, James had

---

* With Mir Alam came the orphaned children of his brother Zein ul-Abidin Shushtari. It is unclear whether the Mir's brother died during the assault on Seringapatam or shortly before it, but Mir Alam henceforth took his Mysore nephews and nieces into his own household.

reported that the Nizam was 'extremely out of humour if not deeply irritated with Meer Allum who has I believe more enemies than friends in the Mahl [*zenana*]'.[89] This was an ominous development, for as James well understood, the Nizam's women – especially the two senior wives, Bakshi Begum and Tînat un-Nissa Begum – had a great deal of influence over the professional life expectancy of the Nizam's advisers and ministers. If they had taken against Mir Alam, then the Mir had cause to worry. But it seems that in the flush of his success he simply did not notice the effect his behaviour was having.

The Nizam and Aristu Jah did in fact both have several good reasons to be exasperated with Mir Alam. Firstly, they were deeply upset with the way that after the victory in May, Tipu's dominions had been carved up by the victorious British. The British feared that the Marathas would be seriously alarmed if the Nizam and the British simply divided Tipu's vast territory between them, thus hugely increasing their power and resources, to the obvious detriment of the Marathas, who had refused to participate in the campaign and were therefore unentitled to any share of the spoils. So a committee which included William Kirkpatrick had come up with an ingenious – if distinctly dishonourable – way of dividing up the state of Mysore without either enraging the Marathas or giving what the British considered to be too much land and power to the Nizam.

Instead of a simple two-way division of Mysore, the British Partition Committee had eventually decided to give relatively modest chunks of land to themselves and the Nizam, while awarding the lion's share to the ancient Hindu Wadyar dynasty of Mysore, whose lands Tipu's father had conquered and whose Rajah he had displaced. The British made sure, however, that the newly reinstated Mysore Rajah would be utterly beholden to his British donors, thus gaining firm indirect control of the land they were purportedly giving back to its rightful former owners. Lord Wellesley thought this a brilliant solution; but the Nizam was appalled, and quite understandably thought that as he had provided half the army which had defeated Tipu, he should by right be rewarded with half the winnings. He was especially angry when he discovered that Mir Alam had weakly agreed to the division, and put his own seal to the Partition Treaty rather than sending it on to the Nizam for his formal ratification.[90] The Nizam's anger with Mir Alam was increased still further when it emerged that the Mir had at the same time accepted a 'very munificent pension' from Wellesley – a monthly allowance which the Nizam and Aristu Jah suspected was more a reward for his feeble acquiescence in this dubious Partition Treaty than for any help he had afforded during the campaign.[91]

More serious for Mir Alam was the Nizam's disapproval of what had happened to Tipu's captured treasure. In India there was no equivalent to the European tradition of formally dividing the spoils not only between the commanders but among the ordinary troops too. When James heard that Harris had authorised the prize committee to reward the sepoys in this manner, he realised straight away that there would be trouble from the durbar: 'When the Nizam and Minister come to know that the whole of the treasure of the Sultaun ... has been shared amongst the army, they will I am certain be ready to break their hearts with grief and disappointment.' He added: 'I shall endeavour to prepare the Minister gradually for the information, which would be too violent a shock to communicate at once to him.'[92]

Worse still for the Mir were the unconfirmed rumours circulating around Hyderabad that during the plundering of Seringapatam he had somehow got his hands on Tipu's finest jewels, including an extraordinary necklace of egg-sized pearls.[93] It was true that he had presented a fine selection of looted gems worth a staggering eleven lakh rupees to the Nizam on his return; but persistent rumours continued to circulate that these were mere baubles compared to the treasures he had secretly seized for himself.[94] There were also stories doing the rounds which suggested that the Mir had embezzled much of the state treasure he carried with him to the war. Aristu Jah was personally affronted by all of this, and was also seriously worried by the close relationship Mir Alam had forged during the campaign with influential British commanders such as Arthur Wellesley, connections the Mir made no effort to hide from his rival.

Nor was Mir Alam the only member of the Shushtari clan to fall under the displeasure of the Nizam. An intriguing incident had taken place a fortnight before the Mir's return. After the fall of Seringapatam, Bâqar Ali Khan had accompanied Mir Alam and John Malcolm to Madras, whence they had been summoned to be presented to Lord Wellesley. But for some reason Bâqar Ali had suddenly made his excuses, deserted the army and headed back two weeks early to Hyderabad. When news of his desertion reached the durbar, Bâqar Ali was severely criticised by Aristu Jah for having left his post without permission, and at first 'was refused admission to the City'; more ominous still, his petitions asking for forgiveness were returned unopened by the Minister.[95] The dispute fizzled on for some time. According to James, 'hurt at this treatment, the old gentleman in the first emotions of anger, wrote an arzee [petition] to the Minister requesting leave to go to Mecca [i.e. to temporarily give up the world and become a pilgrim]. To this arzee he received no answer which provoked him to such a degree that he positively prohibited his wife and family from continuing their attendance in the Minister's Mahl, and it was not until repeated messages and intreaties from the Boo Begum [one of Aristu Jah's wives], between whom and Baukers family a great intimacy exists, that the Minister allowed him to return thither.'[96] This was all extremely odd – and also extremely unwise and uncharacteristic – behaviour by Bâqar Ali Khan. James's letters are the only source for this incident, and naturally they contain no mention of what would be the most obvious explanation of Bâqar Ali's behaviour: that he had somehow heard rumours that something was afoot in his *zenana*, and the women of the family badly needed his supervision.

For all these growing tensions, the popular mood was still one of celebration, and a great round of public entertainments was organised to celebrate the fall of Tipu. The first party – on 18 October, a week after the return of the army – was a huge nautch at Mir Alam's house during which the Mir's mistress, Mah Laqa Bai Chanda, danced for the audience and presented a book of her poems to John Malcolm.[97] Malcolm, who had become close to the Shushtari clan on the Seringapatam campaign, was also invited to a party at Bâqar Ali's *deorhi*, where he was invited to meet the women of the family – an unprecedented honour, tantamount in the etiquette of the day to declaring him an honorary brother of Bâqar Ali. It was a measure of the family's liberal principles, very far, as one observer put it, 'from the usual narrow prejudices of their sect'.[98]

Nautch parties and *mehfils* in Hyderabad at this period, as in Delhi and Lucknow, tended to be held outside at night in the illuminated garden courtyards of the great palaces. Some of the most alluring descriptions of such parties are given by Farzand Begum's grandfather, Dargah Quli Khan, who writes how,

> in the evenings, the courtyards are swept and sprinkled with water and colourful carpets are spread on a raised platform. Then the established poets start the recitation of *ghazals* . . . [sometimes] *shamiana* tents are erected . . . Dancers entertain the people and good looking women gather in such large numbers that the mere sight of them appeases the appetite, although for the lecherous this does not suffice. The illumination of the lamps and candles is akin to the light in the Valley of *Tur*.* The *omrahs* occupy a separate side which is adorned with most beautiful carpets. They are courteously offered fruits and other delicacies along with perfume. Those desirous of wine are also provided with it . . . The sounds emanating from the bow on the strings of the sarangi are like arrows piercing the heart . . . The music makes people listless with ecstasy and the sounds of appreciation rend the air . . .[99]

James enjoyed such entertainments, and usually stayed to the very end. Certainly, his letters to Calcutta during November are full of apologies for being so behind in his work, and after one particularly late night at Aristu Jah's he excuses himself on the grounds that 'in compliment to the Minister I did not take leave until a very late hour . . . [Indeed] I have engaged myself to a regular nightly attendance during the remainder of the festivities – the fatigue from which will I hope plead as an apology for the lateness of my address to your Lordship.'[100]

Just as this circuit of celebratory parties was coming to an end, the announcement of the forthcoming marriage between the Nizam's

* The Koranic name for Mount Sinai.

son and heir apparent, Sikander Jah, and the granddaughter of Aristu Jah, Jahan Pawar Begum,* prompted a whole new round of entertainments. It also provided James with what he regarded as an important diplomatic opportunity. He was very worried by the marked cooling of relations between the durbar and his Residency which had taken place following the announcement of the much-hated Mysore Partition Treaty, and said he saw 'serious inconveniences from the ill humour' of the Nizam, 'which will increase if not soothed in some way or other'.[101]

Up to this point James had been an unqualified admirer of Lord Wellesley, writing to his brother of his veneration for the Governor General in terms that sometimes come close to hero-worship: 'How I long to throw myself at his Lordship's feet and express to him if possible the deep sense of [my gratitude for] all his goodness towards me,' he had written to William at one point in February 1799. 'I earnestly trust this to be not impracticable before his Lordship's return to Bengal. I really think my veneration and attachment to that great and worthy nobleman is only short of what I feel to my beloved Parent, and of course my love and regard for you.'[102]

Now however James's views were beginning to change. For the first time, the Partition Treaty had led him to re-examine his attitude to Wellesley's aggressive and bullying approach to Indian princes. The Nizam had unflinchingly stuck to his commitments in the 1798 Preliminary Treaty and had provided a huge army at very short notice to fight alongside the British at Seringapatam. The reward of the Hyderabadis was to be cheated of their full share in the division of the spoils. Irritated by this, and by the damage it had done to his carefully nurtured relations with the Hyderabad durbar, James now wrote to his friend General William Palmer, the Resident in Pune, openly criticising the Governor General's policy: 'I perfectly concur in the justness of your reflexions respecting our late dictatorialness of spirit. Our success indeed appears to me to have somewhat intoxicated us.'[103] It was a view that James would hold more and more strongly over the following months.

---

* Jahan Pawar Begum was the daughter of Sharaf un-Nissa's great friend Farzand Begum. Her father was Ma'ali Mian, Aristu Jah's son, who had died on the way to the Battle of

In order to try to undo some of the damage done by this Treaty, he now wrote to Calcutta for permission to lay on a major *jashn* (the word means simply 'party', but in this case refers to a post-marriage feast) – for Aristu Jah and the Nizam, during which generous presents could be presented to all the members of the Nizam's and the Minister's families, including the key members of both *zenanas*, and so pour oil on the troubled waters.[104]

James realised that it was not going to be easy to sell such massive expenditure to a thoroughly sceptical Lord Wellesley, who would never be particularly enamoured of the idea of spending so much money on 'natives', least of all in making donations to the women of various harems, troupes of *nautch* girls and a series of Hyderabadi Sufi shrines. In his letter, therefore, James acknowledged that from the point of view of Calcutta 'the time is no doubt gone by when the friendship or enmity of this state was an object of serious importance to us, and nothing but some strange vicissitude can hereafter render its smiles or its frowns of much consequence to us. Nevertheless you will no doubt agree with me that harmony and good understanding are at all times desirable things between states in alliance and that it is better if possible to maintain our ascendancy and influence in this by conciliatory acts than by any other means.'[105]

In the event Lord Wellesley refused to countenance James's initial estimate of over three lakh rupees for the *jashn*, but he did finally authorise him to throw a more modest party costing one lakh. A date in April 1800 was set, as custom dictated, five months after Sikander Jah's marriage.

As the great state marriage grew imminent, gatherings of the durbar were increasingly marred by clashes between Aristu Jah and Mir Alam. 'Meer Allum and Solomon have been sparring a great deal of late,' James wrote on 1 November, 'so much so, indeed, that the Meer has sent his son Meer Dauran twice to me, to request my advice or interposition on the occasion . . . candidly acknowledging at the same time, that the open declaration of my readiness to take his part to the extent required would in all probability enable him to carry the

Khardla, after which she and her mother Farzand Begum had continued to live in the Minister's *zenana*.

points [with Aristu Jah] he was contending for'.[106] When James politely declined to intervene, Mir Alam let it be known – to James's surprise and mild alarm – that he regarded it as a personal insult.

The real crisis point was however reached two days later on 3 November, during the middle of the wedding celebrations. Aristu Jah had thrown the wedding party at Purani Haveli, one of his residences which he had just gifted to his granddaughter as part of her dowry. James had arrived with the senior Residency staff and some of the more senior army officers led by James Dalrymple, along with 'the trays containing dresses and jewels for the brides principal male and female relatives'. They had sent 'various trays of viands together with a large assortment of confectionary into the female apartments for distribution', and had themselves been 'regaled agreeably, as is the usage on such occasions, with sherbet'. Moreover each British officer was presented with a valuable *sarpèche* or turban jewel. Aristu Jah, huge bearlike man though he was, spent much of the party in tears, 'so great is his grief in parting with his granddaughter in whom all his affections centre'.[107]

Later that night, very publicly, in front of the gathered Hyderabadi nobles, a tearful Aristu Jah challenged Mir Alam as to the whereabouts of Tipu's state jewels. Mir Alam denied all knowledge of them and after a moment's silence and extreme embarrassment the festivities continued; but everyone realised that a point of no return had been reached in the relationship between the two most powerful officials in Hyderabad.

Even so, when Mir Alam left Hyderabad a few days later to take up his post as Governor of the newly conquered Mysore district of Rydroog, few could have guessed how swift, complete and ingenious Aristu Jah's retribution would be.

Mir Alam was the Nizam's official *vakil* to the Company, effectively his Minister for British Affairs. Ever since his three-year stay in Calcutta with Bâqar Ali Khan from 1787 the Mir had had excellent contacts with the senior Company staff in Calcutta, and Aristu Jah realised that if he wished to disgrace him, he would have first to alienate him from his British supporters. He now set about using James and Khair un-Nissa as the unwitting agents of this revenge. His plan was as brilliant as it was simple.

Mir Alam had already heard rumours about James's infatuation with his cousin, and according to James had joshed him good-naturedly on the subject before he left Hyderabad again at the end of December.[108] The Mir clearly had no idea, however, how far the relationship had progressed. So, shortly after Mir Alam arrived at his new posting in January 1800, Aristu Jah hit on the simple but ingenious ruse of leaking the news to a Hyderabadi newswriter, but in a deliberately exaggerated form.

The two resulting newsletters – or *akhbars* – accused James not just of sleeping with Khair un-Nissa but of raping her, and of using his position to force her mother and grandfather to hand the girl over to him for his pleasure. Moreover, the *akhbar* included several titbits of gossip about James's previous revelries in Hyderabad, including a long and complicated tale of how James had 'debauched a brazier's wife', leaving the cuckolded husband to attempt to commit suicide at the most public place in Hyderabad, directly in front of the Char Minar. There was a kernel of truth behind the story: there was a brazier's wife, and she had indeed attempted to take shelter from her abusive husband with her mother who worked in the Residency; but James had never seen her, and when the woman was called in front of the Hyderabad durbar, her far from attractive physical features were enough to convince the court of James's complete innocence.[109]

There was however a much more serious charge contained in the newsletters. Sharaf un-Nissa's brother, and Khair un-Nissa's uncle, Mahmud Ali Khan had died soon after Mir Alam's departure for Rydroog, after a gun he was playing with – part of the loot from Seringapatam – had exploded in his face.[110] Bâqar Ali Khan had testified that 'the gun accidentally burst as he [Mahmud] discharged it . . . he retained his sense and talked until 9pm in the night and himself mentioned that this had happened in consequence of the trait which he had always had since his infancy of amusing himself with fireworks'.[111] But according to the scurrilous newsletter, the story was much darker: the uncle had strongly opposed Khair un-Nissa's relationship with James, and had been quietly assassinated on the Resident's orders so as to remove the one remaining obstacle to him attaining his wicked ends. As James reported to William, the *akhbar* maintained 'that I sent or hired people to despatch him as an obstacle to my views on his Niece, or as other [gossips] related it, that I presented him with the fatal weapon, from the extreme badness of which I foresaw all that actually followed'.[112]

Beyond the central undeniable truth that James had been sleeping with Khair un-Nissa, none of these charges had any basis in fact; but they were sufficiently credible for Mir Alam – already angry with James for failing to take his side with Aristu Jah – to believe them. Once they had been published, according to the historian Ghulam Husain Khan's contemporary account, the *Gulzar i-Asafiya*, 'Aristu Jah wrote all the details of this affair [in an anonymous letter] and sent it to Mir Alam at Krapa . . . So it was that he [Mir Alam] wrote to Calcutta to the Lord Bahadur [Wellesley] demanding that the scandalous behaviour of Hushmat Jang [Kirkpatrick] should be punished as it deserved, to be a warning to others. Mir Alam acted according to the suggestion, and wrote a fulminating letter demanding Hushmat Jang's execution.'[113]

Mir Alam had fallen straight into Aristu Jah's trap. As Aristu Jah had guessed he would, Wellesley reacted to Mir Alam's letter by writing immediately to the Nizam and Aristu Jah, demanding to know the truth about Mir Alam's charges.

He sent the letter via James. On the morning of 7 March 1800, James received in the weekly *dak* (post) what was probably the single most terrifying missive he was ever to be sent by Wellesley. There were none of the pleasantries or compliments he was used to. Instead the letter was as abrupt as it was menacing. It simply instructed James that

as soon as you shall have read the [enclosed] papers [i.e. copies of the *akhbars*] you will lay them before His Highness

and Azim ul-Omrah [Aristu Jah]. You will in my name request
H.H. & the Minister to insert on the blank margins of the
papers such observations as may occur to them on the allega-
tion contained in the papers. I request HH and the Minister
will authenticate their respective observations under their
hands and seals. You will add such explanations as may appear
necessary to vindicate your character against the heavy charges
which these papers contain. In the meantime my judgement
on the matter of those charges will remain suspended & the
subjects will be preserved in the strictest secrecy.[114]

At this point, according to the usually very reliable *Gulzar i-Asafiya*,
Aristu Jah called in James. 'After some cockfighting' he made it clear
how serious the charges were, pointed out that James's fate rested
in his hands, and outlined what James's fate would be if he chose to
corroborate Mir Alam's charges.[115] Then he effectively offered to cut
a deal. If James sacked Mir Alam as the Company's *vakil* and was
prepared to work with Aristu Jah for the best interests of Hyderabad,
then in return the Minister would make sure that James's name was
completely cleared. He would personally persuade the Nizam to write
to Wellesley, telling him that the charges were a malicious invention
of Mir Alam. The dialogue put into James's mouth in the *Gulzar
i-Asfiya* is presumably invented, but the substance of the conversation
has the clear ring of truth and tallies with all the other evidence:

> Kirkpatrick went to have a private interview with Aristu Jah
> to beg for his life and his position, saying: 'It was the girl who
> became obsessed with me. I did nothing; it was she who came
> and threw herself at me. I used no force. If you write this to
> Lord Bahadur, my life will be safe. In recognition for this
> great help, as long as I remain Resident here, I shall never
> forget the debt I owe, *I shall strive for the best interests of your
> government and will obey all your orders.*' [My italics.]
>
> Aristu Jah replied: 'If I did try my utmost to have your life
> spared, I wonder whether you would be willing or able to do
> that service that I would require of you in return?'
>
> Hushmut Jung [Kirkpatrick] asked: 'And what is that?'
>
> Aristu Jah made Hushmut Jung swear to total and utter

secrecy, then said: 'To have Mir Alam dismissed from the service of the English Resident and that I might succeed him in that office so that the Nizam's Prime Minister and the English political agent will be as one – if you could persuade Calcutta to instruct the Nizam accordingly?'

Hushmut Jung accepted with all his soul, and swore to keep his part of the bargain.

Then Aristu Jah went into the presence of the Nizam and presented the case according to Hushmut Jung's version, that he was completely innocent . . . [and Mir Alam was guilty of wilfully wrecking relations with the British by making unsubstantiated allegations against the blameless British Resident]. They sent the letter making this point to Calcutta, and the English notables, after due consideration, wrote that: 'If Hushmat Jang is not guilty, and if the Nizam's government is content to have him still as Resident, then let him keep his position. We are only concerned to secure the satisfaction of the Nizam's government.'

In addition, about the dismissal of Mir Alam, they added: 'The Nizam is master of his servants, and is free to choose and appoint as he wishes. We are happy to rely on his choice. However, if Aristu Jah is appointed, what could be better, on condition that Mir Alam's life and honour and property are all safe!'

When this letter with its welcome answer reached Hyderabad, Hushmat Jang attended court, and Mir Alam was dismissed from his post as *Vakil* to the English, and also from the lucrative post of overseeing the newly conquered territories. He was imprisoned in isolation in Rudrur fort without the right to meet anyone else.'[116]

How seriously can this evidence be taken? Did Aristu Jah really succeed in using Khair un-Nissa not only as a way of disposing of his increasingly dangerous rival Mir Alam, but also as a way of 'turning' Kirkpatrick? And what exactly did Kirkpatrick's promise to *'strive for the best interests of your government and obey all your orders'* actually entail? Was he really promising to betray his country and become some sort of double-agent – a late-eighteenth-century Philby, Burgess or Maclean? Or was he expressing a more general sympathy with – and affection for – Hyderabad, and saying that in gratitude for Aristu Jah's intervention he would always be willing to help the Minister whenever he could?

With the evidence available, so long after the event, this question is now almost impossible to answer. Certainly James had always been sympathetic to Hyderabad, and became more so the longer he stayed in the town. He also grew increasingly outraged by what he believed to be the completely unacceptable threats and aggression used by Wellesley to put pressure not only on his Hyderabadi allies, but on several other independent Indian princes, to enter into ever more unequal treaties with the British. James was also appalled by Wellesley's failure to honour his obligations in those treaties he had signed. It is difficult, however, to know now how much this was due to his own increasingly anti-Imperial political views and his longstanding fondness for Hyderabad, and how much to the fact that Aristu Jah now had a lever with which he could put pressure on James. For, by strenuously denying to the Governor General Mir Alam's charges that he had raped Khair un-Nissa and murdered her uncle, James had been able to skate over the fact that there was a real basis to the scandal which underlay these stories, and that he had indeed been sleeping with Mir Alam's teenage cousin. He had not told any blatant lies to the Governor General; but nor had he come completely clean. This was a grey area which left James extremely vulnerable, and open to further manipulation by the wily Minister.

The question as to the reliability of the evidence is easier to answer. On its own perhaps the *Gulzar* would not necessarily carry much weight, though it is in general an unusually accurate and well-informed record of the period. But the same story is repeated in two other independent Hyderabadi histories – the *Tarikh i-Asaf Jahi* and the slightly later *Tarikh i-Nizam*[117] – as well as in an investigation into the affair commissioned by the Residency after James's death, which concluded that he had 'ingratiated himself into the good graces of Aristu Jah, and by promising to stand by him in all his straits he succeeded in the fulfilment of his desires'.[118]

Much more importantly, Mir Alam himself clearly believed that Aristu Jah had succeeded in blackmailing James, and that together the two had conspired to ruin him. Certainly he told this story to Arthur Wellesley six months later, in September 1800. The Mir had just been released from imprisonment but was still in deep disgrace, and had been banned from returning to the city of Hyderabad. Arthur Wellesley wrote immediately to his brother the Governor General to pass on what Mir Alam had told him, and his evidence is important as it is the earliest and most direct version of the story which later appears in a much fuller version in the *Gulzar*.

It is unclear if Arthur Wellesley ever met James; but it is quite apparent in his writings that he actively disliked William Kirkpatrick, whom he did know, and nothing he had heard about James did anything to alter his decided prejudice against both Kirkpatrick brothers. Moreover, he had come to rather admire the efficient, intelligent and unemotional Mir Alam, with whom he had worked closely during the campaign against Tipu. So when Mir Alam and his followers, newly released from captivity and heading into internal exile, fortuitously bumped into the future Duke of Wellington and his regiment in the middle of rural Karnataka in September 1800, Arthur was quite prepared to give the Mir's version of events the benefit of the doubt.

On 21 September, the day after their chance meeting, Mir Alam laid on a nautch performance for Wellesley and his officers in a garden close to the fort of Koppal, just to the north-west of the ruins of the great Hindu capital of Vijayanagar (modern Hampi). 'During the noise of the nautch,' Arthur wrote in a memorandum which he sent Lord Wellesley in an official despatch written a few days later, 'Meer Allum took the opportunity of entering into conversation with Col W[ellesley – i.e. himself] regarding his exile and disgrace. He began by saying that the fountain of justice no longer flowed towards him; that it was stopped by William Kirkpatrick in Bengal and his brother at Hyderabad, and that he depended solely on Col W for a representation of his case to the Governor-General.'[119]

Mir Alam then told the whole story to Arthur: how Aristu Jah had long wanted to have him disgraced, but finally succeeded in his object by using Kirkpatrick; how Kirkpatrick had wickedly seduced Khair un-Nissa; how Aristu Jah 'had known of the affair from its commencement', and tried to put the family of Ahmed Ali Khan off the idea of their son marrying Khair un-Nissa; how at first no one had dared to tell him – Mir Alam – about the developments; and how he, having at length been informed of the disgraceful behaviour of Kirkpatrick, wrote at once to the Governor General telling him what had happened; but that the Governor General – not knowing Aristu Jah's close involvement with the affair –

> thought the enquiry belonged to the Nizam's government, and referred it to the Nizam ... [whereupon Aristu Jah] reported upon it that there was no ground whatever of complaint; that the whole story was a fabrication ... He [Mir Alam] then contended that the whole had been a plan of Azim ul-Omrahs [Aristu Jah's] to ruin Mir Alam; that he knew that as long as Meer Allum was supported by Kirkpatrick it would be impossible to disgrace him, but that the moment he could deprive him of that support he was undone; that he had availed himself of the passions of Hushmut Jung [Kirkpatrick] to make it impossible that Meer Allum could ever connect himself with him in politics again.[120]

All the other Hyderabadi accounts that refer to Kirkpatrick's use of Hyderabadi clothes and customs speak of how much the people of the city were pleased and even flattered by his fondness for their culture, but on this occasion the Mir

> launched into abuse of Kirkpatrick [saying] ... that he had long respected the English for their steadiness and their adherence to their own manners and customs in private life, and their respect upon all occasions for the manners and customs of Hindustan, particularly those relating to women ... but

that Kirkpatrick, by dressing himself in the garb of a native and by the adoption of their manners, had made himself ridiculous, and was detested for his interference with their women. He said that if Col W did not believe him, he begged that he would send an hircarrah [messenger] to Hyderabad and desire him only to bring news of Hushmut Jung . . .[121]

In the context of his dismissal and disgrace, Mir Alam's claims that James's crossing of cultures was regarded as 'ridiculous' can be taken with a fair pinch of salt, especially as we know from a note by Kirkpatrick – on the back of the only surviving miniature which shows him in Hyderabadi dress – that the clothes he is depicted wearing were actually given to him by Mir Alam so that he could wear them at the marriage of Mir Alam's son Mir Dauran in November 1799.* But the remark nevertheless provides a fascinating counterpoint to the view of, for example, the historian Ghulam Imam Khan who in his *Tarikh i-Khurshid Jahi* stresses on several occasions that James's adoption of Hyderabadi manners had made him especially popular in the city. It would be fascinating to know whether Mir Alam's remarks reflected a widespread view in Hyderabad, or merely the Mir's own anger and bitterness at losing his job.[122] The remark does certainly highlight the contradictions and limitations to James's transculturation: he might wear Indian dress, have an Indian lover and embrace Indian customs; but he remained – at least in the eyes of his political enemies – a *firangi* interloper and the official representative of an alien power.

Mir Alam concluded his tirade by asking Arthur Wellesley to 'represent his case to the Governor General in order that Kirkpatrick might be removed' and that he 'be allowed to return to his house and family'. He also warned that Kirkpatrick was now 'so completely under the

* The miniature is still in the possession of Kirkpatrick's descendants. The inscription in his hand is on the reverse of the image and reads in full: 'This was copied from a sketch taken of me in the Hindostanny dress presented me by Meer Allum & which I wore at his particular request at his son Meer Dowraun's nuptials; with this difference, that the original drawing which was made by old Shah Tajully was a more flattering – and according to the opinion of those who saw it a more faithful – likeness in a sitting posture and the coloured dress which I had on at the time and which was *nah firmaun* [more appropriate].' The inscription on the front reads in Persian: 'Mutamin ul-Mulk, Fakhr ud-Dowlah Bahadur, Hushmat Jung'.

influence of the Minister that it was to be expected that he would attend more to the objects of the Nizam's court than those of his own government'.[123] As Wellesley noted in his memo to his brother, 'if it were true that the Minister had told a falsehood to screen Kirkpatrick from disgrace, he must be a very convenient Resident to the Nizam's Government'.

The day after the nautch, Arthur Wellesley wrote to his friend Colonel Barry Close: 'It will be impossible in my opinion to do anything for Mir Alam. The strong desire of Aristoojah to get rid of him is the cause of his removal . . . [and] Hushmut Jung's passions have thrown him into the hands of Aristoojah and he could do nothing . . .' He added, in a tone of characteristic understatement, 'It is a curious story altogether.'[124]

In the months which followed, Mir Alam, now unprotected by the British, underwent a series of further misfortunes.

Aristu Jah's spies had confirmed the rumours that the Mir had secretly acquired a set of spectacular gems at the sack of Seringapatam. Now that the Mir was under arrest, the Minister was determined to find where he had hidden them all. He questioned Mir Alam's son, Mir Dauran, and his brother-in-law, Mustaqim ud-Daula. Both denied all knowledge of the stones. So Aristu Jah sent in a force of soldiers to Mir Alam's mansion and ransacked it. They also tortured his *khansaman* or steward. When none of these measures had any effect, they burned the steward's house down.[125]

Khair un-Nissa's grandfather Bâqar Ali Khan had, meanwhile, become deeply unpopular with all his kinsmen, who regarded him as indirectly responsible for Mir Alam's disgrace. As the story of James's affair spread, Bâqar Ali was jeered 'in the streets [and accused of] having prostituted his grand daughter to the Resident'. At one point 'abusive papers' were stuck up around the Char Minar insulting him.[126]

Sometime in June, Lieutenant Colonel James Dalrymple, now the most senior British soldier in Hyderabad, was out on a hunting expedition with Lieutenant Colonel Bowser a day's journey from the city, when a message 'was delivered by a servant of Bauker Aly, requesting us as his oldest and best friends to pay him a visit the next morning in order that he might consult with us on an affair of importance'. Dalrymple loved his *shikar* (hunting) – his will is full of detailed instructions for the disposal of his beloved 'Arab horse, the little horse called Mamoola, and all my hounds' – but realised something important was up and immediately turned back to the city.[127]

James Dalrymple had been a close friend of Bâqar Ali for at least five years, and the two had fought side by side at the capture of Raichur during the rebellion of the Nizam's son-in-law Dara Jah in 1796.[128]* Now, so it seemed to Dalrymple, Bâqar Ali Khan's friendliness and hospitality had been badly abused, causing his old friend to be almost outcast from his clan. Dalrymple went to see Bâqar Ali first thing the following morning, and found the old man to be in a state of considerable agitation.

Four months earlier, in March, Bâqar Ali had helped Kirkpatrick out of his troubles by writing a signed statement to Wellesley declaring that the claims in the scandalous *akhbars* were nonsense: that James had neither raped his granddaughter nor murdered his son, that the charges were 'an absolute falsehood & a mere calumny', and that towards James he felt nothing but 'gratitude and obligation'.[129] Since then, however, the old man had clearly heard many more of the rumours linking Kirkpatrick with his granddaughter, and he needed Dalrymple to help him put a stop to it all.[130] Moreover, Khair un-Nissa was still firmly refusing to marry the son of Ahmed Ali

---

* After this engagement, Dalrymple had organised a joint letter from all the officers to be sent to James Kirkpatrick, then newly appointed as Resident in place of his brother William, testifying to Bâqar Ali's bravery and kindness: 'We cannot in justice withhold our warmest acknowledgements, nor omit declaring that no man whatever could have excited himself with more warmth or attachment, or have accorded himself with more gentlemanly acquiescence to our differing habits and customs, than he has done.' OIOC, Kirkpatrick Papers, Mss Eur F228/83, f.1, Camp at Rachore, 1 May 1796, James Dalrymple et al to James Kirkpatrick.

Khan, to whom she continued 'to testify an unequivocal aversion'.[131] Bâqar Ali – so it seems – had been the last to discover about his granddaughter's 'partiality' for Kirkpatrick, and apparently still did not know quite how far the relationship had gone; but he was – albeit belatedly – well aware that there was a great deal of gossip linking the two, as the insults and bill-posters had made plain. Khair un-Nissa's engagement to the son of Ahmed Ali Khan had still not been formally broken off, but Bâqar realised it was likely to be if there were any more scandals associated with her. Bâqar said he wanted Dalrymple to talk to Kirkpatrick, and tell him firmly to keep away from Khair un-Nissa. His granddaughter, he told Dalrymple,

> had been demanded in marriage by a Mussulman of great respectability, and he was desirous of concluding that alliance. But the Resident had been using every means in his power to impede the marriage, and had sent repeated messages and communications with that view to the females of his family ... [He] expressed an indignation approaching to phrenzy at the indignity offered to the honour of his family by such proceedings, and he declared his intention of proceeding to the Mecca Masjid (the principal mosque of the city) and stating the fact to the Mussulmen assembled: I will march, said he, at their head to take vengeance on the person of your Resident, and we will see what opposition his escort can make against the indignation and fury of the whole Mussulman body.[132]

This was looking very bad indeed. Hyderabad was a vital ally and a crucial strategic asset for the British. There was still a French army at large in Egypt, and there was still, in the Marathas, an Indian army on the borders of Hyderabad that was quite capable of joining a disaffected Hyderabad and together turning the British out of India once and for all. Now, so it seemed, Kirkpatrick's libido was endangering everything, and causing a major anti-British uprising in the Deccan. Faced with this potentially catastrophic turn of events, Dalrymple read the riot act to James: 'Colonel [Dalrymple] represented to the Resident the fatal consequences not only to his own personal safety but to the public interests which must result in persevering in a conduct so improper.'[133] He demanded, in short, that James stop seeing Khair un-Nissa.*

James was forced to agree to keep his distance from the girl – at least for the time being, at least until the scandal blew over. After all, his own position was far from secure. He had very nearly lost his job over the affair already, and realised that he simply could not afford to ignore the explicit wishes of both Bâqar Ali and Dalrymple. His failure to come completely clean to Lord Wellesley about Khair un-Nissa had left him very vulnerable to gossip, especially from the British military in Hyderabad, over whom he had limited authority; and there was every reason to believe that having excused him once, Wellesley would not take it very kindly if further complaints about James's womanising were made; still less would he sit back if James's adventures were to lead to an anti-British rebellion. So James really had no choice: he gave Dalrymple 'a solemn promise ... that he would refrain from all intercourse with Bauker's family'.

By the mid-summer of 1800, therefore, it appeared that the brief affair between James and Khair un-Nissa, which had already caused so much havoc, was over; or so at least it must have seemed to Kirkpatrick, Dalrymple and Bâqar Ali Khan.

None of them could have guessed that the real trouble was in fact just beginning. For what none of these three men knew, and what the women in Bâqar Ali's *zenana* must have been all too aware of, was that Khair un-Nissa was now three months pregnant with James Kirkpatrick's child.

---

* James Dalrymple was himself married to the daughter of the Nawab of Masulipatam and had five children by her, so he was in a good position to understand the finer points in the etiquette of dealing with such interracial relationships. Scottish Records Office, Edinburgh, GD135/2086, The Will of Lieutenant Colonel James Dalrymple, Hussein Sagar, 8 December 1800.

V

TOWARDS THE END OF NOVEMBER 1800, James wrote to Calcutta to report that 'The annual *'urs* [festival] to Mawlah Ali is close at hand, and I propose going there and staying in my tents in a few days, for the benefit of fresh air and recreation.'[1]

It was not just James who planned to leave the city for the *'urs*. Great swathes of the population of Hyderabad took the opportunity to break from their routine for ten days and to set off twenty miles to the north on a short pilgrimage whose attractions mixed the satisfaction of piety with the pleasures of novelty and a change of air. It was at once a pilgrimage and a pageant, a sacred festival and what James described in one letter as a 'tenting holiday'.[2]

The festival commemorated a vision of Ali, the Prophet's son-in-law, granted two hundred years earlier to a senior eunuch in the Qutb Shahi court named Yaqut ('Ruby'). One night Ruby the Eunuch was asleep when a man in green came to him in a dream, and told him he was being called by Maula Ali,* the husband of the Prophet's daughter Fatima, and the most revered figure in Shi'a devotion. Ruby followed the mysterious figure in green and was led to a place where Maula Ali was seated on the summit of a hill, with his right hand resting upon a rock. Ruby fell down before the figure, but before he could say anything, he awoke. The following morning, Ruby set off from Golconda in his palanquin and went up the hill, where he found the mark of Maula Ali's hand branded on the stone where it

* Maula in this context meaning 'My Lord'.

had rested during the night. Ruby ordered the handmark to be hewn out of the stone and placed in a great arch he built on the site.

The rock soon became a popular centre of devotion for Sufis, mystics and ascetics, and after one of the Golconda princesses renounced the world and became a hermit on the hill, the Shi'a Qutb Shahi sultans began leading an annual pilgrimage to the site on the anniversary of Ruby's vision. After the conquest of Hyderabad by the Sunni Mughals in 1687 the festival went into temporary decline, and it was only after the Nizam's family began to patronise the 'urs from the 1780s onwards that the pilgrimage again grew to become one of the two great national festivals of Asaf Jahi Hyderabad. The women of the Nizam's zenana seem to have particularly welcomed the opportunity to escape from the city for a few days, and one of the Nizam's two most influential wives, Tînat un-Nissa Begum, gave her blessing to the 'urs by building a garden complex not far from the shrine which she named Tînat Nagar; here she and the Nizam stayed for the festival as well as for occasional winter hunting expeditions.[3] Word spread among the townspeople that Maula Ali himself could be seen wandering around the shrine on his birthday, and such was the popularity of the 'urs that rather than being celebrated on a single day as in Qutb Shahi times, the festival gradually became extended: 'The coming and going of visitors increased constantly, the 'Urs grew accordingly, and all the distinguished citizens of the town came out for rest and recreation and stayed to enjoy the long nights of revelry.'[4]

A line of lamps was lit on either side of the road all the way from the Char Minar to Koh e-Sharif, the shrine of Maula Ali. Haloed in dust, much of the population of the city, and indeed of the surrounding towns and villages, of whatever faith, would set off on foot, on bullock cart, in palanquins and on elephant-back to a lush green stretch of country enclosed in a bend in the Musi, and bounded by a group of three smooth volcanic hills, one large, two slightly smaller. By 1800 the festival lasted from Ali's birthday, on the thirteenth of Rajab,* to the anniversary of the vision on the seventeenth, and many

* In the Islamic lunar calendar.

of the people, from stallholders to great *omrahs*, stayed in the area for as long as ten days.[5] Amid the smell of sweat and spices, elephant dung and the wafts of hot cooking from the roadside stalls, the highest officials of the Deccan rubbed shoulders with trinket-sellers and stable boys, soldiers and sepoys, diamond merchants, senior courtiers and, in particular, the courtesans.

For in that strange link between piety and prostitution that existed all over India at this period – both among the *devadasis** of the great Hindu temples and the Muslim courtesans who used to pick up their clients in the great Sufi shrines† – this was a festival especially associated with the *tawaif*, the cultivated and urbane dancing girls who were such a central feature of late Mughal society. Across India at this most libertine moment in the country's recent history, such festivals, with their music and high spirits and unrestricted mixing of men and women, had become notoriously convenient occasions to meet lovers. One young Hyderabadi of the period described the scene at an *'urs* as follows:

> Chandeliers of all kinds are hung [inside the shrine], and the artisans come and give the lamps the shape of trees which when lighted put to shame even the cypresses. When the place is fully lighted, it dazzles like sunlight and over-shadows the moon ... Hand in hand lovers roam the streets [around the shrine], while the debauched and drunken, unmindful of the *kotwal* [police] revel in all kinds of perversities. There are beautiful faces as far as the eye can see. Whores and winsome lads entice more and more people to this atmosphere of lasciviousness. Nobles can be seen in every nook and corner [of the shrine] while the singers, *qawals* and beggars outnumber even the flies and the mosquitoes. In short both the nobles and plebeians quench the thirst of their lust there.[6]

The link between the *tawaifs* and the Maula Ali festival was especially strong due to the influence of the greatest of all the *tawaifs* of

---

* Literally 'slave girls of the gods': temple dancers, prostitutes and courtesans who were given to the great Hindu temples, usually in infancy.
† See for example the use of Delhi Sufi shrines as places to meet lovers and pick up prostitutes, as recorded by Dargah Quli Khan (trans. Chander Shekhar), in *The Muraqqa' e-Dehli* (New Delhi, 1989), e.g. p.7.

the Deccan, Mah Laqa Bai Chanda. Her mother, Raj Kanwar Bai, who was also a celebrated courtesan, was six months into her pregnancy when, in the spring of 1764, she went on a pious outing to the shrine with James's friend, the Nizam's court historian and painter, Tajalli Ali Shah. Just as they were approaching the Koh e-Sharif, Raj Kanwar Bai began bleeding and appeared to be suffering a miscarriage. Tajalli Shah took her straight up to the shrine, where they bought some sacred threads to tie around Raj Kanwar's waist and ate the *prasad** given to them by the *pirzadas* (officials). Raj Kanwar Bai miraculously recovered and Mah Laqa was born a beautiful and healthy child three months later.[7]

In gratitude, the family became prominent donors to the shrine, and due to their influence and prestige the Nizam and his family began attending the *'urs* of Maula Ali. Mah Laqa's uncle, the assassinated Prime Minister Rukn ud-Daula,† was buried just below the shrine, and in 1800, the year James first attended the *'urs*, Mah Laqa herself had just begun building a magnificent garden tomb at its base, where she laid her mother and where, in due course, she too would be buried, under a Persian inscription that described her as a 'cypress of the garden of grace and rose tree of the grove of coquetry'.[8]

Other *tawaifs*, and the musicians who worked with them, donated guest houses for the pilgrims, mosques, ceremonial arches and *naqqar khanas* (drum houses), as well as pools and fountains and pleasure gardens in the countryside nearby. According to Ghulam Husain Khan, 'There are on the upper slopes of the Koh e-Sharif, many buildings commissioned by the courtesans. This is where they congregate during the *'urs*. There they serve delicious foods, have fireworks

* Temple sweets given to devotees in exchange for offerings – a tradition that was transferred from Hindu to Islamic practice in many Sufi shrines.
† According to the biography commissioned by Mah Laqa, the *Hyat-e-Mah-e-Laqa*, towards the end of his life the Prime Minister Mir Musa Khan, entitled Rukn ud-Daula, married his courtesan mistress, Mahtab Kanwar, who was the sister of Raj Kanwar Bai, and the aunt of Mah Laqa. Mahtab Kanwar also appears to have been the mistress of Aristu Jah at some point in her career. Ghulam Samdani Gohar, *Hyat-e-Mah-e-Laqa* (Hyderabad, n.d.), and Rahat Azmi, *Mah-e-laqa* (Hyderabad, 1998). The source of this information – in a book personally commissioned by Mah Laqa – may mean that it should be treated with a certain scepticism. It was most unusual for courtesans formally to marry into the nobility (though it was their stock in trade to have affairs with them); but then, Mah Laqa's dynasty does appear to have been unusual in almost all respects.

and illuminations, adding to all these pleasures the delights of musical *raags*.' During the *'urs*, in these illuminated gardens the *tawaifs* would give dance displays far into the night, as well as – presumably – providing all the other services that made them so sought-after among the Hyderabadi nobility.[9]

As well as being a popular excuse for a holiday, the festival played an important political role, by allowing the Nizams to reach out across the sectarian divide in the Hyderabadi aristocracy, a divide that split the nobles of the kingdom straight down the middle. The old Qutb Shahi élite, as well as the other old Deccani families from towns such as Aurangabad and Bidar, had been almost entirely Shi'a. Their numbers had been augmented by the large numbers of new Shi'a Persian immigrants welcomed to Hyderabad by a succession of Shi'a Ministers including Aristu Jah and Mir Alam.[10] The Nizams were however themselves solidly Sunni, as were the nobles of the élite Paigah clan and most of the Mughal soldiers and courtiers who had emigrated from Delhi to join them in the Deccan.* The two groups regarded each other with suspicion, and as James's Assistant Henry Russell later wrote, 'a considerable degree of jealousy subsists between the two sects, and they seldom intermarry'.[11] Yet despite its Shi'a inspiration, the festival of Maula Ali was celebrated by both Sunni and Shi'a with equal enthusiasm; moreover the popular devotion to holy relics which formed the centrepiece of the festival was also accessible to Hyderabad's Hindus, both high and low; indeed, as today, Hindus often outnumbered Muslims at a shrine which in any other country might have become a centre for exclusively Shi'a sectarian devotion.

Indeed the people of Hyderabad – of whatever sect or religion – were proud of their festival, and the Deccani historian Munshi Khader Khan Bidri boasted patriotically in his *Tarikh i-Asaf Jahi* that 'during the *'urs* the place was so crowded that wise and elderly people were of the opinion that no place in Delhi, or indeed anywhere else in India had such a vast crowd on any occasion'.[12] They certainly did

---

* Nizam ul-Mulk had led the newcomer 'Turkish' faction at the Mughal court in Delhi, and almost all those Sunni nobles who had joined their fortunes to his accompanied him to Hyderabad.

not like it when Middle Eastern Shi'as hinted that Najaf and Karbala and any of the other shrines in Iraq associated with the historic Ali were in any way more authentic or powerful than the Hyderabadis' own home-grown Shi'ite holy site. In this context Mir Alam used to tell a story about a Shi'ite Mongol Hazara from Afghanistan, who had

recently arrived from Iran, and came to my house just as I was preparing to go to the Koh-e Sharif to give an ex-voto picnic. I invited the Mongol to join me on this pious visit. He answered: 'I'm afraid you'll have to excuse me, I've already visited Najaf [the premier Shi'ite pilgrimage site in Iraq] many times, so I hardly feel any need to visit your little shrine here!'

At last I persuaded him to mount the bullock-cart in the middle of my household and took him with me to the Koh-e Sharif. When we halted, as he was coming down off the bullock cart, and unused to such transport, he slipped his leg in between the supports of the cart and a sudden movement of the bullocks made the wheels turn and snapped his shin-bone. He screamed and wailed and then fainted, so I was forced to throw him back in the middle of the cart and proceed to the top of the mountain, while sending servants to fetch a surgeon. The Mongol, coming to, shouted: 'I never have and never will give up my leg to a surgeon, never, ever! Just as He (Praise Be Upon Him) broke my leg upon this hilltop, so He will mend it!'

So the Mongol spent the whole night, without medicaments or surgery, weeping and tossing on his bedding, crying out: 'Ya Maula! Ya Maula' 'O my Lord 'Ali, O my Lord 'Ali!' At last, in the last watch of the night before morning, sleep overtook him. He dreamed he saw His Holiness of Manifest Wonders [i.e. Maula Ali] graciously appearing and approaching him. As He laid His hand on the Mongol's broken leg, He cried: 'Arise and walk!'

The Mongol awoke and no longer felt any pain; he stretched out his leg, and drew it up and stretched it again, sat up, stood, walked, came back to sit again, and saw no trace of any fracture. So he prostrated himself in grateful prayer, and called out by name each of his dependants to show them his miraculously healed leg. He entered the shrine and recited the *Fatiha** and circled the holy rock-print seven times.

As long as he remained in Hyderabad, this Mongol never failed to visit the shrine each Thursday, convinced that this sacred place was quite especially acceptable to Maula 'Ali.[13]

The *'urs* could not have been better-timed for James. He badly need a break, for it had been a terrible few months – the worst since he became Resident – and his nerves were frayed and his health in tatters; indeed he worried at times that he was approaching the point of total physical breakdown.

For weeks now he had been forced to work from his bed; at other times his letters were written from 'a warm bath' into which he had been ordered by George Ure, the Residency quack, who thought this the best cure for the crippling headaches to which James was increasingly prone.[14] On occasion his symptoms seemed closer to dysentery, and at one particularly embarrassing moment he was forced to take his own thunderbox tent into the Nizam's palace as he was suffering from a 'very bad bowel and stomach disorder – or rather I think a complication of all the disorders the human frame is subject to. I got very well through my visit to the Minister, though I had such a looseness in me as obliged me to take a necessary tent with me to the durbar.'[15]

Both in his public and his private life, the pressure was now on. The *jashn* party James had thrown to celebrate the marriage of Sikander Jah to Aristu Jah's granddaughter had gone well, clearing the air after the unpleasantness of the Mysore Partition Treaty, and for a while he was able to report that 'I am grown a prodigious

---

* The short opening chapter of the Koran, which is part of the ritual prayer and is also read in all sorts of ceremonial contexts.

favourite and Pett' of the Minister.[16] But Calcutta had been pressing him to force a further treaty of alliance on the Nizam, by which the size of the British military mission in Hyderabad (known as the Subsidiary Force) would be increased, so providing a strong protection for the Nizam against any potential invasion – but only in return for some very large land concessions by the Nizam to the Company.

This of course suited the Company, which still retained ultimate control of the troops lent to the Nizam – and which indeed could use them to gently pressurise Hyderabad if ever the Nizam should prove less pliable than usual – while gaining a profitable way of financing its own forces. The benefits of the deal were less obvious to the Hyderabadi durbar, especially now that the threat of an attack by the Marathas seemed to have receded: as James told William at a particularly trying moment in the negotiations, 'Though Solomon [Aristu Jah] is inclined to concede a great deal to us, I begin to doubt whether he will concede all we require, unless really frightened from the Poonah quarter.'[17] Yet Wellesley would brook no watering-down of the terms he had set, which were weighed heavily in the Company's favour. He ordered James to get the Hyderabadis to sign, whatever it took.

Wellesley was in fact in a particularly foul and uncompromising mood that season. After conquering Seringapatam and 'Taming the Tiger' (as he euphemistically referred to the killing of Tipu) he had assumed that he would be lavishly rewarded by his masters in London, and wrote to his French wife Hyacinthe that 'I don't see how one can deserve honours more than by such feats, and if there is any justice in England they must send me the Garter by an express courier . . . I don't care about any honour except the Garter.'[18] When he was offered instead a mere Irish marquessate, which did not even give him the right to sit in the House of Lords in London, Wellesley almost had a nervous breakdown. He took to his bed for ten days, unable to eat or sleep, raging at the perceived insult of what he called this 'double gilt potato' and working himself into such a state that he 'broke out into enormous and painful boils'.

Nor was there anything in Calcutta that might cheer him up or lure him out of his bedroom. Calcutta society, Wellesley had decided, was boring and vulgar: 'the men are stupid, are coxcombs, are uneducated; the women are bitches, are badly dressed, are dull', and he raged to Hyacinthe about 'the stupidity and ill-bred familiarity' of the Company merchants he was meant to govern and control: 'They are so vulgar, ignorant, rude, familiar & stupid as to be disgusting and intolerable; especially the ladies, not one of whom, by the bye, is even decently good looking.'[19]

In misery, the highly-strung Wellesley wrote to Hyacinthe: 'I have been reduced to a skeleton, yellow, trembling, too weak to walk around my room . . . In my mind I suffer martyrdom . . . I am ruined here, everyone feels my degradation.'[20] Hyacinthe, like his staff in Calcutta, was mystified by her husband's almost psychotic vanity and conceit, and especially the degree to which he cared about the most arcane gradations in the British honours system. Baffled by his behaviour, she wrote gently to her husband pointing out the absurdity that 'he . . . before whom all the rulers of Asia tremble [lies] stretched on his bed, devoured by fury, without sufficient philosophy and courage to look on honours and decorations with an indifferent eye . . . Dear, dear soul you are not a child – your accursed head destroys your body.'[21]

None of this of course made Wellesley any more pliable, and it was certainly no moment for one of his staff to take issue with his orders or to fail to achieve all that the Governor General expected of him. William Kirkpatrick wrote urgently to James to tell him to try his very utmost to bring his negotiations to a successful conclusion at least if he wanted to have any chance of retaining his position. Already, he said, Wellesley had been muttering about replacing James with his own brother Arthur.*

To add to his difficulties, James's able and hard-working Assistant, John Malcolm, had left Hyderabad in the summer of 1799 on an embassy to the Shah of Persia. His place had been filled by one of

---

* It is interesting to speculate on the difference it might have made to subsequent European history had Wellesley persevered with this plan, and moved Arthur, the future Duke of Wellington, away from the military and into the diplomatic line of the Company's service.

Malcolm's protégés, an elderly Scottish soldier named Captain Leith. James had been suspicious of Leith's abilities from the beginning, and had noted laconically to William that 'Malcolm, like a true good Scotchman, [always] has a happy knack at discerning the special merits in those born North of the Tweed.'[22] Leith's arrival in Hyderabad had been delayed – ominously – by his bad health and an attack of dysentery, and when three months had passed and he had still yet to leave Madras, James wrote in some irritation that 'If Capt Leith does not soon get into motion for this quarter I shall begin to think that he has no bowels.'[23] When Leith did finally make it to Hyderabad, he proved more of a hindrance than a help: 'The new assistant is a disaster,' James wrote to William in January 1800. 'He can barely read or speak Hindoostany – indeed he can barely converse in it so as to be intelligible – or Persian [for that matter], and has taken three days to translate a letter with Amaun Oollah [Aman Ullah, the younger brother of James's very able *munshi**] the whole time by his side.'[24]

The following month, around the time of the wedding of Sikander Jah, James's own health had begun to fail, yet at this vital moment Leith was unable to assist in any way. James wrote: 'I have been tormented for this week past to an unusual degree with bile which has at length brought on a fever and ague which I am at this moment suffering under. Pray heavens that the physic which Ure has just given me may afford me some relief! For I plainly see that it will be a *long* time indeed 'ere my present assistant [Leith] gives me any. He is slow beyond anything I had conception of . . . He is almost deaf and blind, and upon the plea of candlelight burning his eyes, has requested me to excuse his attendance at the durbar . . .'[25]

Over the course of the year, as the treaty negotiations wound their interminable way through successive drafts, proposals and counter-proposals, Leith disappeared from his office for weeks at a time on

---

* *Munshis* were highly educated Indian assistants who specialised in helping Euopeans surmount their language difficulties. They could sometimes act merely as language teachers, but in the British Residencies they were much grander figures who often acted as confidential advisers and private assistants, and in some instances – such as here with Munshi Aziz Ullah – would even perform such important and delicate tasks as negotiating treaties and dispensing bribes to the appropriate officials in the durbar.

a variety of excuses: 'I am almost at my wits end with this strange assistant of Malcolm's recommendation,' James wrote in February. 'I have not set eyes upon him for this last fortnight, he being laid up with worms in his feet, and in a deep salivation in consequence of attempting to kill them with mercury. If ever his finger aches he fancies himself terribly out of order and declares his incapacity to attend the office; though from the specimens [of his work] he has hitherto given, I can't say I suffer much inconvenience from his absence. I am obliged as hitherto to attend to, and to carry, all the detail [i.e. humdrum] business of the Residency, which the assistant surely ought to ease his principal of. Ure says Leith is constantly whimsical and hypochondriacally inclined.'[26] Captain Leith finally took fright at the danger Hyderabad posed to his delicate health and fled back to his regiment in Madras later in the year.[27]

This left James to deal with the entire business of the treaty negotiation with only his highly intelligent and wily Delhi-born *munshi*, Aziz Ullah, to help him.[28] In order to lure the Hyderabadis into a closer embrace with the Company, James and Aziz Ullah were forced to use every stratagem they could think of, and Aziz Ullah spent many hours at Aristu Jah's *deorhi* trying to find ways of making the Minister more pliable. Day after day he would go to sit with him smoking a hookah in the summerhouse of the Minister's garden, or to fly pigeons, or to watch cockfights; on one occasion the grave *munshi* even reported in his official record of a meeting that Aristu Jah had invited him to continue their discourse in his personal *hamam* (Turkish bath), where they could talk without being overheard.[29]

On Aziz Ullah's advice, James tried buttering up Aristu Jah by sending to Madras for 'a curious piece or two of mechanism in the clock work way' which he believed 'will go a great way to clinching the treaty now brought on the carpet.'[30] The Nizam was likewise deluged with presents, including a new set of winter woollies to keep him from the worst of the December cold.[31] James also spent huge sums bribing both Aristu Jah and the women in the Nizam's *zenana*, writing to William in code that he had promised Aristu Jah a pension of one thousand rupees a month if he could get the Nizam to agree to the treaty, and remarking that the 'citadel of negotiation' might yet be taken 'by a well directed fire of gold shot'.[32]

Later, when William asked for details, James wrote – again in code – revealing exactly how he went about the difficult art of bribing the Prime Minister:

> The affair of the bribe . . . only occurred to me when every other means seemed to fail, but I should probably not have had recourse to it if you had not repeatedly called my attention to this mode of accomplishing difficult points, or at least not to the extent I did . . . Bribery effected the objects, viz removing Solomon's and the Nizam's objections to certain points [in the treaty]. The number of persons bribed is of no consequence at a court like this and will seldom if ever do any harm even if it reaches the ears of the Principal, except in cases very different from the present one. The principal channel of my bribes in Nizam's mahl [zenana] was Fihem Bhye, a woman of the most inordinate avarice . . .[33]

The Subsidiary Treaty of 1800, dubbed 'The Perpetual Alliance', was finally signed on 12 October after nearly a year of negotiations. The Company agreed to increase the British forces in Hyderabad by an additional two thousand infantry and a thousand cavalry, in return for which the Nizam handed over to the British the Mysore provinces he had won after the fall of Seringapatam eighteen months earlier – provinces that were of course worth a huge multiple of the actual cost of maintaining a few thousand sepoys.

Diplomatically, it was another triumph, and Wellesley wrote to congratulate James in fulsome terms; indeed when the Governor General had his portrait painted by Robert Home the following year he asked to have himself depicted with his hand resting on the Subsidiary Treaty, as if he regarded it as his greatest achievement to date in India.[34] The Nizam also seemed pleased, and gave James the title 'Beloved Son' as well as an enormous gem attached to a gold ring. 'Solomon [Aristu Jah] for some time past had dropped obscure hints to Munshi Uzeez Oollah of having something in store for me,' wrote James on the day the treaty was signed, which he thought would be highly acceptable, but could not be brought to tell him plainly what that something was . . . The day before yesterday however I was partly enabled to form a guess as to what was intended, by His Highness requesting me to send him a ring as the measurement of my finger; and this morning on my arrival at Durbar, Solomon signified to me His Highness's intention of distinguishing me by the appellation of his Son!!! an honour never hitherto conferred on anyone *whatsoever* but himself [Aristu Jah]. It was in vain for me to protest so high an honour utterly exceeded my merits, pretensions, or most sanguine expectations . . . The ring is a very shewy one, and the diamond a pretty large one. Young Sydenham [one of the junior Residency staff] thinks it may be worth from fifteen hundred to two thousand pagodas. Were I to guess, I should say a thousand pounds . . .[35]

Nevertheless, the whole affair left a nasty taste in Kirkpatrick's mouth. He was particularly disgusted by the degree to which he had had to bully and bribe the durbar to get his way, and he had more than a sneaking suspicion that the treaty was not at all in the best interests of Hyderabad. To his friend General William Palmer in Pune he wrote in full agreement with the latter's view that the Company was becoming dangerously grasping and over-confident.[36] When he finally wrote to his brother to tell him of the imminently successful result, the letter contained no hint of triumph. Instead he revealed his growing unease at the ruthlessness with which Wellesley had pursued his objects, telling William that Aristu Jah had told Munshi Aziz Ullah 'that our avidity had no bounds, that we required everything while we would concede nothing and that we seemed determined in short, to have everything our own way'. He added as a P.S.: 'My mind is just now in too perturbed a state to answer the private matter contained in your letter, even if I had time to do so.' Instead he simply asked his brother 'whether I ought not in justice to myself and to the public to request permission to resign the station'.[37]

This 'private matter' over which he was considering resignation was, of course, Khair un-Nissa.

The affair was now a continual source of pain and worry to James. In May, the growing unrest in Hyderabad over rumours about his seduction of a Sayyida had surfaced dramatically when, on his usual early-morning ride along the banks of the River Musi, James was ambushed: 'I had a narrow escape from being shot, having been twice fired at by two sepoys of the old French Party, within twenty yards,' he reported to William the following day. 'One of the balls passed very near to my head. I had some difficulty suppressing the indignation of the troopers who attend me; but the offenders were sent bound to me soon after by Solomon, with a request that I would hang them up. I contented myself however (after asking if they had been sent by anyone, which they positively denied) with cautioning them against ball firing in future, except against enemies of the state.'[38] Hyderabad gossip, of course, immediately linked the shooting to the growing disquiet caused by James's affair.

But it was not the gossip and signs of anger in the old city that really worried James. He knew now that Khair un-Nissa was pregnant. He also knew that her family were trying to force her into aborting their child.

Little is known about abortion in India and the Islamic world at this time, but the practice was clearly widespread. Islamic jurists had ruled early on that abortion in the early stages of pregnancy was not *haraam* (forbidden); indeed they laid down that it was permissible, in exceptional medical circumstances connected with the health of the mother, up to the fourth month, at which point the foetus was deemed to have become fully 'ensouled', and so a human being. Niccolao Manucci, who attended Aurangzeb's Imperial Mughal harem in Delhi, asserts that abortions were common there, and medieval Islamic texts are full of unusual suggestions for herbs and medicines that either prevented conception or aborted any foetus that might accidentally be conceived.

Birth-control methods varied widely around the Islamic world, and there are a great number of texts suggesting a variety of techniques, ranging from *coitus interruptus* to more bizarre solutions such as suppositories containing rennet of rabbit, 'broth of wall flower and honey' and 'leaves of weeping willow in a flock of wool' (a popular option in early medieval Persia). But birth control was not just the woman's business: male contraceptive techniques included 'drinking juice of watermint at coitus', rubbing the juice of an onion or a solution of rock salt onto the end of the penis, or, more alarmingly, smearing the entire penis with tar.* Other mysterious solutions to the problems of Islamic family planning included 'fumigation with elephant's dung' and, stranger still, 'jumping backwards'.†

Much less is known about the always sensitive subject of abortion, but the great medical authority Ibn Sina (known in the West as Avicenna), writing in early-eleventh-century Bokhara, suggested the following methods in his *Canon of Medicine*, all of which sound fairly unpleasant, as well as being (one would have thought) notably risky for the mother's health:

> Abortion may be performed by movements or by medicine. Medicines work by killing the foetus and causing the menses to flow ... Movements include phlebotomy [blood-letting], starvation, [bodily] exercise, frequent jumping, carrying of heavy loads and loud sneezing.
>
> A good procedure is to insert in the *os uteri*, a rolled piece of paper, a feather, or a stick cut to the size of a feather made of salwort, rue, cyclamen, or male fern. This will definitely work, especially if it is smeared with abortifacient medicine such as tar, the water of colocynth pulp, or some other abortifacient.

Other widely-used abortifacients in the medieval Islamic world included drinking potions of 'myrrh in lupine water, pepper, laurel seeds, cinnamon, madder, juice of absinthe, cardomum, water mint, roots of sweet basil, candy carrot and luffa seeds in vinegar', which

---

* It is unclear from the sources at what temperature the tar was meant to be applied. One presumes that if applied hot it would make a very effective contraceptive indeed.
† All of which makes the Vatican-endorsed rhythm method seem the height of reliability and sophistication.

methods could be combined with rubbing the navel with the gall bladder of a cow, fumigation with roots of cyclamen and the use of suppositories containing roots of wild carrot and 'the juice of squirting cucumber'.

It is not known what methods late-Mughal midwives favoured, still less what were those common in Hyderabad, but the midwives concerned, the family and Kirkpatrick all clearly regarded the act as well within their competence. Just as Indian women were regarded throughout the Middle East as being especially sophisticated in the arts of love, so they were believed to be especially skilled in the art of preventing pregnancy, and if all else failed, in assisting at births.[39]

Abortion was nevertheless a dangerous operation, and apart from wishing to keep the child, Khair un-Nissa must have been alarmed at the sheer risk involved in undergoing a termination: after all, her half-sister had died only a few months before, in March 1800, after going through a presumably much less dangerous operation to help her conceive.[40]

Not surprisingly, this unpleasant saga was not something James felt able to confide to his brother. Indeed he always tried to tell William as little as possible about his Hyderabadi lover, and even avoided revealing to him that she was pregnant – but a brief reference was made to the abortion attempt in the Clive Report, when Colonel Bowser testified that Kirkpatrick had personally told him that

> in consequence of this intercourse the young lady became pregnant, and to conceal her disgrace they [her family] wished to marry her to the Mussulman formerly alluded to [the son of Ahmed Ali Khan], but the lady herself had positively refused, had threatened if compelled to put an end to her existence, and declared that she would marry no person but Hushmut Jung (Major Kirkpatrick). Finding that they could not prevail upon her, they wished to give her medicine to procure an abortion, but that he (the Resident) had sent for the principal midwives of the city and deterred them from an attempt of that nature. He concluded with declaring that whatever might be the ultimate result of these investigations he was determined never to desert the lady or her offspring.[41]

Yet while James may have been determined not to abandon Khair un-Nissa in the long term, in the short term he was unable to meet her or even regularly answer her letters, due to the vigilance of her grandfather Bâqar Ali Khan and, more importantly for his own security, his recent promise to James Dalrymple. Instead he was forced to sit impotently in the Residency gazing over the Musi to the old city where Khair un-Nissa lived, forbidden to contact her or reply to her letters. To William he wrote in cipher: 'I have long since desisted from all intercourse with the females of B[âqar] A[li]'s family ... [But] it is generally reported that the young girl is pining miserably, and that her parents have by way of soothing her distress of mind come to a determination not to marry her to any one.'[42]

He then, for the first time, hinted to his brother that he was a lot more serious about the affair than he had previously made out. Up to now he had grudgingly admitted to William that he had slept with Khair un-Nissa but denied that he was planning to marry her, or indeed that he regarded his connection with her as anything more than a regrettable lapse of self-control. Now however he made it clear that in fact he was far, far more deeply involved than this. He wrapped up the revelation in the language of honour and duty so as to make it seem less objectionable to his brother, and still pretended that the connection was forced upon him; but the import was exactly the same: that he was prepared to resign from his job and abandon his entire East India Company career before he gave up the girl: 'I should not be astonished,' he wrote on 17 August,

> if they [Khair un-Nissa's family] were sooner or later to implore me to renew a connexion with her in my own terms. I will tell you however with the same un-reserve I have hitherto practised, how I should in all probability act in such a predicament. I would first endeavour by every means in my power to decline the offer, but if I found that this could not be done without danger of more than one kind, I would feel the pulse of the Nizam and Solomon, and if they proved not averse to the business, I would, as in duty bound, have the matter submitted to Lord W who from my public statement of the case is well acquainted with the young girl's sentiments respecting me.

[But] if his Lordship should from reasons of political expediency or from any other consideration prove decidedly hostile to any arrangement whatever, my feelings will in all probability compel me to request permission to resign my situation in order that I may be more at liberty to consult them and my inclinations, than I can do as a public man. Various considerations no doubt will make this alternative a most painful one indeed, but it will be the only one left me, to extricate myself with honour from as cruel a dilemma as perhaps any man was ever placed in . . . [43]

If James had hoped to escape from the shadow of the affair during his trip to Maula Ali, he was mistaken.

He set off north on 1 December, and took with him Leith's replacement as Residency Assistant, a talented, vain and cocky young Oriental scholar named Henry Russell. Russell was a fluent Hindustani speaker, though his Persian was not up to scratch, and he probably got the job as much from his connections as his skills. His father, Sir Henry Russell senior, was the Chief Justice of Bengal, an honest, clever but coarse man whose *nouveau riche* manners appalled the profoundly snobbish Lord Wellesley: 'I know not where you picked up Sir Henry Russell,' Wellesley wrote to the Company Board of Control's President Henry Dundas in London when he first heard hints about Sir Henry's appointment. 'He is a vulgar, ill-bred, violent and arrogant brute; he gives universal disgust. I hope you will never allow him to be Chief Justice . . . at all events do not place that brute in a station which his manners and conduct will disgrace.'[44]

But while abhorring the father, Wellesley admired Russell's son, whom he regarded as 'the most promising young man' he knew.[45] James agreed, and wrote to William that Russell 'cannot, I think, fail to be an acquisition to me in every point of view. As yet, he has not,

I perceive, made much progress in the Persian but he is a very tolerable Hindwy [i.e. Hindustani/Urdu] scholar through the medium of which he will make himself useful to me in the translating turn, and thus by degrees gain himself a knowledge of the language.'[46] He also personally liked the boy, whom he found lively, intelligent and companionable, and a welcome relief after the dour and heavy presence of the self-pitying Leith.

By the time Russell, Kirkpatrick and the Residency party arrived at Koh e-Sharif the crowds were already immense. Lines of huge silken *shamiana* tents had been erected amid the palm trees at the base of the hill. The pilgrims milled around, shopping in the temporary bazaars and eating the food and drinking the sherbet provided to everyone free of charge in the huge kitchen erected by Mah Laqa Bai and maintained at her own expense.[47] Hindus came with coconuts to bring as offerings to the shrine; Muslims brought sheep to slaughter; beggars lined up for alms. According to Ghulam Husain Khan:

> All of God's people go, from the Nizam and his Ministers to the poor, the soldiers and the entertainers – even old women, of 90 or 100 years old, who hardly have the strength to walk, yet still drag themselves to the festivities. About 5 lakhs of people – Muslims and Hindus, followers of Vishnu and Shiva, Brahmins and *sadhus* and Marwaris, as well as foreigners from Iran, Central Asia and Turkestan, Ottoman Turkey and Syria, Arabs and non-Arabs, and even the English – all of them come to this *'urs* which none will willingly miss. They erect countless tents, and those that have built lodgings decorate them with carpets and candles . . . Each of the major nobles endows mansions that are named after them.*
>
> Some 3,000 elephants, as well as some 50,000 horses and load-bearing camels, with stalls selling fresh and dried fruit, clothes and fine woollen *pashmina* shawls: as far as the eye can see, immense crowds appear, of buyers and sellers, riders and dancers, glorious tents and mountainous elephants, and

---

* Around the base of the shrine of Maula Ali there still survives a great spread of crumbling mansions dating back to around 1800. It is probably the single place in Hyderabad that is least changed and which would today be most immediately recognisable to Kirkpatrick.

with tall buildings erected continuously on either side from the Musi river to the foot of Koh-e Sharif, hung with silk and adorned with chandeliers . . .

Beautiful dancers with variously painted faces and rich jewels and bright coloured dresses entertain joyful gatherings where they astonish listeners with their ravishing music; there are fireworks, various delicious dishes of food and drinks beyond counting. When His Highness the Nizam enters, the celebrations and illuminations begin . . .[48]

The centrepiece of the festivities – in a syncretic Hindu touch to a nominally Shi'a Muslim ceremony – was the moment at midnight on the sixteenth of Rajab when the tray of holy sandalwood was carried with great pomp on the back of a camel from the graveyard of Takia Rang Ali Shah; after this a second piece of sandal was sent to Koh e-Sharif from Punja Shah, and a third from Malajgiri. The pilgrims surged up to the top of the hill and, according to Ghulam Husain Khan, 'the crowds are such, that it is difficult to reach the shrine, unless, pushed by the repeated shoving of the strong young men behind you, drenched in sweat, you finally come into the shrine chamber'. Here they bowed or prostrated themselves before the holy handprint found by Ruby the Eunuch more than two hundred years earlier.

Yet James found that even here, in the middle of the vast anonymous crowds that thronged to the festival, he still could not escape the scandal that was rapidly enveloping him. Wherever he went – up to the shrine, on a hunting trip, or to one of the dance displays – he found himself being shadowed by Mir Abdul Lateef Shushtari and his cousin Mir Dauran, the plump, spoilt and deeply unattractive teenage son of Mir Alam.* Both were intent on trying to persuade James to intercede for their disgraced and exiled kinsman, who was now approaching Hyderabad on his way from Rudroor to his chosen place of internal exile, his estates in Berar, a hundred miles north-east of the city; both men refused to believe James's protestations that he

---

* Some later Hyderabadi sources maintain that Mir Alam had considered marrying Mir Dauran to his cousin Khair un-Nissa, and that the frustration of this plan added to Mir Alam's dislike of James. This is not, however, mentioned in any contemporary source, and Mir Alam succeeded in marrying his son to the daughter of a far more powerful Hyderabadi *omrah* than Bâqar Ali Khan, Bahram ul-Mulk.

was unable to exert any influence on Mir Alam's behalf. James was particularly irritated when the two suggested a deal: that if they got Khair un-Nissa for him, could he agree to get permission for Mir Alam to return home? As James reported to William,

> Abdul Lateef is frequently with me, and to all appearances very candid and *vastly* communicative. His complaisance indeed knows no bounds, for like Meer Dowraun he has not hesitated to offer his services to me very unreservedly in a *certain quarter* where he assured me there would be no difficulty in effecting in my own terms all my wishes – whatever they might be. You may easily suppose how I received and answered such meanness and impertinence ... I suspect he [Mir Dauran] has been tampering with old Bauker [Khair's grandfather, Bâqar Ali Khan], and that he has been pumping him, as the old man has unreservedly declared to me.[49]*

As James knew very well, now that Khair un-Nissa was seven months pregnant and clearly in no state to marry Ahmed Ali Khan's son, Bâqar Ali and the Shushtari clan were less the problem than Lieutenant Colonel Dalrymple. For Dalrymple could still make Kirkpatrick's life very difficult, especially if he reported to Calcutta that James had broken his solemn undertaking and was again seeing Khair un-Nissa, despite the clear dangers this presented to the British position in Hyderabad.

So when on 9 December, just three days after the end of the Maula Ali festival, news arrived at the Residency that Lieutenant Colonel Dalrymple had caught a sudden fever and died in his tent, James must have felt a very mixed series of emotions. Dalrymple was a close acquaintance, and James wrote warmly of his 'mild, conciliating

---

* James was especially angry as this was Mir Dauran's second attempt at trying to win him over to Mir Alam's cause by dishonest means. Eight months earlier, in March, he attempted quite blatantly to bribe James, who had reported to William: 'I rejected with disdain a bribe which he offered me in his fathers name of a lakh of rupees in jewels and another in money. He had the meanness to hint pretty plainly to me, that he was ready to assist in any views that I might have in a certain quarter, if I would, upon the principle of give and take, promote those of his father. I could not help telling him in reply, that though I did not immediately understand what quarter he alluded to, yet I could never think of disgracing him so far as employing his services in any unsuitable way.' OIOC, Kirkpatrick Papers, Mss Eur F228/11, p.338, 9 March 1800, James to William Kirkpatrick.

manners', of his humility and 'the heavy loss we have just experienced in the death of my invaluable friend'.[50] Indeed, he personally conducted the funeral service at the Parade Ground Cemetery just beside the new British cantonments, and showed every sign of grief as he read the funeral oration. But part of him must have quietly rejoiced. For according to Bâqar Ali Khan's later testimony, less than two days after the death of Dalrymple, James again began secretly visiting Khair un-Nissa with 'more eagerness than ever'.[51]

Just over two weeks later a mysterious *harkarra* (messenger) appeared at Aristu Jah's palatial courtyard house. He entered the Minister's durbar and in front of the assembled crowds loudly demanded in the name of Hushmut Jung Kirkpatrick that Khair un-Nissa should be immediately handed over to the British Resident. Before he could be questioned, the man slipped out into the crowded street.[52]

That same evening Sharaf un-Nissa, accompanied by her mother Durdanah Begum, burst crying and weeping into the quarters of her father, Bâqar Ali Khan. The old man was sitting alone and he anxiously asked what was wrong. Sharaf un-Nissa claimed that she had in the past fortnight received a whole series of threatening messages from the Minister's house. The first two messages, she said, had come from Aristu Jah's daughter-in-law, Farzand Begum. Then, 'the day following the Festival of the Birth of Christ', another had arrived from Mama Salaha, an *aseel** in Farzand Begum's service. Mama Salaha had told her that 'as the Resident had for the Six months past become a real Mussulman [Muslim] she ought therefore to give her Daughter; but that if she did not Comply, ruin would fall on her Father and his Family'.

Sharaf un-Nissa said she had ignored these threats, but then, only

---

* In this context, a maidservant.

three hours earlier, 'Mama Nuddeem, another of the Minister's *Aseels*, brought a message from Furzund Begum, to the following purport, "That if I did not immediately give up my Daughter to the Resident, his eagerness & desire to have her was so violent, that he would Cut off his hair & come & sit down at Bauker Ally Khan's Door." '[53] Bâqar Ali Khan was understandably aghast at these threats, as was Durdanah Begum, who, 'tearing open her garment and throwing a winding sheet over her shoulders, said "Now I am a fakeer and renounce the world."' She then gave him another winding sheet, saying, 'Take this and having gone before the [British] battalions, throw it over your shoulders and before the whole of the English gentlemen declare that it is your wish to become a fakeer and to relinquish the world' – turning mendicant being in her view the only sure way to save the family both from such threats and such irreparable dishonour.[54]

Early the following morning, 28 December, Bâqar Ali Khan did indeed visit the British camp, but not to turn fakir. Instead he sought out Colonel Bowser, who was thought likely to succeed Dalrymple as the commander of the Subsidiary Force, and urgently begged him for his help and protection against both Kirkpatrick and the Minister. Bowser was at breakfast when the Khan entered, and as he did not speak either Persian or Hindustani, and realised the importance of the matter, he agreed with Bâqar Ali that it would be best to go and find the force's fluent-Persian-speaking doctor. Dr Kennedy was at home, and once the three were gathered behind closed doors, Bâqar Ali explained the 'delicate' matter he had come to discuss with them. He described how

> for a long time past attempts had been made by the Resident, and backed by the Minister, to get possession of his Grand Daughter; but that he had hitherto resisted all their importunities, and had in this been supported by the Late Lt Col Dalrymple, who had exacted a solemn declaration upon honour from the Resident, that he should desist in future from any attempt of the kind. Only two days after the death of Colonel Dalrymple however, these attempts were again renewed ... and were very lately accompanied by threats from the Minister, of ruining him & his Whole Family if he did

not comply with what was required of him – 'To every impor-
tunity and to every threat,' the Khan observed, 'he had
returned for answer that he was resolved never to yield; that
they might deprive him of his jaghire [estates], his pension,
and even his life; but that he would never consent to the
Dishonor of his Family.

'They were pushing him now,' the Khan continued, 'so very
hard, that he saw no other way of saving his Honor than by
demanding the protection of Col. Bowser; and that to make
the matter appear in the most serious light, he would instantly
retire, and get a [formal] letter [of complaint] written to
Colonel Bowser on the subject.'

The Khan then went out & returned shortly with a letter,
which he immediately carried in his own hand to Colonel
Bowser:

After the usual compliments – 'Since the death of Colonel
Dalrymple, a business of oppression has come upon me, on
account of which my character & reputation will be ruined if
I remain any longer at Hyderabad – I request therefore that
you will allot to me some habitation in the English Lines, in
which I may remain with all my Dependants, or, if this cannot
be done, that you will give me a Guard of Seypoys to escort
me & my dependants into the Company Territories.'[55]

With this formal public complaint of Bâqar Ali's, the dice were
thrown. From this point, the affair clearly had to be properly investi-
gated, and what had been up to this point a very private matter
suddenly became very public indeed.

That evening Bowser sent a note to James, telling him about the very
serious charges Bâqar Ali had made against him. He suggested that
all the parties in the dispute should meet face to face at the Residency
two days later on the morning of the thirtieth so that they could

attempt to find out the truth of the accusations and to settle the matter in as civilised a manner as possible.

James agreed to the meeting, and in the meantime, the following morning, the twenty-ninth, sent Munshi Aziz Ullah straight over to Aristu Jah's *deorhi* to tell him what had happened, and to show him Bowser's note. He particularly wanted Aziz Ullah to find out whether it was true that the Minister's daughter-in-law, Farzand Begum, had been sending threatening messages to Bâqar's womenfolk as the old man had claimed.

By chance, Munshi Aziz Ullah arrived just five minutes after Mir Abdul Lateef Shushtari had turned up to petition the Minister on behalf of his exiled cousin, Mir Alam. The two men were friends – Shushtari talks warmly of Aziz Ullah in his memoirs, saying what an excellent Urdu poet and sympathetic companion the *munshi* was[56] – and a full account of what transpired survives from Shushtari's pen:

> This day, the 13th of Shabaun [29 December], I happened to wait upon the Minister and had only set down a moment when Moonshee Uzeez Oolla arrived and gave a note straight into his hands. The Minister while reading it underwent many changes of countenance and two or three times exclaimed, 'I declare to God that it is false!' After having read it he turned to me and said 'God is my witness that this is an egregious calumny.'[57]

Aristu Jah then gave the paper detailing Bâqar's charges to Shushtari to read, muttering that Bâqar Ali Khan deserved to have his nose cut off for spreading such damaging and obviously untrue libels. As Shushtari read it, Aristu Jah sent to his harem summoning his daughter-in-law, Farzand Begum and the two *aseels* whom Bâqar said had threatened Sharaf un-Nissa. One by one they were brought and questioned in front of Shushtari and the *munshi*. According to the former, 'they severally declared, with a hundred oaths, that they were entirely ignorant of the circumstance, and that it was a calumny on them'.[58]

This only deepened the confusion – had they or had they not threatened Sharaf un-Nissa? – but James took it as a vindication of his innocence. He knew he had threatened no one, and he believed that Bâqar Ali was not as ignorant as he made out of his wife and daughter's concerted attempts to draw Khair un-Nissa and himself together. He therefore assumed that Bâqar Ali was up to something, and suspected that it might not be unconnected to Mir Alam's exile and the manoeuvres of the Shushtari clan to get their kinsman returned to power.

For Mir Alam was now encamped just thirty miles to the north of Hyderabad and was making one last desperate attempt to be returned to favour before he set off into exile and obscurity in Berar. He even wrote to James attempting to make up, saying that 'the silly reports relating to the family of Aukul Oo Dowlah [Bâqar Ali Khan] are now entirely effaced from my mind by the discovery of their falsity ... Friends cannot harbour malice against one another any more than a drop of rain can remain on the surface of the water.'[59] Mir Alam also sent to the Nizam claiming that he was suffering from extreme ill health and begging the Nizam to take pity on him; though Abdul Lateef Shushtari 'had the candour to acknowledge [privately to James] that it is more a pretext than anything else, observing that a man cannot well be at death's door who like M.A. travels with a seraglio of *fifty five* concubines with one or other of whom he is said to have daily or nightly connection'.[60] Though this made James warm to Abdul Lateef, whom he had begun to like and even trust, it made him all the more suspicious of the motives of Bâqar Ali.

So when, on the following morning, 30 December 1800, Colonel Bowser, Dr Kennedy and Bowser's Persian interpreter Captain Orr rode into the Residency gardens as agreed, they found James angry, suspicious and in no mood for compromise. The soldiers had gone over Bâqar Ali's claims as they cantered the seven miles from the cantonments, and had come to the conclusion that 'some gross mistake or deception existed between the parties'; but James was convinced that there was more to Bâqar's absurd story than met the eye. He told Bowser that he believed

the Khan was wilfully misrepresenting matters for some sinister purpose. This opinion he founded both upon a Conviction that the messages which the Khan complained as coming from the Minister's family had never been sent (in as much as the Minister, when informed of the subject had expressed the utmost astonishment *&* anger at so bare faced assertions), and also because he was Convinced that [Bâqar Ali] Khan's family was by no means in the state of mental distress represented.

This opinion he founded upon communications with which the females of that family troubled him too frequently. From this channel he was well assured that there was no such distress, and thence seemed persuaded, that the [story of the women's] Lamentations, [and adoption of] *Cuffunies* [winding sheets] *etc* were all a Deception. From these considerations the Resident seemed to have no doubt that he should be able to demonstrate to us, that all the grievances complained of were fictitious, and the complaints fabricated for some sinister view, to which he seemed to believe that the Khan was privy.[61]

Shortly afterwards, Bâqar Ali Khan arrived at the Residency gardens. He had barely dismounted and been ushered into the Residency before James had angrily confronted him, asking 'how he came to involve his name in such a business, and demanded that he should produce proofs of what he had alleged. To this the Khan replied by asserting, that the [threatening] messages he complained of had indeed been sent from the Minister's family, and added "If you were not the cause of them, how could they have been sent?" '[62] Munshi Aziz Ullah was then called for, who relayed verbatim what had transpired at Aristu Jah's the day before, and how Farzand Begum and her *aseels* had all denied sending any threats or messages to the Khan's house. This only added to the confusion. As Bowser later wrote in his report of the meeting:

The Khan persevered in asserting his belief of the messages and affirming that all the distress in his family had been occasioned by them ... Hitherto nothing had appeared to throw any light on the subject, and each Party seemed positive that the other was wrong. We therefore reverted to what had been affirmed of the distressed state of the Khan's family in consequence of the messages in question and wished to find means of satisfying ourselves whether the Family had assumed

Mourning Dress as the Khan had affirmed, or whether they were (excepting a family quarrel) in their usual state of Composure, and only astonished at the Khan's behaviour . . .'[63]

They were still arguing the point when there was a knock, and 'a Person presented himself at the door. Upon seeing him the Resident said, that a message from the Begum [Sharaf un-Nissa] must have been brought. He went out immediately, and on his return observed that he had just received a message of a complexion very different from the Khan's story.'

At this the three British soldiers agreed that there could be only one solution to the mystery: they would have to send someone to Sharaf un-Nissa's *zenana* to question her and find out her version of events. The question was who? Bâqar Ali suggested Mrs Ure, the doctor's amply proportioned wife, 'who, from speaking the Hindostany language, might be able to satisfy herself of what the females had to say'; but this proposal was vetoed by Lieutenant Colonel Bowser, who said the matter was too delicate to involve a European woman. Sending all three of the soldiers with Bâqar Ali was then suggested, but vetoed on the grounds that it would make too public a spectacle, and also that, as James pointed out, 'by the Khan being present also, the women might be overawed from declaring themselves, or even find themselves under the necessity of saying whatever he might wish them. The Khan objected to Captain Orr or Dr. Kennedy going to his *zenana* unless he himself was with them: and Dr. Kennedy objected to going alone unless the Khan gave his assent to the enquiry being made in this way, which he would not do.'

At this point of impasse, it occurred to them all to question the messenger who had just delivered the message from Sharaf un-Nissa; but he had just left, so a boy was sent to fetch him back. While they waited they went through to eat at the Residency dining hall, where, according to Bowser, 'The necessity of ascertaining the points in question became every moment more evident. It was accordingly proposed that Dr. Kennedy as a medical man & less liable to excite observation, should visit Sheriffe ul Nissa Begum [alone], and enquire about the [threatening] message and the [story of the fakir's] *cuffuny*.'

This seemed an especially suitable solution, as apart from anything else Dr Kennedy had been to Sharaf un-Nissa's mansion before: a year earlier Khair un-Nissa had been struck down with what appeared to be smallpox, and her horrified mother had prevailed on Bâqar Ali to consult an English physician. Kennedy had paid a visit to the family *deorhi*, after which Khair un-Nissa made a full recovery.[64] Bâqar Ali finally agreed to send Dr Kennedy to his women, and a note was duly dispatched to Aristu Jah requesting permission for the doctor to enter the city. While they were waiting,

> the Resident being out on the verandah, Dr. Kennedy [discreetly] asked the Khan what steps he had taken to satisfy himself that the women of his family were not [in fact] deceiving him. He said that he had ... stated the matter to his wife and daughter, and entreated them to declare themselves, telling them at the same time, that if they were inclined to forward what he was resolved never to consent to [i.e. marrying his granddaughter to Kirkpatrick] they had only to say so, and that he would leave the matter entirely to themselves; but that he was resolved also to leave with them the disgrace, and retire to his own country [Persia], or turn *fakeer*. The Females declared upon this that they had no such inclinations, & that they were resolved to share his fortunes & turn fakeers also. He then pointed out to us, that this proposal was in him an instance of great forbearance, as much harsher measures were commonly adopted by men of his cast upon similar occasions.
>
> [At this point] we were informed that the Begum's messenger had returned, & was in the bungalo behind. Thither we went, and Dr. Kennedy recognised the man as an old servant of the Khan's. The purport of the message [he had brought] was, 'that the Begum wished to inform the Resident, that the Khan had been making a great deal of disturbance in the family, and was no doubt gone to the Residency to expose himself still further by telling a very idle story; but that she hoped the Resident would keep him quiet (*sumjow*)'.[65]

Bâqar Ali was both angry and astonished at this, but agreed that the only solution now was for Dr Kennedy to proceed with his mission and to question Sharaf un-Nissa directly, which he did as soon as the permission to enter the old city had arrived from Aristu Jah.

He set off, as agreed, within a covered palanquin, in order to preserve – as far as possible – his anonymity. But while no one could see in, it also meant that Kennedy could not see out, and isolated as he was inside the lattices of the litter, he was unaware that he was in fact being followed, not by one but by two shadowy but entirely separate figures, who themselves were apparently unaware that they were not alone in tailing their quarry.[66]

In December, travelling on horse- or elephant-back, it was usually possible to ford the Musi in the shallows immediately below the Residency; but a team of palanquin-carriers would probably have opted to keep their feet dry and cross the river a mile further upstream by the old, low Qutb Shahi Bridge. This would have taken them along a bank filled with a line of Mughal water-gardens and then past the bustling city ghats, 'always a stirring sight, with its countless groups of people bathing, washing clothes, or carrying away water from holes scooped in the sand; elephants being washed or scrubbed with sand by their keepers, and evidently enjoying the operation'.[67] From there Kennedy and his palanquin-bearers would have entered the city by the great Banjara Gate.

Although the staff of the Residency regularly visited the old city, they rarely ventured off the main roads; in general, the British simply paid brief visits to the durbar, shopped in the main jewel bazaars or took visitors to see the Char Minar and the Mecca Masjid. As a result, Western observers who penetrated deeper into the city were often struck by the contrast between the magnificent prospect of the city from afar, and the squalor of its back alleys. As one English resident of Hyderabad described it, your first glimpse of the city from the high ground of the Banjara Hills just to the north of the Residency was always unforgettable. It was, after all,

the first city of the Dukhun . . . Before me, on the gentle rise of
the valley [stood a jumble of] white terraced houses gleaming
brightly in the sunlight amidst from what seemed to me at a
distance, almost a forest of trees. The Char Minar and the
Mecca Masjid rose proudly from the masses of buildings by
which they were surrounded; and here and there a white
dome, with its bright gilt spire, marked the tomb of some
favourite or holy saint, while smaller mosques, I might say in
hundreds, were known by their slender white minarets.

. . . The city seemed to be of immense extent; but I thought
from the number of trees, that it was comprised principally of
gardens and enclosures, and was much surprised afterwards,
when I entered it, to find its streets so filled with houses, and
the whole so thickly populated . . . It was altogether a most
lovely scene: the freshness of the morning, the pureness of the
air, and the glittering effect of the city and its buildings caused
an impression which can never be effaced from my memory.

When the traveller passed through the gates, and left the main
ceremonial avenues, there was always, however, something of a feeling
of anti-climax:

It had been a late Monsoon and the streets were narrow and
dirty, and the interior of the city certainly did not answer
the expectations we had formed from its outside and distant
appearance; still there were evident tokens of its wealth in the
numbers of elephants, on the backs of which, in canopied
umbaras, sat noblemen or gentlemen, attended by their armed
retainers. Crowds of well dressed persons paraded the streets
and . . . we made our way as well as we could through the throng,
and our attendants were often obliged to clear us a passage . . .[68]*

It is not known for certain where Bâqar Ali Khan's *deorhi* lay, but
in all probability it was beside his cousin Mir Alam and the other

---

* The streets appear to have been particularly muddy and smelly in December 1800:
North Dalrymple, the nephew of James, had arrived in Hyderabad on the very day his
uncle lay dying in his tent, and visiting the old city immediately after the funeral had
found the back streets 'extremely narrow and full of mud, so that gentlemen are obliged
to go in mounted on elephants'. Scottish Record Office, Edinburgh, GD135/2904, pp.30–
6, 'Diary of North Dalrymple of the 22nd Dragoons'.

Persian émigrés in Irani Gulli. This lay half a mile from the Char Minar, in the warren of alleys behind the Burkha Bazaar, where the women of Hyderabad came to buy their clothes and bangles.

Aristocratic *deorhis* of the period were often very substantial complexes of buildings. You would enter through the great double gates of a whitewashed *naqqar khana*, from the first floor of which musicians would beat their drums and sound fanfares to announce the arrival of any important visitor. Inside were a succession of courts filled with slowly dripping fountains and enclosing small Mughal *char bagh* gardens. These would give onto a series of low, open *baradari* pavilions with their ornate arcades of cusped Mughal arches, as well as a few more substantial two-storey Mughal townhouses with latticed windows and intricately carved wooden balconies.

The *zenana* courtyard was usually a separate enclosure, the exclusive preserve of the women, at the rear of a *deorhi* complex. In the case of the clearly very substantial *deorhi* of Bâqar Ali Khan, the *zenana* courtyard contained two entirely separate mansions, one for Sharaf un-Nissa and her daughters, and the other for her mother Durdanah Begum.[69] A separate gatehouse would give access, and in Hyderabad at this period it was usually watched over by a small guard of armed women *aseels*, described by one rather superior Englishman of the time as 'low caste women who are armed, accoutred and disciplined like our sepoys. They make a ridiculous appearance.'[70]

It was into such a courtyard, and past such guards, that Dr Kennedy would have stepped, before clambering out of his palanquin to seek an audience with Sharaf un-Nissa. The etiquette for such visits was well-established. Watched over by a trusted servant, the visitor would converse through a lattice or a roll of reed *chicks*. Even on a medical visit – as this purported to be – face-to-face contact was not permitted, though in exceptional emergencies the doctor was permitted to put his hand through the lattice to feel the pulse of the patient.*

---

* Such tantalising contact led to a whole raft of erotic stories told by European doctors, though it is impossible now to say whether they are true or imagined. The Italian quack and confidence trickster Niccolao Manucci, who occasionally attended the ladies of Aurangzeb's harem, maintained that 'there are some [women] who from time to time affect the invalid simply that they may have the chance of a conversation with and have

This occasion was no different. When Sharaf un-Nissa eventually appeared, attended by a maidservant, she 'sat during the conversation inside of a Door, before which hung a bamboo blind'.[71] According to Dr Kennedy's account of the meeting, he 'began by telling her, that I was a friend of her Father's, and had come to her to ascertain the truth of certain points which seemed doubtful, but which it was necessary to verify – She desired me to proceed & to say what these points were, and that she would speak the truth.'

Seated on the veranda of Sharaf un-Nissa's pavilion, Dr Kennedy then relayed the confused nexus of charges and suspicions that they had spent the morning discussing at the Residency: how her father had claimed that Farzand Begum and her household were pressurising her to marry Khair un-Nissa to Kirkpatrick, and that her father suspected that the Resident was ultimately behind these messages and threats. Kennedy finished telling his story and asked the shadowy figure behind the blind what she thought of all this. There was a moment's silence. Then the figure began to speak. What she said changed everything. For Sharaf un-Nissa decided to come completely clean, and admitted unreservedly that in fact

> no such message had ever been sent to her, that no communication had been held on the subject with the Minister's family since the Month of Suffer [two months earlier], about which time, or previous to which, she had been sent for by Farzund Begum, and had discussed upon the point, but that she [Sharaf] had refused either to give her own consent, or to permit the matter to be submitted to decision of her daughter, as Farzund Begum wished.

Dr Kennedy then pointed out that Bâqar Ali Khan believed there had been a whole series of more recent threats, 'and that it appeared strange how so much uneasiness could have been occasioned, if no such message had been delivered'. But Sharaf un-Nissa said, quite clearly and explicitly,

---

their pulse felt by, the physician who comes to see them. The latter stretches out his hand inside the curtain; they lay hold of it, kiss it, and softly bite it. Some out of curiosity apply it to their breast . . .' Niccolao Manucci (trans. William Irvine), *Storia do Mogor, or Mogul India, 1653–1708* (London, 1907, 2 vols), Vol. 2, p.353.

that she had *herself* delivered the message to Akul ud-Dowlah, and that she had done so without any such message being brought to her; that she herself was the contriver of the message, and had fabricated it with a certain view. I asked what her intention in it could be, as her father seemed much afflicted at the Circumstance, and affirmed, that both his Wife and Daughter were equally distressed – She then proceeded to say, that in consequence of what had passed between Hashmut Jung and her Daughter, the Daughter's character had been ruined in the eyes of the world, but that since what had passed could not be recalled, and a fault (*gonah**) had been committed, that she could not think of adding to the crime by marrying her daughter to anyone else, and therefore wished that she should be given to Hushmut Jung, and that it was this view that the message was framed.

Kennedy then asked if it was true that the women had been wearing 'Fakeer's dress', and if so, why? Sharaf un-Nissa replied that 'the message had occasioned a great deal of discussion & high words; that her father was much incensed at her avowing to him the sentiments she had just expressed to me; and that he had struck her & drawn his sword upon her, with an intention of killing her; that he had [only] been prevented [from doing so] by her mother stepping in & mitigating his anger, as well as threatening to accuse him herself of murder before the Nizam'.

At this crucial moment, said Sharaf un-Nissa, her mother had ordered her maidservant to bring in mourning rags, known as the *kafan* (or, as Kennedy spelled it, *cuffuny*), as a distraction. When they arrived the old woman immediately put them on as a symbol of her disgust with the situation, and signalling her intention to leave her worldly life and turn ascetic. Terrified that her father might still try to kill her, Sharaf un-Nissa also put on the rags, 'overcome by fear & apprehension, [in order] to pacify my father, but from no other motive'. She also told Dr Kennedy that she was not wearing the fakir's rags now. According to Kennedy,

Sheriffe ul Nissa then disclaimed strongly and pointedly her ever having made any Complaint of Oppression by Hushmut Jung

* *Gonah* (more usually spelled *gunah*) in fact means a sin rather than a fault.

[Kirkpatrick], or of any Compulsion of any measure whatever being used by him; that there never had been any, nor had she ever said so. She said that for the space of a Year she had been against her daughter being sent to Hushmut Jung; but that within the last five or six days she had changed her opinion, and now wished that Hushmut Jung had her – 'I wish he had her,' she repeated, 'in the same manner that he might have had her, before the Distinctions introduced by Moosa [Moses], Issa [Jesus] and Mahomed were known in the world.'

I observed that since matters had gone so far & were so public, it seemed strange that Akul ud-Dowlah [Bâqar] should be ignorant of them; and, if he knew them, it seemed still more difficult to understand, why he should be so much distressed upon the subject now. She replied, that it was all the fault of herself & her mother, and must rest on their heads. I observed that keeping him in ignorance occasioned much trouble, and that it would be better to inform him at once how matters really were – She said, she believed it would be better, but that he had been so much incensed regarding the honor of the family, that they were afraid to let him know what had actually happened, but wished much that the matter might be broken to him by some of his English friends – She added, that we might assure him also, that his good name ought not to suffer, as whatever fault there was, was the fault of herself and her mother, & that he was altogether ignorant and blameless. She also observed, that she ought to have more to say in the disposal of her daughter than Akul ud-Dowlah [Bâqar], who was only the girl's grandfather.[72]

With that Dr Kennedy thanked the figure behind the blind, made his *salaams* and stepped backwards, only to find 'that a man, whom I knew to be a Boy Servant of Akul ud-Dowlahs, had come in and was listening to what had been said'. Worried about the possible safety of the three Begums if Sharaf un-Nissa's words were relayed straight back to Bâqar Ali, Kennedy got straight into his palanquin and set off back into the crowded streets, when,

reflecting upon the extraordinary & unexpected nature of the conversation which had just passed I began to think that I

might be disbelieved in relating it, and that it might be better
if I could remove all ambiguity about the Person who had
spoken to me behind the Blind – I therefore returned, and
being admitted to the same place, informed the Lady, that as
Akul ud-Dowlah [Bâqar] was so much in the dark, that it was
more than possible that he might not believe what he must
now have upon my authority – that though I was perfectly
satisfied that I had been conversing with Akul ud-Dowlah's
daughter there was still room for him to say that I had been
deceived, and been addressed by someone who only imperson-
ated her – that therefore I wished that she would give me a
Ring or any other trinket known to Akul ud-Dowlah to be
her's, as a token that what I had to say came actually from
herself – This however, she declined, and I then proposed,
that she should permit me to leave something of mine with
her, to be shewn to her father, in order to convince him that
his own daughter had actually received it from me –

   To this she consented, and I took from my watch chain a
seal with my name in Persian characters, and gave it to her,
to be produced to her father.[73]

   This time, as Dr Kennedy stepped back, he found that as well as
the eavesdropping boy-servant of Bâqar Ali, his conversation had
also been listened to by 'a servant of the Resident' who had clearly
tailed him to Bâqar Ali's *deorhi* and somehow slipped in at the same
time as his palanquin. The two eavesdroppers had, wrote Kennedy,
'heard all that had passed'.

For Bâqar Ali Khan, this was in every way the worst possible outcome,
a total collapse, a complete humiliation. He had been outwitted
and completely outmanoeuvred by his womenfolk. They had taken
matters into their own hands, and not only had they successfully
opposed a marriage alliance he had forced upon them and to which

his granddaughter had expressed an 'unequivocal aversion', he had been fooled by them into thinking that they were planning to turn fakir, and so had successfully protected themselves from his wrath. By themselves sending threatening messages to Bâqar Ali which purported to come from James, and by inventing a series of intimidating visits from the *aseels* of the Prime Minister's *zenana*, the women had hoped to induce Bâqar Ali to back down quietly and to hand Khair un-Nissa over to James without a struggle. That plan had gone wrong, and Bâqar Ali had instead taken the complaint to his British friends in the Subsidiary Force; but though their various tricks had now been exposed, the women still ended by getting their way.

Two days later, on the morning of 1 January 1801, Sharaf un-Nissa and her mother, Durdanah Begum, were summoned to Aristu Jah's *deorhi*. There they were asked to confirm what they had told Dr Kennedy. They did so, and were warned that they had behaved disgracefully, even if Bâqar had drawn a sword on them and they had been forced to invent these stories to save their lives. But the Minister's real wrath was reserved for Bâqar Ali. He told James's *munshi*, Aziz Ullah, that Bâqar had been given the wrong title – instead of Akil ud-Daula, 'The Wisest of the State', he should be renamed Ahmuk ud-Daula, 'The State Fool' – and that the old man should be banished or imprisoned. Aziz Ullah replied that Bâqar's public humiliation was probably more than punishment enough.[74]

That same day, at three in the afternoon, a grave and embarrassed Bâqar Ali appeared at the Residency and asked to see James. He apologised for falsely accusing him of issuing secret threats, and said it was clear that he could no longer stand in James's way. As long as Khair un-Nissa's paternal uncle, Mir Asadullah, also gave his assent, as the law required, he withdrew all his objections to James marrying his granddaughter if he still wished to do so; but he was not prepared to attend the *nikah* (marriage ceremony) in person. Instead, 'with a view of not being a witness to the ceremony he would quit the city and take up his abode 10 or 12 coss* from it; but that he would leave his seal in the house and that they might execute

---

* One *coss* is just over two miles.

what they pleased in his name and apply his seal to it'. With that he set off north in a *dhoolie* or covered litter, towards where his cousin Mir Alam was still temporarily encamped. James later wrote that he believed the old man was 'more to be pitied than blamed' for the confusion, adding that he was 'defective in sight and hard of hearing [so] the females might [easily] have succeeded in deceiving him'.[75]

Two men had stood between Khair un-Nissa and James: one of these two, Lieutenant Colonel Dalrymple, was now dead, while the other, Bâqar Ali, had formally withdrawn his objections. But there was still one further obstacle to James's marriage. For all that he wore Hyderabadi clothes and had embraced Hyderabadi customs, and indeed for all that he was widely believed in Hyderabad to be a Muslim, he was nonetheless still technically a Christian, and so strictly forbidden by Sharia law from marrying a Muslim woman. There was only one way around this: he had to be circumcised, and then formally to convert to Islam.

According to a later report prepared by a Residency *munshi* after consulting with Khair un-Nissa's family, 'As a marriage was impossible without professing Islam he [James] promised to embrace that faith at the time of marriage ... Hashmat Jang [therefore] secretly embraced Islam before a Shi'a *Mujtahid* [cleric] and presented a certificate from him to Khair-un-Nisa Begum, who sent it to her mother.'[76]

As the conversion is never referred to in Kirkpatrick's own writings, it is difficult to guess at his feelings about taking this major and irrevocable step. Was it a nominal conversion, taken only in order to give him access to his pregnant lover? Or did his 'partiality' to Muslim culture extend to the religion itself? At this distance, with the nature of the sources that exist, it is impossible to say. What is certain, however, is that if it *was* a real conversion, then it seems to have been Khair un-Nissa who brought him to Islam, rather than the other way around.

James having produced his certificate of conversion, it was agreed that the marriage could go ahead, and 'accordingly, the marriage tie was bound by the said Shi'a *Mujtahid* and all the ceremonies incident there to were performed in accordance with the customs in vogue with the Mohamadans'.[77] As Sharaf un-Nissa makes clear in a letter she

wrote much later, the ceremony did however take place in the greatest
secrecy,* and there was no public *shadi*, or marriage party† – not least,
presumably, because Khair un-Nissa was heavily pregnant by this stage.
According to Sharaf:

> Colonel James Kirkpatrick sought my daughter from Nizam
> Ali Khan as also from Aristojah. Nizam Ali Khan and Aristojah
> communicated the request to my father, who at last, after
> much demur, gave his consent, that the ceremony of the *Nikah*
> should take place, and expressed his willingness that the rites
> should be performed according to the customs of our tribe.
>
> To this also Nizam Ali Khan assented, and honoured Col
> James Kirkpatrick at the same time with the designation of
> his son. His Highness also desired that he should stand as
> father for the approaching marriage to Col James Kirkpatrick
> in the bonds of love and that Aristojah should take the place
> of my daughter's [dead] father . . . In consequence of some
> disruptions [i.e. Bâqar Ali's complaint and the scandal this
> had caused] the marriage ceremonies were not performed in
> the usual manner, though the marriage contract was gone
> through according to Mahommedan rites. In proof of this a
> learned man named Meer Ahmed Ali Khan[78] attended on the
> part of Aristojah and two of his confidential servants were
> also present in the capacity of witnesses. Syed ood Dowlah[79]
> was my representative on this occasion when they all
> assembled in my house, and performed the ceremony of the
> marriage contract only.[80]

This, in Islamic law, involved fixing the bride's dowry and the
amount that would be given back to her in the event of a divorce.
In Khair un-Nissa's case it was clearly a large sum, as James refers
in his will to his wife's private fortune and says that he need not
provide for her as she was 'amply provided for by Jaghiers [estates]

---

* Even Henry Russell, who was by this stage becoming James's closest friend in the
Residency, later claimed in a letter of 30 March 1848 that he never once heard James
mention his marriage, though both Khair un-Nissa and Sharaf un-Nissa confirmed to
him that it had taken place.
† A Muslim marriage traditionally has two parts, the *nikah* and the *shadi*. When the
nikah is performed the marriage becomes legal. The *shadi* is the public and ceremonial
portion of the marriage, but is not essential for the consummation of a marriage.

and other possessions both hereditary and acquired, independent of her personal property and jewels, which cannot amount to less than half a lakh of rupees', a very large sum indeed, perhaps £300,000 in today's currency.[81] Khair un-Nissa's *jagirs* were presumably the gift of Aristu Jah, implying that he stood in for her dead father in more ways than one. The marriage, in other words, made James not only a very happy man, but a very rich one too.*

If Sharaf un-Nissa's account of the marriage is read in this way, it might be taken to indicate the degree to which – in the eyes of the Nizam and Aristu Jah at least – this was a political marriage, and a variation on the traditional courtly way of concluding alliances: first you signed a treaty, then organised a marriage between the two parties to seal the alliance. Khair un-Nissa was not of course an Asafiya princess, but for the purpose of this wedding she had become the Minister's adopted daughter, while James was now the Nizam's adopted son. In this way Aristu Jah believed he had finally succeeded in binding the British Resident through marriage into obedience and gratitude to the Nizam. No wonder the Nizam and Aristu Jah had been so angry at Bâqar Ali's attempts to wreck so useful an alliance. It gave the two men a considerable degree of leverage on the Resident sent to keep an eye on them.

Whatever sensations of relief and elation James might have felt at the happy conclusion of eighteen months of often desperate hopelessness, he left no surviving record of his emotions at the moment of the marriage. For despite the fact that everyone in Hyderabad who needed to give their assent to the marriage had now done so, James continued to pretend to his brother William – and to everyone else in Calcutta – that the affair was over.[82] On 16 January 1801 he wrote William a letter that veered further from the truth than any he had

---

* All these details would seem to confirm that the marriage was a 'permanent' one, not a 'temporary' marriage, which was an option in Shi'a law, and which some Hyderabadi scholars have suggested to me in conversation might have been available to Kirkpatrick had he wanted it. But James showed great fidelity to Khair un-Nissa, and there is absolutely no suggestion that he went into the marriage intending to divorce his wife soon afterwards – quite the opposite. He was taking a considerable political risk by marrying Khair un-Nissa, and the only reason to have done so would have been his own desire to permanently legitimise the relationship in the eyes of her family.

ever written, telling him that he had forbidden all messages from Khair's family, despite their continual entreaties that he should marry her.[83] James now clearly believed that with his conversion to Islam he had moved far beyond a position that he could ever explain to William; and so rather than telling the truth he began creating a whole Pandora's box of lies and half-truths which once opened and exposed would come back to haunt him at intervals over the next few years. James also thought – presumably for safety's sake – that for the time being it was better for Khair un-Nissa to continue in her house in the old city, at least until memory of the scandal had passed. So it was that less than two months later Khair un-Nissa gave birth to their first child, a little boy, in the family *deorhi* in the shadow of the Char Minar, the principal symbol of old Hyderabad.

James was in the house for the birth, and the note he wrote that night on a tiny scrap of paper still survives in the private archive of their descendants. It reads as follows:

> On Wednesday the
> 4th of March, 1801
> answering to ye 10th
> Shuwaul AH
> 1215, at about
> four o clock in the
> morning a Son was
> born to me in the
> City of Hyderabad.
> His mother from a
> Dream she had, wishes
> Him to be named Meer
> Goolam Ali,* to which
> I mean to add that of Saheb
> Aallum [Lord of the World].

* i.e. She had had a dream in which Maula Ali had appeared to her.

VI

IN THE SUMMER OF 1800 – at around the time Khair un-Nissa became pregnant – James's friend and closest political ally, General William Palmer, the liberal and sympathetic British Resident at the Maratha court in Pune, found that he had become a victim of Lord Wellesley's new, harsher political order.

In late June, Palmer had received a letter from the Governor General giving him notice that in due course he would be removed from his important and 'arduous public station' on the ostensible grounds of his 'precarious state of health and advanced time of life'. The true reason for his removal, as Palmer immediately realised, was that he represented exactly the sort of tolerant, Indophile white Mughal that Wellesley most abhorred, and which he was determined to weed out of the Company's service.[1]

General Palmer was married to Fyze Baksh, a beautiful Mughal Begum from Delhi. He was a gentle, thoughtful and highly intelligent man, who was openly sympathetic to Indian fears and aspirations: Abdul Lateef Shushtari, who stayed with the Palmers at the Pune Residency, called him 'almost angel-like in his good nature'.[2] General Palmer was, moreover, a man of firm principles, and had stated publicly to Calcutta that he refused to engage in 'practices against the Peishwa [the Maratha leader] in any degree incompatible with [the] good faith . . . [or] candour and rectitude so essential to confidence and harmony in the public intercourse of nations' – in other words, he resolutely refused to obey Calcutta's orders to bully, bribe and browbeat the Maratha durbar into a treaty which could reduce them to a state of subservience and which they had not the slightest wish to sign.³ This was not the sort of man who could expect to flourish in Wellesley's India.

Palmer's replacement, it was announced, was to be William Kirkpatrick, whom Wellesley knew would bring a much tougher and more inflexible approach to British relations with Pune. Nana Phadnavis, the great Maratha Minister and Aristu Jah's former rival, had died just three months earlier, and without him to hold it together, the Maratha Confederacy began to unravel at speed, as rival chieftains and warlords jockeyed for power. Wellesley knew that unlike Palmer, William Kirkpatrick would be quite prepared to take full advantage of what the Governor General described as 'the critical state of affairs in the Mahratta Empire [which] becomes hourly more interesting', adding, ominously for the Marathas: 'opportunities [for British intervention] appear likely to open up . . .'⁴

The idea that William Kirkpatrick's health was in any way better than Palmer's was laughable: while Palmer was a fit, active man of sixty, Kirkpatrick, fourteen years his junior, was almost an invalid: his 'cure' at the Cape had been of short duration, and he spent much of his time in Calcutta prostrate with both severe rheumatism and a serious bladder complaint, the pain from which he attempted to alleviate with larger and larger doses of opium. Nevertheless, publicly at least, Palmer accepted his enforced 'retirement' with good grace, replying to Wellesley: 'I am perfectly sensible, My Lord, that the cares and fatigues of an arduous public station may require powers of mind and strength of constitution that it cannot be expected I still possess.'⁵

Privately, however, Palmer was outraged at his 'removal from office without the slightest public pretext' after a lifetime of highly distinguished service to the Company.⁶ He would not normally be expected to retire from the Residency for many years, unless he actually wished to do so: twenty years later, for example, the Delhi Resident, Sir David Ochterlony, was still busily at work at the time of his death aged sixty-seven. Writing to his old friend and patron Warren Hastings, now retired into the depths of the Gloucestershire countryside, Palmer maintained that he had 'preserved the best understanding

with the [Maratha] durbar during my Residency, and have experienced more attention & cordiality from the Peishwa & his principal
servants than any of my predecessors ... Perhaps my disposition is
not thought suitable to the management of our concerns, and if
alliances are [now] to be obtained by menace & intimidation instead
of argument & persuasion & conciliation, then it is certain that a
fitter person than I may easily be found.'[7]

Palmer was one of the last survivors of an earlier generation of
East India Company scholar-officials. His career had flourished under
Hastings, who had shared his love of, and interest in, all things
Indian. For four years between 1776 and 1785 Palmer had been Hast-
ings' Military Secretary in Calcutta, before being sent up-country
as his personal agent (or representative) at the sybaritic court of
Lucknow.

While performing his diplomatic duties, Palmer had spent his
leisure hours busily searching around for interesting Sanskrit and
Mughal manuscripts, often for Hastings, to whom he wrote a long
series of enthusiastic, scholarly letters about his quest.* Palmer also
formed his own extensive collection of ancient Indian coins, and
took a scholarly interest in the traditions of the eighteenth-century
military adventurers.[8]

With these interests and enthusiasms, the General soon grew to
love the highly cultured city of Lucknow. In the late eighteenth
century, with Mughal Delhi sinking into headlong decline, Lucknow
was at the height of its golden age and had usurped the great Mughal

---

* 'I applied to the Shah [Alam II, the blind Mughal Emperor] in your name for permission
to transcribe his copy of the *Mahbharrut*,' he wrote at one point. 'I was assured that it
would have been most cheerfully granted if the book had been in his possession, but his
library had been totally plundered & destroyed by that villain Ghullam Khauder Khan
[who had also blinded the prostrate Emperor with his own thumbs]. He [Shah Alam]
added, not without some degree of indignation, that part of the books had been purchased
at Lucknow, that is by the Vizier [i.e. the Nawab]; & upon enquiry find this to be the
case, for his Excellency [the Nawab] produced some of them to the English Gentlemen,
boasting that they were the 'King's'. Amongst them were two volumes beautifully painted
& illuminated for which he gave 10,000 Rs.' This is probably a reference to the most
beautiful of all Mughal manuscripts, the great *Padshahnama*, which the Nawab soon
afterwards sent to London as a gift for George III. Hastings Papers, BL Add Mss
29,172, Vol. XLI, 1790, p.184, 21 November 1790, Agra. The *Padshahnama* is now one of
the principal treasures of the Windsor Castle Library.

capital to become indisputably the largest, most prosperous and most civilised pre-colonial city in northern India. The city's courtly Urdu diction and elaborate codes of etiquette were renowned as the most subtle and refined in Hindustan;* its dancers admired as the most accomplished; its cuisine famous as the most flamboyantly baroque. According to one historian, this hedonistic city resembled an Indian version of '[pre-Revolutionary] Teheran, Monte Carlo and Las Vegas, with just a touch of Glyndebourne for good measure'.⁹ It was here, in this Bacchanalian atmosphere that Palmer met his lifelong love, and the woman who in due course would become Khair un-Nissa's closest friend, Begum Fyze Baksh.

Palmer was, in fact, already married at the time he met Fyze. As a young man he had been sent as a soldier in the 70th Foot to the West Indies. There, in 1761, on the island of St Kitts, he had married Sarah Hazell, a Creole beauty, by whom he had three boys and two girls.¹⁰ But when Palmer was posted to India six years later, Sarah opted to stay in St Kitts with her daughters while her husband and three boys caught ship to India. The boys continued to write to their mother,¹¹ and after she left the Caribbean and moved to Greenwich, the permanently impecunious Palmer tried to persuade his friends in Britain to send her money;† but there seems to have been no question of Sarah ever intending to

---

* Hindustan at this period was a geographically vague term that encompassed that part of northern India which lay around the Ganges and the Jumna and formed the hinterland to Delhi and Agra – roughly the western half of modern Uttar Pradesh plus Haryana.

† William rather unwisely looked to his Scottish friend David Anderson for money for Sarah's maintenance, writing in March 1792 that 'the heavy losses and disappointments which I have sustained, compel me to lay a small tax upon your friendship and generosity. Having been for some time past utterly unable to make any Remittance to my Mother and Wife if it will not be at all inconvenient to your affairs, you will most essentially serve to oblige me by an advance of Two Hundred pounds towards their support to be paid into the hands of my friend Mr Cooke of Greenwich Hospital. I make no apology for this liberty being convinced that you will rather thank me for the confidence which I place in you on so delicate an occasion.' Anderson, a careful Scotsman and notably tight with his purse-strings, was most put out by the request, pointedly telling his friend in his reply from Edinburgh that he had to learn to manage his financial affairs better, and that he himself had recently had to give up his much-loved beagle pack for reasons of economy. He did however send the money, later writing to his brother: 'I am almost angry at my friend Palmer for his thoughtlessness ... but as he has trusted to me for this advance for the support of his Wife and Mother, I cannot (whatever inconvenience it may be attended with to myself) suffer his expectations to be disappointed ... at the

join him in Lucknow, nor of William planning to return to England to see either her or the two girls who had remained with her.[12] The marriage, one can only assume, had collapsed – or at least jaded into mutual distaste – in the West Indies, and the two had agreed to separate, though there was no divorce and Palmer continued to refer to Sarah as his 'wife'. Either way, by 1779 Palmer had met and married Fyze, according to Muslim law;[13] and the following year the couple had their first child, named William Palmer after his father. In due course the boy's destiny was to be closely – and tragically – interwoven with that of James Kirkpatrick, Khair un-Nissa and her mother.

Palmer's young bride had been born in Mughal Delhi. She was the daughter of 'a Persian captain of cavalry' formerly in the service of the Emperor Shah Alam II, who had emigrated to Lucknow where he rose to prominence in the Nawab's service, and where he later married Fyze's Lucknavi mother.[14] Fyze also had a sister, Nur Begum,[15] who having been married as a child to the Nawab of Pundri, to the west of Delhi, found herself widowed at the age of fifteen, before the marriage could be consummated, and who thereafter seems to have spent much of her time with Fyze in her house in Lucknow. Over the next few years, with Nur on hand to play the role of maiden aunt, Fyze produced child after child on an almost annual basis, until the couple had produced a brood of six – four boys and two girls – in just eight years.

Both Fyze and her children figure prominently in Palmer's letters. 'Your little friend Fyze sends Bunder-gee and bote bote Salaam [many good wishes and may peace be with you],' he wrote to David Anderson in 1781. 'She brought me a little boy soon after you left Lucknow and another here last year, but born dead. I expect another in about four months.'[16] In May 1783, William was outside Lucknow,

---

same time I must request that you will tell Palmer that he must not impose such a Duty on me again.' British Library, Anderson Papers, Add Mss 45,427. p.203, March 1792. Anderson had a point: for all his debts, Palmer enjoyed a princely salary of £22,000 a year – which would make him almost a millionaire in today's currency (though that sum was also supposed to cover all his Residency expenses). As Anderson suggested, Palmer's permanent lack of cash had more to do with his celebrated extravagance than with any lack of resources.

unable to return home due to an epidemic that had attacked his children. 'It is my intention to proceed to the residency as soon as I can move my little family,' he reported. 'The boy is just recovered from Small Pox and a Girl which Fyze brought me six months ago is still ill of it.'[17] A year later 'poor Fyze' was pregnant yet again, and 'has been for this month past so unwieldy that she [cannot make it to their first-floor bedroom and] has been obliged to sleep below stairs'.[18]

A picture of the family painted between April and July 1785 by the artist Johan Zoffany* survives today in the India Office library in London.[19] It is one of the most charming images of a family group to survive from the entire Indo–British encounter. Fyze is placed at the centre of the picture, barefoot and dressed in Lucknavi court costume: a magnificent saffron *peshwaz* and *dupatta* over a brief *angia* bodice.[20] She is seated on the ground, surrounded by her children and their *ayahs* and wetnurses, a calm, serene and beautiful young woman in her late teens, modest and maternal, but hung with the finest Mughal jewellery: sparkling diamond earrings, several strings of pearl necklace and silver *payal* anklets. In her lap she lovingly cradles a sleeping newborn infant. This is her third son, later baptised Hastings Palmer, but now still wrapped in swaddling clothes, his head covered with an embroidered Muslim *topi*. Hastings' two elder siblings, William and Mary, then aged five and three respectively, look on engagingly from the sides of the canvas in their long, flowing Lucknavi *jamas*.

To Fyze's left, seated in a European chair and wearing the formal red coat of his British military uniform, is her husband, a dark, thin, still-handsome man in his early forties. He looks down at Fyze with a long gaze that is at once adoring and protective. To his left, kneeling at his feet but with her expression directed at her elder sister, sits Fyze's sister Nur, then a beautiful girl of around sixteen, wearing

---

* The Frankfurt-born Zoffany (1734–1810) lived in Lucknow for two and a half years, staying much of the time with Claude Martin. On his way back to England (where he had settled in the 1750s) he was shipwrecked off the Andaman Islands. Lots having been drawn among the starving survivors, a young sailor was duly eaten. Zoffany may thus be said with some confidence to have been the first and last Royal Academician to become a cannibal.

a thin white veil. Another sister looks on from the right of the painting.[21]

Sometime towards the end of the 1780s Nur married William's friend, the great Savoy-born Maratha General, Benoît de Boigne, and went to live with him in his house in Aligarh, near Agra. The letters between the two brothers-in-law, preserved in the de Boigne family archives in Chambéry, contain many fond references to the two sisters: 'Fyze sends her affectionate salaams to her *bahyne* [sister], to which I add mine,' Palmer writes at one point. 'Give my love to the Begum & kiss the young Baron for me,' he writes again in February 1792; then more unexpectedly two months later, 'Make my affectionate salaams to my sister the Begum.* How will she bear a rival princess?'[22]

This is a reference to one of de Boigne's two other concubines, Mihr un-Nissa and Zeenut,† who were both given to de Boigne as spoils of war, although of at least one of them he swore '*Je ne l'ai jamais touché.*'‡ When de Boigne returned to Europe in November 1796, bringing Nur with him, he left the allowance due to his two other women in the hands of Fyze, and the Chambéry archive contains a fascinating Persian *arzee*, or petition, in Fyze's hand, begging her brother-in-law de Boigne to increase their pensions – a fascinating instance of female solidarity within the *zenana*: after all, Mihr un-Nissa and Zeenut might in other circumstances have been taken to be rivals of Fyze's sister, and therefore hardly eligible for her support. The *arzee* is headed, very grandly:

* The formulation 'my sister the Begum' is of course additional evidence that Palmer did go through some sort of marriage ceremony with Fyze. It is hardly likely he would claim Nur Begum as his sister-in-law if Fyze was merely an unrecognised concubine.
† 'Zeenut' and 'Mihr un-Nissa' would probably be transliterated today as 'Zeenat' and 'Mehr un-Nissa', but I have retained the spelling used in the sources.
‡ Mihr un-Nissa is referred to in letters of de Boigne as the adopted daughter of the powerful Mughal General Najaf Khan and his wife Moti Begum. Moti gave Mihr to de Boigne as a present after he safeguarded her when he stormed a fortress that Moti was defending. The present was not, however, quite as generous as it first appeared. De Boigne later wrote that 'when I got this girl [it was understood that] she would live with me in rather an inferior condition, as being only an adopted girl of this Moti Begum. But she was far from being handsome and of a most violent disposition and temper, as well as bad education, so much so that I could not gain upon her to live with her mother at Delhi, who also did not appear desirous to have her on account of her bad temper'. After his departure, de Boigne left instructions that Mihr un-Nissa was 'free to marry or

Arzee from Lady Fyze un-Nissa Khanum
to the Saheb Kalan [Great Lord] M. Benoît de Boigne.

My Lord Hail!

From the day I parted from you, God and the people are my witness, that I am continually thinking of you, and I hope you will not forget me. The money which you entrusted me to present to Moutie [Mihr un-Nissa's mother], she has refused it; saying, never mind, it is too little to be of consequence. We must think about this. My Lord, she is an influential person; if the sum had been worthy of her position, she would have accepted it; [but she didn't, so] the purse and that sum are returned herewith. Pray do not be offended in the least by my returning the money. You are a great man, and she is likewise very respectable. Perhaps we should consult together on what to offer her. The purse is sent merely to remind you. Forget me not.[23]

The Lucknow that Fyze and Palmer inhabited was every bit as hybrid as their own marriage; indeed Lucknow in many ways pioneered the sort of white Mughal Residency culture which James Kirkpatrick later cultivated at Hyderabad. If the Nawab sometimes amazed foreign visitors by appearing dressed as a British admiral, or even as a clergyman of the Church of England, then the Europeans of Lucknow often returned the compliment.[24] Miniature after miniature from late-eighteenth-century Lucknow shows Europeans of the period dressed in long white Avadhi gowns, lying back on carpets, hubble-bubbles in their mouths, as they watch their nautch girls dance before them. Some Europeans even married into the Nawabi royal family: William Linnaeus Gardner's Anglo-Indian son James, for example, married the Nawab's sister-in-law, Mulka Begum.[25]*

Nor was this sexual curiosity one-way: at least two British memsahibs (or possibly Anglo-Indians) were recruited to join the Avadhi harem, and a mosque survives which was built by the Nawab for one of them, a Miss Walters.[26] Another Englishwoman who was

---

live single just as she pleases'. See Desmond Young, *Fountain of Elephants* (London, 1959), p.146, and the de Boigne archives, Chambéry, *passim*.
* 'Mulka' would probably be transliterated today as 'Malika', but I have retained the spelling used in the sources.

ABOVE: James Achilles Kirkpatrick, the British Resident at Hyderabad, 1799. On the reverse James noted that: '*This was copied from a sketch taken of me in the Hindostanny dress presented me by Meer Allum & which I wore at his particular request at his son Meer Dowraun's nuptials; with this difference, that the original drawing which was made by old Shah Tajully [Ali Shah] was a more flattering – and according to the opinion of those who saw it a more faithful – likeness in a sitting posture and the coloured dress which I had on at the time and which was Nah Firmaun [more appropriate].*' The inscription on the front reads in Persian: 'Mutamin ul-Mulk, Fakhr ud-Dowlah Bahadur, Hushmat Jung', James's principal titles.

OVERLEAF: The Nizam and his durbar ride out on a hunting expedition, *c*.1790, by Venkatchellam. To the right of the picture, the Nizam is seated on his elephant, with a hawk on his wrist; Aristu Jah is seated behind him holding a peacock fan. Above in the top-right hand corner is poet and courtesan Mah Laqa Bai Chanda, carried in her gilded palanquin and accompanied by her hunting cheetah. General Raymond, wearing a black broad-brimmed hat, rides behind the vanguard of the red-jacketed Corps Français de Raymond to the left of the central register. Almost immediately in front of the Nizam's elephant rides the young Mir Alam, who glances back towards the Nizam. The artist has depicted himself riding out holding a paintbrush on the bottom register, far left, accompanied by the small Persian inscription: 'Rai Venkatchellam, *tasvir* [painter]'.

Images of the Hyderabadi durbar by Venkatchellam

ABOVE: Aristu Jah at the height of his powers, *c.*1800, with his ubiquitous golden hookah. Contemporary Hyderabadi chronicles say the Minister never left this pipe for a second, and that 'the smell of his scented tobacco' was one of the great features of his durbar.

OPPOSITE [*clockwise from top left*]: Henry Russell, *c.*1805; the two youngest sons of the Nizam, princes Suleiman Jah and Kaiwan Jah, *c.*1802 (Kaiwan Jah was given to Aristu Jah to adopt following the death of his own son Ma'ali Mian during the Khardla campaign); Nizam Ali Khan consults Aristu Jah and his son and successor Sikander Jah, *c.*1800 (both this picture and that of the two princes are from James's own miniature collection); Ma'ali Mian, Aristu Jah's eldest son and the husband of Farzand Begum, sniffs a flower while admiring a string of pearls and his hunting hawk, sitting amid the parakeets and fountains of his pleasure garden.

LEFT: The young Maratha Peshwa Madhu Rao (*left*) with his guardian and effective jailor, the brilliant and ruthless Maratha Minister Nana Phadnavis. By James Wales, 1792.

ABOVE: Tipu Sultan, the Tiger of Mysore, *c*.1790.

Richard Colley Wellesley, 1st Marquess Wellesley, by J. Pain Davis *c*.1815. 'He is clever but weak [and] proud,' thought one observer, 'and will get himself more looked up to than beloved.'

Mir Alam, Khair un-Nissa's first cousin, and the protégé and later rival and successor of Aristu Jah.

ABOVE: James Achilles Kirkpatrick, *c*.1805, attributed to George Chinnery.

ABOVE RIGHT: General William Palmer in old age, *c*. 1810.

BELOW: The famous Zoffany picture of General William and Fyze Palmer with their young family in Lucknow. It was painted sometime between April and July 1785. The young William Palmer, the future Hyderabadi banker, looks on from the left, Fyze is seated at the centre left of the picture in a red *angia* and *peshwaz*, and the General looks on adoringly from the centre. The two well-dressed women on the right of the picture are presumably Fyze's sisters. The sister kneeling immediately next to the General has traditionally been identified as Nur Begum, later the wife of General Benoît de Boigne.

OVERLEAF: The celebrated portrait by George Chinnery of James and Khair's two children, Sahib Allum and Sahib Begum. Shortly after the picture was painted in August 1805 the children were booked onto the *Lord Hawkesbury* for the passage to England as William George and Katherine Aurora Kirkpatrick, names they would bear for the rest of their lives.

married to a prominent Lucknavi Muslim nobleman at this
wrote a remarkable book entitled, somewhat cumbersomely, *Obse*
tions on the Mussulmauns of India Descriptive of their Mann
Customs, Habits and Religious Opinions Made During Twelve Ye
Residence in their Immediate Society, which she published un
the name Mrs Meer Hassan Ali.[27] After returning to Englan
Mrs Meer Hassan Ali ended her life, bizarrely enough, 'attach
in some capacity to the household of [George III's sister] Prince:
Augusta'.[28]*

Equally integrated into the life of Lucknow was one of Palmer's
best friends, the Swiss-French engineer, businessman, spy and scholar,
Colonel Antoine Polier. On his *jagir* near Agra or in his *haveli* in
Lucknow, Polier lived entirely like a Mughal nobleman, as his
voluminous Persian correspondence, now in the Bibliothèque
National in Paris, shows. One day he might instruct his agents to

---

* Intellectually too, there seems to have been a remarkable degree of intercourse between
the more enlightened Europeans and the scholars and poets of Lucknow. The greatest
collection of Oriental manuscripts in Britain – now the core of the India Office collection
– was formed by Richard Johnson while he was the Deputy to the British Resider
Lucknow. During his years in Avadh he mixed with the poets, scholars and calligra
of Lucknow, discussing Sanskrit and Persian literature, and forming long-lasting f
ships with many of them. One of these scholars, Abu Talib Tafazul, was an old
both of the Palmers and of Khair un-Nissa's cousin, Abdul Lateef Shushtari; in
was probably the man Shushtari most admired in India. In the *Tuhfat al-'Alam S*
described Tafazul as a 'pious Shiite, who also knew, apart from Persian an
English and the Roman tongue which they call Latin, which is the learned ton
Europeans in which they write their scholarly books, and which has the sam
among them as Arabic among non-Arab Muslims. Tafazul even knew Gre
translated several books by European scholars into Arabic, apart from his c
on algebra and jurisprudence. India should be proud to have brought forth s
... however much his position gave him the attributes of wealth and sta
changed his courteous and egalitarian behaviour towards the poor and the
Abd al-Latif Shushtari, *Kitab Tuhfat al-'Alam* (written Hyderabad, 180
Bombay, 1847), p.450. Johnson and Palmer also greatly admired Tafaz
welcome him to their houses, where they would discuss mathematics, as
and Greek. Palmer even took Tafazul with him to help negotiate a trea
of Gohud, and persuaded him to help with the drafting of letters to t'
Toby Falk and Mildred Archer, *Indian Miniatures in the India Offic*
1981), pp.14–20. For Tafazul see Gulfishan Khan, *Indian Muslim Pe*
During the Eighteenth Century (Karachi, 1998). Writing to Warrer
also fond of the old scholar, Palmer called him the embodiment
learned and good among the Mussulmans'; Hastings Papers, BL
XLVII, 1801–02, 10 July 1801, pp.61–3, William Palmer to Hastir

find him betel-leaf holders, hookahs and luxurious palanquins; the next he would send for the great Lucknavi painter Mir Chand and order an album-ful of miniatures of his wives and dancing girls; a third he might send out for his favourite green mango pickle or a particular type of scented tobacco. He had two Indian wives (one senior, one junior, who were deeply jealous of each other and fought incessantly), a large number of half-Indian children (one of whom, George, later went to live with Palmer's sister-in-law Nur Begum in Sussex[29]), and a vast collection of rare Mughal manuscripts (which mostly ended up in Paris).[30]*

In his letters to Hastings from this tolerant and hedonistic oasis, Palmer's letters mixed happy expressions of pleasure in the life he lived in Lucknow with darker passages recording his growing horror at the ever-increasing arrogance and indeed naked racism of the Company's government in Calcutta from the late 1790s onwards. When Wellesley arrived in 1798 things rapidly went from bad to worse, and Palmer's correspondence shows that he intensely disliked the new Governor General from the start; he wrote perceptively to Hastings of Wellesley's 'inordinate love of pomp, and a Vanity which almost surpasses conception'. He added, equally perceptively, 'It is sincerely to be lamented that such weakness should accompany and defeat the effects of talents of the first order.' A couple of years later, Palmer had become firmly convinced that Wellesley's policies were bringing disaster to India, and permanently estranging Indians from the British. 'I do not take His Lordship's patriotism to be of the first order,' he wrote to Hastings after a trip to Calcutta.

> The desire of fame is his ruling passion & it is insatiable, too often indeed ridiculous. His state maxims are those audacious one's of Mr. Pitt's that the end justifies the means & convenience sanctifies the ends . . . Little or no attention is [now] paid to those [of your friends] who are *Vakils* [ambassadors] of the Native Courts by Lord Wellesley. They are not permitted

er years of agonising as to whether he should stay in India or not, Polier finally
ed to return to France and buy a château – with exquisite bad timing – in 1788.
ttled near Avignon and was duly lynched and stabbed on 9 February 1795 in the
that accompanied the French Revolution.

to pay their respects to him oftener than two or three times a year which I think is as impolitic as it is ingracious . . .

I observe with great concern the system of oppressing them adopted by the present government and imitated in the manners of almost every European. They are excluded from all posts of great respectability or emolument, and are treated in society with mortifying hauteur and reserve. In fact they now have hardly any social intercourse with us. The functions of magistrate and judge are performed by Europeans who know neither the laws nor the language of the country, and with an enormous expense to the Company. The Head Molavy in each court, on whose information and explanation the judges must decide, has a salary of Rs.50 a month. And this I believe one of the most trustworthy and lucrative employments which a Native is allowed to hold in the Company's service. What must be the sensations of this people at our thus starving them in their native land?[31]

A couple of months on, Palmer was gloomier still: 'Our weakness, arrogance & injustice cannot fail to draw upon us the vengeance of a united India,' he wrote prophetically. 'Already there have been insurrections . . .'[32] Against this background of growing British conceit, and with Palmer feeling increasingly isolated as he saw successive new generations of British officials behaving with ever greater *hauteur* to his Indian friends, he quickly realised that James Kirkpatrick represented a kindred spirit. As soon as he arrived in Pune in 1798, Palmer jumped to befriend his counterpart over the border in Hyderabad.

In a series of increasingly warm letters, the General did his best to establish a close friendship with James, though they had yet to meet face to face. Among their many shared enthusiasms, it turned out in the course of their correspondence, was a passionate love of mangoes: 'The mango season has been late but tolerably abundant & of no bad flavour,' wrote James in one of the first letters, whereupon Palmer offered to send him a selection of mango grafts for his orchards; the two were soon comparing notes on their favourite varieties, agreeing – sensibly enough – that Alphonsos were hard to bcat. When Mir Alam complained to Calcutta about James, Palmer was quick to offer support, and when the Mir finally fell from grace after Aristu Jah managed to get him sacked and arrested, Palmer wrote a characteristically discerning letter about him to James:

> I confess I feel no compassion for Mir Alam. His malice and ingratitude to you deserve much severer retribution than has yet fallen upon him, and his mind is so sordid as to render him unworthy of confidence or esteem. All his zeal in our cause was excited by his persuasion of its carrying him, by the nearest road, to reputation & fortune, and if these objects could have been obtained by opposing our interests, or even by exterminating us, I have no doubt he would have laboured to that effect. His firmness and abilities certainly make him a valuable acquisition to any cause he thinks it in his interest to support; but unbounded sacrifices to his avarice must be made to retain him ... He well knows that Aristu Jah has never forgiven his conduct towards him while he was prisoner here, and to expose himself to the consequences of it, and of your resentment, by acting upon the silly stories which were framed of you in the hope of injuring you, shows that his rancour had quite subdued his reason.[33]

Other letters expressed both men's growing disillusion with Wellesley, and in this Palmer led the way, encouraging his younger colleague to express openly what he really thought about the vain and aggressive Governor General. Letter by letter, Palmer openly voiced the heresies that James had up to now only expressed tentatively to his elder brother: of Wellesley's personal arrogance, his imperious way of behaving both to his own colleagues and to Indian rulers and ambassadors, his ruinous overspending, and his habit of making appointments and decisions without even summoning the Council through whose majority vote all his predecessors had filtered their decisions.[34]

Throughout June 1801, James was already becoming more and more disgusted with Wellesley's bullying approach to Indian rulers, when an order came from Calcutta commanding him to renegotiate the solemn Subsidiary Treaty Wellesley and the Nizam had signed only the previous year. In that treaty, the chunk of Tipu's territory won by the Nizam after the fall of Seringapatam had been surrendered to the Company in return for the British agreeing to send a large number of extra troops to increase the size of the Subsidiary Force in Hyderabad. The extra troops had yet to arrive, indeed they had not yet left Madras, but when Wellesley discovered that the revenue of the area handed over to the Company had fallen far short of what he expected, he wrote to James demanding that he get the Nizam to make up the shortfall, despite the fact this was specifically forbidden in the small print of the treaty.[35] Wellesley had no leg to stand on: he was manifestly bullying an important and friendly ally into handing over large sums of cash without any legal pretext, and in direct contravention of a treaty he had signed only eight months earlier. The fact that no new troops, and only a limited quantity of artillery, had yet arrived in Hyderabad made the blatant injustice of Wellesley's position all the more glaring.

Palmer was quite clear what this would mean for British relations with Hyderabad: due to these 'hard exactions . . . I fear our harmony with the court of Hyderabad will be completely interrupted'.[36] James was even more baffled by Wellesley's 'cruel' instructions, and wrote privately to his elder brother in a state of deep depression: 'My dear Will, the more I reflect on these secret commands, the more deeply they fill me with regret, astonishment and alarm . . . [they are a] glaring attempt at infringement on a recent advantageous treaty with an old and highly useful ally and [if they should] get abroad nothing on earth could save his Lordship from impeachment [back in Britain].'[37]

It was a turning point for James. From this moment, he wrote to William, it was 'no longer in my power to cherish that high awareness of his [Wellesley's] political wisdom and integrity that I hitherto did'.[38] James had his opinion of Wellesley's rapaciousness confirmed in November 1801, when the Governor General sent his youngest brother Henry to Lucknow to extract massive territorial concessions from the hapless Nawab. Having bullied and threatened Nawab Saadat Ali Khan into signing over more than half of his dominions to the Company, including most of the rich and fertile Doab region, worth a total annual revenue of more than thirteen million rupees, Henry Wellesley was then given charge of the newly seized territories.[39]

James could not believe what was happening, all of it without any legal justification, and wrote to Palmer that he was again half-considering resignation rather than continue to serve such a master:

> I am, my dear Sir, so heartily sick (between ourselves) of witnessing such disgraceful doings that I do not think it at all impossible but I may keep you company from hence [when Palmer's successor arrived in Pune], as far as our two routes be together, yours to Calcutta, mine to Madras [where James could catch ship to England]. [It is scarcely possible to credit] the extraordinary threats said to have been held out to the Nabob [Nawab] by Mr [Henry] Wellesley, who I understand is to enjoy the fruits of his labours in some great office of controul over the countries thus wrested from their rightful owner.[40]

In the meantime James had to decide how to react to Lord Wellesley's instructions to renegotiate his Subsidiary Treaty. He wrote in despair to Palmer, saying that 'the Dispatch of the Gov General almost sets me frantic. How, after all the assurances that I gave Solomon [Aristu Jah] in the course of the late Negotiations, can I show my face to him with such demands as I am now ordered to bring forward, and how will he, poor man, be able to shew his face to his master?'[41] In the end, screwing up his courage, James wrote back to Wellesley and told him that he thought the orders he had received were frankly unreasonable, and clearly contrary to the stipulations of the treaty he, Wellesley, had signed less than a year earlier. It was a major mistake, at least as far as James's future career was concerned: Wellesley was never one to take criticism lightly, and his attitude towards James, and the language in which his letters were phrased, grew progressively more hostile and adversarial from this point onwards.

James's letters to Palmer strayed, however, far beyond their shared political beliefs, hopes and fears: the pair also discussed the less upsetting and more intimate subject of Palmer's Anglo-Indian children, who had all been educated in England and were now returning to try to make lives for themselves in India. In 1799, James had found a job for William, Fyze's eldest son, in the Nizam's irregular cavalry, and he now offered to look after their daughter Mary on her return from England as she made her way from Madras to Pune (an offer that in the end was not taken up, as Mary chose instead to join her half-brother John Palmer, a successful Calcutta banker known as 'The Prince of Merchants', and so did not in the end pass through James's Residency*). The offer was greatly appreciated by Fyze and the General: at a time of growing prejudice against Anglo-Indians, the Palmers felt sure that they could trust James to be friendly to their beloved daughter.

Soon Palmer was writing to James that he planned to visit Hyderabad himself once he had finally been relieved of his duties. He would return to Calcutta via Hyderabad and Masulipatam, and would it be possible for him to stay at the Residency?[42] James replied that he was delighted at the prospect: 'I have a large bangaloe prepared, which will I think accomadate you and your entire family,' he wrote. 'There is a zennanah, though rather a small one, attached to it.'[43] This, it soon became apparent, was not going to be by any means sufficient. As James wrote in a letter shortly afterwards, the General's 'suite is rather numerous and includes at least a dozen females'.[44]

The Palmers – especially Fyze, now honoured as an 'adopted daughter' of the Mughal Emperor, and known by the title Sahib Begum – clearly liked to travel in style.[45]

* John Palmer was the youngest child of General Palmer's first wife Sarah Hazell. Since leaving the navy in 1783, he had joined the Calcutta agency house of Burgh, Barber & Co. In the mid-1790s he became sole manager under the name Palmer & Co. Shortly before this, according to his obituary in the *Englishman and Military Chronicle*, he used all the capital he had saved to bail his impecunious father out of a short period in jail, whence he had been thrown for bad debts: '. . . At the very early period of his career, his father, General Palmer, an extravagant man, was arrested for debt which he was

In that long, hot summer of 1801, James had also found his own *zenana* rather too small for his needs. For sometime in late August, he had decided to throw caution to the winds, and formally to invite Khair un-Nissa and their little baby Sahib Allum (and also, so it seems, James's mother-in-law, Sharaf un-Nissa) to come and live in his *zenana* in the Residency, apparently displacing, if they had not done so already, James's existing concubines.

The reason he later gave for taking this risky decision was that he 'did hearken to the voice of nature, pleading eloquently in the engaging form of an helpless and innocent infant', and this may well have been partly true.[46] The child was considered by everyone who saw him 'a most lovely infant', and 'by his female connexions as a downright prodigy of loveliness of every kind'.[47] James also remarked that 'among other circumstances which render this child peculiarly dear and interesting to me is the striking resemblance which he bears to my dear father [the Handsome Colonel], which has been remarked by all his female attendants who have seen the picture [of the Colonel] hanging up in my room, and which Ure and his wife (who are the only Europeans who have seen him) declare to be uncommonly strong. He is indeed, in every respect, a most lovely infant, the most so, if their declarations can be relied upon, that Ure or his good wife, ever in their lives saw.'[48]

Later, discussing with William the distant prospects for following Palmer's lead and sending the boy to England to be educated, James admitted, 'it will go to my soul to part with him, to say nothing of the opposition I may expect to meet with on this point in another quarter'.[49] But it clearly was not just because he had fallen in love with his baby son that the proud father finally invited his family onto the British Residency compound; he was badly missing Khair un-Nissa too. He knew he was risking everything by allowing his aristocratic Muslim wife into the Residency when he was yet to admit to Calcutta that there was any truth at all in the stories of their liaison, and when that liaison had

entirely without means of defraying. His son had just at the same time formed arrangements for concerting a commercial partnership, for which he had realized a capital not more than sufficient; this he instantly sacrificed to liberate his father, and by so doing created a general feeling of respect and confidence, which greatly contributed to advance his future prospects.' *Englishman and Military Chronicle*, 23 January 1836, p.157.

already caused him so much grief with his masters. The fact that he willingly took that risk – as he had already taken so many others – is a measure of the strength of his commitment to his young wife.

Now he directed all his energies into building Khair a *zenana*-palace that would meet her expectations and requirements. That month he began work constructing the Mughal-style 'Hindoostanee House' or 'Rang Mahal' ('Palace of Colours'), which was later described as 'a very elegant and highly finished specimen of Hindustan architecture'.[50] James never describes the building himself in his letters, but according to an impressed visitor who was allowed to look around it in 1809, it was 'built according to the native fashion & I have been assured that no Indian prince has so elegant a zenana. It would be reckoned a most beautiful set of apartments in Europe. It is situated in a garden. Within the court is a parterre. Round the interior of the court is a verandah of which the walls and ceilings are painted & gilded with great brilliancy & taste. The principal bedroom is larger than the Asiatics are accustomed to construct. The dressing room and baths are exactly the size they prefer.'[51] At the centre of the principal courtyard was a large marble basin of water, fed by numerous fountains and lined by stately cypress trees. The arcades and terraces surrounding the court were gilded and richly ornamented with trellised *jail* screens and paintings of birds, flowers and beasts. Here Khair would entertain the ladies while Kirkpatrick received their husbands in the main Residency building.[52]

Seventy years later, almost the entire structure was destroyed and levelled by a shocked Victorian Resident who believed that it smacked of 'native immorality'.* All that remains now is the beautifully built and decorated gatehouse, and some fragments of the interior including what appears to be Khair's *kabooter khana*, or pigeon house. Dilapidated and overgrown as these fragments are, lying at the rear of a space still known as 'the Begum's Garden', the quite exceptional finish and beauty of their construction hint at just how fine was the palace that James built for his beloved Khair un-Nissa, and for their son, Sahib Allum, the little Lord of the World.

* The *mahal* was pulled down by Sir George Yule in 1860. See *Bengal Past and Present*, Vol. 27, January–June 1924, No. 53, p.120.

Wellesley had given Palmer notice that he was to be replaced in June 1800, but a year later he was still in place, thanks to the increasing illness of his putative successor, William Kirkpatrick.

William did not set off from Calcutta until March 1801, and far from getting better on the voyage, as he had hoped, instead found his condition rapidly worsening. He arrived in Madras 'in a grievous state of health', with his agonising bladder condition greatly inflamed and much more painful. James immediately sent Dr Ure off to Madras to try to treat his elder brother – Ure had, after all, tended to William throughout his time as Resident in Hyderabad, especially after his health broke down during the siege of Khardla – and for once, Ure's treatment seemed to work.

On 5 April 1801, James was able to write that he had just heard of the improvement in William's condition: 'I may consequently 'ere long have the happiness of embracing you at Hyderabad.' But he went on to tell William that if things got worse again, Ure had been clear that 'you should return home without further delay, [and] for heavens sake let no [financial] consideration prevent your doing so by the very next opportunity from Madras.'[53]

Twelve days later, however, while staying in Madras with William Thackeray, the uncle of the novelist, William Kirkpatrick's health had once again broken down. The Madras doctor had made him drink 'caustic' in an attempt to unblock his urethra, with drastic results: 'I am glad you did not attempt to give me an idea of the sufferings you have laboured under, as they have already by a sort of sympathy affected me more than I can describe,' wrote James. 'Heaven grant that my dearest brother may never again be exposed to them . . . I perfectly concur with you in thinking that the caustic ought not to have been applied until the irritation of your body had somewhat more subsided, and I earnestly trust that this opinion will prevent you from submitting to any further operations until your strength shall enable you to bear them, and your habit be in a proper condition to meet them.' James also promised to search Hyderabad for some presents for Thackeray's boys and nephews as a way of rewarding him for his care: 'I will enquire for toys for Thackeray's children immediately,' he wrote on the seventeenth. 'What is there indeed that I would not most heartily make him an offer of, within the compass of my means and ability, if he returns my beloved William to the full enjoyment of health again, which I am now sanguine enough to expect he will.'[54]*

William's health continued to fluctuate, but he remained far too ill to proceed in the direction of Pune, and as the omens grew less and less encouraging, James began encouraging him to think seriously about retiring to England, though he was only forty-six: 'you must now consult your own preservation, my dearest Will, and the well-being of your family in preference to every other consideration', he wrote at the end of April. 'These, in my opinion, loudly call for your early return to your native country.'[55] He also made it clear that he would consider it his duty to support his elder brother in his retire-ment: 'My purse, as you well know, and as I have so often told you, is most entirely at your service, and must be considered in fact as your own.'[56]

In early May, when William's health suddenly dipped again, Ure despatched some new 'electuary', while James scoured the Deccan to find some 'very fine fresh figs and prunes' in order that Ure could 'compose an electuary that you will approve of both for its taste and its effects. Ure is however decidedly of the opinion that you ought on no account allow of any further operation being performed upon you until you have completely recovered your strength.'[57]

This never happened; instead William's health complications

---

* The toys were found, but only got to Thackeray as late as mid-September that year, after a mix-up when 'the crate of toys sent for Thackeray's children got swapped for one containing Lord Clive's collection of arms and armour [intended for Powys Castle, where they remain], to the latter's amazement when he opened it and found playthings instead'. OIOC, Kirkpatrick Papers, F228/13, p.164, 16 September 1801. It is interesting to think of the nappy-clad author of *Vanity Fair* growing up playing with Mughal rattles sent by James Kirkpatrick and Khair un-Nissa from the bazaars of Hyderabad.

became more and more serious, and the pain almost unbearable.*
By the beginning of June, he was forced to accept that his career in
India was over, at least for the time being. He wrote to Calcutta for
permission to leave India on account of his health, and at the end
of the month received the brief chit from Wellesley allowing him to
head 'for the Cape, and eventually to Europe on Furlough should
the state of your health render a voyage to Europe necessary'.[58]†

All that remained now was for William to find a ship to take him
home. James wrote: 'I must still insist on your embarking on none but
an Indiaman with a *good* surgeon on board: these you know, are *sine
qua nons* to my hearty acquiescence in the step, and if you cannot get
such a passage at Madras you should go to Bengal in search of one.'[59]

While William lingered prostrate in the Thackerays' house in Madras,
the two young Assistants who had accompanied him from Calcutta
were told to proceed on their way to Pune, via Mysore and Hyderabad, where they would in due course be joined by a Resident, once
one had been appointed to replace William.

Edward Strachey and Mountstuart Elphinstone were, James
thought, 'two very superior young men';[60] and the *double entendre*
of this phrase was entirely deliberate. Strachey was twenty-six, Elphinstone barely twenty-one. Both were highly intelligent and capable;
but they made little effort to hide the fact that they knew it, or that
they clearly believed they were destined for great things.

---

* Some of William's symptoms sound suspiciously like a severe case of mercury poisoning, which no doubt exacerbated the pain and seriousness of his bladder complaint.
† With it came an official certificate, also dated 20 June 1801, computing the length of
William's service in India to date. It stated that he had been admitted as a cadet on 26
September 1771, resigned 18 December 1783; was readmitted 25 July 1785, and that he had
therefore spent a total of twenty-nine years, eight months and twenty-four days in India,
on the basis of which the Company intended to calculate his pension. OIOC, Kirkpatrick
Papers, F227/25, p.30, 20 June 1801, Lord Wellesley to William Kirkpatrick.

As there was no need for them to rush to their new appointment in Pune, they took their time about it, zigzagging across almost the whole of India and spending nearly a year *en route*. They travelled in great state with a *sawaree* of eight elephants, eleven camels, four horses and ten bullocks, not to mention the horses and ponies of their servants, of whom there were between 150 and two hundred, together with an escort of twenty sepoys and, later, what Elphinstone described as 'a Mahratta condottiere of 30 to 40 men'. One elephant was reserved entirely for carrying their books, including a history of the Bengal Mutiny by Edward's father, Henry Strachey, as well as volumes of the Persian poets, and editions of Homer, Horace, Hesiod, Herodotus, Theocritus, Sappho, Plato, *Beowulf*, Machiavelli, Voltaire, Horace Walpole, Dryden, Bacon, Boswell and Thomas Jefferson. As they ambled across India at the Company's expense, they read aloud to each other, sketched, practised their Persian and Marathi grammar, went shooting and played the flute by the light of the moon. They also kept diaries.[61]

Diaries – and especially travel diaries – often reveal as much about the writer as the place or person written about. In his trip to Hyderabad, the French jeweller Tavernier noticed mainly the gold and diamonds in the bazaars, while the anonymous French soldier-gourmet who wrote an account of Hyderabad in 1750 was transfixed by the city's celebrated cooking, especially the famous Hyderabad biryani. Edward Strachey, brought up at the height of the fashion for the Picturesque, saw instead a City of Ruins. Elphinstone, meanwhile, raised his nose at so extreme an angle he missed much that was of interest; but what he did record, he noted down with a waspish wit.

The two young Englishmen arrived at the outskirts of Hyderabad on the evening of 22 August 1801. As Strachey noted:

> Near the city the grounds are more bare, rugged and rocky than before . . . Hyderabad is surrounded by a stone wall the extent of which is I am told nearly seven miles. This defence would be sufficient to keep off predatory incursions of horse, but would not stand an hour against our artillery. From a distance [you can see over the walls] . . . a great many white buildings much hid among trees with some lofty buildings and

minarets rising above them . . . Wretched and ruinous as the
scene is now where the walls are cracked and decayed, the cor-
nices broke and different parts of the building overgrown with
grass and weeds, I can easily conceive that in better times it must
have been in a high degree splendid and magnificent . . .[62]

The two diaries, with their detailed record of five months in Hyderabad, form one of the most graphic and immediate sources for the city
in the early nineteenth century. From the comments they make, both
Strachey and Elphinstone clearly thought they were making a record
of a timeless India that had not changed for centuries; but in actual fact
the diaries are important and observant records of Hyderabad at a time
of massive and rapid change: the ruins Strachey so lovingly describes
were irrigated pleasure gardens when Tavernier passed through the city
shortly before the Mughal invasion, while a few years later they would
be swallowed up in the bustling commercial quarter that quickly grew
up around Kirkpatrick's Residency.

Likewise the picture of their visit to the Hyderabad durbar given
by Elphinstone a month after his arrival is a record not of medieval
continuity or the timeless customs of 'Oriental Despotism', as he and
Strachey thought, but an interesting snapshot of ceremonial in a
period of transformation, when the old ways copied from the Mughal
emperors of the Delhi Red Fort were slowly becoming mixed with
new forms imported from Europe: 'Major K[irkpatrick] goes [to the
durbar] in great state and has several elephants, a state palankeen,
led horses, flags, long poles with tassels &ca and is attended by ten
companies of infantry & a troop of cavalry,' recorded Elphinstone.

> . . . We passed through several courts in going to His High-
> ness's presence, the gates surrounded by armed men some of
> them with beards one or two with steel caps [i.e. helmets]
> and gauntlets, some of them very picturesque . . . At the last
> courtyard, the minister Azim ul Omrah [Aristu Jah] met us
> & embraced us. He led us though a court to a *diwan khaneh*
> where the Nizam was sitting. I went up to him and presented
> my nuzzar [ceremonial gift]. Major K's munshi [Aziz Ullah]
> showed me how to hold it and a man prest me down to the

proper stoop; His Highness took my nuzzar smiling. I retired and made a low salaam.

The Nizam was drest in brocade. He kept his right arm, which is palsied, within his gown; he wore a cap with a shawl twisted round it. The whole headress was shaped like a cone. He is a good looking old man [and . . .] wore many splendid jewels. There were many other people some sitting & some standing. Among the latter were several female women sentries, dressed something like Madras seypoys. More were on guard before the doors & about 20 or 30 more women were drawn out before [the] guardroom in sight. Many women sat in the back part of the room where we were.

The Nizam showed us many clocks & curious pieces of mechanism some of them very obscene . . . I did not hear him say a word – he was most of the time amusing himself with laughing at the little machinery of the watches etc . . . Major K behaved like a native & with great propriety. The Nizam gave [us] sirpèches [turban jewels] for each donation [nuzzar]. Eventually we made a low bow then we withdrew into a room on one side of a passage.

[Here] we stopt to talk with the Minister [Aristu Jah] . . . He looks much younger than the Nizam & was plainly dressed. His only ornaments were a gold belt & dagger with a diamond buckle. He talked familiarly with a favourite old *aseel*, Mama Barun . . .[63]

[Afterwards] the Resident told us of an event which had just happened, and which shows strongly the nature of the Nizam's Govt. There had been many robberies committed in the city within a short time and the Nizam declared that if there were any more he would make an example of some of the offenders. One morning the *Kotwal* brought three men to the Nizam declaring that he had seized them drunk in the street late at night. The Nizam simply ordered them to be blown from a gun. The sentence had just been put in execution when one of the chief *Omrahs* of the court came in and said that the men were honest men servants of his, returning from a merry meeting where they had been drinking. The Minister [Aristu Jah] took advantage of the *Kotwals* having occasioned, by his careless report, the execution of the three innocent men, and fined him 30,000 rupees . . .[64]

It is a fascinating moment: the old Mughal ceremonial – the giving and receiving of nuzzars – and the tradition of instant 'justice' has survived, despite the intrusion of growing Company power and a profusion of new European knick-knacks such as the 'very obscene' clocks (a matter in which the Nizams seem to have pre-empted the tastes of the later Victorian maharajahs). The description is also interesting for what it shows of the sudden and unexpected power and prominence of women in the Hyderabad durbar at this period, and the degree to which Mama Barun, one of the two senior *aseels* – former wetnurses of the royal family who had also been commanders of the Zuffur Plutun women's battalion at Khardla five years earlier – now acted as the principal master of ceremonies, while their women sepoys acted as the Nizam's bodyguards.*

But perhaps the biggest and most significant change recorded by Strachey and Elphinstone in their accounts of Hyderabad, and something which no previous traveller had described, is the picture they give of the new British cantonments, ten miles to the north of the old city, just over the Banjara Hills.

---

* There are pictures of Mama Barun and her formidable colleague Mama Champa surviving from an album of Henry Russell's in the India Office (OIOC, Add Or. 1946, 1947). As well as commanding the Zuffur Plutun, and acting as MCs during the durbar, they were put in charge of sensitive state matters regarding women, such as searching *zenanas* for stolen jewels and conducting the inquiry into the scandal of the brazier who claimed that James Kirkpatrick had abducted his wife. In the pictures both women are wearing the same court uniform of flowing white robes with gilt edges worn over a pink *choli* and covered with strings of pearls; but they are very different figures, and the artist has almost caricatured these differences. Mama Champa is a tall, large-breasted and large-bottomed woman shown in her late fifties with powerful, masculine hands and an extremely fearsome expression on her face. Mama Barun is a little older, and more stooped and emaciated, with her face speckled by smallpox; but she is made to appear wise and canny, with a hooked nose and the hint of a smile at the edges of her mouth. She holds a kerchief in one hand and a narcissus in the other, while on her head she wears a loose turban. Neither woman has her face covered. According to the *Tarikh i-Yadgar i-Makhan Lal*: 'Mama Champa was a purchased slave girl. She was the nurse of His Highness. As she was very intelligent, therefore His Highness of Illuminated Glory entrusted many of the works of state to her. Her monthly salary from twelve rupees was raised up to rupees forty and she was awarded a palanquin. She was also granted the land of Champ Paith. His Highness arranged her marriage with Fojdar Khan, who is the master of elephant fighting in Hyderabad. Fojdar Khan was also honoured with the

These cantonments were vast tent cities which housed the now very substantial British military contingent that had arrived in the area following the two treaties James had signed with the Nizam. Strachey talks of the cantonments as 'already extending near 2 miles (I guess) and there is a considerable town formed by the huts of the troops and camp followers. The situation is very high and airy commanding a fine view of the Hoosn Sagoor [the huge man-made lake north of the old city].'[65] Elphinstone adds that the tent city was 'very neat'; he also implies that, in a way the Residency had never been – located as it was in an old Qutb Shahi *baradari* pavilion within a walled pleasure garden – the cantonments were intrusions of unadulterated Englishness in the utterly Indian landscape. Here the two youths went shopping in a 'Europe Shop' – an emporium which sold only imported luxury goods from Europe – consulted a European doctor (about Elphinstone's severe clap) and went to see an English farce at a makeshift open-air regimental theatre. They went shooting (though apparently only hit an owl), attended regimental balls, gambled and played whist, billiards and backgammon in the officers' mess.[66] It was not much yet, but these cantonments were the embryo that would soon grow to become Secunderabad, Hyderabad's twin city and a conurbation that is today as large as Hyderabad itself. Moreover, their growth was rapid: only eighteen months later, by the autumn of 1804, the cantonments were already 'like a large regular town reckoned equal in extent to [the large north Indian station of] Cawnpore'.[67]

The cantonment was a rival centre of power not only to the Nizam and his durbar, but also to James and the Residency, whose writ ran uncertainly in the army lines. James certainly believed – with reason – that he was head of the British community in Hyderabad; but his authority was tacitly resisted by his former army colleagues. After all, James was still a humble major, while the commander of the Subsidiary Force was a lieutenant colonel. Moreover, among the troops in the force were a number of James's former colleagues who resented his rapid promotion to a senior position in the Company's

military command of the late His Highness [Nizam Ali Khan]. Mama Champa died in the year 1237 A.H./1821 A.D.'

diplomatic corps, when they remembered him only eight years earlier as a fairly undistinguished junior lieutenant. His swift rise from commander of an obscure tribal fort to one of the most lucrative positions in the Company's service was attributed less to his own merits than to the influence of his powerful half-brother William. Moreover, James's adoption of Muslim clothes, and the stories circulating about his partiality to Hyderabadi customs, did not go down well with his former army colleagues either, especially as some of them – like the late Colonel James Dalrymple – had been prisoners of Tipu, and had seen a number of their colleagues convert to Islam and adopt Decanni Muslim clothes, turbans and moustaches in return for easier conditions. A few of the prisoners had even agreed to help drill Tipu's troops in modern European military techniques, in exchange for Mysorean wives and positions as officers and drill sergeants in Tipu's army.[68] The soldiers in the cantonments therefore tended to look on all converts and Islamophiles as turncoats, and regarded the thoroughly assimilated James with the deepest suspicion.

This dislike and distrust of James was something that Strachey and Elphinstone had picked up when they stayed with Arthur Wellesley and his garrison at Seringapatam on their way to Hyderabad. According to their diaries, Wellesley had 'rowed Hushmut Jung' [i.e. joked about Kirkpatrick], and Elphinstone certainly arrived in Hyderabad thoroughly prejudiced against James. When a messenger from him came out to meet them on their way to Hyderabad, generously offering them accommodation at the Residency, his initial reaction to his diary was: 'Bore! Who would like to live with Hushmut Jung?'[69] On arrival he was clearly surprised to be received 'very civilly', and to discover that 'in most respects' James was 'like an Englishman'.[70] It was only after James had lavished his hospitality on the pair for several weeks that Elphinstone began to write warmly about his host, although what seemed to impress the twenty-one-year-old most was James's shooting skills: 'Major K is a capital shot,' he wrote admiringly after an expedition looking for sand grouse in the Banjara Hills.[71]

In August 1801, when Strachey and Elphinstone arrived in Hyderabad, the nascent tensions between the Subsidiary Force and the Residency were evident, if still unspoken. But even before the pair had left the city three months later, it was out of these innocent-looking lines of regimental tents that the next great storm to shake Kirkpatrick was to emerge.

The rumblings of discontent with James were brought out into the open by events during the Muharram festivities in the old city in September; and in many ways it was James who brought the storm down upon himself.

'As soon as the crescent new moon of the sacred month of Muharram is sighted over the city, the Standard of Hussain, the Blessed Horse-shoe, and innumerable flower-garlands are sent by the Minister to the Palace to ensure the good fortune of the Nizam's thousand-year rule,' wrote Ghulam Husain Khan in his history of Hyderabad, the *Gulzar i-Asafiya*.

> It is an ancient custom that when the garlands arrive, at the second watch of the night, with the Nizam's guards all present, the Nizam – duly bathed and perfumed, dressed in green with a multitude of gems, and hair anointed – reverently takes the garland container on his head and carries it step by step, bare-foot, among crowds of people, along with goblets of sherbet and cauldrons of food offerings, into the place where the standards are erected in the great Husaini 'Alam shrine. There he ties the garlands [to the standards] while reciting the Fatiha [the opening chapter of the Koran].[72]

So, every year, began the great ten-day-long festival of Muharram. If the festival of Maula Ali was one of the two great celebrations of the Hyderabadi year, then Muharram was the other. Despite both being ostensibly Shi'a celebrations, the two were very different events. For if Maula Ali was essentially a pleasurable holiday, an escape from the teeming lanes and alleys of the old city of Hyderabad, then

Muharram was a celebration of the city itself, and especially of its internal divisions and diversity.

The festivities were organised – like the Palio of Siena, or the mystery plays of medieval York – by the rival quarters (or *mohallas*) of the city, who all competed with each other over the size and splendour of their devotional processions. The Sufis, the fakirs and the ascetics in particular tended to take a factional attitude to the celebrations, and 'massed under the sun banners distinct to each *mohalla*', ready to defend its honour and prestige against that of its neighbours: 'Thus they all come from their own quarter and according to custom rank by rank, they join the processions. But if they try to get into any position other than that sanctified by custom, there will be quarrels and feuds, and the troublemakers will be arrested. In the past many were killed in this way until the Nizam issued strict orders against the wearing of weapons and the shedding of blood.'[73]

Muharram was supposedly a time of mourning. It marked the anniversary of the defeat and death of Imam Hussain, the son of Maula Ali and the Prophet's grandson, at the Battle of Karbala on the tenth day of the month of Muharram, AD680. The standards – or *alams* as they were called – were stylised representations of the standards carried by Hussain at Karbala.* The beautiful elegies – or *marsiyas* – that were sung evoked the thirst of Hussain and his entourage of women and children, and their sufferings at the hands of the Ummayad Caliph al-Yazid, an event considered by Shi'as as the most tragic martyrdom in history.

---

* *Alams* were usually either tear-shaped, or fashioned in the form of a hand. They are often highly ornate and beautiful objects, and the best of them are among the greatest masterpieces of medieval Indian metalwork. Chroniclers speak of gold *alams* studded with gems, but most of those that survive are cast either in bronze or silver. According to the most literate of all the art historians of the Deccan, the late Mark Zebrowski, 'the most remarkable thing [about *alams*] is the spell of mystery and miracle they cast upon the spectator. Islam abhors idols, but these banners are objects of devotion with their outstretched protective hands or writhing bands of serpents intertwined with snake-like Arabic script. Their power is immense . . . [and they] move the strongest men to tears . . . They remind one of the statues and crucifixes in Catholic churches completely covered in purple cloth during the sorrowful period of Lent, to be uncovered at long last only at Easter, on the Day of Resurrection. They are symbols of pain, death and rebirth.' See Mark Zebrowski, *Gold, Silver and Bronze from Mughal India* (London, 2000).

Black was worn, and meat, smoking, sex and *paan*-chewing were all strictly forbidden, while the usual half-hearted ban on alcohol was more seriously observed than usual. Men went through the streets barefoot. Women unloosed their tresses, removed their bangles and put on mourning clothes. Charpoys were removed from the *zenana* wings so that even the grandest begum would have to spend Muharram sitting on the floor like the servants. Day after day, processions of pious Shi'ite men beat their chests and flagellated themselves in sorrow at the sufferings of the man they regarded as the legitimate heir of the Prophet: 'The spectators are roused to an unbearable pitch of grief and the women shriek and wail as if it were indeed the end of the world, crying, Lord save us! Lord save us! *Ma'adh Allah! Ma'adh Allah!*'

Singers and reciters of the *marsiyas* would come in succession around those houses which had their own private *ashur khanas* (mourning halls), competing with each other to reduce their audiences to tears, or to raise them to such extremes of devotional hysteria that they would wail and beat their chests. In some houses the women would organise their own *majlis* (or assembly) in which women singers would sit on carpets in the illuminated *zenana* courtyards and sing devotional elegies; sometimes aristocratic women would even perform their own compositions.[74]

Aristu Jah and Mir Alam, both of whom competed to be the most cultured of the Hyderabadi *amirs*, were especially keen to be seen promoting and patronising the most talented young Hyderabadi poets to excel in the art of *marsiya*-writing. Each year James and his Residency Assistants would visit the *ashur khanas* of both rivals to hear the works that they had commissioned. As one historian put it, Aristu Jah

> was very keen on such gatherings, and he organised many, mostly at night. [Such was the reputation of the poets who attended Aristu Jah's *ashur khanas* that] other reciters and chanters would come secretly and listen to the most popular chants and learn them to perform at their own gatherings, which inevitably led to many quarrels and literary feuds among the town's poets. Indeed the Nizam and his Minister

showed such a passion for these recitations that it became quite the fashion for the nobles to compete in bringing poets and reciters even from as far away as Delhi and Lucknow, and they were all kept busy. One year, Aristu Jah organised 17 such soirées and the Nizam 20. Even more modest *amirs* had two or three such events each.[75]

The grandest and most magnificent of the *ashur khanas* was, however, that used by Nizam Ali Khan, the ancient Badshahi Ashur Khana, which the Nizam had recently renovated and enlarged after Aurangzeb had used it as a stable for his horses, as a way of deliberately humiliating the conquered Hyderabadi Shi'as. This beautiful Safavid-style mourning hall, which would not have looked out of place in the centre of Isfahan, was filled with some of the most exquisite tilework in India: great intricate swathes of startling parrot-blue, canary-yellow and egret-white, containing delirious swirls of roaring dragons and flame-like clouds.[76] Here, each Muharram, every one of the fourteen brass and silver *alams* (representing the Prophet, his daughter Fatima and the twelve imams, beginning with Ali) was 'clothed' by the Nizam's family in gold brocade on which Koranic verses had been woven. Like Christianity, Shi'a Islam has at its core the story of the scandalously unjust suffering of innocents. Just as relics – especially relics of the True Cross – acted as devotional focuses for the meditations of medieval Christians, so the *alams* acted for Shi'a Muslims.

The walls of the Badshahi Ashur Khana and its forecourt were lined with arched recesses. The lowermost thousand rows were lit with small earthen lamps on the first night of Muharram, and the rows above each successive evening until, on the evening of the tenth of Muharram, each wall glowed with the light of ten thousand lamps – 'a flaming garden of Ali', as one poet put it, 'lit up by ten thousand burning, grieving hearts'. In addition a circular pit was dug in the centre of the forecourt and filled with incense sticks, so that a great fragrant cloud rose from the building as a long procession of black-clad mourners reciting the elegies and holding the *alams* high circled around the complex.[77]

For all the sadness of Muharram, and of the events it commemorated, there was nevertheless a carnival element in the festival. There were fireworks every night. Houses were decorated and lit up with oil lamps, as at the Hindu festival of Diwali. As so often in India, and especially in the Deccan, Islam found itself unwittingly absorbed, transformed and assimilated by its overwhelmingly Hindu environment. Indian Muharram processions are unique in that large wooden models of the mausoleum of Hussain at Karbala, called *ta'ziyas*, are borne through the streets by devotees; sometimes in Hyderabad as many as two hundred *ta'ziyas* would be carried in succession. This practice was almost certainly modelled on the Hindu tradition of temple chariots, such as the famous Jagannath* car at Puri in Orissa.[78] Even more Hindu was the practice of placing 'on the *ta'ziyas* small portions of corn, rice, bread, fruit, flowers, cups of water &c', offerings to Hussain derived from the Hindu custom of leaving flour balls (or *pinda*) for the spirits of the dead.[79]

Certainly the Hyderabad Muharram celebrations witnessed by Abdul Lateef Shushtari in September 1801 bore hardly any resemblance to the festivities he had grown up with in the solidly Sh'ia environment of Iran. Instead they had been transformed into a sort of syncretic Indo-Islamic saturnalia which had almost as much in common with Hindu river festivals such as the Kumbh Mela as it did with the purely Islamic Muharram he knew from home: 'I have seen with my own eyes how the Muslims in India copy Hindu styles of mourning, fasting and prostrating themselves in the Ashur Khanas,' wrote a shocked Shushtari in his *Tuhfat al-'Alam*.

> The two groups compete in self-mortification, wounding their chests, and flagellating themselves till the blood flows and they fall unconscious . . . More bizarrely still, the lower orders disguise themselves, going around in animal skins, some as camels, some as lions and so on, making grotesque gestures and setting up at crossroads and passages a standard [of their quarter], under which they light a great fire: there both men and women and these strange apparitions beat their breasts

---

* From which, of course, the modern English word 'juggernaut' derives, though a belching lorry does little honour to the intricately carved chariot of Puri after which it is named.

and dance   but never do they give any food to the hungry
nor any drink to the thirsty![80]*

Ghulam Husain Khan also describes this strange, almost animist
tradition of dressing up in animal skins during Muharram, adding
that some of the 'lions'

> take sheep by the throat and bite through their jugular veins
> so that blood spurts out and adds to their image of a fierce
> blood-covered lion. In the city and Begum Bazaar [immedi-
> ately behind Khair un-Nissa's townhouse] ... there are not
> less than 200 of them.
>
> On the [tenth, the] day of the martyrdom, most of them
> gather under the Purana Pul, the Old Bridge. Some go mad
> and wear large hats with multicoloured paper streamers, and
> others put bells around their wastes like *harkarra* messengers.
> As they wander around the town banging their tambourines,
> quarrels and fights arise between them which threaten to
> become serious disturbances if it were not for the policing by
> the state.
>
> At this time, two Ethiopians, young and well built, gild
> their bodies with gold leaf, and wearing only a turban, rush
> out into the streets with 25 other Ethiops and Arabs fully
> armed. All the other would-be lions become timorous foxes
> and pull in their codpieces not daring to confront these two.
> If any dare to they cut off his wooden tail ...
>
> In these celebrations both Muslims and Hindus take part
> together, and on the tenth, the actual day of the martyrdom,

---

* Shushtari was not being completely accurate here. There was a tradition of the Nizam
distributing *naan* bread and *halwa* to the poor on the fifth and also the tenth day of
Muharram, after the singing of the last *marsiyas* of the year, while on the same days the
women of Hyderabad would set up stalls to distribute milk, sherbet and scented water
while their menfolk gave out money and clothes. Moreover, free food was available
throughout Muharram at the Hussaini Alam shrine, thanks to the endowment left for
this purpose by a Qu'tb Shahi queen whose son was carried off by a mad elephant during
the celebrations, and who vowed to feed the poor of the city if he was brought back
safely. Two hundred years later the free *langar* was still being distributed according to
her wishes. Ghulam Husain Khan went as far as suggesting that 'for nine days there is
nothing but this rushing from one langar to the next, all spectators, rich and poor, Hindu
and Muslim alike abandoning all their worldly pursuits and busying themselves only
with mourning and free meals'. Nevertheless, in the eyes of Shushtari, the giving of food
and alms was clearly a less central part of the festivities in Hyderabad than in Iran.

all the alam standards and ta'zya models and life size wooden images of *buraq* flying horses* go down the Hussaini Alam street to the Musi, accompanied by elephant standards and fanfares and guards of Arabs and Western trained sepoys . . . Hindus and Muslims go by the thousands, all bare-headed and bare-foot, beating their chests and crying Hussain! Hussain! The Hindus in particular participate with full reverence tying onto the alam standards garlands of flowers with their own hands . . . From houses rich and poor, as many as can manage stream out of the old Bridge Gate. The mendicants in their two processions under their two rival leaders, the dervishes, the madmen dressed as runners, the lions and so on all go down to the river, chanting praises to Ali, and stay there overnight. The number of people is fifty thousand, not to mention the elephants, some of which carry perfume to spray over the crowd, and horses beyond counting, and all the tents which those who can bring and set up on the bank. There is no more wonderful sight in all Hyderabad!

The difficulty of maintaining order during this frenzy is a constant theme of Ghulam Husain Khan's account, and he emphasises how in the past, many died during clashes, especially as rival processions of the fakirs of the different quarters of the city would clash, usually when they converged on the ghats of the Musi, where they would go to wash the *alams* in the river – a direct echo of the ceremony of washing and garlanding the standards of the different orders of sadhus that takes place every twelve years at the Kumb Mela, also with traditionally bloody results: 'unfortunately,' he adds, 'when thousands and thousands of people are scrabbling in the sand on the ghats there are many injured in the shoving and fighting that ensues . . .'

* These winged horses were images whose artistic ancestry goes back to the images of flying horses and winged bulls in ancient Assyria and Persia. They were sanctified in Islam as being images of the mount who took the Prophet Mohammed on his night journey from the Dome of the Rock in Jerusalem to heaven and back again. They are usually shown with crowns, a woman's head, a deer's feet and a peacock's breast and tail. In an image of the Muharram processions in Patna at this period, now in the India Office, pairs of huge flying horses support the *ta'ziya* shrines, and are themselves carried on poles by teams of devotees turned for the day into voluntary palanquin-bearers.

Keeping some semblance of order over this mystical Saturnalia was also the matter most firmly on James Kirkpatrick's mind throughout the 1801 Muharram celebrations.

During a particularly bad bout of violence one night between the ecstatic mourners of two rival quarters, the Nizam had called him to the palace and asked if the Subsidiary Force might be brought in to restore order, and James had agreed. The order was sent up to the cantonments, but only a fraction of the required men had turned up. As James wrote to William ten days later, 'the last Mohurram festival, having occasion for a strong battalion to go into the city at the Nizam's application, and having consequently desired Col. Vigors [the new commander] to send me the very strongest [battalion available], one of [only] seven hundred and eighty firelocks was with some difficulty produced! And I have heard it said that if the Sub[sidiar]y Force were to be required to move tomorrow, not more than the above number could be reckoned upon.'[81]

A day later, having made a few more enquiries, James was shocked to have his first suspicions confirmed: a major fraud appeared to be taking place in the cantonments. Writing to William, who was still bedridden in Madras, he reported: 'The more I reflect on the matter the more I am persuaded that there must be some serious abuses going on in the corps, which cannot too soon be put a stop to . . .'

James had suspected that the officers were pocketing most of the allowances the Nizam had given them to provide for their weapons, equipment, tents and carriage. Not only were there not enough guns and artillery, there were hardly any tents.[82]

Further investigations over the days that followed revealed the situation to be even worse than James had feared: his inquiries showed that, 'if my information is correct' there could not have been more than four thousand guns when there should have been, according to the treaty, 7200 – in other words 'little more than half of what [the Nizam] pays for'. This, James realised, put him in an impossible position, as he would

> be under the unavoidable necessity of bringing [corruption] to public notice 'ere long . . . a great deal of dishonest conceal-ment must be going on, for all the corps are returned as complete or nearly so [in their official accounts]. At this rate what terrible abuses must be going in the Subsidiary Force! And how much are both our own government and this state imposed upon, and what a consequent load of responsibility will fall upon my shoulders if it should ever come out that I know, or even suspected, the serious deception going on, without taking any steps to remedy it?
>
> Col Vigors faculties, I am sorry to say, both bodily and mental appear to be rapidly in decline, and he seems to possess in no small degree a defect common more or less to all who have attained to his rank in our service by the usual gradual rise, I mean the defect of winking at abuses, which they are probably conscious of having themselves in similar situations practised. The muster of the troops also must, I fear, be taken in a very slovenly way.

James's sources, one of whom was almost certainly Fyze's son, the young Captain William Palmer, who was now attached to the Nizam's irregular cavalry and so had easy access to the British cantonments while remaining distinct from the regular soldiers, had informed him that the male children of the sepoys were being produced at parade to artificially inflate the numbers in the muster rolls.[83]

Yet again, James found himself in a hopeless quandary, caught between his conscience and his sense of duty, between the British and Hyderabad, unsure whether to honour his residual loyalties to his old army colleagues and 'wink' at their clear corruption, or to honour his commitments to the Nizam under the treaty he had signed. In the end, aware of the unpopularity and odium it would bring down upon him, James eventually wrote to William that, after much hesitation, he was clear where his duty lay, and that he was intent on rooting out the abuses.

What he did not know when he wrote this was that his inquiries had already been noticed in the cantonments; and the suspicions of the senior officers were confirmed when William Kirkpatrick wrote to the commander asking for details of muster rolls and the amount of equipment available, saying that he had received a worrying letter from someone in Hyderabad: 'They [now] know they are being watched,' wrote James to William in early October.[84] He was also unaware that the senior officers in the force had already acted to defend themselves – by turning the spotlight back on him.

Sometime towards the end of September, an anonymous letter was sent from Hyderabad to the Governor General, detailing all the facts about Khair un-Nissa and her child and their move to the Residency that James had so far managed to keep concealed from Calcutta. The letter reached Wellesley in Patna at the very end of the month. Only a week later, having first checked the facts with James's former Assistant John Malcolm, who had accompanied Wellesley on his journey, the Governor General picked up his pen and wrote an ominous letter to William Kirkpatrick as follows:

> PRIVATE AND SECRET
> PATNA OCTOBER 7th 1801
>
> My dear Sir,
> It is with the utmost degree of pain and sorrow that I inform you that intelligence has reached me from various quarters which leaves no doubt on my mind that your brother the Resident at Hyderabad has abused my confidence in the most criminal manner and has deceived both me and yourself with respect to his conduct towards the granddaughter of Bauker Alli under circumstances of the most aggravated guilt.
> The accusation originally came before me as a charge against the Resident of having employed the authority of his station to compel the family of this unfortunate woman to grant her to him in marriage. This charge led to a reference to the Nizam himself & I thought your brother fully acquitted himself by his Highnesses reply, and by the report of some respectable gentlemen then at Hyderabad. But it now appears evident that whether Kirkpatrick ever attempted to force such a marriage

or not, he has debauched the granddaughter of Bauker Alli, he has a child born of this woman and he now lives with her.

The effect at Hyderabad is mischievous in the extreme as might be expected from such an outrage upon the general principles of normality & upon the most revered prejudices of the Musselmans. I will not press the aggravations of the most hideous crime to the extent which they would bear because I know the justice, honor & purity of your mind too well to suppose that you do not anticipate every topic which I could devise from the principles of public duty, or private gratitude. I will therefore only add the determination which I have formed upon this case.

Although thoroughly convinced of the bulk of the charges preferred against Major Kirkpatrick, it is not my intention to proceed to extremities until they shall have been verified by evidence regularly taken by competent authority. When I shall have reduced the facts alleged to regular form, I shall remove the Resident from his station and I shall afford him the fullest opportunity of entering upon any species of defence which can tend to exempt him from any more severe punishment. This course appears to me to be the most just, & expedient; the facts now alleged, when stated in a solemn manner by credible and respectable evidence will require the immediate removal of the person representing me at Hyderabad.

As if all this was not bad enough, the letter grew worse. Having stated his belief that James was guilty of gross deception, Wellesley then asked William to disown and publicly denounce his brother if he wanted to save his own reputation:

Now my dear sir, I wish to call your attention to the situation in which the offences of Major Kirkpatrick against me and against the State have placed (what I know you value more than life) against your character & honor. I know that your brother has deceived you even more flagrantly than he has deceived me and the Government, but the World is ignorant of this fact, the Court of Directors & the Government at home must be ignorant of it, & may continue in error unless you shall resort to some effectual mode of manifesting to the

World what is evident to me that you have been as much injured by this nefarious transaction as I have been.

I therefore most earnestly represent to you the absolute necessity of your remaining in India while the whole enquiry into your brothers conduct shall be concluded and until a regular opportunity shall be afforded to you of furnishing me with the means of recording such materials as shall preserve the actual lustre of your character from blemish.

You shall receive full information of every proceeding respecting Major Kirkpatrick; in the meanwhile I desire that you will not open the subject to him until you shall have received further intimation from me. His eminent public services & his connection with you have rendered me slow to credit the charges against him, until the truth became too manifest to justify hesitation; I must therefore proceed to the execution of the most painful part of my public Duty, in the instance in which that duty will be most painful; but I shall proceed with calmness & deliberation.

Believe me, Dear Sir, with the greatest regard & respect always your faithful & obliged friend and servant –

Wellesley[85]

By the time William received the letter, the order had already arrived in Hyderabad for Lieutenant Colonel Bowser and Major Orr to head straight for Madras to report to Lord Clive on a matter of the greatest secrecy and importance. Unknown to James, his investigations of the Subsidiary Force had brought down on his head the most serious threat yet to his life and career in India.

By the time he became aware that things were amiss towards the end of November, the investigation was already well under way.

VII

AT THE VERY END OF DECEMBER 1801 – the most beautiful time of year in the Deccan, when the light is oblique, the evenings cool and the shadows long – William and Fyze Palmer finally packed up their household and set off for the last time from the Residency in Pune, heading off towards Hyderabad by the old Golconda road.

Their convoy moved slowly down through the then thickly wooded foothills of the Western Ghats, and out into the open farmland that lay in the plains beyond: rich, well-watered black earth where bullocks ploughed flat fields edged with palm groves and mango orchards. By 4 January 1802, the Palmers had made good progress and reached the dusty cotton-town of Tuljapur on the border with the Nizam's dominions. James was there to meet them, but Khair un-Nissa stayed behind in the newly completed *mahal* at the Hyderabad Residency. There was a good reason for this: though James had yet to tell anyone about it, Khair was now five months pregnant with their second child.[1]

Pune had been the Palmers' home for four years, and the elegant British Residency at the confluence of the rivers Moota and Mula, opposite the ghats where *sati* (widow burning) was performed, was filled with the treasures they had accumulated in the course of their life together in Lucknow, Delhi, Agra and Pune itself. Yet even by the standards of the time the Palmers travelled heavily, and James was astonished by the sheer number of bullock carts, transport cattle, elephants, baggage camels, syces, sepoys, bearers and Fyze's 'dozen females' (presumably her attendants) that turned up at the Maratha–Hyderabad border.[2]

The Palmers had originally planned to spend only a week or so resting in Hyderabad, before continuing their journey to Calcutta overland along the new military road which had recently been constructed up the length of the east coast. But so well did the two families get on, and so well matched were both the men and the women, that James tried to persuade his guests to stay on, arguing that if they waited for spring they could then catch a fast boat from Masulipatam and reach Calcutta just as quickly, and with much less effort, than by lumbering slowly over the Eastern Ghats. The General was won over, and in the end he and Fyze did not set off on the road again until April had come, and with it the height of the summer heat.[3]

Over their three months together Fyze and Khair un-Nissa struck up a close friendship, despite the fifteen-year difference in their ages. They spent their days in each other's company, and in that of Sharaf un-Nissa, playing with Khair's little boy Sahib Allum, now one year old and, according to James, beginning 'to prattle very prettily'.[4] Fyze introduced Khair un-Nissa to her twenty-two-year-old son William, for whom James had found a job in the Nizam's irregular cavalry, while Khair introduced Fyze to the women of both the Minister's and the Nizam's *zenanas*. With them came Fanny Khanum, Fyze's adopted daughter, who was probably the General's child by a concubine whom Fyze had taken into the family, as was the tradition at that period in both East and West.*

On these visits Fanny, who must then have been aged about ten, played happily with Prince Sulaiman Jah, the Nizam's nine-year-old son.† After the Palmers had set off to Calcutta, James wrote to William, 'Pray do not omit presenting my kindest remembrances to

---

* Fanny was later sent to England to be educated, which means she must almost certainly have had some English blood, and so was in all probability William's daughter – as would seem to be implied by James calling her 'your darling little Fanny'. OIOC, Kirkpatrick Papers, F228/58, p.73, 10 December 1802, James Kirkpatrick to William Palmer.
† Mir Jehangir Ali Khan, Rais ul-Mulk, Sulaiman Jah, was born in 1793 and died in 1862. He was the Nizam's seventh son, out of eight. (Nizam Ali Khan also fathered twelve daughters.)

Fyze and her little daughter by adoption, with whom the little Prince Sulaiman Jah[5] was so smitten, that he himself begged the females of my family to intercede on his behalf. They all join in sending kind wishes to Fyze . . .'[6] Later, James talked of Fanny as she 'whom the young Prince Sulaiman Jah wished for his bride. By the bye, the impression she made was deeper than could be supposed, as he never fails to ask after her.'[7] At the end of April, after Fanny had recovered from a serious illness, James promised the General that Khair would pass the news of her recovery on to Aristu Jah's women, and assured him that Fanny's 'rapid improvements when mentioned by my family in their occasional visits to the Minister's, will fire the breast of her young princely lover'.[8]

A miniature by the Hyderabad court artist Venkatchellam of the young Sulaiman Jah, with his younger brother Kaiwan Jah, still remains in the possession of James and Khair's descendants. It shows the two boys, aged about seven and eight, sitting on superbly inlaid chairs on a marble terrace next to the Hussain Sagar lake, being fanned by barefoot attendants. Sulaiman Jah wears a suit of child's toy armour; Kaiwan Jah, Nizam Ali Khan's youngest son, who was given to Aristu Jah to adopt following the death of the latter's only son in 1795, wears orange pyjamas, is hung with pearls and holds a sarpeche.* Presumably Sulaiman Jah was regularly brought to the Minister's *zenana* to play with his younger brother Kaiwan, and it was no doubt there that Fanny and Fyze first met the young prince.†

The friendship between Khair and Fyze grew very deep indeed. They had much in common: both were of Persian extraction and spoke Persian as their first language; both were second-generation immigrants to India who had grown up with fathers in senior positions in the armies of Shi'a Indian courts, and with local Indian mothers. Moreover, both had faced the same challenges in that they had fallen in love with, and eventually married, Englishmen from a

---

* Adoption was a common practice in princely India, and rulers without an heir frequently adopted one. It was however unusual for a princely ruler to give his son for adoption to a non-royal, and a measure of the deep trust and affection felt by the Nizam for his oldest and closest adviser, Aristu Jah.

† Kirkpatrick's descendants also own a second Venkatchellam image, of the young Prince Sulaiman riding out with a company, perhaps on a hunting expedition.

very different world to their own. Fyze perhaps acted as older, wiser adviser to Khair, but she was clearly as fond of Khair un-Nissa as Khair was of her. From the day the Palmers left Hyderabad, letters and parcels passed between the two women, both of whom were literate and keen letter-writers.[9] Although their letters have since disappeared – or in the case of Khair un-Nissa's apparently been deliberately destroyed[10] – something of their contents can be gauged from the accompanying letters written by their husbands, most of which are still intact.

Two days after Fyze and the General had left for the coast, James was writing that 'My little Boy's Mother and Grandmother return with interest and affectionate ardour the kisses imprinted on their infant in the name of Begum [Fyze], to whom I beg my best remembrances.'[11] The following morning Khair un-Nissa, attended by James and her mother Sharaf un-Nissa, and presumably also by Dr Ure, gave birth to a baby girl. James recorded the exact time and date on a small scrap of paper that he kept next to the piece on which he had recorded Sahib Allum's birth only thirteen months previously:

On Friday the
9th (ninth) of April
AD 1802 answering
to the 5th Zehidge A.H
1216, between 8 & 9 clock
in the morning a
Daughter was born to
Me in my House at
The Residency (Hyderabad)
She has been named
By her female parents
Noor oon Nissa
– Saheb Begum[12]

Noor un-Nissa means 'the Light of Women'; the title Sahib Begum, 'Lady of High Lineage', was a reference to the child's godmother, Fyze.* Soon James was ending a letter to the General with the post-

---

* Sahib Begum was the title given to Fyze by the Mughal Emperor Shah Alam.

script: 'The females of my family all join in [sending their] kind wishes to Fyze, including her little namesake Sahib Begum who is improving daily.'[13] A few days later James was telling William that 'my family here both great and small are all well, and as many as can speak for themselves, beg to be remembered most kindly to Fyze, for whom the young Begum has made up a set of *choorys* [bangles] which I propose forwarding under cover to you, when I have got a smaller sett ready for my little ward [Fanny Khanum]'.

By the end of April, Khair had made still more *choories* for her friend, and James wrote to William that 'as I find the choorys for Fyze and your little darling are not admissible in the dawke,* I shall commit them to the charge of [John] Malcolm and request you will assure the Begum with my best remembrances of my readiness to furnish her with further supplies as occasions may offer.† There are four setts for her, and two for Fanny Khanum.'[14]

So strong was Khair un-Nissa's relationship with Fyze that it out-lasted her marriage to James, and many years later, as Khair lay dying, Fyze was beside her bed, holding her hand. Six weeks after Khair's death, according to James's Assistant Henry Russell, Fyze was still, 'I fear, in great distress . . . She says she has lost the only real friend she ever had; and I suspect from what I have heard of her disposition and habits, that it is truly the case . . .'[15]

---

* The *dak* (as it is usually spelled) was the Indian despatch system, adopted by the British from the Mughals. It comprised a network of interlocking runners and horses.
† James's former Assistant (later Sir John Malcolm, though he was at this period usually referred to as 'Boy' Malcolm), now the Governor General's Private Secretary, was passing through Hyderabad on his way to Bombay. His feelings at being turned into a purveyor of Mughal women's bangles and trinkets are not recorded. He did however remain friends with Fyze after the delivery, and many years later, on a visit to Hyderabad in 1818, recorded: 'I paid a visit to Fyze Begum, the celebrated lady of the late General Palmer, and was received with Oriental magnificence.' See J.W. Kaye, *The Life and Correspondence of Sir John Malcolm GCB* (2 vols, London, 1856), Vol. 2, p.163.

James and the General also got on as well as, if not better than, both had hoped and expected. They visited court together, went hawking and hunting, and spent long nights talking over their mutual despair at the direction in which Wellesley was taking the Company in India. When the General finally left Hyderabad, James wrote him an emotional letter, telling him of the 'gloom and vacuity' into which he had fallen since his departure, and of the 'gratitude and exultation' the memory of their friendship brought to him.[16]

James also sent Palmer a revealing letter that openly acknowledged the degree to which both men had become Indianised. Soon after he left, James wrote to advise him that 'With regard to your eventual intention respecting a trip to England . . . I am not sure that your well wishers – that is those who wish you many long years of life and happiness – would rejoice at such a measure, after a residence of more than half your life in the sultry climes of India.'[17] At this stage, he gives no hint as to exactly what his worries for the General are; but in a later letter he enlarges on this: 'I am glad to hear that your darling little Fanny Khanum is to be sent to England,' he wrote towards the end of the year, 'but I cannot say I am quite reconciled to the idea of your accompanying her, and I do not know if it depended on me, whether I should not vote for you in preference some snug sinecure in this country where you have passed so large a portion of your life. Recollect my dear friend, that you were long ago yourself doubtful how far you could stand the rigour of an English *summer*, how then can you think of braving an English winter?'[18]

James, it seems, was thoroughly convinced that the General no longer truly belonged to Britain: India was now his real home, and as far as James was concerned, it would only lead to trouble and serious health problems if he were to return to the West. This was a very different attitude to that of the late-nineteenth-century sahib dreaming of drizzle in Tunbridge Wells while complaining about the bloody awful climate in India. In James's view, his friend had much more to fear from the chill winds of a British midwinter. India had transformed both him and his friend, the old General. It was one thing for the children to go back to Europe to get a good education; it was quite another for him or Palmer to retire there.[19] Possibly James also

wanted to protect the eccentric old General from the taunts he suspected a white Mughal such as he might attract in the crowded streets
of Piccadilly.

The letters James wrote to Palmer show his love, respect and
concern for his friend, and these were feelings that the General clearly
reciprocated. The Palmers had come to stay at a particularly stressful
and upsetting time for James, and their presence calmed and cheered
him at one of his lowest points. James had first learned that he was
in trouble with Calcutta again when William sent him a frantic note
in cipher at the end of October 1801. William had given his word to
Wellesley that he would not tell James of the secret investigation
about to convene in Madras, but his note was intended to alert
his brother to the fact that something was afoot without explicitly
mentioning the Clive Enquiry. The letter contained none of William's
usual gossip, but went – starkly – straight to the point: 'My dear
James,' it read,

> When I lately put a question to you respecting the state of
> your intercourse with a certain female you satisfied yourself
> with answering that I might be perfectly easy on that subject.
> This, though not an explicit answer, I construed into such an
> appearance as I wished for.
>
> I trust I did not deceive myself on this occasion: yet it
> would be a great comfort to me to know for certain that the
> woman in question does not now and has not at any time
> lived with you.
>
> My solicitude on this subject is not idle. You have enemies.
> Who they are God knows – *where* they are is not difficult to
> guess [i.e. in the Subsidiary Force cantonments]. Whether in
> writing or in conversation, on whatever subject, I must relate
> personally to yourself to be at this time peculiarly guarded,
> reserved and temperate as well as collected. When I rec-
> ommend reserve I mean especially those about yourself.*

---

* James was beginning to suspect – correctly as it turned out – that two members of
his own staff, Thomas Sydenham and Captain William Hemming, the commander of
his bodyguard, were not as loyal as they professed to be, and these appear to be the
characters 'about yourself' that his brother William is referring to in this letter. On 17
December 1801 James had written to William in cipher: 'A variety of concurring circumstances compel me, however reluctantly, to doubt the sincerity of Sydenham's professions

James immediately accepted; but the inspection was a disaster. James was not greeted with his usual seventeen-gun salute, no guard of honour was there to receive him, and no Union Flag was raised.[26] Worse still, he was treated with disdain by the officers of the men he came to examine. On his return to the Residency he wrote a formal complaint, and copied it to Calcutta. He also picked up his pen to report to William what had happened, informing him that Vigor's

> avarice is of the most extreme and sordid kind, and not to be equalled by his avidity to amass money which by all accounts is boundless. It is the check which I have lately given to this gratification by requiring him to send me a monthly *nerak* [tariff rate] in order to set some bounds to his enormous and undue bazaar gains* that has excited (I have no doubt) the spirit of opposition which lately manifested itself. Though all this is bad enough, yet it is quite venial in comparison with his unreserved disclosure to all who would listen to him of the subject of my late [private] letter, his boastful account of his *manly* reply, and discussion of various points touching on our relative situations . . . The Colonel has certainly deceived me not a little.[27]

Things had not improved by the following spring, and there was an unpleasant incident soon after the Palmers left Hyderabad when James reported that some of the Subsidiary Force officers let it be known that they would be 'refusing to subscribe to a certain [Regimental] Ball, if I was invited'. Moreover, James's letters continue to contain frequent references to his enemies in the cantonments, who 'have been so busy in defaming and misrepresenting me'. He was also aware that these enemies 'would scarcely have dared, I think, to indulge so freely as [they have done] had not the too prevalent idea of my disgrace and approaching end have encouraged them to perseverance'.[28]

There was also the issue of James's relations with General Palmer's

---

* In other words, Vigors was buying supplies cheaply in the bazaar and charging the Nizam for them at a much higher rate, so grossly inflating his expenses claims, and his personal profits.

successor at Pune, Colonel Barry Close, an Anglo-Irish friend of Arthur Wellesley who very much took the Wellesleys' line in his attitude to Indians in general and Indian princes in particular. Palmer had been astonished when Close turned up to replace him in Pune without any official instructions or credentials, so breaking all the most elementary courtesies of diplomacy: 'If the Peishwa had a grain of spirit he would not receive him,' the General had written to James in December, just before leaving for Hyderabad, 'and callous as he [the Peishwa] may be, he must feel the contempt implied in appointing an Ambassador to his court and sending him thither without a letter of introduction.'[29]

But it was not just the Peishwa that Close showed contempt for. By the spring of 1802, as James's fate still remained uncertain, Close had begun sending his Calcutta despatches, which came via Hyderabad, sealed rather than open, so that James was unable to read the contents. This was an important change from the existing system and usages, which had allowed the Hyderabad Resident to brief himself on developments over the Maratha border.

Close's actions clearly implied that he felt James was somehow unreliable, or untrustworthy, or a straightforward security risk. After hundreds of copies of James's Residency correspondence had turned up in Tipu Sultan's palace chancellery at Seringapatam in 1799, Close had good reason to suspect that security at Hyderabad was not all that it might be.[30] But the 'mole' responsible for those leaks – the Residency 'intelligencer' Laxmi Narayan – had been exposed and sacked three years earlier; and the clear implication was that Close was dubious about James's own reliability. He had, after all, been privy to what Mir Alam had told Arthur Wellesley of James's alleged deal (or accommodation) with Aristu Jah; he also knew about Khair un-Nissa, and might have suspected that her discretion was not to be relied upon, and that James's pillow talk might easily make its way into other Hyderabad *zenanas*. Whatever his reservations were, they remained unarticulated. Even though James wrote formally to Close to protest, his appeal had no effect. The Pune *dak* continued to arrive in Hyderabad with its seals firmly attached.[31]

In the end it was William Kirkpatrick who saved James from this extended limbo and who rescued his career, just as nine years earlier it was he who had first kick-started it. Although officially William was just off to the Cape to recover his health, it was now very clear to him that his condition was too serious to be healed by a few weeks at the mineral baths. Deep down he knew that his career was over, and that if he stayed in India, or indeed ever returned to it, he would probably die. He therefore decided to do all he could to save the career of his half-brother, even if it meant sacrificing his own reputation with Wellesley in the process.

From what John Malcolm had told him in his letters, William knew that James had been cleared of the charge of raping Khair un-Nissa or of using force or threats to pressurise her family to hand her over: the Clive Enquiry had accepted that unusual though it was, the women of Khair un-Nissa's family appeared to have set out to seduce the Resident, rather than the other way around.

Only one serious political charge remained unresolved: that of concealment. The Governor General was quite willing to forgive James for his moral lapse in sleeping with Khair un-Nissa, and was even prepared to overlook his failure of judgement (as Wellesley saw it) in allowing himself to be dragged, through his marriage, into a position where he was open to manipulation by the Hyderabadi durbar: Malcolm had written to William that Wellesley thought James 'highly culpable considering his station, to have an intrigue at a native court with a woman of such rank'.[32] Yet while James may have been culpable, the offence; Malcolm had also hinted, was not unforgivable, and certainly not enough in itself for James to lose his job. But what Wellesley was not prepared to put up with – reasonably enough – was his senior officials deliberately withholding vital political information from him. At the end of the Clive Enquiry, the charge remained that James had knowingly concealed important details about his affair from his superiors, and that his despatches and submissions on the subject had been deliberately misleading.

These charges were in fact unanswerable – James had indeed told barefaced lies to almost everyone, including his own brother, about the degree to which he had become entangled with Khair un-Nissa. William nonetheless took it upon himself to risk a reputation he had spent twenty years building up, and to write to John Malcolm telling him that James – very properly hesitating to explain such delicate matters in a public despatch – had made a full confession to William in his private letters, expecting him to pass it on discreetly to the Governor General; but that he, William, had hesitated to do so, as 'I did not consider myself at liberty, or view it in any light as necessary, to betray the confidence which [James] had reposed on me on the occasion.'[33] It was, in other words, William's failure, not James's, that had caused the misunderstanding.

This story was not strictly truthful, but it nevertheless provided James with the perfect cover, and put the onus for failing to reveal the full truth about the affair firmly onto his elder brother. As John Malcolm eventually wrote to William, 'in consequence of your communication [Lord Wellesley has finally] acquitted your brother of the charge of improper concealment & [has] therefore resolved to continue him in the station which he has filled with so much credit'.[34] The latter somewhat unexpected compliment was in part a reference to the fact that James had just successfully persuaded the Nizam to sign a third treaty with the Company, this time one that dealt with matters of commerce* – yet another sign of James's unusual degree of influence with the Nizam, and his continuing value to the Company.

After five months of uncertainty, and three inquiries, James had again been forgiven for an affair which over and over again had come close to wrecking his career and reputation. But it was a short-lived respite. No sooner had Wellesley decided to forgive James than another anonymous letter arrived in Calcutta. This time it was a letter of support for James; but one which had a much more damaging effect than any letter of criticism.

Not only did it attack Wellesley in terms that the Governor General regarded as 'very violent, menacing and indelicate' as well as libellous, its inside knowledge of the case showed that it was written by a close friend or associate of Kirkpatrick. Its postmark showed moreover

---

* The Commercial Treaty of April 1802 laid down that free transit of all goods was now permitted between Company territory and that belonging to the Nizam, all local duties were to be abolished, and a flat rate of 5 per cent would be paid on all goods imported into the territories of either party.

that it had been posted in the Residency, and must thus have been written by one of the very few people in Hyderabad who had access to the Residency post room. In the covering letter which Wellesley sent to James along with the offending tract, he demanded that Kirkpatrick immediately track down and unmask 'Philothetes', the author of a piece of invective which according to Wellesley 'violated the Laws of respect and Subordination, by an injurious and dictatorial stile of address to the Supreme Authority in India'.[35]

This was another scandal, and it broke at exactly the moment James least needed it. Worse still for him, the author – as must have been apparent to James as soon as he opened the package – was none other than the son of his closest and most intimate friends and allies, General Palmer and Fyze.

'Philothetes' was quite clearly the young Captain William Palmer, of the Nizam's irregular cavalry.[36]

William Palmer had been born in Lucknow in 1780, a year after Fyze had moved in with the General.

In Zoffany's celebrated portrait of the family, painted when William was five, he is shown wearing a white Avadhi *jama*. His early years were spent in the cosmopolitan environment of Lucknow, then at the height of its golden age as the centre of north Indian courtly culture. At some point William was shipped off to England to be educated, and ended up completing his schooling at the Vanbrugh-designed Royal Military Academy at Woolwich.* When he returned

---

* Nothing at all is known about where William was sent to school prior to Woolwich; but when his Anglo-Indian cousins – the children of his aunt Nur Begum (Fyze's sister) – arrived in London a little later, they attended two small private schools in London: Miss Eliza Barker's School in Hammersmith for the girls, and Mr Clarke's for the boys. It is quite possible that Mr Clarke's was where William was educated, and that Nur placed her son Charles in the school following recommendations from her sister Fyze. General Palmer's mother, his first wife Sarah, and his two daughters from his first

to India in 1798, aged eighteen, and briefly moved in with his half-brother John Palmer, by now a successful Calcutta banker, he was able to speak English and Persian with equal fluency, and to operate in aristocratic English and Mughal environments with equal ease.[37]

By the early years of the nineteenth century, many Anglo-Indians were beginning to find their mixed racial inheritance a major drawback: William's contemporary Lieutenant Colonel James Skinner of Skinner's Horse, for example, felt that his mixed blood, 'like a two edged blade, was made to cut both ways against him'.[38] But unlike Skinner – and indeed unlike most Anglo-Indians – William was born into the upper echelons of both British and Mughal society, and his father made sure that every resource was available so that he could take advantage of both sides of his ethnic identity and find his mixed blood a boon and a blessing rather than the insuperable obstacle it became to so many other mixed-race children. As William caught ship to India at the end of his English education, the General wrote proudly to his old friend Warren Hastings boasting about his children's achievements, and how they were all now well set up and provided for.[39]

Palmer's first appointment, which James Kirkpatrick had arranged for him, was in the Finglas Brigade of the Nizam's army, which he joined just in time to see action at the storming of Seringapatam in

---

marriage were all living at Greenwich at this time, intermittently supported by the General, and as Woolwich is immediately adjacent to Greenwich it seems unlikely that they would not have looked after William while he was in London, in the same way as the Handsome Colonel took in all his Indian grandchildren, legitimate, illegitimate, English and Anglo-Indian. If so, it is interesting to speculate how the General's Creole first wife, Sarah, treated the son of his Indian second wife, Fyze. The Royal Military Academy was founded in the Woolwich Arsenal buildings in 1721. Vanbrugh's celebrated domes – once regarded as the epitome of Englishness – have recently been shown to have been heavily influenced by the Mughal domes of the Muslim-style mausolea built for Indianised East India Company factors at Surat, where Vanbrugh worked for two years as a young man, and where, in his spare time, he would go off to sketch the tombs and local palace architecture. (For Mr Clarke's school, see the box 'London Receipts' in the de Boigne archive, Chambéry. For Sarah in Greenwich, and William's attempts to get David Anderson to send her some money, see Anderson Papers, BL Add Mss 45,427, p.203, March 1792, Gualiar. For Woolwich Military Academy and the Royal Arsenal see Ben Weinreb and Christopher Hibbert (eds), *The London Encyclopaedia* (London, 1983). For Vanbrugh in Surat see Christopher Ridgeway and Robert Williams (eds), *Sir John Vanbrugh and Landscape Architecture in Baroque England* (London, 1999).

May 1799.* Thereafter he rose rapidly through the ranks, so that before long he was commanding a battalion and was in charge of collecting taxes across several Hyderabadi districts.[40] This was his position when his parents arrived in Hyderabad in January 1802.

Soldiering was not, however, what William intended to do with his life. In the course of his duties with the Nizam's forces he had served in the devastated but fertile and potentially rich district of Berar, an area that had been badly scarred by nearly a century of intermittent warfare between the Mughals and the Marathas. Berar's well-watered soils were however clearly capable of being profitably developed. As he rode around gathering taxes, William – perhaps inspired by the entrepreneurial example of his elder half-brother John – dreamt of somehow repopulating the area, opening it up and planting cotton, indigo and opium there. This, he realised, was quite feasible, as the harvest could be easily transported down to the coast if the Wardha and Godavari rivers were made navigable.

On his visits to Hyderabad, William would have heard James talking about other schemes which were then being provisionally floated to exploit the vast untapped resources of the Nizam's dominions. One in particular seems to have made an impression on him: a scheme suggested by a private trader named Ebeneezer Roebuck to log the inaccessible malarial jungles and teak forests in the remote reaches of the Upper Godavari. The scheme never came off, but it was the cause of much discussion and correspondence at the Residency at exactly the time when William would have been present: during the visit of his parents in March 1802.[41]

Certainly the idea must have fermented in William's head, because in due course he raised considerable capital – some of it from his half-brother John in Calcutta, then at the height of his reputation as the

* Michael Finglas (see Chapter Three) was an ineffective Irish soldier of fortune who Aristu Jah brought back from Pune to found a European brigade in Hyderabad as a counterbalance to that of Raymond. His brigade was made up of a roguish bunch of European and American vagabonds and ne'er-do-wells, as well as a fairly sizeable contingent of Anglo-Indians. Finglas himself was 'possessed of very little talent or education', according to James, but Aristu Jah liked him and gave him the inappropriate title of Nawab Khoon Khar Jung, 'the Falcon'. He died on 7 July 1800.

'Prince of Merchants' – for a major logging and shipbuilding scheme to exploit the extraordinary mineral, timber and agricultural riches of the wilder reaches and jungles of the Nizam's vast state.

Moreover, at some point William seems to have realised that he had a major advantage over other businessmen that he could use to enormous effect. Because of his birth in India to an Indian mother, he was classified by the Company's bureaucracy as an 'East Indian', not as a British subject. As such he was permitted to engage in banking operations within the Nizam's dominions, something that was strictly forbidden to British subjects under the terms of the various treaties James had signed. He was also free to charge any rate of interest that he wished, unlike bankers in British India who were compelled by law to charge no more than 12 per cent. Untrammelled by Company regulations, within a few years William had put in place ambitious plans to open a merchant house that would engage in 'banking and agency transactions' while also

> supplying the timber of the forests, on the banks of the Godavery, for the purpose of ship-building; these forests abounding in timber of a superior size and quality. We entertain the most sanguine hopes that we shall be able to open a navigation of four hundred miles, during four months of the year, on that river and the Wurda. The opening of this navigation will also facilitate the commercial intercourse subsisting between [the interior of] Berar and the coast.[42]

The scale of William's ambitions has echoes of the world of Conrad, with its steamships, up-country logging stations, ivory hunters, uncharted malarial forests and riverboats. Yet, driven forward with an almost manic energy, it was not long before many of these schemes had been realised: by 1815 William Palmer & Co. had grown to be the richest and most important commercial operation in the subcontinent outside British-controlled India; it also ended up bankrolling the Nizam and 'acquired an ascendancy over the Minister that rendered him a creature of their will'.[43]

In many ways William Palmer can be said to have brought nineteenth-century Western entrepreneurial capitalism to the late-

Mughal world of the Deccan; but what is remarkable is that he did so in a way that was not entirely Western, and which was certainly quite independent of the East India Company. He used local bankers and, mostly, local money, and seems to have operated, at least partly, according to traditional Indian modes of doing business. Moreover, he sought influence and gained patronage by using time-honoured Mughal techniques of giving gifts and seeking favours from his mother's friends in the Nizam's *zenana*: according to a later British Resident, if William met any opposition to his plans, 'the Women of the Palace would be brought over to favour the application'.[44]

In 1802 this all lay in the future. But throughout the time William was establishing himself in Hyderabad, he had continued to live the hybrid Anglo-Mughal lifestyle which had been such a distinguishing mark of his parents' home. His house in Hyderabad gradually became a celebrated gathering place where the British and Hyderabadis met on equal terms. A revealing portrait of his domestic arrangements is given by an anonymous English traveller who visited him there in about 1810:

> I passed one morning and took tiffin with a famous English merchant, who holds a singular sort of durbar every morning at which you may see shroffs [moneylenders] and merchants, officers and nobles, coming to beg, borrow, lend or transact business; all of which is done according to native customs. These Mr. P observes in everything connected with his establishment; even when alone, sitting on the floor to a dinner served in their fashion; reading the Arabian nights with his Moorish wives; presiding at nautches; and (*de gustibus non est disputandum*) listening with pleasure to the musical sound of the native tom-tom.
>
> He is a man of uncommon talent and great information – very popular among the natives of course, and with the British also, for his liberality, ready and obliging politeness, and unbounded hospitality to all: to the poor man also he is very charitable. The choice of an Eastern mode of life is with him not altogether unnatural. He was born of a native mother, a female of Delhi of good descent.[45]

William Palmer had been baptised a Christian, but Fyze had kept her cultural and religious identity as a Muslim, and it was to Indian Muslim women, not to British ones, that William naturally looked for love and companionship. At home in both worlds, he found the perfect arena for his talents where he could straddle Mughal and British society, in the shadow of James Kirkpatrick's Hyderabad Residency.

Like the rest of his family, William clearly felt a marked kinship to and warmth for James, whose domestic arrangements so closely resembled his own; he also felt intense gratitude to a man who had helped him get started both as a soldier and as a businessman.* The exact relationship between James and William Palmer at this period is unclear, but James had certainly aided the younger man in a variety of ways, and by 1805, if not before, had allowed him the use of some of the Residency buildings as an office for his new business; this not only provided a useful base but also lent William's business operations the appearance of having the East India Company's *imprimatur*, something it did not in reality in any way possess.[46] In return William had done errands and 'confidential work' for James, including finding out the details of the arms and corruption scandal going on in the cantonments.

For all these reasons William leapt to James's defence when he saw that his patron was under attack from his enemies; but he could not have done it in a more damaging manner had he tried. His letter written under the pseudonym of 'Philothetes' was an extraordinary production: a fifteen-page rant in fantastically overblown prose, packed full of inappropriate classical references, passionately defending not just James, but the general right of English officials to marry and cohabit with Indian women, and remarking at the climax of its invective that its author could not 'recollect any institution by which Residents are denied the Enjoyment of female society in the courts of eastern princes: nor a precedent by whose establishment such an Indulgence may be deemed criminal'.[47]

---

* James also worked strenuously to keep William rising in the ranks. On 10 December 1802, for example, he wrote to the General: 'Your son William is just now on command somewhere. When he returns, which I believe will be soon, I shall exert myself strenuously to get him placed near [the Crown Prince] Secunder Jah.' OIOC, Kirkpatrick Papers, F228/58, p.73, James Kirkpatrick to William Palmer.

For all its extravagant phrasing, the letter is fascinating for the light it sheds on the way James was then regarded in the cantonments: 'In the Camp at Hyderabad,' maintains 'Philothetes', 'there is a factious party, whose very counsels are the Springs of Mischief.' This party, he asserts, is eaten up with jealousy of James's rapid rise: 'On the elevation of Captain Kirkpatrick to the Representation of your Lordship at the Court of the Deccan, the companions of his youthful days offered their congratulations at the Mansion of the Resident. But, my Lord, their congratulations were chilled by Envy and their offerings disquieted by prejudice.' So envious were Kirkpatrick's former companions that when 'Philothetes' first came to Hyderabad, 'my Ears were frequently regaled with anecdotes of the personal Eccentricities of Hushmut Jang'. Yet when he actually met him, 'Gracious God! Affability, Politeness, and Hospitality smiled on his every countenance. The film dropped from my eyes.'

Nor, claimed 'Philothetes', was he alone in being impressed by James's 'engaging address and captivating manners'. James, he says, was exceptionally popular at the Hyderabadi durbar, and even Khair un-Nissa's cousin Abdul Lateef Shushtari ('a respectable mussulman, to whose Name and Circumstances, your Lordship is not a stranger') believed him to be entirely innocent in the matter of his relationship with Khair:

> with the most pleasing satisfaction, I have learned that the Connection of Major Kirkpatrick with a female of that House arose in the warmest attachment of her heart, and has been cemented by the most liberal conduct on his part. He never aspired to her Seduction, nor ever sought an illicit enjoyment of her person. The Gratification of her fondest desire was her determined resolution. The disappointment of her wish would have closed her existence. In whatever point of view, my Lord, this Circumstance may be considered to the Character of Major Kirkpatrick no Crime can be attached; but the deviation from the Rules of morality according to its Restrictions only in the more polished societies of Europe.

He adds that the only reason the soldiers in the Subsidiary Force were unaware of this was that 'throughout the Camp at Hyderabad there is not one man who possesses a sufficient knowledge of the Deckanee or Persian to open and support a conversation to whose result the stamp of precision can be legally applied'. Only James could properly speak the languages, and Wellesley should realise, says 'Philothetes', that 'to the Resident of Hyderabad there is due from your Lordship the most Unlimited Confidence'. He then suggests that Wellesley seek confirmation of all this from 'the late Resident of Poonah [i.e. the General, William's father]', who he says 'will give you every Information. In a few days he will be at Calcutta.'

All this, though strangely and sometimes tactlessly expressed, would in itself have done James no harm. But where 'Philothetes' went badly wrong was to ask, in a manner that was deemed threatening and indeed containing hints of blackmail by Wellesley, whether the Governor General was himself entitled to criticise such amorous adventures: 'To such an Imputation is the Character of your Lordship invulnerable? Has the daring insolence of curiosity presumed to explore the Mysteries of your secret apartments? In the inmost Recesses of your mind, are the Motives of all your actions opened to public inspection and public censure?'

The answer to this was of course no. For all his evident indignation at James's conduct, Wellesley was no puritan. Indeed he was notoriously highly-sexed, telling his wife Hyacinthe in London that if she did not join him in Calcutta it was inconceivable that he would remain faithful, as 'I assure you that this climate excites one sexually most terribly.' Later he repeated the same belief, simultaneously confessing that he had been true to his threat and was indeed indulging in every sort of vice: 'As for sex, one must have it in this climate . . . *je vais pralaquer dix fois au moins*!!!!!!'*

---

* Wellesley seems to have begun philandering even before he reached India, apparently seducing Anne Barnard's cousin 'the fair Anne Elizabeth' on his stopover at the Cape. His gargantuan sexual appetite became a major problem after his return to London, where there was a series of semi-public incidents with prostitutes. Moreover, after his break-up with Hyacinthe he employed a live-in *accoucheur* who provided 'useful' services to his seraglio of concubines. It was partly rumours of this sort of thing that in due course blocked Wellesley from becoming Prime Minister: his younger brother Arthur firmly believed that it was his 'fornication rather than indolence that has kept him out of office . . . I wish that Wellesley was *castrated*; or that like other people attend to his business and perform too.' See Iris Butler, *The Eldest Brother* (London, 1973), pp.157, 230, 386.

The Governor General tended to take grave offence at the mildest criticism. A letter such as that written by 'Philothetes' – in Wellesley's eyes impudent, ignorant and threatening – sent him into a towering rage; and his response, dictated the same day to his long-suffering secretary Neil Edmonstone, rings with outraged viceregal indignation. While admitting that James was in no way responsible for what his anonymous supporter had written, Wellesley quite unreasonably went on to use the letter as a pretext for savaging James's diplomatic record, claiming that 'so far from possessing any claim to that elevated and commanding situation which this letter arrogates for you in a tone of such ridiculous pomp, your conduct in the execution of orders has frequently and on the most important occasions, required the direct interposition' of Calcutta. He also reminded James that 'you owe your continuance in your present station and the credit which you possess in it, at least as much to his Excellency's forbearance and to his desire of forgiving occasional indiscretions, as to his love of justice'.[48]

The only way James could regain the Confidence of Lord Wellesley, concluded the tirade, was immediately to 'employ your utmost endeavours for the discovery of the author of this anonymous Libel . . . His Excellency is confident that your zeal for the public service, together with your sense of your own character, will urge you to exert every degree of activity in discovering, and enabling His Excellency to bring to justice, a Criminal whose attempt requires the severe punishment of the Law.'

This, James realised immediately, he could never do. His response to Wellesley was measured and dignified, defending his exceptional record as Resident by mentioning merely that 'the detail of my diplomatic services, and Lord Wellesley's opinions on them, have long been upon record'. But he then wrote that, much as he regretted the upset the letter had caused and the insults it contained, he could in no way be expected to carry out a witch-hunt to discover the identity of 'Philothetes', or to be 'instrumental in the disgrace and ruin of a person, who though he has undoubtedly merited his Lordship's highest indignation, would be considered by the World at large as having incurred it by his zeal and attachment – however deplorable & mistaken – to my cause'.[49]

This politely defiant reply fell far short of promising the sort of action Wellesley demanded. By early May, less than a month after being cleared of the charges contained in the Clive Report, and having survived one of the most thorough investigations ever mounted by the East India Company into the private life of one of its servants, James found that he was again back in the doghouse.

This time, however, he was too weary and disgusted with it all to really care. Frustrated in his career and his public life, but confident that Wellesley could not sack him for refusing to track down the writer of an anonymous letter of support, James retreated into the happiness of domesticity and fatherhood. Mentally withdrawing from the political front line, and more or less ignoring Lord Wellesley's hurt pride, he began to focus instead on his wife and children – 'my dear little ones', as he described them repeatedly to his brother William.

Though he continued as Resident, James's letters show how pleasing his masters in Calcutta gradually grew less and less central to his daily concerns. By conciliation and friendship with the Nizam and the Hyderabadi durbar, he had pulled off a series of mutually beneficial treaties which set the relationship between Hyderabad and the Company on a permanent and sustainable footing. If Wellesley wished to wreck all that for the sake of greed, pride and out-and-out belligerency, then that, believed James, was his problem.

As so many have done since in the same situation, James Kirkpatrick effectively drew back, 'to spend more time with his family'; he even took up home improvements and gardening. He went about these endeavours, however, on a rather different scale to most of his modern successors, beginning work on building what John Malcolm would later describe as a dream palace that was 'surpassed in splendour and magnitude only by the Government House at Calcutta . . . [The Governor's House] at Madras cannot even be compared to it.'

As James realised at the time, the palatial Residency that he planned, a perfect fusion of British and Mughlai tastes, and financed by the Nizam, would be a monument not only to himself, but to the close relations between Britain and Hyderabad that he had worked so hard to build, and which were now in danger of being soured for ever.[50]

The British Residency in Hyderabad that James inherited from William was, as Mountstuart Elphinstone memorably pointed out in 1801, 'laid out partly in the taste of Islington & partly in that of Hindostan'.[51]

Ever since John Holland, the first British Resident, arrived in Hyderabad in 1779, the British had rented a beautiful but half-ruined Qutb Shahi riverside garden in which was situated 'the house of a native gentleman, which was pleasant from being surrounded by small gardens and fountains'.[52] This house – an open *baradari* pavilion lying at the centre of the rambling garden complex – had been turned into the principal dining hall and reception area of the Residency. Around it had grown up a spread of new neo-classical bungalows and mansions to house the Residency staff, many of which commanded views over the low garden wall to the waters of the Musi and the domes and minarets of the great city beyond.*

The Hyderabad Residency complex may have been a wonderful

---

* This was an arrangement not uncommon among Indophile Europeans of the period: the chief general of the Sikh leader Ranjit Singh, Claude Auguste Court, built his residence inside the walled formal garden enclosing Asaf Khan's tomb by the river Ravi on the edge of Lahore. (A picture of the house is reproduced in Jean-Marie Lafont, *Maharaja Ranjit Singh: Lord of the Five Rivers* (New Delhi, 2002), p.99.) Just outside the walls of Delhi at the same time, Sir David Ochterlony was building a very similar spread of neo-classical bungalows amid the rills of Shah Jehan's beautiful Shalimar Gardens, the spot where Aurangzeb had been made Mughal Emperor in 1657. Towards the end of his life Ochterlony also began to construct an extraordinary garden tomb in the Mughal garden he had had built for his most senior wife, Mubarak Begum, a short distance from Shalimar Bagh. The Ochterlonys' tomb is a wonderfully hybrid monument, whose central dome was modelled on that of the Delhi church, St James's, and was surmounted by a cross, while the side wings are enclosed in a forest of small minarets – the perfect architectural expression of the religious fusion Ochterlony seems to have achieved in his marriage. In the event, Ochterlony died away from Delhi and was buried in Meerut, and the empty tomb was destroyed during the Mutiny, in which Mubarak Begum, by then remarried to a Mughal nobleman, fought on the Mughal side. It is an extraordinary and completely forgotten moment in architectural history: the last of the great Mughal garden tombs – a tradition that reached its finest moment in the Taj Mahal – being built not

architectural expression of the cultural hybridity of its inhabitants; but in practical terms it was by 1800 a fairly ramshackle collection of buildings. James's bungalow leaked, and attempts at patching it up had failed to stop the damp and decay. In August 1800, James had written to William that the upper half was 'scarcely habitable'.[53] Two wet monsoon months later, the building had nearly collapsed, and James was forced to write to Calcutta to apply for funds as several of the Residency buildings were 'now perfectly uninhabitable. Their condition indeed is such that they have with difficulty been prevented from falling so that their being taken down altogether is a matter of absolute necessity.'

Nor was decay the only problem. With the growing size of the Residency staff and the vast number of British soldiers coming to live in Hyderabad, the old Qutb Shahi pavilion which formed the centrepiece of the garden was no longer remotely adequate for throwing parties. As James wrote to Calcutta,

> the Mussulman building which has always been used as a dining hall and place of public entertainment is both uncomfortable and inconvenient in a very great degree, from its being open and exposed to the South and from its roof being supported on large Gothic pillars which fill so considerable a space in the centre of the room that on particular public days I find it impossible to accommodate as I could wish the numerous guests which the increased and still increasing state of the Subsidiary Force renders me liable to.

James planned as a first improvement to 'add a spacious Hall or Dining Room to the South or open side of [the pavilion] and immediately connected with it'. He also asked for permission to construct 'a suite of apartments consisting of a sitting room for the reception of occasional visitors, a bed chamber and two smaller rooms for writing in or as temporary bedrooms – the whole to be sheltered by a verandah on the two sides most exposed to the weather'.[54]

---

by the last of the Mughals, but by a Scottish-American general. There is a picture of the tomb in Emily Bayley's *The Golden Calm: An English Lady's Life in Moghul Delhi* (London, 1980), p.181.

There was another reason for James's sudden interest in rebuilding the Residency. In the summer of 1800, around the time he was negotiating the Subsidiary Treaty with the Nizam, his landlord, a venerable Hyderabadi *amir* named Nawab Shumshair Jung, had died of old age. Realising the opportunity this provided, James had asked the Nizam for both the Residency compound and some of the fields that immediately surrounded it, to be thrown in with the other land handed over to the British in the treaty.[55] The Nizam had agreed, and James's letter asking Calcutta for funds to begin the rebuilding was written only four days after the treaty was signed. James was no longer a tenant: he was now the effective owner of the Residency, and while he had to wait for Calcutta's say-so to rebuild the house, there was nothing to stop him immediately improving and replanning the gardens around him.

James already had the beginnings of a wonderful mango orchard thanks to the trees sent from Pune by General Palmer. Now he asked his brother William to help to procure some first-class peach trees and, a little later, enough orange trees to plant a decent orange grove. The detail of his requirements demonstrates the degree to which James was becoming a connoisseur in such matters: 'I wish you would endeavour,' he asked William, who was just about to catch ship back home,

> to procure [in England], and send out to me under the charge of some careful trusty friend or acquaintance, a few well grown orange trees, the fruit of which can be warranted excellent of its kind. The best are, I imagine, those that are brought from Portugal. The Malta orange indeed is reckoned the highest flavoured fruit in Europe, and from its juice being red is supposed to be a graft on the Pomegranate.* It may be diffi-cult, if not absolutely impracticable perhaps, to procure plants of this last . . .
>
> You must know that I am turned a great gardener of late, and from what I have heard of the vast superiority of the Portuguese orange over any in this country, have a great notion that I could improve the fruit very much, by having

---

* The sanguinello or blood orange is not in fact any relation to the pomegranate.

a few European standards to engraft from. General Martin,*
I am told, had *one* European orange tree at Lucknow the
fruit of which was so vastly superior to anything of the kind
cultivated there (where they pique themselves on the goodness
of their fruit) as to render the best flavour of the best oranges
of Lucknow growth perfectly insipid.

He added: 'By the means of a few Alphonso and Massagon plants
which I got from our friend [General Palmer] I hope in a few years
to improve the mangoes here wonderfully . . .'[56] A year later, James
was still searching for more varieties of mango, and told his agent
in Bombay that he was 'desirous if it is practicable to have an orchard
of those fine fruits at once, and I have now in my garden an avenue
of many trees of six years growth that will I think all yield fruit next
season, if only I could engraft them all from mature grafts'.[57]

In the months following James's rupture with Wellesley over the
'Philothetes' letter, his correspondence became more and more
centred on the 'improvements' he was planning at the Residency.
Disillusioned with diplomacy and the Company's ambitions, which
he now saw were in danger of destroying a world and a civilisation
he had come to love, he concentrated instead on building a nest for
his little family, and living with his wife and children in a style which
mixed Mughal tastes with the ambitions of a Georgian gentleman
'improving' his estates.

One day he would write to his agent in Madras asking for 'a
handsome house clock', some good 'wheels for my chariot' and 'three
pipes of the very best Madeira together with twelve dozen of choice

---

* General Claude Martin (1735–1800) was General Palmer's old friend from Lucknow
and the founder of the La Martinière schools in Lucknow, Calcutta and Lyon. See Rosie
Llewellyn-Jones, *A Very Ingenious Man: Claude Martin in Early Colonial India* (New
Delhi, 1992).

Malmsey wine'; the next, he sought out the type of Mughal goods which catered to his more Indianised tastes: from Lucknow he ordered a set of best-quality hookah snakes, a large pack of scented Lucknavi tobacco and some *soorayes* (or *surahis*) – the traditional north Indian water-coolers which he believed were of much better quality than those made in Hyderabad.[58]

A consistent worry was the lack of any decent china or table linen for entertaining visitors, and for years James kept writing to his various agents with requests for 'creditable table ware, equipment I consider requisite to the station I fill, and yet it is what this Residency certainly has not had to boast of since I have been at the head of it. My table cloths and napkins I have hitherto had made up from such cloth as bazaars here afford, that is very flimsy and extravagantly dear; and my China ware is a motley collection of occasional auctions'.[59]*

A flourishing vegetable garden was another persistent goal of James's: to one friend in Calcutta he asked for seeds of peas, French beans, lettuce, endive and celery, 'to which may be added a little choice cabbage and cawliflower seed'.[60] In return for these, all he could offer were seeds of aubergines, which appears to have been very much the Hyderabadi vegetable of choice in the late eighteenth century. James particularly pined for 'a good supply of potatoes, being a vegetable which I like much but have not tasted for these two years and more' – interesting evidence that at this period the potato was only grown around the three Presidency towns – Calcutta, Bombay and Madras – though it is hard now to imagine Indian cooking without *aloo*.[61]

James even tried breaking the ice with General Palmer's uncommunicative successor in Pune, Colonel Barry Close, with some fruit-tree diplomacy. In the course of an exchange of elephants between the two men, James took up an offer from the bluff soldier of some saplings from the General's old peach trees: 'The Ceylon Elephant shall be sent off to you in the course of a few days,' wrote James,

---

* A lack of good-quality china seems to have remained a consistent grouse of the English in India throughout the nineteenth century. During the Raj it became a custom in the remoter stations to invite guests to dinner 'camp fashion', which meant they had to bring not just their own servants and their own chair, but their own plates, cutlery and glasses. In 1868 an anonymous army officer wrote in *Life in the Mofussil* that 'it was amusing to see three pretty girls, daughters of an indigo planter of a remote part of the district,

and I will readily avail myself by this opportunity of your kind offer of a few Peach Plants, which will be highly acceptable. I have now in my Garden . . . three very fine ungrafted China Peach Trees sent to me with several other kinds of China Fruit Trees from the botanical garden [in Calcutta] by Doctor Roxburgh.* If these China plants thrive – and many of them are as yet in good health, I shall be able to add three or four very fine fruits to your present stock at Poonah – The peaches you have been so good as to promise a small supply of, will also be very acceptable if not as an immediate relish, at least as the source at least of much future Enjoyment to the palate.[62]†

Within two years, James had arranged all these fruit trees into a huge orchard and kitchen garden 'about half a mile in circumference, completely walled in, and abounding in the choicest Grapes, Mangoes (from Bombay), Peaches, Apples, Oranges, Pine Apples, Strawberries, Raspberries, together with all the horticultural productions of the best sort peculiar to Indian Gardens, or introduced into them of late years from Europe'.[63]

He also tried to acquire a variety of gardeners from different horticultural traditions. In May 1802 he sent requests to his agent in Madras to try to find a good English gardener; five months later he was writing to Bombay trying to find one from China, having heard that Chinese gardeners were to be found in that city, and that they were particularly skilled in the growing of vegetables. For entertainments he also wished to buy

a large assortment of coloured lamps, such as are used in illuminations, and are I understand to be had in ever such quantities in and at very reasonable rate in China . . . [There

drinking champagne out of three-pint pewters, which they had brought with them as safer than glass. They were clearly accustomed to camp fashion.'

* Dr William Roxburgh (1751–1815), a Scot from Edinburgh, started his career on the Andhra coast and published *The Plants of the Coast of the Coromandel* from his time in the vicinity of Hyderabad. In 1793 he was appointed the East India Company's Chief Botanist and the first Superintendent of the Calcutta Botanic Gardens. He was the first botanist to attempt to draw up a systematic account of the plants of India, published posthumously as *Flora Indica*.

† i.e. They would probably be rotten by the time they arrived, but it would be possible to plant the stones.

are] two kinds, one, large lamps for hanging in trees, the other small and globular, in use for common illuminations such as emblematic figurines and mottos which they are made to represent by judicious arrangement and disposition – of the former a few hundred – or perhaps even one hundred would be sufficient for my purpose, but of the latter, a great many thousand will I imagine be requisite for an illumination or anything of a grand scale. The price of these things I am utterly unacquainted with . . . but if they can be procured at a moderate rate, that is a sum which would not absolutely ruin me, I should esteem it as a particular favour if you would commission such a supply for me from China.[64]

Part of James seems to have felt a faint homesickness for England. Certainly, at the other side of his estate from the Mughal watercourses of 'the Hindoostanny Garden', in the farmland he had acquired in the treaty of 1800, he wished to create the sort of gentle, informal park that William Kent, Capability Brown and Humphrey Repton had made fashionable in the England of his youth: an arrangement that had become as central to British conceptions of peaceful, civilised refinement, as cool rippling waters and the shade of overarching broadleaf trees was to that of the Mughals. For this purpose he got teams of men to lay out, on the main axis of the Mughal pavilion, 'Pleasure Grounds, and a paddock well stocked with Deer, of nearly a mile in circumference'.[65] To keep the deer company, he ordered from Bombay some elk and a herd of 'Abyssinian sheep'.[66]*

Creating an expanse of pseudo-English parkland was not, however, without its problems in the middle of India, and by the end of the year James had had to send to Bombay for 'a fire engine, or even two, to water my trees and Pleasure Grounds' to prevent the grass withering in the intense Deccani heat.[67]

---

* Writing to his brother's old friend (and his own former patron) Sir John Kennaway a little later, James mentioned how the park had been constructed from areas outside the original garden perimeter: 'These in your time were all Paddy Fields, but are now partly converted to the aforementioned use and partly covered with handsome bungalows, regular sepoy barracks for my escort, stabling and farm yards, while a lofty and well constructed Flag Staff which I have erected in a centrical and appropriate spot serves at once to convey an idea of Security and Grandeur.' OIOC, Kirkpatrick Papers, F228/59, p.31, 24 October 1804, James Kirkpatrick to Kennaway.

Visitors to the Residency make it clear, however, that the overall style of James's very extensive gardens remained principally Indian in inspiration: according to Malcolm, for example, they were 'laid out more in the Oriental than European style'. Moreover, James told Kennaway that 'the Hindoostanny Garden' was still as he would remember it, and that he had deliberately kept it unchanged. This 'Hindoostanny Garden' appears to have been a typical irrigated Mughal *char bagh* with rippling rills, thickets of fruit trees and flowing fountains; it lay in the corner of the compound beside Khair un-Nissa's Rang Mahal.

With James's clear fondness for Indian paradise gardens in mind,* it is intriguing to wonder how much he discussed gardening with the Nizam, Aristu Jah and his friends in the Hyderabad durbar. For just as Nizam Ali Khan's highly cultured reign had led to a revival of Hyderabad as a centre of Deccani literary and artistic endeavour, so the Nizam's interest in the art of gardening led to a revival of the Deccan's remarkable traditions of Indo-Islamic horticulture.

The court chronicles of Nizam Ali's reign from the 1790s onwards are suddenly full of references to visits to gardens, and to new gardens being built around Hyderabad: for example Aristu Jah's chief wife, Sarwar Afza Begum, built a huge new *char bagh* named Suroor Nagar, where the Minister used to go to relax. Beside it she created a deer park where Aristu Jah, the Nizam and the men of their families would hunt black buck.[68] Mir Alam was also a passionate lover of gardens, and was so proud of his creations that towards the end of his life he opened his *char bagh* to the public in spring; according to the *Gulzar-i-Asafiya* people would flock there to relax and to fly kites.[69] The Hyderabadi miniatures of the period, especially those by the court artist Venkatchellam, are particularly concerned with the cultivated Arcadia of the pleasure garden, and the fountains and ranked cedar trees of the irrigated garden became the standard background to all Hyderabadi portraits of the time.[70] The famous

---

* The English word 'paradise' derives from the walled Eastern garden, or enclosed hunting park – specifically from the Persian words *pairi* (around) and *daeza* (a wall). The word passed into English via the Greek *paradeisoi*. See Elizabeth B. Moynihan, *Paradise as a Garden in Persia and Mughal India* (New York, 1979).

Venkatchellam image of Aristu Jah's son Ma'ali Mian, for example, shows him sitting in a garden sniffing a flower and admiring a tame hawk as five small fountain jets play amid the roses and dragonflies at his feet, and clouds of rosy parakeets fly to roost in the banana trees and toddy palms that frame the scene.[71]

Moreover, it was during Nizam Ali's reign that a great number of gardening books came to be written, translated and copied: one particularly influential manual named the *Risala i-Baghbani* was written in Golconda at the beginning of Nizam Ali's reign in 1762. These books contain wonderful passages of advice to Hyderabadi gardeners which mix the scientific with the pseudo-scientific, the useful and well-observed with more eccentric – and probably rather less useful – items of *mali's* lore and old wives' tales. The *Risala*, for example, recommends that melons can be made especially sweet and tasty if, before planting, their seeds are stored in mounds of fresh rose petals, and if honey, dates, cows' milk and chopped liquorice are dug into the plants' roots. Bananas meanwhile can be encouraged to elongate to become as long and as firm as elephant tusks 'if an iron bar dipped in a steamy mix of animal wastes' is used to 'scorch' the tree.[72]

The *Khazan wa-Bahar*, another contemporary Deccani gardening treatise, contains a great deal of detailed information which would have been of interest to James. This is especially so in the section on the planting of fruit trees, which it recommends should be done by the light of the waning moon if the gardener wishes to promote the growth of fruit rather than the trees' size. To prevent disease the earth should be fertilised with pigeon dung and olive-leaf extract, while wild onions should be planted around the tree's base. The anonymous writer also has advice to those, like James, who had problems getting their mango trees to fruit. A barren tree, he advises, will suddenly spring into life if it is loudly threatened with the axe, or if the appropriate Koranic verses are tied to its branches.[73] Had James read the *Khazan wa-Bahar* he would have learned that he could have produced seedless grapes by applying musk and opium to the roots of his vines; grow bright-red apples by pegging down the lower branches with an iron bar; and stimulate his peach trees to fruit by inserting pine or willow cuttings in the roots. He would also have learned of some intriguing methods of ecologically sound pest control: black hellebore and mustard planted at the entrance of a garden would keep away snakes, while filling his vegetable patch with turnips, cabbage, radish and broad beans would free the garden from mosquitoes.

Another concept that James would have come across among the garden connoisseurs of Hyderabad was the lovely idea of the evening garden. By day, the 'flowers of the sun' were there to be admired for their beauty; but as the sun set at the end of the day, other 'flowers of the night' came to the fore, to be enjoyed for their scent or for the glow of their foliage in the light of the moon. In these specially planted areas, marble pavilions would be arranged with bolsters and carpets for nights of wine, music, poetry and the company of women, all surrounded by beds of carefully selected night flowers. Here the heady perfume of tuberose would mix with that of *chandni*, the moon-flower, said to diffuse the sweetest perfume on nights when the moon shone brightly. The importance of such scents was a central concept in Islamic thought, an idea which derived from the Hadith, attributed to the Prophet: 'Scent is the food of the soul, and the soul is the vehicle of the faculties of man.'[74]

It is impossible now to say whether James was familiar with the finer points of the aesthetics of the Deccani garden, and whether he made an attempt to maintain his Residency *char bagh* according to these traditions. However, given what is known about his fondness for Hyderabadi food, architecture, clothes, poetry and women, and given his feeling for plants and gardening, it would be extraordinary if he did not. Certainly there are two clear hints that he was indeed as *au fait* with current fashions in Hyderabadi garden design as one would have expected. The first is his eclectic choice of trees for the Residency, many of which are still alive and which show a close similarity to those selected at the same time by Mah Laqa Bai Chanda in the shady walled garden she built to surround her mother's tomb below the hill of Maula Ali, notably the extensive use of the relatively rare *mulsarry* (or Indian medlar).*

* The *mulsarry* (or *maulshree* in Sanskrit) was unusual in the Deccan, though it was extensively used by the Mughals in Delhi and Agra as its neat crown lent itself to formal

The second hint is the Residency pigeon tower, and the pigeon pots which still survive in the ruins of Khair un-Nissa's *mahal*. Pigeon-fancying was never a feature of the Georgian gentleman's house, and no other examples are known in British India. It was however central to the idea of refinement in the social life of a Mughal nobleman, with flying pigeons regarded as an essential part of the cultivated enjoyment of a gentleman's pleasure garden. This seems to have been especially the case in Hyderabad: the *Khazan wa-Bahar* dedicates a whole chapter to the subject of the pigeon and its place in the garden of a civilised Hyderabadi *amir*.

Not only were pigeons supposed to keep snakes away, and their excrement deemed ideal for the cultivation of fruit trees; their voices – or rather their billing and cooing – were believed to be stimulating for the human intellect. The anonymous author of the *Khazan* advises his reader to burn incense and to mix *mastaki* (mastic or terbinth) and honey in the pigeons' water, in order to keep them content and happy in the garden.[75]

Somehow, it seems impossible to imagine that James and Khair un-Nissa did not closely follow this advice.

After the departure of the Palmers in April 1802, explicit details of the daily life and routine of James's two children and their young mother become frustratingly elusive. It is as if they have retreated out of the sudden shaft of sunlight provoked by the visit of Fyze and the General, and disappeared back into the shadows. We know they are there, and it is clear that James is increasingly spending his time with them; but only occasionally do the clouds roll back to let the sun briefly break through once more. One day Khair and Sahib Allum are glimpsed sending their greetings and more parcels of bangles to Fyze and Fanny

planting arrangements. (I would like to thank Pradip Krishen for his help with this intriguing tree.)

Palmer; on another the two children are being sent off to Dr Ure to be inoculated against smallpox, or possibly cholera: as James reported to the General in October 1802, 'Both my little ones here have been *vaccinated*, and are enjoying excellent health and spirits . . . By the bye, I have prevailed on Nizzy and Solomon to render vaccination general, by introducing the practice into their own families.'[76]

Nevertheless, reading carefully between the lines, it is possible to piece together some fairly detailed information about James's domestic life and the choices that he made as to the upbringing of his young family. It is quite clear, for example, that the children were brought up by Khair and her mother – assisted by a great retinue of serving girls, *aseels* and wetnurses – in a more or less entirely Hyderabadi environment. They were raised as Muslims, had Mughal names, spoke Persian (or possibly Deccani Urdu) as their first language (Khair un-Nissa spoke no English[77]) and wore typical aristocratic Hyderabadi dress. They do not seem to have been introduced to the Europeans of the Residency,[78] and given their aristocratic status were probably not encouraged to play with the other Anglo-Indian children on the campus, such as Henry Russell's child by his unnamed (and therefore probably non-aristocratic) mistress.[79] All the indications are that the *mahal* was like a detached fragment of the old city dropped into the middle of the semi-Anglicised world of the Residency, and that James's children mixed mainly with the children of the *zenanas* of other Hyderabadi nobles, and especially with the inhabitants of Aristu Jah's mansion.[80]

Held firmly within the cultural and religious embrace of Mughlai Hyderabad, the children must presumably have undergone the normal cycle of ceremonies and initiations that would mark the childhood of any other Deccani Muslim child of their rank and status. The birth itself was the first staging-post on this ceremonial journey. On the day of delivery, almost as soon as the baby had been cleaned and swaddled, the call to prayer, the *Azan*, would be recited into the babe's right ear, followed by the *Kalima* (or creed), which would be read into the left. The idea was to introduce the holy words into the ears of the child as it first opened its eyes, after which *paan* would be distributed among eagerly waiting friends and relatives. Then a little piece of dried date, chewed by a respected scholar or *qazi*, would be inserted into the child's mouth, followed shortly afterwards by a little honey water, sucked through a piece of clean, soft cloth – the former being a Middle Eastern custom, the latter a Hindu one, both of which were absorbed into and became part of the composite Deccani Mughal culture. After this, the child would be applied to the breast for the first time. As was the custom among aristocratic Mughal women, Khair un-Nissa did not breastfeed her children herself, instead giving them to a wetnurse, who in some Mughal *zenanas* could continue feeding the child up to the age of three or even four.[81]

The choice of a wetnurse was considered a matter of the greatest importance, as it was believed that with her milk were transferred some of her spiritual and moral qualities. Honest, pious, good-tempered women of unimpeachable reputation were sought out for the job, especially those from grand or Sayyid families who had for one reason or another fallen into poverty; after they had finished suckling, they and their own children were brought to live in the family mansion as honoured and respected members of the household.[82]* Nothing is known of the family backgrounds of Sahib Allum and Sahib Begum's wetnurses, Ummat ul-Fatimeh and Maham Aloopaim[?],† but both continued to live in Sharaf un-Nissa's household, with their sons and daughters, and were still there forty years later when Sharaf un-Nissa sent their greetings to her two beloved grandchildren.[83]

Two or three days into breastfeeding a girl, another small rite of passage took place. In India it has always been the custom – though the practice is completely unknown in the West – to squeeze the nipples of a suckling child so that small 'milkdrops' emerge. This is

---

* Indeed, in the Imperial Mughal court, the wetnurses of the Mughal emperors often became important figures of state: Maham Anaga, Akbar's wetnurse, was one of the most powerful figures in sixteenth-century India, and her eldest son, Akbar's foster-brother, the cruel and unprincipled Adham Khan, grew so influential and unruly that he became a major threat to the stability of the Empire. Adham Khan eventually became so uncontrollable that in 1561 he killed the Mughal Prime Minister, Atagha Khan, before being himself despatched by Akbar, who in a fit of anger following the murder knocked him out and then threw him from a second-floor palace window. Filled with remorse after the event, Akbar did penance and built a magnificent tomb for Adham Khan that still stands above the Qutb complex and the walls of Lal Kot in south Delhi. See Abu'l Fazl, *Ain i-Akbari* (Calcutta, 1873–94), Vol. 2, pp.269–71.

† This name is corrupted in the source document which is almost illegible at this point.

believed to be of great medicinal value, and is said to ensure the future well-being of the breast. In the case of female babies of Mughal families, the brother of the infant was asked to suckle the 'milkdrop' so produced; this was believed to create a deep bond of love between a brother and his sister, as the Emperor Jehangir recorded in his diaries. His sister Shakar un-Nissa Begum was, he writes,

> of good disposition and naturally compassionate towards all people. From infancy and childhood she had been extremely fond of me, and there can be few such close relationships between a brother and a sister. The first time when, according to the custom of pressing the breast of a child and a drop of milk is perceptible, they pressed my sister's breast and a drop of milk appeared, my revered father [the Emperor Akbar] said to me: 'Baba! Drink this milk that in truth this sister may be to thee as a mother.' God the Knower of Secrets, knows that from that day forward, after I drank that drop of milk, I have felt love for my sister such as children have for their mothers . . .[84]

The custom is still current among many Indian families – Hindu and Muslim – today. It was certainly the practice in Mughal families of James Kirkpatrick's period, and the women of Khair un-Nissa's *mahal* would no doubt have expected Sahib Allum to taste his sister's 'milkdrops' in just this manner.[85]*

On the sixth, seventh or ninth day after the birth, a Mughal family would normally hold the *chatthi*, or birth celebration, when the mother and child would be bathed and clothed in costly new dresses – another Mughal borrowing from Hindu tradition. The same day, the *aqiqa*, or the first shaving of the child's head, would take place with a silver razor; the shaved head was rubbed in saffron, and goats sacrificed (two for a boy, one for a girl) to remove impurities and preserve against the evil eye. Alms would then be distributed among the poor.

The evening of the *chatthi*, tradition dictated that the house would

---

* Modern Indian doctors frown on the practice, which can lead to breast abscesses forming. Full-term babies, both male and female, have palpable mammary glands and breast engorment can occur after three days, leading to the secretion of a milky substance called 'witch's milk' by modern doctors. This is due to maternal hormone withdrawal. (I would like to thank Dr Prita Trehan for help on this matter.)

be cleaned and illuminated, and guests entertained by fireworks, singers and dancing girls, as well as feasted with the most precious and costly food. Guests would present gifts of infants' clothes, such as embroidered *kurtas* and *topis* (long shirts and skullcaps), with further trunkloads of presents – jewels, toys and sweetmeats – being presented by the mother's relations. Finally, at the climax of the *chatthi*, the mother of the child, along with her girlfriends, would carry the infant into an open courtyard and then, for the first time, '*tare dikhana*', show the child the stars in the night sky. While this was happening, so the Mughals believed, the child's destiny was written by the angel whose duty it was to record a person's fate.[86]

Khair un-Nissa, one can presume, would have insisted on all the basic traditional ceremonies being performed for her children: the remark in Sahib Allum's birth note, that Khair called her son Ali after dreaming of the Prophet's son-in-law, would seem to point to her particular piety. Nor does James seem likely to have opposed his children being brought up as Muslims. He had, after all, been prepared himself to undergo a formal conversion ceremony to marry Khair, and although there is no unequivocal evidence that he regularly practised his new faith, or regarded himself as an active Muslim, his mother-in-law, who lived closely with him, certainly believed him to be such, as did his Munshi, Aziz Ullah.*

What is certain is that James respected Islam and made sure, for example, that the Residency gave money to Hyderabad Sufi shrines. But his attraction to the faith is likely to have been as much cultural as religious. His own letters to Europeans deliberately use vague and Deist terms for God – he refers at one stage for example to 'Bounteous

---

* Sharaf un-Nissa refers to James as a practising Muslim in her evidence to Dr Kennedy published in the Clive Enquiry, where she mentions that 'the Resident had for the Six months past become a real Mussulman'. This is corroborated by Munshi Aziz Ullah, who in a Persian letter to Sharaf un-Nissa after James's death prays for his soul using a very specific construction that would only be used of a *pukka* Muslim, 'may Allah illumine his dust and grant him abode in heaven'. Letter from Munshis Aziz Ullah and Aman Ullah to Sharaf un-Nissa, 25 August 1810. The letter is in a bound volume of Russell's Persian correspondence in the Bodleian Library. These letters somehow became detached from Russell's well-catalogued English correspondence and languished uncatalogued in a box in the library's Persian Department. I am extremely grateful to Doris Nicholson for finally locating the vital folder of correspondence.

Providence'[87] – rather than more specifically sectarian terms such as 'Christ' or 'Allah', and this vague approach to religious boundaries would seem to have fitted in well with the widespread Indian belief, very much lying at the heart of Deccani culture with its strong Sufi and Bhakti influences, that all faiths were really one, and that there were many different paths up the mountain. Hyderabad's principal festivals, after all, were Shi'ite but were attended by Sunni Muslims, Christians and Hindus alike. Clear European ideas of the firm and heavily defended frontiers separating different religions were quite alien to Hyderabadi culture, and in this fluid and porous atmosphere James's broadly Deist approach to his faith would have fitted in easily both with those Europeans who had embraced the ideas of the eighteenth-century Enlightenment and with the general outlook of the Hyderabadis around him.*

Even so, it would be intriguing to know if James would have been confident enough to hold such large and public non-Christian ceremonies as the *chatthi* for his wife and babies in the Residency compound, within view of his less open-minded colleagues. If not, might he have held them in Bâqar Ali Khan's mansion in the old city? It is clear that Khair and Sharaf un-Nissa kept their *deorhi* townhouse in use, frequently visiting Sharaf's mother Durdanah Begum who was still residing there, while living principally at the Residency *mahal*. We also know, intriguingly, that James used to keep 'three or four [spare] setts' of his Mughal robes, cummerbunds and turbans there, including some of the especially fine quality normally used by nobles at the durbar.[88] This then was perhaps the most likely place for him to have held the *chatthi*, in a venue that Khair's relations could have more easily reached and felt at ease within –

---

* Whatever his own views, James was however quite clear – both in a letter to his father and in his will – that his children should be baptised 'as soon as possible after their arrival in England', just as General Palmer had had William baptised before his English schooling, and without which both fathers must have feared – probably correctly – that their children would never be accepted in Britain. See OIOC, F228/84, 'The Last Will and Testament of James Achilles Kirkpatrick', and Kirkpatrick Papers. See also the fascinating letter (F228/59, p.27) of 24 October 1804, James to William Kirkpatrick, where James seems to imply that it would not be possible to baptise the children on a trip to Madras as Khair un-Nissa would be there (and, implicitly, either she would not allow it, or he did not want to offend her by performing the ceremony in her presence).

though even so the ceremonies would have doubtless appeared a little strange to Hyderabadis, as James had no female family relations on his side to host the *zenana* celebrations as in a normal Mughal family.

In the weeks and months that followed the birth of James's children, a further succession of rites and ceremonies would continue to mark the babies' progress to health and toddlerhood. Most of these took place in the *zenana* wing with only women invited, and commemorated various significant mileposts in the child's life: the *chillah*, marking the child's fortieth day and the mother's release from confinement;* the ceremony attendant on the first piercing of a girl's ears by a barber to allow her to wear earrings;† or the moment when a little girl's hair was plaited for the first time,‡ all of which were followed by a small celebration and a general distribution of sweets.

The final ceremony of early childhood was the *bismillah*, when a child's education would begin, usually at the age of three or (more usually) four.¶ A girl was dressed as a bride and a special scented powder was rubbed over her body; boys were dressed as grooms. They were then presented to their tutor in the presence of guests, after which they recited, following the tutor's instruction, the whole of the ninety-sixth chapter of the Koran, the Surah Iqra. After this their study of the Arabic alphabet would begin.

* According to custom, it also marked the moment that the child could be placed in a *gahwarah* (swinging cradle).

† Known as the *kanchhedan* ceremony. Sahib Begum's ears were pierced by July 1805 when, at the age of three, she was painted by George Chinnery wearing a pair of large pearl earrings.

‡ Known as the *bal gunthan*.

¶ In some families it was a tradition to celebrate the *bismillah* on the fourth day of the fourth month of the child's fourth year.

342

Throughout her children's childhood, we catch only fleeting glimpses of Khair un-Nissa.

Though she was the central figure in the life of James's family, and clearly a quietly forceful personality, the loss of her letters means that today we can see her only obliquely, reflected through the eyes of her lover, her husband, her mother and her children. Only rarely – and then indirectly – are her own words recorded. Nevertheless, through the impressions of her family and her own actions, a coherent mosaic does emerge.

Khair was clearly a pious, impulsive and emotional woman, as well as being a remarkably brave and determined figure when the need arose, and few people – certainly not her mother, grandmother or husband – seemed willing or able to stand in her way once she had made up her mind about something.* She was educated and literate and wrote frequent letters. She was also very generous – constantly loading her friends with presents of clothes and jewellery – and had the gift of friendship: she is frequently recorded as being surrounded by her friends.[89] Her children remembered her as a gentle and loving mother, and a much milder figure than James, whom Sahib Allum recalled, surprisingly perhaps, as a slightly stern father – at least initially: many years later he wrote to his sister that he had discovered some copies of James's old letters to the Handsome Colonel in which it was clear that 'you [Sahib Begum] were allowed to be over indulged in consequence of my father having found the ill-effect of over-severity to me, and the terror of which severity he says all his subsequent kindness could hardly soothe me out of'.[90]

We do catch the occasional glimpse of Khair un-Nissa's hobbies and pastimes. The evidence of the pigeon pots in her *mahal* would seem to indicate that she liked flying pigeons, as did many other Hyderabadi Begums, judging by the frequency with which it appears as a motif of Hyderabadi painting at this time. She was also creative, amusing herself making (or at least designing) jewellery and bangles,

---

* One of the advantages for Khair in marrying James was that she would never have had to contend with the will of a mother-in-law, as would almost certainly have been the case had she married within Hyderabadi society. Instead, at the age of sixteen she found herself mistress of her own *zenana*. See p.178n.

and together she and James developed an interest in precious stones. In a postscript to one of his letters to William, James lets slip that he and Khair 'have discovered here by mere accident that the opal which turns opaque in the hot winds completely recovers its clearness and colour by immersion in water, for a greater or less time according to their size and degree of opacity. The opal must therefore be classed among the Hydrophanous gems.'[91] It is a lovely image: Khair un-Nissa busily creating her jewellery; James looking on, the amateur Georgian gemmologist scratching his head as the opals change colour and trying to work out his geological classifications.

One set of her jewel creations Khair sent as a present for her nieces, William Kirkpatrick's daughters. Many years later a necklace from this consignment found its way back to Sahib Begum, who treasured it as a rare memento of her long-dead mother. In a letter to Sharaf un-Nissa she wrote: 'I possess a necklace & bracelets of beads inter-weaved with small pearls made by my mother & sent by my mother to one of my cousins – as it has passed through my mother's fingers, it is the possession I treasure the most.'[92] Khair also made (or, again, at least designed) clothes, which she sent as presents to her family and friends, embroidery being one of the traditional pursuits of Mughal Begums, and a skill in which Nur Jehan (and many other imperial princesses such as Aurangzeb's daughter Zeb un-Nissa) was especially accomplished. As an adult, one of Sahib Begum's strongest memories of her Hyderabadi childhood was 'the place [presumably just outside the *mahal*] where the tailors worked'.[93]

As to the games and the toys with which Khair played with her children, Sahib Begum later remembered some sort of slide on the flat roof of the *mahal*, while we know that James asked his agent to send out from England 'a few Europe dolls in high Court Dress' for the children to play with – possibly as a way of familiarising them with European dress and complexions.

As a home for the dolls, James built a four-foot-high model of his planned new Residency mansion. The model still lies (albeit now in a ruinous state) immediately behind the remains of Khair un-Nissa's *mahal* and within its old enclosure wall. Later tradition in the Residency has it that it was built for Khair, who was locked so deep in purdah that she could not go around the front of the house to see what it looked like – but this story (still current in the town) clearly has no basis in reality, as there is ample evidence that Khair frequently and freely travelled around Hyderabad to visit her friends and family. It would also have been normal for aristocratic Mughal women in purdah to travel out from their mansions for picnics, pilgrimages, visits to shrines and hunting expeditions.[94] The model is much more likely to be a dolls' house which James constructed, possibly as a birthday present, for one or both of his beloved children.*

It was some time before a reply was received from Calcutta in response to James's request for money to repair and rebuild his collapsing Residency. Funds were sanctioned, but they fell far short of what James wanted or needed: a ceiling of twenty-five thousand rupees† was put on the expenditure.

This far from generous offer was particularly mean coming from Wellesley, who had just earmarked the most colossal sum for building himself a vast new Government House in Calcutta, in order, so he said, to protect him from the 'stupidity and ill-bred familiarity' of

---

* That the model was once a dolls' house was also the conclusion reached independently by preservationist Elbrun Kimmelman and her student team. In the summer of 2001 they began work restoring the model, and reached their conclusions partly by comparisons with other eighteenth-century dolls' houses of similar dimensions. The fact that Kirkpatrick was ordering dolls from Europe at the same time as he was building the replica – a fact unknown to Kimmelman – can be taken as clinching evidence of their speculations. Intriguingly, in *Palaces of the Raj*, Mark Bence-Jones notes that 'the miniature palace, complete with portico and balustrade, remained a feature of the Begum's Garden, a delight to future generations of Residency children who were, however, discouraged from playing with it since it harboured snakes and insects'. That the model predates the completed building is clear from various differences between the two, and a number of small architectural features included on the model that were never actually constructed on the Residency proper. Work conducted by Kimmelman on the dolls' house resulted in a successful application to the World Monuments Fund for the entire Residency complex to be selected for the Fund's Hundred Most Endangered Sites list in 2001.

† Perhaps £150,000 in today's currency.

Calcutta society; at the end of four years, the house, modelled on Keddlestone Hall in Derbyshire, had cost a colossal £63,291.* Visitors certainly admired the new building, designed by Lieutenant Charles Wyatt of the Bengal Engineers, and Lord Valentia famously observed that it was better that 'India be ruled from a palace than a counting house'; but it was this spendthrift use of Company funds that more than anything gradually eroded Wellesley's support among the Company Directors, and put in train a series of decisions in London that ended with his recall in 1805.[95]

Already, by early 1803, the Directors of the Company were sending shots across Wellesley's bows, fiercely attacking Lord Clive's far less grand constructions in Madras, and making it quite clear that 'it by no means appears to us essential to the well-being of our Government in India that the pomp, magnificence and ostentation of the Native Governments should be adopted by the former; the expense that such a system would naturally lead to must prove highly injurious to our commercial interests.'[96] But no one in London, it seems, had the slightest idea of the scale of the building Wellesley was engaged in constructing, and when the bill arrived at the Company headquarters in Leadenhall Street, the Directors were appalled by 'this work of unexampled extent and magnificence . . . undertaken without any previous or regular communication with us'.[97]

It is not clear whether James hinted about the Residency's financial straits to Aristu Jah, or whether the Minister came to learn of the state of the Residency buildings by direct observation. Whatever the truth, sometime in 1802 he suggested to James that in the absence of Company funds he might apply to the Nizam for money, an offer which James immediately took up. According to the story which James later told John Malcolm, he

> requested the Engineer of the English force stationed at Hyderabad to make an exact survey of the spot, and when this was finished upon a large sheet carried to the Durbar, where showing it to the Nizam, requested he would give the English Government a grant of the land. The Prince, after

* Perhaps £3.8 million today.

gravely examining the survey, said he was sorry he could not comply with the request.

When the Resident was retiring, not a little disconcerted at the refusal of a favour which seemed so trifling, the Minister[98] said to him with a smile, 'Do not be annoyed. You frightened the Nizam with the size of the plan you showed him. Your fields were almost as large as any of the maps of his Kingdom he had yet seen. No wonder,' said he, laughing, 'that he did not like to make such a cession. Make a survey upon a reduced scale, and the difficulty will vanish.' The Resident could hardly believe this would be the case. But when, at his next interview, he presented the same plan upon a small card, the ready and cheerful assent of the Prince satisfied him that the [Minister] had been quite correct in his guess of the cause of the former failure.[99]

In his youth Nizam Ali Khan had won himself the throne by a combination of ruthlessness and charisma; he was also a notable orator.* But by 1802 this once formidable warrior was a toothless sixty-eight-year-old, and after a lifetime of energetic activity had recently suffered not one but two debilitating strokes, which had left him weak, listless and partly paralysed. He now spent his days sipping camels' milk (the cure his *unani* doctors had recommended for his paralysed right arm and leg) and fishing for tame carp in the pools of the palace, a diversion in which he sometimes invited James to join him. His other great passions were flying pigeons,

---

* In 1761, for example, he led the army of Hyderabad into battle against a vastly superior Maratha army, telling his troops, 'In this life, which is like a bubble of water and which vanishes like the scent of a flower, to leave behind a reputation for cowardice is against all honour. He who does not mind losing his life and wants to sacrifice himself, can come with me and meet the challenge of the swords. Otherwise everybody is permitted to go . . .' The victory which followed was one of the greatest ever won by the Hyderabadis. See *Gulzar i-Asafiya*, pp.121–34.

evenings of music and poetry, and disembowelling European clocks.

Over his years in Hyderabad James had grown very fond of the Nizam, and not only indulged all his whims, but went out of his way to please 'the old gentleman' (as he usually called him in his letters). James had been present at the late-night music party when the Nizam had had his first stroke after becoming over-excited by the dancing of Mah Laqa Bai Chanda. Subsequently he had gone out of his way to find him a pair of 'prodigious' spice island doves, 'each as large as a goose', as ornaments for his pigeon collection, and a young lioness for his menagerie. These presents were not just a function of James's undoubted generosity; they were useful policy, and James privately believed that he might never have pulled off the Subsidiary Treaty of 1800 had he not found the Nizam three items for which he had especially asked: a particularly intricate piece of clockwork 'with cascades and fountains represented by glass set in motion', 'an artificial singing bird . . . an automaton, set with jewels . . . representing the plumage [and] thirdly a fur cloak . . . from Nepaul . . . a most acceptable present to the old gentleman, who even in this hot weather is always wrapped up in a fur dress or shawls'.[100]

James also did his best to protect the Nizam from the host of dubious magicians, faith-healers and Dervish quacks who, at Aristu Jah's bidding, tended to collect around his sickbed (Aristu Jah being, according to James, 'besotted with astrology and necromancy'[101]). He was able to arrest English quacks who had manoeuvred their way into the Nizam's presence – in May 1802 he expelled from Hyderabad 'an imposter who had passed himself off with the Nizam and the Minister as a famous alchemist'[102] – but he had less influence with local Hyderabadi faith-healers and medicine men, and was particularly worried by one 'wizard' who began feeding the 'old gentleman' large quantities of mercury. As James told William:

> I must inform you that the Nizam though he looked so much better at my late visit has taken it into his head to try a medicine which if he continues (as I understand he means to do) for any considerable time, will, by all I can learn, send him to a certainty to his eternal home in a twelve month or

less. This medicine is neither more or less than an amalgam
of mercury recommended to him by an ambitious quack as
an infallible cure for the palsy, and so it certainly is in one
sense . . . By way of having company in the shades below, he
kindly associates Solomon [Aristu Jah], and the Bakshi
Begum [his senior wife] in this regimen, and I saw Solomon
and himself take their prescribed doses together, at my late
audience.[103]

Six months later, James was surprised to discover that the Nizam
was still taking the mercury, and yet showing remarkably few signs
of its ill-effects, though James hoped that he was beginning to tire
of the 'wizard' who was feeding it to him: 'His Highness certainly
has, as Colonel Palmer observes, as many lives as a cat,' he wrote,

> or he surely what with age, infirmity, debauchery and quackery
> would have been numbered 'ere this year with his forefathers.
> He is now taking mercury again (which once was so near
> doing his business*) under the direction of the Wizard, intro-
> duced to him by Conjuror Solomon, who still has great faith
> in his diabolic medical skills. The wizard himself however
> disclaims infallibility, and if my private information can be
> relied upon, is preparing, probably from fear, to vanish: having
> already by way of preparation declared, that when the foul
> fiend, or *djinn* whom he avows to converse with, takes a stick
> into his hand, he thinks nothing of seizing and transporting
> him in the twinkling of an eye to the antipodes.[104]

James's affection for the increasingly eccentric Nizam was more
than returned. The Nizam used to address him as 'Beloved Son', and
once the plan for the Residency had been reduced to the size of a
card he had been happy to authorise not only the handing over of
the adjacent fields, but had generously offered to cover the cost of
the rebuilding himself.

No sooner had the Nizam agreed to pay for the building than
James set to work planning a Residency mansion rather larger and
more substantial than he had originally envisaged when applying for

---

* i.e. Finishing him off.

funds from Calcutta. The magnificent Residency at Hyderabad has traditionally been attributed to Samuel Russell, and there is no doubt that Russell oversaw the last part of the building's completion, and may have added to or refined the final plan. But equally it is quite clear from James's letters that the initial plans, and the beginning of construction, were undertaken by James himself with the help of an anonymous Indian 'maistry'* architect, who was apparently trained in Mughal methods before being taught a basic grammar of contemporary neo-classical forms by the British. James's letters reveal that behind the construction of the apparently perfect European classical form of the Palladian Hyderabad Residency lay a Mughal-trained architect. As with so many features of life in the East India Company, look under an apparently English veneer and one finds a more complicated, hybrid Anglo-Mughal reality.

In October 1802, some six months after the storm over the 'Philothetes' letter, James wrote to James Brunton, a friend in Madras, with a set of detailed instructions and a request for him to start work collecting the men and materials that would be needed to begin work on his great project. Very little is known about the details of the architecture of the East India Company at this period, as buildings tended to be erected in a fairly *ad hoc* fashion by military engineers rather than trained architects. Most buildings in the three British Presidency towns were copies of originals in England, constructed from plates in books like Robert Adam's *Works of Architecture* or Colin Campbell's *Vitruvius Britannicus*, although they were given a superficial gloss of Oriental features, such as blinds and verandahs, essential for the climate. Few original plans, or correspondence, survive to indicate the ideas, conceptions and ambitions that lay behind these buildings, and in this – as in so many other areas – James's letters are unusually illuminating and well worth quoting in full: 'Being about to build a new mansion at this Residency,' he wrote to Brunton on 6 October 1802,

and desirous of it being erected both with taste and solidity,

---

* 'Maistry' (or the modern Hindi *mistri*) means a highly skilled foreman or 'master' craftsmen. According to *Hobson-Jobson* the word, 'a corruption of the Portuguese *mestre* has spread into the vernaculars all over India and is in constant Anglo-Indian use'.

I could wish to have the advice and aid of a Madras Native Architect, and a few artisans, such as Maistry Bricklayers, Smiths and Carpenters. You will therefore oblige me by setting on foot enquiries immediately and procuring me one of the first description, two or three of the second, and one of each of the latter, taking particular care that they are each sufficiently expert in their respected professions, and that their monthly wages shall be on as reasonable a scale as possible.

I am willing to pay them their travelling expenses and to make such addition to the wages which Men of their description earn at Madras as you may deem liberal; and maybe a sufficient encouragement to them to undertake the journey with perhaps one half or two thirds more than they got in their own country – with an engagement of one year certain.

What I mean by a native architect, is what is termed here a *Ruaz* or an expert accomplished mason, conversant in the different orders of European architecture. The Maistry bricklayers I require must work themselves in brick and mortar as an example to the native Hyderabad bricklayers who will work under them, and be masters of the art of laying on fine *chunam* [polished lime plaster]. The maistry smith and carpenter must also be expert in handicrafts, and well acquainted with house timber work – such as ceiling, flooring, door and window making; which the smiths and carpenters here are but rough workmen in.[105]

In a final, characteristically thoughtful postscript, James said he was happy to arrange for part of the workmen's wages to be paid direct to their families in Madras.

Within a few months the masons and architects had been found and duly despatched to Hyderabad. By the early summer of 1803, the foundations were already being laid for one of the most ambitious buildings to be erected in the Deccan for over a hundred years. James's main concern now was to remain in his post long enough to complete this project; and on this score he had good reason to worry.

Not only was he completely and irreparably out of favour with Lord Wellesley, his health was in decline too. His rheumatism grew worse over the course of 1802, and towards the end of the year he developed some severe hepatitic complaint that left him bedridden for a month, and very weak for the entire first quarter of 1803. He never entirely recovered from the disease and suffered from intermittent relapses the rest of his life. For the first time, Dr Ure began to mutter about James considering following his half-brother William back to Europe.

England was no longer the place that James really considered to be his home. He had been born in India, and had spent all but eleven years of his life there. Like General Palmer, he felt most himself in India, and returning to England was the last thing he wanted. But as his health continued to decline, it increasingly became a prospect he was forced to hold in reserve, to consider as a final option, if the worst came to the worst.

VIII

O N 6 AUGUST 1803 Nizam Ali Khan died in his sleep, at the age of sixty-nine. That same day Lord Wellesley declared war on the Maratha Confederacy, and sent his younger brother Arthur into battle. James had long predicted both events, and had dreaded the prospect of either.

For years he had worried about the Nizam's death and the possibility of the major upheavals that might follow it. He had good reason to do so: almost every Mughal Emperor had come to power in a fratricidal bloodbath, and the same pattern had shown every sign of developing in the Mughal satellite of Hyderabad: when Nizam Ali's father, Nizam ul-Mulk, had died in 1748, Hyderabad had been engulfed in fourteen years of disastrous civil war as the Nizam's six sons fought for control. Moreover, Nizam Ali's own progeny had already demonstrated their capacity for internecine anarchy: in 1795 and 1796 the Nizam's eldest son Ali Jah, and his ambitious son-in-law Dara Jah, had both revolted. Although the two rebellions had been quickly crushed (and Ali Jah despatched in an apparent suicide, while under Mir Alam's charge), fear of the Nizam's sudden death had kept James in Hyderabad, or its immediate vicinity, for most of the previous two years. This worry was the reason he had been unable to go to Madras to see his brother William off to England – a meeting both knew might well have been their last.*

In the event, however, to the surprise of most observers, the

---

* William finally set off from Madras for England on 18 February 1802. He never saw James again.

transition of power was completely smooth. The Nizam had had another stroke in early June 1803, after which James had reported sadly to Calcutta that 'his whole appearance is now [suddenly] emaciated in the extreme, his eyesight dim and drowsy, his countenance worn, his speech feeble and inarticulate, and his faculties in short greatly impaired'.[1] A month later, 'Old Nizzy's' condition had worsened further: 'The very dangerous state of the Nizam's health continues to be such as to leave very little hope of his Recovery,' James reported, 'the Palsey having spread to his left side, and deprived him nearly of the use of his left arm and leg . . .'[2] As the old man's end was clearly approaching, James and Aristu Jah – who was the grandfather of the Crown Prince Sikander Jah's wife and so, like James, firmly committed to his swift accession – were both able to make minute arrangements for ensuring a peaceful handover of power.

The Nizam finally passed away in the Chaumhala Palace in the early morning of 6 August, and was buried that evening beside his mother in the great marble forecourt of the Hyderabad Mecca Masjid.* The following day James was able to report to Arthur Wellesley that 'nothing has hitherto occurred beyond that sort of stir and commotion in the capital usually attendant on such an event, and I have little doubt that I shall have it in my power to announce to you in the course of tomorrow, the Prince Secunder Jah's peaceable succession'.[3]

This was indeed the case. Remarkably, the thirty-one-year-old Sikander Jah was able to take over the reins of government without a single sword being removed from its scabbard. The following evening James picked up his pen to report: 'I am just returning from witnessing and assisting in the ceremony of His Highness Secunder Jah's installation on the vacant *musnud* [throne] of the Deccan. This was conducted in the due forms, but with little if any pomp or ceremony, owing to the very recent death of the late sovereign.' To mark the

---

* The Nizam's austere father, Nizam ul-Mulk, had chosen to be buried near his hero Aurangzeb at the Chisti Sufi shrine of Shaykh Burhan ud-Din Gharib at Khuldabad near Aurangabad, at the other end of the Deccan. All the subsequent Nizams, however, followed Nizam Ali Khan's lead and were buried in Hyderabad under a succession of surprisingly modest and unostentatious cenotaphs in the forecourt of the Mecca Masjid, where they still lie.

accession of Sikander Jah guns were fired in the cantonments, from the city walls and from the parapets of Golconda, while (somewhat bizarrely) James gravely reported that 'extra butter [was] served to the Europeans' of the Subsidiary Force as part of the celebrations; but otherwise 'the utmost tranquillity reigns, both within and without the city, and I see no probability of its meeting with the smallest interruption'.[4]

It was only in the period that followed the carefully stage-managed succession that James realised how much he found himself missing his old friend, the eccentric but kindly Nizam: 'His memory will be ever dear to me,' he wrote to William a week after the death. 'His eldest son, the Prince Secunder Jah ascended the *musnud* on the 8th amid the universal acclamation of the people. I all along assured the GG [Wellesley] that the succession would be a peaceable one, and I think myself particularly fortunate that it has so turned out. I have reason to believe that some doubts on this head were entertained in other quarters, so that if my prediction had not been verified, I should have been subjected to, and no doubt have met with, considerable reproach, if not something worse . . .'[5]

Privately, however, James had few illusions about Nizam Ali Khan's successor. Five years earlier, in his first major report from Hyderabad, he had written to Wellesley of Sikander Jah's 'unpopularity and sordid avarice', remarking that he was 'not extolled for the brightness of his talents nor the strength of his judgement', though he also remarked that, 'inclined to corpulency though he may be, yet [Sikander] is not ungraceful . . . His deportment is easy and affable, and in his placid well-favoured countenance, mildness, diffidence and good nature, are conspicuously enough depicted.'[6] This, it soon became clear, was wishful thinking: reports quickly began to circulate of the new Nizam publicly kicking his concubines and even attempting to hang various members of his family with silk handkerchiefs. Soon there were mutterings that he was suffering from bouts of insanity. According to Henry Russell, James's assistant, Sikander Jah's

> expression is dull, melancholy and care-worn . . . and he looks much older than he is. He has been supposed in some degree

insane, and certainly [his behaviour] has countenanced the suspicion ... He is subject both to the delusion of his own fears and jealousies, and to the pernicious influence of those low senseless creatures that are about him ...

The Nizam leads a life of almost total seclusion. He hardly ever appears in public, and seldom even sees his Ministers. What little intercourse he has with them is sometimes by notes, but generally by messages conveyed through female servants. His time is passed either in his private apartments where he sits quite alone, or with a few personal attendants of profligate character and low habits who flatter his prejudices, and poison his mind with stories of the treachery of his Ministers. He has no domestic intercourse even with his nearest male relations. Neither his brothers nor his sons ever visit him, except on the great festivals, and even then they are admitted to him in public, where he generally receives their *nuzzurs* [ceremonial offerings] and then dismisses them without speaking to them ...[7]

The days when James could rely on a friendly and sympathetic figure on the throne of Hyderabad were clearly over.

At the same time as the Nizam's dominions were experiencing a moment of unexpected tranquillity, the Marathas territories to the north and west of Hyderabad were given over to a war of quite extraordinary violence.

Wellesley's intricate manoeuvres to divide and subjugate the Marathas – the last great military force in India really able to take on the British – were now reaching their head. With the death of the great Minister Nana Phadnavis, as General Palmer put it, 'all the wisdom and moderation of the Mahratta government departed', and Wellesley could sit back in Calcutta and watch as the great Confederacy unravelled.[8] In Nana's absence, rival warlords conspired and intrigued against each other in a welter of mutual distrust.

The young Peshwa, Baji Rao II, had proved wholly unequal to the challenge of holding together the different factions that made up his power base. In particular he had alienated the powerful Holkar clan, watching with glee as one of the senior males of the family was trampled to death on his orders by an elephant. The dead man's brother, Jaswant Rao Holkar, duly attacked Pune, and took the city by surprise.* Jaswant Rao fired the town and ravaged the vicinity so as to leave 'not a stick standing at a distance of 150 miles' from Pune.[9] Fleeing the violence, the Peshwa was driven into exile in British territory at Bassein, a former Portuguese city a little to the north of Bombay, full of crumbling Jesuit churches and Dominican convents.

There Wellesley succeeded where General Palmer had failed, and forced the now powerless Peshwa to sign a humiliating Subsidiary Treaty. This document, known as the Treaty of Bassein, was ratified on 31 December 1802. With it, Wellesley believed he had at last succeeded in turning the Marathas into dependants of the British, with a huge British garrison installed, according to the terms of the treaty, to overlook the Peshwa's palace in Pune, into which British arms would now reinstall him.

As soon as he heard the details of the treaty, James knew that this was never going to work, and he had the courage to speak out and say so. In an official despatch in March 1803 he warned that not one of the Maratha warlords – the real powers in the Peshwa's dominions – would sit back and allow the English to control Baji Rao as their puppet and in this way attempt to subvert and undermine the Maratha Empire. Moreover he predicted that Wellesley's actions would only succeed in uniting the Marathas where Baji Rao had

---

* Among Jaswant Rao's commanders at this point was the freebooter William Linnaeus Gardner, the husband of Begum Mâh-Manzel ul-Nissa of Cambay, and the former friend of both James and General Palmer. Gardner had left the Hyderabad Finglas Battalion and joined Jaswant Rao's service in 1799, his place being taken by the newly arrived Captain William Palmer. Shortly after the capture of Pune, he was falsely accused by Jaswant Rao of collaboration with the British, and tied to a cannon to await execution. He managed to escape, however, and took his wife and family to Jaipur, where he briefly became commander of the Maharajah's irregular cavalry, before resigning to found his own regiment in the Company's forces, Gardner's Horse.

failed, and that together the Maratha armies would mass in a great 'hostile confederacy' to fight the Company.

Wellesley was predictably furious at what he regarded as James's impertinence, and wrote his most intemperate despatch yet to Hyderabad, saying that any sort of united Maratha resistance was now 'categorically impossible' and that Kirkpatrick was guilty of 'ignorance, folly, and treachery' in suggesting otherwise. But James held his ground, replying that his sources of intelligence indicated that 'such a confederacy was highly probable', that Jaswant Rao was even now on his way to reoccupy Pune, and that one of the leading Maratha chieftains, the Rajah of Berar, was planning to join him there. He also defended his action in sending notice of his intelligence to Arthur Wellesley and Colonel Close, arguing that it was his clear duty to 'prepare men's minds for an event which by coming unexpectedly might be apt to excite temporary alarm and inconvenience'. He concluded the letter by challenging Wellesley to sack him if he was wrong:

> If the explanations I have here offered should fail of their expected effect, and the unfavourable impressions which his Excellency seems to have received of my character and conduct should unfortunately not be removed, it will rest with his Excellency to determine on the steps proper in such an event to be pursued. Whatever they may be, I shall be found I trust ready to submit to them with a resignation and a fortitude arising from conscious rectitude of intention.[10]

Having sent the despatch off, James sat down to await his removal from office, which he thought could not be far away. His job was, however, narrowly saved yet again when all his predictions about the Marathas proved entirely correct. Within eleven days of accusing James of being an incompetent fool, Wellesley had his secretary write to him again, this time (as James later told William) 'apprising me, that the Gov Genl had selected me as *peculiarly qualified* for the task [of leading] an immediate Deputation to the Rajah of Berar's Camp, for the express purpose of preventing if possible the very Confederacy which a few days before his Ldship pronounced to be impracticable, and which I was charged with folly and ignorance or something worse for stating the possibility of'.[11]

It was however too late now to undo the damage Wellesley's aggressive policies had done. In August, hostilities were opened, with five British armies converging from different directions on the huge and now united Maratha Confederacy. In a bloody five-month campaign, the Marathas were defeated in a succession of brilliant victories by Arthur Wellesley, the future Duke of Wellington, one of which, the Battle of Assaye, was reckoned by him the finest in his entire military career. But there was a huge cost. At Assaye alone, Arthur Wellesley left a quarter of his army dead on the battlefield; as one of his senior officers wrote to him soon afterwards: 'I hope you will not have occasion to purchase any more victories at such a high price.'[12]

James Kirkpatrick, who believed the entire conflict unnecessary and misconceived, was more acerbic: 'oceans of blood and treasure have been wasted in his [Lord Wellesley's] pretended plan of general pacification which was [in fact] a mere pretence for the general subjugation [of India ... the completion of which] we appear to be as far from as ever, and [which has] roused a restless uneasy spirit of dread and animosity against us' amongst all the other Indian princes.[13]

As far as James was concerned this only added to the intense dislike he felt for his master, and he wrote to William (now reunited with his daughters in England and 'taking the waters' at Bath), of the 'contempt and abhorrence' with which he now regarded the Governor General.[14] He added, in a rare show of anger with his beloved elder brother, 'I am concerned to find that you retain your former sentiments regarding the public principles and conduct of a Certain Person [i.e. Lord Wellesley] as it must occasion a difference of political opinion at least between us, which there seems to be no prospect of reconciling.'[15]

He also told William of the callous manner in which Lord Wellesley had broken all his most solemn promises to General Palmer. Having eased the old General out of his Residency in Pune with the promise of a generous pension and a prominent position by his side in Calcutta, Wellesley had completely neglected and ignored Palmer since his arrival in Bengal. Not only had he failed to produce the promised job or indeed any sort of financial compensation, he had insulted him by failing to summon him even once for consultation during the course of the Maratha War, despite the fact that there was no Englishman in Calcutta, or indeed anywhere else in India, who knew the mind of the Peshwa or his warlords as Palmer did. As Palmer wrote helplessly to his old patron Warren Hastings, 'Lord W has totally discontinued his levées, and as he has not invited me to dinner I have no means of access to him.'[16]

Throughout the course of the Maratha War James's letters are full of concern for the General's 'cruel situation' and his 'continued slight and ill treatment, which afflict me much more than they frankly surprise me'.[17]

For James the sky darkened even further seven months later. For on 9 May 1804, his other great friend and ally in Hyderabad, the Minister Aristu Jah, died, and was buried the same day in his Suroor Nagar garden.

Unlike the Nizam's death, which had been long expected, Aristu Jah's end came as a complete surprise. Although he was a direct contemporary of Nizam Ali Khan, the Minister had always seemed far stronger and more active and robust; well into his mid-sixties he would take regular exercise, notably with his daily gallop on the fine Arab stallions whose breeding and maintenance he minutely oversaw. At the end of April he had caught a fever which for a week had looked serious, but after ten days he had appeared to be pulling through. As James reported to Calcutta:

> after having been pronounced out of danger yesterday by his Physicians, [Aristu Jah] relapsed towards the evening, and after a continued fever and delirium during the whole course of the night, this morning early breathed his last. His remains

have just been interred with considerable funereal Pomp, at the family Vault, about a mile from the City; the procession being attended by most of the principal *Omrahs* at Court and a vast concourse of Inhabitants.[18]

Worse yet for James, while he was still recovering from the shock of the loss of his friend, it became clear within a few days that Nizam Sikander Jah's preferred candidate to replace Aristu Jah as Minister was none other than James's bitterest old enemy, Mir Alam. Moreover, it soon became equally apparent that Mir Alam's candidacy was fully supported by Wellesley from Calcutta.

The person responsible for Wellesley's decision to support Mir Alam's return to power was Henry Russell. Russell had been James's Assistant in Hyderabad since the end of 1801 and, with James's recommendation, had recently, at the age of only twenty-one, been promoted to the job of the Residency's Chief Secretary. He had also become James's main friend and ally among the British in Hyderabad: James wrote to William that 'young Henry Russell continues as much as ever attached to me', and was 'my most valuable young friend'.[19]

Despite the nineteen-year age gap between them, the two men had much in common, and James found Russell a lively and interesting companion. Moreover, like James, Russell showed every sign of appreciating Hyderabadi culture, and he kept an Indian *bibi* by whom he had had a child of about the same age as Sahib Begum.[20] A picture of him at this period by an Indian miniaturist survives in a private collection. It shows an alert, neat, handsome young man with close-cropped hair and elongated muttonchop whiskers of a style very similar to those then being sported by Lord Wellesley. He is dressed in a hybrid uniform of an embroidered black jacket of a vaguely English cut, but below it he wears cool white Indian pyjama bottoms and Hindustani slippers.[21]

Russell had one major flaw, though James never mentions it, and it is apparent more in his own letters than in the comments others made about him. This was an unusual vanity and conceit about himself, his looks and his intelligence. The eldest of ten children, Russell was regarded as a child prodigy by his adoring father, and he grew up patronising his younger brother Charles, as he would later patronise his staff, his colleagues, his lovers and his wives. His early letters to Charles, written when he was eighteen and had only just arrived in Hyderabad, are very much those of an experienced man of the world (as he clearly saw himself) attempting to help his little brother fathom the mysteries of adulthood.

In 1802 Charles had recently arrived in Calcutta, and Henry puts pen to paper to advise him: 'I need not direct your attention to the ladies – follow my footsteps and you will be a favourite; the society of females improves the mind as much as the manners of a gentleman, but avoid becoming that detestable or rather negative, contemptible character "a ladies man".' He adds, 'I passed most of the day in the society of a lovely little female friend for whose name and description I refer you to my late Chowringhee correspondence . . . Have you brought me nothing from Europe? [Not even] a fashionable article of dress?'

A month later, Henry takes his younger brother to task for failing to have mastered the art of flattering the women of Calcutta: 'Flattery is only to be administered through the medium of a third person,' he advises. 'If you assure a woman that she is handsome she will doubtless believe you but she will not obtain a favourable impression of your sincerity (a virtue you *must* make a woman believe you possess whether you do or not). But if another man tells her that he has heard you deliver a favourable opinion both of her beauty and her understanding (the two weakest points of a female) she will be upon as good terms with you as she no doubt is with herself . . .' This advice appears to have been of little use to Charles, as a month later Henry writes again in exasperation, 'can it really be possible that a gentleman of your pretensions should not be able to discover a single person through whom to administer the flattery?'[22]

Although now permanently based in Hyderabad, Russell had happened to be in Calcutta visiting his father and stepmother when the news of the death of Aristu Jah reached Bengal. He had been immediately summoned to Government House and consulted by Wellesley about who the British should recommend as a replacement. Unable to resist such red-carpet treatment, Russell had dashed off a short report for the Governor General in which he mentioned in passing that Mir Alam – whom he had never met – was probably the most pro-British of the nobles of the durbar. Wellesley had seized on the line and used it to overrule the various detailed recommendations made by James Kirkpatrick in his despatch on the subject. Mir Alam was the only Hyderabadi noble Wellesley had ever met, and he made his decision in an instant. In the margins of Russell's report he wrote: 'This Paper is extremely creditable to Mr Russell's Judgement, Diligence, and Knowledge of the affairs of the Court of Hyderabad. Meer Allum is the only person qualified for the office or disposed (according to our best information) to exercise it in the Spirit of the Alliance. He must therefore be recommended.'[23]

Thereafter, supported by both the new Nizam and by Wellesley, Mir Alam's appointment was assured. The decision was made even while the Mir was still under house arrest on his country estates, whence he had been banished by Aristu Jah and had yet to return to the city of Hyderabad.

There was however one major problem that no one had anticipated. Mir Alam had now been in internal exile for four years, and in that time had not once been seen in Hyderabad. What no one in the city (or in Calcutta) knew was that during that time the Mir had been very ill indeed. The leprosy which had first made its appearance in 1799 was now far advanced. On arrival in Hyderabad, the Mir turned out to be not only embittered, twisted and bent on revenge; he had also suffered a more or less complete physical collapse. On his first visit to greet the newly returned Mir, James was horrified, writing to William: 'The man's mental faculties appear to have nearly kept pace in decay with his Body, which with his fallen-in nose, is now the most hideous lump of corruption and deformity that was ever beheld.'[24]

Nor was James the only one to be alarmed at the sight of the Mir. According to the *Tarikh-i-Asaf Jahi*,

> [On his return to Hyderabad] Mir Alam had become hideously afflicted by leprosy, so much so that secretions oozed from his body. Many Indian and British doctors tried to cure him, but it was of no use. At last [at the suggestion of an ayurvedic doctor] a very dangerous and angry snake was brought and put on his bed, for it was said that if a snake bit a leper he would be

cured. But the snake did not bite him. Instead, it took one look
at the Mir and slithered away as fast as it could.[25]

It was now, however, too late to do anything. Mir Alam was
confirmed as the First Minister of Nizam Sikander Jah in a ceremony
on 13 July 1804. It was not long before he demonstrated the degree
to which he was willing to pursue his quest for vengeance on those
who had, in his eyes, tricked and humiliated him four years earlier.
On 20 October, James was horrified to hear that in the early morning
the women soldiers of the Zuffur Plutun had surrounded the mansion
of Aristu Jah's senior widow, Sarwar Afza Begum, and then ransacked
the place. As he reported to Calcutta:

> Meer Allum in order to secure the good favour of His High-
> ness told him that [Aristu Jah] had taken jewels worth 12 lakhs
> [which rightly belonged to the government]. These he said
> the Sarwar Afza Begum had [in her Residence], & that they
> should be confiscated. They could not be got easily and His
> Highness sent five guards of females with some of his *asseels*
> to the Begum's house. Much violence was used. They dragged
> the Begum by her arms into the courtyard & dug up the floor,
> removed the jewels & took that with a list to HH. They found
> jewels estimated at 12 lacs & a pearl *buzuband* [armband]
> belonging to the Begum [worth] one lakh, 35,000 gold mohurs,
> 50,000 pagodas, 7 lacs and 92 thousand rupees, gold vessels
> including one [bejewelled elephant] howdah with pearls esti-
> mated at one lakh [rupees] . . .[26]

Despite her pleas, the new Nizam did nothing to help Sarwar Afza
Begum, who was his senior wife's grandmother. Instead, to add to
her sufferings, he publicly humiliated his wife, Jahan Pawar Begum,
Aristu Jah's beloved granddaughter, at whose wedding the old Minister had wept and who now, exposed and unprotected since the death
of Aristu Jah, began to be subjected to the same indignities as Sikander
Jah's other women. He also remained silent as Mir Alam ransacked
in turn the houses and personal properties of each of Aristu Jah's closest
political associates, starting with his deputy Raja Ragotim Rai.*

---

* Rajah Ragotim Rai appears frequently in James's correspondence with William, usually
under the pet name 'Ragged Tim'.

By the middle of 1804, James's position must have seemed weaker than ever. Not only was he still effectively *persona non grata* in Calcutta, in the space of twelve months he had lost his two closest friends and allies in Hyderabad. In their place was the paranoid, sadistic and intermittently insane Sikander Jah, and James's sworn enemy, the embittered and malevolent Mir Alam. Yet James's position was actually a lot stronger than he might have believed.

Unknown to him, the Company's Court of Directors in London increasingly shared his feelings about the unnecessary and wasteful belligerency of Wellesley's policies, though their concerns were motivated more by the crippling cost of the Governor General's constant wars than by any ethical or moral considerations: while Wellesley's conquests had annexed a wider swathe of territory than had the whole of Napoleon's conquests at the same time in Europe, the effect was only to increase the Company's deficits, which at this point were running at around £2 million a year.* Indeed the Company's overall debt, which had stood at £17 million when Wellesley first arrived in India, was now rising towards £31.5 million.† The news of the cost of Lord Wellesley's colossal new Government House in Calcutta was the final straw. Under Wellesley, the government of India, declared the Directors, had 'simply been turned into a despotism'.

The pressure was building up, and by the autumn of 1804 the final decision had been taken: Wellesley was to be recalled, and Lord Cornwallis sent out to India for a second term, at the advanced age of sixty-seven.[27] He left England towards the end of 1804, although it not until May 1805 that Wellesley received the news from London that he had been dismissed from office.

---

* Around £120 million a year in today's currency.
† Around £1.8 billion.

One of the principal problems that had developed under Wellesley, as even his supporters acknowledged, was that no one now ever dared to cross the Governor General. As his brother Arthur put it to Henry Wellesley, the third of the brothers in India, 'Who will speak his mind to the Governor-General? Since you and [John] Malcolm have left him, there is nobody about him who has the capacity to understand these subjects, who has nerves to discuss them with him, and to oppose his sentiments when he is wrong.'[28]

Of his senior officials only one man had dared to stand up to Wellesley, and even before Cornwallis had arrived in Calcutta, the new Governor General had been fully briefed about James Kirkpatrick's principled stand against the worst excesses of Wellesley's expansionist policies. Cornwallis instructed his assistants to arrange an interview with the brave and sensible Resident in Hyderabad as soon as possible. He also let it be known that he wished to see old General Palmer, whom he remembered well from his first term in India and whom he had reason to believe had also stood up to Wellesley on the Maratha business.[29]

After five years of investigations, hostility and isolation, James's ideas of co-existence and his more conciliatory approach to British–Indian relations were suddenly being looked at with new eyes. True, Cornwallis was no liberal, and he had been responsible for beginning the erosion of the social and economic status of Indians and Anglo-Indians,* a process that had merely accelerated throughout Wellesley's governor generalship. Nevertheless, the old Marquis did not believe in threats and belligerence as an instrument of policy, and saw no need for the sort of naked imperialism imposed by Wellesley; moreover he was appalled by the needless bloodshed and expenditure it had caused. His job, as he saw it, was to 'avoid war [and] to establish perfect confidence [among Indian princes] in the Justice and Moderation' of the British – the very policies James had pursued since becoming Resident at Hyderabad.[30]

Though he did not know it, James's future, contrary to all the indications, had in fact never been brighter.

* See pp.50–1.

As the dolls'-house model of James's new Residency building was being completed in the *mahal*, the real mansion was slowly beginning to rise from its groaning foundations a short distance to the north. Month by month throughout 1802, James had corresponded frantically with his friend James Brunton in Madras, making the final arrangements for the workmen he needed to build his new house. At the beginning of November there was still no sign of them, and James wrote to Brunton begging news of their progress, as he said he was 'very anxious for the arrival of the architect & mechanics'.[31] By the end of the month the first of the builders had begun to appear up the road from the port of Masulipatam, but many of the more skilled craftsmen were still missing: 'despatch hither immediately,' he begged Brunton in one letter, 'one Head Maistry Bricklayer, one ditto Carpenter and one ditto Smith ... Their wages are certainly high, but then I conclude that they are each perfect masters of their respective professions, and the head Maistry bricklayer is a tolerable architect.'[32]

Steadily, one by one, the skilled *maistry* craftsmen arrived, and by the beginning of 1803 they had set to work building foundations. Over the course of the year, successive layers of stonework slowly begun to rise from the cat's cradle of scaffolding and the piles of raw stonework which now lay about the bungalows of James's garden. Amid the cries of the mynah birds and parakeets calling from the Residency *char bagh* came the more insistent tap-tap-tap of chisels on stone, the cries of the coolies and their wives swaying along narrow wooden walkways, and the yelling of the bellows boys and hammermen trying to be heard above the noise of the forge.

As the pillars of the Residency portico slowly rose above the runnels of the Mahal and the Mughal garden, and as in due course the sculptors began to carve the arms of the East India Company on the grcat triangular pediment overlooking the new deerpark, filled now with elk and black buck, James looked on with ever growing satisfaction. Judging from his letters, the new Residency was an achievement of which he was hugely proud, though he always recognised how much he owed to his departed mentors, Nizam Ali Khan and Aristu Jah. In one letter to his old patron Sir John Kennaway he wrote how, having been awarded the land by the old Nizam with the assistance of Aristu Jah,

> It would of course still have been out of my power to have converted their liberal grant to any permanent or splendid use, had they not with still greater liberality readily undertaken to defray the expense of all the improvements which ensued, and which will, I trust, remain a lasting Monument to their generosity and munificence. They are now sadly succeeded by two men who are the very reverse of their regretted Predecessors and vie with each other in meanness and penury.[33]

It was to Kennaway that James wrote the fullest description of his Residency 'improvements'. His brother William, he seemed to accept, was not an aesthete, and would not have appreciated the labours he had undertaken to turn 'one of the most dreary spots [in Hyderabad] into one of the most delightful in the whole Deckan'.[34] Indeed in his letters to William, James describes his 'improvements' as rarely as he once described the progress of his *amours*. But Sir John Kennaway was a man of taste who understood the business of building a country house, as he had demonstrated on his return to Britain when he tastefully extended and beautified the exquisite Inigo Jones mansion of Escot near Exeter that he had bought with his Indian fortune.[35] James knew about this, and with Kennaway he was not ashamed to show his pleasure and pride in what he had brought into being: 'It would be as little in your power to recognise the place where you once resided, as it is out of the power of all who now see it to withhold their surprise and admiration,' he wrote proudly in October 1804, as the building was nearing completion.

> Of the old plan, nothing now remains but the Hindoostanny Garden, which with great improvements, and an entire restor-

ation of the Cypress Avenues that were cruelly condemned to the axe in my Brother's time, now flourishes in renovated bloom. The *bârâhdurry* [the Mughal pavilion] where you used to dine, together with the Mahl or Sleeping Apartment that were behind it on the other side of the square fountain (now an octagonal one) are levelled to the ground, and in their place a Grand Mansion, erected according to the Chastest Rules of Architecture, and two stories high, now rears its proud head on the site of the antient Mahl, and is surrounded in front, and on its Eastern and Western Faces, with Pleasure Grounds, and a paddock well stocked with Deer, of nearly a mile in circumference.

Of the magnificent new Residency House, he told Sir John:

I will just inform you, that the House which the last Minister built for me, has a Grand Salon with a Gallery and Painted Ceiling, a Portico to the North of nearly the same dimensions, a verandah to the south, with two grand public staircases, and twelve Private Apartments, the whole finished and furnished in a stile suitable to the magnificence of the Structure and the Rank of the Princely Donors. Besides the above numerated apartments, there is an arched ground floor, some of the apartments of which are particularly cool and pleasant during the hot winds.*

Before the North Front of the House, there is an extensive oval sheet of water, which is constantly full, and round which a wide gravel walk with lamps at proper distances meet and terminate at the foot of a most stately flight of granite steps that lead up to the portico.

As an accompaniment to this description – or rather as a corrective to its lameness – I propose furnishing you by the bye with views of all the Principal Buildings and Grounds at the Residency, which are even now being taken, by the Gentleman who most ably assisted me in laying them out.[36]†

---

* In other words, in the basement of his Georgian mansion James built a Mughal-style *tykhana*, or cool house.
† Presumably Samuel Russell – but it is important and significant that James says Russell only 'assisted' in the building, and was not the principal architect, as has been traditionally believed.

This palace was to be James's home, and he tried to persuade William to send his eldest daughter Isabella, now aged sixteen, out to him so that he could bring her 'back with me to the Residency, which by that time will perhaps be one of the most delightful spots in India, as I think Isabella herself will allow when she has once seen it; and where I trust you will ultimately find yourself greatly mistaken in supposing that she cannot meet with an eligible match – while at all events, there can be no harm in trying the experiment'. James also insisted that he would pay Isabella's Indian costs, whether she came to see him or just went to straight to Calcutta as part of the British 'fishing fleet' of girls who sailed out every year on the lookout for an eligible husband:* 'Isabella, you know, is my daughter by adoption, and as such I beg you will make her over entirely to my management. It shall be my business and my delight, to defray her expenses . . .'[37]

As the Residency rose higher and higher, and the prospect of actually moving into it grew closer, James began to think about how he would furnish his huge new mansion. He started by ordering an

---

* Unsuccessful members of the fishing fleet who failed to land their fish and had to return to England single were (rather cruelly) described as 'returned empties'. This seems to have been the fate of many of the fleet at this period: 'Hindoo Stuart' in his extraordinary book *A Ladies Monitor* quotes a conversation he had at a Calcutta dinner party attended by a whole group of 'returned empties' who complained that Englishmen in India all preferred Indian women to Europeans, and that few were interested in marrying a white girl, everyone being more than happy with their *bibis*: 'One of the ladies observed, that it were better they had staid at home; that marriages were little in fashion now-a-days; and that the bad taste of the men rendered unnecessary the introduction of any more foreign beauty; at least, until that desire for novelty, which scarcity ever produces, should induce gentlemen to incline to their own country-women, as an agreeable change, enhanced by the pleasure of variety.' Stuart believed that half the problem was the unattractive busks and corsets worn by English women at the period, and suggested they might have more chance of competing with the *bibis* if they all adopted the sari, which he clearly regarded as the sexiest garb imaginable (and to promoting which he dedicates many thousands of words). The change in morality brought about by the rise of the Evangelicals in the 1830s and 1840s seems to have radically improved the fishing fleet's chances of success, as it became increasingly unacceptable to take an Indian *bibi*. See Hindoo Stuart's anonymously published *A LADIES' MONITOR Being a series of letters first published in Bengal on the subject of FEMALE APPAREL Tending to favour a regulated adoption of Indian Costume; and a rejection of SUPERFLUOUS VESTURE By the ladies of this country: with Incidental remarks on Hindoo beauty; whale bone stays; iron busks; Indian corsets; man-milliners; idle bachelors, hair powder, side saddles, waiting-maids; and footmen. By the author of A VINDICATION OF THE HINDOOS* (Calcutta, 1809), pp.16, 21.

enormous carpet, sixty feet long by thirty wide, to be woven for the main durbar hall.[38] He also purchased an enormous chandelier which the Company had bought from the ever impecunious Prince of Wales, and which had once hung in the Royal Pavilion in Brighton. At the same time, thinking of the entertainments he could hold in the house, James asked his Madras agent to try to find him a bandmaster and 'twelve lads from the orphan school' to be trained up as musicians.[39] He also got a job lot of music and musical instruments sent up, along with twenty cartloads of his much-missed potatoes, plus 'a few armed peons to guard them on the road', one of his odder consignments.[40]

At the same time James continued sending orders to Europe for other more rare and valuable items that would allow him to fulfil his great dream of combining the lifestyle of a Mughal prince, the landed pursuits of a Georgian gentleman and the interests of a Renaissance man. Over the course of 1803 and 1804, these interests seem to become increasingly scientific, and James's letters are suddenly full of requests for 'a good Electrifying Machine with a curious apparatus such as would surprise and delight' the nobles of the durbar, as well as a 'box of chemical preparations'. The electrical apparatus apparently got lost in transit, but the 'chemical box' duly appeared.*

James's interest in chemistry, however, seems to have been soon overtaken by his growing fascination with astronomy. He hatched an ambitious plan to build an observatory on the roof of the Residency, and towards the end of 1804 he asked William to send out to him 'a capital telescope for astronomical observations . . . The terrace

---

* It was, thought James, 'curious and amusing, but upon too small a scale, and extremely defective moreover from the awkward circumstances of the ingredients in the bottles'. The perils of mail order seem to have been at the root of the problem, and James struggled to reconcile the box in front of him with the instruction booklet: 'No. 28 [does not correspond] to the printed list in the Book of Experiments that accompanied the box and thus rendering *all* the experiments that require ingredients *beyond* what are contained in the phials up to No.28 impracticable. I will thank you therefore to send me as soon as possible a similar chemical apparatus but upon a much larger scale; and above all, with a more faithful & correct correspondence between the articles in the respective phials, and what is laid down in the printed list in the accompanying Book of Experiments. Let the supply both of solid and liquid phosphorus in particular be as abundant as possible.' This last, presumably, was to impress Hyderabadi *omrahs* with bright flashes of spectacular chemical efflorescence.

of my new house is a noble observatory, and there is a gentleman here who has inspired me with a great love and admiration of the noble science of astronomy.'[41]

This was none other than James's old friend and now relation by marriage, Khair's first cousin, Abdul Lateef Shushtari. At the end of 1804, Shushtari had taken advantage of the death of Aristu Jah and Mir Alam's return to power to come back to Hyderabad from Bombay (where he had been briefly engaged in the textile trade[42]), to complete the writing of his great memoir, the *Kitab Tuhfat al-'Alam*. Astronomy, like philosophy and jurisprudence, was one of the traditional accomplishments of Abdul Lateef's polymathic branch of the Shushtari sayyids, and before coming to India he had spent several years studying the stars with one of his many learned cousins, Sayyid Ali Shushtari. Sayyid Ali, as remarkable a scholar as the rest of his clan, had been the chief astronomer in Baghdad when the young Abdul Lateef came to him for instruction.*

Shushtari came to recognise that not only were the British more knowledgeable than Persians on some astronomical matters, so, to his surprise, were the Indians: 'Copernicus was more exact in astronomical observation than the traditional Muslim astronomers which makes the Muslim *zij* tables and our astronomers' predictions less reliable. What appears to onlookers as the movement of the sun is in reality the movement of the earth ... Moreover, the English reject the idea of astral influences ... Even the Hindus have more knowledge than us in some matters of astronomy and mathematics' – a virtually unprecedented admission for the often Indophobic Abdul Lateef.[43]

In some matters, however, Islamic astronomy was still well ahead

---

* What seems to have most impressed the young traveller was the way Sayyid Ali combined in one man the callings of poet and astronomer, spending nights gazing at the stars while 'every afternoon he held at home a *majlis* [gathering] of poets where they would present their new work. The author [Abdul Lateef] studied astronomy with him until his death.' Over the years Shushtari grew increasingly interested in astronomy. At the same time, partly under the influence of the British during his time in India, he seems to have become increasingly sceptical of the traditional idea of using the stars as a means of predicting the future: as he wrote in the *Tuhfat*, he later came to regard as wasted the years he spent in the Middle East studying astral influences, because after a while 'I had no belief in the influence of the stars and the predictions of astrology, yet in those days, I spent much of my time calculating and casting horoscopes.' See *Kitab Tuhfat al-'Alam*, p.145.

of European learning, as other British amateur astronomers in India had learned to their surprise. Thomas Deane Pearse, who acted as Warren Hastings' second during his famous duel with Philip Francis in 1780, developed an interest in astronomy in the late 1770s and regularly sent his observations to Nevil Maskelyne, the Astronomer Royal at Greenwich.* In September 1783 a conversation with 'a learned Musulman' directed Pearse's attention to a Persian text, *The Wonders of Creation*, which showed that Saturn (as Pearse wrote excitedly to the Secretary of the Royal Society in a long letter of the twenty-second of that month) was 'possessed of what, till very lately, we were utterly ignorant of, I mean his satellites or ring. Hitherto only five satellites have been seen by Europeans, [but in this text] he is there represented as having seven ... I am much inclined to believe that the [medieval Arabs] had better instruments than we have.' The seventh satellite of Saturn was only formally 'discovered' by the astronomer Sir William Herschel (1738–1822) in 1789, six years after this correspondence.[44] For the next few years Pearse's letters contain intermittent references to his conversations with pundits and 'learned Mussulmen' on astronomical matters.†

---

* Maskelyne (1732–1811) will be familiar to anyone who has read Dava Sobel's *Longitude*, where he is the villain of the piece – something Pearse would have sympathised with, as he later ceased to send his observations to Greenwich, believing that 'Maskelyne has suppressed all my astronomical observations, and has not had the civility even to answer my letters to him.'

† Thomas Deane Pearse (1738–89) not only shared the same astronomical interests as James, he seems to have lived a similar lifestyle. According to his will, Pearse had long been secretly married to 'Punna Purree a native of Hindostan who since the said marriage is become Punna Purree Pearse and I do firmly believe that our marriage, tho' for many years kept secret was in every respect Lawfull, and if it were not so I most assuredly would have gone through every possible form to have made it so. By my wife Punna Purree Pearse I have only one son Thomas Deane Mahomet Pearse' – who, it turns out, they somewhat surprisingly sent to Harrow. Whether Tommy Mahomet Pearse told his English public-school chums about his Indian mother is unknown; or indeed for that matter whether he told them that also living in the house and helping to bring him up was his father's Hindu mistress, Murtee. Both, incidentally, seem to have been women of means – and thus presumably from an élite background – since in Pearse's will he repays large sums of money to each which, so he writes, he borrowed from them to buy land in Chowringhee. It is also clear from the will that his wife, Punna Purree, seems to have brought to the marriage her own Mughal garden, Purree Bagh. Pearse's will, written in Purree Bagh, is an extraordinary document in which he divides his property between his Harrovian son, his Muslim Bengali wife and his Hindu concubine – except for his chemical and astronomical instruments, which he leaves to the Royal Observatory at

In a similar manner, although the exact details are now sadly lost, James and Abdul Lateef Shushtari seem to have been spending their nights on the Residency roof, busy comparing notes to see how Indian, Islamic and European astronomical systems could be reconciled, and what each could learn from the other. Certainly James's letters between 1804 and 1805 become full of requests for such objects as 'A Compleat Planetarium, Tellurian and Lunerian, all in brass showing the motions completely by wheel work, packed in a portable mahogany case', and 'a pair of 18 inch terrestrial and celestial globes'. But over and again his letters come back to the matter of the telescope, which he repeatedly tells William he should spare no expense upon, instructing him to take the very greatest care in shipping:

No pains indeed should be spared in the package of the [telescope] and on the skill and judgement employed in the packing of the *speculum* of the telescope depends entirely the value of this instrument, which will be useless and of course worth not *one farthing* if the least injury befalls the speculum either from *damp* or from any other cause ... It is of great importance that these packages should be stowed in some very dry and commodious part of the ship in some snug corner of the gun room, for instance. Pray let this point be carefully attended to, and the packages recommended if possible to the particular care and charge of the Captain and Chief Mate, or of both together ... [If properly packed the telescope will] enable me to descry clearly and distinctly the spots on the sun's dish, and the mountains and even the volcanoes on the

---

Greenwich. There also survive amid Warren Hastings' papers two of Punna Pearse's own letters to Hastings, in which she talks of her difficulties since her husband's death, and asks him to use his influence to help her get her full allowance, which the executors appear to have cut down: all Pearse's estates are now 'in the hands of Captain Grace', she writes, 'but he won't do according to the Colonel's Will – and he lessen'd my allowance so that I cannot be maintain'd by it. As you are like my protector – therefore I informs of it to you.' Finally she asks Hastings to favour her son, now in England: 'I beg you will be pleased to favor Mr. Tommy.' There is no record of Hastings' reply, or of the result of Punna's pleading, and at this point the historical record goes silent. For Thomas Deane Pearse's will see Bengal Wills for 1787–1790, 1789, OIOC, L/AG/34/29/6, No. 26, The Will of Col. Thomas Deane Pearse. For Punna Pearse's letters to Warren Hastings, see Hastings Papers, BL Add Mss 29,172, Vol. XLI, 1790, pp.317, 410.

Moon, Jupiter's belts and Saturn's ring, as plain as you can
see the cross on the top of St. Paul's . . .[45]

James seems to have been determined that not only would the
Residency become a place where British and Mughal ideas of civilised
refinement would be fused, it would also be a place where, albeit in
a typically amateur Enlightenment way, the intellectual life of the
two peoples might begin to meet and enrich each other, to the mutual
benefit and fascination of both.

At about this time, James entrusted a small confidence to Sir John
Kennaway: that despite his fears for the way India was going under
Wellesley, and despite his professional difficulties, surveying his creation and the life he had made for himself in Hyderabad, he was
now 'as happy and comfortable' as he could ever imagine himself
being. In a rare letter to his elder brother George Kirkpatrick, with
whom he had little contact,* he echoed his feelings of intense happiness and fulfilment, noting, as he signed off:

> I shall just say that my health, though not very robust, is upon
> the whole as good as can be expected after a Residence of

---

* Though George was James's full brother and was also based in India, the two were
never close and kept in only intermittent contact. William Kirkpatrick had even less
contact with his other half-brother. George sounds a slightly hopeless figure – stiff, pious,
unimaginative and somewhat lacking in charm – whose career in India never took off,
despite the best efforts of James and William to use their influence on his behalf. When
he finally returned home in 1803 he was unable to afford even to pay his passage, as
James described to William in a letter of June of that year: 'I must not omit noticing
the lamentable case of poor George, who is gone home in the *Travers* so miserably
poor after twenty years service in the Civil Line that his agents have applied to me for
reimbursement of a balance due on account of his passage money. I enclose you his
letter to me from Calicut, which will enable you to form some idea of the wretch'd
forlorn situation of this excellent worthy fellow, who shall not however want either the
comforts or conveniences of life, as long as it may please God to continue to me the
means of enabling him to command them.' OIOC, Kirkpatrick Papers, F228/59, 11 June
1803, James Kirkpatrick to William Kirkpatrick.

near 25 years in this Climate; that my circumstances (thanks
to a bounteous Providence* are flourishing beyond my most
sanguine wishes; that my two children are daily improving
in mind and body; and that I want nothing to complete
my happiness, but the much coveted society of my absent
friends and far removed but dearly beloved kindred and
relations . . .'[46]

Yet amid the now Eden-like idyll of the magnificent new Residency
and its observatory, the elk and the grazing Abyssinian sheep, the
laughing children playing with their ayahs, the gardens and the park,
the Rang Mahal with its frescoed walls and its gently falling fountains
– amid all this, there always lay a great unspoken sadness: the knowledge of the egg-shell fragility of this creation, and the growing realis-
ation that it could not last.

Towards the end of January 1805, James's health had suddenly
gone into rapid decline. In July, Dr Ure wrote out a medical certificate
for James to send to Calcutta. It read:

This is to certify that Lieutenant Colonel Kirkpatrick, Resident
at the Court of His Highness the Soubah of the Deccan, has
been for the last eighteen months subject to severe Hepatic
and Rheumatic Complaints, & although the disease of the
Liver has always hitherto yielded to a course of Mercury, yet
the attacks of late have been so frequent (almost every two
months) and so much more difficult to remove than formerly
that I solemnly & sincerely declare that according to the best
of my judgement a change of air is essentially necessary to
his recovery, and do therefore recommend that he may be
permitted to go to the sea coast; & if necessary after his arrival
on the coast eventually to proceed to sea.

> George Ure
> Surgeon to the Residency at Hyderabad
> Hyderabad 13th July 1805[47]

---

* An interesting and typically non-sectarian Deist usage of James's, and one that would
work equally well in a Christian and a Muslim context. For similar reasons many Muslims
living in the West today sometimes choose to use terms such as 'the Almighty' rather
than the more specifically Islamic 'Allah' (though 'Allah' is also used by Arab Christians
as their word for God).

James hoped that a quick sea voyage would do the trick and restore him to health; but he feared that, realistically, it was unlikely to do more than 'patch up my constitution to a certain degree'.[48] He was sufficiently worried to write a will, dividing his now considerable fortune between his children, his nieces and 'the excellent and respectable . . . Kheir oon Nissah Begum'.[49] Moreover he realised that if the voyage failed to cure him, in the medium term the only other two options were dying (pretty promptly) in India, or retiring to England. His spirit might feel completely at home in India; but his wretched body, less malleable, seemed to need England.

In which case, he wondered, what would happen to his beloved Khair un-Nissa? Most Indian wives and consorts did not accompany their husbands back to Britain when they left the subcontinent at the end of their service, though there was no law preventing it. When the Mughal travel writer Mirza Abu Taleb Khan visited London at about this time he described meeting several completely Anglicised Indian women who had returned with their husbands and children. One of them in particular, Mrs Ducarrol, especially impressed him: 'She is very fair,' he wrote, 'and so accomplished in all the English manners and language, that I was some time in her company before I could be convinced that she was a native of India.' He added: 'The lady introduced me to two or three of her children, from sixteen to nineteen years of age, who had every appearance of Europeans.'[50]

But other attempts to take Indian wives back to England ran into disastrous and tragic problems. Another Indian woman who Mirza Abu Taleb Khan met and admired in London was Fyze Palmer's younger sister from Lucknow, Nur Begum: 'Noor Begum who accompanied General de Boigne from India . . . was dressed in the English fashion, and looked remarkably well,' he wrote. 'She was much pleased with my visit, and requested me to take charge of a letter for her mother, who resides at Lucknow.'[51] But Khan was being discreet here, for he does not say what James and Khair knew well, and what he must have known too: that Nur's marriage had not survived the transition to England, and though she might look 'remarkably well', her life was in ruins.

Within a few months of General de Boigne's arrival in England in

May 1797, Nur had been dumped out of sight in the tiny village of Enfield, outside London, with her two small children Anne and Charles, to which she voluntarily added the extra burden of the orphaned half-Indian son of Antoine Polier, General Palmer's white Mughal friend from Lucknow who had been killed two years earlier, soon after his return from India, in the terror that followed the French Revolution. De Boigne, meanwhile, had taken up with a beautiful and spirited young French émigrée aristocrat (and, though he only discovered this later when it was too late, a completely unprincipled fortune-hunter), Adèle d'Osmond, whom he married in June 1798, thirteen months after arriving in England with Nur.

Nur's household receipts, which survive in de Boigne's family archive in Chambéry, make painful reading: at the same time that 'Mrs. Begum' (as she is referred to in the accounts) was expected to subsist on an allowance of £200 a year – with which she had to live, pay her rent, the children's school fees and all other expenses – de Boigne was cruising around Britain spending, in a single weekend, £78 on necklaces, clasps, bracelets and earrings for his youthful new European wife.* Fyze and the General had been deeply dismayed to

* Nur kept careful accounts, which typically read as follows:
18 requests for pocket money.....3.0 [?shillings]
a pair of gloves.....3.0
a pen knife.....1.0
a great coat for Geo Polier: 1.1
a silver spoon for Miss AB: 14.6
25 × coach to take Miss AB to school: 10.613 × bisquits from Miss AB: 1.0
25 Oranges for GP: 1.0,
Prayer books and Christian doctrine for Miss AB: 1.6
Blossoms of Morality, slate and Spelling book.....8.3.
At the same time de Boigne, is spending a king's ransom doing up his lodgings at 47 Portland Place: £73 for the carpenters' work in the house, £39 for the painters, £32 for the plasterers, and £28 for the bricklayers' work on the chimney in the stables – a total of £254 – with £42.19s. for the removal bill alone. In September 1799 de Boigne paid £169 for a travelling chaise, and in February 1799 he paid J. Hatchett and Co., His Majesty's Coachmaker, £82.5s. for painting his chariot. He also spent a fortune on his new Countess: £20.13s on a trip to an Edinburgh jeweller, John White of South Bridge, on 14 July 1801 to buy Madam earrings, necklaces and a gold brooch. This clearly wasn't enough: the following day he was back in the same shop buying more necklaces, clasps, bracelets and earrings for a further £58. After de Boigne asked for his children to be sent to him in France a decade later, Nur Begum lived the rest of her life on her own in Horsham in Sussex, where she converted to Christianity, took the name Helena Bennet (an improvement on 'Mrs Begum') and inspired Shelley, who saw the woman known locally as 'The

hear of Nur's fate, and had told James about it. This cannot but have added to his worries about how Khair would fare if a return to England was forced upon him.

There was at least some hope that James's uncertain health could recover; but there was another, greater, sadness in the air, and from this it seemed that there was no escape. Almost from the day of her children's birth, Khair un-Nissa had known that they would be taken from her when Sahib Allum reached the age of five, and sent away over the Black Water* to England. There they would spend the rest of their childhood away from her, receiving an English education – an idea to which she was instinctively and bitterly opposed. James looked forward to the children's departure with as much dread as she did, but thought that it had to be. In 1801, soon after the birth of Sahib Allum, he wrote to William: 'I will certainly endeavour to send my little *Hyderabadi* to England as soon as possible: but it will go to my soul to part with him, to say nothing of the opposition I may expect to meet with cn this point in another quarter in spite of any agreements.'52

In sending his little Hyderabadi Muslim children to Britain without either of their parents, James was not (at least in his own eyes) acting heartlessly: on the contrary, he believed he was making a considerable sacrifice for the sake of his children. It was widely and probably correctly believed at the time that the only way Anglo-Indian children had the chance of making something of their lives was if they received a *pukka* English public-school education. English racism against 'country born' Anglo-Indian children was now becoming so vicious

Black Princess' wandering lonely and forlorn around St Leonard's Forest. She died on 27 December 1853, aged eighty-one. Her former housekeeper, Mrs Budgen, remembered her as 'sallow in complexion with strange dark eyes. She would sometimes stay in bed until noon and often kept her nightcap on when at last she got up. She took no trouble at all about her dress but wore magnificent rings. She smoked long pipes [presumably a hookah], lost her temper very easily and could not be bothered with anything.' She attended mass at the local Catholic church in Horsham, but her grave is aligned quite differently from the others in the cemetery, possibly indicating that at her death she had hedged her bets and tried to have it aligned in the Muslim fashion. See Rosie Llewellyn-Jones's sad and fascinating piece on Nur/Helena in her book *Engaging Scoundrels: True Tales of Old Lucknow* (New Delhi, 2000), pp.88–93.

* An Indian expression for the sea. According to tradition, Hindus lost caste if they 'crossed the Black Water'.

in India as to make this provision very necessary. Without it, their options were limited in the extreme, and they were condemned to sink to the margins, pushed away and ostracised by both British and Indian society.

One of the most moving testaments to this is General Sir David Ochterlony's letters concerning his two daughters by Mubarak Begum. These were written around 1803, and in them he discusses the question of whether it would be better to bring the girls up as Anglo-Indian Christians and attempt to integrate them into British society, or instead to educate them as fully Muslim Indians, and to propel them as best he could into the parallel world of late-Mughal society. 'My children are uncommonly fair,' wrote Ochterlony, 'but if educated [in India] in the European manner they will in spite of complexion labour under all the disadvantages of being known as the NATURAL DAUGHTERS OF OCHTERLONY BY A NATIVE WOMAN – In that one sentence is compressed all that ill nature and illiberality can convey, of which you must have seen numerous instances during your Residence in this country.'[53]

If he were to make his daughters Christian and keep them in British company, argues Ochterlony, they would be constantly derided for their 'dark blood'; but he hesitates to bring them up as Muslims, with a view to them marrying into the Mughal aristocracy, as 'I own I could not bear that my child should be one of a numerous haram* even were I certain that no other Disadvantages attended this mode of disposal & were I proof against the observations of the world who tho' unjust to the children, would not fail to comment on the Conduct of a father who educated his offspring in Tenets of the Prophet.' The letter to Major Hugh Sutherland, another Scot in a similar position who had eventually opted to bring up his children as Muslim,† ends rather movingly: 'In short my dear M[ajor] I

---

* This was rather rich coming from Ochterlony, who, it should be remembered, was reputed to have thirteen wives, all of whom took the evening Delhi air with the Resident, each on the back of her own elephant.

† Sutherland (1766–1835), from Tain in Invernesshire, was the Maratha *qiladar* or fort-keeper at Agra (and as such would shortly face Ochterlony in battle). In old age both he and his Begum returned to Britain, where they settled on Stockwell Green. Sutherland died in 1835, but his Begum, who eventually converted to Christianity (in contrast to her

have spent all the time since we were parted in revolving this matter in my mind but I have not yet been able to come to a positive Decision.'[54]

A similar dilemma faced James. Six months after Sahib Allum's birth, James had written to his brother in Madras asking him to take especial care to look after his other unnamed 'Hindustani' son when William arrived in England. In the course of the letter James reflects with pain on the racism then prevalent among the British in India, which he well knew to be especially harsh towards children of mixed race, and he writes of the worries this causes him for his young baby's future.* At first he believed the solution to the problem lay in sending Sahib Allum to join his cousins in Britain, where colour prejudice was still much less prevalent than among Company servants in India: 'I still retain the opinion I expressed to my father,' he wrote to William in September 1801,

> of [the Hindustani boy's] future happiness and perhaps suc-
> cess in life, being best consulted by providing for him if poss-
> ible in the country he is now in [i.e. England], rather than in
> his native one [India]. And that for the very same reason –
> namely the illiberal prejudices entertained [by the British in

---

daughters, who remained Muslims) lived on until the age of eighty, finally passing away in 1853. Two cousins of Sutherland's also married Indians or Anglo-Indians: Lieutenant Colonel John Sutherland (1793–1838), who briefly commanded the Nizam's irregular horse, married Usrat Hussaini, 'a Persian Princess, in the principal mosque at Bhurtpore', while another ne'er-do-well member of the clan was Robert Sutherland (c.1768–1804), who had been cashiered from the Company's forces and joined the mercenary army of Scindia under Benoît de Boigne. There he was known as 'Sutlej Sahib', married the Anglo-Indian daughter of George Hessing, another Maratha freelance, and had a whole tribe of Anglo-Indian mercenary children. He and many of his brood (and those of his Hessing in-laws) are buried in domed Mughal tombs in the Roman Catholic cemetery at Agra.

* In his early letters James himself was not above making disparaging comments about Anglo-Indians. His attitudes to mixed-race children – as to so many other aspects of Indo–British relations – seem to have been radically changed by his falling in love with and marrying Khair un-Nissa, and he writes of his two children by her in an utterly different and infinitely more compassionate way than that in which he once wrote about his first 'Hindustani' boy. This could, however, have had as much to do with class as race: in India, as in Britain, illegitimate children born to lower-class mistresses were treated in a very different way to children of aristocratic women, whether born in or out of wedlock.

India] against children born of native mothers, be their colour ever so fair, their conduct ever so correct, or their spirit ever so indomitable.

In point of complexion my little boy *here* has greatly the advantage over his brother in England being as fair as it is possible I conceive for the offspring of any European female to be, and yet [here James scored out his first attempt to express himself] I would be loathe to think, that he may be one day [before beginning again:] he would I have no doubt, be exposed to the same illiberal objection and obloquy, should he ever be obliged to seek his fortunes in the country which gave him birth. Among other circumstances which render *this* child peculiarly dear and interesting to me is the striking resemblance which he bears to my dear father. He is indeed, in every respect, a most lovely infant . . .[55]

Over time, however, with the example of the Anglo-Indian Captain William Palmer's growing power and success in Hyderabad before him, James seems to have reconsidered his assumption that his children's future necessarily lay in Britain. Without an élite British education, and the *éclat* that brought, Anglo-Indian children would almost certainly suffer from the worst prejudices of both races, just as James feared; but with it, as Palmer's career seemed to show, it might be possible for his children to use both sides of their racial inheritance to their advantage, and to be equally at ease in both worlds. With due preparation, in other words, their future might well lie in India.

For this reason, by the beginning of 1804 James had begun to write to the Handsome Colonel to find out if the old man was still active and energetic enough to add two more grandchildren to his collection, and to explain in some detail his hopes and ideas for their education: 'On the subject of the girl's education,' he wrote to his father in October 1804,

I shall at present content myself with expressing a wish that it should be private – that is not carried on through the means of a boarding school. But with regard to the Boy, in whose infantine lineaments I delight in tracing your likeness, which to me appears very striking, he cannot perhaps be sent too early to a public seminary, where I shall be happy to learn that he emulates the good example which I have no doubt will be set him by his kinsman the young stranger announced to me in your letter.[56]

This latter clause seems to be a reference to what must have been the last of the Handsome Colonel's many illegitimate children, fathered – if this is the correct interpretation – while the old Lothario was in his early seventies. In the same letter, James explained that when he sent the children to England, 'as my own state of health has long required a temporary change at least of climate, I propose if I can obtain leave of absence for the purpose, to accompany them myself to the Presidency in December or January next, and after seeing them safe on board, to take a cruise to sea, as the most likely means of recovering a sufficient stock of health to enable me to return to my station'.[57]

Eight months later, by June 1805, James's plans had solidified, and bookings had been made. Dr Ure had, like him, decided to send his two-year-old boy to England, but with the difference that in the Ures' case, Mrs Ure was to go with the boy on the journey. James realised that this was an excellent chance for the children to be accompanied by a woman they knew and who also spoke Urdu. As he wrote to William:

They leave this, please God for Madras, early in August, to embark for England on board (I believe) the *Hawkesbury* Indiaman, which is expected to sail with the rest of the Fleet early in September. They will be under the immediate charge of Mrs. Ure conjointly with whom I have bespoken about half the [ship's] Round House [the most comfortable and spacious berths in the ship] and they will besides have for their immediate attendant a very careful, attentive European Woman of the name of Perry, the wife of one of the musicians of my Band, and whom I have hired for the trip to England. Supposing the Fleet to sail in September, you may reasonably expect them all March next, that is in about three or four months as I guess after your receipt of this letter.[58]

The original plan had been for James and Khair un-Nissa to escort the children to Madras, 'whither their respectable and amiable mother insists on accompanying them', as James explained to William.[59] Having said goodbye to the children, James and Khair would then travel on together to Calcutta for the marriage of William's eldest daughter Isabella, who had not, as her father had feared, ended up a 'returned empty' but instead had been snapped up almost before she had left the gangplank by an ambitious young Company servant, Charles Buller.* Buller had just been appointed Secretary to the Revenue Board, an important and powerful position, and the wedding, which was clearly going to be quite a grand one, was set for 26 August.

But at the last minute there was a hitch: James appears to have been struck down by some sort of fever, in addition to which he seems to have suffered a recurrence of his hepatitis. Together, the two complaints relegated him to his bed and prevented him from travelling. Moreover, there was a political crisis brewing in Hyderabad due to the famine spreading across the Deccan that had followed close on the devastation left by Wellesley's Maratha War. From his sickbed, James was determined to do what he could in the way of famine relief. As he reported in early August to an old childhood friend,

> in addition to the hardships and calamities of war, we have
> now to struggle against the horrors of famine which has
> already desolated the greatest part of the Dekkan, and is now
> advancing with rapid strides to this capital where the scarcity
> has for some time past been so great as to amount nearly to
> downright want and starvation. Shocking as such calamities
> are, they do not of course materially affect the higher classes
> of society, but it must be a hard and unfeeling heart that can
> witness such scenes without sharing in the misery and woe
> which they occasion, or without feeling a wish at least to fly

---

* Isabella was the most beautiful of William Kirkpatrick's daughters, and quickly became famous in Calcutta for her startling blue eyes and her grace of movement. According to the *Calcutta Review* of April 1899, 'even so critical a genius as John Leyden made her the theme of his verse, as befitted one who was known on the banks of the Hooghly as "Titania" and who had been compared for her stately beauty to Madame Récamier'.

from them, when relief as in the present case, is nearly fruitless
and unavailing.

Though thousands are daily fed from the fragments of my
table, and from the pecuniary relief which is bestowed by
my orders, still I am surrounded, whenever I go abroad, by
multitudes of the most ghastly and pitiable objects of both
sexes and of all ages that your affrighted fancy could
picture . . .[60]

As part of the famine-relief programme, the Nizam and Mir Alam
had embarked, on James's recommendations, on a grand programme
of public works and construction as a way of providing employment
and money to the starving famine refugees who now flooded into
Hyderabad. As James explained to William:

By the much admired style of my improvements at the Residency, I have awakened a passion for architectural improvement in the Meer [Alam] and Secunder Jah, both of whom I
have persuaded to lay out a little of their enormous hoards
in public and private works, both within and without the City
. . . [These are] of considerable extent and some degree of
Taste, which at one and the same time improves the Interior
of Hyderabad, and gives bread to thousands of Poor, who
would otherwise have starved in these dreadful times of
scarcity.

Among other works carrying on, and which are imitated
on a humbler scale by rich Mussulman and Hindoo individuals, Meer Allum has constructed under the super-
intendence of an Engineer Lieut Russell* a canal which
supplies the whole city with water and is about to repair the
Hoossein Sagar Bank, and restore the ancient canal that
brought water to it from the River. He has also nearly completed a neat square of upstairs houses in front of his own
mansion with a stone tank in the centre, a mosque, *hammaum*
[Turkish bath] and madrassah [religious school] on one face,

---

* This is the first and only explicit reference in James's letters to Lieutenant Samuel
Russell, to whom the Residency is usually attributed – I think wrongly. On the evidence
of James's letters his contribution seems to be limited to finishing the building off – and
even that possibly only after James's death.

and a wide and long street of shops with upper apartments
leading to this square, the *tout ensemble* effect of which is
striking enough.*

Secunder Jah has begun something on a similar plan around
his old abode, besides having a large Garden House in hand,
partly European and partly Asiatic, upon the site of an ancient
Garden at Lingumpilly. I shall endeavour in conclusion to get
him to build a Bridge at the Residency end of the City, by
way of a match to the Bridge at the West or Upper end of
Hyderabad.[61]

The famine crisis and his dangerously fragile health prevented
James from leaving as planned throughout the early summer, and in
the end Khair un-Nissa opted to stay in Hyderabad too, nursing her
ailing husband – though James still hoped to recover sufficiently to
rush to the coast and join the children in Madras for a few days
before their scheduled embarkation in late August.

So it was in late June that James and Khair un-Nissa began sadly
to pack up for the children and to make preparations for them to
set off from Hyderabad. They were then just five and three years old.
Their parting from Khair un-Nissa was a terrible thing. She well
knew how slim the chances were of her ever seeing them again, and
of how changed they would necessarily be – both in their ways and
attitudes and in their love for her – if she ever did. For the children,
who were now old enough to understand that they were soon to be
taken away from everything they had ever known, it was more traumatic still. Forty years later, Sahib Begum could still recall every
detail of the separation:

> My mother has never had any rival in my affections. I can
> well recollect her cries when we left her & I can now see the
> place in w[hich] she sat when we parted – her tearing her
> long hair† – what worlds would I give [now] to possess one
> lock of that beautiful and loved hair. Since I have been a
> mother myself how often have I thought of the anguish

---

* This square, still known as the Mir Alam Mandi, survives in the old city of Hyderabad,
albeit in a pretty ruinous and derelict state.
† A mourning ritual in Mughal society, and the most extreme expression of grief Khair
un-Nissa could have made.

she must have endured in seeing us forced away from her . . .[62]

In Madras, James arranged for the children to stay with his maternal uncle and aunt, Mr and Mrs William Petrie, the former of whom had just been appointed as Senior Member of the Council there. Without telling Khair, he had also organised for another man to visit the Petries while the children were staying with them: the Anglo-Irish painter George Chinnery.

Chinnery, who went on to become one of the greatest of British Imperial artists, had been in Madras two and half years when he undertook James's commission to paint a life-size portrait of the children for Khair. It was his biggest commission yet: probably his first full-length portrait since he had arrived in Madras to stay with his brother, and certainly his largest. Chinnery was a strange, volatile man, high-spirited and depressive by turns, and a certain emotional fragility seems to have been a family trait: his brother ended his life in a Madras madhouse.* Thanks partly to his commission from James, Chinnery went on the following year to paint Henry Russell's father, Sir Henry Russell senior, the portly and bewigged Chief Justice of Bengal. While doing so he found himself closely watched by Sir Henry's attorney, the diarist William Hickey, who left a perceptive pen-portrait of the painter at work:

> Mr Chinnery, like so many other men of extraordinary talent, was extremely odd and eccentric, so much so as at times to make me think him deranged. His health certainly was not good; and he had a strong tendency to hypochondria which made him ridiculously fanciful, yet in spite of his mental and bodily infirmities, personal vanity shewed itself in various ways. When not under the influence of low spirits, he was a cheerful, pleasant companion, but if hypochondriacal was melancholy and dejected to a degree.[63]

---

* The surgeon in charge of the Madras Lunatic Hospital certified that John Chinnery 'has entirely lost . . . his judgement and [his] memory is so impaired that he cannot recognise his nearest relatives – he is in fact in the most lamentable state of mental fatuity'. See Patrick Conner, *George Chinnery 1774–1852: Artist of India and the China Coast* (London, 1993), p.87.

James's son and daughter cannot have been in Madras for longer than three weeks, and children are always notoriously difficult sitters. Yet the completed painting is one of the masterpieces of British painting in India. In the richest and most gorgeous of colours, Chinnery presents the two small children in their Hyderabadi court dress, standing at the top of a flight of steps engulfed by the swags of a huge dark curtain. Sahib Allum – an exceptionally beautiful, poised, dark-eyed child – wears a scarlet *jama* trimmed with gilt brocade, and a matching gilt cummerbund; he has a glittering *topi* on his head and crescent-toed slippers. Round his neck hangs a string of enormous pearls. His little sister, who is standing one step up from Sahib Allum, and has her arm around her big brother's shoulders, is discernibly fairer-skinned, and below her *topi* is a hint of the red hair that would be much admired in the years to come.

Yet while Sahib Allum looks directly at the viewer with an almost precocious confidence and assurance, Sahib Begum looks down with an expression of infinite sadness and vulnerability on her face, her little eyes dark and swollen with crying. Chinnery clearly understood the intense sadness of separation that this family were going through: six months earlier his own brother had sent his three young children back to England, and he well knew the empty grief and silence that now filled the Chinnery house in place of their cries and laughter.[64]

It was just after his children had arrived to stay with the Petries in late July that James learned the news of his sudden and rather unexpected popularity with the new regime in Calcutta.

In the middle of the month, the new Governor General, Lord Cornwallis had landed at Madras. There he had been briefed by Petrie on the state of politics in India, and especially on James's single-handed resistance to Wellesley's more aggressive policies, particularly his creation and subsequent mishandling of the Maratha crisis. As Petrie duly reported to James, he had told Cornwallis how none of Wellesley's senior officials had had the courage to question the Governor General's policies, but 'that impartial justice and the love of truth obliged me to make an exception in favor of the Resident at Hyderabad who was the only one of all the Diplomatic Corps who had ventured to speak his sentiments freely upon the consequences he apprehended from Marquis Wellesley's Political system respecting the Mahrattas'.[65]

Cornwallis landed at Calcutta to replace Wellesley on 30 July 1805. He immediately made it clear that he wanted none of the Imperial paraphernalia Wellesley had insisted was his right. As he landed, according to William Hickey who was in the crowd massed on the shore to greet him, the bluff old soldier 'looked surprised and vexed at the amazing cavalcade that was drawn up to greet him' – carriages, an escort, bands, staff officers, ADC and servants. 'Too many people,' said Cornwallis. 'I don't want them, don't want one of them. I have not yet lost the use of my legs, hey? Thank God I can walk, walk very well, hey!'

And walk he did. The following evening, according to Hickey, 'while I was out taking my airing, I met Lord Wellesley in his coach and six, preceded by a party of Dragoons and a number of outriders, and in about ten minutes afterwards I met our new Governor General, Marquis Cornwallis, driving himself in a phaeton with a pair of steady old jogtrot horses, accompanied his Secretary, Mr Robinson, and without a single attendant of any description whatsoever'.[66]

Less than a week later, soon after Wellesley had slipped off back to England,* James received a note from this same Mr Robinson, inviting him to come straight up to Calcutta to meet the new Governor General and to give him a full briefing. The note was written in

---

* Further personal, political and economic disappointments awaited Lord Wellesley in England, and though he rose to become Foreign Secretary (1809–12) and later Lord Lieutenant of Ireland (1821–28 and again 1833–34), he never fulfilled his remarkable early promise. His marriage broke up almost immediately on his return to Britain, and in later years he suffered the additional humiliation of watching his younger brother Arthur eclipse him both as a politician and a national hero. He died disappointed and embittered (though still remarkably self-regarding) on 26 September 1842. See Iris Butler, *The Eldest Brother: The Marquess Wellesley 1760–1842* (London, 1973), passim.

a very different tone to the sort of despatches he had become used to receiving from Wellesley's Bengal staff. Robinson assured James that:

> His Lordship will ... be very desirous of availing himself of your long experience, and intimate knowledge of the real state of the Nizam's mind, in respect to the existing connection between the two Courts, as well as of the disposition of his Minister and principal advisers ... [He hopes] to benefit by the continuance of the zeal for the public interest which, from the favourable terms in which you have been mentioned to him by Mr Petrie, he has every reason to suppose has ever been the rule of your conduct in the important station you have so long filled.[67]

Robinson went on to hint that Cornwallis intended to bring about a radical change from Wellesley's aggressive policies, saying that the new Governor General's principle aim was to 'establish perfect confidence in the Justice and Moderation' of the British among Indian princes, and that 'conciliation and kindness [were] the likeliest means of producing this impression on them'. He wanted 'to avoid war' and 'to give every possible degree of facility' to enable peace to return to India. With that view, he was planning to leave Calcutta as soon as was practicable to see for himself 'the upper stations' where the war against the Marathas had just burst into flame again. This was a new round of hostilities between the Company and the most powerful of the remaining Maratha leaders, Jaswant Rao Holkar, who at the end of August 1804 had succeeded in ambushing and wiping out a retreating British force on the modern Rajasthan–Gujerat border.* Among the others Cornwallis wished to meet 'up the country' was General Palmer, who had recently been put out to grass in the badly-paid position of commander of a garrison at Monghyr, on the banks of the Ganges in Bengal.[68]

A copy of the letter was sent by Robinson to Petrie, who wrote by

---

* Holkar eventually made peace with the British, only to lapse into insanity shortly afterwards. According to one authority, 'out of remorse he took to drink, consuming vast quantities of cherry and raspberry brandy, and in 1808 went mad. From then on until his death in 1811 he was kept tied up with ropes and fed on milk.' See Sir Penderel Moon, *The British Conquest and Dominion of India* (London, 1989), p.347.

express to James advising him not to delay. This, he implied, was James's big chance. Petrie had, he said, given Lord Cornwallis all his 'confidential notes and memorandums which I have taken over the last 3 years . . . In that detailed narrative you are particularly mentioned . . . The Marquis at this interview more particularly than before, desired that you would come to Calcutta and [said that] if he had left the place that you should follow him up the country . . . in great confidence I give you my opinion that there will be great changes . . .'[69]

James was still very ill, and Dr Kennedy* advised him to stay in bed. But it was clear to James that his duty, both political and paternal, lay in getting to Madras as quickly as possible. His last piece of work before he left Hyderabad was to patch up some sort of peace with Mir Alam. The conciliatory letter he wrote has disappeared, but the Mir's reply of 20 August acknowledges that James had supported him 'on all occasions, in time of adversity, and in the hour of distress'. Because of this, Mir Alam gave his word that 'I bind myself . . . to maintain and evince, during the remainder of my life, both in your presence, and in your absence . . . a regard to the claims of your amicable aid and assistance . . . I will never adopt any measure which may be inconsistent with the relations of friendship and attachment; or incompatible with your wishes.'[70] The Mir also asked James a favour: that while he was in Madras he should help him purchase a property belonging to the Nawab of Arcot that he, Mir Alam, wanted for his personal use. James agreed to do so.

A week later James kissed goodbye to his Begum and, gathering his strength, galloped off from Hyderabad at speed, hoping above hope that it might still be possible to get to Madras before his children set sail.

* Dr Ure had accompanied his wife to Calcutta a fortnight earlier.

The road from Hyderabad to the port of Masulipatam was one of the most beautiful in the Deccan.

From the Residency it wound up past the great rounded boulders of the Banjara hills towards the tent lines of the Subsidiary Force cantonments. There it snaked alongside the gleaming new obelisks and pyramids of the Parade Ground Cemetery, where Kirkpatrick had buried his friend James Dalrymple five years earlier.

From there the land started to fall, and the road followed the Musi – in August a great, brown, churning torrent newly filled with monsoon rain – steadily down towards the coast, out of the dusty cottonfields around Hyderabad, towards the wetter, greener, muggier expanses of paddy that girded the coast. It was a strange, unearthly landscape that linked the two, the Deccan plateau with the Coromandel coast. At first James passed through flat, newly harvested cotton-scrub dotted with coconut and toddy palms, where the land would erupt suddenly and without warning into low ridges of rock, great spines of tumbled boulders rising like the humps of a camel out of the planisphere plains.

Early in the morning after a night of rain, the scent of flowering *champa* wafting from a roadside tree, James would find that a thin haze veiled the ground like a fine dupatta, blotting out the muddy road ahead but leaving a strangely disembodied forest of palm trunks rising out of the mist, silhouetting the half-naked toddy-tappers shinning up their trunks to harvest their gourds. Roadside caravanserais – strikingly solid and monumental after the floating world of the palms – lay empty but for colonies of monkeys scampering in from the road.

James had not been out of Hyderabad for nearly three years, and as he galloped on towards the coast his eyes and ears would have been sensitive to the contrast with the urban and predominantly Muslim world he had inhabited for so long. Here and there, beside lakes choked with the blossom of kingfisher-blue lotus flowers, he would see the canopy of a *chattri*, or the crumbling *sati* monument marking the burning-place of the wife of some long-dead Hoysala warrior. Occasionally he would pass a Hindu woman with a flower in her hair, or a crocodile of dark-skinned villagers with their short *lungis* tucked up above the

knee, all a reminder of just how fragile and isolated an Islamic island
the city of Hyderabad really was. For this was Telengana, a fragment of
the rural Hindu world that existed before the Muslim invasions, and
which, in these more remote outposts, seemed unchanged and
untouched by five hundred years of Muslim rule.

At first, despite the rains and the muddy roads, the journey went
well. The Krishna was the first major obstacle, for during the monsoon a crossing could sometimes be perilous; but James made it over
without mishap. On 9 September, a week after James had set off,
Henry Russell – left in charge at the Residency in his absence –
picked up his pen to report the news from Hyderabad. He wrote:

> I was glad to hear from Addison [one of the junior Residency
> staff], who arrived here the day before yesterday, that you had
> nearly completed your journey to the River, without having
> experienced any serious inconvenience from fatigue.
>
> Noor ool Omrah [also] sent me a long account which he
> had received of your progress from his manager at Nilgoonda,
> and which conveyed the first intelligence that we had received
> of your having actually crossed the Kistnah [Krishna River].
>
> I know not whether to wish you should still be at Madras
> when this letter arrives there. If the fleet should not have
> sailed for England, it will be gratifying for you to pass a few
> days with the little ones; but otherwise, I think it will be
> desirable for you to reach Calcutta as soon as possible.
>
> Having just sent to the *Mahl* to say that I was writing to
> you, and to know if the Begum had any message to send –
> she has desired, in reply, that I will convey to you her Salaam;
> and that I will assure you she is perfectly well, and anxiously
> hoping to hear of your safe arrival at Madras.[71]

This was the last communication that would ever take place
between James and his Begum. It is unclear exactly what happened
after he crossed the Krishna, but he arrived in Madras much later
than expected with his health in tatters, having missed the fleet by
three days. When the town finally hove into view on 12 September,
there was none of the hoped-for thicket of tall masts rising over the
walls of the fort and the spire of St Mary's church. The *Lord*

Hawkesbury had set sail for England, with the rest of the convoy, on 9 September. On board, according to the passenger list published a week later in the *Calcutta Gazette*, were Mrs Ure and Master John Ure, Miss Katherine Kirkpatrick and Master William George Kirkpatrick. It was the first time that James's children had been referred to by their new Christian names, names which they would bear for the rest of their lives. Never again would they be called Sahib Allum and Sahib Begum. The Lady of High Lineage and the little Lord of the World had shed their Muslim identities as finally and conclusively as a snake sheds its first skin.[72]

James had missed his beloved children, and his body was badly weakened by the exertion of rushing to try to catch them in time. He had simply left it too late, and with the roads boggy, with the incessant late-monsoon rains and the Krishna swollen to its full size, he had missed the chance to say goodbye.

He spent two weeks in Madras trying to regain his strength, but without much success. As there seemed to be no point in waiting any longer, on 22 September he went over to see the Nawab of Arcot, and carried out Mir Alam's errand as he had promised.[73] Despite his fraying health, he then pressed on to Bengal and his appointment with Lord Cornwallis. On 25 September he caught the *Metcalfe* to Calcutta.[74] By the time the ship docked to take on water at Masulipatam, James Achilles Kirkpatrick was very ill indeed.

And then, quite suddenly, nothing.

In a story powered by a succession of extraordinarily detailed and revealing sources – letters, diaries, reports, despatches – without warning the current that has supported this book suddenly flickers and fails. There are no more letters. The record goes dead, with James critically ill, delirious and feverish on the boat. The lights go out and we are left in darkness.

Now and again there is a tiny surge, and the bulb flickers briefly into life. A single item in a newspaper: according to the passenger list published in the *Calcutta Gazette* of 10 October, Dr Ure was with James on the boat. After saying goodbye to his own wife and children, he must have come across James in Madras, seen the state he was in, and offered to accompany him to Calcutta. Also on board, though probably less welcome, were Captain and Mrs Samuel Dalrymple: Sam was a cousin of Kirkpatrick's late friend Lieutenant Colonel James Dalrymple, and in the absence of a clergyman James had married the couple in Hyderabad four years earlier. But as a senior member of the Subsidiary Force, Captain Dalrymple was probably not that well disposed towards James, and his wife Margaret was renowned as one of the biggest shrews in Hyderabad: Mountstuart Elphinstone thought her 'an affected, sour, supercilious woman'.[75] But she was probably too busy nursing her husband to give much offence on this particular journey: Samuel Dalrymple was also ill, and like James was 'proceeding to Bengal on a sick certificate'.[76]

The *Metcalfe* reached Calcutta on Monday evening, 7 October, and James was carried ashore, now clearly dying. He was taken to the house of his niece Isabella, whom he had probably never met before. The last-minute delay in Hyderabad meant that he had just missed not only his children's departure but also Isabella's grand wedding to Charles Buller, which had taken place in St John's church shortly before.

Nursed by his niece and by Dr Ure, James clung on for another week – long enough to learn the bitter news that his last journey had been wasted: Cornwallis, pushing on into the interior of Bengal had also overdone it. He too had become critically ill, and died hours after meeting General Palmer, another loser in the great Indian lottery. As the General wrote to Warren Hastings:

> The poor Marquiss desired me to meet him on the river, so as that he might have one day's conversation with me. I proceeded from Monghyr to Bhaugulpore where I met him, but he was so exceedingly exhausted that he desired Robinson to tell me that he found it impossible to converse with me, and wished to spare us the distress of seeing him in that condition

... He was carried on shore where he has daily become more exhausted. He has lain for the last two days in a state of stupor & total insensibility ... Thus are our fair prospects of rescue from impending ruin, & the restoration of our national character of justice, good faith & moderation blasted in the bud.[77]

By the time Palmer completed his letter on the following day, 5 October, Cornwallis was dead. James need never have bothered leaving Hyderabad; his whole journey had been in vain. On 14 October James recovered sufficiently to add a few codicils to his will, which, fearing the worst, he had secretly carried with him.[78] That night he fell into a coma. He died the early the following morning, 15 October 1805. He was aged only forty-one.

That same evening, as was the custom in Bengal, where putrefaction sets in fast, James Achilles Kirkpatrick was laid to rest amid the obelisks and mausolea of Park Street Cemetery. It was a hurried but formal funeral, with full military honours. The coffin was escorted by His Majesty's 67th Regiment, and Major General Sir Ewen Baillie read an oration recording James's 'meritorious public character' and the 'important services' he rendered to the Honourable East India Company.

But it cannot have been a very emotional affair. For James had died among strangers, away from everyone he loved, and far from everyone who loved him. His beloved wife, his two little children, his brothers, his friends, and his father: as he was laid in the muddy monsoon ground, not one of them even knew that he was dead. In place of tears, there was a cold military salute. The coffin was lowered, and the mud of the grave was filled in.

And that was that. Calcutta was inured to death: as one Company man commented, 'We have known instances of dining with a gentleman [at midday] and being invited to his burial before suppertime.' Nowhere else would a death have caused less stir. As the saying went, two monsoons was the average life-span of a European in Bengal; one year, out of a total European population of 1200, over a third died between August and the end of December. Every year at the end of the monsoon in October, the survivors used to hold thanksgiving

PREVIOUS PAGE: The mercenary Alexander Gardner, one of the last of the white Mughals, in his tartan *salvar kemise*. Gardner had his photograph taken 'clothed from head to foot,' according to his autobiography, 'in the 79th tartan, but fashioned by a native tailor in a garment of his own invention. Even his *pagri* was of tartan, adorned with the egret's plume, only allowed to persons of high rank.'

TOP: The tomb of Michel Joachim Raymond. The complex remained the venue of strange syncretic rituals until it was destroyed by unknown vandals in March 2002.

BELOW: The hill of Maula Ali. The *naqqar khana* gateway at the centre of the picture was erected by the poet-courtesan Mah Laqa Bai Chanda.

Images from Hyderabad in the 1890s

ABOVE: The state executioners.
ABOVE RIGHT: Medicine men.
RIGHT: Amazon harem guards and band members.

RIGHT: French Empire meets the Deccan: Raymond's Bidri ware hookah.

FAR RIGHT: William Kirkpatrick.

CENTRE: William Linnaeus Gardner: 'my having been married some thirty years [to the same begum] and never having taken another wife surprises the Musselmans very much, and the ladies all look upon me as a pattern: they do not admire a system of having three or four rivals, however well pleased the gentlemen may be with the custom'.

BELOW: William Fraser: 'as much Hindoo as Christian'.

BELOW RIGHT: James Achilles Kirkpatrick as a young man.

Mours faithfully,

T. Carlyle

ABOVE LEFT: William Palmer the Hyderabad banker as a disillusioned old man.

ABOVE: Kitty Kirkpatrick, according to Thomas Carlyle 'a strangely complexioned young lady, with soft brown eyes and floods of bronze-red hair, really a pretty-looking, smiling, and amiable though most foreign bit of magnificence and kindly splendour'.

FAR LEFT: Henry Russell on his return to England.

LEFT: Thomas Carlyle.

ABOVE: The south front of the Hyderabad Residency seen looking north from the Musi in 1805.
BELOW: The south front today.

ABOVE: The north front today.

BELOW: The *naqqar khana* gateway into Khair un-Nissa's *zenana*. This is all that remains of the beautiful Rang Mahal built for Khair by James, 'a very elegant and highly finished specimen of Hindustan architecture'. It was pulled down in 1860 by a shocked Victorian Resident who believed that it smacked of 'native immorality'.

OVERLEAF: The Char Minar in the 1890s, the symbolic centre and principal icon of the old city of Hyderabad.

banquets to celebrate their deliverance. In her diary for 1826 a newly arrived Company wife wrote: 'Here people die one day and are buried the next. Their furniture is sold the third. They are forgotten the fourth . . .'[79]

In James's case there was no furniture, but there was, bizarrely enough, the 'Electrifying Machine' which he had ordered to amuse the nobles of the Hyderabad durbar two years previously. It had somehow got lost in the post, and disappeared off to the China coast. The week of James's death, it suddenly reappeared on the quayside at the port of Calcutta. On 28 October, before a single obituary had appeared, the *Calcutta Gazette* contained a large advertisement:

TO BE SOLD AT PUBLIC AUCTION
ON SATURDAY NEXT
AN EXTENSIVE NEW AND VALUABLE
SET OF
APPARATUS FOR EXPERIMENTS ON
ELECTRICITY
MAGNETISM AND MAGIC
BELONGING TO THE ESTATE OF
THE LATE LT COL JAMES ACHILLES KIRKPATRICK

But there is no account of how much it went for; or to whom.[80]

It was eighteen days before the news of James's death reached Hyderabad. According to Henry Russell's official despatch, it was announced to the durbar to 'universal gloom'. There is no record of Khair un-Nissa's reaction to losing her husband, but it can easily be imagined. She was, after all, still only nineteen, and James's death meant that in all likelihood she would never again see her son and daughter. They would now be kept from her, and turned into little English children. This was the loss of everything she had ever worked for, or dreamed of. There was no future, and in such circumstances there could be no comfort.

Her last love letter from her husband – at least the last to have survived – was in effect James's will. Here he makes it clear that Khair had no need of his money: 'The excellent and respectable Mother of my two natural children, who is named Kheir oon Nissah Begum, being amply provided for by Jaghiers and other possessions, both hereditary and acquired, independent of her personal property and jewels, which cannot amount to less than half a lakh of rupees, I have not thought it necessary to provide particularly for her.' But, James implies, this might be misinterpreted, possibly by Khair, possibly by their children, and possibly by his relations. So he added an unequivocal declaration of his love for her: 'By way of proof however of my unbounded love and affection towards her, and as a last token of my Esteem and Remembrance, I hereby will and ordain the sum of ten thousand Hyderabad rupees to be paid to her out of my funds immediately after my demise.'

A further ten thousand rupees was apportioned to Khair un-Nissa should there be any residue left to the estate after the children's legacies had been paid. But Khair did not need such proof of her husband's love for her. Over and over again, James had risked everything for her. Most relationships in life can survive – or not – without being put to any really crucial, fundamental test. It was James's fate for his love to be tested not once, but four times. Four entirely separate inquiries had been carried out into his affair with Khair. At each stage he could easily have washed his hands of his teenage lover. Each time he chose to remain true to her.

That, not the words of any will, was the evidence she could cling to.

And there, abruptly and tragically, the story seemed to end.

In the various short accounts of the romance that have been written

she was in the process of making what must have been for her an epic pilgrimage: a one-thousand-mile journey to the other end of India, at the most inclement time of year, to mourn at her husband's grave. This seemed an unambiguous mark of her fidelity and devotion to James, and a final proof, if proof were needed, that her involvement with him was not just a political ruse dreamt up by her mother and Aristu Jah to entrap the Resident. She loved him, after all.

As the letters unfolded, it was clear that Khair was not alone on her expedition. Apart from the Munshi, Sharaf un-Nissa was coming too, though her mother, Durdanah Begum, now presumably in her seventies or even eighties, had opted to stay behind in the family *deorhi* in the old city. By good fortune, Russell was also in Calcutta at the time, and recorded everything in his letters. He travelled separately, and on separate business, but planned to meet the two Begums in Calcutta: two women beside whom he had lived, and whose notes and messages he had carried, but whose faces he had never yet seen.

There was another plan afoot too: Fyze and General Palmer were going to be in Calcutta to meet the two Begums, as was James's niece Isabella Buller, to whom Khair had sent presents of opal jewellery, but whom she had never met. It sounded as if this expedition was like some sort of rebirth for Khair, an escape from the empty cage of the Residency *mahal*, with all its memories, and perhaps a part of a necessary exorcism.

There was certainly little indication at this stage, with Russell's jaunty letters recording their progress, that the saddest and most tragic part of the whole story was still to come.

IX

WHEN WILLIAM HUNTER SAILED into Calcutta for the first time to take up a job as a Junior Clerk in the Company at the very beginning of the nineteenth century, he wrote home: 'Imagine everything that is glorious in nature combined with everything that is beautiful in architecture and you can faintly picture to yourself what Calcutta is.' And this wasn't just because (as one cruel commentator has suggested) he was in love – and had arrived fresh from Peckham.[1]

In 1806 Calcutta was at the height of its golden age. Known as the City of Palaces or the St Petersburg of the East, the British bridgehead in Bengal was unquestionably the richest, largest and most elegant colonial city in India. Here a Nabob like Philip Francis could boast in the 1770s that he was 'master of the finest house in Bengal, with a hundred servants, a country house, spacious gardens, horses and carriages'. Francis's 'wine book', which survives in the India Office Library, gives an indication of the style in which such men lived: in one typical month, chosen at random, Francis, his family and his guests drank seventy-five bottles of Madeira, ninety-nine bottles of claret, seventy-four bottles of porter, sixteen bottles of rum, three bottles of brandy and one bottle of cherry brandy – some 268 bottles in all, though part of the reason for such consumption was the noxious state of the Calcutta drinking water, and the widespread belief that it should always be 'purified' by the addition of alcohol – and especially by a little tot of brandy.[2]

Nor was it just the British who did well and lived extravagantly:

Bengali merchant dynasties also flourished. The Mullick family, for example, had rambling baroque palaces strewn around the city, and used to travel around Calcutta in an ornate carriage drawn by two zebras.

If Calcutta impressed and surprised the British who sailed out from Georgian London, it amazed Mughal and Persian travellers, for whom it combined the splendour of scale with the novelty of imported notions of European urban management and Palladian architecture.* Khair un-Nissa's cousin, Abdul Lateef Shushtari, first saw Calcutta in 1789 and could not believe his eyes: 'The city now contains around five thousand imposing two or three storey houses of stone or brick and stucco,' he wrote.

> Most are white but some are painted and coloured like marble. Seven hundred pairs of oxen and carts are appointed by the Company to take rubbish daily from streets and markets out of the city and tip it into the river. All the pavements have drains to carry off the rain water to the river and are made of beaten brick so as to absorb water and prevent mud forming. Houses stand on the road and allow passers-by to see what is happening inside; at night camphor candles are burned in upper and lower rooms, which is a beautiful sight. Grain and rice are plentiful and cheap . . .
>
> There is no fear of robbers nor highwaymen, no one challenges where you are going nor where you have come from; all the time, big ships come from Europe and China and the New World filled with precious goods and fine cloths, so that velvets and satins, porcelains and glassware have become commonplace. In the harbour at Calcutta there are over 1000 large and small ships at anchor, and constantly the captains fire cannons to signal arrival or departure . . .[3]

---

* Though even at the best of times, town planning was never one of Calcutta's more obvious virtues: as early as 1768, Mrs Jemima Kindersley thought it 'as awkward a place as can be conceived, and so irregular that it looks as if all the houses had been thrown up in the air, and fallen down again by accident as they now stand: people keep constantly building; and everyone who can procure a piece of ground to build a house upon consults his own taste and convenience, without any regard to the beauty or regularity of the town'. Mrs Jemima Kindersley, *Letters from the East Indies* (London, 1777), p.17.

If Calcutta was a city of trade and business, it was also a place of swaggering excess, famous for being as debauched and dissolute as any port in the world. Forty years earlier, Robert Clive had written that 'corruption, licentiousness and want of principle seem to have possessed the minds of all the Civil Servants'; and he spoke from experience. British Calcutta was a uniquely introverted, self-obsessed and self-regarding society, a little island of Britishness with remarkably few links to the real Indian India beyond. In his decade in the subcontinent, Philip Francis, for example, never ventured more than a mile or two outside Calcutta, and as late as 1793 the artist William Hodges, travelling up the Ganges and Jumna, could express it 'a matter of surprise that a country so closely allied to us should be so little known. Of the face of the country, of its arts and crafts little has yet been said.'⁴

The hundreds of Company servants and soldiers who arrived annually in Calcutta – typically, penniless younger sons of provincial landed families, Scots who had lost their estates or their fortunes (or both) in one of the Jacobite uprisings, squaddies recruited from the streets of the East End, down-at-heel Anglo-Irish landowners and clergymen's sons – were all prepared to risk their lives and travel thousands of miles to the impossible climate of Bengal's undrained marsh and steaming jungle, hazarding what would very probably be an early death, for one reason: if you survived there was no better place in the world to make your fortune.

More clearly and unequivocally than those elsewhere in India, the British inhabitants of Calcutta had come east to amass a fortune in the quickest possible time. For the politically ambitious in the East India Company too, this was the place to be: here, by the side of the Governor General, was somewhere you could make your name, find yourself quickly promoted up the ranks, and, all being well, return home with a Governor's cocked hat and an honour which would allow you to match your elder brother's inherited title. Few in Calcutta seem to have had much interest in either the mores of the country they were engaged in plundering, or in the social niceties of that which they had left behind.

By 1806 William Hickey was an attorney working for Henry

Russell's father, the Chief Justice of Bengal. He had been in Calcutta for thirty years now, but was still appalled by the excesses he saw around him every day in the taverns and dining rooms of the city. In his celebrated diaries he depicts a grasping, jaded, philistine world where bored, moneyed Writers (as the Company called its clerks) would amuse themselves in Calcutta's punch houses* by throwing half-eaten chickens across the tables. Their womenfolk tended to throw only bread and pastry (and then only after a little cherry brandy), which restraint they regarded as the highest 'refinement of wit and breeding'. Worse still was

> the barbarous [Calcutta] custom of pelleting [one's dining companions] with little balls of bread, made like pills, which was even practised by the fair sex. Mr. Daniel Barwell was such a proficient that he could, at a distance, snuff a candle and that several times successively. This strange trick fitter for savages than for polished society, produced many quarrels . . . A Captain Morrison had repeatedly expressed his abhorrence of pelleting, and said that if any person struck him with one he should consider it intended as an insult and resent it accordingly. In a few minutes after he had so said he received a smart blow in the face from one which, although discharged from a hand below the table, he could trace by the motion of the arm from whence it came, and saw that the pelleter was a very recent acquaintance.
>
> He therefore without the least hesitation, took up a dish that stood before him containing a leg of mutton, which he discharged at the offender, and with such well-directed aim that it took him upon the head, knocking him off his chair and giving him a severe cut upon the temple. This produced a duel in which the unfortunate pelleter was shot through the body, lay upon his bed for many months, and never perfectly recovered.[5]

With only 250 European women to four thousand men, and with little else to spend their money on, the young Writers tended to

---

* 'Punch' being of course an Indian word, arriving in the English language via the Hindustani *panch* (five), a reference to the number of ingredients for the drink, which traditionally were (according to *Hobson Jobson*) 'arrack, sugar, lime-juice, spice and water'.

wander the streets of Calcutta, whoring in the city's famous brothels and debauching in its taverns. Even the otherwise admiring Shushtari was horrified by the number of bordellos lining the Calcutta back-streets, and the health problems this caused:

> Brothels are advertised with pictures of prostitutes hung at the door ... *Atashak* – a severe venereal disease causing a swelling of the scrotum and testicles – affects people of all classes. Because so many prostitutes are heaped together that it spreads from one to another, healthy and infected mixed together, no one holding back – and this is the state of even the Muslims in these parts![6]

Even his own cousin, he admits elsewhere, caught something of the sort in Calcutta, 'an itching skin disease called *hakka o jarb* common in Bengal ... It spread to cover his whole body and the itching allowed him no rest, so that he had to employ four servants to scratch and scrub him continually; this they did so vigorously that he often fainted; and he was no longer able to eat or sleep.'[7] That such social diseases were rampant was due at least partly to the fact that the manners and morals of Calcutta's European élite left much to be desired, at least to Shushtari's Persian eyes. It wasn't just the phenomenal consumption of alcohol that worried him: 'No-one eats on his own at home whether by night or by day, and people who know each other go to each others' houses and debauch together ... No man can prevent his wife from mixing with strange men, and by reason of women going unveiled, it is quite the thing to fall in love ...'[8]

All this was, in a way, hardly surprising. The Writers who made up most of the Company's Calcutta employees were little more than schoolboys, sent out from England as young as fifteen. After a dull and uncomfortable six-month voyage they were let loose from the holds and found themselves free from supervision for the first time. One traveller commented how 'the keeping of race horses, the extravagant parties and entertainments generally involve the young Writers in difficulties and embarrassments at an early period of their lives', while according to another observer, 'the costly champagne suppers of the Writers Building were famous, and long did the old walls echo to the joyous songs and loud rehearsing tally-hoes'.

Joyous songs was clearly about as sophisticated as British Calcutta's musical scene got. In 1784 a Danish player of the newly invented clarinet turned up in the city, seeking employment. Joseph Fowke, regarded as one of the more cultured citizens, was appalled: 'This Clarinet D'Amor [is] a coarse instrument,' he wrote in his diary, 'worse to my ears than the grunting of Hogs.' As for the new music of Haydn that the clarinet player had brought with him from Europe, Fowke was quite clear that it was not fit for public performance: '[This] Noisy modern music . . .' he wrote. '[Haydn is] the Prince of Coxcombs.' A John Bull conservative down to his square-toed shoes, Fowke continued, 'Fashion governs the world of Music as it does in dress – Few regulate their taste on the unerring principles of Truth and good Sense.'[9]

Certainly not, so it would seem, the Calcutta clergy. According to Hickey, the army chaplain Mr Blunt, '[an] incomprehensible young man, got abominably drunk and in that disgraceful condition exposed himself to both soldiers and sailors, talking all sorts of bawdy and ribaldry, and singing scraps of the most blackguard and indecent songs, so as to render himself a common laughing stock'.* Even the Calcutta Constabulary were far from paragons of virtue: W.C. Blaquière, the startlingly effeminate police magistrate throughout the 1780s, being a noted cross-dresser who used to leap at any opportunity to adopt female disguises.†

* Blunt was part of a long tradition of dubious English clergymen exported to India after failing to find a living at home. The curate of Madras in 1666, for example, was described as 'a drunken toss-pot', while his counterpart in Calcutta twenty years later was 'a very lewd, drunken swearing person, drenched in all manner of debaucheries, and a most bitter enemy of King William and the present Government'. Back in Madras, Francis Fordyce, padre to the Presidency throughout the 1740s, turned out to have fled his post as chaplain at St Helena after having debauched a planter's daughter. In Madras he fared little better, quarrelling with Clive and being called before the Council to justify his conduct. He refused to attend, but it was declared in his absence that he vowed he would 'pull off his canonicals at any time to do himself justice'. See Henry Dodwell, *The Nabobs of Madras* (London, 1926), pp.19–20.
† So comely was Blaquière's appearance that when Zoffany came to paint a Leonardo-style Last Supper for the altarpiece of St John's church in Calcutta he chose him as the model for the traditionally effeminate-looking apostle John ('the apostle Jesus loved'), and posed him with his long blond tresses tumbling over Jesus' breast. Jesus himself was

Wellesley had made some efforts to reform this dissolution, and in one of his more far-sighted moves had set up Fort William College in an attempt to educate the cleverer of the Writers in the Indian languages that they would need to administer the subcontinent. But the social reforms and stricter Victorian morality that began to establish themselves from the 1830s onwards were still far away, and in 1806, when Khair un-Nissa first arrived in Calcutta, this was still a city of Hogarthian dissipation.

Sometime at the beginning of May 1806, a small boatload of Shi'a Muslims from Hyderabad docked at the Port of Calcutta. Two veiled Begums were accompanied by their ladies-in-waiting and the shrouded ladies of another family, headed by a pair of suave and highly educated brothers, originally from Delhi.* Munshi Aziz Ullah and his younger brother Aman Ullah, and their families, had all made the journey to Calcutta before and knew what to expect. But to Khair un-Nissa and her mother this was all new, foreign territory, to be wondered at with the widest of eyes.

It was not the sailing season: the winds and unpredictable coastal tides of April and May made it too unsafe. So from Masulipatam,

---

modelled by the 'worthy Greek priest, Father Parthenio', while according to Mildred Archer, the auctioneer William Tulloh, who had disposed of James Kirkpatrick's Electrifying Machine, 'was far from pleased to find himself as Judas'. It is certainly an unusual reworking of the familiar scene: as a contemporary critic pointed out, 'Peter's sword hung upon a nail on the wall is a common peon's *tulwaar* [scimitar]: the water ewer standing near the table is copied from a *pigdanny* [a Hindustani spittoon]: and there is a *beesty* bag full of water lying near it.' See Mildred Archer, *India and British Portraiture 1770–1825* (London, 1979), p.158.

* The Begums brought at least one slave girl with them, by name Zora. She appears in Henry Russell's letters as she became pregnant while in Calcutta, and stayed there to give birth to her child, rejoining the Begums the following year. It is unclear from the surviving letters who the father was, though Russell's daughter-in-law Constance, who bound, edited and censored his papers, clearly believed that it might have been Russell. See Bodleian Library, Russell Papers, Ms Eng Letts C155, p.219, 26 January 1807.

the party had skirted the foothills of the Eastern Ghats on elephant-back, then headed on up the east coast as far as the Orissan river port of Cuttack. There they had sent their elephants and the *mahouts* back to Hyderabad, and caught a skiff down to the coast and thence across the Bay of Bengal to Calcutta.

After the relatively dry, equable climate of Hyderabad, the weather in a Bengali May – the hottest and most humid time of the year – would have been something quite new to the two Begums. Certainly, their cousin Abdul Lateef had been amazed by the humid fertility of the Calcutta hinterland – so different from the dusty scrub of Persia or the Deccan plateau: 'The rainy season lasts for up to four months,' he wrote,

> during which time it is difficult for men and animals to pass, the fields and plains are all under water, and the wealthier citizens spend their time on boats as their dwellings are flooded. [In the fields around Calcutta] rice grows up to a hand's breadth overnight when the rains are heavy . . . Agriculture is flourishing here, well-tended and pleasing to the eye, indeed unparalleled in all the world. In all seasons the surrounding country is emerald-green in colour: you cannot find one rock in the mountains nor one handful of earth in the plain which is not green . . .[10]

The Hyderabadi party eventually landed at Beebee Johnson's Ghat, beside the old Customs House, and set off – perhaps carried in closed purdah carriages or covered palanquins – to a rented house in the fashionable district of Chowringhee.[11]

To the two Begums, this city, so different from their own, and indeed from anything they had ever seen, must have been a breath-taking sight. Like their cousin Abdul Lateef Shushtari twenty years earlier, they would have been amazed at their first glimpse of a European town: by the succession of tall, white-porticoed palaces that lined the banks of the Hooghly long before they arrived at the city itself; by the mansions of Garden Reach with their soft lawns and fertile, landscaped grounds leading down to the muddy brown monsoon waters of the river; by the flowerbeds of the riverside gardens full of unfamiliar, imported English blooms; by the star-shaped ramparts of Fort William, then the port with its hundred Indiamen bobbing at anchor; the wide, clean streets leading into the heart of the town, and the buggies and carriages bumping in and out of the potholes on the Esplanade; the top hats and tailcoats of the men about town; the busks, parasols and (inexplicably to Muslim eyes) lapdogs of their ladies; the Governor General's bodyguards in their plumed busbees and 'blazing uniforms'; the ubiquitous storks perched atop Wellesley's new Government House; the gleaming stucco.

It is not clear from Russell's letters that May exactly where either he or the Begums were staying in Chowringhee, or indeed whether he and the families of the two *munshis* were renting the same apartments as the two Begums. But it is apparent that they were all very near each other and that they seemed to spend most of their time in each other's company. Given this, it is perhaps most likely that the entire party from the Hyderabad Residency would have taken a large house in Chowringhee and apportioned the different floors between them, as Hickey had done a few years earlier when he, his *bibi* Jemdanee and their friends had clubbed together to rent a garden house outside town.

Certainly, in his letters from Calcutta, which span the seven months from May to November 1806, Henry Russell writes to his brother Charles in Hyderabad that the Begums and the *munshis* were never far from his side: in one letter, he reports that Munshi 'Uzeez Ullah and his brother desire [to send] their bundagee [greeting] to you'; in another that 'Amaun Oolah, who is at my elbow', wishes to send his salaams. As for Khair un-Nissa, she clearly spent much of her first month or two in Calcutta mourning at her husband's grave;[12] but thereafter – perhaps exhausted with weeping and bewailing her fate amid the mud and puddles, the dripping obelisks and monsoon-stained mausolea of Park Street – she too retreated to Russell's side at the Chowringhee house. A month or so after that, she had gone so far as to remove her veil and show herself for the first time to Russell:* in one letter, which makes this explicit, we learn that the

---

* This was a great honour, which Muslim women in purdah were free to extend only to the most honoured family friends, as for example when the Emperor Jehangir decreed

Begum 'was with me sitting for her picture when your letter arrived'.[13]

In his descriptions of the group's activities, Russell invariably includes himself, and always uses the first person plural. When he hears for example that a false rumour has swept Hyderabad that Khair un-Nissa has died, he asks his brother to 'send the enclosed letter [from Khair] to the old lady [Durdanah Begum] immediately, and, when you see her, tell her how much distressed we all are that she should have suffered so much uneasiness from a groundless report'. Later he asks: 'What is the reason we receive so few letters from the old lady?'[14]

Indeed, so friendly was the relationship between the Begums and the Russell family that in August Henry writes that Khair has even consented to receive and show herself to his younger brother Charles: 'The Begums are both of them very grateful for your constant attentions to their wishes,' Russell told him, 'and frequently speak of you with great warmth and interest. Khyr oon Nissa says she will see you and become personally acquainted with you, whenever she has an opportunity . . .'[15]

The tone Russell adopts with Khair is at times close to that of the bowing and deferential courtier; it is almost as if he sees himself in the role of the Begum's Private Secretary or Personal Assistant. In November, Khair's promise to receive Charles is renewed, and Russell, like a faithful equerry, formally passes the information on in a style that is not far removed from that of a court circular: 'The Begum desires to be kindly remembered to you. She says she should not have had any objection to my sending her picture to you, if she had not herself intended to take round the original; and that as she is so much handsomer than her picture, she wishes you to see her first.'[16]

The new portrait of Khair un-Nissa was not the only picture in the apartment. On elephant-back, all the way from Hyderabad, the grieving Begum had brought with her the huge, life-size Chinnery

---

that his father-in-law, Itmad ud-Daula, had become such 'an intimate friend' that 'the ladies of the harem [were] not to veil their faces to him'. See *Tuzuk i-Jahangiri*, Vol. 1, p.351. One way of getting around the stricture of purdah was for a woman or a group of women formally to adopt the man in question as their 'brother'. Tipu's widows did this to the officer at Vellore who was deputed to look after them following the fall of Seringapatam in 1799, and there is some evidence that this was what Khair did with the Russells: certainly on 29 May, a month after the Begums had arrived in Calcutta, Henry instructs his brother Charles that when writing to Khair, 'you must address her as your elder sister'. Bodleian Library, Russell Papers, Ms Eng Letts C155, p.138.

of her two beloved children, all that she had now to cling onto from her marriage and her former life.

Soon the fame of the wonderful portrait began to spread, and before long strangers were turning up at the house asking to see it. As Russell wrote to his brother, 'Chinnery's picture of the Colonel's children has been universally admired, and has acquired great celebrity for him here.'[17]

This strange, diverse group of people from Hyderabad – a mixed bag of Begums, *munshis*, senior British diplomats and their respective slaves and staff – had more in common than mere geographical proximity. They were all, to different extents, refugees from the new regime at the Hyderabad Residency.

Thomas Sydenham, a Wellesley acolyte, had been appointed Resident soon after James had died. He had immediately set about removing all vestiges of James's approach to Anglo–Hyderabadi relations, quarrelling with Nizam Sikander Jah within days of arriving at the durbar, and convincing Ghulam Imam Khan, author of the *Tarikh i-Khurshid Jahi*, that he was intent on 'ceasing all the work of Hushmut Jung, whose approach he disliked'.[18] At the same time, Khair was given notice to vacate the Rang Mahal, even though Sydenham had an English wife and did not need it for his own use. The strict rules about caste purity in the Residency kitchens (observed, presumably, to reassure Indian guests) were cancelled, and there was a fundamental change in the way the Residency operated.[19]

Sydenham seems in fact to have defined himself and his style in direct opposition to that of James Kirkpatrick.* When he bought

---

* Sydenham had briefly served under James at Hyderabad before being transferred to Pune. James (who called him 'Pontifex Maximus' in his letters) had always been suspicious of him, and speculated that he might have been behind the 'leak' confirming the existence of his child by Khair un-Nissa which, relayed to Calcutta via the Subsidiary Force, had resulted in the 1801 Clive Enquiry.

two of James's silver elephant howdahs which had once belonged to Tipu Sultan's father, Haidar Ali, he felt it necessary to send a despatch to Calcutta explaining that he had no intention of going the way of Kirkpatrick, despite the impression that might have been created by the purchase: 'the dignity and respectability of the British Representative should be made to rest – as indeed it does rest – on more solid foundation than the maintenance of state and splendour borrowed from the manners and habits of the natives of Asia [which are] in great degree inconsistent with our national character', he wrote.[20]

There are also hints that there was some sort of financial scandal in which Sydenham believed the old regime to be indirectly implicated. The exact details are unclear, but Sydenham decided that Munshi Aziz Ullah was responsible and had sacked him on the spot, even before initiating a proper investigation. This summary treatment horrified and disgusted Henry Russell, who had great respect for the *munshi*, admired his negotiating skills, and knew the degree to which he was responsible for the small print of all three of the treaties James had signed. Indeed he described the *munshi* to his brother Charles as 'a man of uncommon character and acquirements, whose abilities did more for the Company than any European unaided could ever have done, and whose integrity was confirmed and secured by his pride ... For all the important measures he [James Kirkpatrick] carried through he was ultimately indebted to Uzeez Oolah; [indeed] no one but himself could have been so indebted with such impunity.'[21]*

---

* This was something James was well aware of, and his extreme admiration and affection for Aziz Ullah is clear throughout the Kirkpatrick Papers. During his time as Resident James wrote constantly to Calcutta demanding pensions, pay rises and honours for his *munshi*, and in his will left him an especially generous bequest: 'Unto my Moonshy, Meer Uzeez Ullah, in Testimony of the high value which I set on his zeal, fidelity, talents and long tried personal attachment to me, I will and bequeath the sum of ten thousand sicca rupees, and my emerald ring with my titles from the King of Delhi engraved in Persian. To his worthy brother Amaun Oollah I bequeath two thousand sicca rupees in testimony of my high approbation of his able and faithful services.' Ten thousand rupees is around £60,000 in today's currency. For James's will see OIOC, Kirkpatrick Papers, F228/84. For a succession of James's letters asking for pensions and pay rises for Munshi Azeez Ullah in view of his exceptional success at negotiating treaties, see OIOC, Kirkpatrick Papers, F228/12, pp.74, 168, 183, 216 and finally p.259, when on 14 November 1800 James finally exploded over Calcutta's continuing neglect of his *munshi*, writing to his brother William: 'So! In return for the highly important services rendered by Uzeez

Russell's theory was that the scandal was the creation of Captain William Hemming, the commander of James's bodyguard, whom he and James had long disliked and distrusted. Moreover, Russell believed that it was part of Hemming's ongoing attempt to smear James's memory:

> If there was reason to suppose that abuses existed in any department of the treasury at H [i.e. the Hyderabad Residency] it was unquestionably wise to institute an enquiry. But whatever may be the result, I am convinced that no imputation of blame can be affixed to the character of Colonel Kirkpatrick. I am almost as much assured of the integrity of Uzeez Ullah . . . It is an extraordinary circumstance that every charge that I have ever heard urged against the Colonel [Kirkpatrick] or the Moonshy, and every suspicion which ever entered my mind against either of them, were communicated to me by Hemming; and its surely honourable to the character of both the Colonel and the Moonshy, that the most unrelenting and virulent malignity has been unable to prove a single instance of his misconduct against either of them . . . I am convinced that we shall be able to defeat all the malice of the poor Colonel's enemies with plain and simple matters of fact.[22]

Russell personally disliked both Hemming and Sydenham, and one of his principal hopes in coming to Calcutta, while ostensibly only taking a short period of leave from the Residency to sort out Kirkpatrick's will, was to find more congenial employment elsewhere in India. To this end he spent many of his evenings in Calcutta away

---

Oolah, and which in conformity to your own express declaration, I encouraged him to expect would be rewarded, for the first treaty [alone], by a *pension* of five hundred rupees per month, his *salary* is to be increased by only one hundred rupees per annum!!! with the pleasing prospect of being a drudge in the office for nearly the remainder of his days. If this really be meant as a favour, I am certain it is one that Uzeez Oolah will humbly beg leave to decline, and in such case, I shall consider myself – after the reiterated and positive assurances I have given him – *most sacredly bound* to make him *full compensation* from my private purse, for the disappointment of his just and well founded expectations in the above score . . . You have met my suggestion with regard to this most invaluable man, in the most extraordinary manner indeed; in a manner that I must say was altogether unexpected; and no less impolitic than unhandsome.' James's constant concern for the well-being of his Indian staff, demonstrated throughout his letters, is one of his most attractive traits and always shows him at his most generous and honourable.

from his Hyderabadi friends, attending a succession of levées and dinners at Government House in an attempt to find a suitable opening.[23]

Russell may have had his faults, but disloyalty was not one of them. For the rest of his life he remained unwaveringly true to James's memory, and vigorously defended him whenever his style or record was attacked. While in Calcutta he was constantly enquiring of his brother Charles in Hyderabad how people were talking about Kirkpatrick and wanting to know how loyal or not James's other old friends were being. In one letter, for example, he asks about 'the Engineer' (as the architect Samuel Russell* was known):

> How does the Engineer conduct himself? And what part does he take in any discussions that arise regarding the Colonel? He is perhaps too weak to persevere in proposing that gratitude which he ought to feel; but it would be painful to me to think that among the many to whom the poor Colonel was kind, you and I are the only two that cherish the memory of his goodness . . .[24]

When Charles replied that the Engineer was indeed joining in the merriment and making jokes about James, Henry was incandescent:

> Your account of the Engineer's conduct has gratified me exceedingly and what you say has caused me more pain than surprise. Perhaps I may be too sanguine, but I cannot help indulging a hope that some day I may be Resident at Hyderabad. If that day should arrive, he will find ample cause to deplore it, for he may be assured that my vengeance shall descend upon him, and that I will give him good reason to know [that] there is no crime which I will [deplore more?] highly, than that of Ingratitude to the Memory of a Benefactor.[25]

Five years later when Russell did indeed become Resident, he made a great point of bringing back all the usages of James's time – includ-

---

* Lieutenant Samuel Russell of the Madras Engineers, the son of the Royal Acadamician John Russell, was (oddly enough) no relation to the brothers Henry and Charles Russell. At this period Samuel Russell was busy finishing off the construction of James's great Residency House.

ing the maintenance of strict caste rules in the kitchens – and kept to his promise to refuse to employ anyone who had been in any way disloyal to his old friend and patron.[26]

By the end of May 1806, once the Hyderabad party were settled in their Chowringhee house, they began to receive visitors.

Fyze and the General were the first to call. The two were now getting older, and beginning to feel their age. The General was also depressed – both by the disappointments that Wellesley had brought to the end of his career, and by the financial constraints that his new, reduced salary had imposed upon him. Throughout his life Palmer had always had debts, and as his worried son John wrote, despite 'knowing the insecurity of his income, he never dreamt of saving one six pence out of it; and he has continued just as careless under the precarious enjoyment of his pension: every dumree of it goes somehow or somewhere'.[27]

Palmer's financial situation was in fact rather worse than John had feared. It was becoming increasingly clear that the old General no longer had the income to service his debts and obligations, and as he wrote to Warren Hastings around this time, 'I sincerely accuse myself for having neglected to secure a provision for my family & repose for my old age.'[28] This was something, naturally enough, that worried his family too, and their anxiety was compounded by both the General and his wife refusing to change their courtly lifestyle to match their newly reduced circumstances. William, Fyze's eldest child, took it upon himself quietly to put money aside for Fyze's old age (as she was twenty years younger than the General it was naturally expected that he would die before her), knowing full well that his father would never have sufficient funds to do so. This was something that his half-brother John agreed was sadly very necessary. Writing to William, John said that he greatly

approve[d] of your proposed plan of making a settlement on
your mother for her life . . . [Perhaps] she should [now] forgo
the allowance of Rs. 700 or more that she receives from the
General and from whom she draws every other supply she
requires . . . I confess however that I despair of the good sense
and the moderation of the one [the General] or the economy
& fortitude of the other [Fyze, who was always regarded as
'magnificent', i.e. enjoying life's little perks] & that your ben-
evolence would be abused without the slightest relief to my
father is my rooted belief . . .

Despite this, John was able to report that both 'the old lady' and
her husband were in fine fettle:

> I have however the happiness of assuring you that his consti-
> tution is nothing impaired & that few men 15 years his junior
> have a fairer chance of life. He sleeps and eats well – and
> though occasionally inconvenienced by a severe *tritius auditus*
> [spells when he heard ringing in his ears], their duration is
> short and a yet shorter time restores his vigor and health.[29]

Staying around the corner from the Hyderabadis in John Palmer's
lavish Loll Bazaar mansion (notorious, incidentally, for its mosquitoes,
which compelled lady supper-guests to cover their legs with thick stockings during dinner),* Fyze and the General came over regularly to see
Khair, though Russell reported to his brother Charles that Fyze was upset
with him for forgetting to bring 'a parcel of soosunee [coloured embroid-
ery] and other things from her son in Hyderabad. I recollect William

---

* According to his friend William Prinsep, John Palmer was 'called the Prince of Merchants from his unbounded liberality, amiability and wealth. He had married a very
handsome woman of an Armenian cast of countenance . . . his house was always open
and a dinner table for nearly twenty always spread and nearly always filled. No stranger
arrived then in Calcutta without dining there as a thing of course . . .' Prinsep adds,
however, that anyone who arrived for dinner wearing silk stockings could never forget
'the torture they suffered under the table' from the mosquitoes. Palmer's style was not
to everyone's liking, and the straitlaced Lady Nugent was alarmed to discover that after
dinner the women all withdrew from the men only to begin smoking an especially noisy
selection of hookahs, 'some deep bass, others a bubbling treble'. She was eventually
persuaded by Mrs Palmer to try it out, 'as she assured me it was only a composition of
spices, but I did it awkwardly, swallowing the smoke and the consequence was I coughed
all night'. See OIOC, Mss Eur D1160/1, 'Memoirs of William Prinsep', pp.251–3. Also
Lady Maria Nugent, *Journal of a Residence in India 1811–15* (2 vols, London, 1839).

telling me he intended giving me a present of that sort; but I cannot find it anywhere, and am strongly inclined to think that he neglected to send it to me. Ask him and let me know what he says.'[30]

Another frequent caller at the house was William Kirkpatrick's beautiful daughter Isabella Buller, in whose home James had died the previous year. Isabella was now heavily pregnant with her first child, and she and the Begum struck up a firm friendship from the moment they first met: 'Since the Begum arrived in Calcutta, Mrs Buller has been extremely civil in calling on her, and paying her every Attention in her power,' wrote Russell in June. '[Khair] is therefore desirous to evince her sense of this kindness, by gratifying Mrs Buller's wishes to get some handsome native dresses, and as she left five very rich suits with her grandmother at Hyderabad, she thinks it is better to get them forwarded to Calcutta, than to incur the expense of making them up here.'[31]

Reverting to his role as the Begum's self-appointed private secretary, Russell went on to give his brother more specific instructions about the consignment:

> The enclosed letter to the old lady points out the things the Begum wishes to be despatched and desires that they may be very carefully packed and sent to you without delay. I will thank you to take it yourself to the old girl [Durdanah Begum], and to desire that she not be any time in complying with her daughter's wish, as the season for sending things by sea is now nearly over. Take care also that they are well packed; and if you should not be satisfied with the Begum's precautions, incur, on my account, any expense that may be requisite to secure the dresses not only from damp, but even from the sea air, which would be apt to tarnish the silver trimmings. When you get them, send them as expeditiously as possible to Alexander [the Company agent at Masulipatam], and check that he will send them consigned to me by the first vessel that may sail for the port of Calcutta.[32]

Many other similar commissions on behalf of Khair un-Nissa soon followed. A week later, for example, after Isabella Buller gave birth to a little girl, Henry was writing to Hyderabad asking Charles to send 'two lots of choorees [bangles], one for Mrs Buller, and the other to accompany whatever *dupatta* the Begum is making up for dear little Rose [Isabella's baby daughter]'.[33]

One thing that comes across very clearly in these letters is the strength of the bonds linking all these women: between Fyze, Isabella Buller and Khair, but also, more intensely and remarkably still, between Khair, her mother and her grandmother. The two Calcutta Begums are constantly writing to Durdanah Begum in Hyderabad, and a whole succession of small domestic requests (and even, apparently, on one occasion, a large helping of *halwa* carrot pudding[34]) go backwards and forwards between Hyderabad and Calcutta, up and down the east coast via the two Russell brothers. The false rumour that Khair has died brings on a further succession of frantic letters. 'I mentioned to the Begum the anxiety which had been caused to her family by the reports that have been prevalent about her illness,' writes Henry in June,

> but her mother is so fidgety, and so much distressed at anything that it is likely to occasion uneasiness to the old Begum, that I did not like to communicate it to her [Sharaf un-Nissa]. The old lady's mind will have been set at ease by so many letters which she must have received before this time; but the Begum and I both thought it would be prudent to express to her grandmother some regret for the distress she has suffered from a premature report.

Russell and Khair 'after consulting together' therefore hatched a small family conspiracy to fake a letter from Sharaf un-Nissa to her mother, something which Russell reported to Charles was easily achieved as 'the old lady always gets her letters written through me, and I had not much difficulty in accomplishing what we wished'.* He goes on: 'Send the enclosed letter to the old lady immediately ... You may also safely assure her that neither her daughter nor her granddaughter were ever in better health in their lives. The season has been uncommonly favourable and mild ...'[35]

---

* Russell was not able to write well in Persian, which implies that the elder two Begums corresponded in the Hyderabadi vernacular, Deccani Urdu (sometimes called Deccani), a close cousin to Hindustani, in which Russell was fluent. Khair un-Nissa on the other hand seems to have been literate only in Persian, something that later caused Russell enormous difficulties when he wished to write to her from Madras and could not find

It is increasingly apparent throughout these letters that it is Khair who seems to be the dominant force among the women. It is she, not her mother, who is writing the letters;* and it is she who is always ordering the various items from Hyderabad. There is absolutely no question of Khair un-Nissa being some sort of powerless ex-concubine: this is a beautiful, charismatic Mughal noblewoman behaving according to her rank, with a pair of senior British officials running around to do her bidding. In her widowhood, she clearly still retained her magnetism and her effortless ability to get her way with all those who were drawn into her orbit. Henry Russell, who treated her both protectively and with the greatest of respect, seemed no more able or willing to resist her requests than her mother, grandmother or late husband had been before him. At times, indeed, Khair seems to treat Russell as if he is some sort of junior milliner's assistant, dictating to him long precise details of her requests which he uncomplainingly passes on to his younger brother at the Residency:

> The enclosed piece of *husmah* [material] was given me with a request that I would get her some of the same pattern. You will oblige me by consulting the old Begum on the subject. I understand that she will be able to extend you useful assist- ance, and that a female servant of hers, named Jagumma is particularly *au fait* at procuring *husmah*. One dress, which is all I want at present, will require six yards ... get it done, that is a great fellow, as soon as you can, and send it to me carefully packed by dawke.[36]

Pages full of further details follow, laying down exactly the measurements, patterns, colour and trimmings that the hapless Charles was supposed to find, and where he should go with Jugumma to get them.

In all ages, in all families, younger brothers are rarely treated with much deference by their elder siblings. Few however can have been so comprehensively patronised as Charles Russell, who was now

a confidential Persian letter-writer there – even though he was clearly quite capable of writing letters himself in Hindustani or Deccani Urdu.
* Unlike Khair, Sharaf un-Nissa seems to have been illiterate and to have been forced to use the services of letter-writers – including, in this instance, Henry Russell.

Assistant Secretary at the Hyderabad Residency and so a diplomat of some standing and seniority in his own right,* but who nevertheless at this stage seems to have spent a great deal of his professional time running errands for the two Begums between the Residency, Durdanah Begum's *deorhi* in Irani Gulli, and the various textile bazaars of the old city of Hyderabad, as well as trotting out to fetch any other personal items that Khair un-Nissa had forgotten to pack before leaving home, such as her *paan* set: 'What is become of the chicknee, suparu and cardamoms [I ordered] for the Begum?' demands Henry at one point. 'I will thank you to send the enclosed letter to the Old Begum,' begins another. 'It contains a desire that she will give you a small box of medicine which her daughter is in the habit of taking, and which she cannot procure in Calcutta. It will be of very small dimensions, and I therefore beg you will forward it to me by dawke . . .'[37]

Intriguingly, amid all these letters between the women, there is never a single mention of Bâqar Ali Khan, nor of Khair's brothers or uncles; and there is certainly no mention of Khair ever writing to them. The strongest bonds, quite clearly, were those within the *zenana* – although it could also be of course that Bâqar and the men of the family had broken off relations with their unusually strong-minded and somewhat ungovernable womenfolk.†

But increasingly – and perhaps inevitably – there is another bond in the air: that between Russell and Khair. Khair had spent eighteen months in mourning. She had lost her children – there is no indication that William Kirkpatrick encouraged them to write to her, though she presumably had news of them via William's daughter Isabella Buller – and she had lost her husband. After the scandal of

---

* Charles Russell's career was from the very beginning less spectacular than that of his elder brother. It had started badly when Sir Henry had failed – despite his best efforts – in his attempts to obtain a writership for Charles, and he had to be content to remain a military ensign. In 1803 he was promoted to the rank of lieutenant, and as such joined Henry at Hyderabad. But even here he rose no higher than Acting Assistant Secretary. Bodleian Library, Russell Papers, Ms Eng Letts C152, 31 July 1803, Henry Russell to Charles Russell. See also Peter Wood, 'Vassal State in the Shadow of Empire' (unpublished Ph.D., University of Wisconsin-Madison, 1981), p.103.

† Or alternatively, Bâqar could be dead. It is unclear when he died; possibly it was in 1808, when there was a dispute over his lands, which the government was attempting to resume.

her affair with James, and the disgrace that Mir Alam had suffered in its wake, she was now very vulnerable to the Mir's vengeance and was completely unprotected. Moreover she was only twenty, still regarded as a great beauty, and there is no stipulation in Islam against the remarriage of widows.* Indeed, Muslim tradition encourages it, and suggests that the late husband's brother is usually the ideal second husband.

James's two brothers were now in England and so unavailable; but his closest friend and Assistant was at hand, and seems to have needed little persuasion to have become more intimate with the 'poor Begum'.

From the start, even before he arrived in Calcutta, Henry Russell had always been extremely solicitous to Khair un-Nissa.

In his letters to Charles on his way to Calcutta, Henry worries that as Ure and the other executors are taking so large a percentage of Kirkpatrick's will as commission, the Begum is unlikely to get her full legacy. He therefore decides to claim his commission and give it straight to Khair, 'both in order to remunerate her for the loss of the provisional bequest, and as the most fair and creditable mode of disposing of that money which nothing but Ure's shabbiness and rapacity would have induced me to have requested from the estate'.†

---

* Another famously strong-willed Mughal beauty who succeeded in remarrying to great advantage was of course Nur Jehan: it is often forgotten that Jehangir was her second husband. See Ellison Banks Findly, *Nur Jehan: Empress of Mughal India* (New Delhi, 1993).

† What Ure had decided to do was apparently a perfectly legal practice, though it was usual only for professional lawyers, and not close friends, actually to claim a commission for acting as executor of a will. Moreover Ure, like the Munshi, received a very generous bequest from Kirkpatrick: 'Mr. George Ure surgeon to the Residency fifty pounds sterling as a token of my esteem and regard . . . and unto my surgeon George Ure Esq I bequeath the [further] sum of five thousand sicca rupees as some reward for his frequent attendance on me in sickness and for all the trouble which I have at times given to him' (OIOC, Kirkpatrick Papers, F228/84). In modern currency, the bequest totalled around £33,000.

Henry also takes it upon himself to get the new *diwan** in Hyderabad, Rajah Chandu Lal, to pay up the money owed to the Begum from her *jagirs* (estates), while he personally advances her the legacy from James's will from his own funds 'in order to prevent the Begum suffering any financial embarrassment'.[38]

The news that Khair had unveiled for Russell is the first hint that the two were becoming intimate. By July they were clearly discussing more personal matters. In the middle of the month, a letter arrived for Henry from Hyderabad telling him that his Hyderabadi concubine, by whom he had a son, had again become pregnant. There seemed to be no suggestion that the father was anyone but him,[†] yet he still wrote a slightly chilling reply to Charles, saying that 'your account of my girls conduct gives me much pain, and I am exceedingly dissatisfied to hear she is with child'. He adds: 'On me she has not many claims, but the Begum has interceded very warmly for her; and at her particular request, I have consented to restore to the girl her full monthly allowance of 30 rupees she originally received from me. I will therefore thank you to pay her that sum in future, and to tell her that I expect her gratitude to the Begum, as well as to me, will induce her to behave better than she has done lately.'[39]

He does not say it here, but the Begum – missing her own children as badly as she clearly did – had in fact offered to bring the child up herself;[‡] something that was in both Mughal and Georgian society

---

Russell tells Charles exactly what he thinks of Dr Ure's decision to pocket his commission: 'when a man appoints a private friend to be his executor and even bequeathes to that friend a legacy . . . it appears to me that, to burden the estate by demanding a percentage, is an act which may be justly reprobated as shabby and rapacious . . . I told Ure very candidly what my sentiments were; but he seemed resolved to maintain and exercise his Right.'

* Effectively Chancellor of the Exchequer to Mir Alam's Prime Minister.

† When the child was born, Russell explicitly called her 'my little girl'. If this is the case, the cause of his anger was not the woman's possible infidelity so much as her failure to employ proper contraception – something Indian prostitutes and courtesans were famously skilled in. See B.F. Musallam, *Sex and Society in Islam* (Cambridge, 1983), p.94.

‡ The baby, a little girl, died soon after her birth the following year, and Russell wrote when he heard the news: 'If the girl had lived she was to have been brought up by the Begum.' Bodleian Library, Russell Papers, Ms Eng Letts C155, p.213, 27 April 1807. In a note attached to this letter, Constance, Lady Russell, Henry's daughter-in-law and the family historian, has scribbled: 'Sir Henry Russell alludes to the death of his little girl and says he shall take the boy [his earlier child by the *bibi*] with him to Hyderabad.'

more normally the response of a long-suffering wife to a husband's infidelities than that of a distant friend or acquaintance. But if Charles Russell, on reading these letters, was growing suspicious of his brother's relationships with the Begum, he does not appear to have voiced it. So it was only in November, as winter was beginning to set in across north India, that Henry brought the matter to a head. He began by telling Charles that he had changed his mind and had now decided to come back to his job beside Charles at the Residency: 'You will be astonished to learn that I have determined to return to Hyderabad,' he wrote.

> The motives which have led to this decision appear to me so prudent and judicious, with a view to your interests, as well as to my own, that I am sure you will not disapprove of them ... the result of my experience during the time I have been in Calcutta, convinces me that no situation in my own line is to be got here, and that Sir George Barlow [the acting Governor General since the sudd·n death of Cornwallis*] is the most unlikely man in the world to make one for me ... It is true that Captain Sydenham is both poor and young, and that he is therefore likely to hold the Residency longer than it may be worth while to wait for it ... [but] painful experience has taught me that in deciding a question like the present, the chance of death ought not to be excluded from the calculation ...†

These apparently are all the children of Zora, the slave of the Begum.' Is this correct? Almost certainly not. Russell's *bibi* may well have had some connection with the Begum, as we know Khair intervened on the girl's behalf when she first became pregnant, but Zora is in Calcutta with the Begums on p.219, where she becomes pregnant, while Russell's 'girl' has apparently remained throughout in Hyderabad. It is quite possible nonetheless that Russell's 'girl' may originally have been a slave of the Begum, before entering his *zenana*. If so, as she was already the mother of his little boy, she must have been given to Russell by the Begum during the lifetime of James. It is all very intriguing. But very unclear.

* Barlow (1762–1847) was the senior member of Wellesley's Council, and enthusiastically supported the latter's aggressive policy, writing: 'No native state should be left to exist in India which is not upheld by the British power, or the political conduct of which is not under its absolute control.' Sir Penderel Moon describes him as 'by nature a time server' and 'lacking in breadth of vision'. *The British Conquest and Dominion of India*, p.347.

† In other words, Russell hoped that Sydenham might die young, as James (and indeed, that very month, Sydenham's English wife) had just done, so allowing Russell to step into his shoes as Resident.

Having tried to explain the purported reason for his sudden change of plan, Russell then, as discreetly as possible, drops a heavy hint about what has happened in his relationship with Khair un-Nissa:

> The Begum having performed her intention of visiting the poor Colonel's tomb, and finding herself melancholy and lonesome without the society of the friends and relations with whom she was accustomed to live, has gladly determined to avail herself of the security of my convoy to return to Hyderabad. After having resided so long among us, and having been accustomed since the poor Colonels death to look up to me entirely for protection and support, she wished, in addition to the house of the family in the city, to have one near me.
>
> I have therefore purchased for her Uzeez Oolah's *Shadee Khana*, the zenana which he gave to his nephew Ibrahim when he was about to leave Hyderabad, and the enclosure near the large mill containing the *Bawuraha Khana*, *Movigh Khana*, and other offices and accommodations for servants. Some or all of these houses are, I believe, occupied by Captain Sydenham's Moonshee or his friends. Tell them I shall be very sorry to put them to any inconvenience, and that they are perfectly welcome to continue in the houses that I have bought until my arrival within a few marches of Hyderabad, when of course it will be necessary to have them cleaned and repaired for the Begum's reception.

Having gently dropped into the middle of the letter the news that he had bought the Begum a *zenana* next to his own Residency bungalow, Russell goes on to reveal that Khair un-Nissa was very nervous about the security of her estates under Mir Alam. Her affair with James had, after all, led to the Mir's disgrace six years earlier, and in his violent treatment of both Aristu Jah's widow and the former Minister's close political allies, the Mir had already shown his appetite for revenging himself on those who had brought exile and disgrace on him at that time. Khair thus had every reason to worry that since James's death she was vulnerable to her cousin's schemes of vengeance, and at the very least could expect that her estates, given to her at the time of her marriage by Aristu Jah, might now be seized by his successor. For this reason, in an earlier letter, she seems to have persuaded Russell to ask Sydenham to use his influence as Resident to guarantee her estates and her income. Sydenham had agreed to this, and Russell now ended the letter by telling Charles:

> I have communicated to the Begum that part of your letter of the 22nd ultimo which contained Captain Sydenham's handsome and satisfactory assurance of protecting her jagheer and property. She is not less sensible of his kindness than I am; and she desires that when you express her gratitude to him, you will assure him that she will never abuse his kindness by troubling him with applications. She [now] does not seem to have any fears that her jaghires and property will be lapsed to the Nizam; and at all events, an attempt to encroach on them would be the only occasion that could induce her to request the interference of Captain Sydenham . . .[40]

The response to this letter was not long in coming. Despite his careful wording, no one in Hyderabad – least of all Sydenham – seems to have had any doubts about the nature of the 'protection' Russell was offering the Begum. Nor did the new Resident have any doubts as to Russell's motives in wanting Khair installed in a *zenana* within easy reach of his bungalow. In both cases Sydenham's suspicions proved entirely correct: though it was not something Russell yet felt able openly to admit, thrown together in the house in Calcutta by James's death, he and Khair un-Nissa had indeed become lovers.

Three weeks later, when Sydenham's reply reached him, Russell had not yet set off from Calcutta and was still making preparations for his overland journey back to Hyderabad. His preparations were not going to plan, and he had been forced to put off his departure as he grappled with the massive task of arranging a full complement of tents, elephants, carriage bullocks and an armed escort. He cannot have been very surprised by what he read in Sydenham's letter, but nevertheless both he and Khair must have been bitterly disappointed by it.

In his reply to Russell, Sydenham makes it quite clear that he does indeed have a 'serious objection' to the plan of the Begum returning

to the Residency, with the political repercussions this could cause.*
He also remarks that Russell's plan would hardly be a very satisfactory
solution to the Begum's needs as, 'after occupying the Rang Mahal
and living in a state of comparative Opulence and Splendour, it
must be distressing to her own feelings to be placed in the local
remembrance of all her former Enjoyment, at one of the Moonshies
dwellings'. It would, in other words, represent a considerable
demotion for the Begum: from Lady of the Manor to what Sydenham
regarded as a residence behind the green baize door. To soften this
blow, the new Resident added:

> At the same time I beg you to assure her that, if she determines
> in returning to Hyderabad, I will consider her under the pro-
> tection and safeguard of the British Residency, that I will pay
> her every Attention and Respect in my Power; & that she may
> depend on my fullest assistance & support in securing her
> from every possible Inconvenience and Danger. If she requires
> any assurances from Mir Allum and his family, I will readily
> procure them, and I will take care that these assurances shall
> be meticulously fulfilled. She has only to point out how I
> can be useful to her, and she may rely on my most zealous
> exertions.[41]

This was an important and unexpectedly explicit guarantee of full
protection, and must have come as a great relief to Khair. However,
Sydenham appears immediately to have copied these letters, or at
least relayed their contents, both to the acting Governor General in
Calcutta and to Mir Alam in Hyderabad. It was at this stage that
Khair un-Nissa's love-life blew up again into yet another full-scale
scandal.

Sir George Barlow was the first to respond. His letters to Russell
on the subject have been lost, but it is clear that he was horrified by
the new development. Worried by the possibility of Khair un-Nissa
causing yet another breach in Anglo–Hyderabadi relations, he went
as far as attempting to forbid the Begum from ever returning to
Hyderabad at all. In a letter to Sydenham he cited the recent mutiny

---

* The first half of this letter has been cut out with a pair of scissors and appears to have
been deliberately censored, either by Russell himself or by his daughter-in-law Constance.

of sepoys at Vellore, and claimed that 'the connexion of native women with European officers having been urged by the troops on the coast as one of the causes of the disaffection, it might be dangerous to recall to their minds so conspicuous an instance as that afforded by the connexion of Col Kirkpatrick with a female of the Begum's rank and family'.[42] This was an extremely dubious assertion, and one that even Sydenham thought stretched credibility.* But the ban on Khair leaving Calcutta remained in place.

A desperate Henry Russell was forced to go to Government House to plead on the Begum's behalf with Barlow's Private Secretary, Neil Edmonstone, himself something of a Persian scholar and (discreetly)

---

* The 1806 Vellore Mutiny was in fact caused by the Madras sepoys' suspicions that there were plans afoot forcibly to convert them to Christianity. Their fears were provoked by a new set of army regulations designed to regularise the appearance of the men, requiring them to shave their beards, trim their moustaches and to give up wearing earrings or painted marks on their foreheads. They were also required to wear a new type of turban, very much resembling a hat, an object closely associated with Europeans and Indian converts to Christianity. The mutiny was quickly put down and the Madras authorities, in an attempt to cover up their own blunders, advanced the theory that it was part of a widespread 'Muhammedan Plot' to expel the British, a claim that was later shown to be an invention (not least because most of the mutineers were Hindu); but thanks to the confusion caused by the idea of the Plot, the new regulations were never rescinded, and similar orders spread across the Company's army. The fear of conversion to Christianity among the Company's sepoys was one of the principal causes of the Great Mutiny (or, to Indians, the First War of Independence) in 1857. The new regulations, incidentally, galvanised 'Hindoo Stuart' into action for the first time when he defended the sepoys' right to appear on parade with their brightly painted caste-marks and full Rajput moustaches. Indeed he had already, in 1798, published a tract calling for all Company troops in India, British and Indian, to adopt a turban, Mughal-style *jama* and curved scimitar as their uniform, as well as growing a proper display of facial hair: 'I dare not yet propose, that our Officers should wear Mustachoes, though they certainly give a very manly air to the countenance;– but as Malborough's are now become very fashionable in the army, I do not despair of soon seeing the hair upon the lip. How often, when passing along in my palankeen, have mendicants supplicated me for charity by the appellation of *Beeby Sauheb* – mistaking my sex, from the smoothness of my face.' The issue was eventually taken up as high as the commander-in-chief, who criticised Stuart for his 'peculiar notions' and for allowing his men to effect a 'preposterous overgrowth of facial hair of Cheek Moustaches and immoderately large whiskers or Malboroughs', which, he maintained, undermined discipline and multiplied the religious prejudices of the sepoys, which 'were already numerous enough and sufficiently embarrassing to the Publick service'. See Hindoo Stuart's anonymously published tract *Observations And Remarks On The Dress, Discipline, &C. Of The Military By A Bengal Officer* (Calcutta, 1798). For his rebuke by the commander-in-chief see OIOC, IOR/P/Ben/Sec/ 253, Fort William, 17 December 1813, No. 39, Re. Regimental Orders By Lt. Col. Stuart, Futtyghur, 2 July 1813. For the Vellore Mutiny see Sir Penderel Moon, *The British Conquest and Dominion of India*, pp.359–61.

the father of an Anglo-Indian family. Russell pointed out 'the painful and cruel situation to which the Begum would be reduced by being detained in Calcutta, and the difficulty she would find in returning to her family at any future time'.[43] This argument had little impact on Edmonstone. As Russell later wrote to his brother, 'All this he acknowledged, but still he said that the objection which had suggested itself to Sir George Barlow's mind being of a public nature he would not suffer any considerations of individual hardship to be opposed to it.' Russell then lost his temper and angrily pointed out that Barlow had no jurisdiction over Khair, a subject of the Nizam of Hyderabad, and so was hardly in any position to order her to remain in Calcutta. Edmonstone coolly replied that he would convey Russell's argument to the Governor General. On Christmas Eve 1806, Russell received a curt note from Government House stating Barlow's conclusion on the matter:

> My dear Sir,
> On a consideration of all the circumstances of the case, the Governor General withdraws his objections to the lady's proceeding to Hyderabad. But he considers it necessary for political reasons that she should not be deemed to be in any way under the immediate protection of the British Government. She may return to Hyderabad and live under the protection of her own family. Any pledge of protection on the part of the British Govt might eventually be productive of great embarrassment. I have instructions to write to Capt Sydenham on the subject,
> > I am ever, dear sir,
> > Yours most sincerely
> > NB Edmonstone[44]

That night Russell finalised his preparations for departure, and scribbled a last, conciliatory note to Sydenham, saying that he wished to

> assure you that neither the Begum nor I will ever trouble you with any Requests which, under the letter you will have received from Mr. Edmonstone, you might think improper. She wishes to live as quietly and as much retired as possible with her mother and grandmother, and she does not appear

to be apprehensive of danger from any quarter. Perhaps indeed
Mir Allum might occasion her some difficulty and uneasiness
if a declaration were explicitly made to him that she would
not receive any protection from you. But such a declaration
cannot under any circumstances be necessary and I am sure
your own kindness and your regard for the memory of Colonel
Kirkpatrick would alone be sufficient to restrain you from
making it.[45]

Khair and Henry bade goodbye to the two *munshis*, Aziz and Aman
Ullah, who were setting off into retirement by the banks of the Ganges
at Benares. The following morning the two lovers nervously set off
on their journey to Hyderabad.

It was a journey that they would never complete.

For over three months, Russell and Khair, accompanied by Sharaf
un-Nissa and the Begum's household, travelled slowly down the now-
familiar spine of the Eastern Ghats, between the teak forests of the
hills and the white breakers of the Bay of Bengal.

With little to look forward to in their return to Hyderabad, they
took their time about the journey. Their progress slowed even further
after an express message from Sydenham reached them on the road
sometime at the end of January. The Resident had received Barlow's
orders, and explained that regrettably he was now forced to withdraw
his offer of protection for Khair. He claimed to have 'rejoiced' that
Russell had been able 'to overcome the Governor General's objections
to the Begum's Return to this Place', adding: 'As a question of mere
policy, I should certainly prefer the Begum to remain in some part
of Company's Territories; but as she felt such repugnance at that
plan, I do not foresee that there will be any unpleasant consequences
to her return to Hyderabad, provided she remains in the City under
the protection of her own Family and Friends . . . I am told that the

houses, both of the mother and Grandmother of the Begum are in good repair and sufficiently convenient; and I should imagine that one of them would be the proper place of Residence for the Begum herself.' But Sydenham then added what was in effect a new condition to Russell's return, further impeding his and Khair's hopes.

> I hope you are prepared to relinquish all personal intercourse with the Begum after her Establishment in the City. I know that Meer Allum will expect that she should not see you, and his objections are natural enough when the customs and prejudices of the Moosulmen respecting their women are considered. I have already informed you that the people in the city of every Description have misconceived notions of the Nature of your Protection which you have afforded to the Begum and there is no doubt that your visits will confirm their notions.[46]

Rather stiffly, the very English Sydenham then added as a post-script: 'P.S.: If such a message be not inconsistent with Propriety I beg you will make my Compliments to the Begum,' before noting that: 'Sir H Russell [Henry's father, the Chief Justice] had once the Goodness to spare me a canister of his excellent snuff. Do you think you could prevail upon his kindness to repeat such a sacrifice?

Just to rub salt in Russell's wounds, there soon appeared a second express letter, this time from his old enemy, Captain Hemming. It was short and to the point. Hemming wrote that he had just had breakfast with the Begum's brother, Dustee Ali Khan,* and he wanted to make a few things quite clear to Russell: 'It is not impertinent curiosity that makes me ask you if you are prepared to take leave of the Begum the day you arrive, probably never to see her again. I don't mean to say that her life would be in any danger residing in the city. But I am sure that all intercourse between you will be interdicted by Meer Alum . . .'[47]

Knowing now for sure that their affair would have to end once

---

* Dustee Ali Khan is not mentioned in any other source, and the *Nagaristan i-Asafiya* explicitly speaks of Sharaf un-Nissa having only two daughters. He was therefore probably Khair un-Nissa's half-brother – in other words Mehdi Yar Khan's son by a different wife or concubine.

they arrived at their destination, the two lovers slowed their progress even further. An express runner could make the journey from Calcutta to Masulipatam in under two weeks (something that amazed Abdul Lateef Shushtari, and which he compared to the old Sufi tales of saints being able to fly at will from one end of India to another*), but on this journey Russell and Khair took over twelve. They were clearly in no hurry to resume their separate lives.

By the end of March the two had passed Masulipatam and were only a week's journey from Hyderabad, when they stopped for three days to allow the Begum's party and Russell's own Muslim servants to celebrate Muharram. Their tents were still pitched by the banks of the Krishna when another express courier cantered into the camp bringing yet another urgent letter, this time from Charles Russell. Again it contained bad news. Mir Alam had at last reacted to the news of Henry's 'protection' of his cousin. In a conversation with Sydenham the new Minister had made it chillingly clear that Khair un-Nissa was a disgrace to her family and that she would not be welcome back in Hyderabad. The vehemence with which the Mir had said this made it quite apparent what it meant. It would not be safe for Khair to return. If she did her life would be in danger.

This was of course the worst possible news; but there seemed no way of getting around it. Now that Sydenham had been forbidden by Calcutta to offer any protection whatsoever to Khair un-Nissa, she had to make a simple choice: either to return and risk Mir Alam's desire for vengeance, or to settle elsewhere. As Russell wrote back to his brother, he had expected that if he had left the Begum alone she would have been

---

* Shushtari once made the journey by the government dak, and was astonished: 'The Governor, as a token of respect, arranged for me to travel by Dak post-horse from Calcutta to Machli-bandar. At every 2 *farsakhs* [leagues] 14 escorts were waiting ready: 8 to carry the litter on their shoulders, travelling faster than a rapidly trotting horse; 2 to carry the food; 2 to carry torches which they lit after dark; 1 guide; and 1 drummer. I reached Machli-bandar from Calcutta in the space of 15 days, a journey which would otherwise have taken two and a half months. In truth, the miracle of *taiy al-arz* [instant global travel] ascribed to the Sufis in the books is to be found here and only in this manner! We travelled mostly at night, but even by day we never stopped, so I found out little about the country through which we passed. Only when the drum sounded did we stop for a picnic, but the movement of the porters had upset my stomach and I had no taste for food, especially not for meat or anything cooked. Everywhere we reached, by

suffered to live quietly and securely with her family, and that she would not have anything to dread from Meer Alum. But I infer from a part of your letter that you apprehend that the spirit of malignity and revenge by which the Meer is still actuated towards the Begum [appears to be] so active as to urge him to the adoption of measures of such severity, that the influence of Capt Sydenham – confined [now] by the restrictions imposed on him by the Gov. General – would be insufficient to protect her ... If I have accurately conceived your meaning, and you still think your apprehensions are well founded, it is absolutely necessary that I should resort to the only means still in my power to preserve the Begum, by recommending her to stay in some part of the Company's Territories.

He then, rather belatedly, apologised to Charles for not having been more open with him about his relationship with Khair: 'You are more than justified in censuring me for not having communicated to you what passed respecting the Begum before I left Calcutta ... I thought it probable that you would not hear that anything had passed until I arrived in Hyderabad, and that I should have had an opportunity of personally talking the matter over with you.'[48]

For three weeks, Russell and Khair remained stationary in their temporary encampment, apparently torn by indecision. Russell wrote to Sydenham and Charles to try to find some way around the impasse. Eventually, however, it became clear that there was no choice. In the second week of April Charles wrote again to Henry. The rumours of Khair un-Nissa's affair with him had been the final straw. The situation was hopeless. Mir Alam's mind was made up. Khair could not return. She had to find somewhere else to live, outside the Nizam's dominions.

The worst had happened. Mir Alam had decided formally to banish Khair un-Nissa from Hyderabad. Already a widow at the age of nineteen, the Begum was now, in addition to that, at twenty, an exile, a refugee.

---

day or by night, the Company's servants were ready to welcome us and offer us repose.'
Abdul Lateef Shushtari, *Tuhfat al-'Alam*, pp.564–70.

On 14 April 1807 Henry wrote back to his brother, telling him of the decision he and Khair had finally made: 'Your letter has convinced me that [Khair un-Nissa] would be exposed to great danger at Hyderabad.' He explained that he read Charles's letter to the two Begums, who 'notwithstanding the desire they had both felt to return to Hyderabad, and the repugnance they had always evinced against remaining in the Company's Territories, both resolved, without any further advice or persuasion from me, to relinquish their original plan, and to settle, for the present at least, at Masulipatam'. He added: 'Whether Residence there, or in any other part of the Company's country, will be permanent, or whether it will continue only during the life of Meer Allum, is a question of which the decision must depend on various circumstances which may hereafter come to pass. At all events they will be secure from danger at Masulipatam; and to that important consideration that of mere comfort must of course be sacrificed.'[49]

Russell went on to say that he had written to the Company's agent in Masulipatam, Major Alexander, 'directing him to prepare the best house that can be got for the reception of the Begum, and I shall myself accompany her to Masulipatam. I shall stay there only a few days, to see her comfortably settled, and to make such arrangements as may be necessary for her establishment, and shall then run on by dawke [i.e. as fast as possible] to Hyderabad ... I hope I shall get [there] during the first week in May.'

He also gave detailed instructions to his brother about how he was to break the news to Durdanah Begum without unduly alarming the old lady:

The enclosed letter will communicate to the old begum the changes which her daughter and grand daughter have made

in their plans; but it would have been improvident to inform
her of their real motives. We have therefore imputed it to a
whimsical spirit of opposition in the poor little Begum, and
have left the letter open, that you may take your line from it.
When you have read it, close it and give it to the old lady.
You must also make the necessary communication to Capt.
Sydenham. I have little doubt that both you and he will
approve of the Begum's determination.

It is at this stage that a note of ambiguity enters Russell's
letter. Up to now, he seems, like James before him, to have been
prepared to risk his career to save his relationship with Khair. He
had, after all, stood up to Neil Edmonstone and made the Governor
General change his ruling that the Begum should remain in exile
in Calcutta. But Henry Russell was a very different man to James
Kirkpatrick. He had clearly been flattered by the Begum's attentions, and had perhaps been mildly surprised to find himself in
bed with his former principal's wife. But there were limits to how
far he was prepared to let such considerations get in the way of his
career.

Such was Russell's conceit that he seemed temperamentally incapable of taking in how culpable he was in the wrecking of Khair's
future: far from dwelling on what he had brought about – the final
destruction of her reputation, her banishment and exile – he instead
wrote to his brother patting himself on the back and remarking: 'It
will be gratifying to me to reflect that I shall have placed the Begum
beyond the Reach of Danger, and myself beyond the necessity of
asking favours from Captain Sydenham. I shall now feel perfectly
independent of him; and I am sure that nothing will contribute so
assuredly of our living on good terms together, as my never having
occasion to ask him for anything.'

Already it was clear that his main concern was less 'the poor little
Begum' than his own ease and reputation. As he explained to Charles:
'the interests of both of us [i.e. the two Russell brothers] require that
we should adopt the most decisive measures in our power to contra-
dict the reports, whether idle or malicious, which seem to prevail so
generally at Hyderabad'.[50]

A week later, Russell, Khair and their attendants had arrived back at the hot, humid harbour town of Masulipatam.

Masulipatam had once been the principal trading station of the Coromandel coast, and in the seventeenth century had grown to become a port of international importance, providing access to the rich bazaars of the kingdom of Golconda at the peak of its power and influence. It was also one of the earliest outposts of both the English and the Dutch East India Companies.* But it had long been overtaken by both Madras and Vizagapatam, and its fate was sealed after it was sacked and burned to the ground first by Aurangzeb in 1661, then again by the Marathas in a raid in the mid-eighteenth century. It was finally overwhelmed by a cataclysmic cyclone which had swept over its sea walls only seven years before Russell and Khair's arrival, during the monsoon of 1800.

By 1807 therefore, this once bustling port had shrunk to a small, ramshackle place, with a crumbling fort, a newly rebuilt English church and a graveyard quickly filling up with the victims of its endemic malarial mosquitoes, inhabitants of the undrained salt marshes to the west of the town.† Three miles to the south, across

---

* And as such, the scene of some of the earliest and wildest English debauches in India. For example, in December 1619 William Methwold reported from Masulipatam that the Company's staff had broken into a series of toddy shacks and port-side bordellos and generally 'behaved [so much] like barbarous outlaws that I feare our nation, formerly well reputed of, will suffer a perpetuall scandal for their most intolerable misdemeanours'. Seven years later, President Hawley, Methwold's successor, finding his Masulipatam staff equally intractable, called for the factory to be 'maintained with civill, sober men', and ordered that 'negligent or debauched persons or common drunkards should be discarded'. See William Foster (ed.), *The English Factories in India* (13 vols, London, 1906–27), Vol. 1, p.153.

† Masulipatam was always a notoriously pestiliential place, and the records of its early factors are full of sad tales of new arrivals dying within weeks of landing: 'This is so sickly a place,' we read, 'that it is very rare to have all of us well at the same time.' Or again: 'The Council taking into consideration the unhealthfulness of the place and the uncertainty of man's frail life and duration in this world, doe order that those who are

the causeway from the English Civil Lines, the port's deep-water harbour was slowly silting up, and was remarkable now less for its trading than its fishing fleet, after which it had become known locally as Machli-patnam, or Fish Town. The name stuck,* partly no doubt because of the strong stench generated by the huge catch brought in every morning by the port's flotilla of small wooden catamaran-canoes, and the overpowering odour of the small fry left out on the sand of its beaches to dry in the sun.

The fishermen here were of the lowest castes, dark-skinned untouchables; the English community was small; and there was no Mughlai society to mention.† Even the town's Nawab, James Dalrymple's brother-in-law, had left the place and settled in the more lively atmosphere of Madras, a hundred miles to the south.[51] A Dutch visitor at about this time reported that in addition to the all-pervading smell of fish, the swampy morass outside the city walls emitted an unbearable stench in dry weather, and the heat was so 'insufferable that one can neither read, nor write, nor think'.[52] Masulipatam was, in short, not a place Khair or her mother would ever naturally have chosen to live, which presumably indicated that both women at this stage believed that their exile would be of short duration.

On arrival, Khair and Russell pitched their tents in a garden belonging to Alexander, the Company's elderly and rather fussy agent (Russell refers to him in his letters as 'Old Mother Alexander'), in the shadow of his two-storey mansion. With Alexander's help they set about trying to find temporary accommodation for Khair, rejecting the Nawab's house as 'too extensive' and settling instead on a more modest bungalow: 'I hope to settle everything about it in

---

in perfect health doe negotiate and carry on the business for those that are indisposed.' See Dodwell, *Nabobs of Madras*, p.109.

* Masulipatam is now officially known as Machlipatnam, which is the name (alternating sometimes with Machlibandar) by which it appears to have been called locally since at least the eighteenth century.

† There were a few Mughal and Persian merchants, generally descendants of old trading families who had lived in Masulipatam for centuries, and who still combined a little Haj traffic from Hyderabad with some textile trade to Jeddah and a few of the Persian ports. See Sinnappah Arasaratnam and Aniruddha Ray, *Masulipatam and Cambay: A History of Two Port Towns 1500–1800* (New Delhi, 1994), p.116. Also Shah Mazur Alam, 'Masulipatam: A Metropolitan Port in the Seventeenth Century', in Mohamed Taher (ed.), *Muslim Rule in the Deccan* (New Delhi, 1997), pp.145–63.

the course of tomorrow,' wrote Russell, 'and the next day, and to have the house cleaned out, and prepared for the Begum's reception, by the first of the month. At all events there is every prospect that she will be comfortably situated; more so perhaps than she would have been at any other place in the Company's territory . . .'

Yet again, Russell's tone seems somehow inadequate to the desperation of the occasion. There are no notes of regret, anguish or contrition in his letters, instead merely the passing observation that 'As far as I can tell the society here is not very good. People live mostly to themselves.' This was an understatement of the first order: there was not one person in Masulipatam with whom either Begum was likely to make friends. There was nothing to do and little to see. It was hot and it smelt. Russell himself seems to have been anxious to leave the town as quickly as possible, and in his letters at least, spares little time worrying about Khair's life in such an unpleasant backwater.

More insensitive still are his remarks to Charles, who had just informed him by despatch that Henry's *bibi* in Hyderabad had given birth to a baby girl prematurely, and that the child looked unlikely to survive. Russell's reaction is chilling: 'I am sorry for the account you give me of the probability of losing my little girl,' he writes, 'but it would be hypocrisy to pretend that it had afflicted me deeply. Even the loss of an infant that we have seen, we lament only in proportion to the love we bear its mother; and the death therefore of a child, whom not only have we never seen, but whose mother was never an object of attachment, cannot be regarded as a misfortune of very serious magnitude.' Then with barely a pause he continues, having apparently dismissed the *bibi*, the dying baby girl and Khair from his mind: 'I have not a book to read in my palanquin between here and Hyderabad. Despatch me one *immediately by dawke* and if you cannot find a better, send me *Madam Europe*.' The letter reveals the small sliver of ice in Russell's heart, a compound of self-centredness, conceit and insensitivity, qualities that became increasingly evident in the months to come.

A week later, Russell had apparently installed the Begum in her new house, looking onto the palms, fishing canoes and breakers of the Coromandel coast; but the only explicit mention he makes of her in his letter to Charles is to note that 'If I can, I shall dispose of some of my bullocks here. The Begum's baggage has left a great many unladen, and it would be a needless expense to feed all the bullocks between here and Hyderabad.'[53]

The next day he was gone, heading back to Hyderabad as fast as his palanquin-bearers could carry him. Behind him he left the weeping Begum, in exile, in a strange town, with only her mother for company, and convinced, from a dream she had had, that she and Russell would never meet again.[54]

And with that, there is a gap in Russell's correspondence for eight whole months. There is no indication of how Khair un-Nissa passed the time, what her feelings were, her mood, or her hopes, or her fears; but it is not difficult to imagine them.

When the letters resume, it is January 1808, and Henry Russell is back in Masulipatam for a fortnight's visit, on his way between Hyderabad and a new posting in Madras. He is flattered and pleased by Khair's rapturous reception of him: 'Dear Khyroo is all kindness and attention,' he tells Charles,

> and seems quite as much delighted to see me as I am to see her; more so she could not be. She is pleased at my appointment to Madras, because it has offered us the opportunity of meeting; and as we have once met after our separation, she appears to have got rid of her superstitious dread she formerly had, that we were not to meet again. I hope therefore that she will not feel my going to Madras so acutely as she felt my going to Hyderabad, and that she will trust to the same good fortune which has brought us together once, bringing us together again.

He goes onto the describe the situation of the two Begums:

I found both the Begum and her mother well. They appear
to be in excellent health, the old lady better perhaps than
when she first came here; and their spirits are as good as
could possibly be expected. The house they moved into after
I left them, is a much better one than [that] in which they
lived at first. They occupy the upper storey only, which makes
them quite private and retired, and gives them the advantage
of fresh air and a good prospect: the whole of their lower
apartments is appropriated to their baggage and servants;
and they have a Havildar's guards, which while perhaps
unnecessary, is so far of use in that it confirms their notion
of security.[55]

Russell's letter also inadvertently reveals why he had had to leave
Hyderabad. In Masulipatam, where he was staying with an old soldier
friend, formerly of the Subsidiary Force, he dines with his host, and
later in the fort, and is pleased and evidently surprised to discover
that 'every lady seems anxious to be as attentive as they can; and
what is very satisfactory, as far as I can judge from appearances, I
am not here a subject of scandal'. This, it is apparent, was a welcome
change from Hyderabad, where his position at the Residency had
become untenable due to the rumours circulating in both the city
and English society about his relationship with the Begum.

All he now wants in Madras, he says, is 'to be as quiet as possible,
and although I cannot lull the tongue of slander, I will not stimulate
it. If any of the reports invented or circulated by my friends at
Hyderabad appear to you to be of such a nature that I ought to
know them, for the reputation of my conduct on any point relating
to the Begum, of course you will mention them to me – otherwise
do not say anything about them. They would irritate and vex me
without doing any good.' In the meantime, he is pleased to discover
that in Masulipatam 'every lady appears to take an interest in the
Begum, and to speak of her with the greatest respect and consideration'.[56]

As for Khair herself, Russell's letter reveals that she is relieved that
she is still getting the money from her estates, and has only one deep
desire: that she should get back the portrait of her children, which

George Chinnery seems to have borrowed in Calcutta, and which, despite her repeated pleas, he is apparently unwilling to send back to her. Russell asks his brother to write to their father, the Chief Justice, then sitting for Chinnery himself, and to tell him 'that the Begum is exceedingly anxious to receive the picture and has written to you very urgently on the subject'. There is no indication that Khair has heard a word from her children since they embarked for England two and half years earlier. The picture is still her only link with what she has lost.

The rest of Russell's letters from Masulipatam are filled with making plans. Sharaf un-Nissa wants to visit Hyderabad over Muharram to petition Mir Alam on her daughter's behalf at that most auspicious time of year, and Russell asks his brother to make the necessary arrangements for an escort: 'She will travel in her palanquin, with a single set of bearers; and as she will be only a few days on the road, she will not encumber herself with any tents or baggage, beyond two or three bungies [wagons].'

Finally he asks Charles to help him keep in touch with the Begum. He anticipates trouble finding a good Persian *munshi* in the very English world of Madras, and certainly no one who could safely be entrusted with the delicate task of writing his love letters to the Begum. He is also keen to avoid any cause for scandal in Madras, and therefore asks his brother a favour. In case he finds writing to Khair impossible, could Charles now begin writing to her, passing on his news? He is worried about Khair, and about her spirits, especially once her mother leaves and she is left on her own. If Charles could write,

> I shall be able to assure the Begum, through you, that I am well, and that my silence does not proceed from any cause that ought to make her uneasy.
>
> On all these accounts it is particularly desirable that from here forward you should continue to correspond with the Begum as regularly as I did; and although the benefits of such rigid punctuality may sometimes prove troublesome, I am sure you will submit to it for the sake of giving the Begum so much comfort and satisfaction as she will derive from it.

I wrote to her every third day, and never on any account allowed an interruption to take place. If I was busy I wrote a single line to say so, and *that* she always thought enough; and if I was to be out all day on the letter day, I wrote a few lines overnight, saying so, and left them to be despatched by the dawke as usual.

Let me intreat you, my dearest Charles, to persevere in this plan; and be assured that constant and persevering regularity in correspondence is the greatest blessing you can confer upon an absent friend. Many people neglect to write at all if they are busy, because they think it indispensable to write a long letter; but this a very erroneous idea. A single hearty line on a regular day to say that you are busy, and cannot write more, is infinitely superior in value to the longest letter on a later day. Bear this in mind, and recollect that the Begum is of that frame of mind, and is so situated, that to her of all people in the world, this principle is most peculiarly applicable.

If he has any trouble, suggests Henry, he should consult Aziz Ullah's old assistant, the Qazi, who is back at work at the Residency, and who

knows my plan of correspondence every bit as much as I knew it myself, and can always tell you what I was accustomed to do on any particular occasion. He is also perfectly acquainted too with the terms and modes of address that you ought to use. I have explained all that I have written to you on this subject to the Begum, who desires me just to add a request from her, that whenever my letters for her reach you from Madras, you will despatch them to Masulipatam by the very first dawke without thinking it necessary to detain them until you have prepared a letter from yourself...

This is a new side to Khair un-Nissa, one we have not seen before. We have seen her strength and resilience, and her warmth and charm; but never has she sounded so vulnerable, so badly in need of reassurance, so badly in need of love.

And with that, again, Russell is gone, and the curtain descends on both him and the Begum for a further three months.

When we next catch a glimpse of Russell, he is in the middle of a very different world.

Madras in 1808 was a somewhat provincial place compared to Calcutta, at least in terms of power and trade; but it nonetheless prided itself on being a politer, more elegant and refined city than its brash, debauched Bengali rival. Its layout was quite different to that of other British cities in India, being spread over a far wider area with low, white, classical garden houses dotted for miles over the plane which lay between the fort and St Thomas's Mount. As one visitor reported a few years later, few Englishmen lived in Madras proper, instead they preferred 'country houses scattered for miles through the interior, and even the shopkeepers who can afford it have detached bungalows for their families'. The hub of the city, around the fort, was a no less singular sight. Thirty years earlier, when the artist William Hodges landed on the surf below Fort George, he wrote that its 'long colonnades, open porticoes and flat roofs offer the eye an appearance similar to what we may conceive of a Grecian city in the age of Alexander. The clear, blue, cloudless sky, the polished white buildings, the bright sandy beach and the dark green sea present a combination totally new to the eye of an Englishman.'

By 1808 Madras had become famous for its social life, and especially for the fact that there seemed to be a much larger proportion of European women to men than at Calcutta. There was the huge new banqueting hall at the Governor's House, with an interior so vast that Lord Valentia thought he and his fellow guests 'looked like pigmies' as they reeled and waltzed. There was the Madras Hunting Society and the annual races below the Mount; a series of good schools, including 'a seminary for young ladies modelled on Miss Pinkerton's in Chiswick Mall', where classes full of young British memsahibs-to-be were taught 'reading, writing, arithmetic, history, the use of globes, French, Greek and Latin'. Even the city's alehouses were relatively respectable places, with *pukka* names like the Old London Tavern and the King's Arms. Not far from the elegant spire of St Mary's, the seventeenth-century fort church, lay for example the celebrated Fort Tavern, which served 'soups every morning, and dinners dressed on the shortest notice, and the very best wines'. It was a far cry from the pelleting punch-houses of William Hickey's Calcutta.[57]*

For the last few years Henry Russell had been enveloped in the Mughal society of Hyderabad. Now he found himself warming to the pleasures of a busy and very British Presidency town like Madras. He was after all intelligent, good-looking and rich; in short a thoroughly desirable bachelor. This was something he was himself only too well aware of: 'I see that the people at Madras have marked me as an eligible object,' he wrote a few weeks after his arrival, 'and that they observe rather minutely to whom my attentions are principally pointed; but I am thoroughly on my guard and always take care to divide my civilities equally.'[58]

By March, Henry was boarding with James Kirkpatrick's aunt and uncle the Petries, while he looked around rather half-heartedly for a house of his own. His letters are now full of dinners, races and horses: 'The Madras plate was won by McDowell's Bacchus, a small bay horse that he got out of Abdool Luteef,' he tells Charles in one letter, adding with some pride, 'With the exception of the three parties Mrs Petrie had at home, I have dined out every night since I arrived here, and frequently I have had three or four invitations for the same day. The dinners are generally pretty good, everybody appears anxious to be as civil and attentive as they possibly can . . .'[59]

In this social swirl, Russell made friends quickly, and took an especial liking, somewhat surprisingly, to the odious Mrs Samuel Dalrymple who had accompanied James on his last boat journey to

---

* Though Madras was certainly not a completely innocent place. There were darker corners of town, such as the Griffin Inn ('Griffin' being eighteenth-century slang for a newcomer to India), where a 'sneaker of grog' could be obtained for as little as three fanams and a bowl of punch for five, and where the Madras press regularly complained about the landlord's 'stale beer, sour claret and rotten hams'. See Dodwell, *Nabobs of Madras*, pp.217–20.

Calcutta: 'Mrs Dal is my prime favourite,' Russell told his brother, 'but I occasionally throw a handkerchief at another object...' As the weeks went by, he threw himself deeper and deeper into the round of parties and dances, and by mid-April wrote to Charles to tell him he had never been happier, or felt more properly appreciated.* At long last he was receiving the attentions and respect that he had been brought up by his adoring father to believe were his by right: 'I become more pleased with Madras every day,' he wrote,

> and the more I see of the society and the people, the more I like them. My situation and my connexions (shall I add my manner and my appearance?) naturally contribute to ensure me a kind and general reception ... In the gaiety and dissipation of an extensive society I do not think that I ever enjoyed myself so much as now I do at Madras. When I find myself laughing, and flirting, and entering heartily into all the fun that is going on, I almost forget the solemn reserve and steadiness of the Secretary. The Dalrymples and all my old friends tell me that I am the most altered being in the world, and Gould says that nothing can be more unlike what I am to the sullen, silent politician that was described to him in Bengal. I now dance, and drink, and laugh and dress, and crack jokes ...

He then makes what is his first reference to the Begum for several weeks:

> However, lest you should entertain any apprehensions of it leading me by the road of flirtation to the temple of love, it may be as well to assure you that my prudence and caution on that subject are unabated, and that any change in my views and sentiments on such a point I should consider a deplorable one indeed. My affections are not, I believe, very

* Russell was especially pleased by the improvements he noticed in his own dancing skills: 'My dancing (though I say it who ought not to say it) appears to me to be as much improved as my manners, and I believe I was as much astonished as everyone else by my own performance. So many fine speeches have been made by the ladies about the acquisition I am to their party, that Gould & Mrs Dal propose to call me "Acquisition Russell".' Bodleian Library, Russell Papers, Ms Eng Letts C156, p.21, 21 April 1808.

easily engaged; but when once fixed, they are steady; and from the quarter where they are at present fixed, I think it would be difficult, I might almost say impossible, to detach them.[60]

Khair had been receiving the odd message from Henry ever since they parted company, but with each month that passed, his letters to Masulipatam were becoming increasingly irregular. Soon there began the first of a succession of complaints from Khair that she was being neglected, complaints that Russell, characteristically, side-stepped, putting the blame on his younger brother and on Sharaf un-Nissa: 'Be very particular too in mentioning me in all your letters to the Begum;' he tells Charles,

> and when you next write say that I am sorry to perceive, from the letters I have lately received from her, that she imputes my silence to forgetfulness. That, she ought to know and believe, is impossible, and she only gives me pain in saying so. She hears of my being well, just as satisfactorily through you as she could hear it from a letter written by any common hand [i.e. professional Persian letter-writer] I could put up here; and it is by no means difficult to imagine that I find it impracticable to get at once a person I could employ to write confidential letters for me.

He goes on to say that Khair is clearly lonely in her mother's absence in Hyderabad, and says that Charles should tell Sharaf un-Nissa to hurry back to her daughter's side in Masulipatam: 'She promised me to stay only a month at Hyderabad, and you must insist on her leaving in the beginning of April. Do not, on any account, permit her to remain beyond that time, even if she should express a desire to do so.'[61]

But despite his protestations to the contrary, there is no doubt that Khair was indeed beginning to move from the centre of Russell's world. It was not just that she appears increasingly infrequently in his letters; there is also a measure of conscious disengagement: when Charles writes to tell his brother that there has been a dispute over the seizure of Bâqar Ali Khan's property – presumably it has been resumed by Mir Alam's government following the old man's death – Henry counsels him not to get involved: 'I do most strongly insist that no consideration whatever may induce you to intervene, on any occasion, on behalf of any member of her family. You would not do so without being liable to a charge of impropriety.'[62]

Henry also fails to react with proper sympathy when Charles and Sharaf un-Nissa both write to tell him that the latter has failed in her attempt to persuade Mir Alam to revoke Khair's banishment. This was a heartbreaking moment for both mother and daughter, the confirmation of all they had feared; but Russell takes it all easily in his stride. Referring to Sharaf's news he remarks merely:

> Her letter was a very good one. It appears she has been kindly received by all those on whose kindness she places any value; and as the coldness and inattention with which the Meer treated her seem not to have given any pain, I am glad that she has been furnished with so strong a practical proof of the insurmountable objections that exist against her daughter's return to Hyderabad. I hope you will take an opportunity of impressing this deeply on her mind, and of inducing her to believe that the Meer still regards even her, as well as her daughter, with sentiments of such virulent and restless asperity as to render their permanent Residence at Hyderabad a source of the most alarming and serious danger to them both.[63]

In a later letter, after Sharaf un-Nissa has headed back to Masulipatam to break the news of Mir Alam's decision to Khair, Russell merely observes: 'I am glad that Shurfoon Nifsa Begum has returned to Masulipatam. The man's conduct towards her has been perfectly consistent, and therefore ought not to cause surprise . . . [and confirms] the necessity of [the Begum] remaining at Masulipatam . . . I think it was discernable [in advance] that the Meer should treat her as he has always done.'[64]

So saying, Russell returns to describing his Madras social life. And as the rounds of parties continue, one figure in particular takes the place of Khair in his correspondence: a beautiful, rich Anglo-Portuguese merchant's daughter. Her name was Jane Casamajor.

Jane is first mentioned as a friend of Thomas Sydenham's younger brother George: 'If George Sydenham is arrived [in Hyderabad],' Henry writes to Charles in March 1808, 'tell him that Jane Casamajor has been alarmingly ill indeed; and though better today, is not yet even pronounced to be out of danger.'[65]

When she recovers, Russell goes to see her: 'Yesterday I called at the Casamajors to congratulate them on the recovery of Jane . . . [She] looked delicate and feeble . . . [and] has been very ill indeed . . . I believe that for several days her medical attendant thought it very precarious which way it would terminate.'[66] Jane eventually made a full recovery, and as March gives way to April she takes up an increasingly large amount of space in Henry's letters. She is, he assures Charles, 'an extremely fine girl and the family is altogether the best at Madras'; but he quickly adds that

> none of their weapons are sharp enough to graze even the surface of my heart . . . I am thoroughly on my guard and always take care to divide my civilities equally so as to prevent them from suspecting that I have a decided preference for anybody . . . At a very pleasant dance at Mrs Oakes's the other night I divided myself between Mrs Dal[rymple] and Jane – while I was with Mrs Dal nobody seemed to observe me particularly; but when I went to Jane, and after flirting an hour with her, handed her to Tupper, I saw a number of sly enquiring looks directed towards me; and the next day a number of people asked me very significantly if I did not think Jane Casamajor a very charming girl.[67]

For the ball, which was a masquerade, Russell had got Charles to send him some of James Kirkpatrick's old Mughal robes, which James had kept at the Begum's house in the old city and which he appears to have worn when he came to relax there, and also at informal occasions at court.[68] There had been moments in Russell's past when it seemed he might have followed James in his journey across cultures; but in the end he was a very different man to his principal. Moreover, and crucially, he was from a very different generation. James was among the last of the English officials in India who found it possible to truly cross cultures. The new Imperial ideas that Wellesley imported from England – ideas which Henry Russell had absorbed when he first arrived in Calcutta – made it increasingly difficult for individuals to make the leap from Britain to India, from Georgian to Mughal, from Christianity to Islam. India was no longer a place to embrace and to be transformed by; instead it was a place to conquer and transform. The British attitudes to Indians and Indian culture that Russell absorbed in the Calcutta of 1800 were never entirely shaken off by his time at James's side in Hyderabad. James had worn his Mughal clothes for everyday use around the Residency and for his other life in Khair un-Nissa's *deorhi* in the old city; now Russell wore them merely as fancy dress. In the brief period separating the two men, an important historical line had been crossed.

Shortly after the ball, Russell writes that he has not visited Jane for nearly a week: 'Excepting once in the evening on the Mount Road, I have not seen Jane since I went there last Sunday. This is Friday. Is not my self command wonderful? But perhaps I shall call there tomorrow morning. It is surely the pleasantest home in Madras . . .'[69]

By the middle of May, rumours about Russell and Jane have reached Charles in Hyderabad, and he writes to his brother to ask if there is any basis in the stories doing the rounds. Henry is horrified, and asks for more information about the detail of this gossip: 'I am now placed in a most cruel and painful predicament; and if her feelings and pride are half so great as mine are I am sure she must feel as distressed as I do' at these stories in circulation, he writes. He goes on to deny having given Jane any grounds for believing he would marry her, and says the rumours Charles has been hearing are wholly incorrect:

You say that you hear that, wherever I dine, Jane Casamajor is invited, that wherever I dance she is my partner; and that in short we are scarcely on any occasion separated from each other ... I shall easily be able to convince you that there is no [basis for any of these stories] ... But how, you will say, if this be correct, is it possible that the report of my having formed an attachment for Jane should have become so prevalent? In the easiest way of the world. My youth, my connexions, my circumstances, and my situation all concur to point me out as the most eligible man in the place (don't laugh) for a woman to marry; and people suppose, naturally enough, that if I admire any lady, I must of course admire the girl who generally speaking is the most admired by everybody else ... to a girl who like Jane who has (whether deservedly or not) the reputation of a leading belle, it is sufficient for me to be a little attentive to set the place agog and to make everybody say it will certainly be a match.[70]

Only a week later, Russell's tone is very different, and he finally admits what has been obvious to everyone in Madras for months. In the middle of a letter to Charles he suddenly bursts out: 'Jane! Dear Jane! What shall I say of her? That I feel my danger growing more imminent every day, and that the swain who deliberates is undone. When I am absent from her I feel that an immediate permanent separation would ultimately eradicate any affection I have formed for her; but in her presence, I am conscious of the influence of a fascination which is altogether irresistible. Of such a separation I see no Prospect.' He tells his brother of a dinner party the night before: 'I said nothing with my tongue that could appear like Love; but I fear my eyes and my manners were beyond my control and that they may have betrayed to anybody who would take the trouble to observe them, that I was far from being insensible to the charms of my companion ... the truth of the matter is that I am in Love ...'

As for the Begum, Henry's mind was clearly made up: 'If anything comes of this flirtation,' he tells Charles breezily, 'I shall request you to take Masulipatam in your way, as you come here; and will, before that time, write to you fully on that subject. The duty you will have to discharge will, I fear, be a very painful and distressing one; but for my sake I am sure you will undertake it.'[71]

Painful and distressing it certainly would be. But not for Henry Russell. The following evening, less than two months after he first met her, he asked Jane Casamajor to marry him.

One month later, on around 20 June 1808, Charles Russell set off from Hyderabad on yet another errand for his brother. This time, however, the task in hand involved a rather longer journey, and a rather more upsetting business, than the fetching and packing of Hyderabadi women's garments, a task on which he had been intermittently engaged on his brother's behalf for the past two years. His job now was to go to Masulipatam and break the news of Henry and Jane's marriage to Khair un-Nissa, a woman he had yet to meet, but with whom (again at his brother's request) he had been corresponding every three days or so since January.

Charles had earlier received a long letter from Henry, telling him that his proposal of marriage had of course been accepted by Jane, and giving him detailed instructions on how he was to deal with the delicate task of informing Khair that she had been abandoned: 'the task you will have to perform will be arduous and painful; most arduous to you, and most painful to me. But it is necessary.'[72] Two days later, obedient as ever, Charles set off to Masulipatam, intending to head on to Madras to meet his future sister-in-law after he had done his brother's bidding.

Unknown to Charles as he cantered down the road to the coast, back in Madras there had been a major hitch in Henry's plans. Quite unexpectedly – at least to Russell – ten days earlier, on 10 June, Jane Casamajor had called him to her house and told him the marriage was off. She gave no reason. Henry returned home, astounded that anyone would or even could turn him down. It was only late the following morning that he remembered that his brother was by now in all probability on his way to Masulipatam to deliver a message that could only come as shattering blow to Khair un-Nissa.

Rushing to his desk, he quickly wrote out two notes. He sent one to Hyderabad and the other direct to Major Alexander at Masulipatam, with urgent orders that it be given to Mr Charles Russell the minute he arrived in the town. Then he sat down to await what would happen.

The express letter to Masulipatam read as follows:

My dear Charles,

I have today written a long letter to you at Hyderabad explaining to you, as far as I could explain them in a letter, and indeed as far as I can myself understand them, the circumstances that have suddenly and unexpectedly occurred finally and, I believe, and even hope, irrevocably to break off the match between me and Jane Casamajor.

I take the precaution of sending these few lines, under cover to Alexander, and I shall desire him to give them to you immediately on your arrival at Masulipatam in order to prevent you from making to the Begum any of the communications described in my long letter of yesterday, in short from saying anything to her about me, except that I am well, that you are coming to pass a month with me and that she may be satisfied, that, notwithstanding that I have not been able to write to her, I still continue to think of her with the former kindness and affection as ever.

I am vexed that anything should have happened to break off a match, on which I had certainly set my Heart more strongly than I ought in prudence to have done, though not perhaps as strongly as I originally imagined. It really is a source of vast comfort to have avoided the necessity of conveying to the poor Begum any communication of so very aggravated and painful a nature, as those contained in my letter to you yesterday. Of course it now becomes totally superfluous to take any measures whatever regarding her. She need not, she *must not* know or suspect that my affections, have ever been diverted from their original direction; and, situated as we now are towards one another, it is better that we should continue on mostly the same footing on which we have hitherto stood.[73]

The letter sent to Hyderabad was longer, more leisurely, and a little more self-aware. It was, Henry acknowledged to Charles, 'impossible to conceal from either you or myself that I am nettled and annoyed at anything like a refusal from any woman whatsoever; but excepting the violence that my pride, or perhaps rather my vanity has sustained, I really am quite astonished at the degree of coldness and apathy with which I have submitted to a separation from a woman to whom I already conceived myself to be irrevocably and eternally united ... be that as it may, my vanity is certainly more deeply injured than my heart'.[74]

He went on to speculate how it was that Jane could possibly have found it in herself to turn down such a splendid chap as himself. In the course of this passage he reveals one reason why his relationship with the Begum had never developed into the marriage that Khair un-Nissa had clearly hoped for and, at least initially, set her heart on. For Russell explained to Charles that the most likely reason for Jane's action was that she had been alarmed by his total refusal to tell his father of their forthcoming marriage, which in turn was due to his father's almost certain refusal to condone it. The reason for this was that Jane had a Malay great-grandmother, and Sir Henry, an ambitious *arriviste* who had closely orchestrated the careers of all his children, had long made it quite clear to them that he would never agree to any of them marrying anyone 'contaminated by one streak of black'.[75] Henry Russell was deeply in awe of his father, who was evidently a very strong personality. It was out of the question that he could ever have dreamed of marrying Khair un-Nissa if he dared not tell his father even about his relatively uncontroversial match with Jane Casamajor.

The letter to Hyderabad arrived too late to catch Charles; he had already set off to Masulipatam to break the news to the Begum. But the express note to Alexander got there just in time. After a week's journey, the ever-obedient Charles read it and headed straight back to Hyderabad without even waiting to pay a courtesy visit to Khair un-Nissa.

But it was only a reprieve, a putting off of the inevitable. Five months later, Charles was back, on the same errand. Jane Casamajor had changed her mind. She eventually married Henry Russell in St Mary's church in Madras on 20 October 1808. 'Dear Jane,' wrote Henry to his brother, 'has made me love her ten times more than I ever did before . . .'[76]

Russell had fully briefed his brother on the story that was to be told to the Begum, and it involved what he described as an 'innocent deception' – perhaps something along the lines that he had been forced into the marriage by his father, and had no option but to submit. Whatever lie it was, it did little to soften the blow, for the news shattered Khair un-Nissa's already fragile composure and self-assurance. Henry was pleased that Charles had kept his description of the encounter to a minimum: 'Your account of what passed between you and the Begum was quite sufficiently full to be satisfactory, and not so detailed as to be unbearably painful to me. The subject is a distressing one; and I shall therefore say as little upon it as I can.' But he still wanted to know one detail more: 'You said that you went to see the Begum again the day you left Masulipatam. Did you see her? Was she more composed and more satisfied of the necessity of submitting to what you had told her the previous day?'[77]

Charles's reply does not survive. But the answer to his question is quite clear, as Khair un-Nissa's subsequent story shows.

With that final conversation, the curtain descends once again on the Begum, but this time not for a month, or a year, or even two years, but for five. In that time Russell wrote thousands of letters, but barely one that mentions Khair un-Nissa. And with his gaze turned elsewhere, she again vanishes from history.

Following his abandonment of the Begum, Russell's own life was engulfed in tragedy. Jane Casamajor died quite suddenly of fever only two months after their marriage. For once something genuinely seemed to have moved Russell, and his grief was absolute. He wrote to his brother Charles: 'Your poor Jane, your poor sister, my wife, my comfort, my darling, my everything, is gone. At ten o'clock this morning her sweet, her heavenly spirit left the frail but lovely tenement it had inhabited; and all hope but her happiness in a better place is now fled. I felt the last vibration of her pulse, I heard the last faint flutter of her breath; and she expired on my arm.'[78]

He tried to continue at Madras, but gave up and returned to England for a year, spending much of the time working on poems to his late wife and writing endless drafts of her epitaph. On his return in 1809 he was appointed briefly to the Pune Residency before, in 1810, finally gaining his long-held ambition of becoming Resident at Hyderabad.

His first act was to summon Aman Ullah from retirement in Benares and to offer him place of honour at the Residency (his elder brother, Aziz Ullah, was now too old to begin work again). The old *munshi* immediately accepted, but died on the journey, just ten days' march from Hyderabad.*

Mir Alam had died of his leprosy on 4 January 1809, and it was at this point that Khair un-Nissa and her mother appear to have limped back to Hyderabad from Masulipatam, and attempted to resume their life in the family *deorhi*. Fyze Palmer also reappears in Hyderabad around this time, spending time with her son William –

---

* Russell was very saddened by Aman Ullah's death, writing to his brother Charles of the 'sudden and melancholy death of poor Amaun Oolah . . . I never thought of him as an ailing man, or doubted that he had many prosperous years to live. Poor creature! He was as faithful, as honest, as affectionate, as unassuming a being who ever lived, very sincerely, I believe attached to me, and possessed of many qualities. How I shall supply his place I do not know, and I question therefore whether it would be best not to fill it at all . . . It was very kind of you to write immediately to Uzeez Oolah, and to attend his brother's funeral. I shall write to Uzeez Oolah myself in few days.' He concludes by saying that he is glad he did not see Aman Ullah again, 'as after seeing my old faithful friend again I should have felt his loss even more deeply than I do now; and my nerves are already so much shaken that I dread anything which would have disturbed them more.' Bodleian Library, Russell Papers, Ms Eng Letts D152, p.72, October 1810. Aman Ullah's Persian letters to Russell written on his journey from Benares survive uncatalogued in the Persian Department of the Bodleian.

and presumably with Khair – in the extensive new Palmer mansion, known as the Kothi, facing the main gate of the Residency.

After the return of the two Begums to Hyderabad, Sharaf un-Nissa makes occasional fleeting appearances in Russell's letters: at one point, for example, he receives a petition from one of Nizam Ali Khan's widows, Pearee Begum, on receiving which he tells Charles: 'Pearee Begum's letter I will answer, if necessary, after my arrival at Hyderabad . . . She is a particular favourite of the Old Begum's, and so . . . I should not like to offend her by shewing any sort of slight to her favourite.'[79] On another occasion Sharaf un-Nissa sends Henry a broken watch and a chipped locket containing James Kirkpatrick's hair. Russell succeeds in mending the watch, but manages to lose the precious locket, telling the old Begum, somewhat insensitively, that 'if she sends some more hair he will have another made'.[80] There are also references to Henry having finally received the Chinnery of the children from Calcutta and promising to send it over to the old Begum. But while Sharaf un-Nissa seems to have intermittently kept in touch with Russell, her daughter – significantly – did not.

It was not until the late summer of 1813 that Khair briefly re-entered Russell's life. The occasion was the visit of an aristocratic Scottish tomboy from the Isle of Lewis named Lady Mary Hood. Mary Hood had temporally deserted her rich, elderly admiral husband and gone off on her own around India, breaking a series of diplomatic hearts as she passed: Mountstuart Elphinstone, William Fraser and Henry Russell himself all seem to have been, to different extents, a little in love with her. During her stay at Hyderabad, Mary had asked Russell if she might meet some 'Hyderabadi women of rank', and he brought Khair and Fyze to see her at the Residency, though whether he attended the meeting and actually saw Khair face to face after all that had passed between them is not clear.

Either way, Lady Hood was entranced by the sadness, beauty and intelligence of the 'poor Begum',* while Khair in turn seems to have

---

* Lady Hood wrote a long letter to Mountstuart Elphinstone describing her meeting with the Begum, but it was sadly destroyed, along with much of the rest of Elphinstone's correspondence, when the Pune Residency was burned down during the Pindari Wars. Elphinstone's reply survives however among Lady Hood's letter books in Edinburgh, and gives an indication of what she had written, implying that the Begum had not only

liked Lady Hood enough to promise to make her a dress. This dress weaves its way in and out of Russell's letters over the following three weeks: initially it was too small, and Lady Hood asked Russell to 'let the Begum be told with my regards & salaams, that if she will allow me I will make a body for the dress myself at Madras to fit me, & send it to her to be trimmed, as I know the one she has kindly made already for me is not large enough for a Scotch princess'.[81] But in all these letters there is no hint of Khair un-Nissa's former engagement with the world. She appears instead like some broken butterfly, wounded, and unhealed by the passage of time.

At her most vulnerable point, she had opened up her heart, only to be seduced, banished and then betrayed. Five years had passed since she had been abandoned by Russell, but despite her beauty and her fortune, she had never remarried.

Khair's last recorded action, towards the end of September 1813, was to send a brief note to her former lover – her first for five years – simply telling Russell that she was dying.

Russell, for once, rose to the occasion. Perhaps struck with remorse he invited the Begum back to the Rang Mahal, to end her life where she had once been happy. By 1813 those days must have seemed far distant to her: it was, after all, eight years since she had been widowed, eight years since she had kissed first her children and then her husband goodbye.

impressed her, but that she was reputed to have totally entranced her late husband James Kirkpatrick. As Elphinstone wrote in his characteristically superior fashion: 'Your account of the Begum is very interesting and new even to me. Her fairness however is owing to her Persian blood. All the native women have good manners to some extent, and some are said to be possessed of great wit, and it would appear, of great powers of fascination, but they have none of the dignity of English women and I fancy very rarely much mind, so that I am astonished when I hear of any of them gaining an ascendancy over a man as the one in question appears to have done.' Scottish Record Office, Edinburgh, GD46/17/42, The Letters of Mountstuart Elphinstone to Lady Hood, 1813–14, p.8, 1813.

Khair un-Nissa – already fading – was duly carried in, and the couch on which she had once given birth to her daughter now became her deathbed. There was no clear cause for her condition: she just seems to have finally turned her face to the wall. Maybe revisiting the Residency – with the flood of memories it must have brought on – had been too painful. But she did not recover, and over a period of two weeks she got weaker and weaker, and her pulse fainter and fainter. She finally slipped away, without pain, on 22 September 1813. She was aged only twenty-seven. By her side, holding her hand to the very end, were Fyze Palmer and Sharaf un-Nissa.

The following morning a clearly shocked Russell picked up his pen to break the news to Lady Hood: 'I am sure you will be very much concerned to hear of the poor Begum's death which happened yesterday morning,' he wrote.

> What her complaint was he [the doctor] hardly knows even now. On the very first day she sent to me to say she was unwell, her hands were cold and clammy, and her pulse so quiet that Mr Currie [the new Residency medic*] could not count it. She was unable to take any sort of nourishment, and said all along that the feelings she had were such as to convince her she would not recover. She died [two weeks later] in the Hindoostanee House [the Rang Mahal].
>
> Her mother and all her relations and friends were with her, and according to Mahommedan customs, must remain in the house in which she died until they have performed some particular ceremony which is observed on the fortieth day.
>
> You cannot imagine anything so distressing as the old lady's situation. More sincere or dignified grief I never witnessed. She was quite wrapped up in her daughter, and seems to feel that the only object she lived for was taken from her; yet her calmness and composure were really admirable. I always thought her a woman of a very superior mind. The Begum was buried by the side of her father, in a garden belonging to

---

* Dr Ure had died in January 1807. Mrs Ure had returned to India from placing her son in school in England to find that her husband was dead and buried, and that she was a widow. She caught the next ship back home.

the family on the opposite side of the city from the Residency, and her funeral was attended by every person of rank in the place.[82]

Six weeks later Russell reported that Fyze (who he calls by her Mughal title, the Sahib Begum) was still 'I fear in great distress. She has shut herself up entirely ever since the Begum's death, and will not see anybody. The people about her have not ventured to tell her of the death of another relation which happened about a fortnight ago, and she has not yet mustered the resolution to see the old lady [Sharaf un-Nissa]. I wish for both their sakes that the first meeting were over. She says she has lost the only real friend she ever had; and I suspect from what I have heard of her disposition and habits, that it is truly the case.'

Sharaf un-Nissa was also completely inconsolable. Russell told Lady Hood that he had shown the letter she had written him about Khair to her mother:

> She was very much affected, but very much gratified, and desired me, with tears running down her cheeks, how deeply she felt the interest and friendship with which you expressed yourself about her daughter . . . I am sure that if you had seen the old lady in the scenes which I have seen her you would think as highly of her as I do. I never saw anybody feel more acutely or make greater efforts to appear composed. She is a woman of a lofty mind, and of a heart and understanding of a very high order indeed. She and her daughter were the only native women of birth I ever had the opportunity of being personally acquainted with. In any country and any class of life they would have been extraordinary persons; and although the women of rank in India are very superior to what Europeans generally think, there are few, I imagine, if any who are equal to them. I never recollect an instance of a death at Hyderabad which exited so general an interest or called forth such marked and universal tributes of respect . . .'[83]

Those are the final words we hear of Khair un-Nissa, the Most Excellent of Women, beloved wife of James Achilles Kirkpatrick, and Henry Russell's rejected lover. She had lived the saddest of lives. At a time, and in a society, when women had few options and choices, and little control over their lives, Khair had defied convention, threatened suicide and risked everything to be with the man she had eventually succeeded in marrying, even though he was from a different culture, a different race, and, initially, from a different religion. Her love affair had torn her family apart and brought her, her mother, her grandmother and her husband to the brink of destruction. Then, just when it seemed that she had, against all the odds, finally succeeded in realising her dream, both her husband and her children were taken from her, for ever, and in her widowhood she was first disgraced, then banished, and finally rejected. When she died – this fiery, passionate, beautiful woman – it was as much from a broken heart, from neglect and sorrow, as from any apparent physical cause.

There is no evidence that Khair un-Nissa received any direct messages from her children after their departure in 1805. It is however recorded that both she and her mother wrote desperate letters to England, begging and pleading for the children to be sent back to her.[84] No reply ever came to these letters, until, ironically enough, six weeks after her death. For in November 1813, a letter and a pair of portraits of her children finally arrived in Hyderabad. It was of course too late for Khair, but Russell recorded the reaction of Sharaf un-Nissa to the pictures of the 'poor Begum's' children: 'I like them very much,' he wrote to Lady Hood,

> and we all think the likeness strong, though it is eight years since the children left us. The girl is handsome, and seems to be getting like her mother, as everybody here who remembered her mother as a child always said she would be. The boy is exceedingly handsome, and very like his father. The old lady is delighted with the picture, and I do not believe her eyes were off it for five minutes during the first day she had it . . . Her notion seems to be that the children when they grow up will themselves come to take up their property [the estates they had now inherited from their mother]. It would be cruel to darken the only bright spot that the prospect of her life affords her . . . The boy was decidedly the grandmother's

favourite, and I confess that I have not the courage to tell her how doubtful I think it whether she will ever see him again . . .[85]

Yet even here the story does not quite end. For after a gap of more than thirty years there is one, final, extraordinary coda.

X

AFTER BEING HELPED INTO the roundhouse of the *Lord Hawkesbury* at Madras, Sahib Allum and Sahib Begum – or, as they were now known, Katherine Aurora and William George Kirkpatrick – had to endure six long months on board ship, most of it out of sight of land.

During the voyage they found themselves under the watchful eyes of a posse of four guardians: the motherly figure of Mrs Ure; an equally well-rounded though rather younger (and unnamed) Indian ayah; Mrs Perry, the elderly wife of one of James's bandsmen; and another faithful Hyderabadi manservant of James whom the children knew from the Residency. As they rounded the Cape, crossed the Equator and headed for the temperate climes of the north, and as the returning English passengers began to relish the familiar sensation of the cool Atlantic climate, the utter strangeness of the bleak, foreign, northern world they were heading towards must have slowly dawned upon the children.

For those Company servants who had spent many years in India, the barren chill of England held in the cold embrace of winter often came as an unexpected shock: after a decade in the East, and after months of longing for an imagined Britain of Eden-like beauty, the Scottish artist James Baillie Fraser had been horrified to find that 'the brown of winter shrouded all, a gloomy welcome to the returned wanderer . . . all about seemed as desolate as a deserted city'.[1] To those brought up in the light and warmth and colour of India, who had never before felt the cold, or seen the thick impenetrable murk of an English fog, the February half-light would have seemed all the more unnerving and uninviting.

The reception that awaited the party at their place of disembarkation 'some four or five miles from Portsmouth' could well have compounded this feeling of loss and despair. According to the somewhat condescending George Elers, a captain in the 12th Regiment of Foot, who happened to be travelling home on the same boat:

> Poor Mrs Ure who had her own infant and the care of Colonel Kirkpatrick's children – together with a faithful old black man (who was very fond of them), a black nurse, and an English maidservant – felt herself in a very helpless and unprotected state; she had, she said, property in shawls, jewels and other valuables to the amount of upwards of £2000 (and the Custom House officers were expected on board at any minute), and all this property was liable to be seized.* We were only allowed to take one trunk each on shore. She began to cry and bewail herself, so I told her to be comforted, that I would not leave her until I saw her safe in London with her friends, and would save all her property if I possibly could, but she must place the whole of it, with the key, under my care.
>
> I had but twenty guineas in my purse to take me to London, and I asked if she had sufficient to pay her expenses to London, for that I should want a good deal to bribe the Customs House officers so as to get her trunk passed. She told me she had plenty of money, and she begged me to arrange everything for her. I then got a large boat and got my black and white party safe on board . . .
>
> When the boat grounded on the beach at Portsmouth, I leaped on shore. The Customs House officers seized our trunks and wheeled them off to the Customs House. Some of the officers seeing the poor fat black nurse, handled her very roughly, thinking from her large size that she had shawls concealed about her person. She poor creature, not speaking a word of English and not understanding their motives, got dreadfully alarmed . . .[2]

---

* These riches presumably belonged to the children, or were presents for William Kirkpatrick and the Handsome Colonel.

Elers bribed the officers with a massive twenty guineas of *baksheesh* and in due course delivered the children to the London townhouse of the Handsome Colonel in Fitzroy Square, an area of the capital perennially popular with returned nabobs and old India hands. The children's uncle William was there to meet them too, luckily perhaps, as it is unclear how much English they would have understood at this stage, and after parting from the bilingual Mrs Ure, William's linguistic gifts may well have been much needed. Less than a month later, the two Muslim children were baptised Christian on 25 March 1806 at St Mary's church, Marylebone Road.[3] Another last link with India was severed.

The children grew up at Hollydale, the Handsome Colonel's rambling country house near Keston in Kent, with frequent visits to Exeter to see their uncle William and all their West Country cousins. But inevitably they 'pined for their native surroundings'; and they were forbidden from writing to their mother, grandmother or any of their Indian family, who in turn 'wrote pathetic appeals to send them [back] out . . . probably it was feared that, if once they went there, the call of the blood might make complications'.[4] Sadder still, 'in after years the daughter told her own children how long she and her brother had pined for the father and mother they remembered, and longed to get away from the cold of England to Hyderabad, and were sad at hearing that they were not to go there again, which was all they could understand of their father's death'.[5]

It was a childhood marred by more of the emotional and physical upheavals that had already scarred their young lives. The first trauma was the increasing incoherence of their uncle William, with whom they seem initially to have spent much of their holidays.[6] William Kirkpatrick had retired to a relatively small but elegant townhouse in Exeter, an easy carriage drive from Sir John Kennaway, his 'oldest and most esteemed friend'.[7] Southernhay House lay in the lee of the crumbling Norman towers of Exeter Cathedral, the centrepiece of the smart new development of Southernhay, which prided itself on being to Exeter what the Royal Crescent was to Bath. The house lay in the middle of the two wings of the crescent, the only detached residence in the whole development. With its pair of side-wings, fluted classical pillars and a pedimented portico, it stood assertively in the middle of the other flat-fronted Georgian townhouses with their fan windows and wooden shutters, somewhat like a miniature redbrick version of the Hyderabad Residency re-erected in Devon. It was also remarkable in the English townscape for one single Oriental flourish that distinguished it from everything around it: a pair of twisted old Indian palm trees standing sentinel in front of the house, presumably planted by William to make the children – or indeed himself – feel at home amid the oaks, chestnuts and holly trees of Southernhay Green.*

William was now an invalid. He had never recovered from either his bowel complaint or his 'rheumatic gout', and by 1809 he was confined to a chair. Judging by the pain he suffered and his increasingly erratic handwriting, he may have been taking large quantities of laudanum to help soothe his condition.[8] But despite his illness, and the laudanum, he worked prolifically at his Oriental studies. He helped select a library for the Company, and wrote an account of his travels in Nepal.[9] Increasingly, however, he became obsessed with the figure of Tipu Sultan. Before William had left India, James had in September 1801 sent him a huge wagonload of documents which had been taken from Tipu's chancellery in Seringapatam.† These documents William now worked up for publication in his 1811 volume *Select Letters of Tippoo Sultaun*, carefully sifting and selecting his material with a view to showing Tipu in the most fearsome light possible.[10]

As the decade progressed, William's interests seem to have centred more and more on Tipu's astronomical and astrological learning. William's letter books in the India Office contain a series of fascinat-

---

* Although much of this part of Exeter was destroyed by bombing in the Second World War, Southernhay House remains. The house once backed onto a deer park, but the land was sold off sometime in the 1980s to be converted into an office development. The house itself now belongs to a group of chartered accountants, and a line of BMWs stand parked in the carriageway from which William Kirkpatrick used to set off to see Kennaway or to take the children on seaside picnics.

† Though James had apologised to William and admitted he had thrown out most of the material that had been salvaged from Tipu's burning palace after Munshi Aziz Ullah had complained that the Residency *daftar* was becoming too crowded, and he had ordered a clear-out. See OIOC, Kirkpatrick Papers, Eur Mss F228/13, p.158, 11 September 1801, James Kirkpatrick to William Kirkpatrick. Among the documents he burned, he says, was a list of the agents Tipu 'employed at this durbar'. He offers to copy others out from the Residency copybooks, but says it will take time 'with such few and indifferent copyists as I have now at my command'.

ing letters that he wrote to Mark Wilks, Lord Clive's Private Secretary during the Clive Enquiry into James's love life, who had gone on to become Resident in Mysore, and the author of a series of important studies of both Mughal metaphysics and the political history of Tipu's reign.[11] William's correspondence with Wilks deals with increasing single-mindedness on Tipu's astrological system, and seems to hint at his growing conviction that Tipu had correctly forecast the time of his own death by a series of esoteric astrological calculations.

In November 1809 Wilks sent William the answer to his query as to the exact moment – according to Tipu's new Mysore calendar – of Tipu's birth 'in the year Angeera on the 17th of the month Margeser. Angeera is the 6th of the cycle and corresponds to 1752–3.'[12] From William's last letters emerges an extraordinary picture of a man, clearly aware that he is dying, taking larger and larger doses of laudanum, obsessively studying the Mysore system of astrology, and all the while (one grows increasingly to suspect) making calculations, casting horoscopes, and believing that he is onto something, that he really does hold, almost within his grasp, some sort of universal Philosopher's Stone. Whether William, in the haze of an opium addiction, really was trying to calculate the date of his own death in the same way that he clearly believed Tipu had succeeded in doing, must remain a matter of speculation; but it is certainly a possibility.[13]

A few weeks before he died in the summer of 1812, William sold up all his possessions from his Exeter townhouse;* and on 22 August he overdosed on laudanum 'near London', aged fifty-eight.[14]

It remains uncertain whether the death was a suicide or not.

---

* The advertisement for the sale in the *Exeter Flying Post* read as follows: 'Southernhay Place: To be SOLD at auction, on Tuesday the 12th day of May next, and following day, on the premises, the NEW and MODERN FURNITURE, of Major General Kirkpatrick, at his late dwelling-house, situated the upper end of Southernhay; comprising mahogany post and other bedsteads, and hangings; hair and wool mattresses; fine seasoned feather beds and bedding; floor and bed carpets; mahogany wardrobe; and all other bedroom requisites; mahogany chairs, with morocco seats; a secretary and book case; revolving library table; Grecian sofa; an eight day clock, in mahogany café; ivory handle knives and forks. The sale to begin by eleven o'clock in the forenoon, and continue until all articles in each days sale are disposed of. NB The goods are of the best quality, and may be viewed the Monday preceding the sale.' This notice, appropriately enough, lies immediately adjacent to an advertisement for 'Trotter's Oriental Dentifrice or Asiatic Tooth Powder'.

Another tragedy followed close on William's overdose.

A month later, while the family was still in mourning, the eleven-year-old Sahib Allum, or William George, as he was now known, fell into 'a copper of boiling water' and was disabled for life, with at least one of his limbs requiring amputation.[15] A letter in shaking old man's handwriting from the Handsome Colonel to Kitty (as Katherine was now known), written immediately after the accident, survives in the archive of their descendants. It shows the closeness of the relationship that had developed between the grieving grandfather and his ten-year-old Anglo-Indian granddaughter:

> My dear Kitty,
> Many affected mourners are joined with you for the calamity which has recently taken place in our Family, but you & I will bewail it together when we meet, for I cannot weep upon paper. I send you a small present which I hope will be to your Taste, and apprise you that I shall send a carriage for you on ye 28th to meet your poor brother. I remain, my dear Kitty
> > Your affectionate grandfather
> > Jas Kirkpatrick
> > Hollydale, 8 Sept 1812[16]

It is the last letter to survive from the Handsome Colonel. Having outlived all but one of his sons he died six years later, in 1818, at the grand old age of eighty-nine.[17] After the funeral, Kitty and William George were shunted off yet again, this time to live in rotation with their various married cousins, William Kirkpatrick's daughters: first Clementina, Lady Louis; then Julia, who had married Edward Strachey (Mountstuart Elphinstone's friend and former travelling companion who had stayed with James at the Hyderabad Residency in 1801); and finally Isabella Buller, who had moved back to England from Calcutta with her husband Charles, become a fervent Evangelical, and set up house on Kew Green. William George begins to fade from the picture at this point: a dreamy, disabled poet, obsessed with Wordsworth and the metaphysics of Coleridge, but sufficiently active (and attractive) to marry at the age of twenty, and to father three girls.

As William George disappears into the background in the 1820s, Kitty begins to takes centre stage. She was already attracting attention as a woman of quite remarkable beauty – as well as one, thanks to her father's generous legacy, of unusual means. In 1822, when Kitty was aged twenty, she met the new tutor Isabella Buller had hired to teach her two sons. He was a young, unknown and struggling Scottish writer and philosopher, three years her senior. His name was Thomas Carlyle. And it was through his pen that Kitty comes suddenly into dazzling focus.

Carlyle had arrived in London off the boat from Edinburgh in the spring of 1822. It was his first visit to the city, and, as he wrote years later in his *Reminiscences:*

> That first afternoon, with its curious phenomena, is still very lively with me . . . Then . . . dash of a brave carriage driving up, and entry of a strangely complexioned young lady, with soft brown eyes and floods of bronze-red hair, really a pretty-looking, smiling, and amiable though most foreign bit of magnificence and kindly splendour, who [was] welcomed by the name 'dear Kitty'.
>
> Kitty Kirkpatrick [was] Charles Buller's cousin . . . her birth, as I afterwards found, an Indian *romance*, mother a sublime *Begum*, father a ditto English official, mutually adoring, wedding, living withdrawn in their own private paradise, a romance famous in the East . . .[18]

Carlyle heard a great deal about Kitty that first week in London. He was staying with his childhood friend, the fiery Evangelical preacher Edward Irving, at 7 Myddelton Terrace. As Irving was too poor to furnish his own house, two of his most ardent admirers had done so for him at a cost of £500, a princely sum in those days. The two 'rich and open-handed ladies' were Mrs Buller's sister, Julia Strachey, and her cousin, Kitty Kirkpatrick.[19] Both were religious – Julia Strachey especially so – and attracted to the Evangelical Clapham Sect, 'whose pious members, it was said, would ask each other at intervals "Shall we Engage?" and drop to their knees'.[20] Irving, with his gaunt features and black broad-brimmed hat, was one of the Sect's star performers, and crowds numbering in the thousands would eagerly squeeze into the Caledonian Chapel to await one of his breathless three-hour sermons.

Over the months that followed Carlyle saw more and more of Kitty, and became increasingly fascinated with her lovely voice, her sense of humour, 'a slight merry curl of the upper lip, the carriage of her head, the quaint little things she said, and her low-toned laugh'.[21] Soon after their first meeting, Carlyle was invited over to Shooter's Hill, the Stracheys' country house. 'I remember entering the little winding avenue,' he later wrote, 'and seeing, in a kind of open conservatory or verandah on our approaching the house, the effulgent vision of "dear kitty" buried among the roses and almost buried under them . . . the before and after and all the other incidents of that first visit are quite lost to me . . .'[22]

Although Carlyle was already involved in an intense (though at this stage largely epistolary) relationship with the formidably clever and acerbic Jane Welsh of Haddington, East Lothian, whom he would later marry, the young philosopher clearly fell a little in love with Kitty. Soon after he got to know her he wrote to Jane:

> This Kitty is a singular and very pleasing creature, a little blackeyed, auburn haired brunette, full of kindliness and humour, and who never, I believe, was angry at any creature for a moment in her life. Tho' twenty one and not unbeautiful, the sole mistress of herself and fifty thousand pounds, she is as meek and modest as a Quakeress . . . Good Kitty, would

you or I were half as happy as this girl. But her Mother was
a Hindoo Princess (whom her father fought for and scaled
walls for); it lies in the blood, and philosophy can do little to
help us.[23]

Jane, predictably enough, grew to become deeply jealous of this
constant talk of Kitty in Carlyle's letters. 'I congratulate you on your
present situation,' she wrote, acid dripping from every stroke of her
pen,

> with such a picture of domestic felicity before your eyes, and
> this 'singular and very pleasing creature' to charm away the
> blue-devils, you can hardly fail to be as happy as the day is
> long. Miss Kitty Kirkpatrick – Lord what an ugly name! Oh
> pretty, dear, delightful, Kitty! I am not a bit jealous of her,
> not I indeed – Hindoo princess though she be! Only you may
> as well never let me hear you mention her name again . . .
> Oh thou Goose! Are you mad? Has Miss Kitty Kirkpatrick
> turned your head?[24]

Jane's jealousy became all the more acute when Kitty, Carlyle and
the Stracheys set off on a trip to Paris in the autumn of 1824, during
which, according to Carlyle's later account, Julia Strachey seems to
have tacitly pushed the two together.[25] Jane's response when she
heard about this trip was characteristically forthright: 'Paris? Art thou
frantic? Art thou dreaming? Or has the Hindoo Princess actually
bewitched thee that thou hast brought thy acid visage into this land
of fops and pastry cooks, where Vanity and Sensuality have set up
their chosen shrine?'[26]

Two years later, with Kitty still very much at the centre of Carlyle's
life and letters, Jane continued to shoot off jealous darts in her
direction: 'Your "Rosy-fingered Morn", the Hindoo Princess, where
is she?'[27] Or: 'There is Catharina Aurora Kirkpatrick for instance, who
has £50,000 and a princely lineage, and "never was out of humour
in her life"; with such a "singularly pleasing creature" and so much
fine gold you could hardly fail to find yourself admirably well
off.'[28]

As Jane Welsh was all too aware, Kitty was indeed a woman of considerable means, and Carlyle was only a tutor. But ironically, despite the former's Indian blood and the latter's subsequent fame, marriage to Carlyle would have been regarded as inappropriate for Kitty, due to the perceived disparity in class and status between the two, though they were clearly and openly attracted to one another.* As Kitty later explained to one of her friends (taking a swipe at Jane in the process), 'He was then the tutor to my cousin, Charles Buller, and had made no name for himself; so of course I was told that any such idea could not be thought of for a moment. What could I do with everyone against it?† Now anyone might be proud to be his wife, and he has married a woman quite beneath him.'[29]

In 1828, Isabella Buller's eldest son Charles wrote to tell Carlyle the news of the latest tragedy in Kitty's life: the death of her beloved brother William George at the age of only twenty-seven: 'We have some expectation of seeing Miss Kirkpatrick soon, but she is in great trouble,' wrote Buller. 'Her brother William, perhaps you already knew, died in May after a painful and lingering illness. His poor young wife has gone mad and Kitty, after all this, has been in a very wearisome dispute with her sister respecting the care of her brother's children.'[30]

A year later, possibly on the rebound, Kitty finally found the love, support and stability that had always eluded her, in the person of a nephew of Sir John Kennaway, the dashing Captain James Winslowe Phillipps of the 7th Hussars.‡ They married on 21 November 1829.[31] Carlyle, himself now clearly jealous, dismissed Phillipps (quite

---

* Indian titles always impressed the British, and Kitty's reputation as the daughter of a 'Hindoo Princess' (Khair un-Nissa was of course neither 'Hindoo' nor a princess) seems to have done as much as her relations, beauty and fortune to ease her passage in English society. Possession of a title remained a trump card for Indians throughout the Raj. As late as the mid-1920s this was something that struck Aldous Huxley as he watched India's Maharajahs assemble in Delhi for a meeting of the Chamber of Princes, a week during which Delhi 'pullulated with Despots and their Viziers'. Proust, he thought, would have enjoyed 'observing the extraordinary emollient effect upon even the hardest anti-Asiatic sentiments of the possession of wealth and a royal title. The cordiality with which people talk to the dear Maharajah Sahib – and even, on occasion, about him – is delightful.' Aldous Huxley, *Jesting Pilate* (London, 1926), pp.106-7.

† So showing, in this quotation at least, a little less spirit than her parents had done in similar circumstances.

‡ At this period, the 7th Hussars had a reputation not dissimilar to that of the modern SAS, and is described in one source as 'Lord Anglesey's crack regiment'.

inaccurately) as 'an idle ex-Captain of Sepoys';[32] but the marriage was a passionate one, and in Phillipps' love letters to Kitty, still in the possession of their descendants, he assures her that 'How sincerely & devotedly I *love* you, words cannot express'.[33]

Shortly after this, Carlyle began work on his celebrated though almost unreadable (and indeed now little-read) novel *Sartor Resartus* ('The Tailor Retailored'). This deeply enigmatic book – even by the standards of the other work produced by the Sage of Ecclefechan – aimed to take on the great issues of Faith and Justice through the curious guise of a History and Philosophy of Clothing by the German Professor of Things in General, the 'Visionary Pedant' Diogenes Teufelsdröckh. At the centre of the narrative of the book lies the story of Professor Teufelsdröckh's relationship with the aristocratic Zähdarm family and his fascination for Blumine, who having made the Professor 'immortal with a kiss' then 'resigned herself to wed some other'. Teufelsdröckh meets Blumine at an 'Aesthetic Tea' in the garden house of Frau Zähdarm, where she sits embowered in a cluster of roses. She is a brunette ('dusky red'), young, hazel-eyed, beautiful and somebody's cousin, 'a many-tinted radiant aurora . . . this fairest of Orient Light bringers . . . his whole heart and soul were hers'.[34]

At the time of publication, and for about forty years after, while the book was still being eagerly read, there was a fierce debate as to the identity of Blumine, with Jane Welsh Carlyle, Margaret Gordon (Carlyle's first love) and Kitty Kirkpatrick all canvassed as potential candidates.[35] No one in the Strachey family, however, had any doubt. As Lady Strachey remarked to her son George on reading it, 'The book is as plain as a pikestaff. Teufelsdröckh is Thomas [Carlyle] himself. The Zähdarmes are your uncle and aunt Buller. Toughgut is young Charles Buller. Philistine is Irving. The duenna cousin is myself. The rose garden is our garden with roses at Shooter's Hill, and the Rose Goddess [Blumine] is Kitty.'[36] According to George Strachey, 'That "Blumine" personified Miss Kirkpatrick has always passed in the family for a certainty, requiring no more discussion than the belief that Nelson stood on the column in Trafalgar Square.'[37]

Kitty herself clearly had no doubt that she was Blumine. Indeed she was once heard to take on an embarrassed Carlyle with the forthright words: ' "You know you were never made immortal in that manner!" . . . where upon they both laughed.'[38]

Six years after finding herself the romantic heroine of one of the most bizarre novels to be written in Victorian England, in May 1841 Kitty was visiting Mrs Duller, a childhood friend, when she was taken to tea with one of Mrs Duller's country neighbours who lived in a grand Berkshire mansion named Swallowfield, to the south of Reading. She had never been to the house before, nor did she know the owners. She can therefore have had little inkling of what she would find inside.

To Mrs Duller's amazement, Kitty walked through the front door of the house and promptly burst 'into floods of tears . . . and was much affected'. On the stairs, instantly recognisable, was the portrait of her and her brother painted by Chinnery just before they left India, thirty-six years earlier.

Swallowfield, it turned out, was the house of Henry Russell, now Sir Henry Russell, a name Kitty may have dimly remembered from her childhood. Russell himself was away in London on business that day, and his second wife, a French woman named Clothilde, gave the ladies tea and promised to find out from her husband how it was that he had somehow acquired the Chinnery portrait.[39]* Russell eventually wrote to Kitty explaining that it had been given to him

---

* Russell married Clothilde Mottet on 13 November 1816. The details are not clear, but she seems to have ousted his then *bibi*, named Luft un-Nissa, who may have been a cousin of Khair's. See Bodleian Library, Russell Papers, Ms Eng Letts C157, p.83, 17 September 1814. See also Sir Richard Temple, *Journals of Hyderabad, Kashmir, Sikkim and Nepal* (2 vols, London, 1887), Vol. 1, p.119. When she first arrived at the Hyderabad Residency, the second Mrs Russell went out to check that the herd of buffaloes, which provided milk for the Residency, were being milked hygienically; '[but] the buffaloes, not used to white faces, charged at her, and she was obliged to take refuge in the kitchen quarters'. See Mark Bence-Jones, *Palaces of the Raj* (London, 1973), p.102.

after Khair un-Nissa's death in 1813, and promised that he would leave her the picture in his will; but he did not offer to hand it over immediately, and seems to have made no attempt to meet the woman whom he must have remembered as a little girl in the Residency *mahal*. His reticence was hardly surprising; after all, there was clearly a limit to how much of the truth he could tell Kitty.

Russell had been back in England for nearly twenty years, having left India in deep disgrace with the Company, but with the redeeming compensation of having hoarded away a phenomenal fortune for his premature retirement. Fearing he might be humiliatingly removed from office, he had resigned as Resident at Hyderabad in 1820, after nine years in the job. Though he did not know it, even as he packed up and headed off towards Masulipatam for the last time, a set of furious letters were in transit from the Court of Directors in London ordering 'that Mr Russell be immediately removed from the Residency of Hyderabad and that he not be employed again at any other court'.[40]

The ostensible reason for Russell's summary removal was the death of two brigands who, without any reference to the Nizam's government, Russell had ordered to be severely flogged; both men had died the following day from the brutality of the wounds inflicted on them. This was however something of a pretext: Russell had become a major embarrassment to the Company, and was widely suspected of massive corruption and bribe-taking, something that the astonishing fortune with which he returned to England would seem to bear out: having come into the job of Resident with total savings of £500, he managed to ship home a fortune of £85,000, which he had impressively succeeded in accumulating in just nine years on an annual salary of £3400.[41]

During his time as Resident, Russell had presided over a dramatic souring of relations between the East India Company and the Hyderabad durbar. Despite a personal fondness for Hyderabad, Russell was always personally ambitious, and in a bid to impress his masters in Calcutta he had imposed a series of damaging new treaties on the Nizam, forcing him to pay for ever larger and more unnecessary numbers of British troops at a total cost of forty lakh rupees a year

– a sum which amounted to nearly half the entire tax revenue of Hyderabad. This vast fortune all went to pay the salaries of the enlarged Subsidiary Force and Russell's new Hyderabad Contingent, for which the Nizam had no use and over which he had in reality little control. Unlike the treaties James had signed, which at least initially were hugely useful to Hyderabad, and which did much to preserve its independence, Russell's not only provided no tangible benefit to the Nizam, they severely undermined and threatened the entire financial stability of his dominions.

Count Edouard de Warren was a French soldier of fortune working for the Nizam and a relation by marriage of Russell's second wife.* He had however little liking for the gross injustices over which Russell presided:

> Thus we see the ruler of a country larger than France . . . the finest jewel in the broken crown of the Moghuls . . . entirely deprived of his liberty, held in utter check-mate, without a soldier of his own worth the name, barely able to count on the loyalty of a few hundred mercenaries, the dregs scraped from distant lands – Sikhs, Arabs, Afghans – who look like robbers lounging at his palace gate, dressed in rags and sporting wretched weapons – is it any surprise then, that the Nizam spends the entire year shut away in his harem, seeking to forget that he is a prince, by drowning himself in vicious pleasures? . . . [Such is the hatred now felt for Europeans in the city] that no European can normally enter Hyderabad dressed in European costume, whether on foot, on horse or in a palanquin, without exposing himself to the insults of yogis, the execrations of fakirs and the real risk of physical harm from the mob.[42]

None of this surprised de Warren, as the British in Hyderabad, especially the soldiers, were now in the habit of behaving with disdain and extreme rudeness to their hosts. He was especially horrified by

---

* De Warren remarks that when he first arrived in Hyderabad he stayed with his 'brother-in-law Captain Mottet who was the last French officer in the Nizam's army who had survived from the days of [James's old rival, Michel Joachim de] Raymond.' This Captain Mottet was presumably the father or the brother of Clothilde Mottet, Russell's second wife.

the behaviour and lack of manners of the British officers at a levée given by the new Minister, Raja Chandu Lal:

> The entertainment was above reproach ... but as a European I was disgusted and ashamed by the lack of refinement, indeed the gluttony, shown by English officers of all ranks and ages: they threw themselves on the French wines, especially the Champagne, with intemperate greed which must have seemed doubly despicable to our native hosts, so sober, grave and courteous, so full of human dignity. Yet again, it was these northern conquerors who were the real barbarians. Even the Resident was aware that his party was transforming itself into a herd of swine, and before the metamorphosis was complete, hurriedly rose from the table and brought the meal to an end.[43]

One person de Warren felt particularly sorry for was Fyze's son, William Palmer. A great deal of Russell's money had come from his secret and illegal partnership in Palmer's extraordinarily successful bank, which by 1815 had grown to become the most successful business operation in India outside British control. Henry and William had initially been friends as well as business partners, and Russell had often dined at Palmer's rambling mansion, known as Palmer's Kothi. There he would pay his respects to Fyze (or the Sahib Begum, as he always referred to her), who had moved in after the old General had died in 1816. Fyze was eventually buried by her son in a pretty Muslim tomb surrounded by gardens and a small mosque a little to the north of the Kothi.* But Russell, worried that his illegal financial links with the bank would be exposed, had eventually fallen out with Palmer, and put in train a series of restrictions on Palmer's business

---

* It still stands, though the fragrant gardens have now been encroached upon by a line of VD clinics, the mosque rebuilt in concrete and the tomb itself has become a motorcycle repair shop. However the owner, Mr Das, voluntarily restricts his motorcycle work to the ambulatory and carefully maintains both the tomb chamber itself and the graves it contains: there are five smaller tombs surrounding the principal one, and they are said in Hyderabad to be the resting place of William's Muslim wives. Mr Das told me he places a new marigold garland on Fyze's tomb every week, and that though he is a Hindu himself, he also maintains and garlands the pictures of the Ka'aba and of the Sacred Heart that he has erected on the wall of the chamber, thus showing himself to be an appropriately syncretic guardian of Fyze's mortal remains.

that eventually brought about its complete and disastrous collapse soon after he left Hyderabad.

De Warren was disgusted by the way Russell and the other British had treated Palmer, and wrote an affectionate description of him in his book *L'Inde Anglaise*, in which he contrasted the starchy manners of the Residency with the elegance and refinement of Palmer's mansion:

> At the Residency, the manners are stiff, cold and polite, and conversation choked in half-whispers, as in a European court; but nearby is the more oriental court of the Palmers, where reigns the politeness of the Persians, the dignity of the Moghuls, the hospitality of the Arabs. At William Palmer's table, there are always some 20 places laid for any visitors who might chance to come by, and at the head of the table presides Palmer himself, who in spite of the original sin of being half-caste, is ennobled by his own genius. Small in stature and as black as the servant standing behind his chair, he calmly smokes his hookha while running his eye over papers written in the Persian or Nagari script and stacked next to the luncheon he barely touches. His two charming nieces sit next to him and do the honours of his table. While they entertain the English guests, the elite of the three cantonments, he receives the humble salutations of the greatest nobles of the city. The learned Pandit, the pious Mulla, the proud Amir all bow with deep reverence before this frail old man.
>
> Messrs Palmer have long served as intermediaries between the Nizam and the British government in India, loyally serving both as the Rothschilds of the Deccan. In any crisis, their honestly acquired wealth came to the rescue of the protectors as well as of the protected. And how were they thanked? Just what one would expect from an ungrateful world: the two governments came to an agreement to strip them bare of their assets . . . and the Palmers lost all their money. Today they have nothing left but a meagre allowance paid at the caprice of [the Minister] Chandu Lal – which is neither reliable nor regular. What they have in undiminished quantity and quality is their honour – the respect of whites as well as of natives will follow them to the grave.

De Warren went on to give a description of the life led by William Palmer and his younger brother Hastings. It is one of the last accounts that would ever be penned of the hybrid white Mughal lifestyle: when de Warren's book went to the press in 1845, British and Indians were drawing fast apart, and Palmer's lifestyle had already become something of an anachronism, a survival from an earlier age. De Warren's tone, with its mid-nineteenth-century racial stereotypes, is another indication of how fast the world was changing:

> The private life of the leaders of this family is overtly epicurian ... Their European education has made them sceptical deists; their oriental upbringing has habituated them to an extreme refinement; their mixed blood has made it impossible for them to find wives who could also be intellectual partners, and so drives them back to unadulterated oriental sensuality. So they each have their harems filled with women of all ages and colours and creeds, all married and divorced according to the whims of favour, but all kept honourably and generously. Their progeny would do honour to King Priam – I have seen there children of all ages and shades. This family has still been able to hold its own against the prejudice that pursues it relentlessly, but woe to them the day William Palmer should die! Only he can face out public opinion, to overwhelm prejudice by the prestige of his genius, his learning, his independent and liberal ideas, his long-term renown, the memory of his boundless generosity, of his immense hospitality in the years of good fortune, which led to his being called 'Prince of Merchants', a title shared with his half-brother in Calcutta.
>
> But William is a frail and elderly man, worn out by the climate and his private griefs. He will not accept the reality of his poverty, nor put a limit to his generous impulses, and still takes care to relieve the miseries of the poor while poverty itself invades his own home. His superb gardens are untended, trees collapse out of sheer old age and are not replanted; the pools without water; even the house itself is crumbling and may well not outlive its aged master. I last visited the garden and its cypresses in 1839 at the moment when I was leaving India for the last time. Poor Palmer, only these trees will

remain after you, and the English whom you have so often hospitably received at your table will repay your generosity by heaping scorn and insults on your children, blocking and refusing them entry into society.[44]

Russell had played his part in Palmer's downfall, and in the inquiry which followed the failure of the bank, which ruined more than 1200 of its investors (who all lost everything), he had not only failed to come to Palmer's defence, he had also resolutely denied having any connection whatsoever with the bank. He even went so far as bribing, at a cost of £60, the printers of the official inquiry report, *The Hyderabad Papers*, in order to make sure that the link between him and Palmer was never published.[45]

It must therefore have been something of a surprise to Russell when in 1841, two years after de Warren's last glimpse of Palmer's crumbling mansion, and a year after Kitty's surprise visit, a letter from Palmer should arrive at Swallowfield. It must have been even more of a surprise that the subject of the letter – after twenty-one years of silence – was none other than Sharaf un-Nissa.

After the death of Khair un-Nissa, her mother Sharaf un-Nissa had hoped that Sahib Allum and Sahib Begum would continue to keep in touch with their Hyderabadi family. At Khair's death they had, after all, inherited not only all Khair's jewels, the value of which was conservatively estimated at £12,000, and which Sharaf had initially put aside for them, but also considerable estates across the Nizam's dominions. As Russell wrote soon after Khair's death, Sharaf un-Nissa's

> own notion seems to be that the children when they grow up will come to take possession of their property . . . I am disposed therefore as far as it depends on me to leave the induce-

ment for the boy at least to visit his grandmother a few years hence. His fortune will be such as to make it unnecessary for him to follow any profession for a livelihood, and when his education has been completed, I don't see how he could employ two or three years better than by coming to India.[46]

Since then, however, things had not gone according to plan. Not only had the children been forbidden from keeping in touch with their grandmother,* as Palmer's letter to Russell revealed, the family's huge and lucrative estates had all been summarily confiscated by the Minister, Rajah Chandu Lal, more than a decade earlier, following the death of Nizam Sikander Jah. For the last twelve years, it now emerged, Sharaf un-Nissa had been living off the charity of William Palmer. Now that Palmer was himself on the verge of destitution, he had suggested that Sharaf had no option but to write a begging letter to Russell, the man who had not only destroyed her beloved daughter three decades earlier, but had also played his part in ruining Palmer himself. Sharaf un-Nissa duly wrote to Russell asking him to use his influence with the Minister, as she was now utterly without means and, having sold her last piece of jewellery, had no one else to appeal to. As she explained through a Persian letter-writer:

> Now in these days I am in debt and helpless. If I were to describe my situation, it would only upset you. In the past 12 years since my jagirs were confiscated, I have had to sell everything that was in my home just in order to be able to buy food for myself – the barest provisions necessary for mere survival – so as not to die. Now there is nothing left. I have nobody to turn to, other than God Himself! This is no longer the time for forgetfulness and neglect. What more can I write, except my prayers . . .[47]

The tone of utter desperation pricked Russell's generally far from over-active conscience, and he wrote back by return, offering to do all he could. In a covering letter to William Palmer, Russell thanked him for getting in touch despite all that had passed between them:

---

* Though clearly she had somehow been informed of the death of Sahib Allum/William George in 1828.

I assure you that I take it very kindly of you to have written
... After the changes of one and twenty years the Begum
would have found it difficult to obtain access to me in any
other way, and I should have had no means of conveying my
answer to her ... The Begum desires nothing more than the
common right of being protected in the enjoyment of that
property which originally and personally belonged to her ...
What has already been done cannot be recalled but I may,
and if I can I will, devise some security for the future. There
is no one for whom I have a stronger respect and affection
than for Shurfoon Nissa Begum, and there is no effort I will
not make to mitigate any difficulties that may press upon
her.[48]

He went on to describe his own growing health problems: a series
of 'paralytic seizures', and a severe infection in his eyes that had
left him all but blind. Via Palmer, he then sent the old lady the
first news of her granddaughter that she had received for many
years:

Col. Kirkpatrick's daughter, Mrs Phillipps, is well & happy.
She lives in Devonshire & I unfortunately missed seeing her
owing to her Residence being in a different part of the country
when I was there on a visit to my sister last year. She was
with Mrs Duller on a visit to a relation in our neighbourhood,
and at Swallowfield when I happened to be in London. As to
the 2000 Rupees which you say is pressing upon her [Sharaf
un-Nissa] and which would remove her difficulty I must beg
of you to pay it for me. I still have a small account with
Binny's House at Madras and I have no doubt they will cash
the bill upon me for the amount.

He saved a more personal request for last:

I am sorry to see a confirmation of what I had before heard
of the Begum having disposed of some of her jewels. Among
them was a *teeka* [forehead jewel] of diamond which I will
be sorry from old association to see pass into the hands of a
stranger. Should you be able to ascertain delicately whether
that was one of the things disposed of & if it was possible to

trace it, I should be thankful to you to repurchase it & send it to me . . .

The tika he refers to must, presumably, have belonged to Khair un-Nissa, and been a jewel he would have known well on the forehead of his old lover. It is always difficult to divine motives, and especially so in this case. Was this the sexual vanity of an old man? Or can one imagine that Russell was perhaps regretful, or remorseful – or even, at some level, still a little in love with the memory of Khair un-Nissa, and the times they had spent together in Calcutta some four decades earlier, in younger, happier days when his future was still bright and his reputation still uncompromised? Russell was, after all, always a weak, rather than a bad man. But it was too late, in every sense, to recapture that moment or to undo what had been done. William Palmer made discreet enquiries, but answered that sadly 'the *teeka* was sold many years ago – & there is no trace left of it'. He added: 'Your assistance came very timely to the poor Begum; she is in great distress. Everything of value has been sold; and a silver chilumchee [basin] was sold through my means a short time back to meet some immediate exigencies. The other things which came with the chilumchee, silver articles of small value, necessitated a breaking up of all that belonged to her establishment . . .'[49]

On hearing this, Russell then did one more thing for the old lady. He finally got directly in touch with Kitty, by return, and told her that her grandmother was in dire need.

Shortly after her visit to Swallowfield, Kitty had had another chance encounter: on a visit to Exmouth in 1841, she had happened to meet the wife of the newly appointed Assistant to the Resident at Hyderabad, Captain Duncan Malcolm, the nephew of James Kirkpatrick's former Assistant, John Malcolm.

Now, alerted by Russell, and using Malcolm as an intermediary and Persian translator, Kitty managed to re-establish contact with Sharaf un-Nissa, the grandmother with whom she had not communicated for nearly forty years. There followed a remarkable and extremely emotional correspondence between the two women, one writing in English from Torquay, the other from Hyderabad dictating in Persian to a scribe who wrote on paper sprinkled with gold dust and enclosed in a *kharita*, a sealed bag of gold Mughal brocade.

Sitting in her villa in Torquay, looking out over the breakers of the same grey northern sea which had brought her to England in 1805, Kitty wrote:

My dear Grandmother,
I received many years ago, your kind letter of condolence with me on the death of my beloved brother. I was very grateful to you for it, tho' by my not having answered it, I am afraid that you may have thought that I little regarded it. But indeed I did, & the more so, because I felt that you too mourned for him I loved so well & that you too were connected with him by the binding ties of blood.

Two years after his death I was married to a nephew of Sir John Kennaway's. My husband is of my own age & is a Captain in the English army.

I have four children living, my eldest daughter is 11 years old. She is exactly like my husband. I have a boy of 8 years & a half, then another girl of 7 and a half who is exactly like my mothers picture & one darling infant of 19 months. I have had seven living children – 1 sweet boy and two sweet girls are gone, but I am blest in those that survive. My boy is so striking an image of my father that a picture that was drawn of my father as a little boy is always taken for my boy. They have a good intellect & are blest with fair skin. I live in a nice pretty house in the midst of a garden on the sea coast. My dear husband is very kind to me & I love him greatly.

I often think of you and remember you and my dear mother. I often dream that I am with you in India and that I see you both in the room you used to sit in. No day of my life has ever passed without my thinking of my dear mother. I can remember the verandah and the place where the tailors worked and a place on the house top where my mother used to let me sit down and slide.

When I dream of my mother I am in such joy to have found her again that I awake, or else am pained in finding that she cannot understand the English I speak. I can well recollect her cries when we left her and I can now see the place where she sat when we parted, and her tearing her long hair – what worlds would I give to possess one lock of that beautiful and much loved hair! How dreadful to think that so many, many years have passed when it would have done my heart such good to think that you loved me & when I longed to write to you & tell you these feelings that I was never able to express, a letter which I was sure would have been detained & now how wonderful it is that after 35 years I am able for the first time to hear that you think of me, and love me, and have perhaps wondered why I did not write to you, and that you have thought me cold and insensible to such near dear ties. I thank God that he has opened for me a way of making the feelings of my heart known to you.

Will this reach you & will you care for the letter of your grandchild? My own heart tells me you will. May God bless you my own dear Grandmother.[50]

The letter ends with a postscript requesting that Sharaf un-Nissa send a lock of her daughter's hair. Sharaf un-Nissa replied in Persian, enclosing the lock of Khair un-Nissa's hair she had kept all that time for Kitty ('a portion of it is plain, the rest is made up'), and saying that when she heard that Kitty was still alive,

Fresh vigour was instilled into my deadened heart and such immeasurable joy was attained by me that it cannot be brought within the compass of being written or recounted. My Child, the Light of my Eyes, the solace of my soul, may God grant you long life!

After offering up my prayers that your days may be lengthened and your dignity increased, let it be known to you that at this moment, by the mercy of God, my health is excellent, and I am at all seasons praying for her welfare at the Threshold of the Almighty. Night and day my eyes are directed to my child.

In compliance with what my child has written, the wife of Captain Duncan Malcolm invited me to her house and told me of the welfare of my child, and of the children of my child. Night and day my eyes are directed to my child. The letter written to me by you is pressed by me sometimes to my head and sometimes to my eyes . . . If I can procure a female artist I will send my child my portrait. My child must send me her likeness and those of her children . . .[51]

The correspondence continued for six years. Spectacles (three pairs in all), pills, money, locks of hair and photographs headed off for Hyderabad; illuminated manuscripts, elaborate pieces of calligraphy and Persian poems came back. On one occasion Kitty recalled:

I have a distinct picture of you in my memory as you were when I was a little child, giving you I am afraid a great deal of trouble. I remember one day when I suppose I had been very naughty you whipped me with your slipper & I was very angry. How often I have been obliged to administer the same correction to my children & then I tell them [']when I was little my grandmother was obliged to whip me'.

This they listen to with great attention & ask me about my grandmother, so I tell them all about you that I can remember. I wish you could see the darling faces of my children especially of the one that I am sure is so like my mother, only not near so beautiful. I have such a dear merry faced little boy who would delight you, in many things he is so like my dear brother. Whilst my brother lived I could talk of you & my mother to him & we could compare our recollections of all we had left in India . . .

Kitty communicated her suspicions about Russell's role in her mother's life to Duncan Malcolm, asking him to find as discreetly as he could whether the Chinnery had really been meant to go to Russell, or to her. This Malcolm tactfully declined to do, remarking in his covering letter that 'The old lady's memory is not good and in this matter I am inclined to trust more to Sir Hy's statement than to your grandmothers account of the transaction of which she does not appear to have a very clear recollection.'*

Kitty also asked her grandmother to send her a full account of her parents' meeting and marriage, which Sharaf duly dictated and sent to Torquay. One thing she could not produce, however. Kitty had laboured all her life in the unenviable position of being regarded as illegitimate. This was because in his will, James Kirkpatrick had referred to both Sahib Allum and Sahib Begum as his 'natural children': contemporary legal terminology for the children of unmarried parents. One of Kitty's principal concerns when writing to her grandmother had been to try to get Sharaf to find a certificate from the Nizam, or a *mujtahid* which formally proved that some sort of legal marriage ceremony had taken place between James and Khair. Sharaf un-Nissa was happy to put on record a formal signed description of James's marriage, but she was unable to produce any document from the time which put the matter beyond legal doubt.

Help on this did, however, come from the rather unexpected quarter of Sir Henry Russell. He had heard of Kitty's worries and the pain they gave her, and feeling that he was one of the last people alive who knew the truth, he finally decided to put the record straight. On a trip to the West Country, he went to see Kitty in Torquay, but finding himself alone with her, and overcome with embarrassment, could not bring himself to broach the subject. Just as before with Kitty's mother, he fell back on his younger brother Charles. Charles was now the rather grand Chairman of Great Western Railways and the MP for Reading,[52] and Henry wrote to him to ask if he would talk to Kitty. He explained that on his visit he had

> hesitated, and was restrained by delicacy from seeming to meddle with a matter which might be said not to belong to me ... Mrs. Phillipps has always passed for an illegitimate

* The picture did go to Kitty on Russell's death in 1852, 'notwithstanding the remonstrances of his family ... an evil day for them', as his daughter-in-law Constance later wrote. See Lady Russell, *The Rose Goddess and Other Sketches of Mystery & Romance* (London, 1910), p.1. It remained in the family until the 1960s when, after 120 years in Britain, it sailed east again. It now hangs in the boardroom of the Hongkong and Shanghai Bank.

child; and is so designated in her father's will; though her birth was as legitimate as yours or mine. Col Kirkpatrick ascribed to her that relation which he supposed her to stand. He knew that he had been married; but he did not think that his marriage was [legally] valid. He supposed, as I did until my father set me right, that a Mahometan marriage was to a Christian null and void; and I conclude he was afraid of invalidating his bequest to his daughter if he designated her in his will by a term which he thought the law would not accord to her.

When, or from whom, I first heard of the marriage, I do not now remember, I think it was soon after Col Kirkpatrick's death in 1805, and that it was told me by his Moonshee Uzeez Oollah, who accompanied me to Calcutta, went on soon after to Benares and I believe finally died there. Certainly I did not hear it from Col Kirkpatrick himself. It was not a subject I ever heard him speak of; nor did I hear in the first instance from Mrs Phillipps' mother, Khyr oon Nifsa Begum, nor from her grandmother, Shurf oon Nifsa, though they both of them often confirmed it to me; and I have and still have such complicit reliance on their word that I am as firmly satisfied that the ceremony which they described did take place, as if I had witnessed it myself.

In 1843, Kitty told her grandmother that William George's eldest daughter was about to go to India and that she planned to visit Sharaf un-Nissa when she got there. This produced an immediate and excited reply:

My heart cannot contain the joy it feels in hearing that the daughter of Sahib Allum is about to visit Hindostan with her husband, and I will without fail cherish that child as the apple of my eye ... May the pure and exalted God speedily lift up the veil of separation from between us, and bringing us all together in person make us happy and gladden us with a meeting.[53]

It is unclear whether Sharaf un-Nissa ever got to see her great-granddaughter; but she certainly never saw her granddaughter Kitty again. Four years later, Henry Russell received another letter from William Palmer. It was dated 27 July 1847:

> My dear Sir,
> I fear the intelligence I have to communicate will distress you. For Shurf oon Nissa Begum died on the 21st Inst [of this month] of dropsy. She was not attended by an English doctor but at her age (over eighty) it would have availed little to arrest the termination common to all. I do not know whether you recollect a relation of hers, Mahmood Ali Khan. He resided with her. There was a mutual confidence & good understanding between them which made him appear (he was her relation) as the son of her adoption. Mahmood Ali Khan married his daughter to Soliman Jah* and the connection so formed has given to Soliman Jah a pretence to put guards on her property, preparatory to its sequestration. Mahmud Ali Khan writes to me that he is distasteful to his son in law & apprehends he will suffer ill usage at his hands. There is no remedy for this. The Govt is too much disordered to give any protection to individuals . . .[54]

Almost exactly ten years later, on 10 May 1857, the great Indian Mutiny broke out in Meerut, north of Delhi.

By that time, the world that gave birth to Kitty Kirkpatrick had disappeared; indeed it had been dead for the best part of two decades. All

---

* i.e. Sulaiman Jah, the then Nizam's uncle, who as a seven-year-old in 1802 had said that he wanted to marry Fyze's adopted daughter, Fanny Khanum.

the white Mughals had long been in their graves: Sir David Ochterlony had died (in Meerut, as it happened) in 1825, heartbroken at a humiliating rebuke from his masters in Calcutta; his friend and protégé William Fraser (whom Lady Nugent had castigated as 'being as much Hindoo as Christian') was assassinated ten years after that in 1835.

The last survivor of the world of James Achilles Kirkpatrick was probably William Linnaeus Gardner, who as a young man had married his Cambay Begum, converted to Islam, and been present as a Hyderabad mercenary in the Nizam's forces at the surrender of the Corps de Raymond in 1798. After years of fighting for different Indian princes, Gardner had finally entered British service in 1803, founding his own regiment of irregular cavalry, Gardner's Horse. His final posting, bizarrely enough, was as deputy to Hindoo Stuart who, despite his many eccentricities, had been given command of the largest cavalry cantonment in central India, at Saugor. It must have been a rather unusual outpost of the East India Company military establishment, commanded as it was by a pair of European converts to India's two rival religions.

Here, throughout the early 1820s, Stuart continued to fight his losing battle to allow his sepoys to wear their caste-marks and their own choice of facial hair on parade, being again reprimanded by the commander-in-chief. His retort that 'A stronger instance than this of European prejudice with relation to this country has never come under my observations' had no effect on his superiors.[55] Stuart's military career thus ended under something of a cloud. As his deputy Gardner put it, 'Poor General Pundit! He is in hot water with almost everyone.'[56] The last glimpse of Stuart in Gardner's correspondence is of him setting off to Calcutta, his Indian *bibi* beside him, his buggy followed by a cavalcade of children's carriages 'and a palkee load of little babes', already a figure who seemed to have survived from a different, more tolerant and open-minded world.

In his last years of retirement, Gardner settled down on his wife's *jagir* at Khasgunge near Agra. His son James had married Mukhta Begum, who was the niece of the Mughal Emperor Akbar Shah as well as being the sister-in-law of the Nawab of Avadh, and together they fathered a noble Anglo-Indian dynasty, half of whose members were Muslim and half Christian; indeed some of them, such as James Jehangir Shikoh Gardner, seem to have been both at the same time. Even those Gardners who were straightforwardly Christian had alternative Muslim names: thus the Rev. Bartholomew Gardner could also be addressed as Sabr, under which name he became a notable Urdu and Persian poet, shedding his clerical dress in favour of Avadhi pyjamas to declaim his love poems at Lucknavi *mushairas*.[57]

Already a museum-piece by the 1830s and the subject of occasional wide-eyed articles in the north Indian press, William Gardner died on his Khasgunge estate on 29 July 1835, at the age of sixty-five. His Begum, whose dark eyes he had first glimpsed through the gap between two curtains in Surat thirty-eight years earlier, could not live without him. As Fanny Parkes wrote,

> my beloved friend Colonel Gardner . . . was buried, according to his desire, near the [domed Mughal] tomb of his son Allan. From the time of his death the poor Begum pined and sank daily; just as he said she complained not, but she took his death to heart; she died one month and two days after his decease. Native ladies have a number of titles; her death, names and titles were thus announced in the papers:– 'On the 31st August, at her Residence at Khasgunge. Her Highness Furzund Azeza Azubdeh-tool Arrakeen Umdehtool Assateen Nuwab Mah Munzil ool Nissa Begum Dehlmi, relict of the late Colonel William Linnaeus Gardner. The sound of *Nakaras* and *Dumanas* [kettle drums and trumpets]* have ceased.'[58]

During the Mutiny, Gardner's Anglo-Indian descendants, like those of all the other white Mughals, were forced to make a final choice between one or other of the two sides – though for many the choice was made for them. Some families, such as the Rottens in Lucknow, and Mubarak Begum, Ochterlony's widow in Delhi, chose the rebels (or, if you like, the freedom fighters). After an attack on their property, the Gardners were forced to take refuge first in Aligarh then in the fort of Agra, and so ended up on the side of the British

---

* A reference to the Begum's rank, by which she was entitled to the use of the *palki* (ceremonial litter), the *morchal*, or fan of peacock feathers, and the *naqqara* and *dumana*, or state kettle drums.

– though given a free hand they might just as easily have lined up behind their Mughal cousins in Delhi and Lucknow.*

The Mutiny led to massive and vicious bloodshed, with great numbers of lives lost on either side. Afterwards, nothing could ever be as it was before; the trust and mutual admiration that the white Mughals had tried to cultivate was destroyed for ever. With the British victory, and the genocidal spate of hangings and executions that followed it, the entire top rank of the Mughal aristocracy was swept away and British culture was unapologetically imposed on India; at the same time the wholesale arrival of the memsahibs, the rise of Evangelical Christianity and the moral certainties it brought with it ended all open sexual contact between the two nations.

In Hyderabad there had been less fighting than in the war-torn north – though there was a half-hearted attack on the Residency by a party of Rohilla horsemen; but the same bitterness and polarisation occurred. William Palmer, one of the last figures to attempt to bridge both worlds, ended up opting for the British. Though he had initially been brought up a Muslim, had married a variety of Muslim wives, and had lovingly cared for his Muslim mother, Fyze Baksh Begum, he ended his days consciously and defiantly a Christian. A year before his death, disillusioned and bankrupt, he wrote a sad letter to an old

---

* Despite possessing a claim to the *pukka* peerage, the Barony of Uttoxeter, over time the family squandered their wealth and became poorer and poorer, less and less British and more and more provincial Indian, gradually losing all touch with their aristocratic English relations. The Vicereine, Lady Halifax, had Gardner blood, and records in her memoirs that she was a little surprised when alighting from the viceregal train on her way from Delhi up to Simla, to see the stationmaster of Kalka break through the ceremonial guard and fight his way up to the red carpet. Shouldering through the ranks of aides and the viceregal retinue, he addressed the Vicereine:

'Your Excellency,' he said, 'my name is Gardner.'

'Of course,' replied Lady Halifax, somewhat to the astonishment of her entourage. 'We are therefore cousins.'

The Gardner dynasty, incidentally, still survives at Khasgunge between Agra and Lucknow, today one of the most violent and backward parts of India (though the picture has been somewhat muddied by an Evangelical missionary from the family who named all his many converts after himself, thus filling Khasgunge with legions of Gardners, many of whom are no genetic relation at all to William Linnaeus). The present claimant to the title Lord Gardner, Baron Uttoxeter, who has never been to England and speaks only faltering English, contents himself with farming his Indian acres and enjoying the prestige of being the village wrestling champion; but until recently he threatened every so often to return 'home' and take up his seat in the House of Lords.

friend and former comrade-in-arms, Major Francis Gresley, who had retired to England. 'My old age,' he wrote,

> eighty-six years old, has left me destitute of friends. I am so infirm that I cannot walk from one apartment to another without some support, and have been almost blind for the last ten or twelve years ... I continue to take an interest in the persons and events around me ... [but] the arrogance and superciliousness of the Mohammedans, and their almost avowed hatred of us have made them detestable to me. There is not a man among them who would not cut our throats, and Briggs [one of the Residency staff] has quaintly expressed himself to the effect that he never sees a Musselman without fancying he sees his assassin. The Residency staff, I understand, now carry loaded pocket pistols about with them.[59]

It was as different a world as could be imagined from that of James Achilles Kirkpatrick, with his family parties in the old-city townhouse and merry nights with Tajalli Ali Shah and the poets of Hyderabad; his evenings spent fishing with the old Nizam for the tame carp in the palace ponds, and afternoons flying pigeons with the Minister in his garden.

William Palmer died on Monday, 25 November 1867. The British Resident, Sir Richard Temple, was one of the few to attend the funeral. But he left early, anxious not to miss the beginning of the Chaddarghat races.[60]

Kitty's husband, Major Phillipps, died in 1864; Kitty survived him. Before she too died, she paid a last visit to Carlyle in his Cheyne Row house, about which visit he quoted from Virgil the lines '*Agnosco veteris vestigia flammae*' (I feel the traces of an ancient flame). Shortly afterwards he wrote to her:

Your little visit did me a great deal of good; so interesting, so strange to see her who we used to call 'Kitty' emerging on me from the dusk of an evening like a dream become real. It sets me thinking for many hours upon times long gone, and persons and events that can never cease to be important and affecting to me . . . All round me is the sound as of evening bells, which are not sad only, or ought not to be, but beautiful also and blessed and quiet. No more today, dear lady: my best wishes and affectionate regards will abide with you to the end.[61]

Kitty lived on quietly in Torquay, finally passing away in 1889 in her house, the Villa Sorrento. Four years afterwards, her cousin Sir Edward Strachey wrote up the first account of James's marriage to Khair, and of Carlyle's fascination with Kitty, for the July 1893 edition of *Blackwood's Magazine*, ending the piece with Kitty's death: 'She was ten years my elder,' he wrote, 'but I remember her from girlhood to old age as the most fascinating of women.'[62]

With the deaths of William Palmer in 1867 and Kitty Kirkpatrick in 1889, an era can truly be said to have come to an end. Although one died in Hyderabad and the other in Torquay, both were buried in Christian cemeteries, with unambiguously Christian inscriptions commemorating them. There was no longer any room for crossover or ambiguity. The day for that had passed.

Their deaths effectively brought to a conclusion three hundred years of fusion and hybridity, all memory of which was later delicately erased from embarrassed Victorian history books, though Khair's posthumous elevation into 'a Hindoo Princess' gave the story of her affair with James an element of 'Oriental Romance' that allowed it to escape the informal censorship that erased so many other similar stories.[63] It would take another seventy years, and the implosion of an empire, before the two races were again able to come into close and intimate contact.

Even today, despite all the progress that has been made, we still have rhetoric about 'clashing civilisations', and almost daily generalisations in the press about East and West, Islam and Christianity, and the vast differences and fundamental gulfs that are said to separate the two. The white Mughals – with their unexpected minglings and fusions, their hybridity and above all their efforts at promoting tolerance and understanding – attempted to bridge these two worlds, and to some extent they succeeded in doing so.

As the story of James Achilles Kirkpatrick and Khair un-Nissa shows, East and West are not irreconcilable, and never have been. Only bigotry, prejudice, racism and fear drive them apart. But they have met and mingled in the past; and they will do so again.

GLOSSARY

Akhbar	Indian court newsletter
Alam	Standard used by Shi'as as a focus for their *Muharram* (qv) venerations. Usually tear-shaped (as illustrated in the text breaks of this book) or fashioned into the shape of a hand, they are stylised representations of the standards carried by Imam Hussain at the Battle of Kerbala in AD680. Often highly ornate and beautiful objects, the best of them are among the greatest masterpieces of medieval Indian metalwork
Amir	Nobleman
Angia	A sensuous, halter-neck version of the *choli* (qv) bodice, usually transparent or semi-transparent, that became very fashionable in Muslim courts in the late eighteenth and early nineteenth centuries. Fyze Palmer is wearing one under her *peshwaz* (qv) in her famous portrait by Zoffany
Apsaras	The courtesans and dancing girls of the Hindu gods; heavenly dispensers of erotic bliss
Arrack	Indian absinthe
Arzee	Persian petition
Aseels	Key figures in a *zenana* (qv). Usually slave girls by origin, they performed a number of essential administrative and domestic tasks within the women's quarters, including that of wetnurse. In the Nizam's *zenana* the senior *aseels* were important figures of state
Ashur khana	Mourning hall for use during *Muharram* (qv)
Avatar	An incarnation
Baksheesh	Tip for services rendered
Banka	Mughal gallant
Baradari	A Mughal-style open pavilion with three arches on each side (lit. 'twelve doors')

Begum	Indian Muslim noblewoman. A title of rank and respect: 'Madam'
Betel	Nut used as a mild narcotic in India, and eaten as *paan*
Bhand	Buffoon, mummer or mimic
Bhisti	Water carrier
Bibi	An Indian wife or mistress
Bibi ghar	'Women's house' or *zenana* (qv)
Bidri	The adjectival form of the place-name Bidar, the capital city of the Islamic Deccan in the fifteenth century. It is normally used to designate metalwork produced in Bidar from an alloy in which zinc predominates, usually decorated with silver or brass inlays in floral patterns against a blackened metal background
Biryani	The rice and meat dish which is the particular speciality of Hyderabadi cuisine
Brahmin	The Hindu priestly caste and the top rung of the caste pyramid
Chamars	Untouchables of the sweeper caste
Char bagh	A formal Mughal garden, named after its division into four (*char*) squares by a cross of runnels and fountains
Chattri	A domed kiosk supported on pillars, often used as a decorative feature to top turrets and minarets (lit. 'umbrella')
Choli	Short (and at this period usually transparent) Indian bodice
Chunam	Polished lime plaster
Coss	Mughal measurement of distance amounting to just over two miles
Daftar	Office, or in the Nizam's palace, chancellery
Dak	Post (sometimes spelt '*dawke*' in the eighteenth and early nineteenth centuries)
Deorhi	Courtyard house or *haveli*
Derzi	Tailor
Devadasi	Temple dancers, prostitutes and courtesans who were given to the great Hindu temples, usually in infancy by their parents (lit. 'slave girls of the gods')

Dharamasala	Rest house
Dhobi	Laundryman
Dhoolie	Covered litter
Dhoti	Loincloth
Divan	Book of collected poetry
Diwan	Prime minister, or the vizier in charge of administrative finance
Dragoman	Interpreter or guide in the Ottoman or Persian Empires
Dubash	Interpreter
Dupatta	Shawl or scarf, usually worn with a *salvar kemise* (lit. 'two leaves or widths'). Also known as a *chunni*
Durbar	Court
Fakir	Sufi holy man, dervish or wandering Muslim ascetic (lit. 'poor')
Fatiha	The short opening chapter of the Koran, read at ceremonial occasions as an invocation
Firangi	Foreigner
Firman	An order of the emperor or sultan in a written document
Ghazal	Urdu or Persian love lyric
Hakim	Physician
Halwa	Pudding made of carrot, or more rarely squash or pumpkin
Hamam	Turkish-style steam bath
Haram	Forbidden
Harkarra	Runner, messenger, newswriter or spy (lit: 'all-do-er') In eighteenth-century sources the word is sometimes spelt *hircarrah*
Havildar	A sepoy (qv) non-commissioned officer, corresponding to a sergeant
Holi	The Hindu spring festival in which participants sprinkle red and yellow powder on one another
Hookah	Waterpipe or hubble bubble
Id	The two greatest Muslim festivals: Id ul-Fitr marks the end of Ramadan, while Id ul-Zuha commemorates the delivery of Isaac. To celebrate the latter a ram or goat is slaughtered, as on the original occasion recorded in both the Old Testament and the Koran

Iftar	The evening meal to break the Ramadan fast
Jagir	Landed estate, granted for service rendered to the state and whose revenues could be treated as income by the *jagirdar*
Jali	A latticed stone or wooden screen
Jashn	Party or marriage feast
Karkhana	Workshop or factory
Khanazad	Palace-born princes
Khansaman	In the eighteenth century the word meant butler. Today it more usually means cook
Khanum	A junior wife or concubine
Kharita	Sealed Mughal brocade bag used to send letters as an alternative to an envelope
Khilat	Symbolic court dress
Kotwal	The police chief, chief magistrate or city administrator in a Mughal town
Lakh	One hundred thousand
Langar	Free distribution of food during a religious festival
Lathi	Truncheon or stick
Lota	Water pot
Lungi	Indian-type sarong, longer version of the *dhoti* (qv)
Mahal	Lit. 'palace', but often used to refer to sleeping apartments or the *zenana* wing of a palace or residence
Maistry	(modern Hindi: *mistri*) A highly skilled foreman or master craftsman. According to *Hobson Jobson* the word, 'a corruption of of the Portuguese *mestre* has spread into the vernaculars all over India and is in constant Anglo-Indian use'
Majlis	Assembly, especially the gatherings during *Muharram* (qv)
Mansabdar	A Mughal nobleman and office-holder, whose rank was decided by the number of cavalry he would supply for battle – for example, a *mansabdar* of 2500 would be expected to provide 2500 horsemen when the Nizam went to war
Marsiya	Urdu or Persian lament or dirge for the martyrdom of Hussain, the grandson of the Prophet, sung in the

	ashur khana (qv) mourning halls during the festival of *Muharram* (qv)
Masnavi	Persian or Urdu love lyric or religious verse
Maula	'My Lord'
Mehfil	An evening of courtly Mughal entertainment, normally including dancing, the recitation of poetry and the singing of *ghazals* (qv)
Mihrab	The niche in a mosque pointing in the direction of Mecca
Mir	Title given before a name usually signifying that the holder is a *sayyed* (qv)
Mirza	Prince or gentleman
Mohalla	A distinct quarter of a Mughal city – i.e. a group of residential lanes, usually entered through a single gate
Muharram	The great Shi'a Muslim festival commemorating the defeat and death of Imam Hussain, the Prophet's grandson. Celebrated with particular gusto in Hyderabad and Lucknow
Mujtahid	A cleric; one who does *ijtehad*, the interpretation of religious texts
Munshi	Indian private secretary or language teacher
Murqana	Stalactite-type decoration over a mosque or palace gateway
Mushaira	Poetic symposium
Musnud	The low arrangement of cushions and bolsters which formed the throne of Indian rulers at this period
Nabob	English corruption of the Hindustani *nawab*, literally 'deputy', which was the title given by the Mughal emperors to their regional governors and viceroys. In England it became a term of abuse directed at returned 'old India hands', especially after Samuel Foote's 1779 play *The Nabob* brought the term into general circulation
Naqqar khana	Ceremonial drum house
Nautch	Indian dance display
Nazr	Symbolic gift given in Indian courts to a feudal superior

Nizam	Part of the title of the first Subedar of the Deccan, Asaf Jah, Nizam ul-Mulk. In the fashion of the time, Asaf Jah became effectively independent of the Mughal government in Delhi, and at his death in 1748 his title was claimed as hereditary by his dynastic successors, starting with his illegitimate younger son and eventual successor, Nizam Ali Khan
Omrah	Nobleman
Palanquin	Indian litter
Peshkash	An offering or present given by a subordinate to a superior. The term was used more specifically by the Marathas as the money paid to them by 'subordinate' powers such as the Nizam
Peshwaz	Long, high-waisted gown
Pikdan	Spittoon
Pir	Sufi holy man
Pirzada	Official at a Sufi shrine, often a descendant of the founding saint
Prasad	Temple sweets given to devotees in exchange for offerings – a tradition transferred from Hindu to Islamic practice at the Sufi shrines of the Deccan
Pukka	Proper, correct
Purdah	Lit. 'a curtain'; used to signify the concealment of women within the *zenana* (qv)
Qawal	A singer of *qawalis* (qv)
Qawalis	Rousing hymns sung at Sufi shrines
Qiladar	Fort keeper
Qizilbash	Lit. 'redheads'. Name given to Saffavid soldiers (and later traders) due to the tall red cap worn under their turbans
Rakhi	Band worn around the wrist as a sign of brotherhood, solidarity or protection
Salatin	Palace-born princes
Sanyasi	Hindu ascetic
Sarpeche	Turban jewel or ornament
Sati	The practice of widow-burning, or the burned widow herself

Sawaree	Elephant stables (and the whole establishment and paraphernalia related to the keeping of elephants)
Sayyed	A lineal descendant of the Prophet Mohammed.
(or f. Sayyida)	Sayyeds often have the title 'Mir'
Sepoy	Indian soldier in the service of the East India Company
Shadi	Marriage feast or party
Shamiana	Indian marquee, or the screen formed around the perimeter of a tented area
Shi'a	One of the two principal divisions of Islam, dating back to a split immediately after the death of the Prophet, between those who recognised the authority of the Medinian caliphs and those who followed the Prophet's son-in-law Ali (*Shi'at Ali* means 'the party of Ali' in Arabic). Though most Shi'ites live in Iran, there have always been a large number in the Indian Deccan, and Hyderabad was for much of its history a centre of Shi'ite culture
Shikar	Hunting
Sirdar	Nobleman
Surahi	Traditional tall, elegant north Indian water and wine cooler/flask
Tawaif	The cultivated and urbane dancing girls and courtesans who were such a feature of late Mughal society and culture
Thali	Tray
'Umbara	Covered elephant howdah
Unani	Ionian (or Byzantine Greek) medicine, originally passed to the Islamic world through Byzantine exiles in Persia and still practised in India today
'Urs	Festival day
Vakil	Ambassador or representative (though in modern usage the word means merely lawyer)
Vilayat	Province, homeland
Yakshi	Female Hindu fertility nymphs, often associated with sacred trees and pools
Zamindar	Landholder or local ruler
Zenana	Harem, or women's quarters

NOTES

INTRODUCTION

1 Mark Zebrowski, *Gold, Silver and Bronze from Mughal India* (London, 1997)

2 Edward Strachey, 'The Romantic Marriage of James Achilles Kirkpatrick, Sometime British Resident at the Court of Hyderabad', in *Blackwood's Magazine*, July 1893.

3 That said, though it has yet to be pulled together into a single coherent thesis, there is a growing body of work which has begun to show the degree to which the East India Company officials of the eighteenth century, like the Portuguese before them, assimilated themselves to Mughal culture. Nearly thirty years ago, Percival Spear's *The Nabobs* (Cambridge, 1963) painted a picture of hookah-smoking eighteenth-century Englishmen with Indian *bibis* living it up in Calcutta, while their counterparts in the backwoods *mofussil* towns and more distant centres of Mughal culture made a more profound transition, dressing in Mughal court dress, intermarrying with the Mughal aristocracy and generally attempting to cross cultural boundaries as part of their enjoyment of, and participation in, late Mughal society.

Subsequent work has refined this picture. Much of this work has centred on Lucknow, where Desmond Young, Rosie Llewellyn-Jones, Seema Alavi, Muzaffar Alam, Jean-Marie Lafont and Maya Jasanoff have between them painted a remarkably detailed picture of a hybrid and inclusive culture where men like Claude Martin, Antoine Polier, Benoît de Boigne, John Wombwell and General William Palmer all, to differing extents, embraced that city's notably hedonistic take on late Mughlai civilisation. Desmond Young, *Fountain of Elephants* (London, 1959); Rosie Llewellyn-Jones, *A Fatal Friendship: The Nawabs, the British and the City of Lucknow* (New Delhi, 1982), *A Very Ingenious Man: Claude Martin in Early Colonial India* (New Delhi, 1992) and *Engaging Scoundrels: True Tales of Old Lucknow* (New Delhi, 2000); Muzaffar Alam and Seema Alavi, *A European Experience of the Mughal Orient: The I'jaz i-Arslani (Persian Letters, 1773–1779) of Antoine-Louis Henri Polier* (New Delhi, 2001); Jean-Marie Lafont, 'The French in Lucknow in the Eighteenth Century', in Violette Graff (ed.), *Lucknow: Memories of a City* (New Delhi, 1997) and *Indika: Essays in Indo–French Relations 1630–1976* (New Delhi, 2000); Maya Jasanoff's essay on art-collecting and hybridity in Lucknow will appear in 2002 in *Past & Present*.

Toby Falk, Mildred Archer and myself have found evidence of a similar process of transculturation in Delhi, particularly in the circle of Sir David Ochterlony, William

Fraser and James Skinner that
formed around the British
Residency from around 1805 until
about the time of Fraser's death in
1835: Mildred Archer and Toby Falk,
*India Revealed: The Art and
Adventures of James and William
Fraser 1801–35* (London, 1989);
William Dalrymple, *City of Djinns*
(London, 1993). Seema Alavi has
also shown the extent to which
James Skinner, half-Scottish, half-
Rajput, mixed both cultures to
create an 'amalgamation of Mughal
and European military ethics', as
well as personally acculturating
himself 'in the manners of high
class Muslim society[, adopting]
many of the customs especially the
hookah and Mughal cuisine': Seema
Alavi, *The Sepoys and the Company:
Tradition and Transition in Northern
India 1770–1830* (New Delhi, 1995),
esp. Chapter 6. Skinner has also
been the subject of study by
Mildred Archer in *Between Battles:
The Album of Colonel James Skinner*
(London, 1982) and Christopher
Hawes in *Poor Relations: The
Making of a Eurasian Community in
British India 1773–1833* (London,
1996).

Chris Bayly has shown how
useful inter-racial sexual
relationships were for gaining
knowledge and information about
the other side, while Durba Ghosh's
important work on the *bibis* has
shown just how widespread this sort
of cross-cultural sexual relationship
was at this period: C.A. Bayly,
*Empire and Information: Intelligence
Gathering and Social Communication
in India 1780–1870* (Cambridge,
1996); Durba Ghosh, 'Colonial
Companions: Bibis, Begums, and
Concubines of the British in North
India 1760–1830' (unpublished
Ph.D., Berkeley, 2000). Ghosh has
also demonstrated the extent to
which this assimilation was a two-

way process, affecting the Indian
women who came into close
contact with Europeans as much as
it did the Europeans themselves.
Meanwhile, Amin Jaffer's work has
shown the degree to which the
domestic material environment
Company servants inhabited tended
to be something of an Anglo-
Mughal amalgam, while in a parallel
study Lizzie Collingham has
emphasised the assimilation of the
British body to its Mughal
environment. Linda Colley has
demonstrated the degree to which
English captives – particularly those
imprisoned by Tipu Sultan at
Seringapatam – embraced Islam by
a combination of force and choice,
and the degree to which they took
on different aspects of Indian ways
of living: Amin Jaffer, *Furniture
from British India and Ceylon*
(London, 2001); E.M. Collingham,
*Imperial Bodies: The Physical
Experience of the Raj* (Cambridge,
2001); Linda Colley, 'Going Native,
Telling Tales: Captivity,
Collaborations and Empire', in *Past
& Present*, No. 168, August 2000,
p.172. Colley's forthcoming work,
Captives, will expand on this theme.

4 Mirza Abu Taleb Khan (trans. C.
Stewart), *The Travels of Mirza Abu
Taleb Khan in Asia, Africa, and
Europe during the years 1799, 1800,
1801, 1802, and 1803* (London, 1810).

5 Michael Fisher, *The Travels of Dean
Mahomet: An Eighteenth Century
Journey Through India* (Berkeley,
1997), p.xxi.

CHAPTER 1

1 'Report of an Examination
instituted by the direction of his
Excellency the most noble Governor
General, Fort St. George 7th Nov
1801' OIOC HM464. For
Government House Madras see Sten

Nilsson, *European Architecture in India 1750–1850* (London, 1968) and Mark Bence-Jones, *Palaces of the Raj* (London, 1973).

2 Mountstuart Elphinstone: OIOC, Mss Eur F88 Box13/16[b], f.92.

3 Annemarie Schimmel, *Islam in the Indian Subcontinent* (Leiden-Koln, 1980), p.111.

4 OIOC HM464, op. cit., f.368.

5 Wellington, *Supplementary Despatches & Memoranda, Vol. II*, p.174, 'Memorandum of Conversations which passed between Seyd–oo-Dowlah, Captain Ogg, and Colonel Wellesley, and between Meer Allum and Colonel Wellesley, Dummul 26th Sept 1800'.

6 Quoted by Sir Penderel Moon, *The British Conquest and Dominion of India* (London, 1989), p.277.

7 Stanley Lane-Poole, *Aurangzeb and the Decay of the Mughal Empire* (London, 1890), p.19.

8 Castanheda, *Historia do Descobrimento e Conquista da India peolos Portugueses*, Vol. I, III–43, p.107, and quoted in Maria A.L. Cruz, 'Exiles and Renegades in Early Sixteenth Century Portuguese India', in *The Indian Economic and Social History Review*, XXIII, 3 (1986), p.9.

9 J.H. Van Linschoten, *The Voyage of John Huyghen Van Linschoten to the East Indies* (2 vols, London, 1885; original Dutch edition 1598), p.205.

10 Ibid., p.213.

11 Jean-Baptiste Tavernier (trans. V. Ball, ed. W. Crooke), *Travels in India* (2 vols, Oxford, 1925).

12 Van Linschoten, op. cit., Vol. 1, pp.207–8.

13 Ibid., pp.206–10, 212–14. See also M.N. Pearson, *The New Cambridge History of India 1.1: The Portuguese in India* (Cambridge, 1987), pp.98–119.

14 Quoted in Pearson, op. cit., p.87.

15 Van Linschoten, op. cit., Vol. 1, p.184.

16 Geoffrey Parker, *The Military Revolution* (Oxford, 1988), p.129.

17 See Cruz, op. cit., p.11.

18 G.V. Scammell, 'European Exiles, Renegades and Outlaws and the Maritime Economy of Asia c.1500–1750', in *Modern Asian Studies*, Vol. 26, No. 4 (1992), pp.641–61.

19 See A.R. Disney, *Twilight of the Pepper Empire: Portuguese Trade in South West India in the Early Seventeenth Century* (Harvard, 1978), p.21.

20 From a manuscript in the OIOC by Mirza Mohd Bux 'Ashoob', '*Tarikh i-Shadaat e Farrukhsiyar va juloos e Mohd Shah*', f.266a, quoted by S. Inayat A. Zaidi, 'French Mercenaries in the Armies of South Asian States 1499–1803', in *Indo–French Relations: History and Perspectives* (Delhi, 1990), pp.51–78.

21 Sanjay Subrahmaniyam, *The Portuguese Empire in Asia: A Political and Economic History* (London, 1993), p.254.

22 William Foster (ed.), *Early Travels in India 1583–1619* (London, 1921) pp.203–4.

23 Nabil Matar, *Islam in Britain 1558–1685* (Cambridge, 1998), p.7.

24 Ibid., p.37.

25 Ms Bodley Or.430, f.47 recto.

26 Thomas Pellow (ed. Robert Brown), *The Adventures of Thomas Pellow, of Penryn, Mariner* (London, 1890), p.103; also quoted in Matar, op. cit., p.39.

27 Samuel C. Chew, *The Crescent and the Rose: Islam and England During the Renaissance* (New York, 1937), pp.373–4.

28 Zaidi, op. cit., p.74, n.112.

29 Nabil Matar, *Turks, Moors and Englishmen in the Age of Discovery* (New York, 1999).

30 Quoted in ibid., p.28.

31 Ibid., p.42.

32 William Foster (ed.), *The English*

Factories in India 1618–1669 (13 vols, London, 1906–27), Vol. 1, pp.vi, 39–40.

33 Dr John Fryer, *A New Account of East India and Persia Letters Being Nine Years Travels Begun 1672 and finished 1681* (3 vols, London, 1698), Vol. 1, p.83.

34 Foster, *English Factories*, op. cit., Vol. 3, p.360.

35 Ibid., Vol. 4, p.99.

36 J.A. de Mandelslo (trans. J. Davis), *The Voyages and Travels of J. Albert de Mandelslo: The Voyages & Travels of the Ambasssadors sent by Frederick Duke of Holstein, to the Great Duke of Muscovy, and the King of Persia* (London, 1662), Vol. 3, p.27.

37 Alexander Hamilton, *A New Account of the East Indies*, (2 vols, London, 1930), Vol. 1, pp.8–9.

38 Foster, *English Factories*, op. cit., quoted in Philip Davies, *Splendours of the Raj: British Architecture in India 1660–1947* (London, 1985).

39 John Jourdain (ed. W. Foster), *Journal of John Jourdain 1608–17* (London, 1905), p.162.

40 Foster, *English Factories*, op. cit., Vol. 8, passim. Also OIOC E/3/21, OC2121 (f126), OC2150 (f221), OC2151 (f224), OC2153 (f228), OC2154 (f232), OC2155 (f234), OC2156 (f236).

41 Foster, *English Factories*, op. cit., Vol. 8, p.304.

42 Ibid., Vol. 3, p.345.

43 Cited in H.D. Love, *Vestiges of Old Madras* (2 vols, London, 1913), Vol. 2, p.299.

44 Scammell, op. cit., pp.643, 646.

45 Philip B. Wagoner, '"Sultan among Hindu Kings": Dress, Titles and the Islamicization of Hindu culture at Vijayanagar', in *Journal of Asian Studies*, Vol. 55, No. 4 (November 1996), pp.851–80.

46 Chester Beatty Library 9.681, 'A Young Prince and his Courtesans', in Linda York Leach, *Mughal and Other Paintings from the Chester Beatty Library* (London, 1995), Vol. 2, pp.948–9.

47 Kirkpatrick's conversion to Islam is the best-attested of such conversions for marriage purposes, but it is clear from his letters that William Gardner also had to undergo a similar ceremony, as, very probably, did William Palmer. The practice was no doubt a great deal more widespread than is apparent from the sources, which only go into detail on such points in exceptional circumstances.

48 Colley, 'Going Native, Telling Tales', op. cit., p.172.

49 P.J. Marshall, 'Cornwallis Triumphant: War in India and the British Public in the Late Eighteenth Century', in Lawrence Freeman, Paul Hayes and Robert O' Neill (eds), *War, Strategy and International Politics* (Oxford, 1992), pp.70–1.

50 James Scurry, *The Captivity, Sufferings and Escape of James Scurry, who was detained a prisoner during ten years, in the dominions of Haidar Ali and Tippoo Saib* (London, 1824), pp.252–3.

51 See Jaffer, op. cit., p.36.

52 Claudius Buchanan, *Memoir on the Expediency of an Eccleciastical Establishment for British India; both as a means of Perpetuating the Christian Religion Among Our Own Countrymen; And as a foundation for the Ultimate Civilisation of the Natives* (London, 1805), pp.15ff.

53 Sadly this much-repeated and thoroughly delightful story may well be apocryphal: I have certainly been unable to trace it back further than Edward Thompson's *The Life of Charles Lord Metcalfe* (London, 1937), p.101, where it is described as 'local tradition . . . this sounds like folklore'. In his will (OIOC L/AG/ 34/29/37), Ochterlony only mentions one *bibi*, 'Mahruttun, entitled Moobaruck ul Nissa Begum and

often called Begum Ochterlony', who was the mother of his two daughters, although his son Roderick Peregrine Ochterlony was clearly born of a different *bibi*. Nevertheless it is quite possible that the story could be true: I frequently found old Delhi traditions about such matters confirmed by research, and several Company servants of the period kept harems of this size. Judging by Bishop Heber's description of him, Ochterlony was clearly Indianised enough to have done so.

54 Reginald Heber, *A Narrative of a Journey Through the Upper Provinces of India from Calcutta to Bombay, 1824–1825* (3 vols, London, 1827), Vol. 2, pp.362, 392.

55 See Herbert Compton (ed.), *The European Military Adventurers of Hindustan* (London, 1943), pp.365–6; Lester Hutchinson, *European Freebooters in Mughal India* (London, 1964), pp.23–6. See also Theon Wilkinson, *Two Monsoons* (London, 1976), p.125.

56 William Francklin, *Military Memoirs of Mr George Thomas Who by Extraordinary Talents and Enterprise rose from an obscure situation to the rank of A General in the Service of Native Powers in the North-West of India* (London, 1805), p.333n.

57 There is a wonderful picture of Jan Thomas in his *banka* kit at the Begun Sumroe's durbar in a miniature in the Chester Beatty Library, 7.121. See Leach, op. cit., Vol. 2, pp.791–5, colour plates 109–110.

58 Cited in John Keay, *India Discovered* (London, 1981), p.21.

59 Hawes, op. cit., p.4.

60 Quoted in Anna A Surorova, *Masnavi: A Study of Urdu Romance* (Karachi, 2000), pp.89–91.

61 Bengal Wills 1782, Number 24, Will of Thomas Naylor, Probate granted 6 August 1782; OIOC L/AG/34/29/4.

62 Bengal Wills 1804, Number 13, Will of Matthew Leslie; OIOC L/AG/34/29/16.

63 Charles D'Oyley, *The European in India* (London, 1813), pp.xix–xx. See also Captain Thomas Williamson, *The East India Vade Mecum* (2 vols, London, 1810; 2nd edition 1825), Vol. 1, p.451.

64 Cited in Fawn M. Brodie, *The Devil Drives: A Life of Sir Richard Burton* (London, 1967), p.51n.

65 See Collingham, *Imperial Bodies*, op. cit., pp.46–7.

66 D'Oyley, op. cit., p.ii.

67 C.A. Bayly, *Imperial Meridian: The British Empire and the World 1780–1830* (London, 1989), p.115.

68 Thomas Medwin, *The Angler in Wales* (London, 1834), pp.4–8.

69 Gardner Papers, National Army Museum, Letter 119, Sekundra, 12 December 1821.

70 Elizabeth Fenton, *The Journal of Mrs Fenton* (London, 1901), pp.51–2.

71 See Bengal Wills 1780–1783. 1782, Number 41, The Will Of A. Crawford, Probate granted 13 November 1782; OIOC L/AG/34/29/4.

72 Williamson, op. cit., Vol. 1, p.412.

73 William Hickey (ed. A. Spencer), *The Memoirs of William Hickey* (4 vols, London, 1925), Vol. 3, p.327.

74 Ibid., Vol. 4, p.100.

75 Ibid., p.89.

76 Ibid., p.6.

77 Ibid., pp.26–7.

78 Ibid., pp.140–1.

79 The text of Halhed's *Code of Gentoo Laws* may be found in P.J. Marshall, (ed.), *The British Discovery of Hinduism* (Cambridge, 1970).

80 Anonymous review of *A Code of Gentoo Laws or Ordinations of the Pundits*, from *Critical Review*, XLIV, September 1777, pp.177–91.

81 Cited in Marshall, *The British Discovery of Hinduism*, op. cit., p.39.

82 Quoted by Michael Edwardes in *King of the Nabobs* (London, 1964).

83 Cited in Marshall, *The British Discovery of Hinduism*, op. cit., p.189, from Hastings' 'Letter to Nathaniel Smith' from *The Bhagavat-Geeta*.

84 Sir William Jones (ed. G. Canon), *The Letters of Sir William Jones* (2 vols, Oxford, 1970), Vol. 2, p.755, 23 August 1787, Sir William Jones to the second Earl Spencer.

85 Ibid., p.766, 4 September 1787, Sir William Jones to the second Earl Spencer.

86 *Asiatic Journal*, Vol. 26, 1828, pp.606–7.

87 See Gardner Papers, National Army Museum: Letter 1, 5 January 1820; Letter 2, 10 January 1820; Letter 110, Saugor, 9 November 1821; Letter 119, 12 December 1821.

88 See Wilkinson, op. cit., p.73.

89 James Morris, *Heaven's Command: An Imperial Progress* (London, 1973), p.75.

90 OIOC Eur Mss, Mackenzie Collection General, XXV, pp.162–3, 'The Culleeka-Pooree-Putna Vrittant Or Memoir Of The Ancient City Of Culleeka-Pooree-Putnam, rendered into Marattas from a Tamil Ms. On Cadjan, in the hands of the Curnam of Culleekapoor, near Tuckolm, in Arcot province, & translated by Sooba Row Bramin, September, 1808'; the original is in the Kalikapurici vrttanta in the Madras List, Marathi Mss, p.1. From the collection catalogue, p.362: 'Next we have what is evidently the record by an eye witness of the visit of General Matthews to Takkolam, which was accompanied by many curious incidents, illustrating the conduct of a European in a Hindu Temple.'

91 Marshall, *The British Discovery of Hinduism*, op. cit., p.42.

92 'British Idolatry in India': a sermon preached by the Rev. R. Ainslie at the monthly meeting of ministers of Congregational Churches, in *The Pastoral Echo: Nineteen Sermons of Eminent Dissenting Ministers and Others* (London, 1837).

93 Rev. A. Thompson, *Government Connection with Idolatry in India* (Cape Town, 1851).

94 *A Vindication of the Hindoos from the Aspersions of the Revd Claudius Buchanan MA by a Bengal Officer* (London, 1808). For Hindoo Stuart's authorship of this work see Jorg Fisch, 'A Solitary Vindicator of the Hindus: The Life and Writings of General Charles Stuart (1757/ 8–1828)', in *Journal of the Royal Asiatic Society*, 4, 2–3, 1985, pp.35–57.

95 See Jorg Fisch, 'A Pamphlet War on Christian Missions in India 1807–9', in *Journal of Asian History*, Vol. 19, 1985, p.22–70.

96 Anon., *Sketches of India Written by an Officer for the Fire-Side Travellers at Home* (London, 1821), p.221–2.

97 Fenton, op. cit., pp.51–2.

98 Wilkinson, op. cit., p.84.

99 Ibid., p.73.

100 R.B. Saksena, *Indo–European Poets of Urdu and Persian* (Lucknow, 1941), p.21. Hawes, op. cit., Chapter 4.

101 See Norman Gash, *Lord Liverpool: The Life and Political Career of Robert Banks Jenkinson, Second Earl of Liverpool, 1770–1828* (London, 1984), p.11.

102 Hastings Papers, BL Add Mss 29,178, Vol. XLVII, 1801–1802, John Palmer to Hastings, 1 January 1802.

103 Anderson Correspondence, BL Add Mss 45,427, William Palmer to David Anderson, 12 November 1786, F196.

104 See Durba Ghosh, op. cit., p.42, for the disappearance of *bibis* from wills, and p.36 for their disappearance from the *East India Vade Mecum*.

105 Major J. Blackiston, *Twelve Years Military Adventures in Hindustan 1802–14* (London, 1829).

106 Williamson, op. cit., Vol. 1, p.501.

107 Emma Roberts, *Scenes and Characteristics of Hindoostan, with sketches of Anglo-Indian Society* (2 vols, 2nd edition, London, 1837), Vol. 1, p.75.

108 D'Oyley, op. cit., Plate X, 'A gentleman with his Hookah-burdar, or Pipe-bearer'.

109 P.J. Marshall, 'British Society under the East India Company', in *Modern Asian Studies*, Vol. 31, No. 1, 1997, p.101.

110 Lady Maria Nugent, *Journal of a Residence in India 1811–15* (2 vols, London, 1839), Vol. 2, p.9.

CHAPTER 2

1 Anne Barnard (ed. A.M. Lewin Robinson), *The Cape Journals of Lady Anne Barnard 1797–98* (Cape Town, 1994), p.263.

2 Quoted in Moon, op. cit., p.341.

3 Anne Barnard (ed. A.M. Lewin Robinson), *The Letters of Lady Anne Barnard to Henry Dundas from the Cape and Elsewhere 1793–1803* (Cape Town, 1973), p.99.

4 Barnard, *Cape Journals*, op. cit., p.266.

5 Now in the National Gallery of Ireland. Illustrated in Mildred Archer, *India and British Portraiture 1770–1825* (London, 1979), pp.226, 152.

6 Richard Wellesley (ed. Edward Ingram), *Two Views of British India: The Private Correspondence of Mr Dundas and Lord Wellesley: 1798–1801* (London, 1970), p.16.

7 OIOC, Kirkpatrick Papers, F228/27, p.26, letter to Lieutenant Colonel John Collins from William Kirkpatrick at the Cape, 11 February 1798.

8 Quoted in Henry Briggs, *The Nizam: His History and Relations with the British Government* (London, 1861), pp.9–10.

9 Strachey Papers, OIOC F127/478a,

'Sketch of the Kirkpatrick Family by Lady Richard Strachey'.

10 Henry Dodwell, *The Nabobs of Madras* (London, 1926), p.113.

11 Ibid., p.122.

12 Kirkpatrick Papers, OIOC F228/13, p.156, James Kirkpatrick to William Kirkpatrick, 8 September 1801.

13 Strachey Papers, OIOC F127/478a, 'Sketch of the Kirkpatrick Family by Lady Richard Strachey'.

14 Kirkpatrick Papers, OIOC F228/96, Letter from Mrs R Strachey (Julia Maria Strachey), 69 Lancaster Gate W, to Sir Edward Strachey, Sutton Court, Pensford, Somersetshire, dated and postmarked 3 April 1886.

15 Kennaway Papers, Devon Records Office, Exeter, B961M ADD/F2.

16 Obituary in the *New Monthly Magazine* for 1836; Rev. George Oliver's 'Biographies of Exonians' in *Exeter Flying Post* 1849–50; and a file on the Kennaway family in the West Country Studies Library.

17 Kennaway Papers, Devon Records Office, Exeter, B961M ADD/F2, William Kirkpatrick to Kennaway, London, July 1784.

18 Anderson Papers, BL Add Mss 45,427, f.198, William Palmer to David Anderson, 12 November 1786.

19 Sir Jadunath Sarkar (ed.), *English Records of Mahratta History: Pune Residency Correspondence Vol. 1 – Mahadji Scindhia and North Indian Affairs 1785–1794* (Bombay, 1936), p.111, Letter 65, James Anderson to William Kirkpatrick, Sindhia's Camp, Shergarh, 5 December 1786.

20 Ibid., p.131, Letter 78, Cornwallis to William Kirkpatrick, Calcutta, 1 March 1787.

21 Kennaway Papers, Devon Records Office, Exeter B961M, ADD/F2, William Kirkpatrick to Kennaway, 24 April 1788.

22 Ibid., John Kennaway to William Kennaway, 23 December 1788.

23 OIOC, Kirkpatrick Papers, F228/1,

p.6, Safdar Jung's Tomb, 20 February 1787, William Kirkpatrick to Shore.

24 Ibid., p.114, 17 February 1794, William Kirkpatrick to Maria Kirkpatrick.

25 Strachey Papers, OIOC F127/478a, 'Sketch of the Kirkpatrick Family by Lady Richard Strachey'.

26 Ibid. The file contains an undated letter from France from Clementina Robinson, a granddaughter of William Kirkpatrick (the daughter of Clementina Louis, m. May 1841 Sir Spencer Robinson), which fills in a lot of the gaps about William Kirkpatrick and Maria, of whom the girls had clearly completely lost track.

27 Kennaway Papers, Devon Records Office, Exeter, B961M ADD/F2, William Kirkpatrick to Kennaway, 31 October 1788.

28 Charles Ross (ed.), *Correspondence of Charles, First Marquis Cornwallis* (3 vols, London, 1859), Vol. 2, p.570.

29 OIOC, Kirkpatrick Papers, F228/1, p.88, 3 March 1793, William Kirkpatrick 'to my dearest Maria'.

30 Ibid., p.92, 4 November 1793, William Kirkpatrick to Maria Kirkpatrick.

31 OIOC, Kirkpatrick Papers, F228/52, p.42, Ellore, 10 May 1792. The letter to the *Madras Courier* is unsigned but is in James Kirkpatrick's handwriting and is clearly autobiographical.

32 Ibid., p.10, James Kirkpatrick to the Handsome Colonel, Camp before Seringapatam, 1 March 1792.

33 Ibid., p.1, James Kirkpatrick to the Handsome Colonel, Camp near Colar, 26 December 1792.

34 William Kirkpatrick, introduction to *Select Letters of Tippoo Sultaun* (London, 1811).

35 OIOC, Kirkpatrick Papers, F228/52, p.42, Ellore, 10 May 1792. See n34, above.

36 Ibid., p.15, James Kirkpatrick to the Handsome Colonel, Camp near Doscottah (?), 1 May 1792.

37 Ibid., p.1, James Kirkpatrick to the Handsome Colonel, Camp near Colar, completed January 1792.

38 Kennaway Papers, Devon Records Office, Exeter, B961M ADD/F2, James Kirkpatrick to Kennaway, 11 August 1793.

39 OIOC, Kirkpatrick Papers, F228/1, p.95, 14 November 1793, William Kirkpatrick to Cornwallis.

40 OIOC, Kirkpatrick Papers, F228/1, p.107, Hyderabad, 29 January, William Kirkpatrick to Gibson [agent] in Calcutta.

41 Bodleian Library, Russell Papers, Ms Eng Letts C151, p.8, Henry Russell to Charles Russell, 2 March 1811.

42 Sayyid Abd al-Latif Shushtari, *Kitab Tuhfat al-'Alam* (written Hyderabad, 1802; lithographed Bombay, 1847), p.156.

43 The uniforms are well illustrated in the great pair of panels of Nizam Ali Khan and his court setting off hunting, in the Salar Jang Museum, Hyderabad.

44 Archives Départmentales de la Savioe, Chambéry, de Boigne archive, bundle AB IIA, Lieutenant William Steuart to 'Mac', Paangul, 30 October 1790.

45 OIOC, Kirkpatrick Papers, F228/1, p.113, William Kirkpatrick to Kennaway, Camp near Bedar, 11 February 1794.

46 De Boigne archive, Chambéry, bundle AB IIA, Lieutenant William Steuart to 'Mac', Paangul, 30 October 1790.

47 M.A. Nayeem, *Mughal Administration of the Deccan under Nizamul Mulk Asaf Jah (1720–48)* (Bombay, 1985), p.87. For the reporting of illicit parties see Lala Mansaram, 'Masir i-Nizami', in P. Setu Madhava Rao, *Eighteenth Century Deccan* (Bombay, 1963), p.112.

48 Nayeem, op. cit., p.95.

49 OIOC, The Hardinge Album, Add Or. 4396–4470.

50 James Achilles Kirkpatrick, 'A View of the State of the Deccan, 4th June 1798', Wellesley Papers, BL Add Mss 13582 f.33.

51 OIOC, Diary of Edward Strachey, Mss Eur F128/196, ff16v–38, p.25v, 17 October 1801.

52 Kennaway Papers, Devon Records Office, Exeter. B961M/M/B9, Kennaway to Cherry, 14 December 1788.

53 Shushtari, op. cit., p.160.

54 Gobind Krishen to Nana Phadnavis, 20 February 1794. Quoted in Sarkar, English Records of Mahratta History, op. cit., p.ix.

55 Quoted in Lafont, Indika, op. cit., p.179.

56 OIOC, Kirkpatrick Papers, F228/3, p.27, William Kirkpatrick to Kennaway, 3 September 1794.

57 OIOC, Kirkpatrick Papers, F228/4, p.3, Kumtaneh, William Kirkpatrick to Shore, 3 December 1794.

58 For the Women's Battalion, see Gavin Hambly, 'Armed Women Retainers in the Zenanas of Indo-Muslim Rulers: The Case of Bibi Fatima', in Gavin Hambly (ed.), Women in the Medieval Islamic World (New York, 1998), esp. p.454. For the Nizam's zenana on campaign in their covered howdahs see William Hollingbery, A History of His Late Highness Nizam Alee Khaun, Soobah of the Dekhan (Calcutta, 1805), esp. p.54.

59 The details about the bribes, and of Mir Alam's treachery, come from the Gulzar i-Asafiya, Chapter 3. The Gulzar was written by Ghulam Husain Khan, whose father, as Nizam Ali Khan's personal physician, accompanied the Nizam to Khardla; this gives some credence to the information.

60 OIOC, Kirkpatrick Papers, F228/3, p.30, William Kirkpatrick to Jack Collins, 2 October.

61 OIOC, Kirkpatrick Papers, F228/4, p.11, Camp Khurdla, 13 March; also p.15, 21 March, to James Duncan.

62 Quoted in G. Kulkarni and M.R. Kantak, The Battle of Kharda: Challenges and Responses (Pune, 1980), p.59.

63 K. Sajun Lal, Studies in Deccan History (Hyderabad, 1951), p.87.

64 OIOC, Kirkpatrick Papers, F228/4, p.11, Camp Khurdla, 13 March.

65 Ibid., p.15, 21 March, William Kirkpatrick to James Duncan.

66 Lal, Studies in Deccan History, op. cit., pp.80–3.

67 OIOC, Kirkpatrick Papers, F228/4, p.20, 30 March, Khurdlah, William Kirkpatrick to Collins (?).

68 Khan, Gulzar i-Asafiya, Chapter 3, notice of Aristu Jah, pp.158–78.

69 OIOC, Kirkpatrick Papers, F228/4, p.28, 13 May, William Kirkpatrick to Shore.

70 OIOC, Kirkpatrick Papers, F228.5, p.2, 24 November 1795, William Kirkpatrick to James Duncan.

71 See Gurbir Mansingh, 'French Military Influence in India', in his Reminiscences: The French in India (New Delhi, 1997), p.58. Also Jadunath Sarkar, 'General Raymond of the Nizam's Army', in Mohammed Taher, Muslim Rule in the Deccan (New Delhi, 1997), pp.125–44. Also Compton, op. cit., pp.382–6.

72 Quoted by Anne Buddle in The Tiger and the Thistle: Tipu Sultan and the Scots in India (Edinburgh, 1999), p.33.

73 Kate Brittlebank, Tipu Sultan's Search for Legitimacy: Islam and Kingship in a Hindu Domain (New Delhi, 1997), p.28. Also Kate Teltscher, India Inscribed: European and British Writing on India 1600–1800 (Oxford, 1995), p.252.

74 OIOC, Kirkpatrick Papers, F228/7, p.43, 16 December 1796, William Kirkpatrick to Shore.

75 OIOC, Kirkpatrick Papers, F228/6, p.14, 9 May, William Kirkpatrick to Shore.

76 Shore cited the India Act of 1784 as the reason for his refusal, explaining that it prohibited alliances in all but a few circumstances. He held that an alliance like that the Nizam sought was illegal under British statute.

77 OIOC, Kirkpatrick Papers, F228/15, p.33, 3 September 1797, William Kirkpatrick to Shore.

78 Ibid.

79 OIOC, Kirkpatrick Papers, F228/12, p.136, 14 August 1797, James Kirkpatrick to William Kirkpatrick.

80 Ibid., p.226, 25 October 1797, James Kirkpatrick to William Kirkpatrick.

81 OIOC, Kirkpatrick Papers, F228/15, p.33, 3 September 1797, William Kirkpatrick to Shore.

82 OIOC, Kirkpatrick Papers, F228/27, p.26, 11 February 1798, William Kirkpatrick to Lieutenant Colonel John Collins at the Cape.

83 OIOC, Kirkpatrick Papers, F228/10, p.87, 4 October 1797, James Kirkpatrick to William Kirkpatrick.

CHAPTER 3

1 J. Pieper, 'Hyderabad: A Qu'ranic Paradise in Architectural Metaphors', in A. Peruccioli (ed.), Environmental Design, pp.46–51.

2 S. Sen, Indian Travels of Thevenot and Careri (New Delhi, 1949), p.135.

3 William Methwold, 'Relations of the Kingdome of Golchonda and other neighbouring Nations and the English Trade in Those Parts, by Master William Methwold', in W.H. Moreland, Relations of Golconda in the early Seventeenth Century (London, 1931).

4 Sir Jadunath Sarkar, 'Haidarabad and Golkonda in 1750 Seen Through French Eyes: From the Unpublished Diary of a French Officer Preserved in the Bibliothèque Nationale, Paris', in Islamic Culture, Vol. X, p.240.

5 See Omar Khalidi, Romance of the Golconda Diamonds (Ahmedabad, 1999), p.66.

6 Many of the items made by Hyderabad jewellers can be seen in Manuel Keene, Treasury of the World: Jewelled Arts of India in the Age of the Mughals (London, 2001).

7 James Mackintosh, Memoirs of Life of The Rt Hon Sir James Mackintosh (2 vols, London, 1835) Vol. 1, p.515.

8 Sarkar, 'Haidarabad and Golkonda in 1750 . . .', op. cit., p.243.

9 De Boigne archive, Chambéry, bundle AB IIA, Lieutenant William Steuart to 'Mac', Paangul, 30 October 1790.

10 Server ul-Mulk (trans. Nawab Jiwan Yar Jung Bahadur), My Life, Being the Autobiography of Nawab Server ul Mulk Bahadur, (London, 1903), p.91.

11 Ali Akbar Husain, Scent in the Islamic Garden: A Study of Deccani Urdu Literary Sources (Karachi, 2000), p.31.

12 Ibid., pp.26–7.

13 Server ul-Mulk, op. cit., p.92.

14 Sarkar, 'Haidarabad and Golkonda in 1750 . . .', op. cit., p.244.

15 Arthur Wellesley to Colonel Close, 22 September 1800. I have been unable to trace the whereabouts of the original letter, only small portions of which are reproduced in Wellington's printed Despatches, but a copy made by Barbara Strachey in the mid-1980s exists in the archives of the Strachey Trust.

16 OIOC, Mountstuart Elphinstone Papers, Mss Eur F88, Box13/16[b], Elphinstone's diary f.93, 23 August 1801, for the henna, moustachios and belching.

17 Ghulam Imam Khan, Tarikh i-Khurshid Jahi, pp.713–14.

18 For Raymond see Mansingh,

'French Military Influence in India', op. cit. For Piron's wish to convert see OIOC, Kirkpatrick Papers, F228/10, p.98, 9 October 1798.

19 Saksena, op. cit., pp.171–85.

20 The large numbers of Hyderabadi women left husbandless after the French were expelled from the city was a major problem for Kirkpatrick, who said he had 'no means of ascertaining now how many wives, concubines or children belong to the Party', but that there were clearly a large number. See OIOC, Kirkpatrick Papers, F228/10, p.165, 4 December 1798.

21 OIOC, Mountstuart Elphinstone Papers, Mss Eur F88, Box13/16[b], Elphinstone's diary, f.92, 23 August 1801.

22 OIOC, Bengal Political Consultations, -P/117/18, 3 June, No. 1: The Residency, Hyderabad, 19 October 1800, James Kirkpatrick to Sir George Barlow. Also OIOC, Kirkpatrick Papers, F228/59, p.36, 24 October 1800, James Kirkpatrick to Sir John Kennaway.

23 OIOC, Edward Strachey's Diaries, Mss Eur F128/196, f.16v.

24 OIOC, Kirkpatrick Papers, F228/12, p.163, 29 August 1800, James Kirkpatrick to William Kirkpatrick.

25 OIOC, Kirkpatrick Papers F228/56, p.14, 10 January, James Kirkpatrick to William Palmer, for the complaint on zenana size, and p.26, 1 February 1802, James Kirkpatrick to John Tulloch, for the number of women in William Palmer's suite. For Kirkpatrick's own mahal having a large staff of aseels and maidservants see for example New Delhi National Archives, Secret Consultations, Foreign Department, 1800, 15 May, No. 20, 'Translation of a Letter from Moonshee Meer Azeez Ooolah to Lieut Col Kirkpatrick', 7 March 1800.

26 OIOC, Mountstuart Elphinstone Papers, Mss Eur F88, Box13/16[b],

Elphinstone's diary, 31 August and 16 October.

27 Scottish Record Office, Edinburgh, GD135/2086, The Will of Lieut Col James Dalrymple, Hussein Sagar, 8 December 1800.

28 Fanny Parkes, Wanderings of a Pilgrim in Search of the Picturesque (London, 1850), Vol. 1, pp.417–18.

29 Gardner Papers, National Army Museum 6305–56, Letter 6, 5 March 1820; Letter 49, Saugor, 6 January 1821, p.131.

30 Cambridge, South Asian Studies Library, Gardner Papers, Letter from W.L. Gardner to his Aunt Dolly Gardner, 25 May 1815.

31 Parkes, op. cit., Vol. 1, p.231.

32 Russell Papers, Bodleian Library, Ms Eng Letts C155, p.15, 9 June 1802.

33 OIOC, Mountstuart Elphinstone Papers, Mss Eur F88, Box13/16[b], Elphinstone's diary, entry for 13 September.

34 For Mrs Ure's appetite see OIOC, Kirkpatrick Papers, Mss Eur F228/11: p.134, 23 April; p.140, 23 April; p.154, 8 May.

35 New Delhi National Archives, Secret Consultations, Foreign Department, 1800, 15 May, No. 23, 'Moonshee Azeez Oolah's Report of a Conversation with Azim ul Omrah and of what passed at the Durbar of His Highness the Nizam on the 9th of March 1800'.

36 Russell Papers, Bodleian Library, Ms Eng Letts D151, p.96, 31 May 1810, Henry Russell to Charles Russell.

37 OIOC, Mountstuart Elphinstone Papers, Mss Eur F88, Box13/16[b], Elphinstone's diary for 15 November 1801, p.111.

38 OIOC, Edward Strachey's Diaries, Mss Eur F128/196, 13 November, p.29.

39 OIOC, Mountstuart Elphinstone Papers, Mss Eur F88, Box13/16[b], Elphinstone's diary for 15 November 1801, p.112.

40 Ibid.

41 OIOC, Kirkpatrick Papers, F228/11, p.192, 5 August 1799, James Kirkpatrick to William Kirkpatrick.

42 Sarojini Regani, *Nizam–British Relations 1724–1857* (New Delhi, 1963), pp.32–4.

43 Kirkpatrick, 'A View of the State of the Deccan', op. cit., f.37.

44 As was in fact often the case in Islamic societies: for the power of post-sexual women in the Imperial Ottoman harem see for example Leslie P. Peirce, *The Imperial Harem: Women and Sovereignty in the Ottoman Empire* (New York, 1993), Chapter 1, esp. p.23.

45 New Delhi National Archives, Hyderabad Residency Records, Vol. 26, pp.46–7, 23 May 1803.

46 Compton, op. cit., pp.382–6.

47 OIOC, Kirkpatrick Papers, F228/10, p.21, 24 August 1797, James Kirkpatrick to William Kirkpatrick.

48 Compton, op. cit., pp.382–6.

49 OIOC, Kirkpatrick Papers, F228/10, p.21, 24 August 1797, James Kirkpatrick to William Kirkpatrick.

50 Wellesley, op. cit., pp.100–1.

51 The full translations of Raymond's correspondence can be found in Sarkar, 'General Raymond of the Nizam's Army', op. cit., pp.125–44.

52 Shushtari, op. cit., p.169.

53 Khan, *Gulzar i-Asafiya*, Chapter 3, notice of Aristu Jah, pp.158–78.

54 Ibid.

55 Nani Gopal Chaudhuri, *British Relations with Hyderabad* (Calcutta, 1964), p.64.

56 Richard Wellesley (ed. M. Martin), *The Despatches, Minutes and Correspondence of the Marquess Wellesley KG during his Administration of India* (London, 1840), Vol. 1, pp.220–1.

57 James Dalrymple, *Letters &c Relative To The Capture of Rachore* (Madras, 1796).

58 New Delhi National Archives, Hyderabad Residency Records, Vol. 15, 19 December 1797, p.15.

59 For Nizam ul-Mulk's use of Sufis, see Rao, op. cit., pp.95–6, 114–15.

60 For the Nizam's intelligencers in villages and Delhi see Dr Zeb un-Nissa Haidar, 'The Glimpses of Hyderabad in the Light of the Tarikh i-Mahanamah' (research project for UGC Grant, Hyderabad, 1998–99). For intelligencers and newswriters in general see the excellent Bayly, *Empire and Information*, op. cit.

61 New Delhi National Archives, Political Consultations, 3 February 1844. No. 182, paras 3–4.

62 I am grateful to Professor Sarojini Regani for this information.

63 OIOC, Mss Eur F228/11, p.287, 25 November, James Kirkpatrick to William Kirkpatrick.

64 OIOC, Mss Eur F228/10, p.4, 7 August 1797, James Kirkpatrick in Hyderabad to William Kirkpatrick.

65 For the spy in the Residency *daftar* see OIOC, F228/11, p.192, 5 August 1799.

66 OIOC, Mountstuart Elphinstone Papers, Mss Eur F88, Box13/16[b], Elphinstone's diary, f.93, 25 August 1801.

67 OIOC, Kirkpatrick Papers, F228/10, p.75, 26 September, James Kirkpatrick to William Kirkpatrick.

68 OIOC, 'Capt GE Westmacott's Ms Travels in India', Mss Eur C29, f.289, 24 December 1833.

69 Compton, op. cit., p.379. See also Bayly, *Empire and Information*, op. cit., p.146.

70 Kirkpatrick, 'A View of the State of the Deccan', op. cit., f.48.

71 John W. Kaye, *The Life and Correspondence of Sir John Malcolm GCB* (2 vols, London, 1856), Vol. 1, p.78n.

72 This information comes from a sheet, 'Finglas Family Records', kindly lent to me by Bilkiz Aladin and given to her by one of Finglas's descendants. There is some dispute as to when Finglas entered

Hyderabadi service, with some secondary authorities assigning him a role at Khardla in 1795. This appears to be an error: no primary source mentions him in Hyderabad before 1797, and it seems likely that he came to the city with Aristu Jah after his return from captivity. See also Kirkpatrick, 'A View of the State of the Deccan', op. cit., f.50.

73 OIOC, Kirkpatrick Papers, F228/10, p.121, 11 November, James Kirkpatrick to William Kirkpatrick.

74 Ibid.

75 For Gardner's American childhood see Narindar Saroop, *A Squire of Hindoostan* (New Delhi, 1983). For James's view of him see OIOC, Kirkpatrick Papers, F228/10, p.72, 27 September 1798.

76 See *The Dictionary of American Biography* and Compton, op. cit., p.340.

77 OIOC, Kirkpatrick Papers, F228/10, p.19, 22 August 1798, James Kirkpatrick to Ulthoff.

78 Compton, op. cit., pp.354, 340.

79 Ibid., p.382.

80 See Saksena, op. cit., p.288; also John Lall, *Begam Samru: Fading Portrait in a Gilded Frame* (Delhi, 1997), p.127.

81 OIOC, Sutherland Papers, Mss Eur D547, p.8, 1801, Pohlmann to Sutherland.

82 OIOC, Kirkpatrick Papers, F228/11, p.75, 26 September 1798, James Kirkpatrick to William Kirkpatrick.

83 OIOC, Sutherland Papers, Mss Eur D547, p.35, undated.

84 OIOC, Kirkpatrick Papers, F228/12, p.166, 31 August.

85 Wellesley, op. cit., Vol. 1, p.209. See also Jac Weller, *Wellington in India* (London, 1972), pp.24–5.

86 OIOC, Kirkpatrick Papers, F228/10, p.75, 26 September, James Kirkpatrick to William Kirkpatrick.

87 Quoted by Andrew Roberts in *Napoleon and Wellington* (London, 2001), pp.16–17. The second quotation in fact dates from 1812, when Napoleon was flirting with launching a second Eastern expedition; but no doubt reflects the ease with which he saw India falling into his hands on the earlier expedition.

88 Quoted in Sir John Malcolm, *Political History of India* (2 vols, London, 1826), Vol. 1, p.310.

89 Louis Bourquien, 'An Autobiographical Memoir of Louis Bourquien translated from the French by J.P. Thompson', in *Journal of the Punjab Historical Society*, Vol. IX, Pt 7, 1923, p.50. For the proposal to land a French force at Cuttack see Iris Butler, *The Eldest Brother* (London, 1973), p.311.

90 OIOC, Kirkpatrick Papers, F228/10, p.92, 6 October, James Kirkpatrick to William Kirkpatrick.

91 For Malcolm see Butler, op. cit., p.157 and J.W. Kaye, op. cit., Vol. 1, Chapter 5. Captain Malcolm was later to be knighted, and is better known as Sir John Malcolm. James later accused him of exaggerating his role in the disarming of the French troops. See OIOC, Kirkpatrick Papers, F228/59, p.6, 16 August 1803 to Petrie.

92 OIOC, Kirkpatrick Papers, F228/10, p.98, 9 October, James Kirkpatrick to William Kirkpatrick.

93 Ibid., p.110, 16 October, James Kirkpatrick to William Kirkpatrick.

94 For the mutiny, see OIOC, Kirkpatrick Papers, F228/11, p.325. For the bullock traces see OIOC, Kirkpatrick Papers, F228/10, p.87, 4 October, 22 February 1799.

95 J.W. Kaye, op. cit., Vol. 1, p.75.

96 Rt Hon. S.R. Lushington, *The Life and Services of Lord George Harris GCB* (London, 1840), p.233.

97 Ibid., p.235.

98 J.W. Kaye, op. cit., Vol. 1, p.78.

99 Ibid., p.78n.

100 OIOC, Kirkpatrick Papers, F228/10, p.195, 25 December, James

Kirkpatrick to William Kirkpatrick.

101 OIOC, Kirkpatrick Papers, F228/7, p.7, 17 October, William Kirkpatrick to Wrangham.

102 The date of Mehdi Yar Khan's death is not known, but he is never referred to in the records of the 1790s, so presumably had died sometime before. His family and his marriage to Sharaf un-Nissa are discussed in the *Nagaristan i-Asafiya* under the entry for Aqil ud-Daula. It is possible that Sharaf un-Nissa never left Bâqar Ali's *deorhi*, and that Mehdi Yar Khan came to live with Bâqar Ali Khan: Karen Leonard's work on the Kayasths of Hyderabad has shown that high-status men would arrange their daughters' marriages with promising and ambitious younger men who would then enter the household as in-married sons-in-law, *khana damad*. Syliva Vatuk has told me in correspondence that she has found the same pattern among the high-status Muslim families she has worked upon. This would help explain why it was Bâqar Ali Khan who arranged his granddaughters' marriages rather than Mehdi Yar Khan's male relations, and especially his elder brother, Mir Asadullah.

103 'Report of an Examination . . .', op. cit., p.364.

104 OIOC, Kirkpatrick Papers, F228/11, p.2, Hyderabad, 2 January 1799, James Kirkpatrick to William Kirkpatrick.

105 This account comes from a translation of Sharaf un-Nissa's letter to her granddaughter Kitty Kirkpatrick, in the private archive of her descendants.

106 OIOC, Kirkpatrick Papers, F228/96, 'Account of the marriage of Sharpun Nisa Begam with Colonel Kirkpatrick called Hashmat Jang, Resident, Hyderabad'. This document was apparently compiled by a *munshi* working for Trevor Plowden, Resident in the early 1890s, after Plowden was asked for information about the romance by Edward Strachey, who was writing his 1893 article for *Blackwood's Magazine*, op. cit. In the event, the information arrived a year after Strachey's article had been published. The anonymous *munshi* states that he got the information from Khair un-Nissa's cousins and an elderly slave girl of Sharif un-Nissa, all of whom were still alive in Hyderabad at the time. It seems generally reliable, with the single major error of calling Khair un-Nissa by her mother's name throughout.

CHAPTER 4

1 Shushtari, op. cit., pp.36, 56.

2 Ibid., pp.82–5, 121–130.

3 Khan, *Gulzar i-Asafiya*, pp.305–15. Also Mohammed Sirajuddin Talib, *Mir Alam*, Chapter 1, passim.

4 Kirkpatrick, 'A View of the State of the Deccan', op. cit., f.45.

5 Khan, *Gulzar i-Asafiya*, pp.305–15.

6 Delhi National Archives, Hyderabad Residency Records, Vol. 57, pp.256–7, Henry Russell to Hastings, 29 November 1819. Also Henry Russell quoted in Talib, op. cit., pp.183–90.

7 Makhan Lal, *Tarikh i-Yadgar i-Makhan Lal* (Hyderabad, 1300 AH/AD1883), p.54. Durdanah Begum was 'from the house of Mir Jafar Ali Khan, son of Benazir Jung'.

8 Abdul Raheem Khan, *Tarikh i-Nizam* (Hyderabad, AH1330/ AD1912), pp.68–9; Anon., *Riyaaz e-Muqtaria Salthanath Asafia*, p.57; Khan, *Gulzar i-Asafiya*, pp.305–15.

9 Shushtari, op. cit., p.485.

10 Ibid., p.427.

11 Ibid., p.153.

12 Ibid., p.257.

13 Ibid., pp.11, 270.

14 Ibid., p.342.

15 Ibid.

16 Ibid.

17 Ibid., p.309.

18 Stephen Blake, 'Contributors to the Urban Landscape: Women Builders in Safavid Isfahan and Mughal Shahjehanabad', in Hambly, op. cit., p.407.

19 Asiya Begum, 'Society and Culture under the Bijapur Sultans' (unpublished Ph.D., University of Mysore, 1983), pp.62–3. There are numerous depictions of Chand Bibi on horseback, many of them from Hyderabad, including one from the collection of Henry Russell now in the India Office Library: OIOC Add Or. 3849.

20 See for example the fascinating comparison in scale of patronage between Mughal and Saffavid women in Blake, op. cit., pp.407–28.

21 Zinat Kausar, Muslim Women in Mediaeval India (Patna, 1992), p.145.

22 For Jahanara see Blake, op. cit., p.416. For Gulbadan see Gulbadan Begum, Humayun Nama, trans. Annette S. Beveridge as The History of Humayun by Princess Rose-Body (London, 1902).

23 Saqi Must'ad Khan, Maasir i-Alamgiri, trans. by Jadunath Sarkar as The History of the Emperor Aurangzeb-Alamgir 1658–1707 (Calcutta, 1946), p.322.

24 Shushtari, op. cit., p.342.

25 Parkes, op. cit., Vol. 1, pp.417–18. For the contemporary Mughal practice of providing girls to Indian rulers as a means of preferment, see Michael H. Fisher, 'Women and the Feminine in the Court and High Culture of Awadh, 1722–1856', in Hambly, op. cit., pp.500–1.

26 Husain, Scent in the Islamic Garden, op. cit., pp.27, 40, 127.

27 Niccolao Manucci, Storia do Mogor, or Mogul India, 1653–1708 (London, 1907), Vol. 1, p.218. For extramarital relations in the Mughal mahal see K. Sajun Lal, The Mughal Harem (New Delhi, 1988), pp.180–2.

28 From a conversation with Dr Zeb un-Nissa Haidar. The records are now in the Andhra Pradesh archives.

29 Dargah Quli Khan (trans. Chander Shekhar), The Muraqqa' e-Dehli (New Delhi, 1989). For Ad Begum, p.107; for Nur Bai, p.110.

30 That Mah Laqa was Mir Alam's mistress is confirmed by James Kirkpatrick in his letters: see for example OIOC, Kirkpatrick Papers, Eur Mss F228/11, p.269, Hyderabad, 12 October 1799.

31 Shushtari, op. cit., p.157.

32 See her entry in the Tazkirah e-Niswan e-Hind (The Biography of Indian Women), by Fasih-ud-Din Balkhi (Patna, 1956).

33 For Mah Laqa's poetry in the Nawab of Avadh's library see A. Sprenger, Catalogue of Arabic, Persian and Hindustany Manuscripts of the libraries of the King of Oudh 1854; for Mah Laqa's status in the durbar see Dr Zeb un-Nissa Haidar, 'A Comprehensive Study of the Daftar i-Dar ul Insha 1762–1803' (unpublished Ph.D., Osmania University, 1978), p.114.

34 Rahat Azmi, Mah e-laqa (Hyderabad, 1998), pp.34, 48–9.

35 Jagdish Mittal, 'Paintings of the Hyderabad School', in Marg, 16, 1962–63, p.44.

36 See Delhi National Archives, Secret Despatches, 1800, p.2491, Fort William, 10 May 1800, No. 3, 'Intelligence from Azim ul Omrah's Household'.

37 Tamkin Kazmi, Aristu Jah, p.38, quoting the Tarikh i-Saltanat i-Khudadad, p.39.

38 At least so Arthur Wellesley was told by Mir Alam; Wellington, 'Memorandum of Conversations . . .

Dummul 26th Sept 1800',
op. cit.

39 Quoted in Butler, op. cit., p.166.

40 Ibid., p.170.

41 Talib, op. cit., p.6.

42 Denys Forrest in *Tiger of Mysore:
The Life and Death of Tipu Sultan*
(London, 1970), pp.227–8.

43 OIOC, Kirkpatrick Papers, Mss Eur
F228/11, p.10, 8 January 1799, James
Kirkpatrick to William Kirkpatrick.

44 Organising the carriage bullocks
and sheep for feeding the army was
one of Kirkpatrick's main concerns
at this period. See OIOC,
Kirkpatrick Papers, Mss Eur F228/11,
pp.14, 15, 28 etc.

45 Wellesley's remark quoted by
Moon, op. cit., p.286; the
subsistence remark quoted by
Buddle, op. cit.

46 For Colonel Bowser see 'Report of
an Examination . . .', op. cit.,
pp.362, 364.

47 OIOC, Kirkpatrick Papers, Mss Eur
F228/83, Hyderabad, 23 May 1800.

48 Ibid.

49 Fyze's *sanad* is in the OIOC,
Persian Mss IO 4440. Mildred
Archer in her magisterial *India and
British Portraiture*, op. cit., wrongly
states that Fyze was from the Delhi
royal house. That she, and her sister
Nur Begum, were the daughters of
a Persian captain of cavalry is clear
from numerous references in the de
Boigne archive, Chambéry.

50 Bengal Wills 1825; OIOC L/AG/34/
29/37, pp.185–205.

51 For Mubarak Begum's background
see the Mubarak Bagh Papers in the
archives of the Delhi
Commissioners Office, DCO F5/
1861. Here it is recorded that
'Mubarik ul Nissa was originally a
girl of Brahmin parentage, who was
brought from Poona in the Deckan
by one Mosst. Chumpa, and
presented or sold by the said
Chumpa to Genl. Ochterlony when
twelve years of age. Mosst. Mubarik

ul Nissa from that time resided in
Genl. Ochterlony's house, and
Mosst. Chumpa resided with her
there, being known by the name of
Banbahi.'

52 Gardner Papers, National Army
Museum, Letter 16, p.42.

53 Ibid.

54 See the Mubarak Bagh Papers in the
archives of the Delhi
Commissioners Office, DCO F5/
1861.

55 According to the evidence Bâqar Ali
Khan gave to Colonel Bowser in
Lord Clive's Report, 'After the
death of Colonel Dalrymple, the
Furzund Begum (Daughter in Law
of the Minister) did twice use
importunities with my Begum,
when on a visit at the Minister's
house, to give up her Grand
Daughter to the Resident.' 'Report
of an Examination . . .', op. cit. As
late as 1802 Khair un-Nissa and her
mother are reported making
'occasional visits' to Farzand
Begum's *zenana* in for example
OIOC, Mss Eur F228/58, p.24, James
Kirkpatrick to William Palmer, 1
April 1802.

56 Wellington, 'Memorandum of
Conversations . . . Dummul 26th
Sept 1800', op. cit.

57 Makhan Lal, *Tarikh i-Yadgar
i-Makhan Lal*, op. cit., p.54. Lal
reports that Bâqar Ali and Sharaf
un-Nissa received *jagirs* and titles
from the Nizam following the
marriage, and that 'Sharaf un-Nissa
Begum is receiving the jagir from
the government until now', i.e.
AD1819/1236AH, the time of
writing.

58 Wellington, op. cit., p.176.

59 See Fisher, 'Women and the
Feminine . . .', op. cit.

60 Wellington, op. cit., p.174.

61 Dhoolaury Bibi appears
intermittently in William
Kirkpatrick's letters, as do her two
children by him, who in Kent were

known by the names Robert and
Cecilia Walker: see OIOC, F228/10,
p.14, 14 September 1797, for James
promising to pay Dhoolaury Bibi
her allowance of one hundred
rupees per month during William's
absence. In William's will,
Dhoolaury Bibi is explicitly referred
to as the mother of Robert Walker,
and receives a legacy of twelve
thousand rupees, a very large sum
considering the ruinous state of
William's finances.

62 OIOC, Kirkpatrick Papers, Eur Mss
F228/13, p.113, 4 August 1801.

63 'Report of an Examination . . .',
op. cit., p.364. Also Khan, *Tarikh
i-Khurshid Jahi*, op. cit., pp.713–14.

64 Arthur Wellesley to Colonel Close,
22 September 1800, op. cit.

65 Wellington, op. cit.

66 OIOC, Kirkpatrick Papers, Eur Mss
F228/13, p.113, 4 August 1801.

67 The letter is now lost but is quoted
by Lady Strachey in a letter.
Kirkpatrick Papers, OIOC, F228/96,
Letter from Mrs R. Strachey [Julia
Maria Strachey], 69 Lancaster Gate
W, to Sir Edward Strachey, Sutton
Court, Pensford, Somersetshire,
dated and postmarked 3 April
1886.

68 OIOC, Kirkpatrick Papers, F228/59,
p.27, 24 October 1804, James
Kirkpatrick to his father, the
Handsome Colonel, on his son's
death.

69 For eighteenth-century English
aristocratic men, treating women
from different classes in utterly
different ways as far as sexual
relations were concerned, see for
example Amanda Foreman,
Georgiana Duchess of Devonshire
(London, 1998), and Stella Tillyard,
*Aristocrats: Caroline, Emily, Louisa
and Sarah Lennox 1740–1832*
(London, 1995), passim.

70 OIOC, Kirkpatrick Papers, Eur Mss
F228/11, p.348, 14 March 1800, James
Kirkpatrick to William Kirkpatrick.

71 Now sadly lost.

72 OIOC, Kirkpatrick Papers, Mss Eur
F228/83, Hyderabad, 23 May 1800.

73 OIOC, Kirkpatrick Papers, Eur Mss
F228/11, p.30, 15 January.

74 Ibid., p.73.

75 Quoted by Buddle, op. cit., p.15.

76 See for example Lord Macartney
quoted in Lafont, *Indika*, op. cit.,
p.158.

77 For the bore of the artillery see
ibid., p.157. For the rockets see
Colley, 'Going Native, Telling
Tales', op. cit., p.190.

78 Lafont, *Indika*, op. cit., p.186.

79 Quoted by Buddle, op. cit., p.34.

80 Weller, op. cit., p.73.

81 Quoted by Moon, op. cit., p.288.

82 See Buddle, op. cit., p.37.

83 OIOC, Kirkpatrick Papers, Eur Mss
F228/11, pp.162–75, 17 and 18 May
1799.

84 Wilkie Collins, *The Moonstone*
(London, 1868).

85 Khan, *Gulzar i-Asafiya*, pp.305–15. A
similar picture is painted by Mehdi
Hasan, Fateh Nawaz Jung, *Muraqq
i-Ibrat* (Hyderabad, 1300AH/
AD1894), p.14.

86 Shushtari, op. cit., p.160.

87 Alexander Walker Papers, NLS
13,601–14, 193, Ms 13,601, f.156,
Madras, 6 August 1799.

88 OIOC, Kirkpatrick Papers, Eur Mss
F228/11, p.321, 7 March 1800.

89 Ibid., p.252, 14 September 1799.

90 Ibid., p.200, 8 August 1799.

91 James was also surprised by the
scale of the 'pension': OIOC,
Kirkpatrick Papers, Eur Mss F228/11,
p.258, 14 September, James
Kirkpatrick to William Kirkpatrick.

92 Ibid., p.174, 22 May.

93 Khan, *Gulzar i-Asafiya*, pp.309–10.

94 OIOC, Kirkpatrick Papers, Eur Mss
F228/11, p.275, 15 October.

95 Ibid., p.262, 26 September, and
p.269, Hyderabad, 12 October 1799,
James Kirkpatrick to William
Kirkpatrick.

96 Ibid., p.269, Hyderabad, 12 October

1799, James Kirkpatrick to William Kirkpatrick.

97 The *divan* given by Mah Laqa Bai Chanda is now in OIOC, Islamic Ms 2768. The book contains an inscription: 'The Diwan of Chanda the celebrated Malaka of Hyderabad. This book was presented as a nazr from this extraordinary woman to Captain Malcolm in the midst of a dance in which she was the chief performer on the 18 October 1799 at the House of Meer Allum Bahadur'.

98 'Report of an Examination . . .', op. cit., p.364.

99 Khan, *The Muraqqa' e-Dehli*, op. cit., p.45–6, 56, 76, 81.

100 New Delhi National Archives, Hyderabad Residency Records, Vol. 20, p.218, 5 November 1799, James Kirkpatrick to Lord Wellesley.

101 OIOC, Kirkpatrick Papers, Eur Mss F228/53, p.16, 24 July 1799, James Kirkpatrick to William Palmer.

102 OIOC, Kirkpatrick Papers, Eur Mss F228/11, p.59, 3 February.

103 OIOC, Kirkpatrick Papers, Eur Mss F228/54, pp.151–2, September, James Kirkpatrick to William Palmer.

104 James's proposal for the *jashn* is a fascinating document, and worth reproducing in full, for it reveals his knowledge both of Mughal etiquette in general and, in particular, of the intimate hierarchy that formed the Nizam's household. At the top of the pile came the Nizam, his three senior wives and the princes, each of whom was to receive the different types of jewels and dresses of honour appropriate to their rank:

Rough Estimate of a great Jushn
His Highness the Nizam and the Begums of his Mahal
To His Highness:

Jewels, nine sorts, viz 1 jiggah [turban ornament in the form of a raised bejewelled flower spray] 1 sarpeich [a different sort of turban jewel] 1 pr dustbund [a jewelled wristband] 1 ditto Bhojbund [armband], 1 ditto bazoobund [an armband formed of especially large jewels], 1 malla of pearls, 1 toorah [another form of turban ornament, round and hung with pearls, associated with the end of the ornament].....60,000 Rs khillut [i.e. a dress of honour, of which in the Mughal court there were five ranks] of Badelah [gold and silver cloth]
khillut of 10 complete dresses
shawls ten pairs
kumkhauls [kincob furs] 10 pieces.........10,000
2 Elephants.....10,000
4 Horses.....4,000
Dinners, pawn &c.........1,000
Rs. 85,000
To the Principal Ladies of the Mahl:
To the Bukshy Begum, 9 sorts of jewels,
1 kuntee [pearl necklace], 1 pair Bhojedbund, 1 ditto bazoobund.....4,000
badelahs, kumhuals and shawls 1,000
Rs. 5,000

To Thyneat un Nisa Begum
The same as Bukshy Begum
Rs. 5,000

To Zeib un Nissa Ditto
Rs. 5,000

To the Princes
Secunder Jah
(As with his Highness, but to the value of only) Rs 45,000

To His Bride
(Jewels as above plus 1 poownchee
['pearls for wrists'].....Rs. 15,000
Feridun Jah, Akbar Jah, Jehander Jah, Jumsheid Jah, Soliman Jah,

Meir Jehunde Ali ('lately born'), Humayoon Jah ('His Highnesses brother) Rs. 5,000 each

Then comes a similar list for the household of Aristu Jah, his two Begums ('To the Begum of his Great Mahl.....5,000 Rs [of jewels and shawls] To the Begum of his Little Mahl.....5,000 Rs ditto', and the same amount to his daughter-in-law Farzund Begum). This is followed by disbursements to the three different ranks of Hyderabadi *omrahs*, and finally the costs of the 'Notch Girls, flower garlands, fireworks, illumination, Donations to shrines and victuals to poor.....15,000 Rs.' OIOC, Kirkpatrick Papers, Eur Mss F228/11, p.259, 14 September, James Kirkpatrick to Lord Wellesley.

105   OIOC, Kirkpatrick Papers, Eur Mss F228/11, p.217, 21 August.

106   Ibid., p.281, 1 November.

107   New Delhi National Archives, Hyderabad Residency Records, Vol. 20, p.218, 5 November 1799, James Kirkpatrick to Lord Wellesley.

108   OIOC, Kirkpatrick Papers, Eur Mss F228/11, p.348, 14 March.

109   The *akhbars* survived in the New Delhi National Archives, Hyderabad Residency Records, where they were copied by Bilkiz Alladin in the 1980s, but have now become unusable since the records were waterlogged sometime between 1999 and 2000. Bilkiz kindly gave me access to her copies and I have worked from them. Some of the correspondence relating to them, however, is still intact in the New Delhi National Archives, Secret Consultations, 1800, Foreign Department, 15 May, No. 14, received from Mir Alam 18 February 1800. Part of the 'Memoranda of the Papers referred

to in the minute of the Rt. Hon. The Gov Gen of the 10th of May 1800'.

110   As above, also OIOC, Kirkpatrick Papers, Eur Mss F228/11, p.338, 9 March.

111   New Delhi National Archives, Secret Consultations, 1800, Foreign Department, 15 May, No. 21, 'Translation of a Letter from Bauker Alli Khaun to Lt Col Kirkpatrick'.

112   OIOC, Kirkpatrick Papers, Eur Mss F228/11, p.338, 9 March.

113   Khan, *Gulzar i-Asafiya*, pp.305–15.

114   New Delhi National Archives, Hyderabad Residency Records – see n109, above.

115   New Delhi National Archives, Secret Consultations, 1800, Foreign Department, 15 May, No. 22, pt 2, 'Meer Uzeez Ollah's report of his conference with Auzim ool Omrah 4 of March'.

116   Khan, *Gulzar i-Asafiya*, pp.305–15.

117   Munshi Khader Khan Bidri (trans. Dr Zeb un-Nissa Haidar), *Tarikh i-Asaf Jahi* (written 1266AH/AD1851, pub. Hyderabad, 1994), p.84. M. Abdul Rahim Khan, *Tarikh e-Nizam* (Hyderabad, 1311AH/AD1896), pp.167–8.

118   OIOC, Kirkpatrick Papers, F228/96, 'Account of the marriage of Sharpun Nisa Begam with Colonel Kirkpatrick called Hashmat Jang, Resident, Hyderabad'. For further details see Chapter 3, n106.

119   Wellington, 'Memorandum of Conversations . . . Dummul 26th Sept 1800', op. cit.

120   Ibid., pp.175–6.

121   Ibid., p.178.

122   Khan, *Tarikh i-Khurshid Jahi*, op. cit., pp.713–14.

123   Wellington, op. cit., p.180.

124   Arthur Wellesley to Colonel Close, 22 September 1800. See Chapter 3, n15.

125   Khan, *Gulzar i-Asafiya*, p.308; Khan, *Tarikh e-Nizam*, op. cit., pp.86, 167–8.

126 See 'Report of an Examination . . .', op. cit., p.374.

127 Scottish Record Office, Edinburgh, GD135/2086, The Will of Lieut Col James Dalrymple, Hussein Sagar, 8 December 1800.

128 Dalrymple, *Letters &c . . .*, op. cit.

129 New Delhi National Archives, Secret Consultations, 1800, Foreign Department, 15 May, No. 8, 'Extract of a Letter from Bauker Alli Khaun, 18 February 1800, part of the Memoranda of the Papers referred to in the minute of the Rt. Hon. The Gov Gen of the 10th of May 1800'.

130 'Report of an Examination . . .', op. cit., p.361.

131 New Delhi National Archives, 1800, Foreign Department, Secret Consultation – 15 May, No. 24, point the 10th.

132 'Report of an Examination . . .', op. cit., p.368.

133 Ibid., p.369.

CHAPTER 5

1 OIOC, Kirkpatrick Papers, Mss Eur F228/12, p.265, 26 November, James Kirkpatrick to William Kirkpatrick.

2 OIOC, Kirkpatrick Papers, Mss Eur F228/13, p.250, 12 November, James Kirkpatrick to William Kirkpatrick.

3 Khan, *Gulzar i-Asafiya*, pp.549–59.

4 Ibid., p.552.

5 Bidri, op. cit., p.154.

6 Khan, in *The Muraqqa' e-Dehli*, op. cit., p.17, the passage about the Urs of Khuld Manzil in Delhi.

7 *Mah e-laqa*, op. cit., p.25.

8 See S.A. Asgar Bilgrami, *The Landmarks of the Deccan: A Comprehensive Guide to the Archaeological Remains of the City and Suburbs of Hyderabad* (Hyderabad, 1927), p.13.

9 Ibid., pp.12ff. The musician Khush-hal Khan – Mah Laqa's dancing instructor – built an arch on the site, while Mah Laqa's daughter Hussun Laqa Bai built a dharamsala.

10 For the make-up of the Hyderabadi ruling class see Karen Leonard, 'The Hyderabad Political System and its Participants', in *Journal of Asian Studies*, XXX, No. 3, 1971, pp.569–82; also Leonard's excellent *Social History of an Indian Caste: The Kayasths of Hyderabad* (Hyderabad, 1994).

11 C. Collin Davies, 'Henry Russell's report on Hyderabad, 30th March 1816', in *Indian Archives*, Vol. IX, No. 2, July–December 1955, pp.123–4.

12 Bidri, op. cit., p.154.

13 Khan, *Gulzar i-Asafiya*, pp.549–59.

14 OIOC, Kirkpatrick Papers, Mss Eur F228/11, p.217, 21 August, James Kirkpatrick to William Kirkpatrick.

15 Ibid., p.191, Hyderabad, 31 July 1799, James Kirkpatrick to William Kirkpatrick.

16 OIOC, Kirkpatrick Papers, Mss Eur F228/12, p.9, 27 April, James Kirkpatrick to William Kirkpatrick.

17 Ibid.

18 Quoted Butler, op. cit., p.182.

19 Ibid., p.70; Bence-Jones, op. cit., p.49; Moon, op. cit., p.312.

20 Butler, op. cit., p.225.

21 Ibid., p.257.

22 OIOC, Kirkpatrick Papers, Mss Eur F228/11, p.217, 21 August 1799.

23 Ibid., p.248, 8 September 1799, and p.291, 29 November 1799.

24 Ibid., p.313, 3 January 1800.

25 Ibid., p.319, 30 January 1800.

26 Ibid., p.329, 27 February 1800.

27 Ibid., p.350, 22 March 1800.

28 For Munshi Aziz Ullah's Delhi background see Shushtari, op. cit., p.591.

29 New Delhi National Archives, Secret Despatches, 1800, p.2491, Fort William, 10 May 1800, No.3, 'Intelligence from Azim ul Omrah's Household', contains a wonderful picture of Aristu Jah's methods of

conducting business: 'On the 7th January Moonshee Azeez Oollah waited upon Azim ul Omrah [AUO] & after being engaged with him in cockfighting told him that he had something of a very urgent nature to communicate with him in private & that he would wait upon him at another time for that purpose to which AUO signified his assent. On the 9th Munshi Azeez Oolah attended at 12 o'clock in the day & was sent for by AUO to the bath. The Moonshee desired Mustaqim un Dowlah not to be present at the conference as he wished to say what he had to state to AUO without any other witnesses. When the Munshi had paid his respects to AUO in the bath, MUD informed the latter that the Moonshee wished to make a secret communication and therefore suggested his returning to the Nawah Khana or Summer House which was done accordingly & AUO continued in conversation with the Moonshee for a whole hour. On the fourteenth Moonshee Azeez Oollah again attended at the diversion of cock fighting.'

30 OIOC, Kirkpatrick Papers, Mss Eur F228/12, p.105, 16 July, James Kirkpatrick to William Kirkpatrick.

31 Ibid., p.226, 25 October, James Kirkpatrick to William Kirkpatrick.

32 Ibid., p.185, 11 September, James Kirkpatrick to William Kirkpatrick.

33 Ibid., p.200, 1 October, James Kirkpatrick to William Kirkpatrick.

34 The picture forms the cover of Iris Butler's *The Eldest Brother*, op. cit. It is also illustrated on p.315, plate 220 of Mildred Archer's *India and British Portraiture*, op. cit.

35 OIOC, Kirkpatrick Papers, Mss Eur F228/12, p.214, 12 October 1800, James Kirkpatrick to William Kirkpatrick.

36 Ibid., p.38, 9 May 1800, William Palmer to James Kirkpatrick.

37 Ibid., p.183, 9 September, James Kirkpatrick to William Kirkpatrick.

38 Ibid., p.17, 2 May 1800, James Kirkpatrick to William Kirkpatrick.

39 These details are all taken from B.F. Musallam's remarkable research published as *Sex and Society in Islam* (Cambridge, 1983). For the Islamic legal view on abortion see p.40. For methods of contraception and abortion see the tables between pp.77–88. For Ibn Sina on abortion see p.69. For the skills of Indian women in methods of birth control see p.94.

40 For the death of Khair un-Nissa's half-sister (Mehdi Yar Khan's daughter by an unnamed wife other than Sharaf un-Nissa) see OIOC, Kirkpatrick Papers, F228/11, p.338, 9 March 1800, James Kirkpatrick to William Kirkpatrick.

41 'Report of an Examination . . .', op. cit., pp.373–4.

42 OIOC, Kirkpatrick Papers, Mss Eur F228/12, p.138, 17 August 1800.

43 Ibid., pp.138–9.

44 Richard Wellesley (ed. Edward Ingram), *Two Views of British India: The Private Correspondence of Mr Dundas and Lord Wellesley: 1798–1801* (London, 1970), p.217.

45 Patrick Cadell, *The Letters of Philip Meadows Taylor to Henry Reeve* (London, 1947), p.62.

46 OIOC, Kirkpatrick Papers, Mss Eur F228/12, p.58, 31 May, James Kirkpatrick to William Kirkpatrick.

47 See Dr Zeb un-Nissa Haidar, 'The Glimpses of Hyderabad', op. cit., Chapters 4 and 5 (no page numbers).

48 Khan, *Gulzar i-Asafiya*, p.305.

49 OIOC, Kirkpatrick Papers, Mss Eur F228/12, p.108, 10 July.

50 OIOC, Kirkpatrick Papers, Mss Eur F228/12, p.275, 9 December, James Kirkpatrick to Webbe.

51 'Report of an Examination . . .', op. cit., p.377.

52 Ibid., pp.382–3.

53 Ibid., pp.378–80.

54 From a document in the private archive of Kirkpatrick's descendants, 'Enclosures from Resident at Hyderabad in a Letter dated 8th January 1801'. Enclosure 2: 'Report of another conversation which took place between Aukil oo Dowlah and Colonel Bowzer on the 29th December 1800'.

55 OIOC HM464, op. cit., pp.377–8.

56 Shushtari, op. cit., p.591.

57 From a document in the private archive of Kirkpatrick's descendants, 'Enclosures from Resident at Hyderabad in a Letter dated 8th January 1801'. Enclosure 3: 'Translation of a Shookha addressed by Abdool Lateef Khaun to the Resident, dated the 3rd January 1801'.

58 Ibid.

59 Delhi National Archives, Foreign Department, Secret Consultations, 16 April. Enclosure 'B' attached to No. 132: 'Translation of a letter from Meer Allum addressed to Major Kirkpatrick dated 10th Jan 1801'.

60 OIOC, Kirkpatrick Papers, Mss Eur F228/13, p.4, 16 January 1801, James Kirkpatrick to William Kirkpatrick.

61 'Report of an Examination . . .', op. cit., pp.380–1.

62 Ibid., p.381.

63 Ibid., p.383.

64 This account comes from a translation of Sharaf un-Nissa's letter to her granddaughter Kitty Kirkpatrick in the private archive of her descendants.

65 'Report of an Examination . . .', op. cit., p.386.

66 Ibid., p.391.

67 Philip Meadows Taylor, *Story of my Life* (London, 1878), p.36.

68 Philip Meadows Taylor, *Confessions of a Thug* (London, 1889), pp.124–6. *Confessions of a Thug* is of course a novel, but this passage clearly draws on Meadows Taylor's many years as a Hyderabadi Resident, where he married the Anglo Indian granddaughter of Khair un-Nissa's best friend, Fyze Baksh Palmer. He gives a fascinating description of his father-in-law, William Palmer, and his house, where he 'met the most intelligent members of Hyderabad society, both native and European, and the pleasant gatherings at his most hospitable house were a great relief from the state and formality of the Residency'. Meadows Taylor, *Story of my Life*, op. cit., p.37.

69 This is made clear in a letter from Thomas Sydenham to Henry Russell when he talks of two different mansions (see Bodleian Library, Russell Papers, Ms Eng Letts C172, p.1, 14 January 1807); but we know from Dr Kennedy's visit that Sharaf un-Nissa's mansion was part of Bâqar Ali Khan's *deorhi* complex. It was clearly a huge campus of buildings.

70 OIOC, Mountstuart Elphinstone Papers, Mss Eur F88 Box13/16[b], p.24. For eighteenth-century *deorhis* see the descriptions given in Sarkar, 'Haidarabad and Golkonda in 1750 . . .', op. cit., p.240. Several *deorhis* of this period still survive in the old city – albeit in a rather run-down state – for example the once lovely Hamid Khan Deorhi behind the Chowk Masjid.

71 'Report of an Examination . . .', op. cit., pp.387–9.

72 Ibid., pp.388–9.

73 Ibid., p.391.

74 From a document in the private archive of Kirkpatrick's descendants, 'Enclosures from Resident at Hyderabad in a Letter dated 8th January 1801': 'Report of a conference which took place on the 1st January between Moonshe Meer Azeez Oolla and Aukil oo Dowlah' and 'Report of Moonshee Aziz Oolah's conference wth Auzim ool Omrah on the 3rd Jan 1801'.

75 OIOC, Kirkpatrick Papers, Mss Eur F228/13, p.1, Hyderabad, 9 January 1801, James Kirkpatrick to William Kirkpatrick. For the details about Bâqar's sight and hearing see Delhi National Archives, Foreign Department, Secret Consultations, 24 April 1800, No. 20, Item No. 66, James Kirkpatrick to Lord Wellesley, 21 January 1800.

76 OIOC, Kirkpatrick Papers, Mss Eur F228/96, 'Account of the marriage of Sharpun Nisa Begam with Colonel Kirkpatrick called Hashmat Jang, Resident, Hyderabad'. This document was apparently compiled by a munshi working for Trevor Plowden, Resident in the early 1890s.

77 Ibid.

78 It is unclear whether this was the same Ahmed Ali Khan whose son was originally engaged to Khair un-Nissa.

79 Syed ood Dowlah seems to have been the mujtahid who converted James. He may or may not have been the same Syed ood Dowlah who was in the train of Mir Alam when he met Arthur Wellelsey on his release from prison.

80 From a translation of Sharaf un-Nissa's letter to Kitty Kirkpatrick in the private archive of her descendants.

81 OIOC, Kirkpatrick Papers, F228/84, Will of James Achilles Kirkpatrick.

82 For all James's secrecy, the fact that he both embraced Islam and formally married Khair un-Nissa according to Shi'a law seems to have been widely known in Hyderabad, judging by the frequency with which the fact is mentioned in Hyderabad chronicles, for example Bidri, op. cit., p.84.

83 OIOC, Kirkpatrick Papers, Mss Eur F228/13, p.4, Hyderabad, 16 January 1801, James Kirkpatrick to William Kirkpatrick.

CHAPTER 6

1 Wellesley, op. cit., Vol. 5, pp.405, 407.

2 Abdul Lateef Shushtari, Tuhfat al-'Alam, 'Dhail al-Tuhfa [the Appendix to the Tuhfat al-'Alam], Being additional notes to 'Abd al-Latif Shushtari's autobiography, about his return to Haidarabad after he had finished writing his book in 1216/1802, these notes were written at the repeated request of Shiite divines, especially the late 'Allama Aqa Muhammad 'Ali son of 'Allama Aqa Muhammad Baqer Behbehani', pp.3–5.

3 G.S. Sardesai (ed.), English Records of Mahratta History: Pune Residency Correspondence Volume 6 – Poona Affairs 1797–1801 (Palmer's Embassy) (Bombay, 1939), p.ii.

4 OIOC, Kirkpatrick Papers, F228/25 p.12, 1 January 1801, Lord Wellesley's offer of the Poona Residency to William Kirkpatrick, a letter to the Board.

5 Sardesai, op. cit., p.571, No. 350A, William Palmer to Lord Wellesley, 'Poona, 27th June 1800'.

6 Hastings Papers, BL Add Mss 29,178, Vol. XLVII, 1801–02, 10 October 1802, pp.277–8, William Palmer to Hastings.

7 Ibid., 10 July 1801, pp.61–3, William Palmer to Hastings.

8 William Palmer was the largest subscriber towards the publication of George Thomas's military memoirs; see William Francklin, Military Memoirs of Mr George Thomas (Calcutta, 1803), p.xiii. For Palmer's coin collection, and its loss during the 1857 Mutiny, see the note in Journal of the Asiatic Society of Bengal, 27, 1858, p.169.

9 Stuart Cary Welch, Room for Wonder: Indian Paintings During the British Period 1760–1880 (New York, 1979).

10 On a visit to St Kitts in 1972, Alex
Palmer, William Palmer's direct
descendant, found the marriage
entry in the Register of St George
and St Peter's church, Basseterre.
See Alex Palmer, 'The Palmer
Family 1740–2000' (unpublished
manuscript). Sarah's family name
given in the register, 'Hazell',
contradicts the evidence contained
in a manuscript written by Edward
Palmer, Alex's grandfather, now in
the India Office Library, entitled
'The Palmers of Hyderabad', OIOC
Mss Eur D443 (1). Edward Palmer
believed that Sarah was called
Melhado or Melkado, but he gives
no authority for this information.

11 In a charming letter from Sarah's
youngest son, now in the Bodleian
Library, the young John Palmer
describes his travels around India to
his mother: 'Wm [Sarah's second
son] and myself are now on a
journey to see my father,' he tells her.
He mentions that his father is now a
major, in a way that implies that he
and Sarah were not in direct contact
and were perhaps estranged. He goes
on to describe his adventures in the
navy, including one engagement with
the French when 'I was stationed in
the quarter deck which place was one
continual scene of slaughter, not
having less than 10 men killed or
wounded,' but says that he finally left
the fleet in August. He has seen his
eldest brother Sam, and wants his
mother to remember him kindly to
all his old friends in St Kitts: 'that
God may grant you health and
prosperity is my prayer'. See Palmer
Papers, Bodleian Library, Ms Eng
Lit C83, p.1, Benares, 16 December
1782.

12 According to Alex Palmer, a
manuscript called the 'Cayon Diary'
bound with the parish register of
Cayon on St Kitts refers to Sarah
staying on in the island after
William's departure. See 'The

Palmer Family', op. cit., p.7 n2. For
John Palmer's letter to his mother,
see Palmer Papers, Bodleian Library,
Ms Eng Lit C83, p.1, Benares, 16
December 1782. For Sarah in
Greenwich, and William's attempts
to get David Anderson to send her
some money, see Anderson Papers,
BL Add Mss 45,427, p.203, March
1792, Gualiar.

13 Palmer is frequently stated to have
married Fyze according to Muslim
law – for example by Count
Edouard de Warren in *L'Inde
Anglaise en 1843* (Paris, 1845), where
he says that the General married his
wife, 'a well-born Indian lady . . .
according to the Koran [i.e. the
rites of her religion]', as is
confirmed by Palmer family
tradition: see letter from Palmer's
great-granddaughter, Mrs Hester
Eiloart, of 15 September 1927, OIOC
L/R/7/49). Given Fyze's social status
this would in turn imply that, like
James Kirkpatrick, Palmer converted
to Islam, which apart from anything
else would have removed the
obstacle of his previous marriage:
Muslims are of course allowed up
to four wives. But unlike the case of
Kirkpatrick there is no firm
evidence either for a conversion or
a Muslim marriage, and in Palmer's
will, Fyze is merely referred to as
'Beby Fize Buksh Saheb a Begum,
who has been my affectionate friend
& companion during a period of
more than thirty five years' (Bengal
Wills 1816, OIOC L/AG/34/29/28,
p.297). This formulation, however,
leaves the question open, and
certainly does not disprove a
Muslim marriage: James Kirkpatrick
used a similar one in his will to
describe Khair un-Nissa, despite
having been legally married in a
Muslim ceremony, because –
according to his friend and
Assistant Henry Russell – he was
worried that English law would not

recognise the Muslim marriage, and he did not wish to endanger his legacy to his children. (See letter from Henry Russell to his brother Charles, Swallowfield, 30 March 1848, in the private archive of James Kirkpatrick's descendants.) It is quite possible that Palmer described Fyze in this way for the same reason.

14 Young, *Fountain of Elephants*, op. cit., pp.99–100. Young quotes from some letters he found in the Chambéry archives, some of which appear to have disappeared since his trawl through the archive in the 1950s. I certainly could not find the one which refers to 'the Persian Colonel', but did find legal documents from Nur Begum's time in Britain which repeatedly state that she was 'of Delhi'. Although Fyze was later made a Begum by the Emperor, there is no contemporary evidence that she was 'a member of the Delhi Royal House', as her grandson-in-law Philip Meadows Taylor seemed to believe.

15 There has long been confusion over the name of Fyze's sister and de Boigne's wife. In an article in *Bengal Past and Present* (Vol. XLIII, p.150), Sir Judunath Sarkar suggested that as she took the name Helena when she later converted to Christianity, she might originally have had some similar Muslim name such as Halima. Since then the name Halima has entered the literature as if it were fact, most recently in Rosie Llewellyn-Jones's fascinating piece on her in her *Engaging Scoundrels*, op. cit., pp.88–93. In actual fact her name was Nur Begum, as was recorded by Mirza Abu Taleb Khan, who writes of his meeting with her in London in *The Travels of Mirza Abu Taleb Khan*, op. cit., pp.198–200: 'Noor Begum who accompanied General de Boigne from India . . . was

dressed in the English fashion, and looked remarkably well. She was much pleased with my visit, and requested me to take charge of a letter for her mother, who resides at Lucknow.'

16 Anderson Papers, BL Add Mss 45,427, p.198v, undated but c.1781.

17 Ibid., p.146, 3 May 1783.

18 Ibid., p.180, 3 October 1784.

19 OIOC, IO Coll 597.

20 For details of the court costume of this period see Ritu Kumar, *Costumes and Textiles of Royal India* (London, 1998). Kumar's book is much the best source for the clothing of the period, but she severely underestimates the degree of intermarriage and cultural cross-dressing that went on.

21 As with much else concerning Palmer's marriage, there has been a great deal of scholarly controversy about the identity of the figures in the picture. A letter written by Palmer's great-great-granddaughter, M.P. Hanley 'of Assam', now in the India Office Library, maintains that 'the General was a "bad old man" and had two wives, the first being the Princess Fyzun Nissa of Delhi, the mother of William Palmer of Hyderabad and the second a princess of Oudh. I have this information from Mr. Charles Palmer who tells me he got it from Miss Meadows Taylor who edited Meadows Taylor's *Story of My Life*' (OIOC, L/R/7/49). This version of events was followed by Mildred Archer in her *India and British Portraiture*, op. cit., pp.281–6, who thought that the figure kneeling to Palmer's left must be the 'Oudh Princess', and that she was 'looking ardently at Palmer and leaning against his knee while he for his part holds her hand' (although this is clearly not the case if you look carefully at the unfinished painting, and represents an almost unique

case of the usually super-scrupulous Mrs Archer failing to look closely at a picture: Nur is in fact neither looking at Palmer nor holding his hand). Archer's reading of the picture has been blindly followed by Beth Toibin in *Picturing Imperial Power: Colonial Subjects in Eighteenth Century British Painting* (Duke, 1999), pp.113–14. The story seems however to have got garbled in the retelling, for while Fyze and her sister appear frequently in Palmer's letters and will, there is never a single mention of a second Indian wife or concubine – though the General did in fact have a second wife, Sarah Hazell, in St Kitts, and here must lie the origin of the confused story. Palmer's 'Begum of Oudh' referred to in a *Times* marriage announcement of 19 February 1925 (taken out by a proud great-grandson of the Begum who was getting married), which Archer believed to be substantiating evidence for a second Indian wife, was of course Fyze herself, who though born in Delhi had long been a Lucknow resident. The beautiful bejewelled figure kneeling beside Palmer in the picture must presumably be Nur Begum, as Mrs Hester Eiloart, another great-granddaughter (who sold the picture to the India Office), always maintained, and as Durba Ghosh also concluded in her investigation of the picture (see 'Colonial Companions', op. cit., p.97, n36). This is also the view of the current Director of the Prints and Drawings Section in the India Office, Dr Jerry Losty, who, just to add to the confusion, has recently re-attributed the picture to the painter Johan Zoffany. (Mildred Archer believed it to be the work of Francesco Renaldi: see her *India and British Portraiture*, op. cit., p.282, and

'Renaldi and India: A Romantic Encounter', in *Apollo*, Vol. 104, July–September 1976, pp.98–105.) The well-dressed female figure standing on the extreme right of the picture must presumably be another of Fyze's sisters.

22 De Boigne archive, Chambéry, letters from William Palmer to Benoît de Boigne, 13 March 1790; Ogeine, 23 April 1792; and 'Friday Evening' (undated but c.1785).

23 De Boigne archive, Chambéry, *arzee* from the Lady Faiz un-Nissa.

24 Dennis Kincaid, *British Social Life in India 1608–1937* (London, 1938).

25 Mulka Begum was also the Mughal Emperor's niece. See Narindar Saroop, *A Squire of Hindustan* (London, 1983), p.149.

26 When she visited the Nawab's harem, Fanny Parkes met one of the Angrezi Begums and writes in detail about her in *Wanderings of a Pilgrim*, op. cit.

27 Mrs B. Meer Hassan Ali, *Observations on the Mussulmauns of India Descriptive of their Manners, Customs, Habits and Religious Opinions Made During Twelve Years Residence in their Immediate Society* (London, 1832).

28 See the Introduction by W. Crooke to the 1917 OUP edition, p.xv.

29 De Boigne archive, Chambéry, 'Mrs Begum's London accounts'.

30 Alam and Alavi, *A European Experience of the Mughal Orient*, op. cit., esp. pp.69–71.

31 Hastings Papers, BL Add Mss 29,178, Vol. XLVII, 1801–02, 10 October 1802, pp.277–8, William Palmer to Hastings.

32 Ibid., 4 December 1802, pp.314–19.

33 OIOC, Kirkpatrick Papers, F228/12, p.30, 5 May 1800.

34 For example ibid., p.179, 16 September 1801, William Palmer to James Kirkpatrick.

35 This had stated that the land handed over was, as William Palmer

reported to Warren Hastings, 'a full and complete equivalent and discharge, whether revenue should exceed or fall short of the estimate, in either of which events neither party was to make any demand on the other'. Hastings Papers, BL Add Mss 29,178, Vol. XLVII, 1801–02, 10 July 1801, pp.61–3.

36 Ibid.

37 OIOC, Kirkpatrick Papers, F228/13, p.70, 23 June 1801, James Kirkpatrick to William Kirkpatrick.

38 Ibid., p.113, 4 August 1801, James Kirkpatrick to William Kirkpatrick.

39 See Moon, op. cit., p.305, and Butler, op. cit., pp.242–51.

40 OIOC, Kirkpatrick Papers, F228/56, p.2, 2 December 1801, James Kirkpatrick to William Palmer.

41 OIOC, Kirkpatrick Papers, F228/13, p.58, 7 June 1801, James Kirkpatrick to William Palmer.

42 Ibid., p.17, 26 January, William Palmer to James Kirkpatrick.

43 OIOC, Kirkpatrick Papers, F228/56, p.13, 4 January 1802, and p.14, 10 January 1802, James Kirkpatrick to William Palmer.

44 Ibid., p.26, 1 February 1802, James Kirkpatrick to John Tulloch.

45 For Fyze's adoption by the Emperor and her title see OIOC, Persian Mss, IO 4440.

46 OIOC, Kirkpatrick Papers, F228/83, pp.19–24, 4 January 1802, James Kirkpatrick to Lord Wellesley.

47 Ibid., p.152, 6 September 1801, and p.166, 21 September 1801, James Kirkpatrick to William Kirkpatrick.

48 Ibid., p.152, 6 September, James Kirkpatrick to William Kirkpatrick.

49 Ibid., p.166, 21 September 1801, James Kirkpatrick to William Kirkpatrick.

50 Thomas Sydenham, quoted in Anon., *Some Notes on the Hyderabad Residency Collected from Original Records in the Residency Office* (Hyderabad, c.1880), p.3.

51 Mackintosh, *Memoirs*, op. cit., Vol. 1, p.511.

52 Julian James Cotton, 'Kitty Kirkpatrick', *Calcutta Review*, April 1899, p.243.

53 OIOC, Kirkpatrick Papers, F228/13, p.35, 5 April 1801, James Kirkpatrick to William Kirkpatrick.

54 Ibid., p.39, 17 April 1801, James Kirkpatrick to William Kirkpatrick. For William Thackeray in Madras see Sir William Hunter, *The Thackerays in India* (London, 1897), pp.111–40. This odd little book also contains (on p.174) an interesting mention of James's now-vanished grave in South Park Street Cemetery, as he was buried adjacent to the grave of Richmond Thackeray, the father of the novelist.

55 OIOC, Kirkpatrick Papers, F228/13, p.40, 22 April 1801, James Kirkpatrick to William Kirkpatrick.

56 Ibid., p.58, 7 June 1801, James Kirkpatrick to William Kirkpatrick.

57 Ibid., p.44, 4 May 1801, James Kirkpatrick to William Kirkpatrick.

58 OIOC, Kirkpatrick Papers, F228/25, p.21, 20 June 1801, Lord Wellesley to William Kirkpatrick.

59 OIOC, Kirkpatrick Papers, F228/13, p.62, 11 June 1801, James Kirkpatrick to William Kirkpatrick.

60 OIOC, Kirkpatrick Papers, F228/55, p.3, 6 December 1801, James Kirkpatrick to William Palmer.

61 There is a wonderful account of the two young men's trip written by Edward's descendant, Barbara Strachey, in *The Strachey Line: An English Family in America, India and at home from 1570 to 1902* (London, 1985), pp.100–5. The diaries of both survive in the India Office Library, though Elphinstone's writing is so scruffy as to be partly illegible. Mountstuart Elphinstone's is in Mss Eur F88 Box13/16[b], and Edward Strachey's in Mss Eur F128/196.

62 OIOC, Edward Strachey's Diary, Mss Eur F128/196, pp.16–20.

63 OIOC, Mss Eur F88 Box13/16[b], entry for 14 September 1801.

64 OIOC, Edward Strachey's Diary, Mss Eur F128/196, p.33.

65 Ibid., p.17.

66 OIOC, Mss Eur F88 Box13/16[b], entry for 13 September 1801.

67 OIOC, Kirkpatrick Papers, F228/58, p.92, 16 October 1802, James Kirkpatrick to to Sir John Kennaway.

68 Colley, 'Going Native, Telling Tales', op. cit., pp.180–1, 184.

69 OIOC, Mss Eur F88 Box 13/16[b], entry for 22 August 1801.

70 Ibid., entry for 23 August 1801.

71 Ibid., entry for 15 November 1801.

72 Khan, Gulzar i-Asafiya, p.560.

73 Ibid., pp.560–5.

74 For this practice in Lucknow see Fisher, 'Women and the Feminine . . .', op. cit., p.507.

75 Khan, Gulzar i-Asafiya, p.588.

76 For this tilework, which has recently been drastically 'renovated' by the Archaeological Survey of India in hideous Disney colours, see the excellent description in Michell and Zebrowski, The New Cambridge History of India 1.7: Architecture and Art of the Deccan Sultanates (Cambridge, 1999), p.138.

77 Husain, Scent in the Islamic Garden, op. cit., p.31.

78 Kausar, op. cit., p.224.

79 Ali, Observations on the Mussulmauns . . ., op. cit., p.51.

80 Shushtari, op. cit., pp.545–8.

81 OIOC, Kirkpatrick Papers, F228/13, p.166, 21 September, James Kirkpatrick to William Kirkpatrick.

82 Ibid., p.168, 22 September, James Kirkpatrick to William Kirkpatrick.

83 Ibid., p.187, 29 September, James Kirkpatrick to William Kirkpatrick.

84 Ibid., p.216, 13 October, James Kirkpatrick to William Kirkpatrick.

85 Wellesley Papers, BL Add Mss 37,282, p.279, 7 October 1801, Lord Wellesley to William Kirkpatrick.

CHAPTER 7

1 OIOC, Kirkpatrick Papers, F228/56, p.13, 4 January 1802, James Kirkpatrick to William Palmer.

2 Ibid., p.26, 1 February 1802, James Kirkpatrick to John Tulloch; also F228/57, p.7, Hyderabad, 5 April 1802, James Kirkpatrick to John Read.

3 OIOC, Kirkpatrick Papers, F228/56, p.25, 1 February 1802, James Kirkpatrick to William Petrie.

4 OIOC, Kirkpatrick Papers, F228/58, p.36, 2 October 1802, James Kirkpatrick to William Palmer.

5 James actually spelt Sulaiman's name 'Sooleymaun', but I have updated the spelling to ease comprehension throughout.

6 OIOC, Kirkpatrick Papers, F228/58, p.23, 6 May 1802, James Kirkpatrick to William Palmer.

7 Ibid., p.15, 24 July 1802, James Kirkpatrick to William Palmer.

8 Ibid., p.24, 1 April 1802, James Kirkpatrick to William Palmer.

9 That Fyze was literate is clear from her letter to de Boigne quoted in Chapter 6. Khair un-Nissa's literacy is alluded to frequently in Henry Russell's letters in the Bodleian Library, which refer to him receiving regular letters from her, although none have survived. Sharaf un-Nissa's letters have survived, however, although they somehow became detached from Russell's well-catalogued English correspondence and languished uncatalogued in the store of the library's Persian Department. I am extremely grateful to Doris Nicholson for finally locating them all. Khair un-Nissa's letters may have been deliberately destroyed, either by Russell himself or by his

daughter-in-law, Lady Russell, who became the family historian. The English correspondence also shows signs of being discreetly pruned, especially of correspondence that might have implicated Russell in the scandal surrounding the collapse of Palmer's bank, about which Russell had to face a formal investigation by the East India Company and which led to his early retirement from India.

10 See previous note. Russell's letters refer to his worries that Palmer might use the matter of 'the Begum' against him in the East India Company inquiry into the collapse of Palmer's bank, and it may have been at this stage that he took the precaution of destroying Khair's letters.

11 OIOC, Kirkpatrick Papers, F228/57, p.8, 8 April 1802, James Kirkpatrick to William Palmer.

12 Both notes are now in the private archive of their descendants.

13 OIOC, Kirkpatrick Papers, F228/58, p.23, 6 May 1802, James Kirkpatrick to William Palmer.

14 OIOC, Kirkpatrick Papers, F228/57, p.24, 1 April 1802, James Kirkpatrick to William Palmer.

15 Scottish Record Office, Edinburgh, Seaforth Muniments, GD46/8/1, Henry Russell to Lady Hood, Hyderabad, 5 November 1813.

16 OIOC, Kirkpatrick Papers, F228/56, p.8, 8 April 1802, James Kirkpatrick to William Palmer.

17 Ibid., p.24, 1 April 1802, James Kirkpatrick to William Palmer.

18 OIOC, Kirkpatrick Papers, F228/58, p.73, 10 December 1802 James Kirkpatrick to William Palmer.

19 Durba Ghosh discusses this letter eloquently in her thesis 'Colonial Companions', op. cit., p.124.

20 OIOC, Kirkpatrick Papers, F228/18, p.30, 31 October, William Kirkpatrick to James Kirkpatrick.

21 OIOC, Kirkpatrick Papers, F228/12,

p.280, 6 December, James Kirkpatrick to William Kirkpatrick.

22 OIOC, Kirkpatrick Papers, F228/18, pp.20–3, from Maula Ali, 23 November 1801, James Kirkpatrick to William Kirkpatrick.

23 Ibid., pp.11–13, John Malcolm to William Kirkpatrick, Patna, 19 October 1801.

24 OIOC, Kirkpatrick Papers, F228/13, p.265, 28 November 1801, James Kirkpatrick to William Kirkpatrick.

25 Ibid., p.222, 19 October 1801, Vigors to James Kirkpatrick.

26 Probably because of this incident, James later wrote a code for etiquette connected to the reception of the British Resident which laid down in minute detail exactly what should be done on the occasion of a visit, including the number of guns which were to make the salute and the size and make-up of the guard of honour with which he was to be met. See New Delhi National Archives, Foreign Department, Secret Consultations, 16 May 1805, No. 89–90.

27 OIOC, Kirkpatrick Papers, F228/13, p.238, 9 November 1801, James Kirkpatrick to William Kirkpatrick.

28 OIOC, Kirkpatrick Papers, F228/58, p.15, 24 July 1802, James Kirkpatrick to William Palmer.

29 OIOC, Kirkpatrick Papers, F228/13, p.282, 7 December 1801, William Palmer to James Kirkpatrick.

30 OIOC, Kirkpatrick Papers, F228/11, p.192, 5 August 1799, William Kirkpatrick to James Kirkpatrick.

31 OIOC, Kirkpatrick Papers, F228/56, p.9, 8 April 1802, James Kirkpatrick to Close.

32 OIOC, Kirkpatrick Papers, F228/18, p.48, 30 November 1801, John Malcolm to William Kirkpatrick.

33 Ibid., pp.24–7, 20 January 1802, William Kirkpatrick to James Kirkpatrick.

34 Ibid., pp.33–7, 20 April 1802, John Malcolm to William Kirkpatrick.

35 OIOC, Kirkpatrick Papers, F228/58, p.27, 25 March 1802, N.B. Edmonstone to James Kirkpatrick.

36 William Palmer's authorship of the letter is clear from its style, its contents, the handwriting, and finally James's remarks on it to William Palmer's father, the General.

37 For William Palmer's stay with his brother John, see the letter from General Palmer to his brother-in-law Benoît de Boigne, Pune, 13 December 1799, in the de Boigne archive at Chambéry.

38 From James Baillie Fraser, *Military Memoirs of Lt. Col. James Skinner C.B.* (2 vols, London, 1851), Vol. 2, p.162.

39 Hastings Papers, BL Add Mss 29,178, pp.240, 254–5.

40 Hawes, op. cit., pp.102–3.

41 OIOC, Kirkpatrick Papers, F228/57, p.1, 14 March 1802, James Kirkpatrick to Ebeneezer Roebuck.

42 East India Company, 'The Hyderabad Papers: Papers Relative To Certain Pecuniary Transactions Of Messrs William Palmer And Co With The Government Of His Highness The Nizam' (London, 1824), letter from William Palmer to Henry Russell, p.2.

43 The Resident Charles Metcalfe, quoted in Hawes, op. cit., p.106.

44 OIOC, HM 743, 'The Affairs Of Messrs Wm Palmer & Co Vol. 2 Extract From Bengal Pol Cons 7th Oct 1825', Point 61–2, (18).

45 Anon., *Sketches of India . . .*, op. cit., pp.325–6.

46 Certainly, William Palmer seems to have been trading in a modest way from at least 1802, when James bought a consignment of camels from him. See OIOC, Kirkpatrick Papers, F228/58, p.22, 8 September 1802, James Kirkpatrick to Charles Farran.

47 OIOC, Kirkpatrick Papers, F228/83, 'The Letter from Philothetes'.

48 OIOC, Kirkpatrick Papers, F228/57, p.27, 25 March 1802, N.B. Edmonstone to James Kirkpatrick.

49 OIOC, Kirkpatrick Papers, F228/27, p.19, 27 April 1802, James Kirkpatrick to N.B. Edmonstone.

50 See J.W. Kaye, op. cit., Vol. 2, p.162.

51 OIOC, Mountstuart Elphinstone Papers, Mss Eur F88, Box13/16[b], Elphinstone's diary, f.92, 23 August 1801.

52 J.W. Kaye, op. cit., p.162. Holland initially resided in the royal palace until he rented the Residency site several months later. See Ashwin Kumar Bakshi, 'The Residency of Hyderabad 1779–1857' (unpublished Ph.D., Osmania University, 1990), p.97.

53 OIOC, Kirkpatrick Papers, F228/12, p.163, 29 August 1800, James Kirkpatrick to William Kirkpatrick.

54 OIOC, Bengal Political Consultations, P/117/18, 19 October 1800; 3 June 1801, No. 1: The Residency, Hyderabad.

55 OIOC, Kirkpatrick Papers, F228/13, p.117, 15 August 1801, for Shumsair Jung.

56 OIOC, Kirkpatrick Papers, F228/12, p.143, 30 August 1801, James Kirkpatrick to William Kirkpatrick. For James's request for peach trees see F228/57, p.33, 27 May 1802.

57 OIOC, Kirkpatrick Papers, F228/58, p.30, 12 September 1802, James Kirkpatrick to Fawcett in Bombay.

58 OIOC, Kirkpatrick Papers, F228/54, p.8, 9 September, James Kirkpatrick to Trail.

59 OIOC, Kirkpatrick Papers, F228/53, p.21, 25 September 1800, James Kirkpatrick to Trail.

60 Ibid., p.31, 25 September 1800, to Richard Chase.

61 OIOC, Kirkpatrick Papers, F228/57, p.16, 29 April 1802, James Kirkpatrick to an unnamed Madras jeweller.

62 Ibid., p.25, 9 May 1802, James Kirkpatrick to Barry Close.

63 OIOC, Kirkpatrick Papers, F228/59, p.31, 24 October 1804, James Kirkpatrick to Kennaway.

64 OIOC, Kirkpatrick Papers, F228/58, p.44, 18 October 1802, to Fawcett.

65 OIOC, Kirkpatrick Papers, F228/59, p.31, 24 October 1804, James Kirkpatrick to Kennaway.

66 OIOC, Kirkpatrick Papers, F228/58, p.67, 3 December 1802, James Kirkpatrick to T.G. Richardson in Madras.

67 OIOC, Kirkpatrick Papers, F228/58, p.77, 21 December 1802, James Kirkpatrick to T.G. Richardson.

68 Anon., *The Chronology of Modern Hyderabad from 1720 to 1890 AD* (Hyderabad, 1954), p.55.

69 Khan, *Gulzar i-Asafiya*, pp.305–15.

70 Jagdish Mittal, 'Paintings of the Hyderabad School', in *Marg*, 16, 1962–63, p.44.

71 This fine image, which James Kirkpatrick's Assistant and successor Thomas Sydenham said he 'procured with much difficulty from the archives of the Nizam's family', is illustrated on p.265 of Mark Zebrowski's *Deccani Painting* (London, 1983).

72 This section is derived from the extraordinary research of Ali Akbar Husain in his important study *Scent in the Islamic Garden*, op. cit., p.108.

73 Ibid., pp.105–6.

74 Ibid., pp.38, 71, 78, 131.

75 Ibid., pp.107–8.

76 OIOC, Kirkpatrick Papers, F228/58, p.3, 2 October 1802, James Kirkpatrick to William Palmer.

77 This is said explicitly in the first letter from Kitty Kirkpatrick to Sharaf un-Nissa, in the private archive of their descendants.

78 James notes in 1801 that of the Residency staff only Dr Ure had seen the children: OIOC, Kirkpatrick Papers, F228/13, p.152, 6 September, James Kirkpatrick to William Kirkpatrick. Later it becomes clear that Henry Russell had also met them. Khair nevertheless kept strict purdah and did not show herself to any of the Europeans: Russell, who had had to deal frequently with her both before and after Kirkpatrick's death, was only permitted to see her unveiled in 1806 in Calcutta, and it was clearly considered a great honour to him that she did so. After her affair with Russell commenced, she promised to show herself to his brother Charles, again something that was granted as a special favour in very special circumstances: as Henry explained, 'The Begums are both of them very grateful for your constant attentions to their wishes, and frequently speak of you with great warmth and interest. Khyr oon Nissa says she will see you and become personally acquainted with you, whenever she has an opportunity.' See Bodleian Library, Russell Papers, Ms Eng Letts C155, p.164.

79 Khair un-Nissa did however seem to have met Russell's mistress, who is never named and remains only 'my girl'. Russell's relationship with the girl does not appear to have been a very serious or affectionate one: in 1806, during his long absence in Calcutta, she became pregnant, to Russell's fury, though he was sure that he was the father and wrote to his brother Charles: 'Your account of my girls conduct gives me much pain, and I am exceedingly dissatisfied to hear she is with child. On me she has not many claims, but the Begum has interceded very warmly for her; and, and at her particular request, I have consented to restore to the girl her full monthly allowance of 30 rupees she originally received from me. I will therefore thank you to pay her that sum in future, and to tell her that I expect her gratitude to the Begum, as well as to me, will

induce her to behave better than she has done lately.' See Bodleian Library, Russell Papers, Ms Eng Letts C155, p.155, Calcutta, 18 June. One child the children might have met was young John Ure, the doctor's son, who was the same age as Sahib Begum.

80 Judging by the evidence of Khair and Sharaf un-Nissa taking Fanny and Fyze to the Minister's and Nizam's *zenanas*.

81 This section is derived from the extraordinary research of Zinat Kausar in her wonderful *Muslim Women in Mediaeval India*, op. cit., esp. Chapter 1.

82 I am grateful to Dr Ruby Lal for her help on the role of wetnurses in the Mughal harem.

83 Letter from Sharaf un-Nissa to Kitty Kirkpatrick, undated but c.1840, in the private archives of their descendants.

84 Jehangir (trans. Alexander Rodgers, ed. Henry Beveridge), *The Tuzuk i-Jehangiri or Memoirs of Jehangir* (London, 1909–14), p.36.

85 Kausar, op. cit., p.11.

86 Ibid., p.14.

87 OIOC, Kirkpatrick Papers, F228/59, p.33, 24 October 1804, James Kirkpatrick to George Kirkpatrick.

88 Bodleian Library, Russell Papers, Ms Eng Letts C156, p.21, 21 April 1808. After James's death and Khair un-Nissa's exile to Masulipatam, Henry Russell sent his brother Charles to Khair's townhouse to fetch him some of James's Mughal clothes that he kept there and which Henry needed for a masquerade in Madras. He told his brother to take 'as many of the poor Colonels Hindoostanee dupes[?] [Indian clothes] that I might wish', asking him to go to the house and 'see if you can solicit[?] a complete dup, if there be one, and if not take what articles are sufficient, and what will be the expense of purchasing them.

There should be a *jama* complete, with *sunjaf*[?] and *kinaree*; a pair of rich *kumkhand* turbauns; a turban of Umjud Ally Khan's shape; and a rich *putka* or cummarbund for the court[?] – all these things I believe you will find at least three or four setts of in the Begum's House, except perhaps the turbun and cummerbund; but you can soon ascertain and let me know'.

89 In Henry Russell's correspondence from Calcutta, he records Khair writing letters not only to her grandmother but to her friends 'Chistan and Hyatee's mother'. Bodleian Library, Russell Papers, Ms Eng Letts C155, p.150, Chowringhee, 4 July 1806. When Khair died, 'her mother [Sharaf un-Nissa] and all her relations and friends were with her'. Among those gathered around her bed was Fyze. In the days that followed, huge crowds turned up at her funeral, 'which was attended by every person of rank in the place'. See Scottish Record Office, Edinburgh, GD46/15/3/1–30, Henry Russell to Lady Hood, Hyderabad, 23 September 1813.

90 Letter from William George Kirkpatrick (Sahib Allum) to Kitty Kirkpatrick (Sahib Begum), dated 1 March 1823, in the private archive of Kirkpatrick's descendants.

91 OIOC, Kirkpatrick Papers, F228/59, p.4, 11 June 1803, James Kirkpatrick to William Kirkpatrick.

92 Letter from Kitty Kirkpatrick to Sharaf un-Nissa, undated but c.1840, in the private archives of their descendants.

93 Ibid. For one among many instances of Khair un-Nissa making dresses for a friend see Bodleian Library, Russell Papers, Ms Eng Letts C172, p.67, 7 June 1813, Masulipatam, from Lady (Mary) Hood.

94 Kausar, op. cit., pp.194–8.

95 For an excellent account of

Wellesley's rebuilding of Government House in Calcutta see Bence-Jones, op. cit., Chapter 2.

96 Quoted in Davies, *Splendours of the Raj*, op. cit., p.35.

97 Quoted by Moon, op. cit., p.340

98 Malcolm makes the error, in his telling of the story, of calling the Minister 'Meer Allum'. As the Mir was in 1802 under house arrest and Aristu Jah was the Minister at the time, I have corrected the mistake in the quotation to avoid confusion.

99 J.W. Kaye, op. cit., Vol. 2, p.100.

100 For the Nizam's toothlessness see de Boigne archive, Chambéry, bundle AB IIA, Lieutenant William Steuart to 'Mac', Paangul, 30 October 1790. For the camels' milk see Bidri, op. cit., p.60; for the fishing see New Delhi National Archives, Foreign Department, Secret Consultations, 1800, 15 May, No. 12, 'Moonshee Azeez Oolah's Report of a conversation with AUO and of what passed at the Durbar of HH on 9th March 1800'. For the spice-island pigeons see OIOC, Kirkpatrick Papers, F228/13, p.80, 29 June 1801, James Kirkpatrick to William Kirkpatrick. For the lioness see OIOC, Kirkpatrick Papers, F228/58, p.65, 3 December 1802, James Kirkpatrick to N.B. Edmonstone. For the clock, the automaton and the cloak see OIOC, Kirkpatrick Papers, F228/11, p.332, 5 March 1800, James Kirkpatrick to William Kirkpatrick.

101 OIOC, Kirkpatrick Papers, F228/13, p.292, 17 December 1801, James Kirkpatrick to William Kirkpatrick.

102 OIOC, Kirkpatrick Papers, F228/57, p.35, 23 May 1802, James Kirkpatrick to William Kirkpatrick.

103 OIOC, Kirkpatrick Papers, F228/11, p.287, 25 November 1800, James Kirkpatrick to William Kirkpatrick.

104 OIOC, Kirkpatrick Papers, F228/13, p.47, 6 May 1801, James Kirkpatrick to William Kirkpatrick.

105 OIOC, Kirkpatrick Papers, F228/58, p.38, 6 October 1802, James Kirkpatrick to James Brunton.

CHAPTER 8

1 See Anon., *Some Notes on the Hyderabad Residency*, op. cit., p.29.

2 OIOC, Kirkpatrick Papers, F228/59, p.1, 11 June 1803, James Kirkpatrick to William Kirkpatrick.

3 New Delhi National Archives, Hyderabad Residency Records, Vol. 834, p.178, 6 August 1803, James Kirkpatrick to Arthur Wellesley.

4 Ibid., 7 August 1803, James Kirkpatrick to 'Major Laton commanding the Hyderabad Detachment' for the 'extra butter'; pp.179–80, 8 August, James Kirkpatrick to Arthur Wellesley for the succession of Nizam Sikander Jah.

5 OIOC, Kirkpatrick Papers, F228/59, p.8, 18 August 1803, James Kirkpatrick to William Kirkpatrick.

6 Kirkpatrick, 'A View of the State of the Deccan', op. cit., p.33.

7 From Davies, 'Henry Russell's Report on Hyderabad', op. cit., pp.121–3.

8 Moon, op. cit., p.314

9 Arthur Wellesley quoted in ibid., p.316.

10 Letter from James Kirkpatrick to N.B. Edmonstone, undated but c.May 1803, in the private archive of Kirkpatrick's descendants.

11 OIOC, Kirkpatrick Papers, F228/59, p.1, 11 June 1803.

12 Sir Thomas Munro, quoted in Moon, op. cit., p.321.

13 OIOC, Kirkpatrick Papers, F228/59, p.40, 4 June 1805.

14 Ibid., p.13, 2 October, James Kirkpatrick to William Kirkpatrick.

15 Ibid., p.1, 11 June 1803, James Kirkpatrick to William Kirkpatrick

16 Hastings Papers, BL Add Mss 29,178, Vol. XLVII, 1801–02, 4

December 1802, pp.314–19, William Palmer to Hastings.

17 OIOC, Kirkpatrick Papers, F228/58, p.62, 23 November 1802, and p.67, 1 December 1802, both James Kirkpatrick to William Palmer.

18 New Delhi National Archives, Hyderabad Residency Records, Vol. 634, 9 May 1804, pp.32–3.

19 OIOC, Kirkpatrick Papers, F228/59, p.8, 18 August 1804, and p.40, 4 June 1805, James Kirkpatrick to William Kirkpatrick.

20 Bodleian Library, Russell Papers, Ms Eng Letts C155, p.42, 17 August 1804, Madras, Henry Russell to Charles Russell.

21 I am grateful to Professor Robert Frykenberg for sending me a copy of this image.

22 Bodleian Library, Russell Papers, Ms Eng Letts C155, p.1, 21 February 1802; p.5, 19 March 1802; p.11, 15 April 1802: all Henry Russell to Charles Russell.

23 Quoted in 'A Preliminary Report on the Russell Correspondence Relating to Hyderabad 1783–1816', reprinted in *Indian Archives*, Vol. IX, January–June 1955, No. 1, pp.25–6.

24 OIOC, Kirkpatrick Papers, F228/59, p.40, 4 June 1805, James Kirkpatrick to William Kirkpatrick.

25 Bidri, op. cit., p.83.

26 New Delhi National Archives, Hyderabad Residency Records, Vol. 634, 20 October 1804, 'A Secret Communication', p.85.

27 Moon, op. cit., pp.340–1.

28 Quoted in Butler, op. cit., p.326.

29 Hastings Papers, BL Add Mss 29,180, Vol. XLIX, f.328, October 1804–December 1805, William Palmer to Hastings, Berhampore, 12 October 1805.

30 OIOC, Kirkpatrick Papers, F228/75, p.3, 27 July 1805, Lieutenant Colonel Robinson to James Kirkpatrick.

31 OIOC, Kirkpatrick Papers, F228/58, p.53, 9 November 1802, James Kirkpatrick to James Brunton.

32 Ibid., p.66, 30 November 1802, James Kirkpatrick to James Brunton.

33 Ibid., p.31, 24 October 1804, James Kirkpatrick to Kennaway.

34 OIOC, Kirkpatrick Papers, F228/59, p.8, 18 August 1804, James Kirkpatrick to William Kirkpatrick.

35 See the obituary in the *New Monthly Magazine* for 1836; Rev. George Oliver's 'Biographies of Exonians', in the *Exeter Flying Post* 1849–50; and a file on the Kennaway family in the West Country Studies Library, Exeter.

36 OIOC, Kirkpatrick Papers, F228/59, p.31, 24 October 1804, James Kirkpatrick to Kennaway.

37 Ibid., p.25, 23 July 1804, James Kirkpatrick to William Kirkpatrick. Isabella (who was christened Barbara Isabella Kirkpatrick, but was known as an adult by her more becoming middle name) was born in 1788. See Strachey Papers, OIOC F127/478a, 'Sketch of the Kirkpatrick Family by Lady Richard Strachey'.

38 OIOC, Kirkpatrick Papers, F228/58, p.67, 3 December 1802, James Kirkpatrick to T.G. Richardson in Madras.

39 Ibid., p.53, 8 November 1802, James Kirkpatrick to James Brunton.

40 OIOC, Kirkpatrick Papers, F228/59, p.20, 9 October.

41 Ibid., p.40, 4 June 1805, James Kirkpatrick to William Kirkpatrick.

42 See Khan, *Indian Muslim Perceptions of the West*, op. cit., Chapter 2.

43 Shushtari, op. cit., pp.11, 351, 425.

44 For Thomas Deane Pearse's interests in astronomy see *Bengal Past and Present*, Vol. 2, 1908, pp.304ff, and esp. Vol. 6, 1910, pp.40 and 273–4, part of a long series of articles on Pearse's letters.

45 OIOC, Kirkpatrick Papers, F228/59, p.40, 4 June 1805, James Kirkpatrick to William Kirkpatrick.

46 Ibid., p.33, 24 October 1804, James

Kirkpatrick to George Kirkpatrick.

47 OIOC, Kirkpatrick Papers, F228/82, p.32, 13 July 1805, Dr Ure.

48 OIOC, Kirkpatrick Papers, F228/59, p.40, 4 June 1805, James Kirkpatrick to William Kirkpatrick.

49 OIOC, Kirkpatrick Papers, F228/84, dated 22 March 1805.

50 Mirza Abu Taleb Khan, op. cit., p.197.

51 Ibid., pp.198–200.

52 OIOC, Kirkpatrick Papers, F228/13, p.166, 21 September 1801, James Kirkpatrick to William Kirkpatrick.

53 OIOC, Sutherland Papers, Mss Eur D547, pp.133–4, undated but c.1803.

54 Ibid., p.134.

55 OIOC, Kirkpatrick Papers, F228/13, p.152, 6 September 1801, James Kirkpatrick to William Kirkpatrick.

56 OIOC, Kirkpatrick Papers, F228/59, p.27, 4 October 1804, James Kirkpatrick to the Handsome Colonel.

57 Ibid.

58 Ibid., p.40, 4 June 1805, James Kirkpatrick to William Kirkpatrick.

59 Ibid., p.27, 4 October 1804, James Kirkpatrick to the Handsome Colonel.

60 Ibid., p.35, James Kirkpatrick to Mrs Hooker, c.August 1805.

61 Ibid., p.40, 4 June 1805, James Kirkpatrick to William Kirkpatrick.

62 Letter from Kitty Kirkpatrick to Sharaf un-Nissa, undated but c.1840, in the private archive of Kirkpatrick's descendants.

63 Hickey, op. cit., Vol. 4, p.385.

64 Patrick Conner, *George Chinnery 1774–1852: Artist of India and the China Coast* (London, 1993), p.62.

65 OIOC, Kirkpatrick Papers, F228/75, p.5, 6 August 1805, William Petrie to James Kirkpatrick.

66 Hickey, op. cit., Vol. 4, pp.319–20.

67 OIOC, Kirkpatrick Papers, F228/75, p.3, 27 July 1805, Lieutenant Colonel Robinson to James Kirkpatrick.

68 See Hastings Papers, BL Add Mss 29,180, Vol. XLIX, f.328, October 1804–December 1805, William Palmer to Hastings, Berhampore, 12 October 1805.

69 OIOC, Kirkpatrick Papers, F228/75, p.5, 6 August 1805, William Petrie to James Kirkpatrick.

70 OIOC, Kirkpatrick Papers, F228/68, p.109, 20 August 1805, Mir Alam to James Kirkpatrick, trans. by Henry Russell, First Assistant.

71 OIOC, Kirkpatrick Papers, F228/75, p.13, 9 September 1805, Henry Russell to James Kirkpatrick.

72 *Calcutta Gazette*, 3 October.

73 OIOC, Kirkpatrick Papers, F228/75, p.15, 14 September, James Kirkpatrick to William Bentinck: Passes on Meer Allum's request to buy His Highness of Arcot's house and enclosure in Hyderbad. Also p.18, 22 September: a note from the Nawab of Arcot's secretary giving James Kirkpatrick an appointment at ten the following morning to see the Nawab at Chipauck House, presumably to discuss Mir Alam's proposed purchase.

74 *Calcutta Gazette*, 10 October.

75 OIOC, Elphinstone Papers, Mss Eur F88, Box13/16[b], entry for 13 September 1801.

76 *Calcutta Gazette*, 3 October.

77 Hastings Papers, BL Add Mss 29,180, Vol. XLIX, f.328, October 1804–December 1805, William Palmer to Hastings, Berhampore, 12 October 1805.

78 The codicil lies at the bottom of the will. See OIOC, Kirkpatrick Papers, F228/84, dated 22 March 1805. Among the points James added was a characteristically thoughtful directive that his generous bequests to his nieces should be paid on marriage, and not necessarily to await their twenty-first birthdays.

79 These details are all taken from Theon Wilkinson's wonderful book *Two Monsoons*, op. cit.; n.b. esp. Chapter 1.

80 *Calcutta Gazette*, 28 November.

81 Bodleian Library, Russell Papers, Ms Eng Letts C152, p.50.

CHAPTER 9

1 Denis Kincaid, *British Social Life in India up to 1938* (London, 1938), pp.22, 95.

2 David Burton, *The Raj at Table: A Culinary History of the British in India* (London, 1993), p.208.

3 Shushtari, op. cit., p.427.

4 Quoted in John Keay, *India Discovered* (London, 1981), p.22.

5 Hickey, op. cit., Vol. 2, p.187.

6 Shushtari, op. cit., p.434.

7 Ibid., p.137.

8 Ibid., p.301.

9 OIOC, Fowke Papers, Mss E6.66, Vol. XXVII, J. Fowke to M. Fowke, Calcutta, 12 December 1783.

10 Shushtari, op. cit., p.432.

11 Bodleian Library, Russell Papers, Ms Eng Letts C155, p.128, 9 April 1806, Henry Russell to Charles Russell; and p.176, 30 August 1806, Henry Russell in Calcutta to Charles Russell in Hyderabad.

12 Ibid., pp.190–2, 7 November 1806, Henry Russell to Charles Russell.

13 Ibid., p.138, 9 May; p.152, 11 July; and p.128, 25 June: all three letters from Henry Russell in Calcutta to Charles Russell in Hyderabad.

14 Ibid., p.140, 2 June 1806, Henry Russell to Charles Russell; and p.158, Calcutta, 23 July, Henry Russell to Charles Russell.

15 Ibid., p.164, 16 August, Henry Russell to Charles Russell.

16 Ibid., p.190, 7 November, Henry Russell to Charles Russell.

17 Ibid., p.162, 3 August 1806.

18 Khan, *Tarikh i-Khurshid Jahi*, op. cit., pp.713–14.

19 Bodleian Library, Russell Papers, Ms Eng Letts D151, p.96, Poona, 31 May 1810, Henry Russell to Charles Russell.

20 Quoted in Anon., *Some Notes on the Hyderabad Residency*, op. cit., p.4.

21 Bodleian Library, Russell Papers, Ms Eng Letts D151, p.120, c.June 1810, Henry Russell to Charles Russell.

22 Ibid., p.11, 1 March 1806; and p.126, 24 March: both Henry Russell to Charles Russell.

23 Bodleian Library, Russell Papers, Ms Eng Letts.

24 Ibid., C155, p.155, 18 July 1806.

25 Ibid., p.132, 14 May.

26 Bodleian Library, Russell Papers, Ms Eng Letts D151, p.76, Poona, 19 May 1810, and p.96, Poona, 31 May 1810. For his vow not to employ anyone disloyal to James, see Ms Eng Letts C155, p.132, 14 May.

27 Bodleian Library, John Palmer Papers, Ms Eng Lit C76, pp.82–3, 8 September 1813, John Palmer to William Palmer.

28 Hastings Papers, BL Add Mss 29,180, Vol. XLIX, October 1804–December 1805, f.328, William Palmer to Hastings, Berhampore, 12 October 1805.

29 Bodleian Library, John Palmer Papers, Ms Eng Lit C76, p.115, 25 July 1810, John Palmer to William Palmer.

30 Bodleian Library, Russell Papers, Ms Eng Letts C155, p.138, 29 May 1806, Henry Russell to Charles Russell.

31 Ibid., p.142, 5 June 1806, Henry Russell to Charles Russell.

32 Ibid.

33 Ibid., p.145, 13 June 1806, Henry Russell to Charles Russell.

34 Ibid., p.198, 29 November, Henry Russell to Charles Russell.

35 Ibid., p.140, 2 June 1806, Calcutta, Henry Russell to Charles Russell.

36 Ibid., p.150, 4 July 1806, Henry Russell to Charles Russell.

37 Ibid., p.158, Calcutta, 23 July; and p.150, 4 July: both Henry Russell to Charles Russell.

38 Ibid., p.155, Calcutta, 18 July, Henry Russell to Charles Russell.

39 Ibid.

40 Ibid., pp.190–2, 7 November 1806, Henry Russell to Charles Russell.

41 Bodleian Library, Russell Papers, Ms Eng Letts C172, p.5, 25 November 1806, Thomas Sydenham to Henry Russell.

42 Ibid., p.7, 26 December 1806, Henry Russell to Thomas Sydenham.

43 Ibid.

44 Bodleian Library, Russell Papers, Ms Eng Letts C168, p.1, 24 December 1806, N.B. Edmonstone to Henry Russell.

45 Bodleian Library, Russell Papers, Ms Eng Letts C172, p.7, 26 December 1806, Henry Russell to Thomas Sydenham.

46 Ibid., p.1, 14 January 1807, Thomas Sydenham to Henry Russell.

47 Ibid., p.11, 20 February 1806, Hemming to Henry Russell.

48 Bodleian Library, Russell Papers, Ms Eng Letts C155, pp.205–6, 22 March 1806, Henry Russell to Charles Russell.

49 Ibid., p.207, 14 April 1807, Henry Russell to Charles Russell.

50 Ibid.

51 Scottish Record Office, Edinburgh, GD135/2086, The Will of Lieut Col James Dalrymple, Hussein Sagar, 8 December 1800.

52 Jacon Hafner, from his *Reizen van Jacob Haafner eerste Deel*, pp.112, 135, quoted in Sinnappah Arasaratnam and Aniruddha Ray, *Masulipatam and Cambay: A History of Two Port Towns 1500–1800* (New Delhi, 1994), p.116.

53 Bodleian Library, Russell Papers, Ms Eng Letts C155, p.213, 27 April 1807, Henry Russell to Charles Russell.

54 Ibid., p.216, 14 January 1808, Henry Russell to Charles Russell.

55 Ibid.

56 Ibid.

57 For Madras see Dodwell, op. cit., pp.187, 217, 220. Also Jan Morris, *Stones of Empire: The Buildings of the Raj* (Oxford, 1983), pp.214–15,

Davies, *Splendours of the Raj,* op. cit., p.30.

58 Bodleian Library, Russell Papers, Ms Eng Letts C156, p.4, 7 April 1808, Henry Russell to Charles Russell.

59 Bodleian Library, Russell Papers, Ms Eng Letts C155, pp.226–30, 4 March 1808, Henry Russell to Charles Russell.

60 Bodleian Library, Russell Papers, Ms Eng Letts C156, p.21, 21 April 1808, Henry Russell to Charles Russell.

61 Bodleian Library, Russell Papers, Ms Eng Letts C155, p.31, 7 March 1808, Henry Russell to Charles Russell.

62 Bodleian Library, Russell Papers, Ms Eng Letts C156, p.51, 14 May 1808, Henry Russell to Charles Russell.

63 Bodleian Library, Russell Papers, Ms Eng Letts C155, p.236, 9 March 1808, Henry Russell to Charles Russell.

64 Bodleian Library, Russell Papers, Ms Eng Letts C156, p.29, 29 April 1808, Henry Russell to Charles Russell.

65 Bodleian Library, Russell Papers, Ms Eng Letts C155, p.236, 9 March 1808, Henry Russell to Charles Russell.

66 Ibid., p.244, 10 March 1808, Henry Russell to Charles Russell.

67 Bodleian Library, Russell Papers, Ms Eng Letts C156, p.4, 7 April 1808, Henry Russell to Charles Russell.

68 Ibid., p.18, 19 April 1808.

69 Ibid., p.30, 1 May 1808, Henry Russell to Charles Russell

70 Ibid., p.41, 7 May 1808, Henry Russell to Charles Russell.

71 Ibid., p.51, 14 May 1808, Henry Russell to Charles Russell.

72 Ibid., p.88, June 1808, Henry Russell to Charles Russell.

73 Ibid., p.89, 11 June 1808, Henry Russell to Charles Russell.

74 Ibid., p.91, 11 June 1808, Henry Russell to Charles Russell.

75 Bodleian Library, Russell Papers, Ms Eng Letts C152, undated letter (c.1809), Sir Henry Russell to Charles Russell; also letter from Sir Henry to Henry Russell, 13 November 1818, reprinted in *Indian*

Archives, Vol. VIII, July–December 1954, pp.135–6. See also Peter Wood, 'Vassal State in the Shadow of Empire: Palmer's Hyderabad, 1799–1867' (unpublished Ph.D., University of Wisconsin-Madison, 1981), pp.106–7.

76 Bodleian Library, Russell Papers, Ms Eng Letts C156, p.98, 20 October, Henry Russell to Charles Russell.

77 Ibid., p.102.

78 Ibid., p.107, 29 December 1808, Henry Russell to Charles Russell.

79 Bodleian Library, Russell Papers, Ms Eng Letts D152, p.8, 9 October 1810.

80 Bodleian Library, Russell Papers, Ms Eng Letts C156, p.279, n.d., Henry Russell to Charles Russell.

81 Bodleian Library, Russell Papers, Ms Eng Letts C172, p.67, 7 June 1813, Lady Hood to Henry Russell.

82 Scottish Record Office, Edinburgh, GD46/15/3/1–30, Henry Russell to Lady Hood, Hyderabad, 23 September 1813.

83 Scottish Record Office, Edinburgh, GD46/8/1, Henry Russell to Lady Hood, Hyderabad, 5 November 1813.

84 See Lady [Constance] Russell, *The Rose Goddess and Other Sketches of Mystery & Romance* (London, 1910), pp.1–18.

85 Scottish Record Office, Edinburgh, GD46/8/1, Henry Russell to Lady Hood, Hyderabad, 5 November 1813.

CHAPTER 10

1 Quoted in Archer and Falk, *India Revealed*, op. cit., p.54.

2 Captain George Elers, *Memoirs of George Elers, Captain of the 12th Regiment of Foot* (London, 1903), pp.179–88.

3 I would like to thank Michael Fisher for this information.

4 For the children pining for India see Lady Russell, *The Rose Goddess . . .*, op. cit., pp.1–18. For Kitty apparently referring to a ban

on correspondence with her mother, see letter in the private archive of her descendants, in which in 1841 she tells Sharaf un-Nissa: 'I longed to write to you & tell you these feelings that I was never able to – [express?], a letter w[hich] I was sure wd be detained.'

5 Edward Strachey, 'The Romantic Marriage of James Achilles Kirkpatrick', op. cit., pp.27–8.

6 Certainly it was always William, not the Handsome Colonel, who wrote occasional progress reports on the children to Henry Russell. His letters clearly describe the children from observation rather than report, so it can safely be assumed that they spent a fair amount of time together.

7 As he described Kennaway in his will. I have been unable to trace the whereabouts of the original of this document, and have worked from a copy made by William's descendant Kenneth Kirkpatrick which he sent to Bilkiz Alladin in Hyderabad. I am very grateful to Bilkiz for twice giving me access to this and to her voluminous collection of Kirkpatrick papers.

8 Brendan Carnduff, entry for William Kirkpatrick in *The New Dictionary of National Biography* (forthcoming). Brendan tells me that Kirkpatrick's letters to Kennaway at this period seem to hint at serious opium abuse.

9 The East India Company Collection is now part of the Oriental and India Office Collections in the British Library. William's description of Nepal was published as *An Account of the Mission to Nepaul in 1793* (London, 1811)

10 In *India Inscribed*, op. cit. (p.235), Kate Teltscher comments that in his preface 'Kirkpatrick describes Tipu's epistolary self-portrait in terms drawn largely from the vocabulary of despotism: the cruel enemy,

intolerant fanatic, oppressive ruler, harsh master, the sanguinary and perfidious tyrant ... the final sentence [of the preface] which leaves much inferred rather than stated, suggests that Kirkpatrick is attempting to answer those few writers who depict the sultan in reasonable guise and dismiss the tyrannical image as an exaggeration.' There is a direct parallel to this selective publication of documentation with a view to showing Muslim rulers in the worst possible light in the selective translations from the Arab and Islamic press produced by various pro-Israeli lobbying organisations today.

11 Mark Wilks (1760?–1831), Military and Private Secretary to Lord Clive 1798–1803, Resident in Mysore 1803–08, when he left India. In retirement in England he wrote *Historical Sketches of the South of India in an Attempt to trace the History of Mysore* (London, 1810–14), and an analysis of the *Akhlak i-Nasiri*, a Persian metaphysical treatise.

12 OIOC, Kirkpatrick Papers, F228/21, pp.1, 7; 4 and 12 November 1809, Mark Wilks to William Kirkpatrick.

13 I am very grateful to Brendan Carnduff for his help with William Kirkpatrick, and for his clever and generous suggestions, especially relating to William's possible opium addiction and his obsession with Tipu's astrological systems.

14 For William's overdose see Strachey Papers, OIOC F127/478a, 'Sketch of the Kirkpatrick Family by Lady Richard Strachey'. His granddaughter Clementina Robinson (daughter of Clementina, Lady Louis) wrote: 'I think he suffered from rheumatic gout but he died from drinking laudanum which his servant had put by his bedside believing it to be senna.'

William was buried in St Clement Danes church in the Strand. His death notice in the *Exeter Flying Post* reads: 'Thursday Sept 3rd, 1812: Died, Near London, on the 22nd Ult, most suddenly, Major General Kirkpatrick, of the East India Company's service, late resident in this city. He had long filled high and important public stations in India, and was alike distinguished for his literary attainments, political knowledge, and private virtues.'

15 There is an undated letter in the archive of his sisters' descendants which refers to the amputation he was going to have to undergo, but does not specify which limb was concerned. The accident is mentioned in Sir Edward Strachey's unpublished memoirs, quoted in Charles Richard Sanders, *The Strachey Family 1588–1932: Their Writings and Literary Associations* (New York, 1968), p.122.

16 From the private archive of their descendants. The Handsome Colonel to Katherine Kirkpatrick, Hollydale, 8 September 1812.

17 The Handsome Colonel died at Hollydale and was buried in St Clement Danes church in the Strand. There was a memorial plaque to him and William high on the north wall of the church, but it was lost when the church was burned down in the Blitz.

18 Thomas Carlyle (ed. Charles Eliot Novem), *Reminiscences* (London, 1887), p.243.

19 Ibid., p.244.

20 Barbara Strachey, *The Strachey Line*, op. cit., p.113.

21 Carlyle, *Reminiscences*, op. cit., p.247.

22 Ibid., p.246.

23 Alexander Carlyle (ed.), *Love Letters of Thomas Carlyle and Jane Welsh* (London, 1909), Vol. 2, p.15.

24 Ibid., p.20.

25 Carlyle, *Reminiscences*, op. cit.,

p.247: 'Mrs Strachey took to me from the first, nor ever swerved: it strikes me now, more than it then did, she silently could have liked to see "dear Kitty" and myself come together.'

26 *Love Letters of Thomas Carlyle and Jane Welsh*, op. cit., Vol. 2, p.25.

27 Ibid., pp.50–1.

28 Ibid., p.235.

29 Quoted in 'Carlyle and the "Blumine" of *Sartor Resartus*', *Westminster Review*, CLXLII, August 1894, pp.164–5.

30 Barbara Strachey, *The Strachey Line*, op. cit., p.117.

31 In Sanders, *The Strachey Family 1588–1932*, op. cit., p.134.

32 Carlyle, *Reminiscences*, op. cit., p.248.

33 From the private archive of their descendants, letter from James Phillipps to Kitty dated only 'Friday Night'.

34 Thomas Carlyle, *Sartor Resartus* (London, 1833–34); see Chapter 5, 'Romance', passim.

35 There is a considerable literature on the identity of Carlyle's 'Blumine' and 'The Rose Goddess'. See G. Strachey, 'Carlyle and the Rose Goddess', in *Nineteenth Century*, Vol. 32, July–December 1892, pp.470–86; J.J. Cotton, 'Kitty Kirkpatrick', in *Calcutta Review*, Vol. CCXVI, April 1899, pp236–48; and the follow-up in Vol. CCIXX, December 1899, J.J. Cotton, 'Kitty Kirkpatrick and Blumine', pp.128–35; Henry Strachey, 'Carlyle's First Love', *Spectator*, CIII, 9 October 1909, pp.559–60. See also Lady Russell, *The Rose Goddess . . .*, op. cit., pp.1–18. Other candidates for Blumine include Margaret Gordon and Carlyle's wife, Jane Welsh. See C.F. Harrold (ed.), *Carlyle's Sartor Resartus* (New York, 1937), pp.37–8.

36 G. Strachey, 'Carlyle and the Rose Goddess', op. cit.

37 Ibid.

38 Ibid., p4/5.

39 How he did this is unclear, and Kitty tried to find out by writing to a contact in the Hyderabad Residency. Russell did not give her the picture immediately, but later left it to her in his will, much to the annoyance of his own family. See letter of Henry Russell to William Palmer in Bodleian Library, Russell Papers, Mss Eng Letts C174, 2 October 1841, p.147. This letter contradicts the later and inaccurate account given by Constance Russell in *The Rose Goddess . . .*, op. cit., p.1, where Kitty is said to have first visited Swallowfield in the company of a Mrs Clive in the summer of 1846 – although there may of course have been two different visits to Swallowfield.

40 Anon., *Some Notes on the Hyderabad Residency*, op. cit., p.23.

41 See Wood, op. cit., pp.269–71.

42 De Warren, op. cit., Chapter 9.

43 Ibid., Chapter 10.

44 Ibid.

45 The best account of Palmer's bank, and Russell's secret involvement with it, can be found in Peter Wood's remarkable thesis 'Vassal State in the Shadow of Empire', op. cit., pp.348–61. For Russell bribing the printers of the *Hyderabad Papers* see ibid., p.357. See also the good short account given in Hawes, op. cit., pp.101–9.

46 Scottish Record Office, Edinburgh, GD46/8/1, Henry Russell to Lady Hood, Hyderabad, 5 November 1813.

47 The letter is in the bound volume of Russell's Persian correspondence in the Bodleian Library. See Chapter 7, n9, above.

48 Bodleian Library, Russell Papers, Mss Eng Letts C174, p.147, 2 October 1841, Henry Russell to William Palmer.

49 Ibid., p.154, 15 January 1842, William Palmer to Henry Russell.

50 The letter, which is undated but must presumably be 1842, survives in the private archive of their descendants. The original is in Persian, and Captain D.C. Malcolm's slightly inaccurate translation is attached to it.

51 The correspondence survives in the private archive of Khair un-Nissa's descendants in London. It is not numbered or referenced.

52 See Wood, op. cit., p.362n.

53 The correspondence survives in the private archive of Khair un-Nissa's descendants in London. It is not numbered or referenced.

54 Bodleian Library, Russell Papers, Mss Eng Letts C174, p.174, 27 July 1847, William Palmer to Henry Russell.

55 Bengal Regimental Orders, IOR/P/ Ben/Sec/253, Fort William, 17 December 1813, No. 39, Regimental Orders by Lt. Col. Stuart, Futtyghur, 2 July 1813. Also No. 68.

56 Gardner Papers, National Army Museum, p.206, Letter 81, Babel, 27 June 1821.

57 Saksena, op. cit., pp.100–37.

58 Parkes, op. cit., p.458.

59 Quoted in Alex Palmer's unpublished 'The Palmer Family', op. cit.

60 Temple, *Journals of Hyderabad . . .*, op. cit., Vol. 1, p.240.

61 Quoted by Lady Russell, *The Rose Goddess . . .*, op. cit., p.18.

62 Edward Strachey, 'The Romantic Marriage of James Achilles Kirkpatrick . . .' op. cit., p.29.

63 See for example p.52.

BIBLIOGRAPHY

1. MANUSCRIPT SOURCES IN EUROPEAN LANGUAGES

Oriental and India Office Collections, British Library (formerly India Office Library), London (OIOC)

James Dalrymple Papers, Mss Eur E330
Elphinstone Papers, Mss Eur F88
Fowke Papers, Mss Eur E6.66
Gardner Papers, Mss Eur C304
Kirkpatrick Papers, Mss Eur F228
'Memoirs of William Prinsep', Mss Eur D1160
Strachey Papers, Mss Eur F127
Edward Strachey's Diaries, Mss Eur F128
Sutherland Papers, Mss Eur D547
GE Westmacott's Ms Travels in India, Mss Eur C29
Home Miscellaneous 464, 'Report of an Examination instituted by the direction of his Excellency the most noble Governor General, Fort St. George 7th Nov 1801'
Home Miscellaneous 743, 'The Affairs Of Messrs Wm Palmer & Co, Extract From Bengal Pol Cons 7th Oct 1825'
Bengal Wills 1780–1804, L/AG/34/29/4–16
Madras Inventories, L/AG/34/29/185–210
Bengal Regimental Orders, IOR/P/BEN/SEC
Bengal Political Consultations, IOR/P/117/18

British Library

Warren Hastings Papers, Add Mss 29,172, Vol. XLI, 1790
Anderson Papers, Add Mss 45,427
Brit Mus Egerton MS 2123
Wellesley Papers, Add Mss 13,582–

Bodleian Library, Oxford

Russell Correspondence, Ms Eng Letts C155–7, C174, D150, D151
Palmer Papers, Ms Eng Lit C176
Ms Bodley Or. 430

Devon Records Office, Exeter

Kennaway Papers, B961M, ADD/F2

West Country Studies Library, Exeter

Kennaway Files
Palk Files

Archives Départmentales de la Savioe, Chambéry, France

De Boigne archive

National Army Museum Library, London

Gardner Papers, NAM 6305–56

Scottish Record Office, Registrar House, Edinburgh

The Will of Lieut Col James Dalrymple, Hussein Sagar, 8 December
1800: GD135/2086
Seaforth Papers: GD46 Letters from Henry Russell to Lady Hood

National Library of Scotland

Papers of Alexander Walker, NLS 13,601–14,193,

National Archives of India, New Delhi

Secret Consultations
Political Consultations
Foreign Consultations
Foreign Miscellaneous
Secret Letters to Court
Secret Letters from Court
Political Letters to Court
Political Letters from Court
Hyderabad Residency Records

Delhi Commissioners' Office Archive, New Delhi

Mubarak Bagh Papers, DCO F5/1861

Private Archives

Fraser Papers, Inverness
Kirkpatrick Papers, London
Strachey and Kirkpatrick Papers, Strachey Trust, Oxford

2. UNPUBLISHED MANUSCRIPTS AND DISSERTATIONS

Bakshi, Ashwin Kumar, 'The Residency of Hyderabad 1779–1857'
    (unpublished Ph.D., Osmania University, 1990)
Chander, Sunil, 'From a Pre-Colonial Order to a Princely State:
    Hyderabad in Transition, c1748–1865' (unpublished Ph.D.,
    Cambridge University, 1987)
Ghosh, Durba, 'Colonial Companions: Bibis, Begums, and Concubines
    of the British in North India 1760–1830' (unpublished Ph.D.,
    Berkeley, 2000)
Haidar, Dr Zeb un-Nissa, 'A Comprehensive Study of the Daftar
    i-Dar ul-Insha 1762–1803' (unpublished Ph.D., Osmania University,
    Hyderabad, 1978)
Haidar, Dr Zeb un-Nissa, 'The Glimpses of Hyderabad: In the Light
    of the Tarikh i-Mahanamah' (research project for UGC Grant,
    Hyderabad, 1998–99)
Wood, Peter, 'Vassal State in the Shadow of Empire, Palmer's
    Hyderabad 1799–1867' (unpublished Ph.D., University of
    Wisconsin-Madison, 1981)

3. PERSIAN AND URDU SOURCES

A. Manuscripts

*Oriental and India Office Collections, British Library (formerly India
    Office Library), London*
Diwan e-Chanda Islamic Ms, 2768

Private Collection, Hyderabad
Tamkin Kazmi (ed. and expanded by Laeeq Salah), *Aristu Jah*
    (unpublished Urdu biography, written c.1950 and re-edited by
    Laeeq Salah c.1980)

Oriental Manuscript Library, Hyderabad
Khazan wa Bahar Mutafarriqat Ms, 686
Risala-e Baghbani Mutafarriqat Ms, 164

B. Published Texts

Anon., *The Chronology of Modern Hyderabad from 1720 to 1890AC*
   (Hyderabad, 1954)
Azmi, Rahat, *Mah e-laqa* (Hyderabad, 1998)
Balkhi, Fasih-ud-Din, *Tazkirah e-Niswan e-Hind* (Patna, 1956)
Bidri, Mohammed Khader Khan Munshi (trans. Dr Zeb un-Nissa
   Haidar), *Tarikh i-Asaf Jahi* (written 1266AH/AD1851, pub.
   Hyderabad, 1994)
Fazl, Abu'l (trans. H. Blochman and H.S. Jarrett), *Ain i-Akbari*
   (written c.1590, pub. Calcutta, 1873–94, 3 vols)
Gohar, Ghulam Samdani, *Hyat e-Mah e-Laqa* (Hyderabad, 1240AH/
   AD1825)
Hasan, Mehdi Fateh Nawaz Jung, *Muraqq-Ibrat* (Hyderabad, 1300AH/
   AD1894)
Husain, Saiyyad Iltifat, *Nagaristan i-Asafi* (written c.1816, pub.
   Hyderabad, 1900?)
Jehangir (trans. Alexander Rodgers, ed. Henry Beveridge), *The Tuzuk
   i-Jehangiri or Memoirs of Jehangir* (London, 1909–14)
Kasravi, Ahmad, 'Ham dozd ham dorugh' ('Not Only a Liar but a
   Plagiarist'), in *Peyman*, Vol. 1, No. 3, 1312AH (about Shushtari's
   Tuhfat al-'Alam)
Khan, Dargah Quli (trans. Chander Shekhar), *The Muraqqa' e-Dehli*
   (New Delhi, 1989)
Khan, Ghulam Husain, Khan Zaman Khan, *Gulzar i-Asafiyu*
   (Hyderabad, 1302AH/AD1891)
Khan, Ghulam Imam, *Tarikh i-Khurshid Jahi* (Hyderabad, 1284AH/
   AD1869)
Khan, Ghulam Imam, *Tarikh e-Rasheeduddin Khani* (written
   Hyderabad, 1270AH/AD1855, pub. 1321AH/AD1901)
Khan, M. Abdul Rahim, *Tarikh e-Nizam* (Hyderabad, 1311AH/AD1896)
Khan, Mirza Abu Taleb (trans. Charles Stewart), *The Travels of Mirza
   Abu Taleb Khan in Asia, Africa, and Europe during the years 1799,
   1800, 1801, 1802, and 1803* (London, 1810)

Khan, Muhammed Najmul Ghani, *Tarikh e-Riyasat e-Hyderabad* (Lucknow, 1930)

Khan, Saqi Must'ad, *Maasir i-Alamgiri* (trans. as *The History of the Emperor Aurangzeb-Alamgir 1658–1707*), (Calcutta, 1946)

Lal, Makhan, *Tarikh i-Yadgar i-Makhan Lal* (Hyderabad, 1300AH/ AD1883)

Mansaram, Lala (trans. P. Setu Madhava Rao), *Masir i-Nizami, Eighteenth Century Deccan* (Bombay, 1963)

Ruswa, Mirza Mohammed Hadi Ruswa (trans. Khuswant Singh and M.A. Hussani), *Umrao Jan Ada* (Hyderabad, 1982)

Server ul-Mulk (trans. from the Urdu by his son, Nawab Jiwan Yar Jung Bahadur), *My Life, Being the Autobiography of Nawab Server ul Mulk Bahadur* (London, 1903)

Shushtari, Sayyid Abd al-Latif, *Kitab Tuhfat al-'Alam* (written Hyderabad, 1802; lithographed Bombay, 1847)

Talib, Mohammed Sirajuddin, *Mir Alam* (Hyderabad, n.d.)

Talib, Mohammed Sirajuddin, *Nizam Ali Khan* (Hyderabad, n.d.)

4. CONTEMPORARY WORKS AND PERIODICAL ARTICLES IN EUROPEAN LANGUAGES

Ainslie, Rev. R., ' "British Idolatry in India": A sermon preached by the Rev. R. Ainslie at the Monthly Meeting of Ministers of Congregational Churches', in *The Pastoral Echo: Nineteen Sermons of Eminent Dissenting Ministers and Others* (London, 1837)

Alam, Muzaffar and Alavi, Seema, *A European Experience of the Mughal Orient: The I'jaz i-Arslani (Persian Letters, 1773–1779) of Antoine-Louis Henri Polier* (New Delhi, 2001)

Anon., review of *A Code of Gentoo Laws or Ordinations of the Pundits*, in *Critical Review*, XLIV, September 1777, pp.177–191

Anon., *Sketches of India Written by an Officer for the Fire-Side Travellers at Home* (London, 1821)

Barnard, Anne (ed. A.M. Lewin Robinson), *The Letters of Lady Anne Barnard to Henry Dundas from the Cape and Elsewhere 1793–1803* (Cape Town, 1973)

Barnard, Anne (ed. A.M. Lewin Robinson), *The Cape Journals of Lady Anne Barnard 1797–98* (Cape Town, 1994)

Bayley, Emily, *The Golden Calm: An English Lady's Life in Moghul Delhi* (London, 1980)

Bourquien, Louis, 'An Autobiographical Memoir of Louis Bourquien translated from the French by J.P. Thompson', in *Journal of the Punjab Historical Society*, Vol. IX, Pt 7, 1923

Carlyle, Thomas, *Sartor Resartus* (London, 1833–34)

Carlyle, Thomas, *Reminiscences* (London, 1887)

Dalrymple, James, *Letters &c Relative To The Capture of Rachore* (Madras, 1796)

D'Oyley, Charles, *The European in India* (London, 1813)

East India Company, *The Hyderabad Papers: Papers Relative To Certain Pecuniary Transactions Of Messrs William Palmer And Co With The Government Of His Highness The Nizam* (London, 1824)

Elers, George, *Memoirs of George Elers, Captain of the 12th Regiment of Foot* (London, 1903)

'Ex-Civilian', *Life in the Mofussil* (London, 1878)

Fenton, Elizabeth, *The Journal of Mrs Fenton* (London, 1901)

Foster, William (ed.), *The English Factories in India 1618–1669* (13 vols, London, 1906–27)

Foster, William (ed.), *Early Travels in India 1583–1619* (London, 1921)

Francklin, William, *Military Memoirs of Mr George Thomas Who by Extraordinary Talents and Enterprise rose from an obscure situation to the rank of A General in the Service of Native Powers in the North-West of India* (London, 1805)

Fraser, James Baillie, *Military Memoirs of Lt. Col. James Skinner CB* (2 vols, London, 1851)

Fryer, Dr John, *A New Account of East India and Persia Letters Being Nine Years Travels Begun 1672 and finished 1681* (3 vols, London, 1698)

Hamilton, Alexander, *A New Account of the East Indies* (2 vols, London, 1930)

Heber, Reginald, *A Narrative of a Journey Through the Upper Provinces of India from Calcutta to Bombay, 1824–1825* (3 vols, London, 1827)

Hickey, William (ed. Alfred Spencer), *The Memoirs of William Hickey* (4 vols, London, 1925)

Hollingbery, William, *A History of His Late Highness Nizam Alee Khaun, Soobah of the Dekhan* (Calcutta, 1805)

Jones, Sir William (ed. G. Canon), *The Letters of Sir William Jones* (2 vols, Oxford, 1970)

Jourdain, John (ed. W. Foster), *Journal of John Jourdain 1608–17* (London, 1905)

Kaye, John W., *The Life and Correspondence of Sir John Malcolm GCB* (2 vols, London, 1856)

Kindersley, Mrs Jemima, *Letters from the East Indies* (London, 1777)

Kirkpatrick, William, *Diary and Select Letters of Tippoo Sultan* (London, 1804)

Kirkpatrick, William, *An Account of the Mission to Nepaul in 1793* (London, 1811)

Linschoten, J.H. Van, *The Voyage of John Huyghen Van Linschoten to the East Indies* (2 vols, London, 1885; original Dutch edition 1598)

Lockyer, Charles, *An Account Of The Trade With India Containing Rules For Good Government In Trade, And Tables: With Descriptions Of Fort St. George, Aheen, Malacca, Condore, Anjenjo, Muskat, Gombroon, Surat, Goa, Carwar, Telicherry, Panola, Calicut, The Cape Of Good Hope, And St Helena Their Inhabitants, Customs, Religion, Government Animals, Fruits &C.* (London, 1711)

Lushington, Rt Hon. S.R., *The Life and Services of Lord George Harris GCB* (London, 1840)

Mackintosh, James, *Memoirs of the Life of The Rt Hon Sir James Mackintosh* (London, 1835)

Malcolm, Sir John, *Sketch of the Political History of India from the Introduction of Mr Pitts Bill* (London, 1811)

Malcolm, Sir John, *Political History of India* (2 vols, London, 1836)

Mandelslo, J.A. de (trans. John Davis), *The Voyages and Travels of J. Albert de Mandelslo; The Voyages & Travels of the Ambasssadors sent by Frederick Duke of Holstein, to the Great Duke of Muscovy, and the King of Persia* (London, 1662)

Manucci, Niccolao (trans. William Irvine), *Storia do Mogor, or Mogul India, 1653–1708* (2 vols, London, 1907)

Medwin, Thomas, *The Angler in Wales or Days and Nights of Sportsmen* (2 vols, London, 1834)

Methwold, William, 'Relations of the Kingdome of Golchonda and other neighbouring Nations and the English Trade in Those Parts', in W.H. Moreland, *Relations of Golconda in the Early Seventeenth Century* (London, 1931)

Nugent, Lady Maria, *Journal of a Residence in India 1811–15* (2 vols, London, 1839)

Parkes, Fanny, *Wanderings of a Pilgrim in Search of the Picturesque* (London, 1850)

Peggs, James, *A Voice from India: The British Connection with Idolatry and Mahomedanism, particularly the Government grant to the Temple at Juggarnarta and numerous other temples in India. A letter to Sir J.C. Hobhouse* (London, 1847)

Pellow, Thomas (ed. Robert Brown), *The Adventures of Thomas Pellow, of Penryn, Mariner* (London, 1890)

Pope, Alexander (ed. N. Ault, completed by J. Bull), *Minor Poems* (London, 1954)

Russell, Lady [Constance], *The Rose Goddess and Other Sketches of Mystery & Romance* (London, 1910)

Sarkar, Jadunath (ed.), *English Records of Mahratta History: Poona Residency Correspondence. Vol. 1 – Mahadji Scindhia and North Indian Affairs 1785–1794* (Bombay, 1936)

Sarkar, Jadunath (trans. and ed.), 'Haidarabad and Golkonda in 1750 Seen Through French Eyes: From the Unpublished Diary of a French Officer Preserved in the Bibliothèque Nationale, Paris', in *Islamic Culture*, Vol. X, 1936, p.24

Scurry, James, *The Captivity, Sufferings and Escape of James Scurry, who was detained a prisoner during ten years, in the dominions of Haidar Ali and Tippoo Saib* (London, 1824)

Sen, S., *Indian Travels of Thevenot and Careri* (New Delhi, 1949)

Sprenger, A., *A Catalogue of Arabic, Persian and Hindustany Manuscripts of the libraries of the King of Oudh* (Lucknow, 1854)

Stuart, Charles, *A Vindication of the Hindoos from the Aspersions of the Revd Claudius Buchanan MA with a refutation of the arguments exhibited in his Memoir . . . By a Bengal Officer* (London, 1808)

Tavernier, Jean-Baptiste (trans. V. Ball, ed. William Crooke), *Travels in India* (2 vols, Oxford, 1925)

Taylor, Philip Meadows, *Story of my Life* (London, 1878)

Taylor, Philip Meadows, *Confessions of a Thug* (London, 1889)

Thompson, Alexander, *Government Connection with Idolatry in India* (Cape Town, 1851)

Vitkus, Daniel J. (ed.), *Three Turk Plays from Early Modern England: Selimus, A Christian Turned Turk and The Renegado* (New York, 2000)

Warren, Count Edouard de, *L'Inde Anglaise en 1843* (Paris, 1845)

Wellesley, Arthur, Duke of Wellington (ed. by his son, the 2nd Duke of Wellington), *Supplementary Despatches and Memoranda of Field Marshal Arthur Duke of Wellington* (15 vols, London, 1858–72)

Wellesley, Richard, Marquess Wellesley (ed. Montgomery Martin), *The Despatches, Minutes and Correspondence of the Marquess Wellesley KG during his Administration of India* (5 vols, London, 1840)

Wellesley, Richard, Marquess Wellesley (ed. Edward Ingram), *Two Views of British India: The Private Correspondence of Mr Dundas and Lord Wellesley: 1798–1801* (London, 1970)

Williamson, Captain Thomas, *The East India Vade Mecum* (2 vols, London, 1810; 2nd edition 1825)

Yule, Henry, *Hobson-Jobson: A Glossary of Colloquial Anglo-Indian Words and Phrases* (London, 1903)

5. SECONDARY WORKS AND PERIODICAL ARTICLES

Alam, Shah Manzur, 'Masulipatam: A Metropolitan Port in the Seventeenth Century', in Mohamed Taher (ed.), *Muslim Rule in the Deccan* (New Delhi, 1997)

Alavi, Seema, *The Sepoys and the Company: Tradition and Transition in Northern India 1770–1830* (New Delhi, 1995)

Arasaratnam, Sinnappah and Ray, Aniruddha, *Masulipatam and Cambay: A History of Two Port Towns 1500–1800* (New Delhi, 1994)

Archer, Mildred, *Company Drawings in the India Office Library* (London, 1972)

Archer, Mildred, *India and British Portraiture 1770–1825* (London, 1979)

Archer, Mildred, *Between Battles: The Album of Colonel James Skinner* (London, 1982)

Archer, Mildred and Falk, Toby, *India Revealed: The Art and Adventures of James and William Fraser 1801–35* (London, 1989)

Ballhatchet, Kenneth, *Race, Sex and Class Under the Raj: Imperial Attitudes and Policies and their Critics 1793–1905* (London, 1980)

Bayly, C.A., *Imperial Meridian: The British Empire and the World 1780–1830* (London, 1989)

Bayly, C.A., *Empire and Information: Intelligence Gathering and Social Communication in India 1780–1870* (Cambridge, 1996)

Bence-Jones, Mark, *Palaces of the Raj* (London, 1973)

Bilgrami, S.A. Asgar, *The Landmarks of the Deccan: A Comprehensive Guide to the Archaeological Remains of the City and Suburbs of Hyderabad* (Hyderabad, 1927)

Bilkiz Alladin, *For the Love of a Begum* (Hyderabad, 1989)

Boyd, Elizabeth French, *Bloomsbury Heritage: Their Mothers and their Aunts* (New York, 1976)

Briggs, Henry, *The Nizam: His History and Relations with the British Government* (London, 1861)

Brittlebank, Kate, *Tipu Sultan's Search for Legitimacy: Islam and Kingship in a Hindu Domain* (New Delhi, 1997)

Buddle, Anne, *The Tiger and the Thistle: Tipu Sultan and the Scots in India* (Edinburgh, 1999)

Burton, David, *The Raj at Table: A Culinary History of the British in India* (London, 1993)

Butler, Iris, *The Eldest Brother: The Marquess Wellesley 1760–1842* (London, 1973)

Cadell, Patrick (ed.), *The Letters of Philip Meadows Taylor to Henry Reeve* (London, 1947)

Chatterjee, Indrani, *Gender, Slavery and Law in Colonial India* (New Delhi, 1999)

Chaudhuri, Nani Gopal, *British Relations with Hyderabad* (Calcutta, 1964)

Chew, Samuel C., *The Crescent and the Rose: Islam and England During the Renaissance* (New York, 1937)

Colley, Linda, 'Britain and Islam: Perspectives on Difference 1600–1800', in *Yale Review*, LXXXVIII, 2000

Colley, Linda, 'Going Native, Telling Tales: Captivity, Collaborations and Empire', in *Past & Present*, No. 168, August 2000

Collingham, E.M., *Imperial Bodies: The Physical Experience of the Raj c.1800–1947* (London, 2001)

Compton, Herbert (ed.), *The European Military Adventurers of Hindustan* (London, 1943)

Conner, Patrick, *George Chinnery 1774–1852: Artist of India and the China Coast* (London, 1993)

Cruz, Maria Augusta Lima, 'Exiles and Renegades in Early Sixteenth Century Portuguese India', in *Indian Economic and Social History Review*, XXIII, 3

Dalrymple, William, *City of Djinns* (London, 1993)

Davies, Philip, *Splendours of the Raj: British Architecture in India 1660–1947* (London, 1985)

Disney, A.R., *Twilight of the Pepper Empire: Portuguese Trade in South-West India in the Early Seventeenth Century* (Harvard, 1978)

Dodwell, Henry, *The Nabobs of Madras* (London, 1926)

Eaton, Richard Maxwell, *Sufis of Bijapur 1300–1700* (Princeton, 1978)

Findly, Ellison Banks, *Nur Jehan: Empress of Mughal India* (New Delhi, 1993)

Fisch, Jorg, 'A Solitary Vindicator of the Hindus: The Life and Writings of General Charles Stuart (1757/8–1828)', in *Journal of the Royal Asiatic Society*, 4, 1985, 2–3

Fisch, Jorg, 'A Pamphlet War on Christian Missions in India 1807–9', in *Journal of Asian History*, Vol. 19, 1985, pp.22–70

Fisher, Michael, *The Travels of Dean Mahomet: An Eighteenth Century Journey Through India* (Berkeley, 1997)

Flexner, J.T., *Mohawk Baronet: Sir William Johnson of New York* (New York, 1959)

Forrest, Denys, *Tiger of Mysore: The Life and Death of Tipu Sultan* (London, 1970)

Ghosh, Suresh Chandra, *The Social Condition of the British Community in Bengal* (Leiden, 1970)

Goffman, Daniel, *Britons in the Ottoman Empire 1642–1660* (Washington, 1998)

Grey, C., and Garrett, H.L.O., *European Adventurers of Northern India 1785–1849* (Lahore, 1929)

Hambly, Gavin (ed.), *Women in the Medieval Islamic World* (New York, 1998)

Hawes, Christopher, *Poor Relations: The Making of the Eurasian Community in British India 1773–1833* (London, 1996)

Husain, Ali Akbar, *Scent in the Islamic Garden: A Study of Deccani Urdu Literary Sources* (Karachi, 2000)

Hutchinson, Lester, *European Freebooters in Moghul India* (London, 1964)

Jaffer, Amin, *Furniture from British India and Ceylon* (London, 2001)

Kausar, Zinat, *Muslim Women in Medieval India* (New Delhi, 1992)

Kaye, M.M. (ed.), *The Golden Calm: An English Lady's Life in Moghul Delhi* (London, 1980)

Keay, John, *India Discovered* (London, 1981)

Keene, Manuel, *Treasury of the World: Jewelled Arts of India in the Age of the Mughals* (London, 2001)

Khan, Gulfishan, *Indian Muslim Perceptions of the West During the Eighteenth Century* (Karachi, 1998)

Kincaid, Denis, *British Social Life in India up to 1938* (London, 1938)

Kulkarni, G. and Kantak, M.R., *The Battle of Kharda: Challenges and Responses* (Pune, 1980)

Kumar, Ritu, *Costumes and Textiles of Royal India* (London, 1998)

Lafont, Jean-Marie, 'The French in Lucknow in the Eighteenth Century', in Violette Graff (ed.), *Lucknow: Memories of a City* (Delhi, 1997)

Lafont, Jean-Marie, *Indika: Essays in Indo–French Relations 1630–1976* (Delhi, 2000)

Lafont, Jean-Marie, *Maharaja Ranjit Singh: Lord of the Five Rivers* (New Delhi, 2002)

Lal, John, *Begam Samru: Fading Portrait in a Gilded Frame* (Delhi, 1997)

Lal, K.S., *Studies in Deccan History* (Hyderabad, 1951)

Lal, K.S., *The Mughal Harem* (New Delhi, 1988)

Lane-Poole, Stanley, *Aurangzeb and the Decay of the Mughal Empire* (London, 1890)

Leach, Linda York, *Mughal and Other Paintings from the Chester Beatty Library* (London, 1995)

Llewellyn-Jones, Rosie, *A Fatal Friendship: The Nawabs, the British and the City of Lucknow* (New Delhi, 1982)

Llewellyn-Jones, Rosie, *A Very Ingenious Man: Claude Martin in Early Colonial India* (New Delhi, 1992)

Llewellyn-Jones, Rosie, *Engaging Scoundrels: True Tales of Old Lucknow* (New Delhi, 2000)

Love, H.D., *Vestiges of Old Madras* (2 vols, London, 1913)

Mansingh, Gurbir, 'French Military Influence in India', in Mansingh, G., *Reminiscences: The French in India* (New Delhi, 1997)

Marshall, P.J. (ed.), *The British Discovery of Hinduism* (Cambridge, 1970)

Marshall, P.J., 'Cornwallis Triumphant: War in India and the British Public in the Late Eighteenth Century', in Lawrence Freeman, Paul

Hayes and Robert O'Neill (eds), *War, Strategy and International Politics* (Oxford, 1992)

Marshall, P.J., 'British Society under the East India Company', in *Modern Asian Studies*, 31, 1, 1997, pp.89–108

Matar, Nabil, *Islam in Britain 1558–1685* (Cambridge, 1998)

Matar, Nabil, *Turks, Moors and Englishmen in the Age of Discovery* (New York, 1999)

Michell, George and Zebrowski, Mark, *The New Cambridge History of India 1.7: Architecture and Art of the Deccan Sultanates* (Cambridge, 1999)

Moon, Sir Penderel, *The British Conquest and Dominion of India* (London, 1989)

Moreland, W.H., 'From Gujerat to Golconda in the Reign of Jahangir', in *Journal of Indian History*, Vol. XVII, 1938, pp.139–50

Morris, James, *Heaven's Command: An Imperial Progress* (London, 1973)

Morris, Jan, *Stones of Empire: The Buildings of the Raj* (Oxford, 1983)

Moynihan, Elizabeth B., *Paradise as a Garden in Persia and Mughal India* (New York, 1979)

Moynihan, Elizabeth B., *The Moonlight Garden* (Washington, 2000)

Mukherjee, S.N., *Sir William Jones: A Study in Eighteenth-Century Attitudes to India* (Cambridge, 1968)

Nayeem, M.A., *Mughal Administration of the Deccan under Nizamul Mulk Asaf Jah (1720–48)* (Bombay, 1985)

Nilsson, Sten, *European Architcture in India 1750–1850* (London, 1968)

Parker, Geoffrey, *The Military Revolution* (Oxford, 1988)

Pearse, *Life of Alexander Gardiner* (London, 1920)

Pearson, M.N., *The New Cambridge History of India 1.1: The Portuguese in India* (Cambridge, 1987)

Peirce, Leslie P., *The Imperial Harem: Women and Sovereignty in the Ottoman Empire* (New York, 1993)

Pieper, J., 'Hyderabad: A Qu'ranic Paradise in Architectural Metaphors', in A. Peruccioli (ed.), *Environmental Design*

Priolkar, A.K., *The Goa Inquisition* (Bombay, 1961)

Rao, P. Setu Madhava, *Eighteenth Century Deccan* (Bombay, 1963)

Regani, Sarojini, *Nizam–British Relations 1724–1857* (New Delhi, 1963)

Ridgeway, Christopher and Williams, Robert (eds), *Sir John Vanbrugh and Landscape Architecture in Baroque England* (London, 1999)

Robb, Peter, 'Clash of Cultures? An Englishman in Calcutta', SOAS
    Inaugural Lecture, 12 March 1998 (London, 1998)

Roberts, Andrew, *Napoleon and Wellington* (London, 2001)

Saksena, Ram Babu, *European and Indo-European Poets of Urdu and
    Persian* (Lucknow, 1941)

Sanders, Charles Richard, *The Strachey Family 1588–1932: Their
    Writings and Literary Associations* (New York, 1968)

Sarkar, Jadunath, 'General Raymond of the Nizam's Army', in
    Mohammed Taher (ed.), *Muslim Rule in the Deccan* (Delhi, 1997)

Saroop, Narindar, *A Squire of Hindoostan* (New Delhi, 1983)

Scammell, G.V., 'European Exiles, Renegades and Outlaws and the
    Maritime Economy of Asia c.1500–1750', in *Modern Asian Studies*,
    26, 4, 1992, pp.641–61

Schimmel, Annemarie, *Islam in the Indian Subcontinent* (Leiden-Koln,
    1980)

Shreeve, Nicholas, *Dark Legacy* (Arundel, 1996)

Shreeve, Nicholas (ed.), *From Nawab to Nabob: The Diary of David
    Ochterlony Dyce Sombre* (Arundel, 2000)

Spear, Percival, *The Nabobs* (Cambridge, 1963)

Strachey, Barbara, *The Strachey Line* (London, 1985)

Strachey, Edward, 'The Romantic Marriage of James Achilles
    Kirkpatrick, Sometime British Resident at the Court of Hyderabad',
    in *Blackwood's Magazine*, July 1893

Subrahmanyam, Sanjay, *Improvising Empire: Portuguese Trade and
    Settlement in the Bay of Bengal 1500–1700* (Delhi, 1990)

Subrahmaniyam, Sanjay, *The Portuguese Empire in Asia: A Political
    and Economic History* (London, 1993)

Surorova, Anna A., *Masnavi: A Study of Urdu Romance* (Karachi,
    2000)

Tamaskar, B.G., *Life and Work of Malik Ambar* (Delhi, 1978)

Teltscher, Kate, *India Inscribed: European and British Writing on India
    1600–1800* (Oxford, 1995)

Thompson, Edward, *The Life of Charles Lord Metcalfe* (London, 1937)

Toibin, Beth, *Picturing Imperial Power: Colonial Subjects in Eighteenth
    Century British Painting* (Duke, 1999)

Wagoner, Philip B., ' "Sultan among Hindu Kings": Dress, Titles and
    the Islamicization of Hindu Culture at Vijayanagar', in *Journal of
    Asian Studies*, Vol. 55, No. 4, November 1996, pp.851–80

Weller, Jac, *Wellington in India* (London, 1972)

Wilkinson, Theon, *Two Monsoons* (London, 1976)

Young, Desmond, *Fountain of Elephants* (London, 1959)

Zaidi, S. Inayat, 'European Mercenaries in the North Indian Armies 1750–1803 AD', in *The Ninth European Conference on Modern South Asian Studies*, Heidelberg, 9–12 July 1986

Zaidi, S. Inayat, 'French Mercenaries in the Armies of South Asian States 1499–1803', in *Indo-French Relations: History and Perspectives* (Delhi, 1990)

Zebrowski, Mark, *Deccani Painting* (London, 1983)

Zebrowski, Mark, *Gold, Silver and Bronze from Mughal India* (London, 1997)

INDEX

City of Djinns

A Year in Delhi

William Dalrymple

WINNER OF THE
1994 THOMAS COOK TRAVEL BOOK AWARD AND
SUNDAY TIMES YOUNG WRITER OF THE YEAR AWARD

Alive with the mayhem of the present and sparkling with the author's ubiquitous, irrepressible wit, *City of Djinns* is the fascinating portrait of a city as has never been attempted before. Meeting an extraordinary array of characters, from the city's elusive eunuchs to the embattled descendants of the great Moguls, from the rich Punjabis to the Sufis and mystics, and investigating the resonances of these people and their modern ways with the India of the past, this is a unique and dazzling feat of research and adventure by one of the finest travel writers of his generation.

'A sympathetic and engaging portrait of this age-old city . . . It is fine, entertaining, well-written stuff, thoroughly researched but with none of the stern academic tone that so many historical profiles adopt. What sustains it, apart from his erudite knowledge of Moslem architecture, medicine, music, military architecture, and arcane religious principles, is Dalrymple's sense of historical adventure. Just open your eyes, he says. If you know how to look, even the empty tombs and abandoned ruins of the past are alive . . . '   *Financial Times*

'Unlike much of modern travel writing *City of Djinns* is informative, learned and funny . . . a lively and sometimes profound book.'
Economist

'Scholarly and marvellously entertaining . . . A considerable feat.'
DERVLA MURPHY, *Spectator*

ISBN: 0 00 637595 2

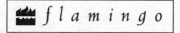

William Dalrymple

In Xanadu

A Quest

'A classic.'   *Sunday Express*

'William Dalrymple's *In Xanadu* carries us breakneck from a
pre-dawn glimmer in the Holy Sepulchre right across Asia to a
bleak wind in Kubla Khan's palace . . . it is learned and comic,
and a most gifted first book touched by the spirits of Kinglake,
Robert Byron and E. Waugh.'

PATRICK LEIGH FERMOR, *Spectator* Books of the Year

'*In Xanadu* is, without doubt, one of the best travel books produced in the last 20 years. It is witty and intelligent, brilliantly
observed, deftly constructed and extremely entertaining . . .
Dalrymple's gift for transforming ordinary, humdrum experience into something extraordinary and timeless suggests that
he will go from strength to strength.'

ALEXANDER MAITLAND, *Scotland on Sunday*

'Exuberant.'   COLIN THUBRON

'Dalrymple writes beautifully, is amazingly erudite, brave and
honest, and can be extremely funny.'

QUENTIN CREWE, *Sunday Telegraph*

'The delightful, and funny, surprise mystery tour of the year.'
SIR ALEC GUINNESS, *Sunday Times*

'Erudite, adventurous and amusing . . . reminded me of Evelyn
Waugh.'   PIERS PAUL READ

0 00 654415 0

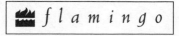

William Dalrymple

From the Holy Mountain

A Journey in the Shadow of Byzantium

'Any travel writer who is so good at his job as to be brilliant, applauded, loved and needed has to have an unusual list of qualities, and William Dalrymple has them all in aces . . . The best and most unexpected book I have read since I forget when.'   PETER LEVI

'Witty, learned and very funny.'   ERIC NEWBY

'Nobody but William Dalrymple – and possibly Patrick Leigh Fermor – could have produced so compulsively readable a book.'   JOHN JULIUS NORWICH, *Observer*

'The future of travel literature lies in the hands of gifted authors like Dalrymple who shine their torches into the shadow hinterland of the human story – the most foreign territory of all.'   SARA WHEELER, *Independent*

'Dalrymple stands out as one of our most talented travel writers. Energetic, thoughtful, curious and courageous.'
                              ANTHONY SATTIN, *Sunday Times*

0 00 654774 5

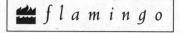

Katie Hickman

Daughters of Britannia

The Lives & Times of Diplomatic Wives

'Fascinating' AMANDA FOREMAN, *Observer*

'This is a lovely book: affectionate, celebratory and as conscious of the glory as the hardship. These women lived; they saw dolphins in the Bosphorus at dawn, took tea with empresses, watched eclipses in Turkistan. And they were so lonely that they wrote it all down.'

LIBBY PURVES, *Sunday Times*

'Absorbing, moving and wonderfully gossipy . . . all of it laced with a good helping of eccentrics and the undeniable glamour of pomp and tradition in far-flung places.'

RUTH GORB, *Guardian*

'This is a delightful and exceptionally well-written book, funny, lively and warm-hearted.'

PHILIP ZIEGLER, *Daily Telegraph*

'Enormously enjoyable, anecdotal and scholarly'

SUE GAISFORD, *Independent*

'Part history, part anecdotal anthology, it makes unputdownable reading as famous names in diplomatic spouse lore like Emma Hamilton and Vita Sackville-West are upstaged by ordinary women faced with extraordinary situations.'

PATRICIA THOMSON, *Evening Standard*

0 00 638780 2

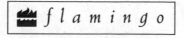